THE ULTIMATE
AIR FRYER
— COOKBOOK —
FOR BEGINNERS
1000

**Easy and Affordable Air Fryer Recipes
for Smart People on a Budget**

ROBBIE B. NEY

Table of Content

Chapter 2 Lunch And Dinner 30

Chapter 5 Poultry 98

Chapter 6 Fish and Seafood   143

Chapter 7 Casseroles, Frittatas, and Quiches 181

Chapter 8 Desserts 184

Chapter 9 Wraps and Sandwiches 212

Chapter 10 Appetizers,Snacks, and Side Dishes.................217

Introduction

I think that much of my childhood memories are built around fried foods. The smell of crispy, battered fish and chips, homemade mozzarella sticks, burgers, shrimp, and so many other delicious fried foods tinge the memory of my mother and grandmother's houses. Many of the recipes that have been passed down through the generations in our family include at least one fried item but this was normal back then.

We didn't yet know how bad excessive amounts of oils, especially saturated fats, are for us. Today we have a huge amount of research and the historical data that is showing us that there is a reason that cardiovascular disease is the biggest cause of death globally—deficient diet. This doesn't just include fried foods, of course, but also all processed and junk foods, but if we cut out processed and junk food and still use a huge amount of bad fats in our cooking process, we aren't helping matters.

As a dietician, this knowledge was imparted on me during my studies, and I realized just how risky my generational family diet had been. It was at this moment I decided to change the way my own family ate. I was determined to send my children out into the world with a different idea about cooking than I had been taught. At first, this meant that we had to cut out many of the foods we enjoyed because there simply wasn't a way to make them without cooking them in some form of fat. Soon, I discovered a kitchen appliance that changed my life—the air fryer. The most amazing thing about this appliance is that it doesn't just replace conventional frying, it also works for food that you would normally cook in an oven and in a fraction of the time!

The United Kingdom is well-known for its love of fish and chips, so it only makes sense that the air fryer was invented there. It was developed in 2008 and is essentially a stand-alone appliance that cooks, fries, bakes, grills, and steams food. Of course, it wasn't long until the United States embraced the air fryer, considering how fast it made cooking and how versatile it is. The air fryer is a compact convection oven that fits on your countertop. It uses superheated air to cook foods that produce results very similar to deep-frying or roasting under high temperatures.

Depending on which brand you buy, the control set-up of your air fryer may differ slightly, but generally, the air fryer has three sets of controls that we need to look at.

▶ The temperature control dial

▶ The control panel

▶ The automatic timer button

The temperature control dial allows you to set the temperature your food will be cooked at. This range is most commonly anywhere between 175°F and 400°F. You can also adjust the cooking temperature during the cooking process. One of the biggest concerns for air fryer beginners is that they won't know what temperature to use and how long to cook. Our recipes and this guide provide you with much of the required information and, it won't be long until you are confidently programming the air fryer yourself.

The control panel on the air fryer has a "heat on" indicator light, illuminating when the inside of the air fryer reaches the temperature you set. It also has a red indicator light indicating the power is running to the air fryer. It illuminates when you plug the appliance in and power it on. Many models of air fryers also have buttons that represent shortcut functions on the control panel. This makes life even easier as you don't need to worry about memorizing all of the cooking times and temperatures for dishes like fish and poultry.

Thirdly, the automatic timer button allows you to select the time you want the air fryer to cook for and automatically counts down while cooking. There is usually an audible signal, like a beeping when the countdown reaches zero. Although many air fryers turn off automatically, for safety reasons, always ensure that the temperature and timer dials are turned back to zero before you walk away from your air fryer.

When I first started my family and realized just how much work meal time was, I developed a bit of a kitchen appliance addiction. I was convinced that every new gadget I purchased was going to change my life. Admittedly, most didn't, but the air fryer has absolutely changed the way I cook and how healthy the meals are that I put in front of my children every day. Most of the kitchen gadgets I have purchased over the years ended up in garage sales because they were just gathering dust. My air fryer will never be one of those, though. It has become as integral a part of food preparation as my microwave, stove, and refrigerator.

When I purchased my air fryer, it was relatively new on the market, so there weren't a ton of options, but if you look for one now, you will find an entire aisle of any given store dedicated to different models of air fryers. The choice can be a bit intimidating. As with anything, your personal needs and preferences are going to determine which model is best for you and your family but there are a few things to look out for.

Budget is always going to be the first consideration, and thankfully, there are models out there with smaller baskets and no extra features that fit well within most budgets. You can pick a fryer that has a digital display or manual. The only difference is one has a digital control panel, and the other has knobs and dials. Although I started out with a manual air fryer, I really enjoy the one I have now, which has a digital display. It shows you the exact temperature that you are cooking at as well as the cooking time. This really helps, in the beginning, to assure you are cooking according to the instructions. The two main considerations when buying an air fryer are size and capacity. The appliance's overall size is a consideration in terms of storage space and operating space in your kitchen. You will need a level, heat-resistant surface in your kitchen with enough space to have at least five inches of clear area around all sides of the fryer for ventilation purposes.

Capacity is the other consideration, and your needs will depend on how many people you are cooking for. The cooking capacity of an air fryer is not enormous, and in general, it is sufficient for a two-person family or slightly larger if you cook in batches. It all depends on what you plan on using it for. Some use the air fryer as their main cooking appliance for most dishes, while others use it to save time and enjoy dishes like roast meats during the week when there is less time available for meal preparation. There are plenty of extra-large air fryers available for larger families. Always open up the display unit in the store you know exactly what capacity you are dealing with. Ask as many questions as possible about the operation of the unit before you purchase. Small things like whether the unit's timer resets itself to zero if you open it during cooking are important considerations. Ideally, you want to be able to check on your food, close the lid, and have it continue from where it left off.

Chapter 1 Breakfast

Egg and Bacon Muffins

Prep time: 5 minutes | Cook time: 15 minutes | Serves 1

2 eggs
Salt and ground black pepper, to taste
1 tablespoon green pesto
3 ounces (85 g) shredded Cheddar cheese
5 ounces (142 g) cooked bacon
1 scallion, chopped

1. Preheat the air fryer to 350ºF (177ºC). Line a cupcake tin with parchment paper.
2. Beat the eggs with pepper, salt, and pesto in a bowl. Mix in the cheese.
3. Pour the eggs into the cupcake tin and top with the bacon and scallion.
4. Bake in the preheated air fryer for 15 minutes, or until the egg is set.
5. Serve immediately.

Parmesan Sausage Egg Muffins

Prep time: 5 minutes | Cook time: 20 minutes | Serves 4

6 ounces (170 g) Italian sausage, sliced
6 eggs
⅛ cup heavy cream
Salt and ground
black pepper, to taste
3 ounces (85 g) Parmesan cheese, grated

1. Preheat the air fryer to 350ºF (177ºC). Grease a muffin pan.
2. Put the sliced sausage in the muffin pan.
3. Beat the eggs with the cream in a bowl and season with salt and pepper.
4. Pour half of the mixture over the sausages in the pan.
5. Sprinkle with cheese and the remaining egg mixture.
6. Bake in the preheated air fryer for 20 minutes or until set.
7. Serve immediately.

Super Easy Bacon Cups

Prep time: 5 minutes | Cook time: 20 minutes | Serves 2

3 slices bacon, cooked, sliced in half
2 slices ham
1 slice tomato
2 eggs
2 teaspoons grated Parmesan cheese
Salt and ground black pepper, to taste

1. Preheat the air fryer to 375ºF (191ºC). Line 2 greased muffin tins with 3 half-strips of bacon
2. Put one slice of ham and half slice of tomato in each muffin tin on top of the bacon
3. Crack one egg on top of the tomato in each muffin tin and sprinkle each with half a teaspoon of grated Parmesan cheese. Sprinkle with salt and ground black pepper, if desired.
4. Bake in the preheated air fryer for 20 minutes. Remove from the air fryer and let cool.
5. Serve warm.

Parmesan Ranch Risotto

Prep time: 10 minutes | Cook time: 30 minutes | Serves 2

1 tablespoon olive oil
1 clove garlic, minced
1 tablespoon unsalted butter
1 onion, diced
¾ cup Arborio rice
2 cups chicken stock, boiling
½ cup Parmesan cheese, grated

1. Preheat the air fryer to 390ºF (199ºC).
2. Grease a round baking tin with olive oil and stir in the garlic, butter, and onion.
3. Transfer the tin to the air fryer and bake for 4 minutes. Add the rice and bake for 4 more minutes.
4. Turn the air fryer to 320ºF (160ºC) and pour in the chicken stock. Cover and bake for 22 minutes.
5. Scatter with cheese and serve.

Breakfast Sausage and Cauliflower

Prep time: 5 minutes | Cook time: 45 minutes | Serves 4

1 pound (454 g) sausage, cooked and crumbled	Cheddar cheese, plus more for topping
2 cups heavy whipping cream	8 eggs, beaten
1 head cauliflower, chopped	Salt and ground black pepper, to taste
1 cup grated	

1. Preheat the air fryer to 350ºF (177ºC).
2. In a large bowl, mix the sausage, heavy whipping cream, chopped cauliflower, cheese and eggs. Sprinkle with salt and ground black pepper.
3. Pour the mixture into a greased casserole dish. Bake in the preheated air fryer for 45 minutes or until firm.
4. Top with more Cheddar cheese and serve.

Onion Omelet

Prep time: 10 minutes | Cook time: 12 minutes | Serves 2

3 eggs	1 large onion, chopped
Salt and ground black pepper, to taste	2 tablespoons grated Cheddar cheese
½ teaspoons soy sauce	Cooking spray

1. Preheat the air fryer to 355ºF (179ºC).
2. In a bowl, whisk together the eggs, salt, pepper, and soy sauce.
3. Spritz a small pan with cooking spray. Spread the chopped onion across the bottom of the pan, then transfer the pan to the air fryer.
4. Bake in the preheated air fryer for 6 minutes or until the onion is translucent.
5. Add the egg mixture on top of the onions to coat well. Add the cheese on top, then continue baking for another 6 minutes.
6. Allow to cool before serving.

Classic British Breakfast

Prep time: 5 minutes | Cook time: 25 minutes | Serves 2

1 cup potatoes, sliced and diced	1 tablespoon olive oil
2 cups beans in tomato sauce	1 sausage
2 eggs	Salt, to taste

1. Preheat the air fryer to 390ºF (199ºC) and allow to warm.
2. Break the eggs onto a baking dish and sprinkle with salt.
3. Lay the beans on the dish, next to the eggs.
4. In a bowl, coat the potatoes with the olive oil. Sprinkle with salt.
5. Transfer the bowl of potato slices to the air fryer and bake for 10 minutes.
6. Swap out the bowl of potatoes for the dish containing the eggs and beans. Bake for another 10 minutes. Cover the potatoes with parchment paper.
7. Slice up the sausage and throw the slices on top of the beans and eggs. Bake for another 5 minutes.
8. Serve with the potatoes.

Golden Avocado Tempura

Prep time: 5 minutes | Cook time: 10 minutes | Serves 4

½ cup bread crumbs	sliced
½ teaspoons salt	Liquid from 1 can white beans
1 Haas avocado, pitted, peeled and	

1. Preheat the air fryer to 350ºF (177ºC).
2. Mix the bread crumbs and salt in a shallow bowl until well-incorporated.
3. Dip the avocado slices in the bean liquid, then into the bread crumbs.
4. Put the avocados in the air fryer, taking care not to overlap any slices, and air fry for 10 minutes, giving the basket a good shake at the halfway point.
5. Serve immediately.

Bacon Hot Dogs

Prep time: 5 minutes | Cook time: 15 minutes | Serves 4

3 brazilian sausages, cut into 3 equal pieces
9 slices bacon
1 tablespoon Italian

herbs
Salt and ground black pepper, to taste

1. Preheat the air fryer to 355ºF (179ºC).
2. Take each slice of bacon and wrap around each piece of sausage. Sprinkle with Italian herbs, salt and pepper.
3. Air fry the sausages in the preheated air fryer for 15 minutes.
4. Serve warm.

Buttermilk Biscuits

Prep time: 5 minutes | Cook time: 5 minutes | Makes 12 biscuits

2 cups all-purpose flour, plus more for dusting the work surface
1 tablespoon baking powder
¼ teaspoon baking soda

2 teaspoons sugar
1 teaspoon salt
6 tablespoons cold unsalted butter, cut into 1-tablespoon slices
¾ cup buttermilk

1. Preheat the air fryer to 360ºF (182ºC). Spray the air fryer basket with olive oil.
2. In a large mixing bowl, combine the flour, baking powder, baking soda, sugar, and salt and mix well.
3. Using a fork, cut in the butter until the mixture resembles coarse meal.
4. Add the buttermilk and mix until smooth.
5. Dust more flour on a clean work surface. Turn the dough out onto the work surface and roll it out until it is about ½ inch thick.
6. Using a 2-inch biscuit cutter, cut out the biscuits. Put the uncooked biscuits in the greased air fryer basket in a single layer.
7. Bake for 5 minutes. Transfer the cooked biscuits from the air fryer to a platter.
8. Cut the remaining biscuits. Bake the remaining biscuits.
9. Serve warm.

Easy Sausage Pizza

Prep time: 10 minutes | Cook time: 6 minutes | Serves 4

2 tablespoons ketchup
1 pita bread
⅓ cup sausage
½ pound (227 g)

Mozzarella cheese
1 teaspoon garlic powder
1 tablespoon olive oil

1. Preheat the air fryer to 340ºF (171ºC).
2. Spread the ketchup over the pita bread.
3. Top with the sausage and cheese. Sprinkle with the garlic powder and olive oil.
4. Put the pizza in the air fryer basket and bake for 6 minutes.
5. Serve warm.

Mushroom and Squash Toast

Prep time: 10 minutes | Cook time: 10 minutes | Serves 4

1 tablespoon olive oil
1 red bell pepper, cut into strips
2 green onions, sliced
1 cup sliced button or cremini

mushrooms
1 small yellow squash, sliced
2 tablespoons softened butter
4 slices bread
½ cup soft goat cheese

1. Brush the air fryer basket with the olive oil and preheat the air fryer to 350ºF (177ºC).
2. Put the red pepper, green onions, mushrooms, and squash inside the air fryer, give them a stir and air fry for 7 minutes or the vegetables are tender, shaking the basket once throughout the cooking time.
3. Remove the vegetables and set them aside.
4. Spread the butter on the slices of bread and transfer to the air fryer, butter-side up. Brown for 3 minutes.
5. Remove the toast from the air fryer and top with goat cheese and vegetables. Serve warm.

English Pumpkin Egg Bake

Prep time: 10 minutes | Cook time: 10 minutes | Serves 2

2 eggs
½ cup milk
2 cups flour
2 tablespoons cider vinegar
2 teaspoons baking powder
1 tablespoon sugar
1 cup pumpkin purée
1 teaspoon cinnamon powder
1 teaspoon baking soda
1 tablespoon olive oil

1. Preheat the air fryer to 300ºF (149ºC).
2. Crack the eggs into a bowl and beat with a whisk. Combine with the milk, flour, cider vinegar, baking powder, sugar, pumpkin purée, cinnamon powder, and baking soda, mixing well.
3. Grease a baking tray with oil. Add the mixture and transfer into the air fryer. Bake for 10 minutes.
4. Serve warm.

Kale and Potato Nuggets

Prep time: 10 minutes | Cook time: 18 minutes | Serves 4

1 teaspoon extra virgin olive oil
1 clove garlic, minced
4 cups kale, rinsed and chopped
2 cups potatoes,
boiled and mashed
⅛ cup milk
Salt and ground black pepper, to taste
Cooking spray

1. Preheat the air fryer to 390ºF (199ºC).
2. In a skillet over medium heat, sauté the garlic in the olive oil, until it turns golden brown. Sauté with the kale for an additional 3 minutes and remove from the heat.
3. Mix the mashed potatoes, kale and garlic in a bowl. Pour in the milk and sprinkle with salt and pepper.
4. Shape the mixture into nuggets and spritz with cooking spray.
5. Put in the air fryer basket and air fry for 15 minutes, flip the nuggets halfway through cooking to make sure the nuggets fry evenly.
6. Serve immediately.

Posh Orange Rolls

Prep time: 15 minutes | Cook time: 8 minutes | Makes 8 rolls

3 ounces (85 g) low-fat cream cheese
1 tablespoon low-fat sour cream or plain yogurt
2 teaspoons sugar
¼ teaspoon pure vanilla extract
¼ teaspoon orange extract
1 can (8 count)
organic crescent roll dough
¼ cup chopped walnuts
¼ cup dried cranberries
¼ cup shredded, sweetened coconut
Butter-flavored cooking spray

Orange Glaze:

½ cup powdered sugar
1 tablespoon orange juice
¼ teaspoon orange extract
Dash of salt

1. Cut a circular piece of parchment paper slightly smaller than the bottom of the air fryer basket. Set aside.
2. In a small bowl, combine the cream cheese, sour cream or yogurt, sugar, and vanilla and orange extracts. Stir until smooth.
3. Preheat the air fryer to 300ºF (149ºC).
4. Separate crescent roll dough into 8 triangles and divide cream cheese mixture among them. Starting at wide end, spread cheese mixture to within 1 inch of point.
5. Sprinkle nuts and cranberries evenly over cheese mixture.
6. Starting at wide end, roll up triangles, then sprinkle with coconut, pressing in lightly to make it stick. Spray tops of rolls with butter-flavored cooking spray.
7. Put parchment paper in air fryer basket, and place 4 rolls on top, spaced evenly.
8. Air fry for 8 minutes, until rolls are golden brown and cooked through.
9. Repeat steps 7 and 8 to air fry remaining 4 rolls. You should be able to use the same piece of parchment paper twice.
10. In a small bowl, stir together ingredients for glaze and drizzle over warm rolls. Serve warm.

Sourdough Croutons

Prep time: 5 minutes | Cook time: 6 minutes | Makes 4 cups

4 cups cubed sourdough bread, 1-inch cubes
1 tablespoon olive oil
1 teaspoon fresh thyme leaves
¼ teaspoon salt
Freshly ground black pepper, to taste

1. Combine all ingredients in a bowl.
2. Preheat the air fryer to 400ºF (204ºC).
3. Toss the bread cubes into the air fryer and air fry for 6 minutes, shaking the basket once or twice while they cook.
4. Serve warm.

Hearty Cheddar Biscuits

Prep time: 10 minutes | Cook time: 22 minutes | Makes 8 biscuits

2⅓ cups self-rising flour
2 tablespoons sugar
½ cup butter (1 stick), frozen for 15 minutes
½ cup grated Cheddar cheese,
plus more to melt on top
1⅓ cups buttermilk
1 cup all-purpose flour, for shaping
1 tablespoon butter, melted

1. Line a buttered 7-inch metal cake pan with parchment paper or a silicone liner.
2. Combine the flour and sugar in a large mixing bowl. Grate the butter into the flour. Add the grated cheese and stir to coat the cheese and butter with flour. Then add the buttermilk and stir just until you can no longer see streaks of flour. The dough should be quite wet.
3. Spread the all-purpose (not self-rising) flour out on a small cookie sheet. With a spoon, scoop 8 evenly sized balls of dough into the flour, making sure they don't touch each other. With floured hands, coat each dough ball with flour and toss them gently from hand to hand to shake off any excess flour. Put each floured dough ball into the prepared pan, right up next to the other. This will help the biscuits rise, rather than spreading out.
4. Preheat the air fryer to 380ºF (193ºC).
5. Transfer the cake pan to the basket of the air fryer. Let the ends of the aluminum foil sling hang across the cake pan before returning the basket to the air fryer.
6. Air fry for 20 minutes. Check the biscuits twice to make sure they are not getting too brown on top. If they are, re-arrange the aluminum foil strips to cover any brown parts. After 20 minutes, check the biscuits by inserting a toothpick into the center of the biscuits. It should come out clean. If it needs a little more time, continue to air fry for two extra minutes. Brush the tops of the biscuits with some melted butter and sprinkle a little more grated cheese on top if desired. Pop the basket back into the air fryer for another 2 minutes.
7. Remove the cake pan from the air fryer. Let the biscuits cool for just a minute or two and then turn them out onto a plate and pull apart. Serve immediately.

Lush Vegetable Omelet

Prep time: 10 minutes | Cook time: 13 minutes | Serves 2

2 teaspoons canola oil
4 eggs, whisked
3 tablespoons plain milk
1 teaspoon melted butter
1 red bell pepper, seeded and chopped
1 green bell pepper, seeded and chopped
1 white onion, finely chopped
½ cup baby spinach leaves, roughly chopped
½ cup Halloumi cheese, shaved
Kosher salt and freshly ground black pepper, to taste

1. Preheat the air fryer to 350ºF (177ºC).
2. Grease a baking pan with canola oil.
3. Put the remaining ingredients in the baking pan and stir well.
4. Transfer to the air fryer and bake for 13 minutes.
5. Serve warm.

Potatoes Lyonnaise

Prep time: 10 minutes | Cook time: 31 minutes | Serves 4

1 Vidalia onion, sliced
1 teaspoon butter, melted
1 teaspoon brown sugar
2 large russet potatoes (about 1 pound / 454 g in total), sliced ½-inch thick
1 tablespoon vegetable oil
Salt and freshly ground black pepper, to taste

1. Preheat the air fryer to 370ºF (188ºC).
2. Toss the sliced onions, melted butter and brown sugar together in the air fryer basket. Air fry for 8 minutes, shaking the basket occasionally to help the onions cook evenly.
3. While the onions are cooking, bring a saucepan of salted water to a boil on the stovetop. Par-cook the potatoes in boiling water for 3 minutes. Drain the potatoes and pat them dry with a clean kitchen towel.
4. Add the potatoes to the onions in the air fryer basket and drizzle with vegetable oil. Toss to coat the potatoes with the oil and season with salt and freshly ground black pepper.
5. Increase the air fryer temperature to 400ºF (204ºC) and air fry for 20 minutes, tossing the vegetables a few times during the cooking time to help the potatoes brown evenly.
6. Season with salt and freshly ground black pepper and serve warm.

All-in-One Toast

Prep time: 10 minutes | Cook time: 10 minutes | Serves 1

1 strip bacon, diced
1 slice 1-inch thick bread
1 egg
Salt and freshly
ground black pepper, to taste
¼ cup grated Colby cheese

1. Preheat the air fryer to 400ºF (204ºC).
2. Air fry the bacon for 3 minutes, shaking the basket once or twice while it cooks. Remove the bacon to a paper towel lined plate and set aside.
3. Use a sharp paring knife to score a large circle in the middle of the slice of bread, cutting halfway through, but not all the way through to the cutting board. Press down on the circle in the center of the bread slice to create an indentation.
4. Transfer the slice of bread, hole side up, to the air fryer basket. Crack the egg into the center of the bread, and season with salt and pepper.
5. Adjust the air fryer temperature to 380ºF (193ºC) and air fry for 5 minutes. Sprinkle the grated cheese around the edges of the bread, leaving the center of the yolk uncovered, and top with the cooked bacon. Press the cheese and bacon into the bread lightly to help anchor it to the bread and prevent it from blowing around in the air fryer.
6. Air fry for one or two more minutes, just to melt the cheese and finish cooking the egg. Serve immediately.

Quick and Easy Blueberry Muffins

Prep time: 10 minutes | Cook time: 12 minutes | Makes 8 muffins

1⅓ cups flour
½ cup sugar
2 teaspoons baking powder
¼ teaspoon salt
⅓ cup canola oil
1 egg
½ cup milk
⅔ cup blueberries, fresh or frozen and thawed

1. Preheat the air fryer to 330ºF (166ºC).
2. In a medium bowl, stir together flour, sugar, baking powder, and salt.
3. In a separate bowl, combine oil, egg, and milk and mix well.
4. Add egg mixture to dry ingredients and stir just until moistened.
5. Gently stir in the blueberries.
6. Spoon batter evenly into parchment-paper-lined muffin cups.
7. Put 4 muffin cups in air fryer basket and bake for 12 minutes or until tops spring back when touched lightly.
8. Repeat previous step to bake remaining muffins.
9. Serve immediately.

Oat and Chia Porridge

Prep time: 10 minutes | Cook time: 5 minutes | Serves 4

2 tablespoons peanut butter	melted
4 tablespoons honey	4 cups milk
1 tablespoon butter,	2 cups oats
	1 cup chia seeds

1. Preheat the air fryer to 390ºF (199ºC).
2. Put the peanut butter, honey, butter, and milk in a bowl and stir to mix. Add the oats and chia seeds and stir.
3. Transfer the mixture to a bowl and bake in the air fryer for 5 minutes. Give another stir before serving.

Ham and Corn Muffins

Prep time: 10 minutes | Cook time: 6 minutes | Makes 8 muffins

¾ cup yellow cornmeal	2 tablespoons canola oil
¼ cup flour	½ cup milk
1½ teaspoons baking powder	½ cup shredded sharp Cheddar cheese
¼ teaspoon salt	½ cup diced ham
1 egg, beaten	

1. Preheat the air fryer to 390ºF (199ºC).
2. In a medium bowl, stir together the cornmeal, flour, baking powder, and salt.
3. Add the egg, oil, and milk to dry ingredients and mix well.
4. Stir in shredded cheese and diced ham.
5. Divide batter among 8 parchment-paper-lined muffin cups.
6. Put 4 filled muffin cups in air fryer basket and bake for 5 minutes.
7. Reduce temperature to 330ºF (166ºC) and bake for 1 minute or until a toothpick inserted in center of the muffin comes out clean.
8. Repeat steps 6 and 7 to bake remaining muffins.
9. Serve warm.

Cornflakes Toast Sticks

Prep time: 10 minutes | Cook time: 6 minutes | Serves 4

2 eggs	6 slices sandwich bread, each slice cut into 4 strips
½ cup milk	
⅛ teaspoon salt	
½ teaspoon pure vanilla extract	Maple syrup, for dipping
¾ cup crushed cornflakes	Cooking spray

1. Preheat the air fryer to 390ºF (199ºC).
2. In a small bowl, beat together the eggs, milk, salt, and vanilla.
3. Put crushed cornflakes on a plate or in a shallow dish.
4. Dip bread strips in egg mixture, shake off excess, and roll in cornflake crumbs.
5. Spray both sides of bread strips with oil.
6. Put bread strips in air fryer basket in a single layer.
7. Air fry for 6 minutes or until golden brown.
8. Repeat steps 5 and 6 to air fry remaining French toast sticks.
9. Serve with maple syrup.

Pita and Pepperoni Pizza

Prep time: 10 minutes | Cook time: 6 minutes | Serves 1

1 teaspoon olive oil	Mozzarella cheese
1 tablespoon pizza sauce	¼ teaspoon garlic powder
1 pita bread	¼ teaspoon dried oregano
6 pepperoni slices	
¼ cup grated	

1. Preheat the air fryer to 350ºF (177ºC). Grease the air fryer basket with olive oil.
2. Spread the pizza sauce on top of the pita bread. Put the pepperoni slices over the sauce, followed by the Mozzarella cheese.
3. Season with garlic powder and oregano.
4. Put the pita pizza inside the air fryer and place a trivet on top.
5. Bake in the preheated air fryer for 6 minutes and serve.

Tomato and Mozzarella Bruschetta

Prep time: 5 minutes | Cook time: 4 minutes | Serves 1

6 small loaf slices	grated
½ cup tomatoes, finely chopped	1 tablespoon fresh basil, chopped
3 ounces (85 g) Mozzarella cheese,	1 tablespoon olive oil

1. Preheat the air fryer to 350ºF (177ºC).
2. Put the loaf slices inside the air fryer and air fry for about 3 minutes.
3. Add the tomato, Mozzarella, basil, and olive oil on top.
4. Air fry for an additional minute before serving.

Creamy Cinnamon Rolls

Prep time: 10 minutes | Cook time: 9 minutes | Serves 8

1 pound (454 g) frozen bread dough, thawed	¾ cup brown sugar
¼ cup butter, melted	1½ tablespoons ground cinnamon

Cream Cheese Glaze:

4 ounces (113 g) cream cheese, softened	1¼ cups powdered sugar
2 tablespoons butter, softened	½ teaspoon vanilla extract

1. Let the bread dough come to room temperature on the counter. On a lightly floured surface, roll the dough into a 13-inch by 11-inch rectangle. Position the rectangle so the 13-inch side is facing you. Brush the melted butter all over the dough, leaving a 1-inch border uncovered along the edge farthest away from you.
2. Combine the brown sugar and cinnamon in a small bowl. Sprinkle the mixture evenly over the buttered dough, keeping the 1-inch border uncovered. Roll the dough into a log, starting with the edge closest to you. Roll the dough tightly, rolling evenly, and push out any air pockets. When you get to the uncovered edge of the dough, press the dough onto the roll to seal it together.
3. Cut the log into 8 pieces, slicing slowly with a sawing motion so you don't flatten the dough. Turn the slices on their sides and cover with a clean kitchen towel. Let the rolls sit in the warmest part of the kitchen for 1½ to 2 hours to rise.
4. To make the glaze, place the cream cheese and butter in a microwave-safe bowl. Soften the mixture in the microwave for 30 seconds at a time until it is easy to stir. Gradually add the powdered sugar and stir to combine. Add the vanilla extract and whisk until smooth. Set aside.
5. When the rolls have risen, preheat the air fryer to 350ºF (177ºC).
6. Transfer 4 of the rolls to the air fryer basket. Air fry for 5 minutes. Turn the rolls over and air fry for another 4 minutes. Repeat with the remaining 4 rolls.
7. Let the rolls cool for two minutes before glazing. Spread large dollops of cream cheese glaze on top of the warm cinnamon rolls, allowing some glaze to drip down the side of the rolls. Serve warm.

Spinach with Scrambled Eggs

Prep time: 10 minutes | Cook time: 10 minutes | Serves 2

2 tablespoons olive oil	1 teaspoon fresh lemon juice
4 eggs, whisked	½ teaspoon coarse salt
5 ounces (142 g) fresh spinach, chopped	½ teaspoon ground black pepper
1 medium tomato, chopped	½ cup of fresh basil, roughly chopped

1. Grease a baking pan with the oil, tilting it to spread the oil around. Preheat the air fryer to 280ºF (138ºC).
2. Mix the remaining ingredients, apart from the basil leaves, whisking well until everything is completely combined.
3. Bake in the air fryer for 10 minutes.
4. Top with fresh basil leaves before serving.

PB&J

Prep time: 5 minutes | Cook time: 6 minutes | Serves 4

½ cup cornflakes, crushed
¼ cup shredded coconut
8 slices oat nut bread or any whole-grain, oversize bread
6 tablespoons peanut butter
2 medium bananas, cut into ½-inch-thick slices
6 tablespoons pineapple preserves
1 egg, beaten
Cooking spray

1. Preheat the air fryer to 360ºF (182ºC).
2. In a shallow dish, mix the cornflake crumbs and coconut.
3. For each sandwich, spread one bread slice with 1½ tablespoons of peanut butter. Top with banana slices. Spread another bread slice with 1½ tablespoons of preserves. Combine to make a sandwich.
4. Using a pastry brush, brush top of sandwich lightly with beaten egg. Sprinkle with about 1½ tablespoons of crumb coating, pressing it in to make it stick. Spray with cooking spray.
5. Turn sandwich over and repeat to coat and spray the other side.
6. Air frying 2 at a time, place sandwiches in air fryer basket and air fry for 6 minutes or until coating is golden brown and crispy.
7. Cut the cooked sandwiches in half and serve warm.

Simple Cinnamon Toasts

Prep time: 5 minutes | Cook time: 4 minutes | Serves 4

1 tablespoon salted butter
2 teaspoons ground cinnamon
4 tablespoons sugar
½ teaspoon vanilla extract
10 bread slices

1. Preheat the air fryer to 380ºF (193ºC).
2. In a bowl, combine the butter, cinnamon, sugar, and vanilla extract. Spread onto the slices of bread.
3. Put the bread inside the air fryer and bake for 4 minutes or until golden brown.
4. Serve warm.

Bacon and Broccoli Bread Pudding

Prep time: 15 minutes | Cook time: 48 minutes | Serves 2 to 4

½ pound (227 g) thick cut bacon, cut into ¼-inch pieces
3 cups brioche bread, cut into ½-inch cubes
2 tablespoons butter, melted
3 eggs
1 cup milk
½ teaspoon salt
Freshly ground black pepper, to taste
1 cup frozen broccoli florets, thawed and chopped
1½ cups grated Swiss cheese

1. Preheat the air fryer to 400ºF (204ºC).
2. Air fry the bacon for 8 minutes until crispy, shaking the basket a few times to help it air fry evenly. Remove the bacon and set it aside on a paper towel.
3. Air fry the brioche bread cubes for 2 minutes to dry and toast lightly.
4. Butter a cake pan. Combine all the ingredients in a large bowl and toss well. Transfer the mixture to the buttered cake pan, cover with aluminum foil and refrigerate the bread pudding overnight, or for at least 8 hours.
5. Remove the cake pan from the refrigerator an hour before you plan to bake and let it sit on the countertop to come to room temperature.
6. Preheat the air fryer to 330ºF (166ºC). Transfer the covered cake pan to the basket of the air fryer, lowering the pan into the basket. Fold the ends of the aluminum foil over the top of the pan before returning the basket to the air fryer.
7. Air fry for 20 minutes. Remove the foil and air fry for an additional 20 minutes. If the top browns a little too much before the custard has set, simply return the foil to the pan. The bread pudding has cooked through when a skewer inserted into the center comes out clean.
8. Serve warm.

Gold Avocado

Prep time: 5 minutes | Cook time: 6 minutes | Serves 4

2 large avocados, sliced
¼ teaspoon paprika
Salt and ground black pepper, to taste
½ cup flour
2 eggs, beaten
1 cup bread crumbs

1. Preheat the air fryer to 400ºF (204ºC).
2. Sprinkle paprika, salt and pepper on the slices of avocado.
3. Lightly coat the avocados with flour. Dredge them in the eggs, before covering with bread crumbs.
4. Transfer to the air fryer and air fry for 6 minutes.
5. Serve warm.

Potato Bread Rolls

Prep time: 15 minutes | Cook time: 20 minutes | Serves 5

5 large potatoes, boiled and mashed
Salt and ground black pepper, to taste
½ teaspoon mustard seeds
1 tablespoon olive oil
2 small onions, chopped
2 sprigs curry leaves
½ teaspoon turmeric powder
2 green chilis, seeded and chopped
1 bunch coriander, chopped
8 slices bread, brown sides discarded

1. Preheat the air fryer to 400ºF (204ºC).
2. Put the mashed potatoes in a bowl and sprinkle on salt and pepper. Set to one side.
3. Fry the mustard seeds in olive oil over a medium-low heat in a skillet, stirring continuously, until they sputter.
4. Add the onions and cook until they turn translucent. Add the curry leaves and turmeric powder and stir. Cook for a further 2 minutes until fragrant.
5. Remove the pan from the heat and combine with the potatoes. Mix in the green chilies and coriander.
6. Wet the bread slightly and drain of any excess liquid.
7. Spoon a small amount of the potato mixture into the center of the bread and enclose the bread around the filling, sealing it entirely. Continue until the rest of the bread and filling is used up. Brush each bread roll with some oil and transfer to the basket of the air fryer.
8. Air fry for 15 minutes, gently shaking the air fryer basket at the halfway point to ensure each roll is cooked evenly.
9. Serve immediately.

Avocado Quesadillas

Prep time: 10 minutes | Cook time: 11 minutes | Serves 4

4 eggs
2 tablespoons skim milk
Salt and ground black pepper, to taste
Cooking spray
4 flour tortillas
4 tablespoons salsa
2 ounces (57 g) Cheddar cheese, grated
½ small avocado, peeled and thinly sliced

1. Preheat the air fryer to 270ºF (132ºC).
2. Beat together the eggs, milk, salt, and pepper.
3. Spray a baking pan lightly with cooking spray and add egg mixture.
4. Bake for 8 minutes, stirring every 1 to 2 minutes, until eggs are scrambled to the liking. Remove and set aside.
5. Spray one side of each tortilla with cooking spray. Flip over.
6. Divide eggs, salsa, cheese, and avocado among the tortillas, covering only half of each tortilla.
7. Fold each tortilla in half and press down lightly. Increase the temperature of the air fryer to 390ºF (199ºC).
8. Put 2 tortillas in air fryer basket and air fry for 3 minutes or until cheese melts and outside feels slightly crispy. Repeat with remaining two tortillas.
9. Cut each cooked tortilla into halves. Serve warm.

Bacon Eggs on the Go

Prep time: 5 minutes | Cook time: 15 minutes | Serves 1

2 eggs
4 ounces (113 g) bacon, cooked

Salt and ground black pepper, to taste

1. Preheat the air fryer to 400°F (204°C). Put liners in a regular cupcake tin.
2. Crack an egg into each of the cups and add the bacon. Season with some pepper and salt.
3. Bake in the preheated air fryer for 15 minutes, or until the eggs are set.
4. Serve warm.

Banana Bread

Prep time: 10 minutes | Cook time: 22 minutes | Makes 3 loaves

3 ripe bananas, mashed
1 cup sugar
1 large egg
4 tablespoons (½ stick) unsalted

butter, melted
1½ cups all-purpose flour
1 teaspoon baking soda
1 teaspoon salt

1. Coat the insides of 3 mini loaf pans with cooking spray.
2. In a large mixing bowl, mix the bananas and sugar.
3. In a separate large mixing bowl, combine the egg, butter, flour, baking soda, and salt and mix well.
4. Add the banana mixture to the egg and flour mixture. Mix well.
5. Divide the batter evenly among the prepared pans.
6. Preheat the air fryer to 310°F (154°C). Set the mini loaf pans into the air fryer basket.
7. Bake in the preheated air fryer for 22 minutes. Insert a toothpick into the center of each loaf; if it comes out clean, they are done.
8. When the loaves are cooked through, remove the pans from the air fryer basket. Turn out the loaves onto a wire rack to cool.
9. Serve warm.

Spinach Omelet

Prep time: 10 minutes | Cook time: 10 minutes | Serves 1

1 teaspoon olive oil
3 eggs
Salt and ground black pepper, to taste
1 tablespoon ricotta

cheese
¼ cup chopped spinach
1 tablespoon chopped parsley

1. Grease the air fryer basket with olive oil. Preheat the air fryer to 330°F (166°C).
2. In a bowl, beat the eggs with a fork and sprinkle salt and pepper.
3. Add the ricotta, spinach, and parsley and then transfer to the air fryer. Bake for 10 minutes or until the egg is set.
4. Serve warm.

Fast Coffee Donuts

Prep time: 5 minutes | Cook time: 6 minutes | Serves 6

¼ cup sugar
½ teaspoon salt
1 cup flour
1 teaspoon baking powder

¼ cup coffee
1 tablespoon aquafaba
1 tablespoon sunflower oil

1. In a large bowl, combine the sugar, salt, flour, and baking powder.
2. Add the coffee, aquafaba, and sunflower oil and mix until a dough is formed. Leave the dough to rest in and the refrigerator.
3. Preheat the air fryer to 400°F (204°C).
4. Remove the dough from the fridge and divide up, kneading each section into a doughnut.
5. Put the doughnuts inside the air fryer. Air fry for 6 minutes.
6. Serve immediately.

Grit and Ham Fritters

Prep time: 15 minutes | Cook time: 20 minutes | Serves 6 to 8

4 cups water
1 cup quick-cooking grits
¼ teaspoon salt
2 tablespoons butter
2 cups grated Cheddar cheese, divided
1 cup finely diced ham
1 tablespoon chopped chives
Salt and freshly ground black pepper, to taste
1 egg, beaten
2 cups panko bread crumbs
Cooking spray

1. Bring the water to a boil in a saucepan. Whisk in the grits and ¼ teaspoon of salt, and cook for 7 minutes until the grits are soft. Remove the pan from the heat and stir in the butter and 1 cup of the grated Cheddar cheese. Transfer the grits to a bowl and let them cool for 10 to 15 minutes.
2. Stir the ham, chives and the rest of the cheese into the grits and season with salt and pepper to taste. Add the beaten egg and refrigerate the mixture for 30 minutes.
3. Put the panko bread crumbs in a shallow dish. Measure out ¼-cup portions of the grits mixture and shape them into patties. Coat all sides of the patties with the panko bread crumbs, patting them with the hands so the crumbs adhere to the patties. You should have about 16 patties. Spritz both sides of the patties with cooking spray.
4. Preheat the air fryer to 400ºF (204ºC).
5. In batches of 5 or 6, air fry the fritters for 8 minutes. Using a flat spatula, flip the fritters over and air fry for another 4 minutes.
6. Serve hot.

Banana Churros with Oatmeal

Prep time: 15 minutes | Cook time: 15 minutes | Serves 2

For the Churros:
1 large yellow banana, peeled, cut in half lengthwise, then cut in half widthwise
2 tablespoons whole-wheat pastry flour
⅛ teaspoon sea salt
2 teaspoons oil (sunflower or melted coconut)
1 teaspoon water
Cooking spray
1 tablespoon coconut sugar
½ teaspoon cinnamon

For the Oatmeal:
¾ cup rolled oats
1½ cups water

To make the churros
1. Put the 4 banana pieces in a medium-size bowl and add the flour and salt. Stir gently. Add the oil and water. Stir gently until evenly mixed. You may need to press some coating onto the banana pieces.
2. Spray the air fryer basket with the oil spray. Put the banana pieces in the air fryer basket and air fry for 5 minutes. Remove, gently turn over, and air fry for another 5 minutes or until browned.
3. In a medium bowl, add the coconut sugar and cinnamon and stir to combine. When the banana pieces are nicely browned, spray with the oil and place in the cinnamon-sugar bowl. Toss gently with a spatula to coat the banana pieces with the mixture.

To make the oatmeal
1. While the bananas are cooking, make the oatmeal. In a medium pot, bring the oats and water to a boil, then reduce to low heat. Simmer, stirring often, until all the water is absorbed, about 5 minutes. Put the oatmeal into two bowls.
2. Top the oatmeal with the coated banana pieces and serve immediately.

Apple and Walnut Muffins

Prep time: 15 minutes | Cook time: 10 minutes | Makes 8 muffins

1 cup flour
1/3 cup sugar
1 teaspoon baking powder
1/4 teaspoon baking soda
1/4 teaspoon salt
1 teaspoon cinnamon
1/4 teaspoon ginger
1/4 teaspoon nutmeg
1 egg
2 tablespoons pancake syrup, plus 2 teaspoons
2 tablespoons melted butter, plus 2 teaspoons
3/4 cup unsweetened applesauce
1/2 teaspoon vanilla extract
1/4 cup chopped walnuts
1/4 cup diced apple

1. Preheat the air fryer to 330ºF (166ºC).
2. In a large bowl, stir together the flour, sugar, baking powder, baking soda, salt, cinnamon, ginger, and nutmeg.
3. In a small bowl, beat egg until frothy. Add syrup, butter, applesauce, and vanilla and mix well.
4. Pour egg mixture into dry ingredients and stir just until moistened.
5. Gently stir in nuts and diced apple.
6. Divide batter among 8 parchment-paper-lined muffin cups.
7. Put 4 muffin cups in air fryer basket and bake for 10 minutes.
8. Repeat with remaining 4 muffins or until toothpick inserted in center comes out clean.
9. Serve warm.

Soufflé

Prep time: 10 minutes | Cook time: 22 minutes | Serves 4

1/3 cup butter, melted
1/4 cup flour
1 cup milk
1 ounce (28 g) sugar
4 egg yolks
1 teaspoon vanilla extract
6 egg whites
1 teaspoon cream of tartar
Cooking spray

1. In a bowl, mix the butter and flour until a smooth consistency is achieved.
2. Pour the milk into a saucepan over medium-low heat. Add the sugar and allow to dissolve before raising the heat to boil the milk.
3. Pour in the flour and butter mixture and stir rigorously for 7 minutes to eliminate any lumps. Make sure the mixture thickens. Take off the heat and allow to cool for 15 minutes.
4. Preheat the air fryer to 320ºF (160ºC). Spritz 6 soufflé dishes with cooking spray.
5. Put the egg yolks and vanilla extract in a separate bowl and beat them together with a fork. Pour in the milk and combine well to incorporate everything.
6. In a smaller bowl mix the egg whites and cream of tartar with a fork. Fold into the egg yolks-milk mixture before adding in the flour mixture. Transfer equal amounts to the 6 soufflé dishes.
7. Put the dishes in the air fryer and bake for 15 minutes.
8. Serve warm.

Nut and Seed Muffins

Prep time: 15 minutes | Cook time: 10 minutes | Makes 8 muffins

½ cup whole-wheat flour, plus 2 tablespoons
¼ cup oat bran
2 tablespoons flaxseed meal
¼ cup brown sugar
½ teaspoon baking soda
½ teaspoon baking powder
¼ teaspoon salt
½ teaspoon cinnamon
½ cup buttermilk
2 tablespoons melted butter
1 egg
½ teaspoon pure vanilla extract
½ cup grated carrots
¼ cup chopped pecans
¼ cup chopped walnuts
1 tablespoon pumpkin seeds
1 tablespoon sunflower seeds
Cooking spray

Special Equipment:
16 foil muffin cups, paper liners removed

1. Preheat the air fryer to 330ºF (166ºC).
2. In a large bowl, stir together the flour, bran, flaxseed meal, sugar, baking soda, baking powder, salt, and cinnamon.
3. In a medium bowl, beat together the buttermilk, butter, egg, and vanilla. Pour into flour mixture and stir just until dry ingredients moisten. Do not beat.
4. Gently stir in carrots, nuts, and seeds.
5. Double up the foil cups so you have 8 total and spritz with cooking spray.
6. Put 4 foil cups in air fryer basket and divide half the batter among them.
7. Bake for 10 minutes or until a toothpick inserted in center comes out clean.
8. Repeat step 7 to bake remaining 4 muffins.
9. Serve warm.

Pretzels

Prep time: 10 minutes | Cook time: 6 minutes | Makes 24 prezels

2 teaspoons yeast
1 cup water, warm
1 teaspoon sugar
1 teaspoon salt
2½ cups all-purpose flour
2 tablespoons
butter, melted, plus more as needed
1 cup boiling water
1 tablespoon baking soda
Coarse sea salt, to taste

1. Combine the yeast and water in a small bowl. Combine the sugar, salt and flour in the bowl of a stand mixer. With the mixer running and using the dough hook, drizzle in the yeast mixture and melted butter and knead dough until smooth and elastic, about 10 minutes. Shape into a ball and let the dough rise for 1 hour.
2. Punch the dough down to release any air and divide the dough into 24 portions.
3. Roll each portion into a skinny rope using both hands on the counter and rolling from the center to the ends of the rope. Spin the rope into a pretzel shape (or tie the rope into a knot) and place the tied pretzels on a parchment lined baking sheet.
4. Preheat the air fryer to 350ºF (177ºC).
5. Combine the boiling water and baking soda in a shallow bowl and whisk to dissolve. Let the water cool so you can put the hands in it. Working in batches, dip the pretzels (top side down) into the baking soda mixture and let them soak for 30 seconds to a minute. Then remove the pretzels carefully and return them (top side up) to the baking sheet. Sprinkle the coarse salt on the top.
6. Air fry in batches for 3 minutes per side. When the pretzels are finished, brush them generously with the melted butter and enjoy them warm.

Ranch Risotto

Prep + Cook Time: 40 minutes | Servings: 2

Ingredients

1 onion, diced
2 cups chicken stock, boiling
½ cup parmesan OR cheddar cheese, grated
1 clove garlic, minced
¾ cup Arborio rice
1 tbsp. olive oil
1 tbsp. unsalted butter

Instructions

1. Set the Air Fryer at 390°F for 5 minutes to heat up.
2. With oil, grease a round baking tin, small enough to fit inside the fryer, and stir in the garlic, butter, and onion.
3. Transfer the tin to the Air Fryer and allow to cook for 4 minutes. Add in the rice and cook for a further 4 minutes, giving it a stir three times throughout the cooking time.
4. Turn the fryer down to 320°F and add in the chicken stock, before gently mixing it. Leave to cook for 22 minutes with the fryer uncovered. Before serving, throw in the cheese and give it one more stir. Enjoy!

Coffee Donuts

Prep + Cook Time: 20 minutes | Servings: 6

Ingredients

1 cup flour
¼ cup sugar
½ tsp. salt
1 tsp. baking powder
1 tbsp. aquafaba
1 tbsp. sunflower oil
¼ cup coffee

Instructions

1. In a large bowl, combine the sugar, salt, flour, and baking powder.
2. Add in the coffee, aquafaba, and sunflower oil and mix until a dough is formed. Leave the dough to rest in and the refrigerator.
3. Set your Air Fryer at 400°F to heat up.
4. Remove the dough from the fridge and divide up, kneading each section into a doughnut.
5. Put the doughnuts inside the Air Fryer, ensuring not to overlap any. Fry for 6 minutes. Do not shake the basket, to make sure the doughnuts hold their shape.

Taco Wraps

Prep + Cook Time: 30 minutes | Servings: 4

Ingredients

1 tbsp. water
4 pc commercial vegan nuggets, chopped
1 small yellow onion, diced
1 small red bell pepper, chopped
2 cobs grilled corn kernels
4 large corn tortillas
Mixed greens for garnish

Instructions

1. Pre-heat your Air Fryer at 400°F.
2. Over a medium heat, water-sauté the nuggets with the onions, corn kernels and bell peppers in a skillet, then remove from the heat.
3. Fill the tortillas with the nuggets and vegetables and fold them up. Transfer to the inside of the fryer and cook for 15 minutes. Once crispy, serve immediately, garnished with the mixed greens.

Bistro Wedges

Prep + Cook Time: 20 minutes | Servings: 4

Ingredients

1 lb. fingerling potatoes, cut into wedges
1 tsp. extra virgin olive oil
½ tsp. garlic powder
Salt and pepper to taste
½ cup raw cashews, soaked in water overnight
½ tsp. ground turmeric
½ tsp. paprika
1 tbsp. nutritional yeast
1 tsp. fresh lemon juice
2 tbsp. to ¼ cup water

Instructions

1. Pre-heat your Air Fryer at 400°F.
2. In a bowl, toss together the potato wedges, olive oil, garlic powder, and salt and pepper, making sure to coat the potatoes well.
3. Transfer the potatoes to the basket of your fryer and fry for 10 minutes.
4. In the meantime, prepare the cheese sauce. Pulse the cashews, turmeric, paprika, nutritional yeast, lemon juice, and water together in a food processor. Add more water to achieve your desired consistency.
5. When the potatoes are finished cooking, move them to a bowl that is small enough to fit inside the fryer and add the cheese sauce on top. Cook for an additional 3 minutes.

Spinach Balls

Prep + Cook Time: 20 minutes | Servings: 4

Ingredients
1 carrot, peeled and grated
1 package fresh spinach, blanched and chopped
½ onion, chopped
1 egg, beaten
½ tsp. garlic powder
1 tsp. garlic, minced
1 tsp. salt
½ tsp. black pepper
1 tbsp. nutritional yeast
1 tbsp. flour
2 slices bread, toasted

Instructions
1. In a food processor, pulse the toasted bread to form breadcrumbs. Transfer into a shallow dish or bowl.
2. In a bowl, mix together all the other ingredients.
3. Use your hands to shape the mixture into small-sized balls. Roll the balls in the breadcrumbs, ensuring to cover them well.
4. Put in the Air Fryer and cook at 390°F for 10 minutes.

Cheese & Chicken Sandwich

Prep + Cook Time: 15 minutes | Servings: 1

Ingredients
⅓ cup chicken, cooked and shredded
2 mozzarella slices
1 hamburger bun
¼ cup cabbage, shredded
1 tsp. mayonnaise
2 tsp. butter
1 tsp. olive oil
½ tsp. balsamic vinegar
1/4 tsp. smoked paprika
¼ tsp. black pepper
¼ tsp. garlic powder
Pinch of salt

Instructions
1. Pre-heat your Air Fryer at 370°F.
2. Apply some butter to the outside of the hamburger bun with a brush.
3. In a bowl, coat the chicken with the garlic powder, salt, pepper, and paprika.
4. In a separate bowl, stir together the mayonnaise, olive oil, cabbage, and balsamic vinegar to make coleslaw.
5. Slice the bun in two. Start building the sandwich, starting with the chicken, followed by the mozzarella, the coleslaw, and finally the top bun.
6. Transfer the sandwich to the fryer and cook for 5 – 7 minutes.

Bacon & Horseradish Cream

Prep + Cook Time: 1 hour 40 minutes | Servings: 4

Ingredients
½ lb. thick cut bacon, diced
2 tbsp. butter
2 shallots, sliced
½ cup milk
1 ½ lb. Brussels sprouts, halved
2 tbsp. flour
1 cup heavy cream
2 tbsp. prepared horseradish
½ tbsp. fresh thyme leaves
1/8 tsp. ground nutmeg
1 tbsp. olive oil
½ tsp. sea salt
Ground black pepper to taste
½ cup water

Instructions
1. Pre-heat your Air Fryer at 400°F.
2. Coat the Brussels sprouts with olive oil and sprinkle some salt and pepper on top. Transfer to the fryer and cook for a half hour. At the halfway point, give them a good stir, then take them out of the fryer and set to the side.
3. Put the bacon in the basket of the fryer and pour the water into the drawer underneath to catch the fat. Cook for 10 minutes, stirring 2 or 3 times throughout the cooking time.
4. When 10 minutes are up, add in the shallots. Cook for a further 10 – 15 minutes, making sure the shallots soften up and the bacon turns brown. Add some more pepper and remove. Leave to drain on some paper towels.
5. Melt the butter over the stove or in the microwave, before adding in the flour and mixing with a whisk. Slowly add in the heavy cream and milk, and continue to whisk for another 3 – 5 minutes, making sure the mixture thickens.
6. Add the horseradish, thyme, salt, and nutmeg and stirring well once more.
7. Take a 9" x 13" baking dish and grease it with oil. Pre-heat your fryer to 350°F.
8. Put the Brussels sprouts in the baking dish and spread them across the base. Pour over the cream sauce and then top with a layer of bacon and shallots.
9. Cook in the fryer for a half hour and enjoy.

Vegetable Toast

Prep + Cook Time: 25 minutes | Servings: 4

Ingredients
4 slices bread
1 red bell pepper, cut into strips
1 cup sliced button or cremini mushrooms
1 small yellow squash, sliced
2 green onions, sliced
1 tbsp. olive oil
2 tbsp. softened butter
½ cup soft goat cheese

Instructions
1. Drizzle the Air Fryer with the olive oil and pre-heat to 350°F.
2. Put the red pepper, green onions, mushrooms, and squash inside the fryer, give them a stir and cook for 7 minutes, shaking the basket once throughout the cooking time. Ensure the vegetables become tender.
3. Remove the vegetables and set them aside.
4. Spread some butter on the slices of bread and transfer to the Air Fryer, butter side-up. Brown for 2 to 4 minutes.
5. Remove the toast from the fryer and top with goat cheese and vegetables. Serve warm.

Cinnamon Toasts

Prep + Cook Time: 15 minutes | Servings: 4

Ingredients
10 bread slices
1 pack salted butter
4 tbsp. sugar
2 tsp. ground cinnamon
½ tsp. vanilla extract

Instructions
1. In a bowl, combine the butter, cinnamon, sugar, and vanilla extract. Spread onto the slices of bread.
2. Set your Air Fryer to 380°F. When warmed up, put the bread inside the fryer and cook for 4 – 5 minutes.

Toasted Cheese

Prep + Cook Time: 20 minutes | Servings: 2

Ingredients
2 slices bread
4 oz cheese, grated
Small amount of butter

Instructions
1. Grill the bread in the toaster.
2. Butter the toast and top with the grated cheese.
3. Set your Air Fryer to 350°F and allow to warm.
4. Put the toast slices inside the fryer and cook for 4 - 6 minutes.
5. Serve and enjoy!

Peanut Butter Bread

Prep + Cook Time: 15 minutes | Servings: 3

Ingredients
1 tbsp. oil
2 tbsp. peanut butter
4 slices bread
1 banana, sliced

Instructions
1. Spread the peanut butter on top of each slice of bread, then arrange the banana slices on top. Sandwich two slices together, then the other two.
Oil the inside of the Air Fryer and cook the bread for 5 minutes at 300°F.

English Builder's Breakfast

Prep + Cook Time: 35 minutes | Servings: 2

Ingredients
1 cup potatoes, sliced and diced
2 cups beans in tomato sauce
2 eggs
1 tbsp. olive oil
1 sausage
Salt to taste

Instructions
1. Set your Air Fryer at 390°F and allow to warm.
2. Break the eggs onto an fryer-safe dish and sprinkle on some salt.
3. Lay the beans on the dish, next to the eggs.
4. In a bowl small enough to fit inside your fryer, coat the potatoes with the olive oil. Sprinkle on the salt, as desired.
5. Transfer the bowl of potato slices to the fryer and cook for 10 minutes.
6. Swap out the bowl of potatoes for the dish containing the eggs and beans. Leave to cook for another 10 minutes. Cover the potatoes with parchment paper.
7. Slice up the sausage and throw the slices in on top of the beans and eggs. Resume cooking for another 5 minutes. Serve with the potatoes, as well as toast and coffee if desired.

Avocado Eggs

Prep + Cook Time: 15 minutes | Servings: 4

Ingredients
2 large avocados, sliced
1 cup breadcrumbs
½ cup flour 2 eggs, beaten
¼ tsp. paprika
Salt and pepper to taste

Instructions
1.Pre-heat your Air Fryer at 400°F for 5 minutes.
2.Sprinkle some salt and pepper on the slices of avocado. Optionally, you can enhance the flavor with a half-tsp. of dried oregano.
3.Lightly coat the avocados with flour. Dredge them in the eggs, before covering with breadcrumbs. Transfer to the fryer and cook for 6 minutes.

Avocado Tempura

Prep + Cook Time: 20 minutes | Servings: 4

Ingredients
½ cup breadcrumbs
½ tsp. salt
1 Haas avocado, pitted, peeled and sliced
Liquid from 1 can white beans or aquafaba

Instructions
1.Set your Air Fryer to 350°F and allow to warm.
2.Mix the breadcrumbs and salt in a shallow bowl until well-incorporated.
3.Dip the avocado slices in the bean/aquafaba juice, then into the breadcrumbs. Put the avocados in the fryer, taking care not to overlap any slices, and fry for 10 minutes, giving the basket a good shake at the halfway point.

English Egg Breakfast

Prep + Cook Time: 25 minutes | Servings: 2

Ingredients
2 cups flour
1 cup pumpkin puree
1 tbsp. oil
2 tbsp. vinegar
2 tsp baking powder
½ cup milk
2 eggs
1 tsp. baking soda
1 tbsp. sugar
1 tsp. cinnamon powder

Instructions
1.Set your Air Fryer at 300°F to pre-heat.
2.Crack the eggs into a bowl and beat with a whisk. Combine with the milk, flour, baking powder, sugar, pumpkin purée, cinnamon powder, and baking soda, mixing well and adding more milk if necessary.
3.Grease the baking tray with oil. Add in the mixture and transfer into the Air Fryer. Cook for 10 minutes.

Pancakes

Prep + Cook Time: 15 minutes | Servings: 2

Ingredients
2 tbsp coconut oil
1 tsp maple extract
2 tbsp cashew milk
2 eggs
2/3 oz/20g pork rinds

Instructions
1.Grind up the pork rinds until fine and mix with the rest of the ingredients, except the oil.
2.Add the oil to a skillet. Add a quarter-cup of the batter and fry until golden on each side. Continue adding the remaining batter.

Breakfast Sandwich

Prep + Cook Time: 10 minutes | Servings: 1

Ingredients
2 oz/60g cheddar cheese
1/6 oz/30g smoked ham
2 tbsp butter
4 eggs

Instructions
1.Fry all the eggs and sprinkle the pepper and salt on them.
2.Place an egg down as the sandwich base. Top with the ham and cheese and a drop or two of Tabasco.
3.Place the other egg on top and enjoy.

Egg Muffins

Prep + Cook Time: 30 minutes | Servings: 1

Ingredients
1 tbsp green pesto
oz/75g shredded cheese
oz/150g cooked bacon
1 scallion, chopped
eggs

Instructions
1.You should set your fryer to 350°F/175°C.
2.Place liners in a regular cupcake tin. This will help with easy removal and storage.
3.Beat the eggs with pepper, salt, and the pesto. Mix in the cheese.
4.Pour the eggs into the cupcake tin and top with the bacon and scallion.
5.Cook for 15-20 minutes, or until the egg is set.

Bacon & Eggs

Prep + Cook Time: 5 minutes | Servings: 1

Ingredients
Parsley
Cherry tomatoes
1/3 oz/150g bacon
eggs

Instructions
1. Fry up the bacon and put it to the side.
2. Scramble the eggs in the bacon grease, with some pepper and salt. If you want, scramble in some cherry tomatoes. Sprinkle with some parsley and enjoy.

Eggs on the Go

Prep + Cook Time: 10 minutes | Servings: 1

Ingredients
oz/110g bacon, cooked
Pepper
Salt
eggs

Instructions
1. You should set your fryer to 400°F/200°C.
2. Place liners in a regular cupcake tin. This will help with easy removal and storage.
3. Crack an egg into each of the cups and sprinkle some bacon onto each of them. Season with some pepper and salt.
4. Bake for 15 minutes, or until the eggs are set.

Cream Cheese Pancakes

Prep + Cook Time: 10 minutes | Servings: 1

Ingredients
2 oz cream cheese
2 eggs
½ tsp cinnamon
1 tbsp coconut flour
½ to 1 packet of Sugar

Instructions
1. Mix together all the ingredients until smooth.
2. Heat up a non-stick pan or skillet with butter or coconut oil on medium-high.
3. Make them as you would normal pancakes.
4. Cook it on one side and then flip to cook the other side!
5. Top with some butter and/or sugar.

Breakfast Mix

Prep + Cook Time: 15 minutes | Servings: 1

Ingredients
tbsp coconut flakes, unsweetened
tbsp hemp seeds
tbsp flaxseed, ground
2 tbsp sesame, ground
2 tbsp cocoa, dark, unsweetened

Instructions
1. Grind the flaxseed and the sesame.
2. Make sure you only grind the sesame seeds for a very short period.
3. Mix all ingredients in a jar and shake it well.
4. Keep refrigerated until ready to eat.
5. Serve softened with black coffee or even with still water and add coconut oil if you want to increase the fat content. It also blends well with cream or with mascarpone cheese.

Breakfast Muffins

Prep + Cook Time: 30 minutes | Servings: 1

Ingredients
1 medium egg
¼ cup heavy cream
1 slice cooked bacon (cured, pan-fried, cooked)
1 oz cheddar cheese
Salt and black pepper (to taste)

Instructions
1. Preheat your fryer to 350°F/175°C.
2. In a bowl, mix the eggs with the cream, salt and pepper.
3. Spread into muffin tins and fill the cups half full.
4. Place 1 slice of bacon into each muffin hole and half ounce of cheese on top of each muffin.
5. Bake for around 15-20 minutes or until slightly browned.
6. Add another ½ oz of cheese onto each muffin and broil until the cheese is slightly browned. Serve!

Spinach Eggs and Cheese

Prep + Cook Time: 40 minutes | Servings: 2

Ingredients
3 whole eggs
3 oz cottage cheese
3-4 oz chopped spinach
¼ cup parmesan cheese
¼ cup of milk

Instructions
1. Preheat your fryer to 375°F/190°C.
2. In a large bowl, whisk the eggs, cottage cheese, the parmesan and the milk.
3. Mix in the spinach.
4. Transfer to a small, greased, fryer dish.
5. Sprinkle the cheese on top.
6. Bake for 25-30 minutes.
7. Let cool for 5 minutes and serve.

Fried Eggs

Prep + Cook Time: 7 minutes | Servings: 2

Ingredients
2 eggs
3 slices bacon

Instructions
1. Heat some oil in a deep fryer at 375°F/190°C.
2. Fry the bacon.
3. In a small bowl, add the 2 eggs.
4. Quickly add the eggs into the center of the fryer.
5. Using two spatulas, form the egg into a ball while frying.
6. Fry for 2-3 minutes, until it stops bubbling.
7. Place on a paper towel and allow to drain.
8. Enjoy!

Potato & Kale Nuggets

Prep + Cook Time: 25 minutes | Servings: 4

Ingredients
1 tsp. extra virgin olive oil
1 clove of garlic, minced
4 cups kale, rinsed and chopped
2 cups potatoes, boiled and mashed
1/8 cup milk
Salt and pepper to taste
Vegetable oil

Instructions
1. Pre-heat your Air Fryer at 390°F.
2. In a skillet over medium heat, fry the garlic in the olive oil, until it turns golden brown. Cook with the kale for an additional 3 minutes and remove from the heat.
3. Mix the mashed potatoes, kale and garlic in a bowl. Throw in the milk and sprinkle with some salt and pepper as desired.
4. Shape the mixture into nuggets and spritz each one with a little vegetable oil. Put in the basket of your fryer and leave to cook for 15 minutes, shaking the basket halfway through cooking to make sure the nuggets fry evenly.

Bread Rolls

Prep + Cook Time: 30 minutes | Servings: 5

Ingredients
5 large potatoes, boiled and mashed
Salt and pepper to taste
1 tbsp. olive oil
½ tsp. mustard seeds
2 small onions, chopped
½ tsp. turmeric
2 sprigs curry leaves
8 slices of bread, brown sides discarded
2 green chilis, seeded and chopped
1 bunch coriander, chopped

Instructions
1. Pre-heat your Air Fryer at 400°F.
2. Put the mashed potatoes in a bowl and sprinkle on salt and pepper. Set to one side.
3. Fry the mustard seeds in a little olive oil over a medium-low heat, stirring continuously, until they sputter.
4. Add in the onions and cook until they turn translucent. Add the curry leaves and turmeric powder and stir. Cook for a further 2 minutes until fragrant.
5. Remove the pan from the heat and combine the contents with the potatoes. Remove from heat and add to the potatoes. Mix in the green chilies and coriander.
6. Wet the bread slightly and drain of any excess liquid.
7. Spoon a small amount of the potato mixture into the center of the bread and enclose the bread around the filling, sealing it entirely. Continue until the rest of the bread and filling is used up. Brush each bread roll with some oil and transfer to the basket of your fryer.
8. Cook for 15 minutes, gently shaking the fryer basket at the halfway point to ensure each roll is cooked evenly.

Veg Frittata

Prep + Cook Time: 35 minutes | Servings: 2

Ingredients
¼ cup milk
1 zucchini
½ bunch asparagus
½ cup mushrooms
½ cup spinach or baby spinach
½ cup red onion, sliced
4 eggs
½ tbsp. olive oil
5 tbsp. feta cheese, crumbled
4 tbsp. cheddar, grated
¼ bunch chives, minced
Sea salt and pepper to taste

Instructions
1. In a bowl, mix together the eggs, milk, salt and pepper.
2. Cut up the zucchini, asparagus, mushrooms and red onion into slices. Shred the spinach using your hands.
3. Over a medium heat, stir-fry the vegetables for 5 – 7 minutes with the olive oil in a non-stick pan.
4. Place some parchment paper in the base of a baking tin. Pour in the vegetables, followed by the egg mixture. Top with the feta and grated cheddar.
5. Set the Air Fryer at 320°F and allow to warm for five minutes.
6. Transfer the baking tin to the fryer and allow to cook for 15 minutes. Take care when removing the frittata from the Air Fryer and leave to cool for 5 minutes.
7. Top with the minced chives and serve.

Maple Cinnamon Buns

Prep + Cook Time: 1 hour 55 minutes | Servings: 9

Ingredients
3/4 cup unsweetened milk
4 tbsp. maple syrup
1 ½ tbsp. active yeast
1 tbsp. ground flaxseed
1 tbsp. coconut oil, melted
1 cup flour
1 ½ cup flour
2 tsp. cinnamon powder
½ cup pecan nuts, toasted
2 ripe bananas, sliced
4 Medjool dates, pitted
¼ cup sugar

Instructions
1. Over a low heat, warm the milk until it is tepid. Combine with the yeast and maple syrup, waiting 5 – 10 minutes to allow the yeast to activate.
2. In the meantime, put 3 tbsp. of water and the flaxseed in a bowl and stir together. This is your egg substitute. Let the flaxseed absorb the water for about 2 minutes.
3. Pour the coconut oil into the bowl, then combine the flaxseed mixture with the yeast mixture.
4. In a separate bowl, mix together one tbsp. of the cinnamon powder and the white and flour. Add the yeast-flaxseed mixture and mix to create a dough.
5. Dust a flat surface with flour. On this surface, knead the dough with your hands for a minimum of 10 minutes.
6. Grease a large bowl and transfer the dough inside. Cover with a kitchen towel or saran wrap. Let sit in a warm, dark place for an hour so that the dough may rise.
7. In the meantime, prepare the filling. Mix the banana slices, dates, and pecans together before throwing in a tbsp. of cinnamon powder.
8. Set the Air Fryer to 390°F and allow to warm. On your floured surface, flatten the dough with a rolling pin, making it thin. Spoon the pecan mixture onto the dough and spread out evenly.
9. Roll up the dough and then slice it in nine. Transfer the slices to a dish small enough to fit in the fryer, set the dish inside, and cook for 30 minutes.
10. Top with a thin layer of sugar before serving.

Taj Tofu

Prep + Cook Time: 40 minutes | Servings: 4

Ingredients
1 block firm tofu, pressed and cut into 1-inch thick cubes
2 tbsp. soy sauce
2 tsp. sesame seeds, toasted
1 tsp. rice vinegar
1 tbsp. cornstarch

Instructions
1. Set your Air Fryer at 400°F to warm.
2. Add the tofu, soy sauce, sesame seeds and rice vinegar in a bowl together and mix well to coat the tofu cubes. Then cover the tofu in cornstarch and put it in the basket of your fryer.
3. Cook for 25 minutes, giving the basket a shake at five-minute intervals to ensure the tofu cooks evenly.

Rice Paper Bacon

Prep + Cook Time: 30 minutes | Servings: 4

Ingredients
3 tbsp. soy sauce or tamari
2 tbsp. cashew butter
2 tbsp. liquid smoke
2 tbsp. water
4 pc white rice paper, cut into 1-inch thick strips

Instructions
1. Pre-heat your Air Fryer at 350°F.
2. Mix together the soy sauce/tamari, liquid smoke, water, and cashew butter in a large bowl.
3. Take the strips of rice paper and soak them for 5 minutes. Arrange in one layer in the bottom of your fryer.
4. Cook for 15 minutes, ensuring they become crispy, before serving with some vegetables.

Posh Soufflé

Prep + Cook Time: 25 minutes | Servings: 4

Ingredients
¼ cup flour
⅓ cup butter
1 cup milk
4 egg yolks
1 tsp. vanilla extract
6 egg whites
1 oz. sugar
1 tsp. cream of tartar

Instructions
1. Set your Air Fryer at 320°F and allow to warm.
2. In a bowl, mix together the butter and flour until a smooth consistency is achieved.
3. Pour the milk into a saucepan over a low-to-medium heat. Add in the and allow to dissolve before raising the heat to boil the milk.
4. Pour in the flour and butter mixture and stir rigorously for 7 minutes to eliminate any lumps. Make sure the mixture thickens. Take off the heat and allow to cool for 15 minutes.
5. Spritz 6 soufflé dishes with oil spray.
6. Place the egg yolks and vanilla extract in a separate bowl and beat them together with a fork. Pour in the milk and combine well to incorporate everything.

7. In a smaller bowl mix together the egg whites and cream of tartar with a fork. Fold into the egg yolks-milk mixture before adding in the flour mixture. Transfer equal amounts to the 6 soufflé dishes.
8. Put the dishes in the fryer and cook for 15 minutes.

Egg Muffin Sandwich

Prep + Cook Time: 15 minutes | Servings: 1

Ingredients
1 egg
2 slices bacon
1 English muffin

Instructions
1. Pre-heat your Air Fryer at 395°F
2. Take a ramekin and spritz it with cooking spray. Break an egg into the ramekin before transferring it to the basket of your fryer, along with the English muffin and bacon slices, keeping each component separate.
3. Allow to cook for 6 minutes. After removing from the fryer, allow to cool for around two minutes. Halve the muffin.
4. Create your sandwich by arranging the egg and bacon slices on the base and topping with the other half of the muffin.

Pea Delight

Prep + Cook Time: 25 minutes | Servings: 2 – 4

Ingredients
1 cup flour
1 tsp. baking powder
3 eggs
1 cup coconut milk
1 cup cream cheese
3 tbsp. pea protein
½ cup chicken/turkey strips
1 pinch sea salt
1 cup mozzarella cheese

Instructions
1. Set your Air Fryer at 390°F and allow to warm.
2. In a large bowl, mix all ingredients together using a large wooden spoon.
3. Spoon equal amounts of the mixture into muffin cups and allow to cook for 15 minutes.

Choco Bars

Prep + Cook Time: 30 minutes | Servings: 8

Ingredients

2 cups old-fashioned oats
½ cup quinoa, cooked
½ cup chia seeds
½ cup s, sliced
½ cup dried cherries, chopped
½ cup dark chocolate, chopped
¾ cup butter
⅓ cup honey
2 tbsp. coconut oil
¼ tsp. salt
½ cup prunes, pureed

Instructions

1. Pre-heat your Air Fryer at 375°F.
2. Put the oats, quinoa, s, cherries, chia seeds, and chocolate in a bowl and mix well.
3. Heat the butter, honey, and coconut oil in a saucepan, gently stirring together. Pour this over the oats mixture.
4. Mix in the salt and pureed prunes and combine well.
5. Transfer this to a baking dish small enough to fit inside the fryer and cook for 15 minutes. Remove from the fryer and allow to cool completely. Cut into bars and enjoy.

French Toast

Prep + Cook Time: 25 minutes | Servings: 2

Ingredients

4 slices bread of your choosing
2 tbsp. soft butter
2 eggs, lightly beaten
Pinch of salt
Pinch of cinnamon
Pinch of ground nutmeg
Pinch of ground cloves
Nonstick cooking spray
Sugar for serving

Instructions

1. In a shallow bowl, mix together the salt, spices and eggs.
2. Butter each side of the slices of bread and slice into strips. You may also use cookie cutters for this step.
3. Set your Air Fryer to 350°F and allow to warm up briefly.
4. Dredge each strip of bread in the egg and transfer to the fryer. Cook for two minutes, ensuring the toast turns golden brown.
5. At this point, spritz the tops of the bread strips with cooking spray, flip, and cook for another 4 minutes on the other side. Top with a light dusting of sugar before serving.

Cheddar & Bacon Quiche

Prep + Cook Time: 30 minutes | Servings: 4

Ingredients

3 tbsp. Greek yogurt
½ cup grated cheddar cheese
3 oz. chopped bacon
4 eggs, beaten
¼ tsp. garlic powder
Pinch of black pepper
1 shortcrust pastry
¼ tsp. onion powder
¼ tsp. sea salt
Some flour for sprinkling

Instructions

1. Pre-heat your Air Fryer at 330°F.
2. Take 8 ramekins and grease with a little oil. Coat with a sprinkling of flour, tapping to remove any excess.
3. Cut the shortcrust pastry in 8 and place each piece at the bottom of each ramekin.
4. Put all of the other ingredients in a bowl and combine well. Spoon equal amounts of the filling into each piece of pastry.
5. Cook the ramekins in the Air Fryer for 20 minutes.

Chorizo Risotto

Prep + Cook Time: 1 hour 20 minutes | Servings: 4

Ingredients

¼ cup milk
½ cup flour
4 oz. breadcrumbs
4 oz. chorizo, finely sliced
1 serving mushroom risotto rice
1 egg
Sea salt to taste

Instructions

1. In a bowl, combine the mushroom risotto rice with the risotto and salt before refrigerating to cool.
2. Set your Air Fryer at 390°F and leave to warm for 5 minutes.
3. Use your hands to form 2 tablespoonfuls of risotto into a rice ball. Repeat until you have used up all the risotto. Roll each ball in the flour.
4. Crack the egg into a bowl and mix with the milk using a whisk. Coat each rice ball in the egg-milk mixture, and then in breadcrumbs.
5. Space the rice balls out in the baking dish of the Air Fryer. Bake for 20 minutes, ensuring they develop a crispy golden-brown crust.
6. Serve warm with a side of fresh vegetables and salad if desired.

Choco Bread

Prep + Cook Time: 30 minutes | Servings: 12

Ingredients
1 tbsp. flax egg [1 tbsp. flax meal + 3 tbsp. water]
1 cup zucchini, shredded and squeezed
½ cup sunflower oil
½ cup maple syrup
1 tsp. vanilla extract
1 tsp. apple cider vinegar
½ cup milk
1 cup flour
1 tsp. baking soda
½ cup unsweetened cocoa powder
¼ tsp. salt
⅓ cup chocolate chips

Instructions
1. Pre-heat your Air Fryer to 350°F.
2. Take a baking dish small enough to fit inside the fryer and line it with parchment paper.
3. Mix together the flax meal, zucchini, sunflower oil, maple, vanilla, apple cider vinegar and milk in a bowl.
4. Incorporate the flour, cocoa powder, salt and baking soda, stirring all the time to combine everything well.
5. Finally, throw in the chocolate chips.
6. Transfer the batter to the baking dish and cook in the fryer for 15 minutes. Make sure to test with a toothpick before serving by sticking it in the center. The bread is ready when the toothpick comes out clean.

Red Rolls

Prep + Cook Time: 45 minutes | Servings: 6

Ingredients
7 cups minced meat
1 small onion, diced
1 packet spring roll sheets
2 oz. Asian noodles
3 cloves garlic, crushed
1 cup mixed vegetables
1 tbsp. sesame oil
2 tbsp. water
1 tsp. soy sauce

Instructions
1. Cook the noodles in hot water until they turn soft. Drain and cut to your desired length.
2. Grease the wok with sesame oil. Put it over a medium-high heat and fry the minced meat, mixed vegetables, garlic, and onion, stirring regularly to ensure the minced meat cooks through. The cooking time will vary depending on the pan you are using – allow 3-5 minutes if using a wok, and 7-10 if using a standard frying pan.
3. Drizzle in the soy sauce and add to the noodles, tossing well to allow the juices to spread and absorb evenly.
4. Spoon the stir-fry diagonally across a spring roll sheet and fold back the top point over the filling. Fold over the sides. Before folding back the bottom point,

brush it with cold water, which will act as an adhesive.
5. Repeat until all the filling and sheets are used.
6. Pre-heat your Air Fryer at 360°F.
7. If desired, drizzle a small amount of oil over the top of the spring rolls to enhance the taste and ensure crispiness.
8. Cook the spring rolls in the fryer for 8 minutes, in multiple batches if necessary. Serve and enjoy.

Chia & Oat Porridge

Prep + Cook Time: 15 minutes | Servings: 4

Ingredients
4 cups milk
2 tbsp. peanut butter
2 cups oats
1 cup chia seeds
4 tbsp. honey
1 tbsp. butter, melted

Instructions
1. Pre-heat the Air Fryer to 390°F.
2. Put the peanut butter, honey, butter, and milk in a bowl and mix together using a whisk. Add in the oats and chia seeds and stir.
3. Transfer the mixture to an fryer-proof bowl that is small enough to fit inside the fryer and cook for 5 minutes. Give another stir before serving.

American Donuts

Prep + Cook Time: 1 hour 20 minutes | Servings: 6

Ingredients
1 cup flour
¼ cup sugar
1 tsp. baking powder
½ tsp. salt
¼ tsp. cinnamon
1 tbsp. coconut oil, melted
2 tbsp. aquafaba or liquid from canned chickpeas
¼ cup milk

Instructions
1. Put the sugar, flour and baking powder in a bowl and combine. Mix in the salt and cinnamon.
2. In a separate bowl, combine the aquafaba, milk and coconut oil.
3. Slowly pour the dry ingredients into the wet ingredients and combine well to create a sticky dough.
4. Refrigerate for at least an hour.
5. Pre-heat your Air Fryer at 370°F.
6. Using your hands, shape the dough into several small balls and place each one inside the fryer. Cook for 10 minutes, refraining from shaking the basket as they cook.
7. Lightly dust the balls with sugar and cinnamon and serve with a hot cup of coffee.

Tofu Scramble

Prep + Cook Time: 40 minutes | Servings: 3

Ingredients
2 ½ cups red potato, chopped
1 tbsp. olive oil
1 block tofu, chopped finely
1tbsp. olive oil
2 tbsp. tamari
1 tsp. turmeric powder
½ tsp. onion powder
½ tsp. garlic powder
½ cup onion, chopped
4 cups broccoli florets

Instructions
1.Pre-heat the Air Fryer at 400°F.
2.Toss together the potatoes and olive oil.
3.Cook the potatoes in a baking dish for 15 minutes, shaking once during the cooking time to ensure they fry evenly.
4.Combine the tofu, olive oil, turmeric, onion powder, tamari, and garlic powder together, before stirring in the onions, followed by the broccoli.
5.Top the potatoes with the tofu mixture and allow to cook for an additional 15 minutes. Serve warm.

Spinach Quiche

Prep + Cook Time: 1 hour 15 minutes | Servings: 4

Ingredients
¾ cup flour
Pinch of salt
½ cup cold coconut oil
2 tbsp. cold water
2 tbsp. olive oil
1 onion, chopped
4 oz. mushrooms, sliced
1 package firm tofu, pressed to remove excess water, then crumbled
1 lb. spinach, washed and chopped
½ tbsp. dried dill
2 tbsp. nutritional yeast
Salt and pepper
Sprig of fresh parsley, chopped

Instructions
1.Pre-heat the Air Fryer at 375°F.
2.Firstly, prepare the pastry. Use a sieve to sift together the salt and flour into a bowl. Combine with the coconut oil to make the flour crumbly. Slowly pour in the water until a stiff dough is formed.
3.Wrap the dough in saran wrap and refrigerate for a half hour.
4.Sauté the onion in a skillet over medium heat for a minute. Add in the tofu and mushroom, followed by the spinach, yeast, and dill.
5.Sprinkle in salt and pepper as desired. Finally add in the parsley. Take the skillet off the heat.
6.Dust a flat surface with flour and roll out the dough until it is thin.
7.Grease a baking dish that is small enough to fit inside the fryer. Place the dough in the tin and pour in the tofu mixture. Transfer the dish to the fryer and cook for 30 minutes, ensuring the pastry crisps up.

Egg Porridge

Prep + Cook Time: 15 minutes | Servings: 1

Ingredients
2 organic free-range eggs
1/3 cup organic heavy cream without food additives
2 packages of your preferred sweetener
2 tbsp grass-fed butter ground organic cinnamon to taste

Instructions
1.In a bowl add the eggs, cream and sweetener, and mix together.
2.Melt the butter in a saucepan over a medium heat. Lower the heat once the butter is melted.
3.Combine together with the egg and cream mixture.
4.While Cooking, mix until it thickens and curdles.
5.When you see the first signs of curdling, remove the saucepan immediately from the heat.
6.Pour the porridge into a bowl. Sprinkle cinnamon on top and serve immediately.

Eggs Florentine

Prep + Cook Time: 20 minutes | Servings: 2

Ingredients
1 cup washed, fresh spinach leaves
2 tbsp freshly grated parmesan cheese
Sea salt and pepper
1 tbsp white vinegar
2 eggs

Instructions
1.Cook the spinach the microwave or steam until wilted.
2.Sprinkle with parmesan cheese and seasoning.
3.Slice into bite-size pieces and place on a plate.
4.Simmer a pan of water and add the vinegar. Stir quickly with a spoon.
5.Break an egg into the center. Turn off the heat and cover until set.
6.Repeat with the second egg.
7.Place the eggs on top of the spinach and serve.

Spanish Omelet
Prep + Cook Time: 15 minutes | Servings: 2

Ingredients
3 eggs
Cayenne or black pepper
½ cup finely chopped vegetables of your choosing.

Instructions
1. In a pan on high heat, stir-fry the vegetables in extra virgin olive oil until lightly crispy.
2. Cook the eggs with one tablespoon of water and a pinch of pepper.
3. When almost cooked, top with the vegetables and flip to cook briefly.
4. Serve

Cristy's Pancakes
Prep + Cook Time: 10 minutes | Servings: 1

Ingredients
1 scoop of genX Vanilla
1 tbsp or hazelnut meal
2 tbsp water
1 egg

Instructions
1. Add the ingredients together in a bowl and mix together.
2. Pour the mixture into a frying pan, cook on a medium heat for approximately 2 to 3 minutes on each side. (Watch carefully as it may burn quickly.)
3. Serve buttered with a handful of mixed berries.

Breakfast Tea
Prep + Cook Time: 5 minutes | Servings: 1

Ingredients
16 oz water
2 tea bags
1 tbsp ghee
1 tbsp coconut oil
½ tsp vanilla extract

Instructions
1. Make the tea and put it to one aside.
2. In a bowl, melt the ghee.
3. Add the coconut oil and vanilla to the melted ghee.
4. Pour the tea from a cup into a Nutribullet cup.
5. Screw on the lid and blend thoroughly.

Sausage Quiche
Prep + Cook Time: 35 minutes | Servings: 4

Ingredients
12 large eggs
1 cup heavy cream

1 tsp black pepper
12 oz sugar-free breakfast sausage
2 cups shredded cheddar cheese

Instructions
1. Preheat your fryer to 375°F/190°C.
2. In a large bowl, whisk the eggs, heavy cream, salad and pepper together.
3. Add the breakfast sausage and cheddar cheese.
4. Pour the mixture into a greased casserole dish.
5. Bake for 25 minutes.
6. Cut into 12 squares and serve hot.

Breakfast Sausage Casserole
Prep + Cook Time: 50 minutes | Servings: 4

Ingredients
8 eggs, beaten
1 head chopped cauliflower
1 lb sausage, cooked and crumbled
2 cups heavy whipping cream
1 cup sharp cheddar cheese, grated

Instructions
1. Cook the sausage as usual.
2. In a large bowl, mix the sausage, heavy whipping cream, chopped cauliflower, cheese and eggs.
3. Pour into a greased casserole dish.
4. Cook for 45 minutes at 350°F/175°C, or until firm.
5. Top with cheese and serve.

Scrambled Mug Eggs
Prep + Cook Time: 5 minutes | Servings: 1

Ingredients
1 mug
2 eggs
Salt and pepper
Shredded cheese
Your favorite buffalo wing sauce

Instructions
1. Crack the eggs into a mug and whisk until blended.
2. Put the mug into your microwave and cook for 1.5 – 2 minutes, depending on the power of your microwave.
3. Leave for a few minutes and remove from the microwave.
4. Sprinkle with salt and pepper. Add your desired amount of cheese on top.
5. Using a fork, mix everything together.
6. Then add your favorite buffalo or hot sauce and mix again.
7. Serve!

Chapter 2 Lunch And Dinner

Sausage Balls

Prep + Cook Time: 25 minutes | Servings: 6

Ingredients
12 oz Jimmy Dean's Sausage
6 oz. shredded cheddar cheese
10 cubes cheddar (optional)

Instructions
1. Mix the shredded cheese and sausage.
2. Divide the mixture into 12 equal parts to be stuffed.
3. Add a cube of cheese to the center of the sausage and roll into balls.
4. Fry at 375°F/190°C for 15 minutes until crisp.
5. Serve!

Bacon Scallops

Prep + Cook Time: 10 minutes | Servings: 6

Ingredients
12 scallops
12 thin bacon slices
12 toothpicks
Salt and pepper to taste
½ tbsp oil

Instructions
1. Heat a skillet on a high heat while drizzling in the oil.
2. Wrap each scallop with a piece of thinly cut bacon—secure with a toothpick.
3. Season to taste.
4. Cook for 3 minutes per side.
5. Serve!

Buffalo Chicken Salad

Prep + Cook Time: 40 minutes | Servings: 1

Ingredients
3 cups salad of your choice
1 chicken breast
1/2 cup shredded cheese of your choice
Buffalo wing sauce of your choice
Ranch or blue cheese dressing

Instructions
1. Preheat your fryer to 400°F/200°C.
2. Douse the chicken breast in the buffalo wing sauce and bake for 25 minutes. In the last 5 minutes, throw the cheese on the wings until it melts.
3. When cooked, remove from the fryer and slice into pieces.
4. Place on a bed of lettuce.
5. Pour the salad dressing of your choice on top.
6. Serve!

Meatballs

Prep + Cook Time: 30 minutes | Servings: 6

Ingredients
1 lb ground beef (or ½ lb beef, ½ lb pork)
½ cup grated parmesan cheese
1 tbsp minced garlic (or paste)
½ cup mozzarella cheese
1 tsp freshly ground pepper

Instructions
1. Preheat your fryer to 400°F/200°C.
2. In a bowl, mix all the ingredients together.
3. Roll the meat mixture into 5 generous meatballs.
4. Bake inside your fryer at 170°F/80°C for about 18 minutes.
5. Serve with sauce!

Fat Bombs

Prep + Cook Time: 100 minutes | Servings: 2

Ingredients
1 cup coconut butter
1 cup coconut milk (full fat, canned)
1 tsp vanilla extract (gluten free)
½ tsp nutmeg
½ cup coconut shreds

Instructions
1. Pour some water into pot and put a glass bowl on top.
2. Add all the ingredients except the shredded coconut into the glass bowl and cook on a medium heat.
3. Stir and melt until they start melting.
4. Then, take them off of the heat.
5. Put the glass bowl into your refrigerator until the mix can be rolled into doughy balls. Usually this happens after around 30 minutes.
6. Roll the dough into 1-inch balls through the coconut shreds.
7. Place the balls on a plate and refrigerate for one hour.
8. Serve!

Cabbage & Beef Casserole

Prep + Cook Time: 40 minutes | Servings: 6

Ingredients
½ lb ground beef
½ cup chopped onion
½ bag coleslaw mix
1-1/2 cups tomato sauce
1 tbsp lemon juice

Instructions
1. In a skillet, cook the ground beef until browned and to the side.
2. Mix in the onion and cabbage to the skillet and sauté until soft.
3. Add the ground beef back in along with the tomato sauce and lemon juice.
4. Bring the mixture to a boil, then cover and simmer for 30 minutes.
5. Enjoy!

Roast Beef Lettuce Wraps

Prep + Cook Time: 10 minutes | Servings: 4

Ingredients
8 large iceberg lettuce leaves
8 oz (8 slices) rare roast beef
½ cup homemade mayonnaise
8 slices provolone cheese
1 cup baby spinach

Instructions
1. Wash the lettuce leaves and sake them dry. Try not to rip them.
2. Place 1 slice of roast beef inside each wrap.
3. Smother 1 tablespoon of mayonnaise on top of each piece of roast beef.
4. Top the mayonnaise with 1 slice of provolone cheese and 1 cup of baby spinach.
5. Roll the lettuce up around the toppings.
6. Serve & enjoy!

Turkey Avocado Rolls

Prep + Cook Time: 10 minutes | Servings: 6

Ingredients
12 slices (12 oz) turkey breast
12 slices Swiss cheese
2 cups baby spinach
1 large avocado, cut into 12 slices
1 cup homemade mayonnaise (see recipe in Chapter 9)

Instructions
1. Lay out the slices of turkey breast flat and place a slice of Swiss cheese on top of each one.

2. Top each slice with 1 cup baby spinach and 3 slices of avocado.
3. Drizzle the mayonnaise on top.
4. Sprinkle each "sandwich" with lemon pepper.
5. Roll up the sandwiches and secure with toothpicks.
6. Serve immediately or refrigerate until ready to serve.

Nearly Pizza

Prep + Cook Time: 30 minutes | Servings: 4

Ingredients
4 large portobello mushrooms
4 tsp olive oil
1 cup marinara sauce
1 cup shredded mozzarella cheese
10 slices sugar-free pepperoni

Instructions
1. Preheat your fryer to 375°F/190°C.
2. De-steam the 4 mushrooms and brush each cap with the olive oil, one spoon for each cap.
3. Place on a baking sheet and bake stem side down for 8 minutes.
4. Take out of the fryer and fill each cap with 1 cup marinara sauce, 1 cup mozzarella cheese and 3 slices of pepperoni.
5. Cook for another 10 minutes until browned.
6. Serve hot.

Taco Stuffed Peppers

Prep + Cook Time: 30 minutes | Servings: 4

Ingredients
1 lb. ground beef
1 tbsp. taco seasoning mix
1 can diced tomatoes and green chilis
4 green bell peppers
1 cup shredded Monterey jack cheese, divided

Instructions
1. Set a skillet over a high heat and cook the ground beef for seven to ten minutes. Make sure it is cooked through and brown all over. Drain the fat.
2. Stir in the taco seasoning mix, as well as the diced tomatoes and green chilis. Allow the mixture to cook for a further three to five minutes.
3. In the meantime, slice the tops off the green peppers and remove the seeds and membranes.
4. When the meat mixture is fully cooked, spoon equal amounts of it into the peppers and top with the Monterey jack cheese. Then place the peppers into your fryer.
5. Cook at 350°F for fifteen minutes.
6. The peppers are ready when they are soft, and the cheese is bubbling and brown. Serve warm and enjoy!

Beef Tenderloin & Peppercorn Crust

Prep + Cook Time: 45 minutes | Servings: 6

Ingredients
2 lb. beef tenderloin
2 tsp. roasted garlic, minced
2 tbsp. salted butter, melted
3 tbsp. ground 4-peppercorn blender

Instructions
1. Remove any surplus fat from the beef tenderloin.
2. Combine the roasted garlic and melted butter to apply to your tenderloin with a brush.
3. On a plate, spread out the peppercorns and roll the tenderloin in them, making sure they are covering and clinging to the meat.
4. Cook the tenderloin in your fryer for twenty-five minutes at 400°F, turning halfway through cooking.
5. Let the tenderloin rest for ten minutes before slicing and serving.

Bratwursts

Prep + Cook Time: 18 minutes | Servings: 4

Ingredients
4 x 3-oz. beef bratwursts

Instructions
1. Place the beef bratwursts in the basket of your fryer and cook for fifteen minutes at 375°F, turning once halfway through.
2. Enjoy with the low-carb toppings and sides of your choice.

Bacon-Wrapped Hot Dog

Prep + Cook Time: 25 minutes | Servings: 4

Ingredients
4 slices sugar-free bacon
4 beef hot dogs

Instructions
1. Take a slice of bacon and wrap it around the hot dog, securing it with a toothpick. Repeat with the other pieces of bacon and hot dogs, placing each wrapped dog in the basket of your fryer.
2. Cook at 370°F for ten minutes, turning halfway through to fry the other side.
3. Once hot and crispy, the hot dogs are ready to serve. Enjoy!

Herb Shredded Beef

Prep + Cook Time: 25 minutes | Servings: 6

Ingredients
1 tsp. dried dill

1 tsp. dried thyme
1 tsp. garlic powder
2 lbs. beefsteak
3 tbsp. butter

Instructions
1. Pre-heat your fryer at 360°F.
2. Combine the dill, thyme, and garlic powder together, and massage into the steak.
3. Cook the steak in the fryer for twenty minutes, then remove, shred, and return to the fryer. Add the butter and cook for a further two minutes at 365°F. Make sure the beef is coated in the butter before serving.

Herbed Butter Rib Eye Steak

Prep + Cook Time: 60 minutes | Servings: 4

Ingredients
4 ribeye steaks
Olive oil
¾ tsp. dry rub
½ cup butter
1 tsp. dried basil
3 tbsp. lemon garlic seasoning

Instructions
1. Massage the olive oil into the steaks and your favorite dry rub. Leave aside to sit for thirty minutes.
2. In a bowl, combine the button, dried basil, and lemon garlic seasoning, then refrigerate.
3. Pre-heat the fryer at 450°F and set a rack inside. Place the steaks on top of the rack and allow to cook for fifteen minutes.
4. Remove the steaks from the fryer when cooked and serve with the herbed butter.

Flank Steak & Avocado Butter

Prep + Cook Time: 40 minutes | Servings: 1

Ingredients
1 flank steak
Salt and pepper
2 avocados
2 tbsp. butter, melted
½ cup chimichurri sauce

Instructions
1. Rub the flank steak with salt and pepper to taste and leave to sit for twenty minutes.
2. Pre-heat the fryer at 400°F and place a rack inside.
3. Halve the avocados and take out the pits. Spoon the flesh into a bowl and mash with a fork. Mix in the melted butter and chimichurri sauce, making sure everything is well combined.
4. Put the steak in the fryer and cook for six minutes. Flip over and allow to cook for another six minutes.
5. Serve the steak with the avocado butter and enjoy!

Monkey Salad

Prep + Cook Time: 10 minutes | Servings: 1

Ingredients
2 tbsp butter
1 cup unsweetened coconut flakes
1 cup raw, unsalted cashews
1 cup raw, unsalted s
1 cup 90% dark chocolate shavings

Instructions
1. In a skillet, melt the butter on a medium heat.
2. Add the coconut flakes and sauté until lightly browned for 4 minutes.
3. Add the cashews and s and sauté for 3 minutes. Remove from the heat and sprinkle with dark chocolate shavings.
4. Serve!

Jarlsberg Lunch Omelet

Prep + Cook Time: 10 minutes | Servings: 2

Ingredients
4 medium mushrooms, sliced, 2 oz
1 green onion, sliced
2 eggs, beaten
1 oz Jarlsberg or Swiss cheese, shredded
1 oz ham, diced

Instructions
1. In a skillet, cook the mushrooms and green onion until tender.
2. Add the eggs and mix well.
3. Sprinkle with salt and top with the mushroom mixture, cheese and the ham.
4. When the egg is set, fold the plain side of the omelet on the filled side.
5. Turn off the heat and let it stand until the cheese has melted.
6. Serve!

Mu Shu Lunch Pork

Prep + Cook Time: 10 minutes | Servings: 2

Ingredients
4 cups coleslaw mix, with carrots
1 small onion, sliced thin
1 lb cooked roast pork, cut into ½" cubes
2 tbsp hoisin sauce
2 tbsp soy sauce

Instructions
1. In a large skillet, heat the oil on a high heat.
2. Stir-fry the cabbage and onion for 4 minutes until tender.
3. Add the pork, hoisin and soy sauce.
4. Cook until browned.
5. Enjoy!

Fiery Jalapeno Poppers

Prep + Cook Time: 40 minutes | Servings: 4

Ingredients
5 oz cream cheese
¼ cup mozzarella cheese
8 medium jalapeno peppers
½ tsp Mrs. Dash Table Blend
8 slices bacon

Instructions
1. Preheat your fryer to 400°F/200°C.
2. Cut the jalapenos in half.
3. Use a spoon to scrape out the insides of the peppers.
4. In a bowl, add together the cream cheese, mozzarella cheese and spices of your choice.
5. Pack the cream cheese mixture into the jalapenos and place the peppers on top.
6. Wrap each pepper in 1 slice of bacon, starting from the bottom and working up.
7. Bake for 30 minutes. Broil for an additional 3 minutes.
8. Serve!

Bacon & Chicken Patties

Prep + Cook Time: 15 minutes | Servings: 2

Ingredients
1 ½ oz can chicken breast
4 slices bacon
¼ cup parmesan cheese
1 large egg
3 tbsp flour

Instructions
1. Cook the bacon until crispy.
2. Chop the chicken and bacon together in a food processor until fine.
3. Add in the parmesan, egg, flour and mix.
4. Make the patties by hand and fry on a medium heat in a pan with some oil.
5. Once browned, flip over, continue cooking, and lie them to drain.
6. Serve!

Cheddar Bacon Burst

Prep + Cook Time: 90 minutes | Servings: 8

Ingredients
30 slices bacon
2 ½ cups cheddar cheese
4-5 cups raw spinach
1-2 tbsp Tones Southwest Chipotle Seasoning
2 tsp Mrs. Dash Table Seasoning

Instructions
1. Preheat your fryer to 375°F/190°C.
2. Weave the bacon into 15 vertical pieces & 12 horizontal pieces. Cut the extra 3 in half to fill in the rest, horizontally.
3. Season the bacon.
4. Add the cheese to the bacon.
5. Add the spinach and press down to compress.
6. Tightly roll up the woven bacon.
7. Line a baking sheet with kitchen foil and add plenty of salt to it.
8. Put the bacon on top of a cooling rack and put that on top of your baking sheet.
9. Bake for 60-70 minutes.
10. Let cool for 10-15 minutes before
11. Slice and enjoy!

Grilled Ham & Cheese

Prep + Cook Time: 30 minutes | Servings: 2

Ingredients
3 low-carb buns
4 slices medium-cut deli ham
1 tbsp salted butter
1 oz. flour
3 slices cheddar cheese
3 slices muenster cheese

Instructions
Bread:
1. Preheat your fryer to 350°F/175°C.
2. Mix the flour, salt and baking powder in a bowl. Put to the side.
3. Add in the butter and coconut oil to a skillet.
4. Melt for 20 seconds and pour into another bowl.
5. In this bowl, mix in the dough.
6. Scramble two eggs. Add to the dough.
7. Add ½ tablespoon of coconut flour to thicken, and place evenly into a cupcake tray. Fill about ¾ inch.
8. Bake for 20 minutes until browned.
9. Allow to cool for 15 minutes and cut each in half for the buns.

Sandwich:
1. Fry the deli meat in a skillet on a high heat.
2. Put the ham and cheese between the buns.
3. Heat the butter on medium high.
4. When brown, turn to low and add the dough to pan.
5. Press down with a weight until you smell burning, then flip to crisp both sides.
6. Enjoy!

Prosciutto Spinach Salad

Prep + Cook Time: 5 minutes | Servings: 2

Ingredients
2 cups baby spinach
1/3 lb prosciutto
1 cantaloupe
1 avocado
¼ cup diced red onion handful of raw, unsalted walnuts

Instructions
1. Put a cup of spinach on each plate.
2. Top with the diced prosciutto, cubes of balls of melon, slices of avocado, a handful of red onion and a few walnuts.
3. Add some freshly ground pepper, if you like.
4. Serve!

Riced Cauliflower & Curry Chicken

Prep + Cook Time: 30 minutes | Servings: 6

Ingredients
2 lbs chicken (4 breasts)
1 packet curry paste
3 tbsp ghee (can substitute with butter)
½ cup heavy cream
1 head cauliflower (around 1 kg)

Instructions
1. In a large skillet, melt the ghee.
2. Add the curry paste and mix.
3. Once combined, add a cup of water and simmer for 5 minutes.
4. Add the chicken, cover the skillet and simmer for 18 minutes.
5. Cut a cauliflower head into florets and blend in a food processor to make the riced cauliflower.
6. When the chicken is cooked, uncover, add the cream and cook for an additional 7 minutes.
7. Serve!

Mashed Garlic Turnips

Prep + Cook Time: 10 minutes | Servings: 2

Ingredients
3 cups diced turnip
2 cloves garlic, minced
¼ cup heavy cream
3 tbsp melted butter
Salt and pepper to season

Instructions
1. Boil the turnips until tender.
2. Drain and mash the turnips.
3. Add the cream, butter, salt, pepper and garlic. Combine well.
4. Serve!

Lasagna Spaghetti Squash

Prep + Cook Time: 90 minutes | Servings: 6

Ingredients
25 slices mozzarella cheese
1 large jar (40 oz) Rao's Marinara sauce
30 oz whole-milk ricotta cheese
2 large spaghetti squash, cooked (44 oz)
4 lbs ground beef

Instructions
1. Preheat your fryer to 375°F/190°C.
2. Slice the spaghetti squash and place it face down inside a fryerproof dish. Fill with water until covered.
3. Bake for 45 minutes until skin is soft.
4. Sear the meat until browned.
5. In a large skillet, heat the browned meat and marinara sauce. Set aside when warm.
6. Scrape the flesh off the cooked squash to resemble strands of spaghetti.
7. Layer the lasagna in a large greased pan in alternating layers of spaghetti squash, meat sauce, mozzarella, ricotta. Repeat until all increased have been used.
8. Bake for 30 minutes and serve!

Blue Cheese Chicken Wedges

Prep + Cook Time: 45 minutes | Servings: 4

Ingredients
Blue cheese dressing
2 tbsp crumbled blue cheese
4 strips of bacon
2 chicken breasts (boneless)
3/4 cup of your favorite buffalo sauce

Instructions
1. Boil a large pot of salted water.
2. Add in two chicken breasts to pot and cook for 28 minutes.
3. Turn off the heat and let the chicken rest for 10 minutes. Using a fork, pull the chicken apart into strips.
4. Cook and cool the bacon strips and put to the side.
5. On a medium heat, combine the chicken and buffalo sauce. Stir until hot.
6. Add the blue cheese and buffalo pulled chicken. Top with the cooked bacon crumble.
7. Serve and enjoy.

'Oh so good' Salad

Prep + Cook Time: 10 minutes | Servings: 2

Ingredients
6 brussels sprouts
½ tsp apple cider vinegar
1 tsp olive/grapeseed oil
1 grind of salt
1 tbsp freshly grated parmesan

Instructions
1. Slice the clean brussels sprouts in half.
2. Cut thin slices in the opposite direction.
3. Once sliced, cut the roots off and discard.
4. Toss together with the apple cider, oil and salt.
5. Sprinkle with the parmesan cheese, combine and enjoy!

'I Love Bacon'

Prep + Cook Time: 90 minutes | Servings: 4

Ingredients
30 slices thick-cut bacon
12 oz steak
10 oz pork sausage
4 oz cheddar cheese, shredded

Instructions
1. Lay out 5 x 6 slices of bacon in a woven pattern and bake at 400°F/200°C for 20 minutes until crisp.
2. Combine the steak, bacon and sausage to form a meaty mixture.
3. Lay out the meat in a rectangle of similar size to the bacon strips. Season with salt/peppe.
4. Place the bacon weave on top of the meat mixture.
5. Place the cheese in the center of the bacon.
6. Roll the meat into a tight roll and refrigerate.
7. Make a 7 x 7 bacon weave and roll the bacon weave over the meat, diagonally.
8. Bake at 400°F/200°C for 60 minutes or 165°F/75°C internally.
9. Let rest for 5 minutes before serving.

Lemon Dill Trout

Prep + Cook Time: 10 minutes | Servings: 1

Ingredients
2 lb pan-dressed trout (or other small fish), fresh or frozen
1 ½ tsp salt
½ cup butter or margarine
2 tbsp dill weed
3 tbsp lemon juice

Instructions
1.Cut the fish lengthwise and season the with pepper.
2.Prepare a skillet by melting the butter and dill weed.
3.Fry the fish on a high heat, flesh side down, for 2-3 minutes per side.
4.Remove the fish. Add the lemon juice to the butter and dill to create a sauce.
5.Serve the fish with the sauce.

'No Potato' Shepherd's Pie

Prep + Cook Time: 70 minutes | Servings: 6

Ingredients
1 lb lean ground beef
8 oz low-carb mushroom sauce mix
¼ cup ketchup
1 lb package frozen mixed vegetables
1 lb Aitkin's low-carb bake mix or equivalent

Instructions
1.Preheat your fryer to 375°F/190°C.
2.Prepare the bake mix according to package instructions. Layer into the skillet base.
3.Cut the dough into triangles and roll them from base to tip. Set to the side.
4.Brown the ground beef with the salt. Stir in the mushroom sauce, ketchup and mixed vegetables.
5.Bring the mixture to the boil and reduce the heat to medium, cover and simmer until tender.
6.Put the dough triangles on top of the mixture, tips pointing towards the center.
7.Bake for 60 minutes until piping hot and serve!

Easy Slider

Prep + Cook Time: 70 minutes | Servings: 6

Ingredients
1 lb Ground Beef
1 Egg

Garlic/salt/pepper/onion powder to taste
Several dashes of Worcestershire sauce
8 oz cheddar cheese (½ oz per patty)

Instructions
1.Mix the beef, eggs and spices together.
2.Divide the meat into 1.5 oz patties.
3.Add a half-ounce of cheese to each patty and combine two patties to make one burger, like a sandwich. Heat the oil on high and fry the burgers until cooked as desired. Serve.

Dijon Halibut Steak

Prep + Cook Time: 20 minutes | Servings: 1

Ingredients
1 6-oz fresh or thawed halibut steak
1 tbsp butter
1 tbsp lemon juice
½ tbsp Dijon mustard
1 tsp fresh basil

Instructions
1.Heat the butter, basil, lemon juice and mustard in a small saucepan to make a glaze.
2.Brush both sides of the halibut steak with the mixture.
3.Grill the fish for 10 minutes over a medium heat until tender and flakey.

Cast-Iron Cheesy Chicken

Prep + Cook Time: 10 minutes | Servings: 4

Ingredients
4 chicken breasts
4 bacon strips
4 oz ranch dressing
2 green onions
4 oz cheddar cheese

Instructions
1.Pour the oil into a skillet and heat on high. Add the chicken breasts and fry both sides until piping hot.
2.Fry the bacon and crumble it into bits.
3.Dice the green onions.
4.Put the chicken in a baking dish and top with soy sauce.
5.Toss in the ranch, bacon, green onions and top with cheese.
6.Cook until the cheese is browned, for around 4 minutes.
7.Serve.

Cauliflower Rice Chicken Curry

Prep + Cook Time: 40 minutes | Servings: 4

Ingredients
2 lb chicken (4 breasts)
1 packet curry paste
3 tbsp ghee (can substitute with butter)
½ cup heavy cream
1 head cauliflower (around 1 kg/2.2 lb)

Instructions
1. Melt the ghee in a pot. Mix in the curry paste.
2. Add the water and simmer for 5 minutes.
3. Add the chicken, cover, and simmer on a medium heat for 20 minutes or until the chicken is cooked.
4. Shred the cauliflower florets in a food processor to resemble rice.
5. Once the chicken is cooked, uncover, and incorporate the cream.
6. Cook for 7 minutes and serve over the cauliflower.

Bacon Chops

Prep + Cook Time: 20 minutes | Servings: 2

Ingredients
2 pork chops (I prefer bone-in, but boneless chops work great as well)
1 bag shredded brussels sprouts
4 slices of bacon
Worcestershire sauce
Lemon juice (optional)

Instructions
1. Place the pork chops on a baking sheet with the Worcestershire sauce inside a preheated grill for 5 minutes.
2. Turnover and cook for another 5 minutes. Put to the side when done.
3. Cook the chopped bacon in a large pan until browned. Add the shredded brussels sprouts and cook together.
4. Stir the brussels sprouts with the bacon and grease and cook for 5 minutes until the bacon is crisp.

Chicken in a Blanket

Prep + Cook Time: 60 minutes | Servings: 3

Ingredients
3 boneless chicken breasts
1 package bacon
1 8-oz package cream cheese
3 jalapeno peppers
Salt, pepper, garlic powder or other seasonings

Instructions
1. Cut the chicken breast in half lengthwise to create two pieces.
2. Cut the jalapenos in half lengthwise and remove the seeds.
3. Dress each breast with a half-inch slice of cream cheese and half a slice of jalapeno. Sprinkle with garlic powder, salt and pepper.
4. Roll the chicken and wrap 2 to 3 pieces of bacon around it—secure with toothpicks.
5. Bake in a preheated 375°F/190°C fryer for 50 minutes.
6. Serve!

Mozzarella Beef

Prep + Cook Time: 30 minutes | Servings: 6

Ingredients
12 oz. beef brisket
2 tsp. Italian herbs
2 tsp. butter
1 onion, sliced
7 oz. mozzarella cheese, sliced

Instructions
1. Pre-heat the fryer at 365°F.
2. Cut up the brisket into four equal slices and season with the Italian herbs.
3. Allow the butter to melt in the fryer. Place the slices of beef inside along with the onion. Put a piece of mozzarella on top of each piece of brisket and cook for twenty-five minutes.
4. Enjoy!

Rosemary Rib Eye Steaks

Prep + Cook Time: 40 minutes | Servings: 2

Ingredients
¼ cup butter
1 clove minced garlic
Salt and pepper
1 ½ tbsp. balsamic vinegar
¼ cup rosemary, chopped
2 ribeye steaks

Instructions
1. Melt the butter in a skillet over medium heat. Add the garlic and fry until fragrant.
2. Remove the skillet from the heat and add in the salt, pepper, and vinegar. Allow it to cool.
3. Add the rosemary, then pour the whole mixture into a Ziploc bag.
4. Put the ribeye steaks in the bag and shake well, making sure to coat the meat well. Refrigerate for an hour, then allow to sit for a further twenty minutes.
5. Pre-heat the fryer at 400°F and set the rack inside. Cook the ribeyes for fifteen minutes.
6. Take care when removing the steaks from the fryer and plate up. Enjoy!

Herbed Butter Beef Loin

Prep + Cook Time: 25 minutes | Servings: 4

Ingredients
1 tbsp. butter, melted
¼ dried thyme
1 tsp. garlic salt
¼ tsp. dried parsley
1 lb. beef loin

Instructions
1. In a bowl, combine the melted butter, thyme, garlic salt, and parsley.
2. Cut the beef loin into slices and generously apply the seasoned butter using a brush.
3. Pre-heat your fryer at 400°F and place a rack inside.
4. Cook the beef for fifteen minutes.
5. Take care when removing it and serve hot.

Lamb Ribs

Prep + Cook Time: 25 minutes | Servings: 4

Ingredients
1 lb. lamb ribs
2 tbsp. mustard
1 tsp. rosemary, chopped
Salt and pepper
¼ cup mint leaves, chopped
1 cup Green yogurt

Instructions
1. Pre-heat the fryer at 350°F.
2. Use a brush to apply the mustard to the lamb ribs, and season with rosemary, as well as salt and pepper as desired.
3. Cook the ribs in the fryer for eighteen minutes.
4. Meanwhile, combine together the mint leaves and yogurt in a bowl.
5. Remove the lamb ribs from the fryer when cooked and serve with the mint yogurt. Enjoy!

Lamb Satay

Prep + Cook Time: 25 minutes | Servings: 2

Ingredients
¼ tsp. cumin
1 tsp ginger
½ tsp. nutmeg
Salt and pepper
2 boneless lamb steaks
Olive oil cooking spray

Instructions
1. Combine the cumin, ginger, nutmeg, salt and pepper in a bowl.
2. Cube the lamb steaks and massage the spice mixture into each one.
3. Leave to marinate for ten minutes, then transfer onto metal skewers.
4. Pre-heat the fryer at 400°F.
5. Spritz the skewers with the olive oil cooking spray, then cook them in the fryer for eight minutes.
6. Take care when removing them from the fryer and serve with the low-carb sauce of your choice.

Italian Lamb Chops

Prep + Cook Time: 20 minutes | Servings: 2

Ingredients
2 lamp chops
2 tsp. Italian herbs
2 avocados
½ cup mayonnaise
1 tbsp. lemon juice

Instructions
1. Season the lamb chops with the Italian herbs, then set aside for five minutes.
2. Pre-heat the fryer at 400°F and place the rack inside.
3. Put the chops on the rack and allow to cook for twelve minutes.
4. In the meantime, halve the avocados and open to remove the pits. Spoon the flesh into a blender.
5. Add in the mayonnaise and lemon juice and pulse until a smooth consistency is achieved.
6. Take care when removing the chops from the fryer, then plate up and serve with the avocado mayo.

Breaded Pork Chops

Prep + Cook Time: 25 minutes | Servings: 4

Ingredients
1 tsp. chili powder
½ tsp. garlic powder
1 ½ oz. pork rinds, finely ground
4 x 4-oz. pork chops
1 tbsp. coconut oil, melted

Instructions
1. Combine the chili powder, garlic powder, and ground pork rinds.
2. Coat the pork chops with the coconut oil, followed by the pork rind mixture, taking care to cover them completely. Then place the chops in the basket of the fryer.
3. Cook the chops for fifteen minutes at 400°F, turning halfway through.
4. Once they are browned, check the temperature has reached 145°F before serving with the sides of your choice.

Juicy Mexican Pork Chops

Prep + Cook Time: 25 minutes | Servings: 2

Ingredients
¼ tsp. dried oregano
1 ½ tsp. taco seasoning mix
2 x 4-oz. boneless pork chops
2 tbsp. unsalted butter, divided

Instructions
1.Combine the dried oregano and taco seasoning to rub into the pork chops.
2.In your fryer, cook the chops at 400°F for fifteen minutes, turning them over halfway through to cook on the other side.
3.When the chops are a brown color, check the internal temperature has reached 145°F and remove from the fryer. Serve with a garnish of butter.

Baby Back Ribs

Prep + Cook Time: 45 minutes | Servings: 2

Ingredients
2 tsp. red pepper flakes
¾ ground ginger
3 cloves minced garlic
Salt and pepper
2 baby back ribs

Instructions
1.Pre-heat your fryer at 350°F.
2.Combine the red pepper flakes, ginger, garlic, salt and pepper in a bowl, making sure to mix well. Massage the mixture into the baby back ribs.
3.Cook the ribs in the fryer for thirty minutes.
4.Take care when taking the rubs out of the fryer. Place them on a serving dish and enjoy with a low-carb barbecue sauce of your choosing.

Pulled Pork

Prep + Cook Time: 30 minutes | Servings: 1

Ingredients
1 lb. pork tenderloin
2 tbsp. barbecue dry rub
1/3 cup heavy cream
1 tsp. butter

Instructions
1.Pre-heat your fryer at 370°F.

2.Massage the dry rub of your choice into the tenderloin, coating it well.
3.Cook the tenderloin in the fryer for twenty minutes. When cooked, shred with two forks.
4.Add the heavy cream and butter into the fryer along with the shredded pork and stir well. Cook for a further four minutes.
5.Allow to cool a little, then serve and enjoy.

Ribs

Prep + Cook Time: 60 minutes | Servings: 4

Ingredients
1 lb. pork ribs
1 tbsp. barbecue dry rub
1 tsp. mustard
1 tbsp. apple cider vinegar
1 tsp. sesame oil

Instructions
1.Chop up the pork ribs.
2.Combine the dry rub, mustard, apple cider vinegar, and sesame oil, then coat the ribs with this mixture. Refrigerate the ribs for twenty minutes.
3.Preheat the fryer at 360°F.
4.When the ribs are ready, place them in the fryer and cook for 15 minutes. Flip them and cook on the other side for a further fifteen minutes. Then serve and enjoy!

Pork Chops

Prep + Cook Time: 15 minutes | Servings: 3

Ingredients
3 pork chops
½ tsp. dried rosemary
1 tsp. garlic salt
1 tsp. peppercorns
1 tbsp. butter

Instructions
1.Pre-heat your fryer to 365°F.
2.Combine the dried rosemary and garlic salt and rub into the pork chops.
3.Place the peppercorns and butter into the fryer and allow the butter to melt.
4.Add in the pork chops and cook for six minutes. Flip them and cook for an additional five minutes before serving.

Sriracha Cauliflower

Prep + Cook Time: 25 minutes | Servings: 4

Ingredients
¼ cup vegan butter, melted
¼ cup sriracha sauce
4 cups cauliflower florets
1 cup bread crumbs
1 tsp. salt

Instructions
1.Mix together the sriracha and vegan butter in a bowl and pour this mixture over the cauliflower, taking care to cover each floret entirely.
2.In a separate bowl, combine the bread crumbs and salt.
3.Dip the cauliflower florets in the bread crumbs, coating each one well. Cook in the Air Fryer for 17 minutes in a 375°F pre-heated Air Fryer.

Ratatouille

Prep + Cook Time: 30 minutes | Servings: 4

Ingredients
1 sprig basil
1 sprig flat-leaf parsley
1 sprig mint
1 tbsp. coriander powder
1 tsp. capers
½ lemon, juiced
Salt and pepper to taste
2 eggplants, sliced crosswise
2 red onions, chopped
4 cloves garlic, minced
2 red peppers, sliced crosswise
1 fennel bulb, sliced crosswise
3 large zucchinis, sliced crosswise
5 tbsp. olive oil
4 large tomatoes, chopped
2 tsp. herbs de Provence

Instructions
1.Blend together the basil, parsley, coriander, mint, lemon juice and capers, with a little salt and pepper. Make sure all ingredients are well-incorporated.
2.Pre-heat the Air Fryer at 400°F.
3.Coat the eggplant, onions, garlic, peppers, fennel, and zucchini with olive oil.
4.Take a baking dish small enough to fit inside the fryer. Transfer the vegetables into the dish and top with the tomatoes and herb puree. Sprinkle on some more salt and pepper if desired, as well as the herbs de Provence.
5.Fry for 25 minutes.

Pesto Stuffed Bella Mushrooms

Prep + Cook Time: 25 minutes | Servings: 6

Ingredients
1 cup basil
½ cup cashew nuts, soaked overnight
½ cup nutritional yeast
1 tbsp. lemon juice
2 cloves of garlic
1 tbsp. olive oil
Salt to taste
1 lb. baby Bella mushroom, stems removed

Instructions
1.Pre-heat the Air Fryer at 400°F.
2.Prepare your pesto. In a food processor, blend together the basil, cashew nuts, nutritional yeast, lemon juice, garlic and olive oil to combine well. Sprinkle on salt as desired.
3.Turn the mushrooms cap-side down and spread the pesto on the underside of each cap.
4.Transfer to the fryer and cook for 15 minutes.

Veg Burger

Prep + Cook Time: 25 minutes | Servings: 8

Ingredients
½ lb. cauliflower, steamed and diced
2 tsp. coconut oil melted
2 tsp. garlic, minced
¼ cup desiccated coconut
½ cup oats
3 tbsp. flour
1 flax egg [1 tbsp. flaxseed + 3 tbsp. water]
1 tsp. mustard powder
2 tsp. thyme
2 tsp. parsley
2 tsp. chives
Salt and pepper to taste
1 cup bread crumbs

Instructions
1.Pre-heat the Air Fryer at 390°F.
2.Drain any excess water out of the cauliflower on a kitchen towel.
3.Combine the cauliflower with all of ingredients bar the breadcrumbs, incorporating everything well.
4.Using your hands, shape 8 equal-sized amounts of the mixture into burger patties. Coat the patties in breadcrumbs before putting them in the basket of the fryer in a single layer.
5.Cook for 10-15 minutes, ensuring the patties crisp up.

Chili Potato Wedges
Prep + Cook Time: 50 minutes | Servings: 4

Ingredients
1 lb. fingerling potatoes, washed and cut into wedges
1 tsp. olive oil
1 tsp. salt
1 tsp. black pepper
1 tsp. cayenne pepper
1 tsp. nutritional yeast
½ tsp. garlic powder

Instructions
1.Pre-heat the Air Fryer at 400°F.
2.Coat the potatoes with the rest of the ingredients.
3.Transfer to the basket of your fryer and allow to cook for 16 minutes, shaking the basket at the halfway point.

Christmas Brussels Sprouts
Prep + Cook Time: 20 minutes | Servings: 2

Ingredients
2 cups Brussels sprouts, halved
1 tbsp. olive oil
1 tbsp. balsamic vinegar
1 tbsp. maple syrup
¼ tsp. sea salt

Instructions
1.Pre-heat the Air Fryer at 375°F.
2.Evenly coat the Brussels sprouts with the olive oil, balsamic vinegar, maple syrup, and salt.
3.Transfer to the basket of your fryer and cook for 5 minutes. Give the basket a good shake, turn the heat up to 400°F and continue to cook for another 8 minutes.

Summer Rolls
Prep + Cook Time: 25 minutes | Servings: 4

Ingredients
1 cup shiitake mushroom, sliced thinly
1 celery stalk, chopped
1 medium carrot, shredded
½ tsp. ginger, finely chopped
1 tsp. sugar
1 tbsp. soy sauce
1 tsp. nutritional yeast
8 spring roll sheets
1 tsp. corn starch
2 tbsp. water

Instructions
1.In a bowl, combine the ginger, soy sauce, nutritional yeast, carrots, celery, and sugar.
2.Mix together the cornstarch and water to create an adhesive for your spring rolls.
3.Scoop a tablespoonful of the vegetable mixture into the middle of the spring roll sheets. Brush the edges of the sheets with the cornstarch adhesive and enclose around the filling to make spring rolls.

4.Pre-heat your Air Fryer at 400°F. When warm, place the rolls inside and cook for 15 minutes or until crisp.

Rice Bowl
Prep + Cook Time: 55 minutes | Servings: 4

Ingredients
¼ cup cucumber, sliced
1 tsp. salt
1 tbsp. sugar
7 tbsp. Japanese rice vinegar
3 medium-sized eggplants, sliced
3 tbsp. sweet white miso paste
1 tbsp. mirin rice wine
4 cups sushi rice, cooked
4 spring onions
1 tbsp. sesame seeds, toasted

Instructions
1.Coat the cucumber slices with the rice wine vinegar, salt, and sugar.
2.Place a dish on top of the bowl to weight it down completely.
3.Pre-heat the Air Fryer at 400°F.
4.In a bowl, mix together the eggplants, mirin rice wine, and miso paste. Allow to marinate for half an hour.
5.Cook the eggplant in the fryer for 10 minutes.
6.Place the eggplant slices in the Air Fryer and cook for 10 minutes.
7.Fill the bottom of a serving bowl with rice and top with the eggplants and pickled cucumbers. Add the spring onions and sesame seeds for garnish.

Asian Tofu Bites
Prep + Cook Time: 20 minutes | Servings: 4

Ingredients
1 packaged firm tofu, cubed and pressed to remove excess water
1 tbsp. soy sauce
1 tbsp. ketchup
1 tbsp. maple syrup
½ tsp. vinegar
1 tsp. liquid smoke
1 tsp. hot sauce
2 tbsp. sesame seeds
1 tsp. garlic powder
Salt and pepper to taste

Instructions
1.Pre-heat the Air Fryer at 375°F.
2.Take a baking dish small enough to fit inside the fryer and spritz it with cooking spray.
3.Combine all the ingredients to coat the tofu completely and allow the marinade to absorb for half an hour.
4.Transfer the tofu to the baking dish, then cook for 15 minutes. Flip the tofu over and cook for another 15 minute on the other side.

Chickpeas

Prep + Cook Time: 20 minutes | Servings: 4

Ingredients
1 15-oz. can chickpeas, drained but not rinsed
2 tbsp. olive oil
1 tsp. salt
2 tbsp. lemon juice

Instructions
1.Pre-heat the Air Fryer at 400°F.
2.Add all the ingredients together in a bowl and mix. Transfer this mixture to the basket of the fryer.
3.Cook for 15 minutes, ensuring the chickpeas become nice and crispy.

Cauliflower Cheese Tater Tots

Prep + Cook Time: 25 minutes | Servings: 12

Ingredients
1 lb. cauliflower, steamed and chopped
½ cup nutritional yeast
1 tbsp. oats
1 flax egg [1 tbsp. desiccated coconuts + 3 tbsp. flaxseed meal
+ 3 tbsp. water]
1 onion, chopped
1 tsp. garlic, minced
1 tsp. parsley, chopped
1 tsp. oregano, chopped
1 tsp. chives, chopped
Salt and pepper to taste
½ cup bread crumbs

Instructions
1.Pre-heat the Air Fryer at 390°F.
2.Drain any excess water out of the cauliflower by wringing it with a paper towel.
3.In a bowl, combine the cauliflower with the remaining ingredients, save the bread crumbs. Using your hands, shape the mixture into several small balls.
4.Coat the balls in the bread crumbs and transfer to the basket of your fryer. Allow to cook for 6 minutes, after which you should raise the temperature to 400°F and then leave to cook for an additional 10 minutes.

Sweet Onions & Potatoes

Prep + Cook Time: 30 minutes | Servings: 6

Ingredients
2 large sweet potatoes, peeled and cut into chunks
2 medium sweet onions, cut into chunks
3 tbsp. olive oil
1 tsp. dried thyme
Salt and pepper to taste
¼ cup s, sliced and toasted

Instructions
1.Pre-heat the Air Fryer at 425°F.
2.In a bowl, combine all of the ingredients, except for the sliced s.
3.Transfer the vegetables and dressing to a ramekin and cook in the fryer for 20 minutes.
4.When ready to serve, add the s on top.

Mushroom Pizza Squares

Prep + Cook Time: 20 minutes | Servings: 10

Ingredients
1 vegan pizza dough
1 cup oyster mushrooms, chopped
1 shallot, chopped
¼ red bell pepper, chopped
2 tbsp. parsley
Salt and pepper

Instructions
1.Pre-heat the Air Fryer at 400°F.
2.Cut the vegan pizza dough into squares.
3.In a bowl, combine the oyster mushrooms, shallot, bell pepper and parsley. Sprinkle some salt and pepper as desired.
4.Spread this mixture on top of the pizza squares.
5.Cook in the Air Fryer for 10 minutes.

Tofu & Sweet Potatoes

Prep + Cook Time: 50 minutes | Servings: 8

Ingredients
8 sweet potatoes, scrubbed
2 tbsp. olive oil
1 large onion, chopped
2 green chilies, deseeded and chopped
½ lb. tofu, crumbled
2 tbsp. Cajun seasoning
cup tomatoes
1 can kidney beans, drained and rinsed
Salt and pepper to taste

Instructions
1.Pre-heat the Air Fryer at 400°F.
2.With a knife, pierce the skin of the sweet potatoes in numerous places and cook in the fryer for half an hour, making sure they become soft. Remove from the fryer, halve each potato, and set to one side.
3.Over a medium heat, fry the onions and chilis in a little oil for 2 minutes until fragrant.
4.Add in the tofu and Cajun seasoning and allow to cook for a further 3 minutes before incorporating the kidney beans and tomatoes. Sprinkle some salt and pepper as desire.
5.Top each sweet potato halve with a spoonful of the tofu mixture and serve.

Risotto
Prep + Cook Time: 40 minutes | Servings: 2

Ingredients
1 onion, diced
2 cups chicken stock, boiling
½ cup parmesan cheese or cheddar cheese, grated
1 clove garlic, minced
¾ cup arborio rice
1 tbsp. olive oil
1 tbsp. butter, unsalted

Instructions
1.Turn the Air Fryer to 390°F and set for 5 minutes to warm.
2.Grease a round baking tin with oil and stir in the butter, garlic, and onion.
3.Put the tin in the fryer and allow to cook for 4 minutes.
4.Pour in the rice and cook for a further 4 minutes, stirring three times throughout the cooking time.
5.Turn the temperature down to 320°F.
6.Add the chicken stock and give the dish a gentle stir. Cook for 22 minutes, leaving the fryer uncovered.
7.Pour in the cheese, stir once more and serve.

Chickpea & Avocado Mash
Prep + Cook Time: 30 minutes | Servings: 4

Ingredients
1 medium-sized head of cauliflower, cut into florets
1 can chickpeas, drained and rinsed
1 tbsp. extra-virgin olive oil
2 tbsp. lemon juice
Salt and pepper to taste
4 flatbreads, toasted
2 ripe avocados, mashed

Instructions
1.Pre-heat the Air Fryer at 425°F.
2.In a bowl, mix together the chickpeas, cauliflower, lemon juice and olive oil. Sprinkle salt and pepper as desired.
3.Put inside the Air Fryer basket and cook for 25 minutes.
4.Spread on top of the flatbread along with the mashed avocado. Sprinkle on more pepper and salt as desired and enjoy with hot sauce.

Fried Potatoes
Prep + Cook Time: 55 minutes | Servings: 1

Ingredients
1 medium russet potatoes, scrubbed and peeled
1 tsp. olive oil
¼ tsp. onion powder
1/8 tsp. salt
A dollop of vegan butter
A dollop of vegan cream cheese
1 tbsp. Kalamata olives
1 tbsp. chives, chopped

Instructions
1.Pre-heat the Air Fryer at 400°F.
2.In a bowl, coat the potatoes with the onion powder, salt, olive oil, and vegan butter.
3.Transfer to the fryer and allow to cook for 40 minutes, turning the potatoes over at the halfway point.
4.Take care when removing the potatoes from the fryer and enjoy with the vegan cream cheese, Kalamata olives and chives on top, plus any other vegan sides you desire.

French Green Beans
Prep + Cook Time: 20 minutes | Servings: 4

Ingredients
1 ½ lb. French green beans, stems removed and blanched
1 tbsp. salt
½ lb. shallots, peeled and cut into quarters
½ tsp. ground white pepper
2 tbsp. olive oil
¼ cup slivered s, toasted

Instructions
1.Pre-heat the Air Fryer at 400°F.
2.Coat the vegetables with the rest of the ingredients in a bowl.
3.Transfer to the basket of your fryer and cook for 10 minutes, making sure the green beans achieve a light brown color.

Black Bean Chili
Prep + Cook Time: 25 minutes | Servings: 6

Ingredients
1 tbsp. olive oil
1 medium onion, diced
3 cloves of garlic, minced
1 cup vegetable broth
3 cans black beans, drained and rinsed
2 cans diced tomatoes
2 chipotle peppers, chopped
2 tsp. cumin
2 tsp. chili powder
1 tsp. dried oregano
½ tsp. salt

Instructions
1.Over a medium heat, fry the garlic and onions in a little oil for 3 minutes.
2.Add in the remaining ingredients, stirring constantly and scraping the bottom to prevent sticking.
3.Pre-heat your Air Fryer at 400°F.
4.Take a heat-resistant dish small enough to fit inside the fryer and place the mixture inside. Put a sheet of aluminum foil on top.
5.Transfer to the air fryer and cook for 20 minutes.
6.When ready, plate up and serve with diced avocado, chopped cilantro, and chopped tomatoes.

Cauliflower

Prep + Cook Time: 20 minutes | Servings: 4

Ingredients

1 head cauliflower, cut into florets
1 tbsp. extra-virgin olive oil
2 scallions, chopped
5 cloves of garlic, sliced
1 ½ tbsp. tamari
1 tbsp. rice vinegar
½ tsp. sugar
1 tbsp. sriracha

Instructions

1.Pre-heat the Air Fryer to 400°F.
2.Put the cauliflower florets in the Air Fryer and drizzle some oil over them before cooking for 10 minutes.
3.Turn the cauliflower over, throw in the onions and garlic, and stir. Cook for another 10 minutes.
4.Mix together the rest of the ingredients in a bowl.
5.Remove the cooked cauliflower from the fryer and coat it in the sauce.
6.Return to the Air Fryer and allow to cook for another 5 minutes. Enjoy with a side of rice.

Tofu Bites

Prep + Cook Time: 65 minutes | Servings: 3

Ingredients

2 tbsp. sesame oil
¼ cup maple syrup
3 tbsp. peanut butter
¼ cup liquid aminos
3tbsp. chili garlic sauce
2 tbsp. rice wine vinegar
2 cloves of garlic, minced
1 inch fresh ginger, peeled and grated
1 tsp. red pepper flakes
1 block extra firm tofu, pressed to remove excess water and cubed
Toasted peanuts, chopped
1 tsp. sesame seeds
1 sprig cilantro, chopped

Instructions

1.Whisk together the first 9 ingredients in a large bowl to well combine.
2.Transfer to an airtight bag along with the cubed tofu.

Allow to marinate for a minimum of a half hour.
3.Pre-heat the Air Fryer to 425°F.
4.Put the tofu cubes in the fryer, keep any excess marinade for the sauce. Cook for 15 minutes.
5.In the meantime, heat the marinade over a medium heat to reduce by half.
6.Plate up the cooked tofu with some cooked rice and serve with the sauce. Complete the dish with the sesame seeds, cilantro and peanuts.

Faux Rice

Prep + Cook Time: 60 minutes | Servings: 8

Ingredients

1 medium-to-large head of cauliflower
½ lemon, juiced
garlic cloves, minced
2 cans mushrooms, 8 oz. each
1 can water chestnuts, 8 oz.
¾ cup peas
½ cup egg substitute or 1 egg, beaten
4 tbsp. soy sauce
1 tbsp. peanut oil
1 tbsp. sesame oil
1 tbsp. ginger, fresh and minced
High quality cooking spray

Instructions

1.Mix together the peanut oil, soy sauce, sesame oil, minced ginger, lemon juice, and minced garlic to combine well.
2.Peel and wash the cauliflower head before cutting it into small florets.
3.In a food processor, pulse the florets in small batches to break them down to resemble rice grains.
4.Pour into your Air Fryer basket.
5.Drain the can of water chestnuts and roughly chop them. Pour into the basket.
6.Cook at 350°F for 20 minutes.
7.In the meantime, drain the mushrooms. When the 20 minutes are up, add the mushrooms and the peas to the fryer and continue to cook for another 15 minutes.
8.Lightly spritz a frying pan with cooking spray. Prepare an omelet with the egg substitute or the beaten egg, ensuring it is firm. Lay on a cutting board and slice it up.
9.When the cauliflower is ready, throw in the omelet and cook for an additional 5 minutes. Serve hot.

Potato Croquettes

Prep + Cook Time: 25 minutes | Servings: 10

Ingredients

¼ cup nutritional yeast
2 cups boiled potatoes, mashed
1 flax egg [1 tbsp. flaxseed meal + 3 tbsp. water]
1 tbsp. flour
2 tbsp. chives, chopped
Salt and pepper to taste
2 tbsp. vegetable oil
¼ cup bread crumbs

Instructions

1.Pre-heat the Air Fryer to 400°F.
2.In a bowl, combine together the nutritional yeast, potatoes, flax eggs, flour, and chives. Sprinkle with salt and pepper as desired.
3.In separate bowl mix together the vegetable oil and bread crumbs to achieve a crumbly consistency.
4.Use your hands to shape the potato mixture into small balls and dip each one into the breadcrumb mixture.
5.Place the croquettes inside the air fryer and cook for 15 minutes, ensuring the croquettes turn golden brown.

Paprika Tofu

Prep + Cook Time: 25 minutes | Servings: 4

Ingredients

2 block extra firm tofu, pressed to remove excess water and cubed
¼ cup cornstarch
1 tbsp. smoked paprika
Salt and pepper to taste

Instructions

1.Cover the Air Fryer basket with aluminum foil and coat with a light brushing of oil.
2.Pre-heat the Air Fryer to 370°F.
3.Combine all ingredients in a bowl, coating the tofu well.
4.Put in the Air Fryer basket and allow to cook for 12 minutes.

Mac & Cheese

Prep + Cook Time: 15 minutes | Servings: 2

Ingredients

1 cup cooked macaroni
½ cup warm milk
1 tbsp. parmesan cheese
1 cup grated cheddar cheese
Salt and pepper, to taste

Instructions

1.Pre-heat the Air Fryer to 350°F.
2.In a baking dish, mix together all of the ingredients, except for Parmesan.
3.Put the dish inside the Air Fryer and allow to cook for 10 minutes.
4.Add the Parmesan cheese on top and serve.

Pasta Salad

Prep + Cook Time: 2 hours 25 minutes | Servings: 8

Ingredients

4 tomatoes, medium and cut in eighths
3 eggplants, small
3 zucchinis, medium sized
2 bell peppers, any color
4 cups large pasta, uncooked in any shape
1 cup cherry tomatoes, sliced
½ cup Italian dressing, fat-free
8 tbsp. parmesan, grated
2 tbsp. extra virgin olive oil
2 tsp. pink Himalayan salt
1 tsp. basil, dried
High quality cooking spray

Instructions

1.Wash and dry the eggplant. Cut off the stem and throw it away. Do not peel the eggplant. Cut it into half-inch-thick round slices.
2.Coat the eggplant slices with 1 tbsp. of extra virgin olive oil, and transfer to the Air Fryer basket.
3.Cook the eggplant for 40 minutes at 350°F. Once it is tender and cooked through, remove from the fryer and set to one side.
4.Wash and dry the zucchini. Cut off the stem and throw it away. Do not peel the zucchini. Cut the zucchini into half-inch-thick round slices.
5.Combine with the olive oil to coat, and put it in the Air Fryer basket.
6.Cook the zucchini for about 25 minutes at 350°F. Once it is tender and cooked through, remove from the fryer and set to one side.
7.Wash the tomatoes and cut them into eight equal slices. Transfer them to the fryer basket and spritz lightly with high quality cooking spray. Cook the tomatoes for 30 minutes at 350°F. Once they have shrunk and are beginning to turn brown, set them to one side.
8.Cook the pasta and drain it. Rinse with cold water and set it aside to cool.
9.Wash, dry and halve the bell peppers. Remove the stems and seeds.
10.Wash and halve the cherry tomatoes.
11.In a large bowl, mix together the bell peppers and cherry tomatoes. Stir in the roasted vegetables, cooked pasta, pink Himalayan salt, dressing, chopped basil leaves, and grated parmesan, ensuring to incorporate everything well.
12.Let the salad cool and marinate in the refrigerator.
13.Serve the salad cold or at room temperature.

Prosciutto & Potato Salad

Prep + Cook Time: 15 minutes | Servings: 8

Ingredients
4 lb. potatoes, boiled and cubed
15 slices prosciutto, diced
15 oz. sour cream
2 cups shredded cheddar cheese
2 tbsp. mayonnaise
1 tsp. salt
1 tsp. black pepper
1 tsp. dried basil

Instructions
1. Pre-heat the Air Fryer to 350°F.
2. Place the potatoes, prosciutto, and cheddar in a baking dish. Put it in the Air Fryer and allow to cook for 7 minutes.
3. In a separate bowl, mix together the sour cream, mayonnaise, salt, pepper, and basil using a whisk.
4. Coat the salad with the dressing and serve.

Chicken Quesadillas

Prep + Cook Time: 20 minutes | Servings: 4

Ingredients
2 soft taco shells
1 lb. boneless chicken breasts
1 large green pepper, sliced
1 medium-sized onion, sliced
½ cup Cheddar cheese, shredded
½ cup salsa sauce
2 tbsp. olive oil
Salt and pepper, to taste

Instructions
1. Pre-heat the Air Fryer to 370°F and drizzle the basket with 1 tablespoon of olive oil.
2. Lay one taco shell into the bottom of the fryer and spread some salsa inside the taco. Slice the chicken breast into strips and put the strips into taco shell.
3. Top the chicken with the onions and peppers.
4. Season with salt and pepper. Add the shredded cheese and top with the second taco shell.
5. Drizzle with another tablespoon of olive oil. Put the rack over the taco to keep it in place.

6. Cook for 4 – 6 minutes, until it turns lightly brown and is cooked through. Serve either hot or cold.

Mozzarella Bruschetta

Prep + Cook Time: 10 minutes | Servings: 1

Ingredients
6 small loaf slices
½ cup tomatoes, finely chopped
3 oz. mozzarella cheese, grated
1 tbsp. fresh basil, chopped
1 tbsp. olive oil

Instructions
1. Pre-heat the Air Fryer to 350°F. Place the bread inside and cook for about 3 minutes.
2. Add the tomato, mozzarella, prosciutto, and a drizzle of olive oil on top.
3. Cook the bruschetta for an additional minute before serving.

Sausage-Chicken Casserole

Prep + Cook Time: 30 minutes | Servings: 8

Ingredients
2 cloves minced garlic
10 eggs
1 cup broccoli, chopped
½ tbsp. salt
1 cup cheddar, shredded and divided
¼ tbsp. pepper
¾ cup whipping cream
1 x 12-oz. package cooked chicken sausage

Instructions
1. Pre-heat the Air Fryer to 400°F.
2. In a large bowl, beat the eggs with a whisk. Pour in the whipping cream and cheese. Combine well.
3. In a separate bowl, mix together the garlic, broccoli, salt, pepper and cooked sausage.
4. Place the chicken sausage mix in a casserole dish. Top with the cheese mixture.
5. Transfer to the Air Fryer and cook for about 20 minutes.

Cashew & Chicken Manchurian

Prep + Cook Time: 30 minutes | Servings: 6

Ingredients

1 cup chicken boneless
1 spring onions, chopped
1 onion, chopped
3 green chili
6 cashew nuts
1 tsp. ginger, chopped
½ tsp. garlic, chopped
1 Egg
2 tbsp. flour
1 tbsp. cornstarch
1 tsp. soy sauce
2 tsp. chili paste
1 tsp. pepper
Pinch MSG
sugar as needed
1 tbsp. oil

Instructions

1. Pre-heat your Air Fryer at 360°F
2. Toss together the chicken, egg, salt and pepper to coat well.
3. Combine the cornstarch and flour and use this to cover the chicken.
4. Cook in the fryer for 10 minutes.
5. In the meantime, toast the nuts in a frying pan. Add in the onions and cook until they turn translucent. Combine with the remaining ingredients to create the sauce.
6. Finally, add in the chicken. When piping hot, garnish with the spring onions and serve.

Cheese & Bacon Rolls

Prep + Cook Time: 25 minutes | Servings: 4

Ingredients

8 oz. refrigerated crescent roll dough [usually 1 can]
6 oz. very sharp cheddar cheese, grated
1 lb. bacon, cooked and chopped

Instructions

1. Roll out the crescent dough flat and slice it into 1" x 1 ½" pieces.
2. In a bowl, mix together the cheese and bacon. Take about ¼ cup of this mixture and spread it across one slice of dough. Repeat with the rest of the mixture and dough.
3. Set your Air Fryer to 330°F and allow to warm.
4. Place the rolls on the Air Fry tray and transfer to the fryer. Alternatively, you can put them in the food basket.
5. Bake for roughly 6 – 8 minutes until a golden brown color is achieved. Watch them carefully to prevent burning, as they may cook very quickly.

Kidney Beans Oatmeal

Prep + Cook Time: 25 minutes | Servings: 2 – 4

Ingredients

2 large bell peppers, halved lengthwise, deseeded
2 tbsp. cooked kidney beans
2 tbsp. cooked chick peas
2 cups oatmeal, cooked
1 tsp. ground cumin
½ tsp. paprika
½ tsp. salt or to taste
¼ tsp. black pepper powder
¼ cup yogurt

Instructions

1. Pre-heat the Air Fryer at 355°F.
2. Put the bell peppers, cut-side-down, in the fryer. Allow to cook for 2 – 3 minutes.
3. Take the peppers out of the Air Fryer and let cool.
4. In a bowl, combine together the rest of the ingredients.
5. Divide the mixture evenly and use each portion to stuff a pepper.
6. Return to the Air Fryer and continue to air fry for 4 minutes. Serve hot.

Chicken Fillets & Brie

Prep + Cook Time: 40 minutes | Servings: 4

Ingredients

4 slices turkey, cured
2 large chicken fillets
4 slices brie cheese
1 tbsp. chives, chopped
Salt and pepper to taste

Instructions

1. Pre-heat Air Fryer to 360°F. Slice each chicken fillet in half and sprinkle on salt and pepper. Coat with the brie and chives.
2. Wrap the turkey around the chicken and secure with toothpick.
3. Cook for 15 minutes until a brown color is achieved.

Cheese & Macaroni Balls

Prep + Cook Time: 25 minutes | Servings: 2

Ingredients
2 cups leftover macaroni
1 cup cheddar cheese, shredded
3 large eggs
1 cup milk
½ cup flour
1 cup bread crumbs
½ tsp. salt
¼ tsp. black pepper

Instructions
1. In a bowl, combine the leftover macaroni and shredded cheese.
2. Pour the flour in a separate bowl. Put the bread crumbs in a third bowl. Finally, in a fourth bowl, mix together the eggs and milk with a whisk.
3. With an ice-cream scoop, create balls from the macaroni mixture. Coat them the flour, then in the egg mixture, and lastly in the bread crumbs.
4. Pre-heat the Air Fryer to 365°F and cook the balls for about 10 minutes, giving them an occasional stir. Ensure they crisp up nicely.
5. Serve with the sauce of your choice.

Cheese Pizza

Prep + Cook Time: 15 minutes | Servings: 4

Ingredients
1 pc. bread
½ lb. mozzarella cheese
1 tbsp. olive oil
2 tbsp. ketchup
⅓ cup sausage
1 tsp. garlic powder

Instructions
1. Using a tablespoon, spread the ketchup over the pita bread.
2. Top with the sausage and cheese. Season with the garlic powder and 1 tablespoon of olive oil.
3. Pre-heat the Air Fryer to 340°F.
4. Put the pizza in the fryer basket and cook for 6 minutes. Enjoy!

Portabella Pizza

Prep + Cook Time: 15 minutes | Servings: 3

Ingredients
3 tbsp. olive oil
3 portobello mushroom caps, cleaned and scooped
3 tbsp. mozzarella, shredded
3 tbsp. tomato sauce
Pinch of salt
12 slices pepperoni
Pinch of dried Italian seasonings

Instructions
1. Pre-heat the Air Fryer to 330°F.
2. Coat both sides of the mushroom cap with a drizzle of oil, before seasoning the inside with the Italian seasonings and salt. Evenly spread the tomato sauce over the mushroom and add the cheese on top.
3. Put the mushroom into the cooking basket of the Air Fryer. Place the slices of pepperoni on top of the portobello pizza after a minute of cooking and continue to cook for another 3-5 minutes.

American Hot Dogs

Prep + Cook Time: 20 minutes | Servings: 4

Ingredients
3 brazilian sausages, cut into 3 equal pieces
9 bacon fillets, raw
Black pepper to taste
Salt to taste

Instructions
1. Pre-heat the Air Fryer for 5 minutes at 355°F.
2. Take a slice of bacon and wrap it around each piece of sausage. Sprinkle with some salt and pepper as desired, as well as a half-teaspoon of Italian herbs if you like.
3. Fry the sausages for 15 minutes and serve warm.

Garlic Bacon

Prep + Cook Time: 40 minutes | Servings: 4

Ingredients
4 potatoes, peeled and cut into bite-size chunks
6 cloves garlic, unpeeled
strips bacon, chopped
1 tbsp. fresh rosemary, finely chopped

Instructions
1. In a large bowl, thoroughly combine the potatoes, garlic, bacon, and rosemary. Place the ingredients in a baking dish.
2. Set your Air Fryer to 350°F and briefly allow to warm.
3. Cook the potatoes for 25-30 minutes until a golden brown color is achieved.

Mexican Pizza

Prep + Cook Time: 15 minutes | Servings: 4

Ingredients
¾ cup refried beans
1 cup salsa
12 frozen beef meatballs, pre-cooked
2 jalapeno peppers, sliced
6 bread
1 cup pepper Jack cheese, shredded
1 cup Colby cheese, shredded

Instructions
1.Pre-heat the Air Fryer for 4 minutes at 370°F.
2.In a bowl, mix together the salsa, meatball, jalapeno pepper and beans.
3.Place a spoonful of this mixture on top of each pita bread, along with a topping of pepper Jack and Colby cheese.
4.Bake in the fryer for 10 minutes. Serve hot.

Pesto Gnocchi

Prep + Cook Time: 30 minutes | Servings: 4

Ingredients
1 package [16-oz.] shelf-stable gnocchi
1 medium-sized onion, chopped
3 cloves garlic, minced
1 jar [8 oz.] pesto
⅓ cup parmesan cheese, grated
1 tbsp. extra virgin olive oil
Salt and black pepper to taste

Instructions
1.Pre-heat the Air Fryer to 340°F.
2.In a large bowl combine the onion, garlic, and gnocchi, and drizzle with the olive oil. Mix thoroughly.
3.Transfer the mixture to the fryer and cook for 15 – 20 minutes, stirring occasionally, making sure the gnocchi become lightly brown and crispy.
4.Add in the pesto and Parmesan cheese, and give everything a good stir before serving straightaway.

Cheeseburger Sliders

Prep + Cook Time: 20 minutes | Servings: 3

Ingredients
1 lb. ground beef
6 slices cheddar cheese
6 dinner rolls
Salt and pepper

Instructions
1.Pre-heat the Air Fryer to 390°F.
2.With your hands, shape the ground beef into 6 x 2.5-oz. patties. Sprinkle on some salt and pepper to taste.
3.Place the burgers in the cooking basket and cook for 10 minutes. Take care when removing them from the Air Fryer.
4.Top the patties with the cheese. Put them back in the Air Fryer and allow to cook for another minute before serving.

Sweet & Sour Tofu

Prep + Cook Time: 55 minutes | Servings: 2

Ingredients
2 tsp. apple cider vinegar
1 tbsp. sugar
1 tbsp. soy sauce
3 tsp. lime juice
1 tsp. ground ginger
1 tsp. garlic powder
½ block firm tofu, pressed to remove excess liquid and cut into cubes
1 tsp. cornstarch
2 green onions, chopped
Toasted sesame seeds for garnish

Instructions
1.In a bowl, thoroughly combine the apple cider vinegar, sugar, soy sauce, lime juice, ground ginger, and garlic powder.
2.Cover the tofu with this mixture and leave to marinate for at least 30 minutes.
3.Transfer the tofu to the Air Fryer, keeping any excess marinade for the sauce. Cook at 400°F for 20 minutes or until crispy.
4.In the meantime, thicken the sauce with the cornstarch over a medium-low heat.
5.Serve the cooked tofu with the sauce, green onions, sesame seeds, and some rice.

Vegetable Salad

Prep + Cook Time: 20 minutes | Servings: 4

Ingredients
6 plum tomatoes, halved
2 large red onions, sliced
4 long red pepper, sliced
2 yellow pepper, sliced
6 cloves of garlic, crushed
1 tbsp. extra-virgin olive oil
1 tsp. paprika
½ lemon, juiced
Salt and pepper to taste
1 tbsp. baby capers

Instructions
1.Pre-heat the Air Fryer at 420°F.
2.Put the tomatoes, onions, peppers, and garlic in a large bowl and cover with the extra virgin olive oil, paprika, and lemon juice. Sprinkle with salt and pepper as desired.
3.Line the inside of your fryer with aluminum foil. Place the vegetables inside and allow to cook for 10 minutes, ensuring the edges turn brown.
4.Serve in a salad bowl with the baby capers. Make sure all the ingredients are well combined.

Mediterranean Vegetables

Prep + Cook Time: 30 minutes | Servings: 4

Ingredients
1 cup cherry tomatoes, halved
1 large zucchini, sliced
1 green pepper, sliced
1 parsnip, sliced
1 carrot, sliced
1 tsp. mixed herbs
1 tsp. mustard
1 tsp. garlic puree
6 tbsp. olive oil
Salt and pepper to taste

Instructions
1.Pre-heat the Air Fryer at 400°F.
2.Combine all the ingredients in a bowl, making sure to coat the vegetables well.
3.Transfer to the fryer and cook for 6 minutes, ensuring the vegetables are tender and browned.

Sweet Potatoes

Prep + Cook Time: 55 minutes | Servings: 4

Ingredients
2 potatoes, peeled and cubed
4 carrots, cut into chunks
1 head broccoli, cut into florets
4 zucchinis, sliced thickly
Salt and pepper to taste
¼ cup olive oil
1 tbsp. dry onion powder

Instructions
1.Pre-heat the Air Fryer to 400°F.
2.In a baking dish small enough to fit inside the fryer, add all the ingredients and combine well.
3.Cook for 45 minutes in the fryer, ensuring the vegetables are soft and the sides have browned before serving.

Sage Chicken Escallops

Prep + Cook Time: 45 minutes | Servings: 4

Ingredients
4 skinless chicken breasts

2 eggs, beaten
½ cup flour
6 sage leaves
¼ cup bread crumbs
¼ cup parmesan cheese
Cooking spray

Instructions
1.Cut the chicken breasts into thin, flat slices.
2.In a bowl, combine the parmesan with the sage.
3.Add in the flour and eggs and sprinkle with salt and pepper as desired. Mix well.
4.Dip chicken in the flour-egg mixture.
5.Coat the chicken in the panko bread crumbs.
6.Spritz the inside of the Air Fryer with cooking spray and set it to 390°F, allowing it to warm.
7.Cook the chicken for 20 minutes.
8.When golden, serve with fried rice.

Fried Pickles

Prep + Cook Time: 30 minutes | Servings: 4

Ingredients
14 dill pickles, sliced
¼ cup flour
1/8 tsp. baking powder
Pinch of salt
2 tbsp. cornstarch + 3 tbsp. water
6 tbsp. bread crumbs
½ tsp. paprika
Cooking spray

Instructions
1.Pre-heat your Air Fryer at 400°F.
2.Drain any excess moisture out of the dill pickles on a paper towel.
3.In a bowl, combine the flour, baking powder and salt.
4.Throw in the cornstarch and water mixture and combine well with a whisk.
5.Put the panko bread crumbs in a shallow dish along with the paprika. Mix thoroughly.
6.Dip the pickles in the flour batter, before coating in the bread crumbs. Spritz all the pickles with the cooking spray.
7.Transfer to the fryer and cook for 15 minutes, until a golden brown color is achieved.

Cauliflower Bites

Prep + Cook Time: 30 minutes | Servings: 4

Ingredients
1 cup flour
⅓ cup desiccated coconut
Salt and pepper to taste
1 flax egg [1 tbsp. flaxseed meal + 3 tbsp. water]
1 small cauliflower, cut into florets
1 tsp. mixed spice
½ tsp. mustard powder
2 tbsp. maple syrup
1 clove of garlic, minced
2 tbsp. soy sauce

Instructions
1. Pre-heat the Air Fryer to 400°F.
2. In a bowl, mix together the oats, flour, and desiccated coconut, sprinkling with some salt and pepper as desired.
3. In a separate bowl, season the flax egg with a pinch of salt.
4. Coat the cauliflower with mixed spice and mustard powder.
5. Dip the florets into the flax egg, then into the flour mixture. Cook for 15 minutes in the fryer.
6. In the meantime, place a saucepan over medium heat and add in the maple syrup, garlic, and soy sauce. Boil first, before reducing the heat to allow the sauce to thicken.
7. Remove the florets from the Air Fryer and transfer to the saucepan. Coat the florets in the sauce before returning to the fryer and allowing to cook for an additional 5 minutes.

Chicken & Veggies

Prep + Cook Time: 30 minutes | Servings: 4

Ingredients
8 chicken thighs
5 oz. mushrooms, sliced
1 red onion, diced
Fresh black pepper, to taste
10 medium asparagus
½ cup carrots, diced
¼ cup balsamic vinegar
2 red bell peppers, diced
½ tsp. sugar
2 tbsp. extra-virgin olive oil
1 ½ tbsp. fresh rosemary
2 cloves garlic, chopped
½ tbsp. dried oregano
1 tsp. kosher salt
2 fresh sage, chopped

Instructions
1. Pre-heat the Air Fryer to 400°F.
2. Grease the inside of a baking tray with the oil.
3. Season the chicken with salt and pepper.
4. Put all of the vegetables in a large bowl and throw in the oregano, garlic, sugar, mushrooms, vinegar, and sage. Combine everything well before transferring to the baking tray.
5. Put the chicken thighs in the baking tray. Cook in the Air Fryer for about 20 minutes.
6. Serve hot.

Falafel

Prep + Cook Time: 30 minutes | Servings: 8

Ingredients
1 tsp. cumin seeds
½ tsp. coriander seeds
2 cups chickpeas from can, drained and rinsed
½ tsp. red pepper flakes
3 cloves garlic
¼ cup parsley, chopped
¼ cup coriander, chopped
½ onion, diced
1 tbsp. juice from freshly squeezed lemon
3 tbsp. flour
½ tsp. salt cooking spray

Instructions
1. Fry the cumin and coriander seeds over medium heat until fragrant.
2. Grind using a mortar and pestle.
3. Put all of ingredients, except for the cooking spray, in a food processor and blend until a fine consistency is achieved.
4. Use your hands to mold the mixture into falafels and spritz with the cooking spray.
5. Preheat your Air Fryer at 400°F.
6. Transfer the falafels to the fryer in one single layer.
7. Cook for 15 minutes, serving when they turn golden brown.

Easy Asparagus

Prep + Cook Time: 10 minutes | Servings: 4

Ingredients
1 lb. fresh asparagus spears, trimmed
1 tbsp. olive oil
Salt and pepper to taste

Instructions
1. Pre-heat the Air Fryer at 375°F.
2. Combine all of the ingredients and transfer to the Air Fryer.
3. Cook for 5 minutes until soft.

Cauliflower Steak

Prep + Cook Time: 30 minutes | Servings: 2

Ingredients
1 cauliflower, sliced into two
1 tbsp. olive oil
2 tbsp. onion, chopped
¼ tsp. vegetable stock powder
¼ cup milk
Salt and pepper to taste

Instructions
1.Place the cauliflower in a bowl of salted water and allow to absorb for at least 2 hours.
2.Pre-heat the Air Fryer to 400°F.
3.Rinse off the cauliflower, put inside the fryer and cook for 15 minutes.
4.In the meantime, fry the onions over medium heat, stirring constantly, until they turn translucent. Pour in the vegetable stock powder and milk. Bring to a boil and then lower the heat.
5.Let the sauce reduce and add in salt and pepper.
6.Plate up the cauliflower steak and top with the sauce.

Rocket Salad

Prep + Cook Time: 35 minutes | Servings: 4

Ingredients
8 fresh figs, halved
1 ½ cups chickpeas, cooked
1 tsp. cumin seeds, roasted then crushed
4 tbsp. balsamic vinegar
2 tbsp. extra-virgin olive oil
Salt and pepper to taste
3 cups arugula rocket, washed and dried

Instructions
1.Pre-heat the Air Fryer to 375°F.
2.Cover the Air Fryer basket with aluminum foil and grease lightly with oil. Put the figs in the fryer and allow to cook for 10 minutes.
3.In a bowl, combine the chickpeas and cumin seeds.
4.Remove the cooked figs from the fryer and replace with chickpeas. Cook for 10 minutes. Leave to cool.
5.In the meantime, prepare the dressing. Mix together the balsamic vinegar, olive oil, salt and pepper.
6.In a salad bowl combine the arugula rocket with the cooled figs and chickpeas.
7.Toss with the sauce and serve right away.

Vegan Ravioli

Prep + Cook Time: 15 minutes | Servings: 4

Ingredients
½ cup bread crumbs
2 tsp. nutritional yeast
1 tsp. dried basil
1 tsp. dried oregano
1 tsp. garlic powder
Salt and pepper to taste
¼ cup aquafaba
8 oz. vegan ravioli
Cooking spray

Instructions
1.Cover the Air Fryer basket with aluminum foil and coat with a light brushing of oil.
2.Pre-heat the Air Fryer to 400°F. Combine together the panko breadcrumbs, nutritional yeast, basil, oregano, and garlic powder. Sprinkle on salt and pepper to taste.
3.Put the aquafaba in a separate bowl. Dip the ravioli in the aquafaba before coating it in the panko mixture. Spritz with cooking spray and transfer to the Air Fryer.
4.Cook for 6 minutes ensuring to shake the Air Fryer basket halfway.

Thanksgiving Sprouts

Prep + Cook Time: 20 minutes | Servings: 6

Ingredients
1 ½ lb. Brussels sprouts, cleaned and trimmed
3 tbsp. olive oil
1 tsp. salt
1 tsp. black pepper

Instructions
1.Pre-heat the Air Fryer to 375°F. Cover the basket with aluminum foil and coat with a light brushing of oil.
2.In a mixing bowl, combine all ingredients, coating the sprouts well.
3.Put in the fryer basket and cook for 10 minutes. Shake the Air Fryer basket throughout the duration to ensure even cooking.

Roasted Garlic, Broccoli & Lemon

Prep + Cook Time: 25 minutes | Servings: 6

Ingredients
2 heads broccoli, cut into florets
2 tsp. extra virgin olive oil
1 tsp. salt
½ tsp. black pepper
1 clove garlic, minced
½ tsp. lemon juice

Instructions
1.Cover the Air Fryer basket with aluminum foil and coat with a light brushing of oil.
2.Pre-heat the fryer to 375°F.
3.In a bowl, combine all ingredients save for the lemon juice and transfer to the fryer basket. Allow to cook for 15 minutes.
4.Serve with the lemon juice.

Pepperoni Pizza

Prep + Cook Time: 15 minutes | Servings: 3

Ingredients
3 portobello mushroom caps, cleaned and scooped
3 tbsp. olive oil
3 tbsp. tomato sauce
3 tbsp. mozzarella, shredded
12 slices pepperoni
1 pinch salt
1 pinch dried Italian seasonings

Instructions
1.Pre-heat the Air Fryer to 330°F.
2.Season both sides of the portobello mushrooms with a drizzle of olive oil, then sprinkle salt and the Italian seasonings on the insides.
3.With a knife, spread the tomato sauce evenly over the mushroom, before adding the mozzarella on top.
4.Put the portobello in the cooking basket and place in the Air Fryer.
5.Cook for 1 minute, before taking the cooking basket out of the fryer and putting the pepperoni slices on top.
6.Cook for another 3 to 5 minutes. Garnish with freshly grated parmesan cheese and crushed red pepper flakes and serve.

Baby Corn Pakodas

Prep + Cook Time: 20 minutes | Servings: 5

Ingredients
1 cup flour
¼ tsp. baking soda
¼ tsp. salt
½ tsp. curry powder
½ tsp. red chili powder
¼ tsp. turmeric powder
¼ cup water
10 pc. baby corn, blanched

Instructions
1.Pre-heat the Air Fryer to 425°F.
2.Cover the Air Fryer basket with aluminum foil and coat with a light brushing of oil.
3.In a bowl, combine all ingredients save for the corn. Stir with a whisk until well combined.
4.Coat the corn in the batter and put inside the Air Fryer.
5.Cook for 8 minutes until a golden brown color is achieved.

Chicken-Mushroom Casserole

Prep + Cook Time: 30 minutes | Servings: 4

Ingredients
4 chicken breasts
½ cup shredded cheese
Salt to taste
1 cup coconut milk
1 cup mushrooms
1 broccoli, cut into florets
1 tbsp. curry powder

Instructions
1.Pre-heat your Air Fryer to 350°F. Spritz a casserole dish with some cooking spray.
2.Cube the chicken breasts and combine with curry powder and coconut milk in a bowl. Season with salt.
3.Add in the broccoli and mushroom and mix well.
4.Pour the mixture into the casserole dish. Top with the cheese.
5.Transfer to your Air Fryer and cook for about 20 minutes.
6.Serve warm.

Chapter 3 Vegetables

Balsamic Brussels Sprouts

Prep time: 5 minutes | Cook time: 13 minutes | Serves 2

2 cups Brussels sprouts, halved
1 tablespoon olive oil
1 tablespoon

balsamic vinegar
1 tablespoon maple syrup
¼ teaspoon sea salt

1. Preheat the air fryer to 375ºF (191ºC).
2. Evenly coat the Brussels sprouts with the olive oil, balsamic vinegar, maple syrup, and salt.
3. Transfer to the air fryer basket and air fry for 5 minutes. Give the basket a good shake, turn the heat to 400ºF (204ºC) and continue to air fry for another 8 minutes.
4. Serve hot.

Lush Summer Rolls

Prep time: 15 minutes | Cook time: 15 minutes | Serves 4

1 cup shiitake mushroom, sliced thinly
1 celery stalk, chopped
1 medium carrot, shredded
½ teaspoon finely chopped ginger

1 teaspoon sugar
1 tablespoon soy sauce
1 teaspoon nutritional yeast
8 spring roll sheets
1 teaspoon corn starch
2 tablespoons water

1. In a bowl, combine the ginger, soy sauce, nutritional yeast, carrots, celery, mushroom, and sugar.
2. Mix the cornstarch and water to create an adhesive for the spring rolls.
3. Scoop a tablespoonful of the vegetable mixture into the middle of the spring roll sheets. Brush the edges of the sheets with the cornstarch adhesive and enclose around the filling to make spring rolls.
4. Preheat the air fryer to 400ºF (204ºC). When warm, place the rolls inside and air fry for 15 minutes or until crisp.
5. Serve hot.

Cauliflower, Chickpea, and Avocado Mash

Prep time: 10 minutes | Cook time: 25 minutes | Serves 4

1 medium head cauliflower, cut into florets
1 can chickpeas, drained and rinsed
1 tablespoon extra-virgin olive oil
2 tablespoons lemon

juice
Salt and ground black pepper, to taste
4 flatbreads, toasted
2 ripe avocados, mashed

1. Preheat the air fryer to 425ºF (218ºC).
2. In a bowl, mix the chickpeas, cauliflower, lemon juice and olive oil. Sprinkle salt and pepper as desired.
3. Put inside the air fryer basket and air fry for 25 minutes.
4. Spread on top of the flatbread along with the mashed avocado. Sprinkle with more pepper and salt and serve.

Lush Vegetables Roast

Prep time: 15 minutes | Cook time: 20 minutes | Serves 6

1⅓ cups small parsnips, peeled and cubed
1⅓ cups celery
2 red onions, sliced
1⅓ cups small butternut squash, cut in half, deseeded

and cubed
1 tablespoon fresh thyme needles
1 tablespoon olive oil
Salt and ground black pepper, to taste

1. Preheat the air fryer to 390ºF (199ºC).
2. Combine the cut vegetables with the thyme, olive oil, salt and pepper.
3. Put the vegetables in the basket and transfer the basket to the air fryer.
4. Roast for 20 minutes, stirring once throughout the roasting time, until the vegetables are nicely browned and cooked through.
5. Serve warm.

Green Beans with Shallot

Prep time: 10 minutes | Cook time: 10 minutes | Serves 4

1½ pounds (680 g) French green beans, stems removed and blanched
1 tablespoon salt
½ pound (227 g)
shallots, peeled and cut into quarters
½ teaspoon ground white pepper
2 tablespoons olive oil

1. Preheat the air fryer to 400ºF (204ºC).
2. Coat the vegetables with the rest of the ingredients in a bowl.
3. Transfer to the air fryer basket and air fry for 10 minutes, making sure the green beans achieve a light brown color.
4. Serve hot.

Ratatouille

Prep time: 20 minutes | Cook time: 25 minutes | Serves 4

1 sprig basil
1 sprig flat-leaf parsley
1 sprig mint
1 tablespoon coriander powder
1 teaspoon capers
½ lemon, juiced
Salt and ground black pepper, to taste
2 eggplants, sliced crosswise
2 red onions, chopped
4 cloves garlic, minced
2 red peppers, sliced crosswise
1 fennel bulb, sliced crosswise
3 large zucchinis, sliced crosswise
5 tablespoons olive oil
4 large tomatoes, chopped
2 teaspoons herbs de Provence

1. Blend the basil, parsley, coriander, mint, lemon juice and capers, with a little salt and pepper. Make sure all ingredients are well-incorporated.
2. Preheat the air fryer to 400ºF (204ºC).
3. Coat the eggplant, onions, garlic, peppers, fennel, and zucchini with olive oil.
4. Transfer the vegetables into a baking dish and top with the tomatoes and herb purée. Sprinkle with more salt and pepper, and the herbs de Provence.
5. Air fry for 25 minutes.
6. Serve immediately.

Rice and Eggplant Bowl

Prep time: 15 minutes | Cook time: 10 minutes | Serves 4

¼ cup sliced cucumber
1 teaspoon salt
1 tablespoon sugar
7 tablespoons Japanese rice vinegar
3 medium eggplants, sliced
3 tablespoons sweet white miso paste
1 tablespoon mirin rice wine
4 cups cooked sushi rice
4 spring onions
1 tablespoon toasted sesame seeds

1. Coat the cucumber slices with the rice wine vinegar, salt, and sugar.
2. Put a dish on top of the bowl to weight it down completely.
3. In a bowl, mix the eggplants, mirin rice wine, and miso paste. Allow to marinate for half an hour.
4. Preheat the air fryer to 400ºF (204ºC).
5. Put the eggplant slices in the air fryer and air fry for 10 minutes.
6. Fill the bottom of a serving bowl with rice and top with the eggplants and pickled cucumbers.
7. Add the spring onions and sesame seeds for garnish. Serve immediately.

Mushroom and Pepper Pizza Squares

Prep time: 10 minutes | Cook time: 10 minutes | Serves 10

1 pizza dough, cut into squares
1 cup chopped oyster mushrooms
1 shallot, chopped
¼ red bell pepper,
chopped
2 tablespoons parsley
Salt and ground black pepper, to taste

1. Preheat the air fryer to 400ºF (204ºC).
2. In a bowl, combine the oyster mushrooms, shallot, bell pepper and parsley. Sprinkle some salt and pepper as desired.
3. Spread this mixture on top of the pizza squares.
4. Bake in the air fryer for 10 minutes.
5. Serve warm.

Mediterranean Air Fried Veggies

Prep time: 10 minutes | Cook time: 6 minutes | Serves 4

1 large zucchini, sliced
1 cup cherry tomatoes, halved
1 parsnip, sliced
1 green pepper, sliced
1 carrot, sliced
1 teaspoon mixed herbs
1 teaspoon mustard
1 teaspoon garlic purée
6 tablespoons olive oil
Salt and ground black pepper, to taste

1. Preheat the air fryer to 400ºF (204ºC).
2. Combine all the ingredients in a bowl, making sure to coat the vegetables well.
3. Transfer to the air fryer and air fry for 6 minutes, ensuring the vegetables are tender and browned.
4. Serve immediately.

Potato and Broccoli with Tofu Scramble

Prep time: 15 minutes | Cook time: 30 minutes | Serves 3

2½ cups chopped red potato
2 tablespoons olive oil, divided
1 block tofu, chopped finely
2 tablespoons tamari
1 teaspoon turmeric
powder
½ teaspoon onion powder
½ teaspoon garlic powder
½ cup chopped onion
4 cups broccoli florets

1. Preheat the air fryer to 400ºF (204ºC).
2. Toss together the potatoes and 1 tablespoon of the olive oil.
3. Air fry the potatoes in a baking dish for 15 minutes, shaking once during the cooking time to ensure they fry evenly.
4. Combine the tofu, the remaining 1 tablespoon of the olive oil, turmeric, onion powder, tamari, and garlic powder together, stirring in the onions, followed by the broccoli.
5. Top the potatoes with the tofu mixture and air fry for an additional 15 minutes. Serve warm.

Crispy Chickpeas

Prep time: 5 minutes | Cook time: 15 minutes | Serves 4

1 (15-ounces / 425-g) can chickpeas, drained but not rinsed
2 tablespoons olive
oil
1 teaspoon salt
2 tablespoons lemon juice

1. Preheat the air fryer to 400ºF (204ºC).
2. Add all the ingredients together in a bowl and mix. Transfer this mixture to the air fryer basket.
3. Air fry for 15 minutes, ensuring the chickpeas become nice and crispy.
4. Serve immediately.

Cauliflower Tater Tots

Prep time: 15 minutes | Cook time: 16 minutes | Serves 12

1 pound (454 g) cauliflower, steamed and chopped
½ cup nutritional yeast
1 tablespoon oats
1 tablespoon desiccated coconuts
3 tablespoons flaxseed meal
3 tablespoons water
1 onion, chopped
1 teaspoon minced garlic
1 teaspoon chopped parsley
1 teaspoon chopped oregano
1 teaspoon chopped chives
Salt and ground black pepper, to taste
½ cup bread crumbs

1. Preheat the air fryer to 390ºF (199ºC).
2. Drain any excess water out of the cauliflower by wringing it with a paper towel.
3. In a bowl, combine the cauliflower with the remaining ingredients, save the bread crumbs. Using the hands, shape the mixture into several small balls.
4. Coat the balls in the bread crumbs and transfer to the air fryer basket. Air fry for 6 minutes, then raise the temperature to 400ºF (204ºC) and then air fry for an additional 10 minutes.
5. Serve immediately.

Russet Potato Gratin

Prep time: 10 minutes | Cook time: 35 minutes | Serves 6

½ cup milk
7 medium russet potatoes, peeled
Salt, to taste
1 teaspoon black pepper
½ cup heavy whipping cream
½ cup grated semi-mature cheese
½ teaspoon nutmeg

1. Preheat the air fryer to 390ºF (199ºC).
2. Cut the potatoes into wafer-thin slices.
3. In a bowl, combine the milk and cream and sprinkle with salt, pepper, and nutmeg.
4. Use the milk mixture to coat the slices of potatoes. Put in a baking dish. Top the potatoes with the rest of the milk mixture.
5. Put the baking dish into the air fryer basket and bake for 25 minutes.
6. Pour the cheese over the potatoes.
7. Bake for an additional 10 minutes, ensuring the top is nicely browned before serving.

Saltine Wax Beans

Prep time: 10 minutes | Cook time: 7 minutes | Serves 4

½ cup flour
1 teaspoon smoky chipotle powder
½ teaspoon ground black pepper
1 teaspoon sea salt flakes
2 eggs, beaten
½ cup crushed saltines
10 ounces (283 g) wax beans
Cooking spray

1. Preheat the air fryer to 360ºF (182ºC).
2. Combine the flour, chipotle powder, black pepper, and salt in a bowl. Put the eggs in a second bowl. Put the crushed saltines in a third bowl.
3. Wash the beans with cold water and discard any tough strings.
4. Coat the beans with the flour mixture, before dipping them into the beaten egg. Cover them with the crushed saltines.
5. Spritz the beans with cooking spray.
6. Air fry for 4 minutes. Give the air fryer basket a good shake and continue to air fry for 3 minutes. Serve hot.

Potatoes with Zucchinis

Prep time: 10 minutes | Cook time: 45 minutes | Serves 4

2 potatoes, peeled and cubed
4 carrots, cut into chunks
1 head broccoli, cut into florets
4 zucchinis, sliced
thickly
Salt and ground black pepper, to taste
¼ cup olive oil
1 tablespoon dry onion powder

1. Preheat the air fryer to 400ºF (204ºC).
2. In a baking dish, add all the ingredients and combine well.
3. Bake for 45 minutes in the air fryer, ensuring the vegetables are soft and the sides have browned before serving.

Mascarpone Mushrooms

Prep time: 10 minutes | Cook time: 15 minutes | Serves 4

Vegetable oil spray
4 cups sliced mushrooms
1 medium yellow onion, chopped
2 cloves garlic, minced
¼ cup heavy whipping cream or half-and-half
8 ounces (227 g) mascarpone cheese
1 teaspoon dried
thyme
1 teaspoon kosher salt
1 teaspoon black pepper
½ teaspoon red pepper flakes
4 cups cooked konjac noodles, for serving
½ cup grated Parmesan cheese

1. Preheat the air fryer to 350ºF (177ºC). Spray a heatproof pan with vegetable oil spray.
2. In a medium bowl, combine the mushrooms, onion, garlic, cream, mascarpone, thyme, salt, black pepper, and red pepper flakes. Stir to combine. Transfer the mixture to the prepared pan.
3. Put the pan in the air fryer basket. Bake for 15 minutes, stirring halfway through the baking time.
4. Divide the pasta among four shallow bowls. Spoon the mushroom mixture evenly over the pasta. Sprinkle with Parmesan cheese and serve.

Gold Ravioli

Prep time: 10 minutes | Cook time: 6 minutes | Serves 4

½ cup panko bread crumbs
2 teaspoons nutritional yeast
1 teaspoon dried basil
1 teaspoon dried oregano
1 teaspoon garlic powder
Salt and ground black pepper, to taste
¼ cup aquafaba
8 ounces (227 g) ravioli
Cooking spray

1. Cover the air fryer basket with aluminum foil and coat with a light brushing of oil.
2. Preheat the air fryer to 400ºF (204ºC). Combine the panko bread crumbs, nutritional yeast, basil, oregano, and garlic powder. Sprinkle with salt and pepper to taste.
3. Put the aquafaba in a separate bowl. Dip the ravioli in the aquafaba before coating it in the panko mixture. Spritz with cooking spray and transfer to the air fryer.
4. Air fry for 6 minutes. Shake the air fryer basket halfway.
5. Serve hot.

Air Fried Brussels Sprout

Prep time: 5 minutes | Cook time: 10 minutes | Serves 1

1 pound (454 g) Brussels sprouts
1 tablespoon coconut oil, melted
1 tablespoon unsalted butter, melted

1. Preheat the air fryer to 400ºF (204ºC).
2. Prepare the Brussels sprouts by halving them, discarding any loose leaves.
3. Combine with the melted coconut oil and transfer to the air fryer.
4. Air fry for 10 minutes, giving the basket a good shake throughout the air frying time to brown them up if desired.
5. The sprouts are ready when they are partially caramelized. Remove them from the air fryer and serve with a topping of melted butter before serving.

Black Bean and Tomato Chili

Prep time: 15 minutes | Cook time: 23 minutes | Serves 6

1 tablespoon olive oil
1 medium onion, diced
3 garlic cloves, minced
1 cup vegetable broth
3 cans black beans, drained and rinsed
2 cans diced tomatoes
2 chipotle peppers, chopped
2 teaspoons cumin
2 teaspoons chili powder
1 teaspoon dried oregano
½ teaspoon salt

1. Over a medium heat, fry the garlic and onions in the olive oil for 3 minutes.
2. Add the remaining ingredients, stirring constantly and scraping the bottom to prevent sticking.
3. Preheat the air fryer to 400ºF (204ºC).
4. Take a dish and place the mixture inside. Put a sheet of aluminum foil on top.
5. Transfer to the air fryer and bake for 20 minutes.
6. When ready, plate up and serve immediately.

Roasted Potatoes and Asparagus

Prep time: 5 minutes | Cook time: 23 minutes | Serves 4

4 medium potatoes
1 bunch asparagus
⅓ cup cottage cheese
⅓ cup low-fat crème fraiche
1 tablespoon wholegrain mustard
Salt and pepper, to taste
Cook spray

1. Preheat the air fryer to 390ºF (199ºC). Spritz the air fryer basket with cooking spray.
2. Place the potatoes in the basket. Air fry the potatoes for 20 minutes.
3. Boil the asparagus in salted water for 3 minutes.
4. Remove the potatoes and mash them with rest of ingredients. Sprinkle with salt and pepper.
5. Serve immediately.

Super Vegetable Burger

Prep time: 15 minutes | Cook time: 12 minutes | Serves 8

½ pound (227 g) cauliflower, steamed and diced, rinsed and drained
2 teaspoons coconut oil, melted
2 teaspoons minced garlic
¼ cup desiccated coconut
½ cup oats
3 tablespoons flour
1 tablespoon flaxseeds plus 3 tablespoons water, divided
1 teaspoon mustard powder
2 teaspoons thyme
2 teaspoons parsley
2 teaspoons chives
Salt and ground black pepper, to taste
1 cup bread crumbs

1. Preheat the air fryer to 390ºF (199ºC).
2. Combine the cauliflower with all the ingredients, except for the bread crumbs, incorporating everything well.
3. Using the hands, shape 8 equal-sized amounts of the mixture into burger patties. Coat the patties in bread crumbs before putting them in the air fryer basket in a single layer.
4. Air fry for 12 minutes or until crispy.
5. Serve hot.

Simple Buffalo Cauliflower

Prep time: 5 minutes | Cook time: 5 minutes | Serves 1

½ packet dry ranch seasoning
2 tablespoons salted butter, melted
1 cup cauliflower florets
¼ cup buffalo sauce

1. Preheat the air fryer to 400ºF (204ºC).
2. In a bowl, combine the dry ranch seasoning and butter. Toss with the cauliflower florets to coat and transfer them to the air fryer.
3. Roast for 5 minutes, shaking the basket occasionally to ensure the florets roast evenly.
4. Remove the cauliflower from the air fryer, pour the buffalo sauce over it, and serve.

Tofu Bites

Prep time: 15 minutes | Cook time: 30 minutes | Serves 4

1 packaged firm tofu, cubed and pressed to remove excess water
1 tablespoon soy sauce
1 tablespoon ketchup
1 tablespoon maple syrup
½ teaspoon vinegar
1 teaspoon liquid smoke
1 teaspoon hot sauce
2 tablespoons sesame seeds
1 teaspoon garlic powder
Salt and ground black pepper, to taste
Cooking spray

1. Preheat the air fryer to 375ºF (191ºC).
2. Spritz a baking dish with cooking spray.
3. Combine all the ingredients to coat the tofu completely and allow the marinade to absorb for half an hour.
4. Transfer the tofu to the baking dish, then air fry for 15 minutes. Flip the tofu over and air fry for another 15 minutes on the other side.
5. Serve immediately.

Herbed Radishes

Prep time: 5 minutes | Cook time: 10 minutes | Serves 2

1 pound (454 g) radishes
2 tablespoons unsalted butter, melted
¼ teaspoon dried oregano
½ teaspoon dried parsley
½ teaspoon garlic powder

1. Preheat the air fryer to 350ºF (177ºC). Prepare the radishes by cutting off their tops and bottoms and quartering them.
2. In a bowl, combine the butter, dried oregano, dried parsley, and garlic powder. Toss with the radishes to coat.
3. Transfer the radishes to the air fryer and air fry for 10 minutes, shaking the basket at the halfway point to ensure the radishes air fry evenly through. The radishes are ready when they turn brown.
4. Serve immediately.

Sweet Potatoes with Tofu

Prep time: 15 minutes | Cook time: 35 minutes | Serves 8

8 sweet potatoes, scrubbed
2 tablespoons olive oil
1 large onion, chopped
2 green chilies, deseeded and chopped
8 ounces (227 g)
tofu, crumbled
2 tablespoons Cajun seasoning
1 cup chopped tomatoes
1 can kidney beans, drained and rinsed
Salt and ground black pepper, to taste

1. Preheat the air fryer to 400°F (204°C).
2. With a knife, pierce the skin of the sweet potatoes and air fry in the air fryer for 30 minutes or until soft.
3. Remove from the air fryer, halve each potato, and set to one side.
4. Over a medium heat, fry the onions and chilies in the olive oil in a skillet for 2 minutes until fragrant.
5. Add the tofu and Cajun seasoning and air fry for a further 3 minutes before incorporating the kidney beans and tomatoes. Sprinkle some salt and pepper as desire.
6. Top each sweet potato halve with a spoonful of the tofu mixture and serve.

Sweet Potatoes with Zucchini

Prep time: 20 minutes | Cook time: 20 minutes | Serves 4

2 large-sized sweet potatoes, peeled and quartered
1 medium zucchini, sliced
1 Serrano pepper, deseeded and thinly sliced
1 bell pepper, deseeded and thinly sliced
1 to 2 carrots, cut into matchsticks
¼ cup olive oil
1½ tablespoons
maple syrup
½ teaspoon porcini powder
¼ teaspoon mustard powder
½ teaspoon fennel seeds
1 tablespoon garlic powder
½ teaspoon fine sea salt
¼ teaspoon ground black pepper
Tomato ketchup, for serving

1. Put the sweet potatoes, zucchini, peppers, and the carrot into the air fryer basket. Coat with a drizzling of olive oil.
2. Preheat the air fryer to 350°F (177°C).
3. Air fry the vegetables for 15 minutes.
4. In the meantime, prepare the sauce by vigorously combining the other ingredients, except for the tomato ketchup, with a whisk.
5. Lightly grease a baking dish.
6. Transfer the cooked vegetables to the baking dish, pour over the sauce and coat the vegetables well.
7. Increase the temperature to 390°F (199°C) and air fry the vegetables for an additional 5 minutes.
8. Serve warm with a side of ketchup.

Creamy and Cheesy Spinach

Prep time: 10 minutes | Cook time: 15 minutes | Serves 4

Vegetable oil spray
1 (10-ounce / 283-g) package frozen spinach, thawed and squeezed dry
½ cup chopped onion
2 cloves garlic, minced
4 ounces (113 g)
cream cheese, diced
½ teaspoon ground nutmeg
1 teaspoon kosher salt
1 teaspoon black pepper
½ cup grated Parmesan cheese

1. Preheat the air fryer to 350°F (177°C). Spray a heatproof pan with vegetable oil spray.
2. In a medium bowl, combine the spinach, onion, garlic, cream cheese, nutmeg, salt, and pepper. Transfer to the prepared pan.
3. Put the pan in the air fryer basket. Bake for 10 minutes. Open and stir to thoroughly combine the cream cheese and spinach.
4. Sprinkle the Parmesan cheese on top. Bake for 5 minutes, or until the cheese has melted and browned.
5. Serve hot.

Super Veg Rolls

Prep time: 20 minutes | Cook time: 10 minutes | Serves 6

2 potatoes, mashed
¼ cup peas
¼ cup mashed carrots
1 small cabbage, sliced
¼ cups beans
2 tablespoons

sweetcorn
1 small onion, chopped
½ cup bread crumbs
1 packet spring roll sheets
½ cup cornstarch slurry

1. Preheat the air fryer to 390ºF (199ºC).
2. Boil all the vegetables in water over a low heat. Rinse and allow to dry.
3. Unroll the spring roll sheets and spoon equal amounts of vegetable onto the center of each one. Fold into spring rolls and coat each one with the slurry and bread crumbs.
4. Air fry the rolls in the preheated air fryer for 10 minutes.
5. Serve warm.

Basmati Risotto

Prep time: 10 minutes | Cook time: 30 minutes | Serves 2

1 onion, diced
1 small carrot, diced
2 cups vegetable broth, boiling
½ cup grated Cheddar cheese
1 clove garlic,

minced
¾ cup long-grain basmati rice
1 tablespoon olive oil
1 tablespoon unsalted butter

1. Preheat the air fryer to 390ºF (199ºC).
2. Grease a baking tin with oil and stir in the butter, garlic, carrot, and onion.
3. Put the tin in the air fryer and bake for 4 minutes.
4. Pour in the rice and bake for a further 4 minutes, stirring three times throughout the baking time.
5. Turn the temperature down to 320ºF (160ºC).
6. Add the vegetable broth and give the dish a gentle stir. Bake for 22 minutes, leaving the air fryer uncovered.
7. Pour in the cheese, stir once more and serve.

Golden Garlicky Mushrooms

Prep time: 10 minutes | Cook time: 10 minutes | Serves 4

6 small mushrooms
1 tablespoon bread crumbs
1 tablespoon olive oil
1 ounce (28 g) onion, peeled and

diced
1 teaspoon parsley
1 teaspoon garlic purée
Salt and ground black pepper, to taste

1. Preheat the air fryer to 350ºF (177ºC).
2. Combine the bread crumbs, oil, onion, parsley, salt, pepper and garlic in a bowl. Cut out the mushrooms' stalks and stuff each cap with the crumb mixture.
3. Air fry in the air fryer for 10 minutes.
4. Serve hot.

Sweet and Sour Tofu

Prep time: 15 minutes | Cook time: 20 minutes | Serves 2

2 teaspoons apple cider vinegar
1 tablespoon sugar
1 tablespoon soy sauce
3 teaspoons lime juice
1 teaspoon ground ginger
1 teaspoon garlic powder

½ block firm tofu, pressed to remove excess liquid and cut into cubes
1 teaspoon cornstarch
2 green onions, chopped
Toasted sesame seeds, for garnish

1. In a bowl, thoroughly combine the apple cider vinegar, sugar, soy sauce, lime juice, ground ginger, and garlic powder.
2. Cover the tofu with this mixture and leave to marinate for at least 30 minutes.
3. Preheat the air fryer to 400ºF (204ºC).
4. Transfer the tofu to the air fryer, keeping any excess marinade for the sauce. Air fry for 20 minutes or until crispy.
5. In the meantime, thicken the sauce with the cornstarch over a medium-low heat.
6. Serve the cooked tofu with the sauce, green onions, and sesame seeds.

Jalapeño Poppers

Prep time: 5 minutes | Cook time: 33 minutes | Serves 4

8 medium jalapeño peppers
5 ounces (142 g) cream cheese
¼ cup grated

Mozzarella cheese
½ teaspoon Italian seasoning mix
8 slices bacon

1. Preheat the air fryer to 400ºF (204ºC).
2. Cut the jalapeños in half.
3. Use a spoon to scrape out the insides of the peppers.
4. In a bowl, add together the cream cheese, Mozzarella cheese and Italian seasoning.
5. Pack the cream cheese mixture into the jalapeño halves and place the other halves on top.
6. Wrap each pepper in 1 slice of bacon, starting from the bottom and working up.
7. Bake for 33 minutes.
8. Serve!

Spicy Cauliflower Roast

Prep time: 15 minutes | Cook time: 20 minutes | Serves 4

Cauliflower:
5 cups cauliflower florets
3 tablespoons vegetable oil
½ teaspoon ground

cumin
½ teaspoon ground coriander
½ teaspoon kosher salt

Sauce:
½ cup Greek yogurt or sour cream
¼ cup chopped fresh cilantro
1 jalapeño, coarsely chopped

4 cloves garlic, peeled
½ teaspoon kosher salt
2 tablespoons water

1. Preheat the air fryer to 400ºF (204ºC).
2. In a large bowl, combine the cauliflower, oil, cumin, coriander, and salt. Toss to coat.
3. Put the cauliflower in the air fryer basket. Roast for 20 minutes, stirring halfway through the roasting time.

4. Meanwhile, in a blender, combine the yogurt, cilantro, jalapeño, garlic, and salt. Blend, adding the water as needed to keep the blades moving and to thin the sauce.
5. At the end of roasting time, transfer the cauliflower to a large serving bowl. Pour the sauce over and toss gently to coat. Serve immediately.

Chermoula Beet Roast

Prep time: 15 minutes | Cook time: 25 minutes | Serves 4

Chermoula:
1 cup packed fresh cilantro leaves
½ cup packed fresh parsley leaves
6 cloves garlic, peeled
2 teaspoons smoked paprika
2 teaspoons ground cumin

1 teaspoon ground coriander
½ to 1 teaspoon cayenne pepper
Pinch of crushed saffron (optional)
½ cup extra-virgin olive oil
Kosher salt, to taste

Beets:
3 medium beets, trimmed, peeled, and cut into 1-inch chunks
2 tablespoons

chopped fresh cilantro
2 tablespoons chopped fresh parsley

1. In a food processor, combine the cilantro, parsley, garlic, paprika, cumin, coriander, and cayenne. Pulse until coarsely chopped. Add the saffron, if using, and process until combined. With the food processor running, slowly add the olive oil in a steady stream; process until the sauce is uniform. Season with salt.
2. Preheat the air fryer to 375ºF (191ºC).
3. In a large bowl, drizzle the beets with ½ cup of the chermoula to coat. Arrange the beets in the air fryer basket. Roast for 25 to minutes, or until the beets are tender.
4. Transfer the beets to a serving platter. Sprinkle with the chopped cilantro and parsley and serve.

Blistered Shishito Peppers

Prep time: 10 minutes | Cook time: 6 minutes | Serves 4

Dipping Sauce:

1 cup sour cream
2 tablespoons fresh lemon juice
1 clove garlic,

minced
1 green onion (white and green parts), finely chopped

Peppers:

8 ounces (227 g) shishito peppers
1 tablespoon vegetable oil
1 teaspoon toasted sesame oil
Kosher salt and

black pepper, to taste
¼ to ½ teaspoon red pepper flakes
½ teaspoon toasted sesame seeds

1. In a small bowl, stir all the ingredients for the dipping sauce to combine. Cover and refrigerate until serving time.
2. Preheat the air fryer to 400ºF (204ºC).
3. In a medium bowl, toss the peppers with the vegetable oil. Put the peppers in the air fryer basket. Air fry for 6 minutes, or until peppers are lightly charred in spots, stirring the peppers halfway through the cooking time.
4. Transfer the peppers to a serving bowl. Drizzle with the sesame oil and toss to coat. Season with salt and pepper. Sprinkle with the red pepper and sesame seeds and toss again.
5. Serve immediately with the dipping sauce.

Cauliflower Faux Rice

Prep time: 15 minutes | Cook time: 40 minutes | Serves 8

1 large head cauliflower, rinsed and drained, cut into florets
½ lemon, juiced
2 garlic cloves, minced
2 (8-ounce / 227-g) cans mushrooms
1 (8-ounce / 227-g) can water chestnuts

¾ cup peas
1 egg, beaten
4 tablespoons soy sauce
1 tablespoon peanut oil
1 tablespoon sesame oil
1 tablespoon minced fresh ginger
Cooking spray

1. Preheat the air fryer to 350ºF (177ºC).
2. Mix the peanut oil, soy sauce, sesame oil, minced ginger, lemon juice, and minced garlic to combine well.
3. In a food processor, pulse the florets in small batches to break them down to resemble rice grains. Pour into the air fryer basket.
4. Drain the chestnuts and roughly chop them. Pour into the basket. Air fry for 20 minutes.
5. In the meantime, drain the mushrooms. Add the mushrooms and the peas to the air fryer and continue to air fry for another 15 minutes.
6. Lightly spritz a frying pan with cooking spray. Prepare an omelet with the beaten egg, ensuring it is firm. Lay on a cutting board and slice it up.
7. When the cauliflower is ready, throw in the omelet and bake for an additional 5 minutes. Serve hot.

Easy Potato Croquettes

Prep time: 15 minutes | Cook time: 15 minutes | Serves 10

¼ cup nutritional yeast
2 cups boiled potatoes, mashed
1 flax egg
1 tablespoon flour
2 tablespoons

chopped chives
Salt and ground black pepper, to taste
2 tablespoons vegetable oil
¼ cup bread crumbs

1. Preheat the air fryer to 400ºF (204ºC).
2. In a bowl, combine the nutritional yeast, potatoes, flax egg, flour, and chives. Sprinkle with salt and pepper as desired.
3. In a separate bowl, mix the vegetable oil and bread crumbs to achieve a crumbly consistency.
4. Shape the potato mixture into small balls and dip each one into the breadcrumb mixture.
5. Put the croquettes inside the air fryer and air fry for 15 minutes, ensuring the croquettes turn golden brown.
6. Serve immediately.

Gorgonzola Mushrooms with Horseradish Mayo

Prep time: 15 minutes | Cook time: 10 minutes | Serves 5

½ cup bread crumbs
2 cloves garlic, pressed
2 tablespoons chopped fresh coriander
$1/3$ teaspoon kosher salt
½ teaspoon crushed red pepper flakes
1½ tablespoons olive oil
20 medium
mushrooms, stems removed
½ cup grated Gorgonzola cheese
¼ cup low-fat mayonnaise
1 teaspoon prepared horseradish, well-drained
1 tablespoon finely chopped fresh parsley

1. Preheat the air fryer to 380ºF (193ºC).
2. Combine the bread crumbs together with the garlic, coriander, salt, red pepper, and olive oil.
3. Take equal-sized amounts of the breadcrumb mixture and use them to stuff the mushroom caps. Add the grated Gorgonzola on top of each.
4. Put the mushrooms in a baking pan and transfer to the air fryer.
5. Air fry for 10 minutes, ensuring the stuffing is warm throughout.
6. In the meantime, prepare the horseradish mayo. Mix the mayonnaise, horseradish and parsley.
7. When the mushrooms are ready, serve with the mayo.

Air Fried Asparagus

Prep time: 5 minutes | Cook time: 5 minutes | Serves 4

1 pound (454 g) fresh asparagus spears, trimmed
1 tablespoon olive
oil
Salt and ground black pepper, to taste

1. Preheat the air fryer to 375ºF (191ºC).
2. Combine all the ingredients and transfer to the air fryer basket.
3. Air fry for 5 minutes or until soft.
4. Serve hot.

Roasted Eggplant Slices

Prep time: 5 minutes | Cook time: 15 minutes | Serves 1

1 large eggplant, sliced
2 tablespoons olive oil
¼ teaspoon salt
½ teaspoon garlic powder

1. Preheat the air fryer to 390ºF (199ºC).
2. Apply the olive oil to the slices with a brush, coating both sides. Season each side with sprinklings of salt and garlic powder.
3. Put the slices in the air fryer and roast for 15 minutes.
4. Serve immediately.

Lemony Falafel

Prep time: 15 minutes | Cook time: 15 minutes | Serves 8

1 teaspoon cumin seeds
½ teaspoon coriander seeds
2 cups chickpeas, drained and rinsed
½ teaspoon red pepper flakes
3 cloves garlic
¼ cup chopped
parsley
¼ cup chopped coriander
½ onion, diced
1 tablespoon juice from freshly squeezed lemon
3 tablespoons flour
½ teaspoon salt
Cooking spray

1. Fry the cumin and coriander seeds over medium heat until fragrant.
2. Grind using a mortar and pestle.
3. Put all of ingredients, except for the cooking spray, in a food processor and blend until a fine consistency is achieved.
4. Use the hands to mold the mixture into falafels and spritz with the cooking spray.
5. Preheat the air fryer to 400ºF (204ºC).
6. Transfer the falafels to the air fryer basket in one layer.
7. Air fry for 15 minutes, serving when they turn golden brown.

Crispy Jicama Fries

Prep time: 5 minutes | Cook time: 20 minutes | Serves 1

1 small jicama, peeled
¼ teaspoon onion powder
¾ teaspoon chili powder
¼ teaspoon garlic powder
¼ teaspoon ground black pepper

1. Preheat the air fryer to 350ºF (177ºC).
2. To make the fries, cut the jicama into matchsticks of the desired thickness.
3. In a bowl, toss them with the onion powder, chili powder, garlic powder, and black pepper to coat. Transfer the fries into the air fryer basket.
4. Air fry for 20 minutes, giving the basket an occasional shake throughout the cooking process. The fries are ready when they are hot and golden.
5. Serve immediately.

Golden Pickles

Prep time: 10 minutes | Cook time: 15 minutes | Serves 4

14 dill pickles, sliced
¼ cup flour
⅛ teaspoon baking powder
Pinch of salt
2 tablespoons cornstarch plus 3 tablespoons water
6 tablespoons panko bread crumbs
½ teaspoon paprika
Cooking spray

1. Preheat the air fryer to 400ºF (204ºC).
2. Drain any excess moisture out of the dill pickles on a paper towel.
3. In a bowl, combine the flour, baking powder and salt.
4. Throw in the cornstarch and water mixture and combine well with a whisk.
5. Put the panko bread crumbs in a shallow dish along with the paprika. Mix thoroughly.
6. Dip the pickles in the flour batter, before coating in the bread crumbs. Spritz all the pickles with the cooking spray.
7. Transfer to the air fryer basket and air fry for 15 minutes, or until golden brown.
8. Serve immediately.

Zucchini Balls

Prep time: 5 minutes | Cook time: 10 minutes | Serves 4

4 zucchinis
1 egg
½ cup grated Parmesan cheese
1 tablespoon Italian herbs
1 cup grated coconut

1. Thinly grate the zucchinis and dry with a cheesecloth, ensuring to remove all the moisture.
2. In a bowl, combine the zucchinis with the egg, Parmesan, Italian herbs, and grated coconut, mixing well to incorporate everything. Using the hands, mold the mixture into balls.
3. Preheat the air fryer to 400ºF (204ºC).
4. Lay the zucchini balls in the air fryer basket and air fry for 10 minutes.
5. Serve hot.

Fig, Chickpea, and Arugula Salad

Prep time: 15 minutes | Cook time: 20 minutes | Serves 4

8 fresh figs, halved
1½ cups cooked chickpeas
1 teaspoon crushed roasted cumin seeds
4 tablespoons balsamic vinegar
2 tablespoons extra-virgin olive oil, plus more for greasing
Salt and ground black pepper, to taste
3 cups arugula rocket, washed and dried

1. Preheat the air fryer to 375ºF (191ºC).
2. Cover the air fryer basket with aluminum foil and grease lightly with oil. Put the figs in the air fryer basket and air fry for 10 minutes.
3. In a bowl, combine the chickpeas and cumin seeds.
4. Remove the air fried figs from the air fryer and replace with the chickpeas. Air fry for 10 minutes. Leave to cool.
5. In the meantime, prepare the dressing. Mix the balsamic vinegar, olive oil, salt and pepper.
6. In a salad bowl, combine the arugula rocket with the cooled figs and chickpeas.
7. Toss with the sauce and serve.

Easy Rosemary Green Beans

Prep time: 5 minutes | Cook time: 5 minutes | Serves 1

1 tablespoon butter, melted
2 tablespoons rosemary
½ teaspoon salt
3 cloves garlic, minced
¾ cup chopped green beans

1. Preheat the air fryer to 390ºF (199ºC).
2. Combine the melted butter with the rosemary, salt, and minced garlic. Toss in the green beans, coating them well.
3. Air fry for 5 minutes.
4. Serve immediately.

Kidney Beans Oatmeal in Peppers

Prep time: 15 minutes | Cook time: 6 minutes | Serves 2 to 4

2 large bell peppers, halved lengthwise, deseeded
2 tablespoons cooked kidney beans
2 tablespoons cooked chick peas
2 cups cooked oatmeal
1 teaspoon ground cumin
½ teaspoon paprika
½ teaspoon salt or to taste
¼ teaspoon black pepper powder
¼ cup yogurt

1. Preheat the air fryer to 355ºF (179ºC).
2. Put the bell peppers, cut-side down, in the air fryer basket. Air fry for 2 minutes.
3. Take the peppers out of the air fryer and let cool.
4. In a bowl, combine the rest of the ingredients.
5. Divide the mixture evenly and use each portion to stuff a pepper.
6. Return the stuffed peppers to the air fryer and continue to air fry for 4 minutes.
7. Serve hot.

Lush Vegetable Salad

Prep time: 15 minutes | Cook time: 10 minutes | Serves 4

6 plum tomatoes, halved
2 large red onions, sliced
4 long red pepper, sliced
2 yellow pepper, sliced
6 cloves garlic, crushed
1 tablespoon extra-virgin olive oil
1 teaspoon paprika
½ lemon, juiced
Salt and ground black pepper, to taste
1 tablespoon baby capers

1. Preheat the air fryer to 420ºF (216ºC).
2. Put the tomatoes, onions, peppers, and garlic in a large bowl and cover with the extra-virgin olive oil, paprika, and lemon juice. Sprinkle with salt and pepper as desired.
3. Line the inside of the air fryer basket with aluminum foil. Put the vegetables inside and air fry for 10 minutes, ensuring the edges turn brown.
4. Serve in a salad bowl with the baby capers.

Potato with Creamy Cheese

Prep time: 5 minutes | Cook time: 15 minutes | Serves 2

2 medium potatoes
1 teaspoon butter
3 tablespoons sour cream
1 teaspoon chives
1½ tablespoons grated Parmesan cheese

1. Preheat the air fryer to 350ºF (177ºC).
2. Pierce the potatoes with a fork and boil them in water until they are cooked.
3. Transfer to the air fryer and air fry for 15 minutes.
4. In the meantime, combine the sour cream, cheese and chives in a bowl. Cut the potatoes halfway to open them up and fill with the butter and sour cream mixture.
5. Serve immediately.

Cheesy Macaroni Balls

Prep time: 10 minutes | Cook time: 10 minutes | Serves 2

2 cups leftover macaroni
1 cup shredded Cheddar cheese
½ cup flour
1 cup bread crumbs
3 large eggs
1 cup milk
½ teaspoon salt
¼ teaspoon black pepper

1. Preheat the air fryer to 365ºF (185ºC).
2. In a bowl, combine the leftover macaroni and shredded cheese.
3. Pour the flour in a separate bowl. Put the bread crumbs in a third bowl. Finally, in a fourth bowl, mix the eggs and milk with a whisk.
4. With an ice-cream scoop, create balls from the macaroni mixture. Coat them the flour, then in the egg mixture, and lastly in the bread crumbs.
5. Arrange the balls in the preheated air fryer and air fry for about 10 minutes, giving them an occasional stir. Ensure they crisp up nicely.
6. Serve hot.

Corn Pakodas

Prep time: 10 minutes | Cook time: 8 minutes | Serves 5

1 cup flour
¼ teaspoon baking soda
¼ teaspoon salt
½ teaspoon curry powder
½ teaspoon red chili
powder
¼ teaspoon turmeric powder
¼ cup water
10 cobs baby corn, blanched
Cooking spray

1. Preheat the air fryer to 425ºF (218ºC).
2. Cover the air fryer basket with aluminum foil and sprtiz with the cooking spray.
3. In a bowl, combine all the ingredients, save for the corn. Stir with a whisk until well combined.
4. Coat the corn in the batter and put inside the air fryer.
5. Air fry for 8 minutes until a golden brown color is achieved.
6. Serve hot.

Sweet Potato Fries

Prep time: 5 minutes | Cook time: 25 minutes | Serves 4

2 pounds (907 g) sweet potatoes, rinsed, sliced into matchsticks
1 teaspoon curry
powder
2 tablespoons olive oil
Salt, to taste

1. Preheat the air fryer to 390ºF (199ºC).
2. Drizzle the oil in the baking pan, place the fries inside and bake for 25 minutes.
3. Sprinkle with the curry powder and salt before serving.

Beef Stuffed Bell Peppers

Prep time: 10 minutes | Cook time: 30 minutes | Serves 4

1 pound (454 g) ground beef
1 tablespoon taco seasoning mix
1 can diced tomatoes and green
chilis
4 green bell peppers
1 cup shredded Monterey jack cheese, divided

1. Preheat the air fryer to 350ºF (177ºC).
2. Set a skillet over a high heat and cook the ground beef for 8 minutes. Make sure it is cooked through and browned all over. Drain the fat.
3. Stir in the taco seasoning mix, and the diced tomatoes and green chilis. Allow the mixture to cook for a further 4 minutes.
4. In the meantime, slice the tops off the green peppers and remove the seeds and membranes.
5. When the meat mixture is fully cooked, spoon equal amounts of it into the peppers and top with the Monterey jack cheese. Then place the peppers into the air fryer. Air fry for 15 minutes.
6. The peppers are ready when they are soft, and the cheese is bubbling and brown. Serve warm.

Sesame Taj Tofu

Prep time: 5 minutes | Cook time: 25 minutes | Serves 4

1 block firm tofu, pressed and cut into 1-inch thick cubes
2 tablespoons soy sauce
2 teaspoons toasted
sesame seeds
1 teaspoon rice vinegar
1 tablespoon cornstarch

1. Preheat the air fryer to 400ºF (204ºC).
2. Add the tofu, soy sauce, sesame seeds, and rice vinegar in a bowl together and mix well to coat the tofu cubes. Then cover the tofu in cornstarch and put it in the air fryer basket.
3. Air fry for 25 minutes, giving the basket a shake at five-minute intervals to ensure the tofu cooks evenly.
4. Serve immediately.

Prosciutto Mini Mushroom Pizza

Prep time: 10 minutes | Cook time: 5 minutes | Serves 3

3 portobello mushroom caps, cleaned and scooped
3 tablespoons olive oil
Pinch of salt
Pinch of dried Italian
seasonings
3 tablespoons tomato sauce
3 tablespoons shredded Mozzarella cheese
12 slices prosciutto

1. Preheat the air fryer to 330ºF (166ºC).
2. Season both sides of the portobello mushrooms with a drizzle of olive oil, then sprinkle salt and the Italian seasonings on the insides.
3. With a knife, spread the tomato sauce evenly over the mushroom, before adding the Mozzarella on top.
4. Put the portobello in the air fryer basket and place in the air fryer.
5. Air fry for 1 minute, before taking the air fryer basket out of the air fryer and putting the prosciutto slices on top.
6. Air fry for another 4 minutes.
7. Serve warm.

Chili Fingerling Potatoes

Prep time: 10 minutes | Cook time: 16 minutes | Serves 4

1 pound (454 g) fingerling potatoes, rinsed and cut into wedges
1 teaspoon olive oil
1 teaspoon salt
1 teaspoon black
pepper
1 teaspoon cayenne pepper
1 teaspoon nutritional yeast
½ teaspoon garlic powder

1. Preheat the air fryer to 400ºF (204ºC).
2. Coat the potatoes with the rest of the ingredients.
3. Transfer to the air fryer basket and air fry for 16 minutes, shaking the basket at the halfway point.
4. Serve immediately.

Ricotta Potatoes

Prep time: 15 minutes | Cook time: 15 minutes | Serves 4

4 potatoes
2 tablespoons olive oil
½ cup Ricotta cheese, at room temperature
2 tablespoons chopped scallions
1 tablespoon roughly chopped fresh parsley
1 tablespoon minced coriander
2 ounces (57 g) Cheddar cheese, preferably freshly grated
1 teaspoon celery seeds
½ teaspoon salt
½ teaspoon garlic pepper

1. Preheat the air fryer to 350ºF (177ºC).
2. Pierce the skin of the potatoes with a knife.
3. Air fry in the air fryer basket for 13 minutes. If they are not cooked through by this time, leave for 2 to 3 minutes longer.
4. In the meantime, make the stuffing by combining all the other ingredients.
5. Cut halfway into the cooked potatoes to open them.
6. Spoon equal amounts of the stuffing into each potato and serve hot.

Air Fried Potatoes with Olives

Prep time: 15 minutes | Cook time: 40 minutes | Serves 1

1 medium russet potato, scrubbed and peeled
1 teaspoon olive oil
¼ teaspoon onion powder
⅛ teaspoon salt
Dollop of butter
Dollop of cream cheese
1 tablespoon Kalamata olives
1 tablespoon chopped chives

1. Preheat the air fryer to 400ºF (204ºC).
2. In a bowl, coat the potatoes with the onion powder, salt, olive oil, and butter.
3. Transfer to the air fryer and air fry for 40 minutes, turning the potatoes over at the halfway point.
4. Take care when removing the potatoes from the air fryer and serve with the cream cheese, Kalamata olives and chives on top.

Marinara Pepperoni Mushroom Pizza

Prep time: 5 minutes | Cook time: 18 minutes | Serves 4

4 large portobello mushrooms, stems removed
4 teaspoons olive oil
1 cup marinara
sauce
1 cup shredded Mozzarella cheese
10 slices sugar-free pepperoni

1. Preheat the air fryer to 375ºF (191ºC).
2. Brush each mushroom cap with the olive oil, one teaspoon for each cap.
3. Put on a baking sheet and bake, stem-side down, for 8 minutes.
4. Take out of the air fryer and divide the marinara sauce, Mozzarella cheese and pepperoni evenly among the caps.
5. Air fry for another 10 minutes until browned.
6. Serve hot.

Sriracha Golden Cauliflower

Prep time: 5 minutes | Cook time: 17 minutes | Serves 4

¼ cup vegan butter, melted
¼ cup sriracha sauce
4 cups cauliflower florets
1 cup bread crumbs
1 teaspoon salt

1. Preheat the air fryer to 375ºF (191ºC).
2. Mix the sriracha and vegan butter in a bowl and pour this mixture over the cauliflower, taking care to cover each floret entirely.
3. In a separate bowl, combine the bread crumbs and salt.
4. Dip the cauliflower florets in the bread crumbs, coating each one well. Air fry in the air fryer for 17 minutes.
5. Serve hot.

Simple Pesto Gnocchi

Prep time: 10 minutes | Cook time: 15 minutes | Serves 4

1 (1-pound / 454-g) package gnocchi
1 medium onion, chopped
3 cloves garlic, minced
1 tablespoon extra-virgin olive oil
1 (8-ounce / 227-g) jar pesto
⅓ cup grated Parmesan cheese

1. Preheat the air fryer to 340ºF (171ºC).
2. In a large bowl combine the onion, garlic, and gnocchi, and drizzle with the olive oil. Mix thoroughly.
3. Transfer the mixture to the air fryer and air fry for 15 minutes, stirring occasionally, making sure the gnocchi become light brown and crispy.
4. Add the pesto and Parmesan cheese, and give everything a good stir before serving.

Roasted Lemony Broccoli

Prep time: 5 minutes | Cook time: 15 minutes | Serves 6

2 heads broccoli, cut into florets
2 teaspoons extra-virgin olive oil, plus more for coating
1 teaspoon salt
½ teaspoon black pepper
1 clove garlic, minced
½ teaspoon lemon juice

1. Cover the air fryer basket with aluminum foil and coat with a light brushing of oil.
2. Preheat the air fryer to 375ºF (191ºC).
3. In a bowl, combine all ingredients, save for the lemon juice, and transfer to the air fryer basket. Roast for 15 minutes.
4. Serve with the lemon juice.

Cashew Stuffed Mushrooms

Prep time: 10 minutes | Cook time: 15 minutes | Serves 6

1 cup basil
½ cup cashew, soaked overnight
½ cup nutritional yeast
1 tablespoon lemon juice
2 cloves garlic
1 tablespoon olive oil
Salt, to taste
1 pound (454 g) baby Bella mushroom, stems removed

1. Preheat the air fryer to 400ºF (204ºC).
2. Prepare the pesto. In a food processor, blend the basil, cashew nuts, nutritional yeast, lemon juice, garlic and olive oil to combine well. Sprinkle with salt as desired.
3. Turn the mushrooms cap-side down and spread the pesto on the underside of each cap.
4. Transfer to the air fryer and air fry for 15 minutes.
5. Serve warm.

Beef Stuffed Bell Pepper

Prep time: 20 minutes | Cook time: 15 minutes | Serves 4

2 garlic cloves, minced
1 small onion, chopped
Cooking spray
1 pound (454 g) ground beef
1 teaspoon dried basil
½ teaspoon chili powder
1 teaspoon black pepper
1 teaspoon garlic salt
2/3 cup shredded cheese, divided
½ cup cooked rice
2 teaspoons Worcestershire sauce
8 ounces (227 g) tomato sauce
4 bell peppers, tops removed

1. Grease a frying pan with cooking spray and fry the onion and garlic over a medium heat.
2. Stir in the beef, basil, chili powder, black pepper, and garlic salt, combining everything well. Air fry until the beef is nicely browned, before taking the pan off the heat.
3. Add half of the cheese, the rice, Worcestershire sauce, and tomato sauce and stir to combine.
4. Spoon equal amounts of the beef mixture into the four bell peppers, filling them entirely.
5. Preheat the air fryer to 400ºF (204ºC).
6. Spritz the air fryer basket with cooking spray.
7. Put the stuffed bell peppers in the basket and air fry for 11 minutes.
8. Add the remaining cheese on top of each bell pepper and air fry for a further 2 minutes. When the cheese is melted and the bell peppers are piping hot, serve immediately.

Chapter 4 Meats

Super Bacon with Meat

Prep time: 5 minutes | Cook time: 1 hour | Serves 4

30 slices thick-cut bacon
4 ounces (113 g) Cheddar cheese, shredded
12 ounces (340 g) steak
10 ounces (283 g) pork sausage
Salt and ground black pepper, to taste

1. Preheat the air fryer to 400ºF (204ºC).
2. Lay out 30 slices of bacon in a woven pattern and bake for 20 minutes until crisp. Put the cheese in the center of the bacon.
3. Combine the steak and sausage to form a meaty mixture.
4. Lay out the meat in a rectangle of similar size to the bacon strips. Season with salt and pepper.
5. Roll the meat into a tight roll and refrigerate.
6. Preheat the air fryer to 400ºF (204ºC).
7. Make a 7×7 bacon weave and roll the bacon weave over the meat, diagonally.
8. Bake for 60 minutes or until the internal temperature reaches at least 165ºF (74ºC).
9. Let rest for 5 minutes before serving.

BBQ Pork Steaks

Prep time: 5 minutes | Cook time: 15 minutes | Serves 4

4 pork steaks
1 tablespoon Cajun seasoning
2 tablespoons BBQ sauce
1 tablespoon vinegar
1 teaspoon soy sauce
½ cup brown sugar
½ cup ketchup

1. Preheat the air fryer to 290ºF (143ºC).
2. Sprinkle pork steaks with Cajun seasoning.
3. Combine remaining ingredients and brush onto steaks.
4. Add coated steaks to air fryer. Air fry 15 minutes until just browned.
5. Serve immediately.

Air Fried Baby Back Ribs

Prep time: 5 minutes | Cook time: 30 minutes | Serves 2

2 teaspoons red pepper flakes
¾ ground ginger
3 cloves minced garlic
Salt and ground black pepper, to taste
2 baby back ribs

1. Preheat the air fryer to 350ºF (177ºC).
2. Combine the red pepper flakes, ginger, garlic, salt and pepper in a bowl, making sure to mix well. Massage the mixture into the baby back ribs.
3. Air fry the ribs in the air fryer for 30 minutes.
4. Take care when taking the rubs out of the air fryer. Put them on a serving dish and serve.

Carne Asada Tacos

Prep time: 5 minutes | Cook time: 14 minutes | Serves 4

$\frac{1}{3}$ cup olive oil
1½ pounds (680 g) flank steak
Salt and freshly ground black pepper, to taste
$\frac{1}{3}$ cup freshly squeezed lime juice
½ cup chopped fresh cilantro
4 teaspoons minced garlic
1 teaspoon ground cumin
1 teaspoon chili powder

1. Brush the air fryer basket with olive oil.
2. Put the flank steak in a large mixing bowl. Season with salt and pepper.
3. Add the lime juice, cilantro, garlic, cumin, and chili powder and toss to coat the steak.
4. For the best flavor, let the steak marinate in the refrigerator for about 1 hour.
5. Preheat the air fryer to 400ºF (204ºC)
6. Put the steak in the air fryer basket. Air fry for 7 minutes. Flip the steak. Air fry for 7 minutes more or until an internal temperature reaches at least 145ºF (63ºC).
7. Let the steak rest for about 5 minutes, then cut into strips to serve.

Beef and Pork Sausage Meatloaf

Prep time: 20 minutes | Cook time: 25 minutes | Serves 4

¾ pound (340 g) ground chuck
4 ounces (113 g) ground pork sausage
1 cup shallots, finely chopped
2 eggs, well beaten
3 tablespoons plain milk
1 tablespoon oyster sauce
1 teaspoon porcini mushrooms
½ teaspoon cumin powder
1 teaspoon garlic paste
1 tablespoon fresh parsley
Salt and crushed red pepper flakes, to taste
1 cup crushed saltines
Cooking spray

1. Preheat the air fryer to 360ºF (182ºC). Sprtiz a baking dish with cooking spray.
2. Mix all the ingredients in a large bowl, combining everything well.
3. Transfer to the baking dish and bake in the air fryer for 25 minutes.
4. Serve hot.

Sun-dried Tomato Crusted Chops

Prep time: 15 minutes | Cook time: 10 minutes | Serves 4

½ cup oil-packed sun-dried tomatoes
½ cup toasted almonds
¼ cup grated Parmesan cheese
½ cup olive oil, plus more for brushing the air fryer basket
2 tablespoons water
½ teaspoon salt
Freshly ground black pepper, to taste
4 center-cut boneless pork chops (about 1¼ pounds / 567 g)

1. Put the sun-dried tomatoes into a food processor and pulse them until they are coarsely chopped. Add the almonds, Parmesan cheese, olive oil, water, salt and pepper. Process into a smooth paste. Spread most of the paste (leave a little in reserve) onto both sides of the pork chops and then pierce the meat several times with a needle-style meat tenderizer or a fork. Let the pork chops sit and marinate for at least 1 hour (refrigerate if marinating for longer than 1 hour).

2. Preheat the air fryer to 370ºF (188ºC).
3. Brush more olive oil on the bottom of the air fryer basket. Transfer the pork chops into the air fryer basket, spooning a little more of the sun-dried tomato paste onto the pork chops if there are any gaps where the paste may have been rubbed off. Air fry the pork chops for 10 minutes, turning the chops over halfway through.
4. When the pork chops have finished cooking, transfer them to a serving plate and serve.

Bacon Wrapped Pork with Apple Gravy

Prep time: 10 minutes | Cook time: 25 minutes | Serves 4

Pork:

1 tablespoons Dijon mustard
1 pork tenderloin
3 strips bacon

Apple Gravy:

3 tablespoons ghee, divided
1 small shallot, chopped
2 apples
1 tablespoon almond
flour
1 cup vegetable broth
½ teaspoon Dijon mustard

1. Preheat the air fryer to 360ºF (182ºC).
2. Spread Dijon mustard all over tenderloin and wrap with strips of bacon.
3. Put into air fryer and air fry for 12 minutes. Use a meat thermometer to check for doneness.
4. To make sauce, heat 1 tablespoons of ghee in a pan and add shallots. Cook for 1 minute.
5. Then add apples, cooking for 4 minutes until softened.
6. Add flour and 2 tablespoons of ghee to make a roux. Add broth and mustard, stirring well to combine.
7. When sauce starts to bubble, add 1 cup of sautéed apples, cooking until sauce thickens.
8. Once pork tenderloin is cooked, allow to sit 8 minutes to rest before slicing.
9. Serve topped with apple gravy.

Bacon and Pear Stuffed Pork Chops

Prep time: 20 minutes | Cook time: 24 minutes | Serves 3

4 slices bacon, chopped
1 tablespoon butter
½ cup finely diced onion
⅓ cup chicken stock
1½ cups seasoned stuffing cubes
1 egg, beaten
½ teaspoon dried thyme
½ teaspoon salt
⅛ teaspoon freshly
ground black pepper
1 pear, finely diced
⅓ cup crumbled blue cheese
3 boneless center-cut pork chops (2-inch thick)
Olive oil, for greasing
Salt and freshly ground black pepper, to taste

1. Preheat the air fryer to 400ºF (204ºC).
2. Put the bacon into the air fryer basket and air fry for 6 minutes, stirring halfway through the cooking time. Remove the bacon and set it aside on a paper towel. Pour out the grease from the bottom of the air fryer.
3. To make the stuffing, melt the butter in a medium saucepan over medium heat on the stovetop. Add the onion and sauté for a few minutes until it starts to soften. Add the chicken stock and simmer for 1 minute. Remove the pan from the heat and add the stuffing cubes. Stir until the stock has been absorbed. Add the egg, dried thyme, salt and freshly ground black pepper, and stir until combined. Fold in the diced pear and crumbled blue cheese.
4. Put the pork chops on a cutting board. Using the palm of the hand to hold the chop flat and steady, slice into the side of the pork chop to make a pocket in the center of the chop. Leave about an inch of chop uncut and make sure you don't cut all the way through the pork chop. Brush both sides of the pork chops with olive oil and season with salt and freshly ground black pepper. Stuff each pork chop with a third of the stuffing, packing the stuffing tightly inside the pocket.
5. Preheat the air fryer to 360ºF (182ºC).
6. Spray or brush the sides of the air fryer basket with oil. Put the pork chops in the air fryer basket with the open, stuffed edge of the pork chop facing the outside edges of the basket.
7. Air fry the pork chops for 18 minutes, turning the pork chops over halfway through the cooking time. When the chops are done, let them rest for 5 minutes and then transfer to a serving platter.

Beef Chuck with Brussels Sprouts

Prep time: 20 minutes | Cook time: 15 minutes | Serves 4

1 pound (454 g) beef chuck shoulder steak
2 tablespoons vegetable oil
1 tablespoon red wine vinegar
1 teaspoon fine sea salt
½ teaspoon ground black pepper
1 teaspoon smoked paprika
1 teaspoon onion powder
½ teaspoon garlic powder
½ pound (227 g) Brussels sprouts, cleaned and halved
½ teaspoon fennel seeds
1 teaspoon dried basil
1 teaspoon dried sage

1. Massage the beef with the vegetable oil, wine vinegar, salt, black pepper, paprika, onion powder, and garlic powder, coating it well.
2. Allow to marinate for a minimum of 3 hours.
3. Preheat the air fryer to 390ºF (199ºC).
4. Remove the beef from the marinade and put in the preheated air fryer. Air fry for 10 minutes. Flip the beef halfway through.
5. Put the prepared Brussels sprouts in the air fryer along with the fennel seeds, basil, and sage.
6. Lower the heat to 380ºF (193ºC) and air fry everything for another 5 minutes.
7. Give them a good stir. Air fry for an additional 10 minutes.
8. Serve immediately.

Kale and Beef Omelet

Prep time: 15 minutes | Cook time: 16 minutes | Serves 4

½ pound (227 g) leftover beef, coarsely chopped
2 garlic cloves, pressed
1 cup kale, torn into pieces and wilted
1 tomato, chopped
¼ teaspoon sugar
4 eggs, beaten
4 tablespoons heavy cream
½ teaspoon turmeric powder
Salt and ground black pepper, to taste
⅛ teaspoon ground allspice
Cooking spray

1. Preheat the air fryer to 360ºF (182ºC). Spritz four ramekins with cooking spray.
2. Put equal amounts of each of the ingredients into each ramekin and mix well.
3. Air fry for 16 minutes. Serve immediately.

Cheddar Bacon Burst with Spinach

Prep time: 5 minutes | Cook time: 60 minutes | Serves 8

30 slices bacon
1 tablespoon Chipotle seasoning
2 teaspoons Italian seasoning
2½ cups Cheddar cheese
4 cups raw spinach

1. Preheat the air fryer to 375ºF (191ºC).
2. Weave the bacon into 15 vertical pieces and 12 horizontal pieces. Cut the extra 3 in half to fill in the rest, horizontally.
3. Season the bacon with Chipotle seasoning and Italian seasoning.
4. Add the cheese to the bacon.
5. Add the spinach and press down to compress.
6. Tightly roll up the woven bacon.
7. Line a baking sheet with kitchen foil and add plenty of salt to it.
8. Put the bacon on top of a cooling rack and put that on top of the baking sheet.
9. Bake for 60 minutes.
10. Let cool for 15 minutes before slicing and serve.

Lamb Meatballs

Prep time: 20 minutes | Cook time: 8 minutes | Serves 4

Meatballs:
½ small onion, finely diced
1 clove garlic, minced
1 pound (454 g) ground lamb
2 tablespoons fresh parsley, finely chopped (plus more for garnish)
2 teaspoons fresh oregano, finely chopped
2 tablespoons milk
1 egg yolk
Salt and freshly ground black pepper, to taste
½ cup crumbled feta cheese, for garnish

Tomato Sauce:
2 tablespoons butter
1 clove garlic, smashed
Pinch crushed red pepper flakes
¼ teaspoon ground cinnamon
1 (28-ounce / 794-g) can crushed tomatoes
Salt, to taste
Olive oil, for greasing

1. Combine all ingredients for the meatballs in a large bowl and mix just until everything is combined. Shape the mixture into 1½-inch balls or shape the meat between two spoons to make quenelles.
2. Preheat the air fryer to 400ºF (204ºC).
3. While the air fryer is preheating, start the quick tomato sauce. Put the butter, garlic and red pepper flakes in a sauté pan and heat over medium heat on the stovetop. Let the garlic sizzle a little, but before the butter browns, add the cinnamon and tomatoes. Bring to a simmer and simmer for 15 minutes. Season with salt.
4. Grease the bottom of the air fryer basket with olive oil and transfer the meatballs to the air fryer basket in one layer, air frying in batches if necessary.
5. Air fry for 8 minutes, giving the basket a shake once during the cooking process to turn the meatballs over.
6. To serve, spoon a pool of the tomato sauce onto plates and add the meatballs. Sprinkle the feta cheese on top and garnish with more fresh parsley. Serve immediately.

Beef Cheeseburger Egg Rolls

Prep time: 15 minutes | Cook time: 8 minutes | Makes 6 egg rolls

8 ounces (227 g) raw lean ground beef
½ cup chopped onion
½ cup chopped bell pepper
¼ teaspoon onion powder
¼ teaspoon garlic powder
3 tablespoons cream cheese
1 tablespoon yellow mustard
3 tablespoons shredded Cheddar cheese
6 chopped dill pickle chips
6 egg roll wrappers

1. Preheat the air fryer to 392ºF (200ºC).
2. In a skillet, add the beef, onion, bell pepper, onion powder, and garlic powder. Stir and crumble beef until fully cooked, and vegetables are soft.
3. Take skillet off the heat and add cream cheese, mustard, and Cheddar cheese, stirring until melted.
4. Pour beef mixture into a bowl and fold in pickles.
5. Lay out egg wrappers and divide the beef mixture into each one. Moisten egg roll wrapper edges with water. Fold sides to the middle and seal with water.
6. Repeat with all other egg rolls.
7. Put rolls into air fryer, one batch at a time. Air fry for 8 minutes.
8. Serve immediately.

Spinach and Beef Braciole

Prep time: 25 minutes | Cook time: 1 hour 32 minutes | Serves 4

½ onion, finely chopped
1 teaspoon olive oil
1/3 cup red wine
2 cups crushed tomatoes
1 teaspoon Italian seasoning
½ teaspoon garlic powder
¼ teaspoon crushed red pepper flakes
2 tablespoons chopped fresh parsley
2 top round steaks (about 1½ pounds / 680 g)
salt and freshly ground black pepper
2 cups fresh spinach, chopped
1 clove minced garlic
½ cup roasted red peppers, julienned
½ cup grated pecorino cheese
¼ cup pine nuts, toasted and roughly chopped
2 tablespoons olive oil

1. Preheat the air fryer to 400ºF (204ºC).
2. Toss the onions and olive oil together in a baking pan or casserole dish. Air fry at 400ºF (204ºC) for 5 minutes, stirring a couple times during the cooking process. Add the red wine, crushed tomatoes, Italian seasoning, garlic powder, red pepper flakes and parsley and stir. Cover the pan tightly with aluminum foil, lower the air fryer temperature to 350ºF (177ºC) and continue to air fry for 15 minutes.
3. While the sauce is simmering, prepare the beef. Using a meat mallet, pound the beef until it is ¼-inch thick. Season both sides of the beef with salt and pepper. Combine the spinach, garlic, red peppers, pecorino cheese, pine nuts and olive oil in a medium bowl. Season with salt and freshly ground black pepper. Disperse the mixture over the steaks. Starting at one of the short ends, roll the beef around the filling, tucking in the sides as you roll to ensure the filling is completely enclosed. Secure the beef rolls with toothpicks.
4. Remove the baking pan with the sauce from the air fryer and set it aside. Preheat the air fryer to 400ºF (204ºC).
5. Brush or spray the beef rolls with a little olive oil and air fry at 400ºF (204ºC) for 12 minutes, rotating the beef during the cooking process for even browning. When the beef is browned, submerge the rolls into the sauce in the baking pan, cover the pan with foil and return it to the air fryer. Reduce the temperature of the air fryer to 250ºF (121ºC) and air fry for 60 minutes.
6. Remove the beef rolls from the sauce. Cut each roll into slices and serve, ladling some sauce overtop.

Beef Egg Rolls

Prep time: 15 minutes | Cook time: 12 minutes | Makes 8 egg rolls

½ chopped onion
2 garlic cloves, chopped
½ packet taco seasoning
Salt and ground black pepper, to taste
1 pound (454 g)

lean ground beef
½ can cilantro lime rotel
16 egg roll wrappers
1 cup shredded Mexican cheese
1 tablespoon olive oil
1 teaspoon cilantro

1. Preheat the air fryer to 400ºF (205ºC).
2. Add onions and garlic to a skillet, cooking until fragrant. Then add taco seasoning, pepper, salt, and beef, cooking until beef is broke up into tiny pieces and cooked thoroughly.
3. Add rotel and stir well.
4. Lay out egg wrappers and brush with a touch of water to soften a bit.
5. Load wrappers with beef filling and add cheese to each.
6. Fold diagonally to close and use water to secure edges.
7. Brush filled egg wrappers with olive oil and add to the air fryer.
8. Air fry 8 minutes, flip, and air fry for another 4 minutes.
9. Serve sprinkled with cilantro.

Pork Chop Stir Fry

Prep time: 10 minutes | Cook time: 20 minutes | Serves 4

1 tablespoon olive oil
¼ teaspoon ground black pepper
½ teaspoon salt
1 egg white
4 (4-ounce / 113-g) pork chops
¾ cup almond flour

2 sliced jalapeño peppers
2 sliced scallions
2 tablespoons olive oil
¼ teaspoon ground white pepper
1 teaspoon sea salt

1. Coat the air fryer basket with olive oil.
2. Whisk black pepper, salt, and egg white together until foamy.
3. Cut pork chops into pieces, leaving just a bit on bones. Pat dry.

4. Add pieces of pork to egg white mixture, coating well. Let sit for marinade 20 minutes.
5. Preheat the air fryer to 360ºF (182ºC).
6. Put marinated chops into a large bowl and add almond flour. Dredge and shake off excess and place into air fryer.
7. Air fry the chops in the preheated air fryer for 12 minutes.
8. Turn up the heat to 400ºF (205ºC) and air fry for another 6 minutes until pork chops are nice and crisp.
9. Meanwhile, remove jalapeño seeds and chop up. Chop scallions and mix with jalapeño pieces.
10. Heat a skillet with olive oil. Stir-fry the white pepper, salt, scallions, and jalapeños 60 seconds. Then add fried pork pieces to skills and toss with scallion mixture. Stir-fry 1 to 2 minutes until well coated and hot.
11. Serve immediately.

Peppercorn Crusted Beef Tenderloin

Prep time: 5 minutes | Cook time: 25 minutes | Serves 6

2 pounds (907 g) beef tenderloin
2 teaspoons roasted garlic, minced
2 tablespoons salted

butter, melted
3 tablespoons ground 4-peppercorn blender

1. Preheat the air fryer to 400ºF (204ºC).
2. Remove any surplus fat from the beef tenderloin.
3. Combine the roasted garlic and melted butter to apply to the tenderloin with a brush.
4. On a plate, spread out the peppercorns and roll the tenderloin in them, making sure they are covering and clinging to the meat.
5. Air fry the tenderloin in the air fryer for 25 minutes, turning halfway through cooking.
6. Let the tenderloin rest for ten minutes before slicing and serving.

Beef and Spinach Rolls

Prep time: 10 minutes | Cook time: 14 minutes | Serves 2

3 teaspoons pesto
2 pounds (907 g) beef flank steak
6 slices provolone cheese
3 ounces (85 g)

roasted red bell peppers
¾ cup baby spinach
1 teaspoon sea salt
1 teaspoon black pepper

1. Preheat the air fryer to 400ºF (204ºC).
2. Spoon equal amounts of the pesto onto each flank steak and spread it across evenly.
3. Put the cheese, roasted red peppers and spinach on top of the meat, about three-quarters of the way down.
4. Roll the steak up, holding it in place with toothpicks. Sprinkle with the sea salt and pepper.
5. Put inside the air fryer and air fry for 14 minutes, turning halfway through the cooking time.
6. Allow the beef to rest for 10 minutes before slicing up and serving.

Pork Chops with Rinds

Prep time: 5 minutes | Cook time: 15 minutes | Serves 4

1 teaspoon chili powder
½ teaspoon garlic powder
1½ ounces (43 g) pork rinds, finely

ground
4 (4-ounce / 113-g) pork chops
1 tablespoon coconut oil, melted

1. Preheat the air fryer to 400ºF (204ºC).
2. Combine the chili powder, garlic powder, and ground pork rinds.
3. Coat the pork chops with the coconut oil, followed by the pork rind mixture, taking care to cover them completely. Then place the chops in the air fryer basket.
4. Air fry the chops for 15 minutes or until the internal temperature of the chops reaches at least 145ºF (63ºC), turning halfway through.
5. Serve immediately.

Beef Chuck Cheeseburgers

Prep time: 10 minutes | Cook time: 15 minutes | Serves 4

¾ pound (340 g) ground beef chuck
1 envelope onion soup mix
Kosher salt and freshly ground black

pepper, to taste
1 teaspoon paprika
4 slices Monterey Jack cheese
4 ciabatta rolls

1. In a bowl, stir together the ground chuck, onion soup mix, salt, black pepper, and paprika to combine well.
2. Preheat the air fryer to 385ºF (196ºC).
3. Take four equal portions of the mixture and mold each one into a patty. Transfer to the air fryer and air fry for 10 minutes.
4. Put the slices of cheese on the top of the burgers.
5. Air fry for another minute before serving on ciabatta rolls.

Greek Lamb Rack

Prep time: 5 minutes | Cook time: 10 minutes | Serves 4

¼ cup freshly squeezed lemon juice
1 teaspoon oregano
2 teaspoons minced fresh rosemary
1 teaspoon minced fresh thyme
2 tablespoons

minced garlic
Salt and freshly ground black pepper, to taste
2 to 4 tablespoons olive oil
1 lamb rib rack (7 to 8 ribs)

1. Preheat the air fryer to 360ºF (182ºC).
2. In a small mixing bowl, combine the lemon juice, oregano, rosemary, thyme, garlic, salt, pepper, and olive oil and mix well.
3. Rub the mixture over the lamb, covering all the meat. Put the rack of lamb in the air fryer. Roast for 10 minutes. Flip the rack halfway through.
4. After 10 minutes, measure the internal temperature of the rack of lamb reaches at least 145ºF (63ºC).
5. Serve immediately.

Avocado Buttered Flank Steak

Prep time: 5 minutes | Cook time: 12 minutes | Serves 1

1 flank steak
Salt and ground black pepper, to taste
2 avocados
2 tablespoons butter, melted
½ cup chimichurri sauce

1. Rub the flank steak with salt and pepper to taste and leave to sit for 20 minutes.
2. Preheat the air fryer to 400ºF (204ºC).
3. Halve the avocados and take out the pits. Spoon the flesh into a bowl and mash with a fork. Mix in the melted butter and chimichurri sauce, making sure everything is well combined.
4. Put the steak in the air fryer and air fry for 6 minutes. Flip over and allow to air fry for another 6 minutes.
5. Serve the steak with the avocado butter.

Chicken Fried Steak

Prep time: 15 minutes | Cook time: 10 minutes | Serves 4

½ cup flour
2 teaspoons salt, divided
Freshly ground black pepper, to taste
¼ teaspoon garlic powder
1 cup buttermilk
1 cup fine bread crumbs
4 (6-ounce / 170-g) tenderized top round steaks, ½-inch thick
Vegetable or canola oil

For the Gravy:
2 tablespoons butter or bacon drippings
¼ onion, minced
1 clove garlic, smashed
¼ teaspoon dried thyme
3 tablespoons flour
1 cup milk
Salt and freshly ground black pepper, to taste
Dashes of Worcestershire sauce

1. Set up a dredging station. Combine the flour, 1 teaspoon of salt, black pepper and garlic powder in a shallow bowl. Pour the buttermilk into a second shallow bowl. Finally, put the bread crumbs and 1 teaspoon of salt in a third shallow bowl.
2. Dip the tenderized steaks into the flour, then the buttermilk, and then the bread crumb mixture, pressing the crumbs onto the steak. Put them on a baking sheet and spray both sides generously with vegetable or canola oil.
3. Preheat the air fryer to 400ºF (204ºC).
4. Transfer the steaks to the air fryer basket, two at a time, and air fry for 10 minutes, flipping the steaks over halfway through the cooking time. Hold the first batch of steaks warm in a 170ºF (77ºC) oven while you air fry the second batch.
5. While the steaks are cooking, make the gravy. Melt the butter in a small saucepan over medium heat on the stovetop. Add the onion, garlic and thyme and cook for five minutes, until the onion is soft and just starting to brown. Stir in the flour and cook for another five minutes, stirring regularly, until the mixture starts to brown. Whisk in the milk and bring the mixture to a boil to thicken. Season to taste with salt, lots of freshly ground black pepper, and a few dashes of Worcestershire sauce.
6. Pour the gravy over the chicken fried steaks and serve.

Herbed Beef

Prep time: 5 minutes | Cook time: 22 minutes | Serves 6

1 teaspoon dried dill
1 teaspoon dried thyme
1 teaspoon garlic
powder
2 pounds (907 g) beef steak
3 tablespoons butter

1. Preheat the air fryer to 360ºF (182ºC).
2. Combine the dill, thyme, and garlic powder in a small bowl, and massage into the steak.
3. Air fry the steak in the air fryer for 20 minutes, then remove, shred, and return to the air fryer.
4. Add the butter and air fry the shredded steak for a further 2 minutes at 365ºF (185ºC). Make sure the beef is coated in the butter before serving.

Air Fried Beef Ribs

Prep time: 20 minutes | Cook time: 8 minutes | Serves 4

1 pound (454 g) meaty beef ribs, rinsed and drained
3 tablespoons apple cider vinegar
1 cup coriander, finely chopped
1 tablespoon fresh basil leaves, chopped
2 garlic cloves, finely chopped
1 chipotle powder
1 teaspoon fennel seeds
1 teaspoon hot paprika
Kosher salt and black pepper, to taste
½ cup vegetable oil

1. Coat the ribs with the remaining ingredients and refrigerate for at least 3 hours.
2. Preheat the air fryer to 360ºF (182ºC).
3. Separate the ribs from the marinade and put them in the air fryer basket. Air fry for 8 minutes.
4. Pour the remaining marinade over the ribs before serving.

Pork Medallions with Radicchio and Endive Salad

Prep time: 25 minutes | Cook time: 7 minutes | Serves 4

1 (8-ounce / 227-g) pork tenderloin
Salt and freshly ground black pepper, to taste
¼ cup flour
2 eggs, lightly beaten
¾ cup cracker meal
1 teaspoon paprika
1 teaspoon dry mustard
1 teaspoon garlic powder
1 teaspoon dried thyme
1 teaspoon salt
vegetable or canola oil, in spray bottle

Vinaigrette:

¼ cup white balsamic vinegar
2 tablespoons agave syrup (or honey or maple syrup)
1 tablespoon Dijon mustard
juice of ½ lemon
2 tablespoons chopped chervil or flat-leaf parsley
salt and freshly ground black pepper
½ cup extra-virgin olive oil

Radicchio and Endive Salad:

1 heart romaine lettuce, torn into large pieces
½ head radicchio, coarsely chopped
2 heads endive, sliced
½ cup cherry tomatoes, halved
3 ounces (85 g) fresh Mozzarella, diced
Salt and freshly ground black pepper, to taste

1. Slice the pork tenderloin into 1-inch slices. Using a meat pounder, pound the pork slices into thin ½-inch medallions. Generously season the pork with salt and freshly ground black pepper on both sides.
2. Set up a dredging station using three shallow dishes. Put the flour in one dish and the beaten eggs in a second dish. Combine the cracker meal, paprika, dry mustard, garlic powder, thyme and salt in a third dish.
3. Preheat the air fryer to 400ºF (204ºC).
4. Dredge the pork medallions in flour first and then into the beaten egg. Let the excess egg drip off and coat both sides of the medallions with the cracker meal crumb mixture. Spray both sides of the coated medallions with vegetable or canola oil.
5. Air fry the medallions in two batches at 400ºF (204ºC) for 5 minutes. Once you have air-fried all the medallions, flip them all over and return the first batch of medallions back into the air fryer on top of the second batch. Air fry at 400ºF (204ºC) for an additional 2 minutes.
6. While the medallions are cooking, make the salad and dressing. Whisk the white balsamic vinegar, agave syrup, Dijon mustard, lemon juice, chervil, salt and pepper together in a small bowl. Whisk in the olive oil slowly until combined and thickened.
7. Combine the romaine lettuce, radicchio, endive, cherry tomatoes, and Mozzarella cheese in a large salad bowl. Drizzle the dressing over the vegetables and toss to combine. Season with salt and freshly ground black pepper.
8. Serve the pork medallions warm on or beside the salad.

Crumbed Golden Filet Mignon

Prep time: 15 minutes | Cook time: 12 minutes | Serves 4

½ pound (227 g) filet mignon
Sea salt and ground black pepper, to taste
½ teaspoon cayenne pepper
1 teaspoon dried basil
1 teaspoon dried rosemary
1 teaspoon dried thyme
1 tablespoon sesame oil
1 small egg, whisked
½ cup bread crumbs

1. Preheat the air fryer to 360ºF (182ºC).
2. Cover the filet mignon with the salt, black pepper, cayenne pepper, basil, rosemary, and thyme. Coat with sesame oil.
3. Put the egg in a shallow plate.
4. Pour the bread crumbs in another plate.
5. Dip the filet mignon into the egg. Roll it into the crumbs.
6. Transfer the steak to the air fryer and air fry for 12 minutes or until it turns golden.
7. Serve immediately.

Marinated Pork Tenderloin

Prep time: 10 minutes | Cook time: 30 minutes | Serves 4 to 6

¼ cup olive oil
¼ cup soy sauce
¼ cup freshly squeezed lemon juice
1 garlic clove, minced
1 tablespoon Dijon mustard
1 teaspoon salt
½ teaspoon freshly ground black pepper
2 pounds (907 g) pork tenderloin

1. In a large mixing bowl, make the marinade: Mix the olive oil, soy sauce, lemon juice, minced garlic, Dijon mustard, salt, and pepper. Reserve ¼ cup of the marinade.
2. Put the tenderloin in a large bowl and pour the remaining marinade over the meat. Cover and marinate in the refrigerator for about 1 hour.
3. Preheat the air fryer to 400ºF (204ºC).
4. Put the marinated pork tenderloin into the air fryer basket. Roast for 10

minutes. Flip the pork and baste it with half of the reserved marinade. Roast for 10 minutes more.
5. Flip the pork, then baste with the remaining marinade. Roast for another 10 minutes, for a total cooking time of 30 minutes.
6. Serve immediately.

Greek Lamb Pita Pockets

Prep time: 15 minutes | Cook time: 6 minutes | Serves 4

Dressing:
1 cup plain yogurt
1 tablespoon lemon juice
1 teaspoon dried dill
weed, crushed
1 teaspoon ground oregano
½ teaspoon salt

Meatballs:
½ pound (227 g) ground lamb
1 tablespoon diced onion
1 teaspoon dried parsley
1 teaspoon dried dill weed, crushed
¼ teaspoon oregano
¼ teaspoon coriander
¼ teaspoon ground cumin
¼ teaspoon salt
4 pita halves

Suggested Toppings:
1 red onion, slivered
1 medium cucumber, deseeded, thinly sliced
Crumbled Feta
cheese
Sliced black olives
Chopped fresh peppers

1. Preheat the air fryer to 390ºF (199ºC).
2. Stir the dressing ingredients together in a small bowl and refrigerate while preparing lamb.
3. Combine all meatball ingredients in a large bowl and stir to distribute seasonings.
4. Shape meat mixture into 12 small meatballs, rounded or slightly flattened if you prefer.
5. Transfer the meatballs in the preheated air fryer and air fry for 6 minutes, until well done. Remove and drain on paper towels.
6. To serve, pile meatballs and the choice of toppings in pita pockets and drizzle with dressing.

Beef Loin with Thyme and Parsley

Prep time: 5 minutes | Cook time: 15 minutes | Serves 4

1 tablespoon butter, melted
¼ dried thyme
1 teaspoon garlic salt

¼ teaspoon dried parsley
1 pound (454 g) beef loin

1. In a bowl, combine the melted butter, thyme, garlic salt, and parsley.
2. Cut the beef loin into slices and generously apply the seasoned butter using a brush.
3. Preheat the air fryer to 400ºF (204ºC).
4. Air fry the beef for 15 minutes.
5. Take care when removing it and serve hot.

Cheese Crusted Chops

Prep time: 10 minutes | Cook time: 12 minutes | Serves 4 to 6

¼ teaspoon pepper
½ teaspoons salt
4 to 6 thick boneless pork chops
1 cup pork rind crumbs
¼ teaspoon chili powder

½ teaspoons onion powder
1 teaspoon smoked paprika
2 beaten eggs
3 tablespoons grated Parmesan cheese
Cooking spray

1. Preheat the air fryer to 400ºF (205ºC).
2. Rub the pepper and salt on both sides of pork chops.
3. In a food processor, pulse pork rinds into crumbs. Mix crumbs with chili powder, onion powder, and paprika in a bowl.
4. Beat eggs in another bowl.
5. Dip pork chops into eggs then into pork rind crumb mixture.
6. Spritz the air fryer with cooking spray and add pork chops to the basket.
7. Air fry for 12 minutes.
8. Serve garnished with the Parmesan cheese.

Italian Lamb Chops with Avocado Mayo

Prep time: 5 minutes | Cook time: 12 minutes | Serves 2

2 lamp chops
2 teaspoons Italian herbs
2 avocados

½ cup mayonnaise
1 tablespoon lemon juice

1. Season the lamb chops with the Italian herbs, then set aside for 5 minutes.
2. Preheat the air fryer to 400ºF (204ºC).
3. Put the chops in the basket and air fry for 12 minutes.
4. In the meantime, halve the avocados and open to remove the pits. Spoon the flesh into a blender.
5. Add the mayonnaise and lemon juice and pulse until a smooth consistency is achieved.
6. Take care when removing the chops from the air fryer, then plate up and serve with the avocado mayo.

Mexican Pork Chops

Prep time: 5 minutes | Cook time: 15 minutes | Serves 2

¼ teaspoon dried oregano
1½ teaspoons taco seasoning mix
2 (4-ounce / 113-g)

boneless pork chops
2 tablespoons unsalted butter, divided

1. Preheat the air fryer to 400ºF (204ºC).
2. Combine the dried oregano and taco seasoning in a small bowl and rub the mixture into the pork chops. Brush the chops with 1 tablespoon butter.
3. In the air fryer, air fry the chops for 15 minutes, turning them over halfway through to air fry on the other side.
4. When the chops are a brown color, check the internal temperature has reached 145ºF (63ºC) and remove from the air fryer. Serve with a garnish of remaining butter.

Lamb Burger

Prep time: 15 minutes | Cook time: 16 minutes | Serves 3 to 4

2 teaspoons olive oil
1/3 onion, finely chopped
1 clove garlic, minced
1 pound (454 g) ground lamb
2 tablespoons fresh parsley, finely chopped
1½ teaspoons fresh oregano, finely chopped
½ cup black olives, finely chopped
1/3 cup crumbled feta cheese
½ teaspoon salt
Freshly ground black pepper, to taste
4 thick pita breads

1. Preheat a medium skillet over medium-high heat on the stovetop. Add the olive oil and cook the onion until tender, but not browned about 4 to 5 minutes. Add the garlic and cook for another minute. Transfer the onion and garlic to a mixing bowl and add the ground lamb, parsley, oregano, olives, feta cheese, salt and pepper. Gently mix the ingredients together.
2. Divide the mixture into 3 or 4 equal portions and then form the hamburgers, being careful not to over-handle the meat. One good way to do this is to throw the meat back and forth between the hands like a baseball, packing the meat each time you catch it. Flatten the balls into patties, making an indentation in the center of each patty. Flatten the sides of the patties as well to make it easier to fit them into the air fryer basket.
3. Preheat the air fryer to 370°F (188°C).
4. If you don't have room for all four burgers, air fry two or three burgers at a time for 8 minutes. Flip the burgers over and air fry for another 8 minutes. If you cooked the burgers in batches, return the first batch of burgers to the air fryer for the last two minutes of cooking to re-heat. This should give you a medium-well burger. If you'd prefer a medium-rare burger, shorten the cooking time to about 13 minutes. Remove the burgers to a resting plate and let the burgers rest for a few minutes before dressing and serving.
5. While the burgers are resting, bake the pita breads in the air fryer for 2 minutes. Tuck the burgers into the toasted pita breads, or wrap the pitas around the burgers and serve with a tzatziki sauce or some mayonnaise.

Kielbasa Sausage with Pierogies

Prep time: 15 minutes | Cook time: 30 minutes | Serves 3 to 4

1 sweet onion, sliced
1 teaspoon olive oil
Salt and freshly ground black pepper, to taste
2 tablespoons butter, cut into small cubes
1 teaspoon sugar
1 pound (454 g) light Polish kielbasa sausage, cut into 2-inch chunks
1 (13-ounce / 369-g) package frozen mini pierogies
2 teaspoons vegetable or olive oil
Chopped scallions, for garnish

1. Preheat the air fryer to 400°F (204°C).
2. Toss the sliced onions with olive oil, salt and pepper and transfer them to the air fryer basket. Dot the onions with pieces of butter and air fry for 2 minutes. Then sprinkle the sugar over the onions and stir. Pour any melted butter from the bottom of the air fryer drawer over the onions. Continue to air fry for another 13 minutes, stirring or shaking the basket every few minutes to air fry the onions evenly.
3. Add the kielbasa chunks to the onions and toss. Air fry for another 5 minutes, shaking the basket halfway through the cooking time. Transfer the kielbasa and onions to a bowl and cover with aluminum foil to keep warm.
4. Toss the frozen pierogies with the vegetable or olive oil and transfer them to the air fryer basket. Air fry at 400°F (204°C) for 8 minutes, shaking the basket twice during the cooking time.
5. When the pierogies have finished cooking, return the kielbasa and onions to the air fryer and gently toss with the pierogies. Air fry for 2 more minutes and then transfer everything to a serving platter. Garnish with the chopped scallions and serve hot with the spicy sour cream sauce below.

Air Fried Lamb Ribs

Prep time: 5 minutes | Cook time: 18 minutes | Serves 4

2 tablespoons mustard	Salt and ground black pepper, to taste
1 pound (454 g) lamb ribs	¼ cup mint leaves, chopped
1 teaspoon rosemary, chopped	1 cup Greek yogurt

1. Preheat the air fryer to 350ºF (177ºC).
2. Use a brush to apply the mustard to the lamb ribs, and season with rosemary, salt, and pepper.
3. Air fry the ribs in the air fryer for 18 minutes.
4. Meanwhile, combine the mint leaves and yogurt in a bowl.
5. Remove the lamb ribs from the air fryer when cooked and serve with the mint yogurt.

Pepperoni and Bell Pepper Pockets

Prep time: 5 minutes | Cook time: 8 minutes | Serves 4

4 bread slices, 1-inch thick	drained and patted dry
Olive oil, for misting	1 ounce (28 g) Pepper Jack cheese, cut into 4 slices
24 slices pepperoni	
1 ounce (28 g) roasted red peppers,	

1. Preheat the air fryer to 360ºF (182ºC).
2. Spray both sides of bread slices with olive oil.
3. Stand slices upright and cut a deep slit in the top to create a pocket (almost to the bottom crust, but not all the way through).
4. Stuff each bread pocket with 6 slices of pepperoni, a large strip of roasted red pepper, and a slice of cheese.
5. Put bread pockets in air fryer basket, standing up. Air fry for 8 minutes, until filling is heated through and bread is lightly browned.
6. Serve hot.

Fast Lamb Satay

Prep time: 5 minutes | Cook time: 8 minutes | Serves 2

¼ teaspoon cumin	black pepper, to taste
1 teaspoon ginger	2 boneless lamb steaks
½ teaspoons nutmeg	Cooking spray
Salt and ground	

1. Combine the cumin, ginger, nutmeg, salt and pepper in a bowl.
2. Cube the lamb steaks and massage the spice mixture into each one.
3. Leave to marinate for 10 minutes, then transfer onto metal skewers.
4. Preheat the air fryer to 400ºF (204ºC).
5. Spritz the skewers with the cooking spray, then air fry them in the air fryer for 8 minutes.
6. Take care when removing them from the air fryer and serve.

Spaghetti Squash Lasagna

Prep time: 5 minutes | Cook time: 1 hour 15 minutes | Serves 6

2 large spaghetti squash, cooked (about 2¾ pounds / 1.2 kg)	1.1-kg) large jar Marinara sauce
4 pounds (1.8 kg) ground beef	25 slices Mozzarella cheese
1 (2½-pound /	30 ounces whole-milk ricotta cheese

1. Preheat the air fryer to 375ºF (191ºC).
2. Slice the spaghetti squash and place it face down inside a baking dish. Fill with water until covered.
3. Bake in the preheated air fryer for 45 minutes until skin is soft.
4. Sear the ground beef in a skillet over medium-high heat for 5 minutes or until browned, then add the marinara sauce and heat until warm. Set aside.
5. Scrape the flesh off the cooked squash to resemble strands of spaghetti.
6. Layer the lasagna in a large greased pan in alternating layers of spaghetti squash, beef sauce, Mozzarella, ricotta. Repeat until all the ingredients have been used.
7. Bake for 30 minutes and serve!

Lollipop Lamb Chops

Prep time: 15 minutes | Cook time: 7 minutes | Serves 4

½ small clove garlic
¼ cup packed fresh parsley
¾ cup packed fresh mint
½ teaspoon lemon juice
¼ cup grated Parmesan cheese
$1/_3$ cup shelled pistachios
¼ teaspoon salt
½ cup olive oil
8 lamb chops (1 rack)
2 tablespoons vegetable oil
Salt and freshly ground black pepper, to taste
1 tablespoon dried rosemary, chopped
1 tablespoon dried thyme

1. Make the pesto by combining the garlic, parsley and mint in a food processor and process until finely chopped. Add the lemon juice, Parmesan cheese, pistachios and salt. Process until all the ingredients have turned into a paste. With the processor running, slowly pour the olive oil in. Scrape the sides of the processor with a spatula and process for another 30 seconds.
2. Preheat the air fryer to 400ºF (204ºC).
3. Rub both sides of the lamb chops with vegetable oil and season with salt, pepper, rosemary and thyme, pressing the herbs into the meat gently with the fingers. Transfer the lamb chops to the air fryer basket.
4. Air fry the lamb chops for 5 minutes. Flip the chops over and air fry for an additional 2 minutes.
5. Serve the lamb chops with mint pesto drizzled on top.

Air Fried London Broil

Prep time: 15 minutes | Cook time: 25 minutes | Serves 8

2 pounds (907 g) London broil
3 large garlic cloves, minced
3 tablespoons balsamic vinegar
3 tablespoons whole-grain mustard
2 tablespoons olive oil
Sea salt and ground black pepper, to taste
½ teaspoons dried hot red pepper flakes

1. Wash and dry the London broil. Score its sides with a knife.
2. Mix the remaining ingredients. Rub this mixture into the broil, coating it well. Allow to marinate for a minimum of 3 hours.
3. Preheat the air fryer to 400ºF (204ºC).
4. Air fry the meat for 15 minutes. Turn it over and air fry for an additional 10 minutes before serving.

Miso Marinated Steak

Prep time: 5 minutes | Cook time: 12 minutes | Serves 4

¾ pound (340 g) flank steak
1½ tablespoons sake
1 tablespoon brown miso paste
1 teaspoon honey
2 cloves garlic, pressed
1 tablespoon olive oil

1. Put all the ingredients in a Ziploc bag. Shake to cover the steak well with the seasonings and refrigerate for at least 1 hour.
2. Preheat the air fryer to 400ºF (204ºC). Coat all sides of the steak with cooking spray. Put the steak in the baking pan.
3. Air fry for 12 minutes, turning the steak twice during the cooking time, then serve immediately.

Cheesy Beef Meatballs

Prep time: 5 minutes | Cook time: 18 minutes | Serves 6

1 pound (454 g) ground beef
½ cup grated Parmesan cheese
1 tablespoon minced
garlic
½ cup Mozzarella cheese
1 teaspoon freshly ground pepper

1. Preheat the air fryer to 400ºF (204ºC).
2. In a bowl, mix all the ingredients together.
3. Roll the meat mixture into 5 generous meatballs.
4. Air fry inside the air fryer at 165ºF (74ºC) for about 18 minutes.
5. Serve immediately.

Mushroom and Beef Meatloaf

Prep time: 10 minutes | Cook time: 25 minutes | Serves 4

1 pound (454 g) ground beef
1 egg, beaten
1 mushrooms, sliced
1 tablespoon thyme
1 small onion,
chopped
3 tablespoons bread crumbs
Ground black pepper, to taste

1. Preheat the air fryer to 400ºF (204ºC).
2. Put all the ingredients into a large bowl and combine entirely.
3. Transfer the meatloaf mixture into the loaf pan and move it to the air fryer basket.
4. Bake for 25 minutes. Slice up before serving.

Vietnamese Pork Chops

Prep time: 15 minutes | Cook time: 12 minutes | Serves 2

1 tablespoon chopped shallot
1 tablespoon chopped garlic
1 tablespoon fish sauce
3 tablespoons lemongrass
1 teaspoon soy
sauce
1 tablespoon brown sugar
1 tablespoon olive oil
1 teaspoon ground black pepper
2 pork chops

1. Combine shallot, garlic, fish sauce, lemongrass, soy sauce, brown sugar, olive oil, and pepper in a bowl. Stir to mix well.
2. Put the pork chops in the bowl. Toss to coat well. Place the bowl in the refrigerator to marinate for 2 hours.
3. Preheat the air fryer to 400ºF (204ºC).
4. Remove the pork chops from the bowl and discard the marinade. Transfer the chops into the air fryer.
5. Air fry for 12 minutes or until lightly browned. Flip the pork chops halfway through the cooking time.
6. Remove the pork chops from the basket and serve hot.

Mongolian Flank Steak

Prep time: 20 minutes | Cook time: 15 minutes | Serves 4

1½ pounds (680 g) flank steak, thinly sliced on the bias into ¼-inch strips
Marinade:
2 tablespoons soy
sauce
1 clove garlic, smashed
Pinch crushed red pepper flakes

Sauce:

1 tablespoon vegetable oil
2 cloves garlic, minced
1 tablespoon finely grated fresh ginger
3 dried red chili peppers
¾ cup soy sauce
¾ cup chicken stock
5 to 6 tablespoons brown sugar
½ cup cornstarch, divided
1 bunch scallions, sliced into 2-inch pieces

1. Marinate the beef in the soy sauce, garlic and red pepper flakes for one hour.
2. In the meantime, make the sauce. Preheat a small saucepan over medium heat on the stovetop. Add the oil, garlic, ginger and dried chili peppers and sauté for just a minute or two. Add the soy sauce, chicken stock and brown sugar and continue to simmer for a few minutes. Dissolve 3 tablespoons of cornstarch in 3 tablespoons of water and stir this into the saucepan. Stir the sauce over medium heat until it thickens. Set this aside.
3. Preheat the air fryer to 400ºF (204ºC).
4. Remove the beef from the marinade and transfer it to a zipper sealable plastic bag with the remaining cornstarch. Shake it around to completely coat the beef and transfer the coated strips of beef to a baking sheet or plate, shaking off any excess cornstarch. Spray the strips with vegetable oil on all sides and transfer them to the air fryer basket.
5. Air fry for 15 minutes, shaking the basket to toss and rotate the beef strips throughout the cooking process. Add the scallions for the last 4 minutes of the cooking. Transfer the hot beef strips and scallions to a bowl and toss with the sauce, coating all the beef strips with the sauce. Serve warm.

Sumptuous Pizza Tortilla Rolls

Prep time: 10 minutes | Cook time: 6 minutes | Serves 4

1 teaspoon butter
½ medium onion, slivered
½ red or green bell pepper, julienned
4 ounces (113 g) fresh white mushrooms, chopped

½ cup pizza sauce
8 flour tortillas
8 thin slices deli ham
24 pepperoni slices
1 cup shredded Mozzarella cheese
Cooking spray

1. Preheat the air fryer to 390ºF (199ºC).
2. Put butter, onions, bell pepper, and mushrooms in a baking pan. Bake in the preheated air fryer for 3 minutes. Stir and cook 3 to 4 minutes longer until just crisp and tender. Remove pan and set aside.
3. To assemble rolls, spread about 2 teaspoons of pizza sauce on one half of each tortilla. Top with a slice of ham and 3 slices of pepperoni. Divide sautéed vegetables among tortillas and top with cheese.
4. Roll up tortillas, secure with toothpicks if needed, and spray with oil.
5. Put 4 rolls in air fryer basket and air fry for 4 minutes. Turn and air fry 4 minutes, until heated through and lightly browned.
6. Repeat step 4 to air fry remaining pizza rolls.
7. Serve immediately.

Orange Pork Tenderloin

Prep time: 15 minutes | Cook time: 23 minutes | Serves 3 to 4

2 tablespoons brown sugar
2 teaspoons cornstarch
2 teaspoons Dijon mustard
½ cup orange juice
½ teaspoon soy sauce
2 teaspoons grated fresh ginger

¼ cup white wine
Zest of 1 orange
1 pound (454 g) pork tenderloin
Salt and freshly ground black pepper, to taste
Oranges, halved, for garnish
Fresh parsley, for garnish

1. Combine the brown sugar, cornstarch, Dijon mustard, orange juice, soy sauce, ginger, white wine and orange zest in a small saucepan and bring the mixture to a boil on the stovetop. Lower the heat and simmer while you air fry the pork tenderloin or until the sauce has thickened.
2. Preheat the air fryer to 370ºF (188ºC).
3. Season all sides of the pork tenderloin with salt and freshly ground black pepper. Transfer the tenderloin to the air fryer basket.
4. Air fry for 20 to 23 minutes, or until the internal temperature reaches 145ºF (63ºC). Flip the tenderloin over halfway through the cooking process and baste with the sauce.
5. Transfer the tenderloin to a cutting board and let it rest for 5 minutes. Slice the pork at a slight angle and serve immediately with orange halves and fresh parsley.

Citrus Pork Loin Roast

Prep time: 10 minutes | Cook time: 45 minutes | Serves 8

1 tablespoon lime juice
1 tablespoon orange marmalade
1 teaspoon coarse brown mustard
1 teaspoon curry powder
1 teaspoon dried

lemongrass
2 pound (907 g) boneless pork loin roast
Salt and ground black pepper, to taste
Cooking spray

1. Preheat the air fryer to 360ºF (182ºC).
2. Mix the lime juice, marmalade, mustard, curry powder, and lemongrass.
3. Rub mixture all over the surface of the pork loin. Season with salt and pepper.
4. Spray air fryer basket with cooking spray and place pork roast diagonally in the basket.
5. Air fry for approximately 45 minutes, until the internal temperature reaches at least 145ºF (63ºC).
6. Wrap roast in foil and let rest for 10 minutes before slicing.
7. Serve immediately.

Char Siew

Prep time: 10 minutes | Cook time: 20 minutes | Serves 4 to 6

1 strip of pork shoulder butt with a good amount of fat

marbling
Olive oil, for brushing the pan

Marinade:

1 teaspoon sesame oil

4 tablespoons raw honey

1 teaspoon low-sodium dark soy sauce

1 teaspoon light soy sauce

1 tablespoon rose wine

2 tablespoons Hoisin sauce

1. Combine all the marinade ingredients together in a Ziploc bag. Put pork in bag, making sure all sections of pork strip are engulfed in the marinade. Chill for 3 to 24 hours.
2. Take out the strip 30 minutes before planning to roast and preheat the air fryer to 350ºF (177ºC).
3. Put foil on small pan and brush with olive oil. Put marinated pork strip onto prepared pan.
4. Roast in the preheated air fryer for 20 minutes.
5. Glaze with marinade every 5 to 10 minutes.
6. Remove strip and leave to cool a few minutes before slicing.
7. Serve immediately.

Pork and Pinto Bean Gorditas

Prep time: 20 minutes | Cook time: 21 minutes | Serves 4

1 pound (454 g) lean ground pork

2 tablespoons chili powder

2 tablespoons ground cumin

1 teaspoon dried oregano

2 teaspoons paprika

1 teaspoon garlic powder

½ cup water

1 (15-ounce / 425-g) can pinto beans, drained and rinsed

½ cup taco sauce

Salt and freshly ground black pepper, to taste

2 cups grated Cheddar cheese

5 (12-inch) flour tortillas

4 (8-inch) crispy

corn tortilla shells

4 cups shredded lettuce

1 tomato, diced

⅓ cup sliced black olives

Sour cream, for serving

Tomato salsa, for serving

Cooking spray

1. Preheat the air fryer to 400ºF (204ºC). Spritz the air fryer basket with cooking spray.
2. Put the ground pork in the air fryer basket and air fry at 400ºF (204ºC) for 10 minutes, stirring a few times to gently break up the meat. Combine the chili powder, cumin, oregano, paprika, garlic powder and water in a small bowl. Stir the spice mixture into the browned pork. Stir in the beans and taco sauce and air fry for an additional minute. Transfer the pork mixture to a bowl. Season with salt and freshly ground black pepper.
3. Sprinkle ½ cup of the grated cheese in the center of the flour tortillas, leaving a 2-inch border around the edge free of cheese and filling. Divide the pork mixture among the four tortillas, placing it on top of the cheese. Put a crunchy corn tortilla on top of the pork and top with shredded lettuce, diced tomatoes, and black olives. Cut the remaining flour tortilla into 4 quarters. These quarters of tortilla will serve as the bottom of the gordita. Put one quarter tortilla on top of each gordita and fold the edges of the bottom flour tortilla up over the sides, enclosing the filling. While holding the seams down, brush the bottom of the gordita with olive oil and place the seam side down on the countertop while you finish the remaining three gorditas.
4. Preheat the air fryer to 380ºF (193ºC).
5. Air fry one gordita at a time. Transfer the gordita carefully to the air fryer basket, seam side down. Brush or spray the top tortilla with oil and air fry for 5 minutes. Carefully turn the gordita over and air fry for an additional 4 to 5 minutes until both sides are browned. When finished air frying all four gorditas, layer them back into the air fryer for an additional minute to make sure they are all warm before serving with sour cream and salsa.

Potato and Prosciutto Salad

Prep time: 10 minutes | Cook time: 7 minutes | Serves 8

Salad:

4 pounds (1.8 kg) potatoes, boiled and cubed
15 slices prosciutto, diced
2 cups shredded Cheddar cheese

Dressing:

15 ounces (425 g) sour cream
2 tablespoons mayonnaise
1 teaspoon salt
1 teaspoon black pepper
1 teaspoon dried basil

1. Preheat the air fryer to 350ºF (177ºC).
2. Put the potatoes, prosciutto, and Cheddar in a baking dish. Put it in the air fryer and air fry for 7 minutes.
3. In a separate bowl, mix the sour cream, mayonnaise, salt, pepper, and basil using a whisk.
4. Coat the salad with the dressing and serve.

Pork with Aloha Salsa

Prep time: 20 minutes | Cook time: 8 minutes | Serves 4

2 eggs
2 tablespoons milk
¼ cup flour
¼ cup panko bread crumbs
4 teaspoons sesame seeds
1 pound (454 g) boneless, thin pork cutlets (⅜- to ½-inch thick)
Lemon pepper and salt, to taste
¼ cup cornstarch
Cooking spray

Aloha Salsa:

1 cup fresh pineapple, chopped in small pieces
¼ cup red onion, finely chopped
¼ cup green or red bell pepper, chopped
½ teaspoon ground cinnamon
1 teaspoon low-sodium soy sauce
⅛ teaspoon crushed red pepper
⅛ teaspoon ground black pepper

1. In a medium bowl, stir together all ingredients for salsa. Cover and refrigerate while cooking the pork.

2. Preheat the air fryer to 390ºF (199ºC).
3. Beat the eggs and milk in a shallow dish.
4. In another shallow dish, mix the flour, panko, and sesame seeds.
5. Sprinkle pork cutlets with lemon pepper and salt.
6. Dip pork cutlets in cornstarch, egg mixture, and then panko coating. Spray both sides with cooking spray.
7. Air fry the cutlets for 3 minutes. Turn cutlets over, spraying both sides, and continue air frying for 5 minutes or until well done.
8. Serve fried cutlets with salsa on the side.

Classic Spring Rolls

Prep time: 10 minutes | Cook time: 8 minutes | Serves 20

⅓ cup noodles
1 cup ground beef
1 teaspoon soy sauce
1 cup fresh mix vegetables
3 garlic cloves, minced
1 small onion, diced
1 tablespoon sesame oil
1 packet spring roll sheets
2 tablespoons cold water

1. Cook the noodle in enough hot water to soften them up, drain them and snip them to make them shorter.
2. In a frying pan over medium heat, cook the beef, soy sauce, mixed vegetables, garlic, and onion in sesame oil until the beef is cooked through. Take the pan off the heat and throw in the noodles. Mix well to incorporate everything.
3. Unroll a spring roll sheet and lay it flat. Scatter the filling diagonally across it and roll it up, brushing the edges lightly with water to act as an adhesive. Repeat until you have used up all the sheets and the filling.
4. Preheat the air fryer to 350ºF (177ºC).
5. Coat each spring roll with a light brushing of oil and transfer to the air fryer.
6. Air fry for 8 minutes and serve hot.

Ritzy Skirt Steak Fajitas

Prep time: 15 minutes | Cook time: 30 minutes | Serves 4

2 tablespoons olive oil
¼ cup lime juice
1 clove garlic, minced
½ teaspoon ground cumin
½ teaspoon hot sauce
½ teaspoon salt
2 tablespoons chopped fresh cilantro
1 pound (454 g) skirt steak
1 onion, sliced
1 teaspoon chili powder
1 red pepper, sliced
1 green pepper, sliced
Salt and freshly ground black pepper, to taste
8 flour tortillas
Toppings:
Shredded lettuce
Crumbled Queso Fresco (or grated Cheddar cheese)
Sliced black olives
Diced tomatoes
Sour cream
Guacamole

1. Combine the olive oil, lime juice, garlic, cumin, hot sauce, salt and cilantro in a shallow dish. Add the skirt steak and turn it over several times to coat all sides. Pierce the steak with a needle-style meat tenderizer or paring knife. Marinate the steak in the refrigerator for at least 3 hours, or overnight. When you are ready to cook, remove the steak from the refrigerator and let it sit at room temperature for 30 minutes.
2. Preheat the air fryer to 400ºF (204ºC).
3. Toss the onion slices with the chili powder and a little olive oil and transfer them to the air fryer basket. Air fry for 5 minutes. Add the red and green peppers to the air fryer basket with the onions, season with salt and pepper and air fry for 8 more minutes, until the onions and peppers are soft. Transfer the vegetables to a dish and cover with aluminum foil to keep warm.
4. Put the skirt steak in the air fryer basket and pour the marinade over the top. Air fry at 400ºF (204ºC) for 12 minutes. Flip the steak over and air fry for an additional 5 minutes. Transfer the cooked steak to a cutting board and let the steak rest for a few minutes. If the peppers and onions need to be heated, return them to the air fryer for just 1 to 2 minutes.
5. Thinly slice the steak at an angle, cutting against the grain of the steak. Serve the steak with the onions and peppers, the warm tortillas and the fajita toppings on the side.

Provolone Stuffed Beef and Pork Meatballs

Prep time: 15 minutes | Cook time: 12 minutes | Serves 4 to 6

1 tablespoon olive oil
1 small onion, finely chopped
1 to 2 cloves garlic, minced
¾ pound (340 g) ground beef
¾ pound (340 g) ground pork
¾ cup bread crumbs
¼ cup grated Parmesan cheese
¼ cup finely
chopped fresh parsley
½ teaspoon dried oregano
1½ teaspoons salt
Freshly ground black pepper, to taste
2 eggs, lightly beaten
5 ounces (142 g) sharp or aged provolone cheese, cut into 1-inch cubes

1. Preheat a skillet over medium-high heat. Add the oil and cook the onion and garlic until tender, but not browned.
2. Transfer the onion and garlic to a large bowl and add the beef, pork, bread crumbs, Parmesan cheese, parsley, oregano, salt, pepper and eggs. Mix well until all the ingredients are combined. Divide the mixture into 12 evenly sized balls. Make one meatball at a time, by pressing a hole in the meatball mixture with the finger and pushing a piece of provolone cheese into the hole. Mold the meat back into a ball, enclosing the cheese.
3. Preheat the air fryer to 380ºF (193ºC).
4. Working in two batches, transfer six of the meatballs to the air fryer basket and air fry for 12 minutes, shaking the basket and turning the meatballs twice during the cooking process. Repeat with the remaining 6 meatballs. Serve warm.

Barbecue Pork Ribs

Prep time: 5 minutes | Cook time: 30 minutes | Serves 4

1 tablespoon barbecue dry rub
1 teaspoon mustard
1 tablespoon apple cider vinegar
1 teaspoon sesame oil
1 pound (454 g) pork ribs, chopped

1. Combine the dry rub, mustard, apple cider vinegar, and sesame oil, then coat the ribs with this mixture. Refrigerate the ribs for 20 minutes.
2. Preheat the air fryer to 360ºF (182ºC).
3. When the ribs are ready, place them in the air fryer and air fry for 15 minutes. Flip them and air fry on the other side for a further 15 minutes.
4. Serve immediately.

Rosemary Ribeye Steaks

Prep time: 10 minutes | Cook time: 15 minutes | Serves 2

¼ cup butter
1 clove garlic, minced
Salt and ground black pepper, to taste
1½ tablespoons balsamic vinegar
¼ cup rosemary, chopped
2 ribeye steaks

1. Melt the butter in a skillet over medium heat. Add the garlic and fry until fragrant.
2. Remove the skillet from the heat and add the salt, pepper, and vinegar. Allow it to cool.
3. Add the rosemary, then pour the mixture into a Ziploc bag.
4. Put the ribeye steaks in the bag and shake well, coating the meat well. Refrigerate for an hour, then allow to sit for a further twenty minutes.
5. Preheat the air fryer to 400ºF (204ºC).
6. Air fry the ribeyes for 15 minutes.
7. Take care when removing the steaks from the air fryer and plate up.
8. Serve immediately.

Easy Beef Schnitzel

Prep time: 5 minutes | Cook time: 12 minutes | Serves 1

½ cup friendly bread crumbs
2 tablespoons olive oil
Pepper and salt, to taste
1 egg, beaten
1 thin beef schnitzel

1. Preheat the air fryer to 350ºF (177ºC).
2. In a shallow dish, combine the bread crumbs, oil, pepper, and salt.
3. In a second shallow dish, place the beaten egg.
4. Dredge the schnitzel in the egg before rolling it in the bread crumbs.
5. Put the coated schnitzel in the air fryer basket and air fry for 12 minutes. Flip the schnitzel halfway through.
6. Serve immediately.

Beef Steak Fingers

Prep time: 5 minutes | Cook time: 8 minutes | Serves 4

4 small beef cube steaks
Salt and ground black pepper, to
taste
½ cup flour
Cooking spray

1. Preheat the air fryer to 390ºF (199ºC).
2. Cut cube steaks into 1-inch-wide strips.
3. Sprinkle lightly with salt and pepper to taste.
4. Roll in flour to coat all sides.
5. Spritz air fryer basket with cooking spray.
6. Put steak strips in air fryer basket in a single layer. Spritz top of steak strips with cooking spray.
7. Air fry for 4 minutes, turn strips over, and spritz with cooking spray.
8. Air fry 4 more minutes and test with fork for doneness. Steak fingers should be crispy outside with no red juices inside.
9. Repeat steps 5 through 7 to air fry remaining strips.
10. Serve immediately.

Smoked Beef

Prep time: 10 minutes | Cook time: 45 minutes | Serves 8

2 pounds (907 g) roast beef, at room temperature
2 tablespoons extra-virgin olive oil
1 teaspoon sea salt flakes
1 teaspoon ground

black pepper
1 teaspoon smoked paprika
Few dashes of liquid smoke
2 jalapeño peppers, thinly sliced

1. Preheat the air fryer to 330ºF (166ºC).
2. With kitchen towels, pat the beef dry.
3. Massage the extra-virgin olive oil, salt, black pepper, and paprika into the meat. Cover with liquid smoke.
4. Put the beef in the air fryer and roast for 30 minutes. Flip the roast over and allow to roast for another 15 minutes.
5. When cooked through, serve topped with sliced jalapeños.

Swedish Beef Meatballs

Prep time: 10 minutes | Cook time: 12 minutes | Serves 8

1 pound (454 g) ground beef
1 egg, beaten
2 carrots, shredded
2 bread slices, crumbled
1 small onion,

minced
½ teaspoons garlic salt
Pepper and salt, to taste
1 cup tomato sauce
2 cups pasta sauce

1. Preheat the air fryer to 400ºF (204ºC).
2. In a bowl, combine the ground beef, egg, carrots, crumbled bread, onion, garlic salt, pepper and salt.
3. Divide the mixture into equal amounts and shape each one into a small meatball.
4. Put them in the air fryer basket and air fry for 7 minutes.
5. Transfer the meatballs to an oven-safe dish and top with the tomato sauce and pasta sauce.
6. Set the dish into the air fryer basket and allow to air fry at 320ºF (160ºC) for 5 more minutes. Serve hot.

Beef and Vegetable Cubes

Prep time: 15 minutes | Cook time: 17 minutes | Serves 4

2 tablespoons olive oil
1 tablespoon apple cider vinegar
1 teaspoon fine sea salt
½ teaspoons ground black pepper
1 teaspoon shallot powder
¾ teaspoon smoked cayenne pepper
½ teaspoons garlic powder

¼ teaspoon ground cumin
1 pound (454 g) top round steak, cut into cubes
4 ounces (113 g) broccoli, cut into florets
4 ounces (113 g) mushrooms, sliced
1 teaspoon dried basil
1 teaspoon celery seeds

1. Massage the olive oil, vinegar, salt, black pepper, shallot powder, cayenne pepper, garlic powder, and cumin into the cubed steak, ensuring to coat each piece evenly.
2. Allow to marinate for a minimum of 3 hours.
3. Preheat the air fryer to 365ºF (185ºC).
4. Put the beef cubes in the air fryer basket and air fry for 12 minutes.
5. When the steak is cooked through, place it in a bowl.
6. Wipe the grease from the basket and pour in the vegetables. Season them with basil and celery seeds.
7. Increase the temperature of the air fryer to 400ºF (204ºC) and air fry for 5 to 6 minutes. When the vegetables are hot, serve them with the steak.

Teriyaki Pork and Mushroom Rolls

Prep time: 10 minutes | Cook time: 8 minutes | Serves 6

4 tablespoons brown sugar
4 tablespoons mirin
4 tablespoons soy sauce
1 teaspoon almond flour
2-inch ginger, chopped
6 (4-ounce / 113-g) pork belly slices
6 ounces (170 g) Enoki mushrooms

1. Mix the brown sugar, mirin, soy sauce, almond flour, and ginger together until brown sugar dissolves.
2. Take pork belly slices and wrap around a bundle of mushrooms. Brush each roll with teriyaki sauce. Chill for half an hour.
3. Preheat the air fryer to 350ºF (177ºC) and add marinated pork rolls.
4. Air fry for 8 minutes. Flip the rolls halfway through.
5. Serve immediately.

Hearty Sweet and Sour Pork

Prep time: 20 minutes | Cook time: 14 minutes | Serves 2 to 4

1/3 cup all-purpose flour
1/3 cup cornstarch
2 teaspoons Chinese five-spice powder
1 teaspoon salt
Freshly ground black pepper, to taste
1 egg
2 tablespoons milk
¾ pound (340 g) boneless pork, cut into 1-inch cubes
Vegetable or canola oil
1½ cups large chunks of red and
green peppers
½ cup ketchup
2 tablespoons rice wine vinegar or apple cider vinegar
2 tablespoons brown sugar
¼ cup orange juice
1 tablespoon soy sauce
1 clove garlic, minced
1 cup cubed pineapple
Chopped scallions, for garnish

1. Set up a dredging station with two bowls. Combine the flour, cornstarch, Chinese five-spice powder, salt and pepper in one large bowl. Whisk the egg and milk together in a second bowl. Dredge the pork cubes in the flour mixture first, then dip them into the egg and then back into the flour to coat on all sides. Spray the coated pork cubes with vegetable or canola oil.
2. Preheat the air fryer to 400ºF (204ºC).
3. Toss the pepper chunks with a little oil and air fry for 5 minutes, shaking the basket halfway through the cooking time.
4. While the peppers are cooking, start making the sauce. Combine the ketchup, rice wine vinegar, brown sugar, orange juice, soy sauce, and garlic in a medium saucepan and bring the mixture to a boil on the stovetop. Reduce the heat and simmer for 5 minutes. When the peppers have finished air frying, add them to the saucepan along with the pineapple chunks. Simmer the peppers and pineapple in the sauce for an additional 2 minutes. Set aside and keep warm.
5. Add the dredged pork cubes to the air fryer basket and air fry at 400ºF (204ºC) for 6 minutes, shaking the basket to turn the cubes over for the last minute of the cooking process.
6. When ready to serve, toss the cooked pork with the pineapple, peppers and sauce. Serve garnished with chopped scallions.

Beef Meatloaf

Prep + Cook Time: 30 minutes | Servings: 4

Ingredients
¾ lb. ground chuck
¼ lb. ground pork sausage
1 cup shallots, finely chopped
2 eggs, well beaten
3 tbsp. plain milk
1 tbsp. oyster sauce
1 tsp. porcini mushrooms
½ tsp. cumin powder
1 tsp. garlic paste
1 tbsp. fresh parsley
Seasoned salt and crushed red pepper flakes to taste
1 cup crushed saltines

Instructions
1. Mix together all of the ingredients in a large bowl, combining everything well.
2. Transfer to the Air Fryer baking dish and cook at 360°F for 25 minutes.
3. Serve hot.

Stuffed Bell Pepper

Prep + Cook Time: 25 minutes | Servings: 4

Ingredients
4 bell peppers, cut top of bell pepper
16 oz. ground beef
2/3 cup cheese, shredded
½ cup rice, cooked
1 tsp. basil, dried
½ tsp. chili powder
1 tsp. black pepper
1 tsp. garlic salt
2 tsp. Worcestershire sauce
8 oz. tomato sauce
2 garlic cloves, minced
1 small onion, chopped

Instructions
1. Grease a frying pan with cooking spray and fry the onion and garlic over a medium heat.
2. Stir in the beef, basil, chili powder, black pepper, and garlic salt, combining everything well. Allow to cook until the beef is nicely browned, before taking the pan off the heat.
3. Add in half of the cheese, the rice, Worcestershire sauce, and tomato sauce and stir to combine.

4. Spoon equal amounts of the beef mixture into the four bell peppers, filling them entirely.
5. Pre-heat the Air Fryer at 400°F.
6. Spritz the Air Fryer basket with cooking spray.
7. Put the stuffed bell peppers in the basket and allow to cook for 11 minutes.
8. Add the remaining cheese on top of each bell pepper with remaining cheese and cook for a further 2 minutes. When the cheese is melted and the bell peppers are piping hot, serve immediately.

Asian Beef Burgers

Prep + Cook Time: 20 minutes | Servings: 4

Ingredients
¾ lb. lean ground beef
1 tbsp. soy sauce
1 tsp. Dijon mustard
Few dashes of liquid smoke
1 tsp. shallot powder
1 clove garlic, minced
½ tsp. cumin powder
¼ cup scallions, minced
⅓ tsp. sea salt flakes
⅓ tsp. freshly cracked mixed peppercorns
1 tsp. celery seeds
1 tsp. parsley flakes

Instructions
1. Mix together all of the ingredients in a bowl using your hands, combining everything well.
2. Take four equal amounts of the mixture and mold each one into a patty.
3. Use the back of a spoon to create a shallow dip in the center of each patty. This will prevent them from puffing up during the cooking process.
4. Lightly coat all sides of the patties with cooking spray.
5. Place each one in the Air Fryer and cook for roughly 12 minutes at 360°F.
6. Test with a meat thermometer – the patties are ready once they have reached 160°F. Serve them on top of butter rolls with any sauces and toppings you desire.

Burger Patties

Prep + Cook Time: 15 minutes | Servings: 6

Ingredients
1 lb. ground beef
6 cheddar cheese slices
Pepper and salt to taste

Instructions
1. Pre-heat the Air Fryer to 350°F.
2. Sprinkle the salt and pepper on the ground beef.
3. Shape six equal portions of the ground beef into patties and put each one in the Air Fryer basket.
4. Air fry the patties for 10 minutes.
5. Top the patties with the cheese slices and air fry for one more minute.
6. Serve the patties on top of dinner rolls.

Beef Rolls

Prep + Cook Time: 30 minutes | Servings: 2

Ingredients
2 lb. beef flank steak
3 tsp. pesto
1 tsp. black pepper
6 slices of provolone cheese
3 oz. roasted red bell peppers
¾ cup baby spinach
1 tsp. sea salt

Instructions
1. Spoon equal amounts of the pesto onto each flank steak and spread it across evenly.
2. Place the cheese, roasted red peppers and spinach on top of the meat, about three-quarters of the way down.
3. Roll the steak up, holding it in place with toothpicks. Sprinkle on the sea salt and pepper.
4. Place inside the Air Fryer and cook for 14 minutes at 400°F, turning halfway through the cooking time.
5. Allow the beef to rest for 10 minutes before slicing up and serving.

Crumbed Filet Mignon

Prep + Cook Time: 20 minutes | Servings: 4

Ingredients
½ lb. filet mignon
Sea salt and ground black pepper, to taste
½ tsp. cayenne pepper
1 tsp. dried basil
1 tsp. dried rosemary
1 tsp. dried thyme
1 tbsp. sesame oil
1 small-sized egg, well-whisked
½ cup friendly breadcrumbs

Instructions
1. Cover the filet mignon with the salt, black pepper, cayenne pepper, basil, rosemary, and thyme. Coat with a light brushing of sesame oil.
2. Put the egg in a shallow plate.
3. Pour the friendly breadcrumbs in another plate.
4. Dip the filet mignon into the egg. Roll it into the crumbs.
5. Transfer the steak to the Air Fryer and cook for 10 to 13 minutes at 360°F or until it turns golden.
6. Serve with a salad.

Grilled Beef Ribs

Prep + Cook Time: 20 minutes + marinating time | Servings: 4

Ingredients
1 lb. meaty beef ribs
3 tbsp. apple cider vinegar
1 cup coriander, finely chopped
1 heaped tbsp. fresh basil leaves, chopped
2 garlic cloves, finely chopped
1 chipotle powder
1 tsp. fennel seeds
1 tsp. hot paprika
Kosher salt and black pepper, to taste
½ cup vegetable oil

Instructions
1. Wash and dry the ribs.
2. Coat the ribs with the rest of the ingredients and refrigerate for a minimum of 3 hours.
3. Separate the ribs from the marinade and put them on an Air Fryer grill pan.
4. Cook at 360°F for 8 minutes, or longer as needed.
5. Pour the remaining marinade over the ribs before serving immediately.

London Broil

Prep + Cook Time: 30 minutes + marinating time | Servings: 8

Ingredients
2 lb. London broil
3 large garlic cloves, minced
3 tbsp. balsamic vinegar
3 tbsp. whole-grain mustard
2 tbsp. olive oil
Sea salt and ground black pepper, to taste
½ tsp. dried hot red pepper flakes

Instructions
1. Wash and dry the London broil. Score its sides with a knife.
2. Mix together the rest of the ingredients. Rub this mixture into the broil, coating it well. Allow to marinate for a minimum of 3 hours.
3. Cook the meat at 400°F for 15 minutes.
4. Turn it over and cook for an additional 10 - 12 minutes before serving.

Smoked Beef Roast

Prep + Cook Time: 45 minutes | Servings: 8

Ingredients
2 lb. roast beef, at room temperature
2 tbsp. extra-virgin olive oil
1 tsp. sea salt flakes
1 tsp. black pepper, preferably freshly ground
1 tsp. smoked paprika
Few dashes of liquid smoke
2 jalapeño peppers, thinly sliced

Instructions
1.Pre-heat the Air Fryer to 330°F.
2.With kitchen towels, pat the beef dry.
3.Massage the extra-virgin olive oil and seasonings into the meat. Cover with liquid smoke.
4.Place the beef in the Air Fryer and roast for 30 minutes. Flip the roast over and allow to cook for another 15 minutes.
5.When cooked through, serve topped with sliced jalapeños.

Vegetables & Beef Cubes

Prep + Cook Time: 20 minutes + marinating time | Servings: 4

Ingredients
1 lb. top round steak, cut into cubes
2 tbsp. olive oil
1 tbsp. apple cider vinegar
1 tsp. fine sea salt
½ tsp. ground black pepper
1 tsp. shallot powder
¾ tsp. smoked cayenne pepper
½ tsp. garlic powder
¼ tsp. ground cumin
¼ lb. broccoli, cut into florets
¼ lb. mushrooms, sliced
1 tsp. dried basil
1 tsp. celery seeds

Instructions
1.Massage the olive oil, vinegar, salt, black pepper, shallot powder, cayenne pepper, garlic powder, and cumin into the cubed steak, ensuring to coat each piece evenly.
2.Allow to marinate for a minimum of 3 hours.
3.Put the beef cubes in the Air Fryer cooking basket and allow to cook at 365°F for 12 minutes.
4.When the steak is cooked through, place it in a bowl.
5.Wipe the grease from the cooking basket and pour in the vegetables. Season them with basil and celery seeds.

6.Cook at 400°F for 5 to 6 minutes. When the vegetables are hot, serve them with the steak.

Beef & Kale Omelet

Prep + Cook Time: 20 minutes | Servings: 4

Ingredients
Cooking spray
½ lb. leftover beef, coarsely chopped
2 garlic cloves, pressed
1 cup kale, torn into pieces and wilted
1 tomato, chopped
¼ tsp. sugar
4 eggs, beaten
4 tbsp. heavy cream
½ tsp. turmeric powder
Salt and ground black pepper to taste
1/8 tsp. ground allspice

Instructions
1.Grease four ramekins with cooking spray.
2.Place equal amounts of each of the ingredients into each ramekin and mix well.
3.Air-fry at 360°F for 16 minutes, or longer if necessary. Serve immediately.

Cheeseburgers

Prep + Cook Time: 15 minutes | Servings: 4

Ingredients
¾ lb. ground chuck
1 envelope onion soup mix
Kosher salt and freshly ground black pepper, to taste
1 tsp. paprika
4 slices Monterey-Jack cheese
4 ciabatta rolls
Mustard and pickled salad, to serve

Instructions
1.In a bowl, stir together the ground chuck, onion soup mix, salt, black pepper, and paprika to combine well.
2.Pre-heat your Air Fryer at 385°F.
3.Take four equal portions of the mixture and mold each one into a patty. Transfer to the fryer and air fry for 10 minutes.
4.Put the slices of cheese on the top of the burgers.
5.Cook for another minute before serving on ciabatta rolls along with mustard and the pickled salad of your choosing.

Simple Beef

Prep + Cook Time: 25 minutes | Servings: 1

Ingredients
1 thin beef schnitzel
1 egg, beaten
½ cup friendly bread crumbs
2 tbsp. olive oil
Pepper and salt to taste

Instructions
1.Pre-heat the Air Fryer to 350°F.
2.In a shallow dish, combine the bread crumbs, oil, pepper, and salt.
3.In a second shallow dish, place the beaten egg.
4.Dredge the schnitzel in the egg before rolling it in the bread crumbs.
5.Put the coated schnitzel in the fryer basket and air fry for 12 minutes.

Meatloaf

Prep + Cook Time: 30 minutes | Servings: 4

Ingredients
1 lb. ground beef
1 egg, beaten
1 mushrooms, sliced
1 tbsp. thyme
1 small onion, chopped
3 tbsp. friendly breadcrumbs
Pepper to taste

Instructions
1.Pre-heat the Air Fryer at 400°F.
2.Place all the ingredients into a large bowl and combine entirely.
3.Transfer the meatloaf mixture into the loaf pan, and move it to the Air Fryer basket.
4.Cook for 25 minutes. Slice up before serving.

Beef Burgers

Prep + Cook Time: 65 minutes | Servings: 4

Ingredients
10.5 oz. beef, minced
1 onion, diced
1 tsp. garlic, minced or pureed
1 tsp. tomato, pureed
1 tsp. mustard
1 tsp. basil
1 tsp. mixed herbs
Salt to taste
Pepper to taste
1 oz. cheddar cheese

4 buns
Salad leaves

Instructions
1.Drizzle the Air Fryer with one teaspoon of olive oil and allow it to warm up.
2.Place the diced onion in the fryer and fry until they turn golden brown.
3.Mix in all of the seasoning and cook for 25 minutes at 390°F.
4.Lay 2 – 3 onion rings and pureed tomato on two of the buns. Place one slice of cheese and the layer of beef on top. Top with salad leaves and any other condiments you desire before closing off the sandwich with the other buns.
5.Serve with ketchup, cold drink and French fries.

Brussels Sprouts & Tender Beef Chuck

Prep + Cook Time: 25 minutes + marinating time | Servings: 4

Ingredients
1 lb. beef chuck shoulder steak
2 tbsp. vegetable oil
1 tbsp. red wine vinegar
1 tsp. fine sea salt
½ tsp. ground black pepper
1 tsp. smoked paprika
1 tsp. onion powder
½ tsp. garlic powder
½ lb. Brussels sprouts, cleaned and halved
½ tsp. fennel seeds
1 tsp. dried basil
1 tsp. dried sage

Instructions
1.Massage the beef with the vegetable oil, wine vinegar, salt, black pepper, paprika, onion powder, and garlic powder, coating it well.
2.Allow to marinate for a minimum of 3 hours.
3.Air fry at 390°F for 10 minutes.
4.Put the prepared Brussels sprouts in the fryer along with the fennel seeds, basil, and sage.
5.Lower the heat to 380°F and cook everything for another 5 minutes.
6.Pause the machine and give the contents a good stir. Cook for an additional 10 minutes.
7.Take out the beef and allow the vegetables too cook for a few more minutes if necessary or desired.
8.Serve everything together with the sauce of your choice.

Swedish Meatballs

Prep + Cook Time: 25 minutes | Servings: 8

Ingredients
1 lb. ground beef
2 friendly bread slices, crumbled
1 small onion, minced
½ tsp. garlic salt
1 cup tomato sauce
2 cups pasta sauce
1 egg, beaten
2 carrots, shredded
Pepper and salt to taste

Instructions
1.Pre-heat Air Fryer to 400°F.
2.In a bowl, combine the ground beef, egg, carrots, crumbled bread, onion, garlic salt, pepper and salt.
3.Divide the mixture into equal amounts and shape each one into a small meatball.
4.Put them in the Air Fryer basket and cook for 7 minutes.
5.Transfer the meatballs to an oven-safe dish and top with the tomato sauce.
6.Set the dish into the Air Fryer basket and allow to cook at 320°F for 5 more minutes. Serve hot.

German Schnitzel

Prep + Cook Time: 15 minutes | Servings: 4

Ingredients
4 thin beef schnitzel
1 tbsp. sesame seeds
2 tbsp. paprika
3 tbsp. olive oil
4 tbsp. flour
2 eggs, beaten
1 cup friendly bread crumbs
Pepper and salt to taste

Instructions
1.Pre-heat the Air Fryer at 350°F.
2.Sprinkle the pepper and salt on the schnitzel.
3.In a shallow dish, combine the paprika, flour, and salt
4.In a second shallow dish, mix the bread crumbs with the sesame seeds.
5.Place the beaten eggs in a bowl.
6.Coat the schnitzel in the flour mixture. Dip it into the egg before rolling it in the bread crumbs.
7.Put the coated schnitzel in the Air Fryer basket and allow to cook for 12 minutes before serving hot.

Steak Total

Prep + Cook Time: 30 minutes | Servings: 4

Ingredients
2 lb. rib eye steak
1 tbsp. olive oil
1 tbsp. steak rub

Instructions
1.Set the Air Fryer to 400°F and allow to warm for 4 minutes.
2.Massage the olive oil and steak rub into both sides of the steak.
3.Put the steak in the fryer's basket and cook for 14 minutes. Turn the steak over and cook on the other side for another 7 minutes.
4.Serve hot.

Betty's Beef Roast

Prep + Cook Time: 65 minutes | Servings: 6

Ingredients
2 lb. beef
1 tbsp. olive oil
1 tsp. dried rosemary
1 tsp. dried thyme
½ tsp. black pepper
½ tsp. oregano
½ tsp. garlic powder
1 tsp. salt
1 tsp. onion powder

Instructions
1.Preheat the Air Fryer to 330°F.
2.In a small bowl, mix together all of the spices.
3.Coat the beef with a brushing of olive oil.
4.Massage the spice mixture into the beef.
5.Transfer the meat to the Air Fryer and cook for 30 minutes. Turn it over and cook on the other side for another 25 minutes.

Beef & Mushrooms

Prep + Cook Time: 3 hours 15 minutes | Servings: 1

Ingredients
6 oz. beef
¼ onion, diced
½ cup mushroom slices
2 tbsp. favorite marinade [preferably bulgogi]

Instructions
1.Slice or cube the beef and put it in a bowl.
2.Cover the meat with the marinade, place a layer of aluminum foil or saran wrap over the bowl, and place the bowl in the refrigerator for 3 hours.
3.Put the meat in a baking dish along with the onion and mushrooms
4.Air Fry at 350°F for 10 minutes. Serve hot.

Chapter 5 Poultry

Herb-Buttermilk Chicken Breast

Prep time: 5 minutes | Cook time: 40 minutes | Serves 2

1 large bone-in, skin-on chicken breast
1 cup buttermilk
1½ teaspoons dried parsley
1½ teaspoons dried chives
¾ teaspoon kosher salt
½ teaspoon dried dill
½ teaspoon onion powder
¼ teaspoon garlic powder
¼ teaspoon dried tarragon
Cooking spray

1. Place the chicken breast in a bowl and pour over the buttermilk, turning the chicken in it to make sure it's completely covered. Let the chicken stand at room temperature for at least 20 minutes or in the refrigerator for up to 4 hours.
2. Meanwhile, in a bowl, stir together the parsley, chives, salt, dill, onion powder, garlic powder, and tarragon.
3. Preheat the air fryer to 300ºF (149ºC).
4. Remove the chicken from the buttermilk, letting the excess drip off, then place the chicken skin-side up directly in the air fryer. Sprinkle the seasoning mix all over the top of the chicken breast, then let stand until the herb mix soaks into the buttermilk, at least 5 minutes.
5. Spray the top of the chicken with cooking spray. Bake for 10 minutes, then increase the temperature to 350ºF (177ºC) and bake until an instant-read thermometer inserted into the thickest part of the breast reads 160ºF (71ºC) and the chicken is deep golden brown, 30 to 35 minutes.
6. Transfer the chicken breast to a cutting board, let rest for 10 minutes, then cut the meat off the bone and cut into thick slices for serving.

Hawaiian Tropical Chicken

Prep time: 10 minutes | Cook time: 15 minutes | Serves 4

4 boneless, skinless chicken thighs (about 1½ pounds / 680 g)
1 (8-ounce / 227-g) can pineapple chunks in juice, drained, ¼ cup juice reserved
¼ cup soy sauce
¼ cup sugar
2 tablespoons ketchup
1 tablespoon minced fresh ginger
1 tablespoon minced garlic
¼ cup chopped scallions

1. Use a fork to pierce the chicken all over to allow the marinade to penetrate better. Place the chicken in a large bowl or large resealable plastic bag.
2. Set the drained pineapple chunks aside. In a small microwave-safe bowl, combine the pineapple juice, soy sauce, sugar, ketchup, ginger, and garlic. Pour half the sauce over the chicken; toss to coat. Reserve the remaining sauce. Marinate the chicken at room temperature for 30 minutes, or cover and refrigerate for up to 24 hours.
3. Preheat the air fryer to 350ºF (177ºC).
4. Place the chicken in the air fryer basket, discarding marinade. Bake for 15 minutes, turning halfway through the cooking time.
5. Meanwhile, microwave the reserved sauce on high for 45 to 60 seconds, stirring every 15 seconds, until the sauce has the consistency of a thick glaze.
6. At the end of the cooking time, use a meat thermometer to ensure the chicken has reached an internal temperature of 165ºF (74ºC).
7. Transfer the chicken to a serving platter. Pour the sauce over the chicken. Garnish with the pineapple chunks and scallions before serving.

Roasted Chicken with Garlic

Prep time: 5 minutes | Cook time: 25 minutes | Serves 4

4 (5-ounce / 142-g) low-sodium bone-in skinless chicken breasts
1 tablespoon olive oil
1 tablespoon freshly squeezed lemon juice

3 tablespoons cornstarch
1 teaspoon dried basil leaves
⅛ teaspoon freshly ground black pepper
20 garlic cloves, unpeeled

1. Preheat the air fryer to 370ºF (188ºC).
2. Rub the chicken with the olive oil and lemon juice on both sides and sprinkle with the cornstarch, basil, and pepper.
3. Place the seasoned chicken in the air fryer basket and top with the garlic cloves. Roast for about 25 minutes, or until the garlic is soft and the chicken reaches an internal temperature of 165ºF (74ºC) on a meat thermometer. Serve immediately.

Chicken and Vegetable Fajitas

Prep time: 15 minutes | Cook time: 23 minutes | Serves 6

Chicken:

1 pound (454 g) boneless, skinless chicken thighs, cut crosswise into thirds
1 tablespoon vegetable oil
4½ teaspoons taco seasoning
Vegetables
1 cup sliced onion
1 cup sliced bell

pepper
1 or 2 jalapeños, quartered lengthwise
1 tablespoon vegetable oil
½ teaspoon kosher salt
½ teaspoon ground cumin

For Serving:

Tortillas
Sour cream
Shredded cheese

Guacamole
Salsa

1. Preheat the air fryer to 375ºF (191ºC).
2. For the chicken: In a medium bowl, toss together the chicken, vegetable oil, and taco seasoning to coat.

3. For the vegetables: In a separate bowl, toss together the onion, bell pepper, jalapeño (s), vegetable oil, salt, and cumin to coat.
4. Place the chicken in the air fryer basket. Air fry for 10 minutes. Add the vegetables to the basket, toss everything together to blend the seasonings, and air fry for 13 minutes more. Use a meat thermometer to ensure the chicken has reached an internal temperature of 165ºF (74ºC).
5. Transfer the chicken and vegetables to a serving platter. Serve with tortillas and the desired fajita fixings.

Chicken with Pineapple and Peach

Prep time: 10 minutes | Cook time: 14 to 15 minutes | Serves 4

1 pound (454 g) low-sodium boneless, skinless chicken breasts, cut into 1-inch pieces
1 medium red onion, chopped
1 (8-ounce / 227-g) can pineapple chunks, drained, ¼ cup juice reserved
1 tablespoon peanut

oil or safflower oil
1 peach, peeled, pitted, and cubed
1 tablespoon cornstarch
½ teaspoon ground ginger
¼ teaspoon ground allspice
Brown rice, cooked (optional)

1. Preheat the air fryer to 380ºF (193ºC).
2. In a medium metal bowl, mix the chicken, red onion, pineapple, and peanut oil. Bake in the air fryer for 9 minutes. Remove and stir.
3. Add the peach and return the bowl to the air fryer. Bake for 3 minutes more. Remove and stir again.
4. In a small bowl, whisk the reserved pineapple juice, the cornstarch, ginger, and allspice well. Add to the chicken mixture and stir to combine.
5. Bake for 2 to 3 minutes more, or until the chicken reaches an internal temperature of 165ºF (74ºC) on a meat thermometer and the sauce is slightly thickened.
6. Serve immediately over hot cooked brown rice, if desired.

Easy Tandoori Chicken

Prep time: 5 minutes | Cook time: 18 to 23 minutes | Serves 4

²/₃ cup plain low-fat yogurt
2 tablespoons freshly squeezed lemon juice
2 teaspoons curry powder
½ teaspoon ground cinnamon
2 garlic cloves, minced
2 teaspoons olive oil
4 (5-ounce / 142-g) low-sodium boneless, skinless chicken breasts

1. In a medium bowl, whisk the yogurt, lemon juice, curry powder, cinnamon, garlic, and olive oil.
2. With a sharp knife, cut thin slashes into the chicken. Add it to the yogurt mixture and turn to coat. Let stand for 10 minutes at room temperature. You can also prepare this ahead of time and marinate the chicken in the refrigerator for up to 24 hours.
3. Preheat the air fryer to 360ºF (182ºC).
4. Remove the chicken from the marinade and shake off any excess liquid. Discard any remaining marinade.
5. Roast the chicken for 10 minutes. With tongs, carefully turn each piece. Roast for 8 to 13 minutes more, or until the chicken reaches an internal temperature of 165ºF (74ºC) on a meat thermometer. Serve immediately.

Roasted Chicken and Vegetable Salad

Prep time: 10 minutes | Cook time: 10 to 13 minutes | Serves 4

3 (4-ounce / 113-g) low-sodium boneless, skinless chicken breasts, cut into 1-inch cubes
1 small red onion, sliced
1 red bell pepper, sliced
1 cup green beans, cut into 1-inch pieces
2 tablespoons low-fat ranch salad dressing
2 tablespoons freshly squeezed lemon juice
½ teaspoon dried basil
4 cups mixed lettuce

1. Preheat the air fryer to 400ºF (204ºC).
2. In the air fryer basket, roast the chicken, red onion, red bell pepper, and green beans for 10 to 13 minutes, or until the chicken reaches an internal temperature of 165ºF (74ºC) on a meat thermometer, tossing the food in the basket once during cooking.
3. While the chicken cooks, in a serving bowl, mix the ranch dressing, lemon juice, and basil.
4. Transfer the chicken and vegetables to a serving bowl and toss with the dressing to coat. Serve immediately on lettuce leaves.

Jerk Chicken Leg Quarters

Prep time: 8 minutes | Cook time: 27 minutes | Serves 2

1 tablespoon packed brown sugar
1 teaspoon ground allspice
1 teaspoon pepper
1 teaspoon garlic powder
¾ teaspoon dry mustard
¾ teaspoon dried thyme
½ teaspoon salt
¼ teaspoon cayenne pepper
2 (10-ounce / 284-g) chicken leg quarters, trimmed
1 teaspoon vegetable oil
1 scallion, green part only, sliced thin
Lime wedges

1. Preheat the air fryer to 400ºF (204ºC).
2. Combine sugar, allspice, pepper, garlic powder, mustard, thyme, salt, and cayenne in a bowl. Pat chicken dry with paper towels. Using metal skewer, poke 10 to 15 holes in skin of each chicken leg. Rub with oil and sprinkle evenly with spice mixture.
3. Arrange chicken skin-side up in the air fryer basket, spaced evenly apart. Air fry until chicken is well browned and crisp, 27 to 30 minutes, rotating chicken halfway through cooking (do not flip).
4. Transfer chicken to plate, tent loosely with aluminum foil, and let rest for 5 minutes. Sprinkle with scallion. Serve with lime wedges.

Lemon Chicken and Spinach Salad

Prep time: 10 minutes | Cook time: 16 to 20 minutes | Serves 4

3 (5-ounce / 142-g) low-sodium boneless, skinless chicken breasts, cut into 1-inch cubes	1 red bell pepper, sliced
5 teaspoons olive oil	1 small zucchini, cut into strips
½ teaspoon dried thyme	3 tablespoons freshly squeezed lemon juice
1 medium red onion, sliced	6 cups fresh baby spinach

1. Preheat the air fryer to 400ºF (204ºC).
2. In a large bowl, mix the chicken with the olive oil and thyme. Toss to coat. Transfer to a medium metal bowl and roast for 8 minutes in the air fryer.
3. Add the red onion, red bell pepper, and zucchini. Roast for 8 to 12 minutes more, stirring once during cooking, or until the chicken reaches an internal temperature of 165ºF (74ºC) on a meat thermometer.
4. Remove the bowl from the air fryer and stir in the lemon juice.
5. Put the spinach in a serving bowl and top with the chicken mixture. Toss to combine and serve immediately.

Almond-Crusted Chicken Nuggets

Prep time: 10 minutes | Cook time: 10 to 13 minutes | Serves 4

1 egg white	g) low-sodium boneless, skinless chicken breasts, cut into 1½-inch cubes
1 tablespoon freshly squeezed lemon juice	
½ teaspoon dried basil	½ cup ground almonds
½ teaspoon ground paprika	2 slices low-sodium whole-wheat bread, crumbled
1 pound (454	

1. Preheat the air fryer to 400ºF (204ºC).
2. In a shallow bowl, beat the egg white, lemon juice, basil, and paprika with a fork until foamy.
3. Add the chicken and stir to coat.

4. On a plate, mix the almonds and bread crumbs.
5. Toss the chicken cubes in the almond and bread crumb mixture until coated.
6. Bake the nuggets in the air fryer, in two batches, for 10 to 13 minutes, or until the chicken reaches an internal temperature of 165ºF (74ºC) on a meat thermometer. Serve immediately.

Barbecued Chicken with Creamy Coleslaw

Prep time: 10 minutes | Cook time: 20 minutes | Serves 2

3 cups shredded coleslaw mix	barbecue sauce, plus extra for serving
Salt and pepper	2 tablespoons mayonnaise
2 (12-ounce / 340-g) bone-in split chicken breasts, trimmed	2 tablespoons sour cream
1 teaspoon vegetable oil	1 teaspoon distilled white vinegar, plus extra for seasoning
2 tablespoons	¼ teaspoon sugar

1. Preheat the air fryer to 350ºF (177ºC).
2. Toss coleslaw mix and ¼ teaspoon salt in a colander set over bowl. Let sit until wilted slightly, about 30 minutes. Rinse, drain, and dry well with a dish towel.
3. Meanwhile, pat chicken dry with paper towels, rub with oil, and season with salt and pepper. Arrange breasts skin-side down in air fryer basket, spaced evenly apart, alternating ends. Bake for 10 minutes. Flip breasts and brush skin side with barbecue sauce. Return basket to air fryer and bake until well browned and chicken registers 160ºF (71ºC), 10 to 15 minutes.
4. Transfer chicken to serving platter, tent loosely with aluminum foil, and let rest for 5 minutes. While chicken rests, whisk mayonnaise, sour cream, vinegar, sugar, and pinch pepper together in a large bowl. Stir in coleslaw mix and season with salt, pepper, and additional vinegar to taste. Serve chicken with coleslaw, passing extra barbecue sauce separately.

Buttermilk Paprika Chicken

Prep time: 7 minutes | Cook time: 17 to 23 minutes | Serves 4

4 (5-ounce / 142-g) low-sodium boneless, skinless chicken breasts, pounded to about ½ inch thick
½ cup buttermilk
½ cup all-purpose flour
2 tablespoons cornstarch
1 teaspoon dried thyme
1 teaspoon ground paprika
1 egg white
1 tablespoon olive oil

1. Preheat the air fryer to 390ºF (199ºC).
2. In a shallow bowl, mix the chicken and buttermilk. Let stand for 10 minutes.
3. Meanwhile, in another shallow bowl, mix the flour, cornstarch, thyme, and paprika.
4. In a small bowl, whisk the egg white and olive oil. Quickly stir this egg mixture into the flour mixture so the dry ingredients are evenly moistened.
5. Remove the chicken from the buttermilk and shake off any excess liquid. Dip each piece of chicken into the flour mixture to coat.
6. Air fry the chicken in the air fryer basket for 17 to 23 minutes, or until the chicken reaches an internal temperature of 165ºF (74ºC) on a meat thermometer. Serve immediately.

Cheesy Chicken Tacos

Prep time: 10 minutes | Cook time: 12 to 16 minutes | Serves 2 to 4

1 teaspoon chili powder
½ teaspoon ground cumin
½ teaspoon garlic powder
Salt and pepper, to taste
Pinch cayenne pepper
1 pound (454 g) boneless, skinless chicken thighs, trimmed
1 teaspoon vegetable oil
1 tomato, cored and chopped
2 tablespoons finely chopped red onion
2 teaspoons minced jalapeño chile
1½ teaspoons lime juice
6 to 12 (6-inch) corn tortillas, warmed
1 cup shredded iceberg lettuce
3 ounces (85 g) cheddar cheese, shredded (¾ cup)

1. Preheat the air fryer to 400ºF (204ºC).
2. Combine chili powder, cumin, garlic powder, ½ teaspoon salt, ¼ teaspoon pepper, and cayenne in bowl. Pat chicken dry with paper towels, rub with oil, and sprinkle evenly with spice mixture. Place chicken in air fryer basket. Air fry until chicken registers 165ºF (74ºC), 12 to 16 minutes, flipping chicken halfway through cooking.
3. Meanwhile, combine tomato, onion, jalapeño, and lime juice in a bowl; season with salt and pepper to taste and set aside until ready to serve.
4. Transfer chicken to a cutting board, let cool slightly, then shred into bite-size pieces using 2 forks. Serve chicken on warm tortillas, topped with salsa, lettuce, and cheddar.

Cranberry Curry Chicken

Prep time: 12 minutes | Cook time: 18 minutes | Serves 4

3 (5-ounce / 142-g) low-sodium boneless, skinless chicken breasts, cut into 1½-inch cubes
2 teaspoons olive oil
2 tablespoons cornstarch
1 tablespoon curry powder
1 tart apple, chopped
½ cup low-sodium chicken broth
¹⁄₃ cup dried cranberries
2 tablespoons freshly squeezed orange juice
Brown rice, cooked (optional)

1. Preheat the air fryer to 380ºF (193ºC).
2. In a medium bowl, mix the chicken and olive oil. Sprinkle with the cornstarch and curry powder. Toss to coat. Stir in the apple and transfer to a metal pan. Bake in the air fryer for 8 minutes, stirring once during cooking.
3. Add the chicken broth, cranberries, and orange juice. Bake for about 10 minutes more, or until the sauce is slightly thickened and the chicken reaches an internal temperature of 165ºF (74ºC) on a meat thermometer. Serve over hot cooked brown rice, if desired.

Tex-Mex Chicken Breasts

Prep time: 10 minutes | Cook time: 17 to 20 minutes | Serves 4

1 pound (454 g) low-sodium boneless, skinless chicken breasts, cut into 1-inch cubes
1 medium onion, chopped
1 red bell pepper, chopped
1 jalapeño pepper, minced
2 teaspoons olive oil
2/3 cup canned low-sodium black beans, rinsed and drained
1/2 cup low-sodium salsa
2 teaspoons chili powder

1. Preheat the air fryer to 400ºF (204ºC).
2. In a medium metal bowl, mix the chicken, onion, bell pepper, jalapeño, and olive oil. Roast for 10 minutes, stirring once during cooking.
3. Add the black beans, salsa, and chili powder. Roast for 7 to 10 minutes more, stirring once, until the chicken reaches an internal temperature of 165ºF (74ºC) on a meat thermometer. Serve immediately.

Piri-Piri Chicken Thighs

Prep time: 5 minutes | Cook time: 25 minutes | Serves 4

1/4 cup piri-piri sauce
1 tablespoon freshly squeezed lemon juice
2 tablespoons brown sugar, divided
2 cloves garlic, minced
1 tablespoon extra-virgin olive oil
4 bone-in, skin-on chicken thighs, each weighing approximately 7 to 8 ounces (198 to 227 g)
1/2 teaspoon cornstarch

1. To make the marinade, whisk together the piri-piri sauce, lemon juice, 1 tablespoon of brown sugar, and the garlic in a small bowl. While whisking, slowly pour in the oil in a steady stream and continue to whisk until emulsified. Using a skewer, poke holes in the chicken thighs and place them in a small glass dish. Pour the marinade over the chicken and turn the thighs to coat them with the sauce. Cover the dish and refrigerate for at least 15 minutes and up to 1 hour.

2. Preheat the air fryer to 375ºF (191ºC). Remove the chicken thighs from the dish, reserving the marinade, and place them skin-side down in the air fryer basket. Air fry until the internal temperature reaches 165ºF (74ºC), 15 to 20 minutes.
3. Meanwhile, whisk the remaining brown sugar and the cornstarch into the marinade and microwave it on high power for 1 minute until it is bubbling and thickened to a glaze.
4. Once the chicken is cooked, turn the thighs over and brush them with the glaze. Air fry for a few additional minutes until the glaze browns and begins to char in spots.
5. Remove the chicken to a platter and serve with additional piri-piri sauce, if desired.

Apricot-Glazed Chicken

Prep time: 5 minutes | Cook time: 12 minutes | Serves 2

2 tablespoons apricot preserves
1/2 teaspoon minced fresh thyme or 1/8 teaspoon dried
2 (8-ounce / 227-g) boneless, skinless chicken breasts, trimmed
1 teaspoon vegetable oil
Salt and pepper, to taste

1. Preheat the air fryer to 400ºF (204ºC).
2. Microwave apricot preserves and thyme in bowl until fluid, about 30 seconds; set aside. Pound chicken to uniform thickness as needed. Pat dry with paper towels, rub with oil, and season with salt and pepper.
3. Arrange breasts skin-side down in air fryer basket, spaced evenly apart, alternating ends. Air fry the chicken for 4 minutes. Flip chicken and brush skin side with apricot-thyme mixture. Air fry until chicken registers 160ºF (71ºC), 8 to 12 minutes more.
4. Transfer chicken to serving platter, tent loosely with aluminum foil, and let rest for 5 minutes. Serve.

Thai Cornish Game Hens

Prep time: 15 minutes | Cook time: 20 minutes | Serves 4

1 cup chopped fresh cilantro leaves and stems
¼ cup fish sauce
1 tablespoon soy sauce
1 serrano chile, seeded and chopped
8 garlic cloves, smashed
2 tablespoons sugar
2 tablespoons lemongrass paste

2 teaspoons black pepper
2 teaspoons ground coriander
1 teaspoon kosher salt
1 teaspoon ground turmeric
2 Cornish game hens, giblets removed, split in half lengthwise

1. In a blender, combine the cilantro, fish sauce, soy sauce, serrano, garlic, sugar, lemongrass, black pepper, coriander, salt, and turmeric. Blend until smooth.
2. Place the game hen halves in a large bowl. Pour the cilantro mixture over the hen halves and toss to coat. Marinate at room temperature for 30 minutes, or cover and refrigerate for up to 24 hours.
3. Preheat the air fryer to 400ºF (204ºC).
4. Arrange the hen halves in a single layer in the air fryer basket. Roast for 20 minutes. Use a meat thermometer to ensure the game hens have reached an internal temperature of 165ºF (74ºC). Serve warm.

Lemon Garlic Chicken

Prep time: 10 minutes | Cook time: 16 to 19 minutes | Serves 4

4 (5-ounce / 142-g) low-sodium boneless, skinless chicken breasts, cut into 4-by-½-inch strips
2 teaspoons olive oil
2 tablespoons cornstarch
3 garlic cloves, minced

½ cup low-sodium chicken broth
¼ cup freshly squeezed lemon juice
1 tablespoon honey
½ teaspoon dried thyme
Brown rice, cooked (optional)

1. Preheat the air fryer to 400ºF (204ºC).
2. In a large bowl, mix the chicken and olive oil. Sprinkle with the cornstarch. Toss to coat.
3. Add the garlic and transfer to a metal pan. Bake in the air fryer for 10 minutes, stirring once during cooking.
4. Add the chicken broth, lemon juice, honey, and thyme to the chicken mixture. Bake for 6 to 9 minutes more, or until the sauce is slightly thickened and the chicken reaches an internal temperature of 165ºF (74ºC) on a meat thermometer. Serve over hot cooked brown rice, if desired.

Curried Orange Honey Chicken

Prep time: 10 minutes | Cook time: 16 to 19 minutes | Serves 4

¾ pound (340 g) boneless, skinless chicken thighs, cut into 1-inch pieces
1 yellow bell pepper, cut into 1½-inch pieces
1 small red onion, sliced

Olive oil for misting
¼ cup chicken stock
2 tablespoons honey
¼ cup orange juice
1 tablespoon cornstarch
2 to 3 teaspoons curry powder

1. Preheat the air fryer to 370ºF (188ºC).
2. Put the chicken thighs, pepper, and red onion in the air fryer basket and mist with olive oil.
3. Roast for 12 to 14 minutes or until the chicken is cooked to 165ºF (74ºC), shaking the basket halfway through cooking time.
4. Remove the chicken and vegetables from the air fryer basket and set aside.
5. In a metal bowl, combine the stock, honey, orange juice, cornstarch, and curry powder, and mix well. Add the chicken and vegetables, stir, and put the bowl in the basket.
6. Return the basket to the air fryer and roast for 2 minutes. Remove and stir, then roast for 2 to 3 minutes or until the sauce is thickened and bubbly.
7. Serve warm.

Air Fryer Chicken Fajitas

Prep time: 15 minutes | Cook time: 10 to 15 minutes | Serves 4

4 (5-ounce / 142-g) low-sodium boneless, skinless chicken breasts, cut into 4-by-½-inch strips
1 tablespoon freshly squeezed lemon juice
2 teaspoons olive oil
2 teaspoons chili powder
2 red bell peppers, sliced
4 low-sodium whole-wheat tortillas
⅓ cup nonfat sour cream
1 cup grape tomatoes, sliced

1. Preheat the air fryer to 380ºF (193ºC).
2. In a large bowl, mix the chicken, lemon juice, olive oil, and chili powder. Toss to coat. Transfer the chicken to the air fryer basket. Add the red bell peppers. Roast for 10 to 15 minutes, or until the chicken reaches an internal temperature of 165ºF (74ºC) on a meat thermometer.
3. Assemble the fajitas with the tortillas, chicken, bell peppers, sour cream, and tomatoes. Serve immediately.

Chicken Manchurian

Prep time: 10 minutes | Cook time: 20 minutes | Serves 2

1 pound (454 g) boneless, skinless chicken breasts, cut into 1-inch pieces
¼ cup ketchup
1 tablespoon tomato-based chili sauce, such as Heinz
1 tablespoon soy sauce
1 tablespoon rice vinegar
2 teaspoons
vegetable oil
1 teaspoon hot sauce, such as Tabasco
½ teaspoon garlic powder
¼ teaspoon cayenne pepper
2 scallions, thinly sliced
Cooked white rice, for serving

1. Preheat the air fryer to 350ºF (177ºC).
2. In a bowl, combine the chicken, ketchup, chili sauce, soy sauce, vinegar, oil, hot sauce, garlic powder, cayenne, and three-quarters of the scallions and toss until evenly coated.

3. Scrape the chicken and sauce into a metal cake pan and place the pan in the air fryer. Bake until the chicken is cooked through and the sauce is reduced to a thick glaze, about 20 minutes, flipping the chicken pieces halfway through.
4. Remove the pan from the air fryer. Spoon the chicken and sauce over rice and top with the remaining scallions. Serve immediately.

Turkey Stuffed Bell Peppers

Prep time: 20 minutes | Cook time: 15 minutes | Serves 4

½ pound (227 g) lean ground turkey
4 medium bell peppers
1 (15-ounce / 425-g) can black beans, drained and rinsed
1 cup shredded reduced-fat Cheddar cheese
1 cup cooked long-grain brown rice
1 cup mild salsa
1¼ teaspoons chili powder
1 teaspoon salt
½ teaspoon ground cumin
½ teaspoon freshly ground black pepper
Olive oil spray
Chopped fresh cilantro, for garnish

1. Preheat the air fryer to 360ºF (182ºC).
2. In a large skillet over medium-high heat, cook the turkey, breaking it up with a spoon, until browned, about 5 minutes. Drain off any excess fat.
3. Cut about ½ inch off the tops of the peppers and then cut in half lengthwise. Remove and discard the seeds and set the peppers aside.
4. In a large bowl, combine the browned turkey, black beans, Cheddar cheese, rice, salsa, chili powder, salt, cumin, and black pepper. Spoon the mixture into the bell peppers.
5. Lightly spray the air fryer basket with olive oil spray.
6. Place the stuffed peppers in the air fryer basket. Air fry until heated through, 10 to 15 minutes. Garnish with cilantro and serve.

Glazed Chicken Drumsticks

Prep time: 5 minutes | Cook time: 20 minutes | Serves 2

4 chicken drumsticks
3 tablespoons soy sauce
2 tablespoons brown sugar
1 teaspoon minced garlic
1 teaspoon minced fresh ginger

1 teaspoon toasted sesame oil
½ teaspoon red pepper flakes
½ teaspoon kosher salt
½ teaspoon black pepper

1. Preheat the air fryer to 400ºF (204ºC).
2. Line a round baking pan with aluminum foil. (If you don't do this, you'll either end up scrubbing forever or throwing out the pan.) Arrange the drumsticks in the prepared pan.
3. In a medium bowl, stir together the soy sauce, brown sugar, garlic, ginger, sesame oil, red pepper flakes, salt, and black pepper. Pour the sauce over the drumsticks and toss to coat.
4. Place the pan in the air fryer basket. Air fry for 20 minutes, turning the drumsticks halfway through the cooking time. Use a meat thermometer to ensure the chicken has reached an internal temperature of 165ºF (74ºC). Serve immediately.

Simple Chicken Shawarma

Prep time: 10 minutes | Cook time: 15 minutes | Serves 4

Shawarma Spice:
2 teaspoons dried oregano
1 teaspoon ground cinnamon
1 teaspoon ground cumin
1 teaspoon ground

coriander
1 teaspoon kosher salt
½ teaspoon ground allspice
½ teaspoon cayenne pepper

Chicken:
1 pound (454 g) boneless, skinless chicken thighs, cut into large bite-size

chunks
2 tablespoons vegetable oil

For Serving:
Tzatziki

Pita bread

1. For the shawarma spice: In a small bowl, combine the oregano, cayenne, cumin, coriander, salt, cinnamon, and allspice.
2. For the chicken: In a large bowl, toss together the chicken, vegetable oil, and shawarma spice to coat. Marinate at room temperature for 30 minutes or cover and refrigerate for up to 24 hours.
3. Preheat the air fryer to 350ºF (177ºC). Place the chicken in the air fryer basket. Air fry for 15 minutes, or until the chicken reaches an internal temperature of 165ºF (74ºC).
4. Transfer the chicken to a serving platter. Serve with tzatziki and pita bread.

Coconut Chicken Meatballs

Prep time: 10 minutes | Cook time: 14 minutes | Serves 4

1 pound (454 g) ground chicken
2 scallions, finely chopped
1 cup chopped fresh cilantro leaves
¼ cup unsweetened shredded coconut
1 tablespoon hoisin sauce

1 tablespoon soy sauce
2 teaspoons sriracha or other hot sauce
1 teaspoon toasted sesame oil
½ teaspoon kosher salt
1 teaspoon black pepper

1. Preheat the air fryer to 350ºF (177ºC).
2. In a large bowl, gently mix the chicken, scallions, cilantro, coconut, hoisin, soy sauce, sriracha, sesame oil, salt, and pepper until thoroughly combined (the mixture will be wet and sticky).
3. Place a sheet of parchment paper in the air fryer basket. Using a small scoop or teaspoon, drop rounds of the mixture in a single layer onto the parchment paper.
4. Air fry for 10 minutes, turning the meatballs halfway through the cooking time. Increase the temperature to 400ºF (204ºC) and air fry for 4 minutes more to brown the outsides of the meatballs. Use a meat thermometer to ensure the meatballs have reached an internal temperature of 165ºF (74ºC).
5. Transfer the meatballs to a serving platter. Repeat with any remaining chicken mixture. Serve.

Garlic Soy Chicken Thighs

Prep time: 10 minutes | Cook time: 30 minutes | Serves 1 to 2

2 tablespoons chicken stock
2 tablespoons reduced-sodium soy sauce
1½ tablespoons sugar
4 garlic cloves, smashed and peeled
2 large scallions, cut into 2- to 3-inch batons, plus more, thinly sliced, for garnish
2 bone-in, skin-on chicken thighs (7 to 8 ounces / 198 to 227 g each)

1. Preheat the air fryer to 375ºF (191ºC).
2. In a metal cake pan, combine the chicken stock, soy sauce, and sugar and stir until the sugar dissolves. Add the garlic cloves, scallions, and chicken thighs, turning the thighs to coat them in the marinade, then resting them skin-side up. Place the pan in the air fryer and bake, flipping the thighs every 5 minutes after the first 10 minutes, until the chicken is cooked through and the marinade is reduced to a sticky glaze over the chicken, about 30 minutes.
3. Remove the pan from the air fryer and serve the chicken thighs warm, with any remaining glaze spooned over top and sprinkled with more sliced scallions.

Crispy Chicken Cordon Bleu

Prep time: 15 minutes | Cook time: 13 to 15 minutes | Serves 4

4 chicken breast fillets
¼ cup chopped ham
1/3 cup grated Swiss or Gruyère cheese
¼ cup flour
Pinch salt
Freshly ground black
pepper, to taste
½ teaspoon dried marjoram
1 egg
1 cup panko bread crumbs
Olive oil for misting

1. Preheat the air fryer to 380ºF (193ºC).
2. Put the chicken breast fillets on a work surface and gently press them with the palm of your hand to make them a bit thinner. Don't tear the meat.
3. In a small bowl, combine the ham and cheese. Divide this mixture among the chicken fillets. Wrap the chicken around the filling to enclose it, using toothpicks to hold the chicken together.
4. In a shallow bowl, mix the flour, salt, pepper, and marjoram. In another bowl, beat the egg. Spread the bread crumbs out on a plate.
5. Dip the chicken into the flour mixture, then into the egg, then into the bread crumbs to coat thoroughly.
6. Put the chicken in the air fryer basket and mist with olive oil.
7. Bake for 13 to 15 minutes or until the chicken is thoroughly cooked to 165ºF (74ºC). Carefully remove the toothpicks and serve.

Parmesan Chicken Wings

Prep time: 15 minutes | Cook time: 16 to 18 minutes | Serves 4

1¼ cups grated Parmesan cheese
1 tablespoon garlic powder
1 teaspoon salt
½ teaspoon freshly ground black pepper
¾ cup all-purpose flour
1 large egg, beaten
12 chicken wings (about 1 pound / 454 g)
Cooking spray

1. Preheat the air fryer to 390ºF (199ºC). Line the air fryer basket with parchment paper.
2. In a shallow bowl, whisk the Parmesan cheese, garlic powder, salt, and pepper until blended. Place the flour in a second shallow bowl and the beaten egg in a third shallow bowl.
3. One at a time, dip the chicken wings into the flour, the beaten egg, and the Parmesan cheese mixture, coating thoroughly.
4. Place the chicken wings on the parchment and spritz with cooking spray.
5. Air fry for 8 minutes. Flip the chicken, spritz it with cooking spray, and air fry for 8 to 10 minutes more until the internal temperature reaches 165ºF (74ºC) and the insides are no longer pink. Let sit for 5 minutes before serving.

Barbecue Chicken

Prep time: 10 minutes | Cook time: 18 to 20 minutes | Serves 4

⅓ cup no-salt-added tomato sauce
2 tablespoons low-sodium grainy mustard
2 tablespoons apple cider vinegar
1 tablespoon honey
2 garlic cloves, minced
1 jalapeño pepper, minced
3 tablespoons minced onion
4 (5-ounce / 142-g) low-sodium boneless, skinless chicken breasts

1. Preheat the air fryer to 370ºF (188ºC).
2. In a small bowl, stir together the tomato sauce, mustard, cider vinegar, honey, garlic, jalapeño, and onion.
3. Brush the chicken breasts with some sauce and air fry for 10 minutes.
4. Remove the air fryer basket and turn the chicken; brush with more sauce. Air fry for 5 minutes more.
5. Remove the air fryer basket and turn the chicken again; brush with more sauce. Air fry for 3 to 5 minutes more, or until the chicken reaches an internal temperature of 165ºF (74ºC) on a meat thermometer. Discard any remaining sauce. Serve immediately.

Israeli Chicken Schnitzel

Prep time: 5 minutes | Cook time: 10 minutes | Serves 4

2 large boneless, skinless chicken breasts, each weighing about 1 pound (454 g)
1 cup all-purpose flour
2 teaspoons garlic powder
2 teaspoons kosher salt
1 teaspoon black pepper
1 teaspoon paprika
2 eggs beaten with 2 tablespoons water
2 cups panko bread crumbs
Vegetable oil spray
Lemon juice, for serving

1. Preheat the air fryer to 375ºF (191ºC).
2. Place 1 chicken breast between 2 pieces of plastic wrap. Use a mallet or a rolling pin to pound the chicken until it is ¼ inch thick. Set aside. Repeat with the second breast. Whisk together the flour, garlic powder, salt, pepper, and paprika on a large plate. Place the panko in a separate shallow bowl or pie plate.
3. Dredge 1 chicken breast in the flour, shaking off any excess, then dip it in the egg mixture. Dredge the chicken breast in the panko, making sure to coat it completely. Shake off any excess panko. Place the battered chicken breast on a plate. Repeat with the second chicken breast.
4. Spray the air fryer basket with oil spray. Place 1 of the battered chicken breasts in the basket and spray the top with oil spray. Air fry until the top is browned, about 5 minutes. Flip the chicken and spray the second side with oil spray. Air fry until the second side is browned and crispy and the internal temperature reaches 165ºF (74ºC). Remove the first chicken breast from the air fryer and repeat with the second chicken breast.
5. Serve hot with lemon juice.

Blackened Chicken Breasts

Prep time: 10 minutes | Cook time: 20 minutes | Serves 4

1 large egg, beaten
¾ cup Blackened seasoning
2 whole boneless, skinless chicken breasts (about 1 pound / 454 g each), halved
Cooking spray

1. Preheat the air fryer to 360ºF (182ºC). Line the air fryer basket with parchment paper.
2. Place the beaten egg in one shallow bowl and the Blackened seasoning in another shallow bowl.
3. One at a time, dip the chicken pieces in the beaten egg and the Blackened seasoning, coating thoroughly.
4. Place the chicken pieces on the parchment and spritz with cooking spray.
5. Air fry for 10 minutes. Flip the chicken, spritz it with cooking spray, and air fry for 10 minutes more until the internal temperature reaches 165ºF (74ºC) and the chicken is no longer pink inside. Let sit for 5 minutes before serving.

Yellow Curry Chicken Thighs with Peanuts

Prep time: 10 minutes | Cook time: 20 minutes | Serves 6

½ cup unsweetened full-fat coconut milk
2 tablespoons yellow curry paste
1 tablespoon minced fresh ginger
1 tablespoon minced garlic
1 teaspoon kosher salt
1 pound (454 g) boneless, skinless chicken thighs, halved crosswise
2 tablespoons chopped peanuts

1. In a large bowl, stir together the coconut milk, curry paste, ginger, garlic, and salt until well blended. Add the chicken; toss well to coat. Marinate at room temperature for 30 minutes, or cover and refrigerate for up to 24 hours.
2. Preheat the air fryer to 375ºF (191ºC).
3. Place the chicken (along with marinade) in a baking pan. Place the pan in the air fryer basket. Bake for 20 minutes, turning the chicken halfway through the cooking time. Use a meat thermometer to ensure the chicken has reached an internal temperature of 165ºF (74ºC).
4. Sprinkle the chicken with the chopped peanuts and serve.

Turkish Chicken Kebabs

Prep time: 15 minutes | Cook time: 15 minutes | Serves 4

¼ cup plain Greek yogurt
1 tablespoon minced garlic
1 tablespoon tomato paste
1 tablespoon fresh lemon juice
1 tablespoon vegetable oil
1 teaspoon kosher salt
1 teaspoon ground cumin
1 teaspoon sweet Hungarian paprika
½ teaspoon ground cinnamon
½ teaspoon black pepper
½ teaspoon cayenne pepper
1 pound (454 g) boneless, skinless chicken thighs, quartered crosswise

1. In a large bowl, combine the yogurt, garlic, tomato paste, lemon juice, vegetable oil, salt, cumin, paprika, cinnamon, black pepper, and cayenne. Stir until the spices are blended into the yogurt.
2. Add the chicken to the bowl and toss until well coated. Marinate at room temperature for 30 minutes, or cover and refrigerate for up to 24 hours.
3. Preheat the air fryer to 375ºF (191ºC).
4. Arrange the chicken in a single layer in the air fryer basket. Air fry for 10 minutes. Turn the chicken and air fry for 5 minutes more. Use a meat thermometer to ensure the chicken has reached an internal temperature of 165ºF (74ºC).
5. Serve warm.

Merguez Meatballs

Prep time: 10 minutes | Cook time: 10 minutes | Serves 4

1 pound (454 g) ground chicken
2 garlic cloves, finely minced
1 tablespoon sweet Hungarian paprika
1 teaspoon kosher salt
1 teaspoon sugar
1 teaspoon ground cumin
½ teaspoon black pepper
½ teaspoon ground fennel
½ teaspoon ground coriander
½ teaspoon cayenne pepper
¼ teaspoon ground allspice

1. In a large bowl, gently mix the chicken, garlic, paprika, salt, sugar, cumin, black pepper, fennel, coriander, cayenne, and allspice until all the ingredients are incorporated. Let stand for 30 minutes at room temperature, or cover and refrigerate for up to 24 hours.
2. Preheat the air fryer to 400ºF (204ºC).
3. Form the mixture into 16 meatballs. Arrange them in a single layer in the air fryer basket. Air fry for 10 minutes, turning the meatballs halfway through the cooking time. Use a meat thermometer to ensure the meatballs have reached an internal temperature of 165ºF (74ºC).
4. Serve warm.

Chicken Burgers with Ham and Cheese

Prep time: 12 minutes | Cook time: 13 to 16 minutes | Serves 4

⅓ cup soft bread crumbs
3 tablespoons milk
1 egg, beaten
½ teaspoon dried thyme
Pinch salt
Freshly ground black pepper, to taste
1¼ pounds (567 g) ground chicken
¼ cup finely chopped ham
⅓ cup grated Havarti cheese
Olive oil for misting

1. Preheat the air fryer to 350ºF (177ºC).
2. In a medium bowl, combine the bread crumbs, milk, egg, thyme, salt, and pepper. Add the chicken and mix gently but thoroughly with clean hands.
3. Form the chicken into eight thin patties and place on waxed paper.
4. Top four of the patties with the ham and cheese. Top with remaining four patties and gently press the edges together to seal, so the ham and cheese mixture is in the middle of the burger.
5. Place the burgers in the basket and mist with olive oil. Bake for 13 to 16 minutes or until the chicken is thoroughly cooked to 165ºF (74ºC) as measured with a meat thermometer. Serve immediately.

Paprika Indian Fennel Chicken

Prep time: 10 minutes | Cook time: 15 minutes | Serves 4

1 pound (454 g) boneless, skinless chicken thighs, cut crosswise into thirds
1 yellow onion, cut into 1½-inch-thick slices
1 tablespoon coconut oil, melted
2 teaspoons minced fresh ginger
2 teaspoons minced garlic
1 teaspoon smoked paprika
1 teaspoon ground fennel
1 teaspoon garam masala
1 teaspoon ground turmeric
1 teaspoon kosher salt
½ to 1 teaspoon cayenne pepper
Vegetable oil spray
2 teaspoons fresh lemon juice
¼ cup chopped fresh cilantro or parsley

1. Use a fork to pierce the chicken all over to allow the marinade to penetrate better.
2. In a large bowl, combine the onion, coconut oil, ginger, garlic, paprika, fennel, garam masala, turmeric, salt, and cayenne. Add the chicken, toss to combine, and marinate at room temperature for 30 minutes, or cover and refrigerate for up to 24 hours.
3. Preheat the air fryer to 350ºF (177ºC).
4. Place the chicken and onion in the air fryer basket. (Discard remaining marinade.) Spray with some vegetable oil spray. Air fry for 15 minutes. Halfway through the cooking time, remove the basket, spray the chicken and onion with more vegetable oil spray, and toss gently to coat. At the end of the cooking time, use a meat thermometer to ensure the chicken has reached an internal temperature of 165ºF (74ºC).
5. Transfer the chicken and onion to a serving platter. Sprinkle with the lemon juice and cilantro and serve.

Crisp Chicken Wings

Prep time: 15 minutes | Cook time: 20 minutes | Serves 4

1 pound (454 g) chicken wings
3 tablespoons vegetable oil
½ cup all-purpose flour
½ teaspoon smoked paprika
½ teaspoon garlic powder
½ teaspoon kosher salt
1½ teaspoons freshly cracked black pepper

1. Preheat the air fryer to 400ºF (204ºC).
2. Place the chicken wings in a large bowl. Drizzle the vegetable oil over wings and toss to coat.
3. In a separate bowl, whisk together the flour, paprika, garlic powder, salt, and pepper until combined.
4. Dredge the wings in the flour mixture one at a time, coating them well, and place in the air fryer basket. Air fry for 20 minutes, turning the wings halfway through the cooking time, until the breading is browned and crunchy.
5. Serve hot.

Thai Curry Meatballs

Prep time: 10 minutes | Cook time: 10 minutes | Serves 4

1 pound (454 g) ground chicken
¼ cup chopped fresh cilantro
1 teaspoon chopped fresh mint
1 tablespoon fresh lime juice
1 tablespoon Thai red, green, or yellow curry paste
1 tablespoon fish sauce
2 garlic cloves, minced
2 teaspoons minced fresh ginger
½ teaspoon kosher salt
½ teaspoon black pepper
¼ teaspoon red pepper flakes

1. Preheat the air fryer to 400ºF (204ºC).
2. In a large bowl, gently mix the ground chicken, cilantro, mint, lime juice, curry paste, fish sauce, garlic, ginger, salt, black pepper, and red pepper flakes until thoroughly combined.
3. Form the mixture into 16 meatballs. Place the meatballs in a single layer in the air fryer basket. Air fry for 10 minutes, turning the meatballs halfway through the cooking time. Use a meat thermometer to ensure the meatballs have reached an internal temperature of 165ºF (74ºC). Serve immediately.

Crisp Paprika Chicken Drumsticks

Prep time: 5 minutes | Cook time: 22 minutes | Serves 2

2 teaspoons paprika
1 teaspoon packed brown sugar
1 teaspoon garlic powder
½ teaspoon dry mustard
½ teaspoon salt
Pinch pepper
4 (5-ounce / 142-g) chicken drumsticks, trimmed
1 teaspoon vegetable oil
1 scallion, green part only, sliced thin on bias

1. Preheat the air fryer to 400ºF (204ºC).
2. Combine paprika, sugar, garlic powder, mustard, salt, and pepper in a bowl. Pat drumsticks dry with paper towels. Using metal skewer, poke 10 to 15 holes in skin of each drumstick. Rub with oil and sprinkle evenly with spice mixture.

3. Arrange drumsticks in air fryer basket, spaced evenly apart, alternating ends. Air fry until chicken is crisp and registers 195ºF (91ºC), 22 to 25 minutes, flipping chicken halfway through cooking.
4. Transfer chicken to serving platter, tent loosely with aluminum foil, and let rest for 5 minutes. Sprinkle with scallion and serve.

Tempero Baiano Brazilian Chicken

Prep time: 5 minutes | Cook time: 20 minutes | Serves 4

1 teaspoon cumin seeds
1 teaspoon dried oregano
1 teaspoon dried parsley
1 teaspoon ground turmeric
½ teaspoon coriander seeds
1 teaspoon kosher salt
½ teaspoon black peppercorns
½ teaspoon cayenne pepper
¼ cup fresh lime juice
2 tablespoons olive oil
1½ pounds (680 g) chicken drumsticks

1. In a clean coffee grinder or spice mill, combine the cumin, oregano, parsley, turmeric, coriander seeds, salt, peppercorns, and cayenne. Process until finely ground.
2. In a small bowl, combine the ground spices with the lime juice and oil. Place the chicken in a resealable plastic bag. Add the marinade, seal, and massage until the chicken is well coated. Marinate at room temperature for 30 minutes or in the refrigerator for up to 24 hours.
3. Preheat the air fryer to 400ºF (204ºC).
4. Place the drumsticks skin-side up in the air fryer basket and air fry for 20 to 25 minutes, turning the drumsticks halfway through the cooking time. Use a meat thermometer to ensure that the chicken has reached an internal temperature of 165ºF (74ºC). Serve immediately.

Nutty Chicken Tenders

Prep time: 5 minutes | Cook time: 12 minutes | Serves 4

1 pound (454 g) chicken tenders
1 teaspoon kosher salt
1 teaspoon black pepper
½ teaspoon smoked paprika
¼ cup coarse mustard
2 tablespoons honey
1 cup finely crushed pecans

1. Preheat the air fryer to 350°F (177°C).
2. Place the chicken in a large bowl. Sprinkle with the salt, pepper, and paprika. Toss until the chicken is coated with the spices. Add the mustard and honey and toss until the chicken is coated.
3. Place the pecans on a plate. Working with one piece of chicken at a time, roll the chicken in the pecans until both sides are coated. Lightly brush off any loose pecans. Place the chicken in the air fryer basket.
4. Bake for 12 minutes, or until the chicken is cooked through and the pecans are golden brown.
5. Serve warm.

Lemon Parmesan Chicken

Prep time: 10 minutes | Cook time: 20 minutes | Serves 4

1 egg
2 tablespoons lemon juice
2 teaspoons minced garlic
½ teaspoon salt
½ teaspoon freshly ground black pepper
4 boneless, skinless chicken breasts, thin cut
Olive oil spray
½ cup whole-wheat bread crumbs
¼ cup grated Parmesan cheese

1. In a medium bowl, whisk together the egg, lemon juice, garlic, salt, and pepper. Add the chicken breasts, cover, and refrigerate for up to 1 hour.
2. In a shallow bowl, combine the bread crumbs and Parmesan cheese.
3. Preheat the air fryer to 360°F (182°C). Spray the air fryer basket lightly with olive oil spray.
4. Remove the chicken breasts from the egg mixture, then dredge them in the bread crumb mixture, and place in the air fryer basket in a single layer. Lightly spray the chicken breasts with olive oil spray. You may need to cook the chicken in batches.
5. Air fry for 8 minutes. Flip the chicken over, lightly spray with olive oil spray, and air fry until the chicken reaches an internal temperature of 165°F (74°C), for an additional 7 to 12 minutes.
6. Serve warm.

Crispy Chicken Strips

Prep time: 15 minutes | Cook time: 20 minutes | Serves 4

1 tablespoon olive oil
1 pound (454 g) boneless, skinless chicken tenderloins
1 teaspoon salt
½ teaspoon freshly ground black pepper
½ teaspoon paprika
½ teaspoon garlic powder
½ cup whole-wheat seasoned bread crumbs
1 teaspoon dried parsley
Cooking spray

1. Preheat the air fryer to 370°F (188°C). Spray the air fryer basket lightly with cooking spray.
2. In a medium bowl, toss the chicken with the salt, pepper, paprika, and garlic powder until evenly coated.
3. Add the olive oil and toss to coat the chicken evenly.
4. In a separate, shallow bowl, mix together the bread crumbs and parsley.
5. Coat each piece of chicken evenly in the bread crumb mixture.
6. Place the chicken in the air fryer basket in a single layer and spray it lightly with cooking spray. You may need to cook them in batches.
7. Air fry for 10 minutes. Flip the chicken over, lightly spray it with cooking spray, and air fry for an additional 8 to 10 minutes, until golden brown. Serve.

Ginger Chicken Thighs

Prep time: 10 minutes | Cook time: 10 minutes | Serves 4

¼ cup julienned peeled fresh ginger
2 tablespoons vegetable oil
1 tablespoon honey
1 tablespoon soy sauce
1 tablespoon ketchup
1 teaspoon garam masala
1 teaspoon ground turmeric
¼ teaspoon kosher salt
½ teaspoon cayenne pepper
Vegetable oil spray
1 pound (454 g) boneless, skinless chicken thighs, cut crosswise into thirds
¼ cup chopped fresh cilantro, for garnish

1. In a small bowl, combine the ginger, oil, honey, soy sauce, ketchup, garam masala, turmeric, salt, and cayenne. Whisk until well combined. Place the chicken in a resealable plastic bag and pour the marinade over. Seal the bag and massage to cover all of the chicken with the marinade. Marinate at room temperature for 30 minutes or in the refrigerator for up to 24 hours.
2. Preheat the air fryer to 350ºF (177ºC).
3. Spray the air fryer basket with vegetable oil spray and add the chicken and as much of the marinade and julienned ginger as possible. Bake for 10 minutes. Use a meat thermometer to ensure the chicken has reached an internal temperature of 165ºF (74ºC).
4. To serve, garnish with cilantro.

Celery Chicken

Prep time: 10 minutes | Cook time: 15 minutes | Serves 4

½ cup soy sauce
2 tablespoons hoisin sauce
4 teaspoons minced garlic
1 teaspoon freshly ground black pepper
8 boneless, skinless chicken tenderloins
1 cup chopped celery
1 medium red bell pepper, diced
Olive oil spray

1. Preheat the air fryer to 375ºF (191ºC). Spray the air fryer basket lightly with olive oil spray.
2. In a large bowl, mix together the soy sauce, hoisin sauce, garlic, and black pepper to make a marinade. Add the chicken, celery, and bell pepper and toss to coat.
3. Shake the excess marinade off the chicken, place it and the vegetables in the air fryer basket, and lightly spray with olive oil spray. You may need to cook them in batches. Reserve the remaining marinade.
4. Air fry for 8 minutes. Turn the chicken over and brush with some of the remaining marinade. Air fry for an additional 5 to 7 minutes, or until the chicken reaches an internal temperature of at least 165ºF (74ºC). Serve.

Chicken Satay with Peanut Sauce

Prep time: 12 minutes | Cook time: 12 to 18 minutes | Serves 4

½ cup crunchy peanut butter
1/3 cup chicken broth
3 tablespoons low-sodium soy sauce
2 tablespoons lemon juice
2 cloves garlic, minced
2 tablespoons olive oil
1 teaspoon curry powder
1 pound (454 g) chicken tenders

1. Preheat the air fryer to 390ºF (199ºC).
2. In a medium bowl, combine the peanut butter, chicken broth, soy sauce, lemon juice, garlic, olive oil, and curry powder, and mix well with a wire whisk until smooth. Remove 2 tablespoons of this mixture to a small bowl. Put remaining sauce into a serving bowl and set aside.
3. Add the chicken tenders to the bowl with the 2 tablespoons sauce and stir to coat. Let stand for a few minutes to marinate, then run a bamboo skewer through each chicken tender lengthwise.
4. Put the chicken in the air fryer basket and air fry in batches for 6 to 9 minutes or until the chicken reaches 165ºF (74ºC) on a meat thermometer. Serve the chicken with the reserved sauce.

Fried Buffalo Chicken Taquitos

Prep time: 15 minutes | Cook time: 5 to 10 minutes | Serves 6

8 ounces (227 g) fat-free cream cheese, softened
⅛ cup Buffalo sauce
2 cups shredded cooked chicken
12 (7-inch) low-carb flour tortillas
Olive oil spray

1. Preheat the air fryer to 360ºF (182ºC). Spray the air fryer basket lightly with olive oil spray.
2. In a large bowl, mix together the cream cheese and Buffalo sauce until well combined. Add the chicken and stir until combined.
3. Place the tortillas on a clean workspace. Spoon 2 to 3 tablespoons of the chicken mixture in a thin line down the center of each tortilla. Roll up the tortillas.
4. Place the tortillas in the air fryer basket, seam-side down. Spray each tortilla lightly with olive oil spray. You may need to cook the taquitos in batches.
5. Air fry until golden brown, 5 to 10 minutes. Serve hot.

Herbed Turkey Breast

Prep time: 20 minutes | Cook time: 45 minutes | Serves 6

1 tablespoon olive oil
Cooking spray
2 garlic cloves, minced
2 teaspoons Dijon mustard
1½ teaspoons rosemary
1½ teaspoons sage
1½ teaspoons thyme
1 teaspoon salt
½ teaspoon freshly ground black pepper
3 pounds (1.4 kg) turkey breast, thawed if frozen

1. Preheat the air fryer to 370ºF (188ºC). Spray the air fryer basket lightly with cooking spray.
2. In a small bowl, mix together the garlic, olive oil, Dijon mustard, rosemary, sage, thyme, salt, and pepper to make a paste. Smear the paste all over the turkey breast.
3. Place the turkey breast in the air fryer basket. Air fry for 20 minutes. Flip turkey breast over and baste it with any drippings that have collected in the bottom drawer of the air fryer. Air fry until the internal temperature of the meat reaches at least 170ºF (77ºC), 20 more minutes.
4. If desired, increase the temperature to 400ºF (204ºC), flip the turkey breast over one last time, and air fry for 5 minutes to get a crispy exterior.
5. Let the turkey rest for 10 minutes before slicing and serving.

Sweet and Spicy Turkey Meatballs

Prep time: 15 minutes | Cook time: 15 minutes | Serves 6

1 pound (454 g) lean ground turkey
½ cup whole-wheat panko bread crumbs
1 egg, beaten
1 tablespoon soy sauce
¼ cup plus 1 tablespoon hoisin sauce, divided
2 teaspoons minced garlic
⅛ teaspoon salt
⅛ teaspoon freshly ground black pepper
1 teaspoon sriracha
Olive oil spray

1. Preheat the air fryer to 350ºF (177ºC). Spray the air fryer basket lightly with olive oil spray.
2. In a large bowl, mix together the turkey, panko bread crumbs, egg, soy sauce, 1 tablespoon of hoisin sauce, garlic, salt, and black pepper.
3. Using a tablespoon, form the mixture into 24 meatballs.
4. In a small bowl, combine the remaining ¼ cup of hoisin sauce and sriracha to make a glaze and set aside.
5. Place the meatballs in the air fryer basket in a single layer. You may need to cook them in batches.
6. Air fry for 8 minutes. Brush the meatballs generously with the glaze and air fry until cooked through, an additional 4 to 7 minutes. Serve warm.

Dill Chicken Strips

Prep time: 15 minutes | Cook time: 10 minutes | Serves 4

2 whole boneless, skinless chicken breasts, halved lengthwise
1 cup Italian dressing
3 cups finely
crushed potato chips
1 tablespoon dried dill weed
1 tablespoon garlic powder
1 large egg, beaten
Cooking spray

1. In a large resealable bag, combine the chicken and Italian dressing. Seal the bag and refrigerate to marinate at least 1 hour.
2. In a shallow dish, stir together the potato chips, dill, and garlic powder. Place the beaten egg in a second shallow dish.
3. Remove the chicken from the marinade. Roll the chicken pieces in the egg and the potato chip mixture, coating thoroughly.
4. Preheat the air fryer to 325ºF (163ºC). Line the air fryer basket with parchment paper.
5. Place the coated chicken on the parchment and spritz with cooking spray.
6. Bake for 5 minutes. Flip the chicken, spritz it with cooking spray, and bake for 5 minutes more until the outsides are crispy and the insides are no longer pink. Serve immediately.

Turkey Hoisin Burgers

Prep time: 10 minutes | Cook time: 20 minutes | Serves 4

1 pound (454 g) lean ground turkey
¼ cup whole-wheat bread crumbs
¼ cup hoisin sauce
2 tablespoons soy sauce
4 whole-wheat buns
Olive oil spray

1. In a large bowl, mix together the turkey, bread crumbs, hoisin sauce, and soy sauce.
2. Form the mixture into 4 equal patties. Cover with plastic wrap and refrigerate the patties for 30 minutes.
3. Preheat the air fryer to 370ºF (188ºC). Spray the air fryer basket lightly with olive oil spray.
4. Place the patties in the air fryer basket in a single layer. Spray the patties lightly with olive oil spray.
5. Air fry for 10 minutes. Flip the patties over, lightly spray with olive oil spray, and air fry for an additional 5 to 10 minutes, until golden brown.
6. Place the patties on buns and top with your choice of low-calorie burger toppings like sliced tomatoes, onions, and cabbage slaw. Serve immediately.

Air Fryer Naked Chicken Tenders

Prep time: 5 minutes | Cook time: 7 minutes | Serves 4

Seasoning:
1 teaspoon kosher salt
½ teaspoon garlic powder
½ teaspoon onion powder
½ teaspoon chili powder
¼ teaspoon sweet paprika
¼ teaspoon freshly ground black pepper

Chicken:
8 chicken breast tenders (1 pound / 454 g total)
2 tablespoons mayonnaise

1. Preheat the air fryer to 375ºF (191ºC).
2. For the seasoning: In a small bowl, combine the salt, garlic powder, onion powder, chili powder, paprika, and pepper.
3. For the chicken: Place the chicken in a medium bowl and add the mayonnaise. Mix well to coat all over, then sprinkle with the seasoning mix.
4. Working in batches, arrange a single layer of the chicken in the air fryer basket. Air fry for 6 to 7 minutes, flipping halfway, until cooked through in the center. Serve immediately.

Sweet-and-Sour Drumsticks

Prep time: 5 minutes | Cook time: 23 to 25 minutes | Serves 4

6 chicken drumsticks
3 tablespoons lemon juice, divided
3 tablespoons low-sodium soy sauce, divided
1 tablespoon peanut oil
3 tablespoons honey
3 tablespoons brown sugar
2 tablespoons ketchup
¼ cup pineapple juice

1. Preheat the air fryer to 350ºF (177ºC).
2. Sprinkle the drumsticks with 1 tablespoon of lemon juice and 1 tablespoon of soy sauce. Place in the air fryer basket and drizzle with the peanut oil. Toss to coat. Bake for 18 minutes or until the chicken is almost done.
3. Meanwhile, in a metal bowl, combine the remaining 2 tablespoons of lemon juice, the remaining 2 tablespoons of soy sauce, honey, brown sugar, ketchup, and pineapple juice.
4. Add the cooked chicken to the bowl and stir to coat the chicken well with the sauce.
5. Place the metal bowl in the basket. Bake for 5 to 7 minutes or until the chicken is glazed and registers 165ºF (74ºC) on a meat thermometer. Serve warm.

Orange and Honey Glazed Duck with Apples

Prep time: 5 minutes | Cook time: 15 minutes | Serves 2 to 3

1 pound (454 g) duck breasts (2 to 3 breasts)
Kosher salt and pepper, to taste
Juice and zest of 1
orange
¼ cup honey
2 sprigs thyme, plus more for garnish
2 firm tart apples, such as Fuji

1. Preheat the air fryer to 400ºF (204ºC).
2. Pat the duck breasts dry and, using a sharp knife, make 3 to 4 shallow, diagonal slashes in the skin. Turn the breasts and score the skin on the diagonal in the opposite direction to create a cross-hatch pattern. Season well with salt and pepper.
3. Place the duck breasts skin-side up in the air fryer basket. Roast for 8 minutes, then flip and roast for 4 more minutes on the second side.
4. While the duck is cooking, prepare the sauce. Combine the orange juice and zest, honey, and thyme in a small saucepan. Bring to a boil, stirring to dissolve the honey, then reduce the heat and simmer until thickened. Core the apples and cut into quarters. Cut each quarter into 3 or 4 slices depending on the size.
5. After the duck has cooked on both sides, turn it and brush the skin with the orange-honey glaze. Roast for 1 more minute. Remove the duck breasts to a cutting board and allow to rest.
6. Toss the apple slices with the remaining orange-honey sauce in a medium bowl. Arrange the apples in a single layer in the air fryer basket. Air fry for 10 minutes while the duck breast rests. Slice the duck breasts on the bias and divide them and the apples among 2 or 3 plates.
7. Serve warm, garnished with additional thyme.

Roasted Cajun Turkey

Prep time: 10 minutes | Cook time: 30 minutes | Serves 4

2 pounds (907 g) turkey thighs, skinless and boneless
1 red onion, sliced
2 bell peppers, sliced
1 habanero pepper, minced
1 carrot, sliced
1 tablespoon Cajun seasoning mix
1 tablespoon fish sauce
2 cups chicken broth
Nonstick cooking spray

1. Preheat the air fryer to 360ºF (182ºC).
2. Spritz the bottom and sides of a baking dish with nonstick cooking spray.
3. Arrange the turkey thighs in the baking dish. Add the onion, peppers, and carrot. Sprinkle with Cajun seasoning. Add the fish sauce and chicken broth.
4. Roast in the preheated air fryer for 30 minutes until cooked through. Serve warm.

Spiced Turkey Tenderloin

Prep time: 20 minutes | Cook time: 30 minutes | Serves 4

½ teaspoon paprika
½ teaspoon garlic powder
½ teaspoon salt
½ teaspoon freshly ground black pepper

Pinch cayenne pepper
1½ pounds (680 g) turkey breast tenderloin
Olive oil spray

1. Preheat the air fryer to 370ºF (188ºC). Spray the air fryer basket lightly with olive oil spray.
2. In a small bowl, combine the paprika, garlic powder, salt, black pepper, and cayenne pepper. Rub the mixture all over the turkey.
3. Place the turkey in the air fryer basket and lightly spray with olive oil spray.
4. Air fry for 15 minutes. Flip the turkey over and lightly spray with olive oil spray. Air fry until the internal temperature reaches at least 170ºF (77ºC) for an additional 10 to 15 minutes.
5. Let the turkey rest for 10 minutes before slicing and serving.

Pecan-Crusted Turkey Cutlets

Prep time: 10 minutes | Cook time: 10 to 12 minutes | Serves 4

¾ cup panko bread crumbs
¼ teaspoon salt
¼ teaspoon pepper
¼ teaspoon dry mustard
¼ teaspoon poultry seasoning
½ cup pecans

¼ cup cornstarch
1 egg, beaten
1 pound (454 g) turkey cutlets, ½-inch thick
Salt and pepper, to taste
Cooking spray

1. Preheat the air fryer to 360ºF (182ºC).
2. Place the panko crumbs, salt, pepper, mustard, and poultry seasoning in a food processor. Process until crumbs are finely crushed. Add pecans and process just until nuts are finely chopped.
3. Place cornstarch in a shallow dish and beaten egg in another. Transfer coating mixture from food processor into a third shallow dish.

4. Sprinkle turkey cutlets with salt and pepper to taste.
5. Dip cutlets in cornstarch and shake off excess, then dip in beaten egg and finally roll in crumbs, pressing to coat well. Spray both sides with cooking spray.
6. Place 2 cutlets in air fryer basket in a single layer and air fry for 10 to 12 minutes. Repeat with the remaining cutlets.
7. Serve warm.

Fajita Chicken Strips

Prep time: 10 minutes | Cook time: 15 minutes | Serves 4

1 pound (454 g) boneless, skinless chicken tenderloins, cut into strips
3 bell peppers, any color, cut into chunks

1 onion, cut into chunks
1 tablespoon olive oil
1 tablespoon fajita seasoning mix
Cooking spray

1. Preheat the air fryer to 370ºF (188ºC).
2. In a large bowl, mix together the chicken, bell peppers, onion, olive oil, and fajita seasoning mix until completely coated.
3. Spray the air fryer basket lightly with cooking spray.
4. Place the chicken and vegetables in the air fryer basket and lightly spray with cooking spray.
5. Air fry for 7 minutes. Shake the basket and air fry for an additional 5 to 8 minutes, until the chicken is cooked through and the veggies are starting to char.
6. Serve warm.

Honey Rosemary Chicken

Prep time: 10 minutes | Cook time: 20 minutes | Serves 4

¼ cup balsamic vinegar
¼ cup honey
2 tablespoons olive oil
1 tablespoon dried rosemary leaves
1 teaspoon salt

½ teaspoon freshly ground black pepper
2 whole boneless, skinless chicken breasts (about 1 pound / 454 g each), halved
Cooking spray

1. In a large resealable bag, combine the vinegar, honey, olive oil, rosemary, salt, and pepper. Add the chicken pieces, seal the bag, and refrigerate to marinate for at least 2 hours.
2. Preheat the air fryer to 325ºF (163ºC). Line the air fryer basket with parchment paper.
3. Remove the chicken from the marinade and place it on the parchment. Spritz with cooking spray.
4. Bake for 10 minutes. Flip the chicken, spritz it with cooking spray, and bake for 10 minutes more until the internal temperature reaches 165ºF (74ºC) and the chicken is no longer pink inside. Let sit for 5 minutes before serving.

Potato Cheese Crusted Chicken

Prep time: 15 minutes | Cook time: 22 to 25 minutes | Serves 4

¼ cup buttermilk
1 large egg, beaten
1 cup instant potato flakes
¼ cup grated Parmesan cheese
1 teaspoon salt
½ teaspoon freshly

ground black pepper
2 whole boneless, skinless chicken breasts (about 1 pound / 454 g each), halved
Cooking spray

1. Preheat the air fryer to 325ºF (163ºC). Line the air fryer basket with parchment paper.
2. In a shallow bowl, whisk the buttermilk and egg until blended. In another shallow bowl, stir together the potato flakes, cheese, salt, and pepper.
3. One at a time, dip the chicken pieces in the buttermilk mixture and the potato flake mixture, coating thoroughly.
4. Place the coated chicken on the parchment and spritz with cooking spray.
5. Bake for 15 minutes. Flip the chicken, spritz it with cooking spray, and bake for 7 to 10 minutes more until the outside is crispy and the inside is no longer pink. Serve immediately.

Roasted Chicken Tenders with Veggies

Prep time: 10 minutes | Cook time: 18 to 20 minutes | Serves 4

1 pound (454 g) chicken tenders
1 tablespoon honey
Pinch salt
Freshly ground black pepper, to taste
½ cup soft fresh bread crumbs

½ teaspoon dried thyme
1 tablespoon olive oil
2 carrots, sliced
12 small red potatoes

1. Preheat the air fryer to 380ºF (193ºC).
2. In a medium bowl, toss the chicken tenders with the honey, salt, and pepper.
3. In a shallow bowl, combine the bread crumbs, thyme, and olive oil, and mix.
4. Coat the tenders in the bread crumbs, pressing firmly onto the meat.
5. Place the carrots and potatoes in the air fryer basket and top with the chicken tenders.
6. Roast for 18 to 20 minutes or until the chicken is cooked to 165ºF (74ºC) and the vegetables are tender, shaking the basket halfway during the cooking time.
7. Serve warm.

Mayonnaise-Mustard Chicken

Prep time: 10 minutes | Cook time: 15 minutes | Serves 4

6 tablespoons mayonnaise
2 tablespoons coarse-ground mustard
2 teaspoons honey (optional)
2 teaspoons curry

powder
1 teaspoon kosher salt
1 teaspoon cayenne pepper
1 pound (454 g) chicken tenders

1. Preheat the air fryer to 350ºF (177ºC).
2. In a large bowl, whisk together the mayonnaise, mustard, honey (if using), curry powder, salt, and cayenne. Transfer half of the mixture to a serving bowl to serve as a dipping sauce. Add the chicken tenders to the large bowl and toss until well coated.
3. Place the tenders in the air fryer basket and bake for 15 minutes. Use a meat thermometer to ensure the chicken has reached an internal temperature of 165ºF (74ºC).
4. Serve the chicken with the dipping sauce.

Turkey, Hummus, and Cheese Wraps

Prep time: 10 minutes | Cook time: 3 to 4 minutes | Serves 4

4 large whole wheat wraps
½ cup hummus
16 thin slices deli turkey

8 slices provolone cheese
1 cup fresh baby spinach, or more to taste

1. Preheat the air fryer to 360ºF (182ºC).
2. To assemble, place 2 tablespoons of hummus on each wrap and spread to within about a half inch from edges. Top with 4 slices of turkey and 2 slices of provolone. Finish with ¼ cup of baby spinach, or pile on as much as you like.
3. Roll up each wrap. You don't need to fold or seal the ends.
4. Place 2 wraps in air fryer basket, seam-side down.
5. Air fry for 3 to 4 minutes to warm filling and melt cheese. Repeat step 4 to air fry the remaining wraps. Serve immediately.

Turkey and Cranberry Quesadillas

Prep time: 7 minutes | Cook time: 4 to 8 minutes | Serves 4

6 low-sodium whole-wheat tortillas
⅓ cup shredded low-sodium low-fat Swiss cheese
¾ cup shredded cooked low-sodium turkey breast

2 tablespoons cranberry sauce
2 tablespoons dried cranberries
½ teaspoon dried basil
Olive oil spray, for spraying the tortillas

1. Preheat the air fryer to 400ºF (204ºC).
2. Put 3 tortillas on a work surface.
3. Evenly divide the Swiss cheese, turkey, cranberry sauce, and dried cranberries among the tortillas. Sprinkle with the basil and top with the remaining tortillas.
4. Spray the outsides of the tortillas with olive oil spray.
5. One at a time, air fry the quesadillas in the air fryer for 4 to 8 minutes, or until crisp and the cheese is melted. Cut into quarters and serve.

Mini Turkey Meatloaves with Carrot

Prep time: 6 minutes | Cook time: 20 to 24 minutes | Serves 4

⅓ cup minced onion
¼ cup grated carrot
2 garlic cloves, minced
2 tablespoons ground almonds
2 teaspoons olive oil

1 teaspoon dried marjoram
1 egg white
¾ pound (340 g) ground turkey breast

1. Preheat the air fryer to 400ºF (204ºC).
2. In a medium bowl, stir together the onion, carrot, garlic, almonds, olive oil, marjoram, and egg white.
3. Add the ground turkey. With your hands, gently but thoroughly mix until combined.
4. Double 16 foil muffin cup liners to make 8 cups. Divide the turkey mixture evenly among the liners.
5. Bake for 20 to 24 minutes, or until the meatloaves reach an internal temperature of 165ºF (74ºC) on a meat thermometer. Serve immediately.

Apricot Glazed Turkey Tenderloin

Prep time: 20 minutes | Cook time: 30 minutes | Serves 4

¼ cup sugar-free apricot preserves
½ tablespoon spicy brown mustard
1½ pounds (680 g) turkey breast
tenderloin
Salt and freshly ground black pepper, to taste
Olive oil spray

1. Preheat the air fryer to 370ºF (188ºC). Spray the air fryer basket lightly with olive oil spray.
2. In a small bowl, combine the apricot preserves and mustard to make a paste.
3. Season the turkey with salt and pepper. Spread the apricot paste all over the turkey.
4. Place the turkey in the air fryer basket and lightly spray with olive oil spray.
5. Air fry for 15 minutes. Flip the turkey over and lightly spray with olive oil spray. Air fry until the internal temperature reaches at least 170ºF (77ºC), an additional 10 to 15 minutes.
6. Let the turkey rest for 10 minutes before slicing and serving.

Tex-Mex Turkey Burgers

Prep time: 10 minutes | Cook time: 14 to 16 minutes | Serves 4

¹/₃ cup finely crushed corn tortilla chips
1 egg, beaten
¼ cup salsa
¹/₃ cup shredded pepper Jack cheese
Pinch salt
Freshly ground black pepper, to taste
1 pound (454 g) ground turkey
1 tablespoon olive oil
1 teaspoon paprika

1. Preheat the air fryer to 330ºF (166ºC).
2. In a medium bowl, combine the tortilla chips, egg, salsa, cheese, salt, and pepper, and mix well.
3. Add the turkey and mix gently but thoroughly with clean hands.
4. Form the meat mixture into patties about ½ inch thick. Make an indentation in the center of each patty with your thumb so the burgers don't puff up while cooking.

5. Brush the patties on both sides with the olive oil and sprinkle with paprika.
6. Put in the air fryer basket and air fry for 14 to 16 minutes or until the meat registers at least 165ºF (74ºC).
7. Let sit for 5 minutes before serving.

Easy Asian Turkey Meatballs

Prep time: 10 minutes | Cook time: 11 to 14 minutes | Serves 4

2 tablespoons peanut oil, divided
1 small onion, minced
¼ cup water chestnuts, finely chopped
½ teaspoon ground
ginger
2 tablespoons low-sodium soy sauce
¼ cup panko bread crumbs
1 egg, beaten
1 pound (454 g) ground turkey

1. Preheat the air fryer to 400ºF (204ºC).
2. In a round metal pan, combine 1 tablespoon of peanut oil and onion. Air fry for 1 to 2 minutes or until crisp and tender. Transfer the onion to a medium bowl.
3. Add the water chestnuts, ground ginger, soy sauce, and bread crumbs to the onion and mix well. Add egg and stir well. Mix in the ground turkey until combined.
4. Form the mixture into 1-inch meatballs. Drizzle the remaining 1 tablespoon of oil over the meatballs.
5. Bake the meatballs in the pan in batches for 10 to 12 minutes or until they are 165ºF (74ºC) on a meat thermometer. Rest for 5 minutes before serving.

Chicken Breasts & Spiced Tomatoes

Prep + Cook Time: 40 minutes | Servings: 1

Ingredients
1 lb. boneless chicken breast
Salt and pepper
1 cup butter
1 cup tomatoes, diced
1 ½ tsp. paprika
1 tsp. pumpkin pie spices

Instructions
1.Preheat your fryer at 375°F.
2.Cut the chicken into relatively thick slices and put them in the fryer. Sprinkle with salt and pepper to taste. Cook for fifteen minutes.
3.In the meantime, melt the butter in a saucepan over medium heat, before adding the tomatoes, paprika, and pumpkin pie spices. Leave simmering while the chicken finishes cooking.
4.When the chicken is cooked through, place it on a dish and pour the tomato mixture over. Serve hot.

Fennel Chicken

Prep + Cook Time: 40 minutes | Servings: 4

Ingredients
1 ½ cup coconut milk
2 tbsp. garam masala
1 ½ lb. chicken thighs
¾ tbsp. coconut oil, melted

Instructions
1.Combine the coconut oil and garam masala together in a bowl. Pour the mixture over the chicken thighs and leave to marinate for a half hour.
2.Pre-heat your fryer at 375°F .
3.Cook the chicken into the fryer for fifteen minutes.
4.Add in the coconut milk, giving it a good stir, then cook for an additional ten minutes.
5.Remove the chicken and place on a serving dish. Make sure to pour all of the coconut "gravy" over it and serve immediately.

Roasted Chicken

Prep + Cook Time: 90 minutes | Servings: 6

Ingredients
6 lb. whole chicken
1 tsp. olive oil
1 tbsp. minced garlic
1 white onion, peeled and halved
3 tbsp. butter

Instructions
1.Pre-heat the fryer at 360°F.
2.Massage the chicken with the olive oil and the minced garlic.
3.Place the peeled and halved onion, as well as the butter, inside of the chicken.
4.Cook the chicken in the fryer for seventy-five minutes.
5.Take care when removing the chicken from the fryer, then carve and serve.

Chicken & Honey Sauce

Prep + Cook Time: 20 minutes | Servings: 4

Ingredients
4 chicken sausages
2 tbsp. honey
¼ cup mayonnaise
2 tbsp. Dijon mustard
1 tbsp. balsamic vinegar
½ tsp. dried rosemary

Instructions
1.Pre-heat your Air Fryer at 350°F.
2.Place the sausages on the grill pan of your fryer and grill for about 13 minutes, flipping them halfway through the cooking time.
3.In the meantime, make the sauce by whisking together the rest of the ingredients.
4.Pour the sauce over the warm sausages before serving.

Penne Chicken Sausage Meatballs

Prep + Cook Time: 20 minutes | Servings: 4

Ingredients
1 cup chicken meat, ground
1 sweet red pepper, minced
¼ cup green onions, chopped
1 green garlic, minced
4 tbsp. friendly bread crumbs
½ tsp. cumin powder
1 tbsp. fresh coriander, minced
½ tsp. sea salt
¼ tsp. mixed peppercorns, ground
1 package penne pasta, cooked

Instructions
1.Pre-heat the Air Fryer at 350°F.
2.Put the chicken, red pepper, green onions, and garlic into a mixing bowl and stir together to combine.
3.Throw in the seasoned bread crumbs and all of the seasonings. Combine again.
4.Use your hands to mold equal amounts of the mixture into small balls, each one roughly the size of a golf ball.
5.Put them in the fryer and cook for 15 minutes. Shake once or twice throughout the cooking time for even results.
6.Serve with cooked penne pasta.

Tarragon Chicken

Prep + Cook Time: 40 minutes | Servings: 4

Ingredients
2 cups roasted vegetable broth
2 chicken breasts, cut into halves
¾ tsp. fine sea salt
¼ tsp. mixed peppercorns, freshly cracked
1 tsp. cumin powder
1 ½ teaspoons sesame oil
1 ½ tbsp. Worcester sauce
½ cup of spring onions, chopped
1 Serrano pepper, deveined and chopped
1 bell pepper, deveined and chopped
1 tbsp. tamari sauce
½ chopped fresh tarragon

Instructions
1.Cook the vegetable broth and chicken breasts in a large saucepan for 10 minutes.
2.Lower the heat and simmer for another 10 minutes.
3.Let the chicken cool briefly. Then tear the chicken into shreds with a stand mixer or two forks.
4.Coat the shredded chicken with the salt, cracked peppercorns, cumin, sesame oil and the Worcester sauce.
5.Transfer to the Air Fryer and air fry at 380°F for 18 minutes, or longer as needed.
6.In the meantime, cook the remaining ingredients over medium heat in a skillet, until the vegetables are tender and fragrant.
7.Take the skillet off the heat. Stir in the shredded chicken, incorporating all the ingredients well.
8.Serve immediately.

Pizza Stuffed Chicken

Prep + Cook Time: 20 minutes | Servings: 4

Ingredients
4 small boneless, skinless chicken breasts
¼ cup pizza sauce
½ cup Colby cheese, shredded
16 slices pepperoni
Salt and pepper, to taste
1 ½ tbsp. olive oil
1 ½ tbsp. dried oregano

Instructions
1.Pre-heat your Air Fryer at 370°F.
2.Flatten the chicken breasts with a rolling pin.
3.Top the chicken with equal amounts of each ingredients and roll the fillets around the stuffing. Secure with a small skewer or two toothpicks.
4.Roast in the fryer on the grill pan for 13 - 15 minutes.

Special Maple-Glazed Chicken

Prep + Cook Time: 20 minutes | Servings: 4

Ingredients
2 ½ tbsp. maple syrup
1 tbsp. tamari soy sauce
1 tbsp. oyster sauce
1 tsp. fresh lemon juice
1 tsp. minced fresh ginger
1 tsp. garlic puree
Seasoned salt and freshly ground pepper, to taste
2 boneless, skinless chicken breasts

Instructions
1.In a bowl, combine the maple syrup, tamari sauce, oyster sauce, lemon juice, fresh ginger and garlic puree. This is your marinade.
2.Sprinkle the chicken breasts with salt and pepper.
3.Coat the chicken breasts with the marinade. Place some foil over the bowl and refrigerate for 3 hours, or overnight if possible.
4.Remove the chicken from the marinade. Place it in the Air Fryer and fry for 15 minutes at 365°F, flipping each one once or twice throughout.
5.In the meantime, add the remaining marinade to a pan over medium heat. Allow the marinade to simmer for 3 - 5 minutes until it has reduced by half.
6.Pour over the cooked chicken and serve.

Turkey Quinoa Skewers

Prep + Cook Time: 15 minutes | Servings: 8

Ingredients
1 cup red quinoa, cooked
1 ½ cups water
14 oz. ground turkey
2 small eggs, beaten
1 tsp. ground ginger
2 ½ tbsp. vegetable oil
1 cup chopped fresh parsley
2 tbsp. seasoned friendly bread crumbs
¾ tsp. salt
1 heaped tsp. fresh rosemary, finely chopped
½ tsp. ground allspice

Instructions
1.In a bowl, combine all of the ingredients together using your hands, kneading the mixture well.
2.Mold equal amounts of the mixture into small balls.
3.Pre-heat your Air Fryer to 380°F.
4.Place the balls in the fryer basket and fry for 8 - 10 minutes.
5.Skewer them and serve with the dipping sauce of your choice.

Potato Cakes & Cajun Chicken Wings

Prep + Cook Time: 40 minutes | Servings: 4

Ingredients
4 large-sized chicken wings
1 tsp. Cajun seasoning
1 tsp. maple syrup
¾ tsp. sea salt flakes
¼ tsp. red pepper flakes, crushed
1 tsp. onion powder
1 tsp. porcini powder
½ tsp. celery seeds
1 small-seized head of cabbage, shredded
1 cup mashed potatoes
1 small-sized brown onion, coarsely grated
1 tsp. garlic puree
1 medium whole egg, well whisked
½ tsp. table salt
½ tsp. ground black pepper
1 ½ tbsp. flour
¾ tsp. baking powder
1 heaped tbsp. cilantro
1 tbsp. sesame oil

Instructions
1. Pre-heat your Air Fryer to 390°F.
2. Pat the chicken wings dry. Place them in the fryer and cook for 25 - 30 minutes, ensuring they are cooked through.
3. Make the rub by combining the Cajun seasoning, maple syrup, sea salt flakes, red pepper, onion powder, porcini powder, and celery seeds.
4. Mix together the shredded cabbage, potato, onion, garlic puree, egg, table salt, black pepper, flour, baking powder and cilantro.
5. Separate the cabbage mixture into 4 portions and use your hands to mold each one into a cabbage-potato cake.
6. Douse each cake with the sesame oil.
7. Bake the cabbage-potato cakes in the fryer for 10 minutes, turning them once through the cooking time. You will need to do this in multiple batches.
8. Serve the cakes and the chicken wings together.

Provençal Chicken

Prep + Cook Time: 25 minutes | Servings: 4

Ingredients
4 medium-sized skin-on chicken drumsticks
1 ½ tsp. herbs de Provence
Salt and pepper to taste
1 tbsp. rice vinegar
2 tbsp. olive oil
2 garlic cloves, crushed
12 oz. crushed canned tomatoes
1 small-size leek, thinly sliced
2 slices smoked bacon, chopped

Instructions
1. Season the chicken drumsticks with herbs de Provence, salt and pepper. Pour over a light drizzling of the rice vinegar and olive oil.
2. Cook in the baking pan at 360°F for 8 - 10 minutes.
3. Pause the fryer. Add in the rest of the ingredients, give them a stir, and resume cooking for 15 more minutes, checking them occasionally to ensure they don't overcook.
4. Serve with rice and lemon wedges.

Gourmet Chicken Omelet

Prep + Cook Time: 15 minutes | Servings: 2

Ingredients
4 eggs, whisked
4 oz. ground chicken
½ cup scallions, finely chopped
2 cloves garlic, finely minced
½ tsp. salt
½ tsp. ground black pepper
½ tsp. paprika
1 tsp. dried thyme
Dash of hot sauce

Instructions
1. Mix together all the ingredients in a bowl, ensuring to incorporate everything well.
2. Lightly grease two oven-safe ramekins with vegetable oil. Divide the mixture between them.
3. Transfer them to the Air Fryer, and air fry at 350°F for 13 minutes.
4. Ensure they are cooked through and serve immediately.

Peppery Turkey Sandwiches

Prep + Cook Time: 25 minutes | Servings: 4

Ingredients
1 cup leftover turkey, cut into bite-sized chunks
2 bell peppers, deveined and chopped
1 Serrano pepper, deveined and chopped
1 leek, sliced
½ cup sour cream
1 tsp. hot paprika
¾ tsp. kosher salt
½ tsp. ground black pepper
1 heaping tbsp. fresh cilantro, chopped
Dash of Tabasco sauce
4 hamburger buns

Instructions
1. Combine all of the ingredients except for the hamburger buns, ensuring to coat the turkey well.
2. Place in an Air Fryer baking pan and roast for 20 minutes at 385°F.
3. Top the hamburger buns with the turkey, and serve with mustard or sour cream as desired.

Chicken Wings & Piri Piri Sauce

Prep + Cook Time: 1 hr. 30 minutes | Servings: 6

Ingredients
12 chicken wings
1 ½ oz. butter, melted
1 tsp. onion powder
½ tsp. cumin powder
1 tsp. garlic paste
For the Sauce:
2 oz. piri piri peppers, stemmed and chopped
1 tbsp. pimiento, deveined and minced
1 garlic clove, chopped
2 tbsp. fresh lemon juice
⅓ tsp. sea salt
½ tsp. tarragon
¾ tsp. sugar

Instructions
1. Place the chicken wings in a steamer basket over a saucepan of boiling water. Lower the temperature and steam the chicken for 10 minutes over a medium heat.
2. Coat the wings with the butter, onion powder, cumin powder, and garlic paste.
3. Allow the chicken wings to cool slightly. Place them in the refrigerator for 45 - 50 minutes.
4. Pre-heat your Air Fryer at 330°F.
5. Roast the chicken wings in the fryer for 25 - 30 minutes, turning them once halfway through the cooking time.
6. In the meantime make the Piri Piri sauce. Blend together all of the sauce ingredients in a food processor.
7. Coat the chicken wings in the sauce before serving.

Goulash

Prep + Cook Time: 20 minutes | Servings: 2

Ingredients
2 chopped bell peppers
2 diced tomatoes
1 lb. ground chicken
½ cup chicken broth
Salt and pepper

Instructions
1. Pre-heat your fryer at 365°F and spray with cooking spray.
2. Cook the bell pepper for five minutes.
3. Add in the diced tomatoes and ground chicken. Combine well, then allow to cook for a further six minutes.

4. Pour in chicken broth, and season to taste with salt and pepper. Cook for another six minutes before serving.

Garlicky Meatballs

Prep + Cook Time: 20 minutes | Servings: 2

Ingredients
½ lb. boneless chicken thighs
1 tsp. minced garlic
1 ¼ cup roasted pecans
½ cup mushrooms
1 tsp. extra virgin olive oil

Instructions
1. Preheat your fryer to 375°F.
2. Cube the chicken thighs.
3. Place them in the food processor along with the garlic, pecans, and other seasonings as desired. Pulse until a smooth consistency is achieved.
4. Chop the mushrooms finely. Add to the chicken mixture and combine.
5. Using your hands, shape the mixture into balls and brush them with olive oil.
6. Put the balls into the fryer and cook for eighteen minutes. Serve hot.

Cilantro Drumsticks

Prep + Cook Time: 30 minutes | Servings: 4

Ingredients
8 chicken drumsticks
½ cup chimichurri sauce
¼ cup lemon juice

Instructions
1. Coat the chicken drumsticks with chimichurri sauce and refrigerate in an airtight container for no less than an hour, ideally overnight.
2. When it's time to cook, pre-heat your fryer to 400°F.
3. Remove the chicken from refrigerator and allow return to room temperature for roughly twenty minutes.
4. Cook for eighteen minutes in the fryer. Drizzle with lemon juice to taste and enjoy.

Poppin' Pop Corn Chicken

Prep + Cook Time: 20 minutes | Servings: 1

Ingredients
1 lb. skinless, boneless chicken breast
1 tsp. chili flakes
1 tsp. garlic powder
½ cup flour
1 tbsp. olive oil cooking spray

Instructions
1.Pre-heat your fryer at 365°F. Spray with olive oil.
2.Cut the chicken breasts into cubes and place in a bowl. Toss with the chili flakes, garlic powder, and additional seasonings to taste and make sure to coat entirely.
3.Add the coconut flour and toss once more.
4.Cook the chicken in the fryer for ten minutes. Turnover and cook for a further five minutes before serving.

Crispy Chicken

Prep + Cook Time: 10 minutes | Servings: 2

Ingredients
1 lb. chicken skin
1 tsp. butter
½ tsp. chili flakes
1 tsp. dill

Instructions
1.Pre-heat the fryer at 360°F.
2.Cut the chicken skin into slices.
3.Heat the butter until melted and pour it over the chicken skin. Toss with chili flakes, dill, and any additional seasonings to taste, making sure to coat well.
4.Cook the skins in the fryer for three minutes. Turn them over and cook on the other side for another three minutes.
5.Serve immediately or save them for later – they can be eaten hot or at room temperature.

Southern Fried Chicken

Prep + Cook Time: 30 minutes | Servings: 2

Ingredients
2 x 6-oz. boneless skinless chicken breasts
2 tbsp. hot sauce
½ tsp. onion powder
1 tbsp. chili powder
2 oz. pork rinds, finely ground

Instructions
1.Cut the chicken breasts in half lengthwise and rub in the hot sauce. Combine the onion powder with the chili powder, then rub into the chicken. Leave to marinate for at least a half hour.
2.Use the ground pork rinds to coat the chicken breasts in the ground pork rinds, covering them thoroughly. Place the chicken in your fryer.
3.Set the fryer at 350°F and cook the chicken for 13 minutes. Flip the chicken and cook the other side for another 13 minutes or until golden.
4.Test the chicken with a meat thermometer. When fully cooked, it should reach 165°F. Serve hot, with the sides of your choice.

Jalapeno Chicken Breasts

Prep + Cook Time: 25 minutes | Servings: 2

Ingredients
2 oz. full-fat cream cheese, softened
4 slices sugar-free bacon, cooked and crumbled
¼ cup pickled jalapenos, sliced
½ cup sharp cheddar cheese, shredded and divided
2 x 6-oz. boneless skinless chicken breasts

Instructions
1.In a bowl, mix the cream cheese, bacon, jalapeno slices, and half of the cheddar cheese until well-combined.
2.Cut parallel slits in the chicken breasts of about ¾ the length – make sure not to cut all the way down. You should be able to make between six and eight slices, depending on the size of the chicken breast.
3.Insert evenly sized dollops of the cheese mixture into the slits of the chicken breasts. Top the chicken with sprinkles of the rest of the cheddar cheese. Place the chicken in the basket of your air fryer.
4.Set the fryer to 350°F and cook the chicken breasts for twenty minutes.
5.Test with a meat thermometer. The chicken should be at 165°F when fully cooked. Serve hot and enjoy!

Fajita Style Chicken Breast

Prep + Cook Time: 35 minutes | Servings: 2

Ingredients
2 x 6-oz. boneless skinless chicken breasts
1 green bell pepper, sliced
¼ medium white onion, sliced
1 tbsp. coconut oil, melted
3 tsp. taco seasoning mix

Instructions
1. Cut each chicken breast in half and place each one between two sheets of cooking parchment. Using a mallet, pound the chicken to flatten to a quarter-inch thick.
2. Place the chicken on a flat surface, with the short end facing you. Place four slices of pepper and three slices of onion at the end of each piece of chicken. Roll up the chicken tightly, making sure not to let any veggies fall out. Secure with some toothpicks or with butcher's string.
3. Coat the chicken with coconut oil and then with taco seasoning. Place into your air fryer.
4. Turn the fryer to 350°F and cook the chicken for twenty-five minutes.
5. Serve the rolls immediately with your favorite dips and sides.

Lemon Pepper Chicken Legs

Prep + Cook Time: 30 minutes | Servings: 4

Ingredients
½ tsp. garlic powder
2 tsp. baking powder
8 chicken legs
4 tbsp. salted butter, melted
1 tbsp. lemon pepper seasoning

Instructions
1. In a small bowl combine the garlic powder and baking powder, then use this mixture to coat the chicken legs. Lay the chicken in the basket of your fryer.
2. Cook the chicken legs at 375°F for twenty-five minutes. Halfway through, turn them over and allow to cook on the other side.
3. When the chicken has turned golden brown, test with a thermometer to ensure it has reached an ideal temperature of 165°F. Remove from the fryer.
4. Mix together the melted butter and lemon pepper seasoning and toss with the chicken legs until the chicken is coated all over. Serve hot.

Greek Chicken Meatballs

Prep + Cook Time: 15 minutes | Servings: 1

Ingredients
½ oz. finely ground pork rinds
1 lb. ground chicken
1 tsp. Greek seasoning
1/3 cup feta, crumbled
1/3 cup frozen spinach, drained and thawed

Instructions
1. Place all the ingredients in a large bowl and combine using your hands. Take equal-sized portions of this mixture and roll each into a 2-inch ball. Place the balls in your fryer.
2. Cook the meatballs at 350°F for twelve minutes, in several batches if necessary.
3. Once they are golden, ensure they have reached an ideal temperature of 165°F and remove from the fryer. Keep each batch warm while you move on to the next one. Serve with Tzatziki if desired.

Buffalo Chicken Tenders

Ingredients: Prep + Cook Time: 20 minutes | Servings: 4

Ingredients
1 egg
1 cup mozzarella cheese, shredded
¼ cup buffalo sauce
1 cup cooked chicken, shredded
¼ cup feta cheese

Instructions
1. Combine all ingredients (except for the feta). Line the basket of your fryer with a suitably sized piece of parchment paper. Lay the mixture into the fryer and press it into a circle about half an inch thick. Crumble the feta cheese over it.
2. Cook for eight minutes at 400°F. Turn the fryer off and allow the chicken to rest inside before removing with care.
3. Cut the mixture into slices and serve hot.

Buffalo Chicken Strips

Ingredients: Prep + Cook Time: 30 minutes | Servings: 1

Ingredients
¼ cup hot sauce
1 lb. boneless skinless chicken tenders
1 tsp. garlic powder
1 ½ oz. pork rinds, finely ground
1 tsp chili powder

Instructions
1. Toss the hot sauce and chicken tenders together in a bowl, ensuring the chicken is completely coated.
2. In another bowl, combine the garlic powder, ground pork rinds, and chili powder. Use this mixture to coat the tenders, covering them well. Place the chicken into your fryer, taking care not to layer pieces on top of one another.
3. Cook the chicken at 375°F for twenty minutes until cooked all the way through and golden. Serve warm with your favorite dips and sides.

Chicken & Pepperoni Pizza

Ingredients: Prep + Cook Time: 20 minutes | Servings: 6

Ingredients
2 cups cooked chicken, cubed
20 slices pepperoni
1 cup sugar-free pizza sauce
1 cup mozzarella cheese, shredded
¼ cup parmesan cheese, grated

Instructions
1. Place the chicken into the base of a four-cup baking dish and add the pepperoni and pizza sauce on top. Mix well so as to completely coat the meat with the sauce.
2. Add the parmesan and mozzarella on top of the chicken, then place the baking dish into your fryer.
3. Cook for 15 minutes at 375°F.
4. When everything is bubbling and melted, remove from the fryer. Serve hot.

Italian Chicken Thighs

Ingredients: Prep + Cook Time: 30 minutes | Servings: 4

Ingredients
4 skin-on bone-in chicken thighs
2 tbsp. unsalted butter, melted
3 tsp. Italian herbs
½ tsp. garlic powder
¼ tsp. onion powder

Instructions
1. Using a brush, coat the chicken thighs with the melted butter. Combine the herbs with the garlic powder and onion powder, then massage into the chicken thighs. Place the thighs in the fryer.
2. Cook at 380°F for 20 minutes, turning the chicken halfway through to cook on the other side.
3. When the thighs have achieved a golden color, test the temperature with a meat thermometer. Once they have reached 165°F, remove from the fryer and serve.

Teriyaki Chicken Wings

Ingredients: Prep + Cook Time: 45 minutes | Servings: 4

Ingredients
¼ tsp. ground ginger
2 tsp. minced garlic
½ cup sugar-free teriyaki sauce
2 lb. chicken wings
2 tsp. baking powder

Instructions
1. In a small bowl, combine together the ginger, garlic, and teriyaki sauce. Place the chicken wings in a separate, larger bowl and pour the mixture over them. Toss to coat until the chicken is well covered.
2. Refrigerate for at least an hour.
3. Remove the marinated wings from the fridge and add the baking powder, tossing again to coat. Then place the chicken in the basket of your air fryer.
4. Cook for 25 minutes at 400°F, giving the basket a shake intermittently throughout the cooking time.
5. When the wings are 165°F and golden in color, remove from the fryer and serve immediately.

Chicken Pizza Crusts

Ingredients: Prep + Cook Time: 35 minutes | Servings: 1

Ingredients
½ cup mozzarella, shredded
¼ cup parmesan cheese, grated
1 lb. ground chicken

Instructions
1.In a large bowl, combine all the ingredients and then spread the mixture out, dividing it into four parts of equal size.
2.Cut a sheet of parchment paper into four circles, roughly six inches in diameter, and put some of the chicken mixture onto the center of each piece, flattening the mixture to fill out the circle.
3.Depending on the size of your fryer, cook either one or two circles at a time at 375°F for 25 minutes. Halfway through, turn the crust over to cook on the other side. Keep each batch warm while you move onto the next one.
4.Once all the crusts are cooked, top with cheese and the toppings of your choice. If desired, cook the topped crusts for an additional five minutes.
5.Serve hot, or freeze and save for later!

Crispy Chicken Thighs

Ingredients: Prep + Cook Time: 35 minutes | Servings: 1

Ingredients
1 lb. chicken thighs
Salt and pepper
2 cups roasted pecans
1 cup water
1 cup flour

Instructions
1.Pre-heat your fryer to 400°F.
2.Season the chicken with salt and pepper, then set aside.
3.Pulse the roasted pecans in a food processor until a flour-like consistency is achieved.
4.Fill a dish with the water, another with the flour, and a third with the pecans.
5.Coat the thighs with the flour. Mix the remaining flour with the processed pecans.
6.Dredge the thighs in the water and then press into the -pecan mix, ensuring the chicken is completely covered.
7.Cook the chicken in the fryer for twenty-two minutes, with an extra five minutes added if you would like the chicken a darker-brown color. Check the temperature has reached 165°F before serving.

Marrod's Meatballs

Prep + Cook Time: 15 minutes | Servings: 6

Ingredients
1 lb. ground turkey
1 tbsp. fresh mint leaves, finely chopped
1 tsp. onion powder
1 ½ teaspoons garlic paste
1 tsp. crushed red pepper flakes
¼ cup melted butter
¾ tsp. fine sea salt
¼ cup grated Pecorino Romano

Instructions
1.In a bowl, combine all of the ingredients well. Using an ice cream scoop, mold the meat into balls.
2.Air fry the meatballs at 380°F for about 7 minutes, in batches if necessary. Shake the basket frequently throughout the cooking time for even results.
3.Serve with basil leaves and tomato sauce if desired.

Turmeric & Mustard Chicken Thighs

Prep + Cook Time: 20 minutes | Servings: 6

Ingredients
1 large egg, well whisked
2 tbsp. whole-grain Dijon mustard
¼ cup of mayonnaise
¼ cup of chili sauce
½ tsp. sugar
1 tsp. fine sea salt
½ tsp. ground black pepper, or more to taste
½ tsp. turmeric powder
10 chicken thighs
2 cups crushed saltines

Instructions
1.In a large bowl, combine the egg, mustard, mayonnaise, chili sauce, sugar, salt, pepper, and turmeric, incorporating everything well.
2.Coat the chicken thighs with the mixture. Place a layer of aluminum foil over the bowl, transfer it to the refrigerator and allow the chicken to marinate for at least 5 hours or overnight.
3.Pre-heat the Air Fryer to 360°F.
4.Separate the chicken from the marinade.
5.Put the crushed saltines into a shallow dish and use them to coat the chicken.
6.Place the chicken in the fryer and cook for 15 minutes, ensuring the thighs are cooked through.
7.Serve with the rest of the marinade as a sauce.

Roasted Turkey Thighs

Prep + Cook Time: 1 hr. 15 minute | Servings: 4

Ingredients
1 red onion, cut into wedges
1 carrot, trimmed and sliced
1 celery stalk, trimmed and sliced
1 cup Brussels sprouts, trimmed and halved
1 cup roasted vegetable broth
1 tbsp. apple cider vinegar
1 tsp. maple syrup
2 turkey thighs
½ tsp. mixed peppercorns, freshly cracked
1 tsp. fine sea salt
1 tsp. cayenne pepper
1 tsp. onion powder
½ tsp. garlic powder
⅓ tsp. mustard seeds

Instructions
1. Put the vegetables into a baking dish small enough to fit inside your Air Fryer and add in the roasted vegetable broth.
2. In a large bowl, pour in the rest of the ingredients, and set aside for 30 minutes.
3. Place them on the top of the vegetables.
4. Roast at 330°F for 40 - 45 minutes.

Vegetables & Italian Turkey Sausage

Prep + Cook Time: 40 minutes | Servings: 4

Ingredients
1 onion, cut into wedges
2 carrots, trimmed and sliced
1 parsnip, trimmed and sliced
2 potatoes, peeled and diced
1 tsp. dried thyme
½ tsp. dried marjoram
1 tsp. dried basil
½ tsp. celery seeds
Sea salt and ground black pepper to taste
1 tbsp. melted butter
¾ lb. sweet Italian turkey sausage

Instructions
1. Cover the vegetables with all of the seasonings and the melted butter.
2. Place the vegetables in the Air Fryer basket.
3. Add the sausage on top.
4. Roast at 360°F for 33 - 37 minutes, ensuring the sausages are no longer pink, giving the basket a good shake halfway through the cooking time. You may need to cook everything in batches.

Ricotta Wraps & Spring Chicken

Prep + Cook Time: 20 minutes | Servings: 12

Ingredients
2 large-sized chicken breasts, cooked and shredded
⅓ tsp. sea salt
¼ tsp. ground black pepper, or more to taste
2 spring onions, chopped
¼ cup soy sauce
1 tbsp. molasses
1 tbsp. rice vinegar
10 oz. Ricotta cheese
1 tsp. grated fresh ginger
50 wonton wrappers

Instructions
1. In a bowl, combine all of the ingredients, minus the wonton wrappers.
2. Unroll the wrappers and spritz with cooking spray.
3. Fill each of the wonton wrappers with equal amounts of the mixture.
4. Dampen the edges with a little water as an adhesive and roll up the wrappers, fully enclosing the filling.
5. Cook the rolls in the Air Fryer for 5 minutes at 375°F. You will need to do this step in batches.
6. Serve with your preferred sauce.

Cajun-Mustard Turkey Fingers

Prep + Cook Time: 20 minutes | Servings: 4

Ingredients
½ cup cornmeal mix
½ cup flour
1 ½ tbsp. Cajun seasoning
1 ½ tbsp. whole-grain mustard
1 ½ cups buttermilk
1 tsp. soy sauce
¾ lb. turkey tenderloins, cut into finger-sized strips
Salt and ground black pepper to taste

Instructions
1. In a bowl, combine the cornmeal, flour, and Cajun seasoning.
2. In a separate bowl, combine the whole-grain mustard, buttermilk and soy sauce.
3. Sprinkle some salt and pepper on the turkey fingers.
4. Dredge each finger in the buttermilk mixture, before coating them completely with the cornmeal mixture.
5. Place the prepared turkey fingers in the Air Fryer baking pan and cook for 15 minutes at 360°F.
6. Serve immediately, with ketchup if desired.

Honey Glazed Turkey Breast

Prep + Cook Time: 55 minutes | Servings: 6

Ingredients
2 tsp. butter, softened
1 tsp. dried sage
2 sprigs rosemary, chopped
1 tsp. salt
¼ tsp. freshly ground black pepper, or more if desired
1 whole turkey breast
2 tbsp. turkey broth
¼ cup honey
2 tbsp. whole-grain mustard
1 tbsp. butter

Instructions
1. Pre-heat your Air Fryer to 360°F.
2. Mix together the 2 tbsp. of butter, sage, rosemary, salt, and pepper.
3. Rub the turkey breast with this mixture.
4. Place the turkey in your fryer's cooking basket and roast for 20 minutes. Turn the turkey breast over and allow to cook for another 15 - 16 minutes.
5. Finally turn it once more and roast for another 12 minutes.
6. In the meantime, mix together the remaining ingredients in a saucepan using a whisk.
7. Coat the turkey breast with the glaze.
8. Place the turkey back in the Air Fryer and cook for an additional 5 minutes. Remove it from the fryer, let it rest, and carve before serving.

Chicken Curry

Prep + Cook Time: 60 minutes | Servings: 2

Ingredients
2 chicken thighs
1 small zucchini
2 cloves garlic
6 dried apricots
3 ½ oz. long turnip
6 basil leaves
1 tbsp. whole pistachios
1 tbsp. raisin soup
1 tbsp. olive oil
1 large pinch salt
Pinch of pepper
1 tsp. curry powder

Instructions
1. Pre-heat Air Fryer at 320°F.
2. Cut the chicken into 2 thin slices and chop up the vegetables into bite-sized pieces.
3. In a dish, combine all of the ingredients, incorporating everything well.
4. Place in the fryer and cook for a minimum of 30 minutes.
5. Serve with rice if desired.

Marjoram Chicken

Prep + Cook Time: 1 hr. | Servings: 2

Ingredients
2 skinless, boneless small chicken breasts
2 tbsp. butter
1 tsp. sea salt
½ tsp. red pepper flakes, crushed
2 tsp. marjoram
¼ tsp. lemon pepper

Instructions
1. In a bowl, coat the chicken breasts with all of the other ingredients. Set aside to marinate for 30 – 60 minutes.
2. Pre-heat your Air Fryer to 390 degrees.
3. Cook for 20 minutes, turning halfway through cooking time.
4. Check for doneness using an instant-read thermometer. Serve over jasmine rice.

Hoisin Glazed Turkey Drumsticks

Prep + Cook Time: 40 minutes + marinating time | Servings: 4

Ingredients
2 turkey drumsticks
2 tbsp. balsamic vinegar
2 tbsp. dry white wine
1 tbsp. extra-virgin olive oil
1 sprig rosemary, chopped
Salt and ground black pepper, to taste
2 ½ tbsp. butter, melted
For the Hoisin Glaze:
2 tbsp. hoisin sauce
1 tbsp. honey
1 tbsp. honey mustard

Instructions
1. In a bowl, coat the turkey drumsticks with the vinegar, wine, olive oil, and rosemary. Allow to marinate for 3 hours.
2. Pre-heat the Air Fryer to 350°F.
3. Sprinkle the turkey drumsticks with salt and black pepper. Cover the surface of each drumstick with the butter.
4. Place the turkey in the fryer and cook at 350°F for 30 - 35 minutes, flipping it occasionally through the cooking time. You may have to do this in batches.
5. In the meantime, make the Hoisin glaze by combining all the glaze ingredients.
6. Pour the glaze over the turkey, and roast for another 5 minutes.
7. Allow the drumsticks to rest for about 10 minutes before carving.

Turkey Sliders & Chive Mayonnaise
Prep + Cook Time: 20 minutes | Servings: 6

Ingredients
For the Turkey Sliders:
¾ lb. turkey mince
¼ cup pickled jalapeno, chopped
1 tbsp. oyster sauce
1 – 2 cloves garlic, minced
1 tbsp. chopped fresh cilantro
2 tbsp. chopped scallions
Sea salt and ground black pepper to taste
For the Chive Mayo:
1 cup mayonnaise
1 tbsp. chives
1 tsp. salt
Zest of 1 lime

Instructions
1.In a bowl, combine together all of the ingredients for the turkey sliders. Use your hands to shape 6 equal amounts of the mixture into slider patties.
2.Transfer the patties to the Air Fryer and fry them at 365°F for 15 minutes.
3.In the meantime, prepare the Chive Mayo by combining the rest of the ingredients.
4.Make sandwiches by placing each patty between two burger buns and serve with the mayo.

Thai Turkey Wings
Prep + Cook Time: 40 minutes| Servings: 4

Ingredients
¾ lb. turkey wings, cut into pieces
1 tsp. ginger powder
1 tsp. garlic powder
¾ tsp. paprika
2 tbsp. soy sauce
1 handful minced lemongrass
Sea salt flakes and ground black pepper to taste
2 tbsp. rice wine vinegar
¼ cup peanut butter
1 tbsp. sesame oil
½ cup Thai sweet chili sauce

Instructions
1.Boil the turkey wings in a saucepan full of water for 20 minutes.
2.Put the turkey wings in a large bowl and cover them with the remaining ingredients, minus the Thai sweet chili sauce.
3.Transfer to the Air Fryer and fry for 20 minutes at 350°F, turning once halfway through the cooking time. Ensure they are cooked through before serving with the Thai sweet chili sauce, as well as some lemon wedges if desired.

Stuffed Turkey Roulade
Prep + Cook Time: 50 minutes | Servings: 4

Ingredients
1 turkey fillet
Salt and garlic pepper to taste
⅓ tsp. onion powder
½ tsp. dried basil
⅓ tsp. ground red chipotle pepper
1 ½ tbsp. mustard seeds
½ tsp. fennel seeds
2 tbsp. melted butter
3 tbsp. coriander, finely chopped
½ cup scallions, finely chopped
2 cloves garlic, finely minced

Instructions
1.Flatten out the turkey fillets with a mallet, until they are about a half-inch thick.
2.Season each one with salt, garlic pepper, and onion powder.
3.In a small bowl, mix together the basil, chipotle pepper, mustard seeds, fennel seeds and butter.
4.Use a pallet knife to spread the mixture over the fillets, leaving the edges uncovered.
5.Add the coriander, scallions and garlic on top.
6.Roll up the fillets into a log and wrap a piece of twine around them to hold them in place.
7.Place them in the Air Fryer cooking basket.
8.Roast at 350°F for about 50 minutes, flipping it at the halfway point. Cook for longer if necessary. Serve warm.

Mac's Chicken Nuggets
Prep + Cook Time: 40 minutes | Servings: 4

Ingredients
2 slices friendly breadcrumbs
9 oz. chicken breast, chopped
1 tsp. garlic, minced
1 tsp. tomato ketchup
2 medium egg
1 tbsp. olive oil
1 tsp. paprika
1 tsp. parsley
Salt and pepper to taste

Instructions
1.Combine the breadcrumbs, paprika, salt, pepper and oil into a thick batter.
2.Coat the chopped chicken with the parsley, one egg and ketchup.
3.Shape the mixture into several nuggets and dredge each one in the other egg. Roll the nuggets into the breadcrumbs.
4.Cook at 390°F for 10 minutes in the Air Fryer.
5.Serve the nuggets with a side of mayo dip if desired.

Colby's Turkey Meatloaf

Prep + Cook Time: 50 minutes | Servings: 6

Ingredients

1 lb. turkey mince
½ cup scallions, finely chopped
2 garlic cloves, finely minced
1 tsp. dried thyme
½ tsp. dried basil
¾ cup Colby cheese, shredded
¾ cup crushed saltines
1 tbsp. tamari sauce
Salt and black pepper, to taste
¼ cup roasted red pepper tomato sauce
1 tsp. sugar
¾ tbsp. olive oil
1 medium egg, well beaten

Instructions

1.Over a medium heat, fry up the turkey mince, scallions, garlic, thyme, and basil until soft and fragrant.
2.Pre-heat the Air Fryer to 360°F.
3.Combine the mixture with the cheese, saltines and tamari sauce, before shaping it into a loaf.
4.Stir together the remaining items and top the meatloaf with them.
5.Place in the Air Fryer baking pan and allow to cook for 45 - 47 minutes.

Chicken Drumsticks

Prep + Cook Time: 35 minutes | Servings: 4

Ingredients

8 chicken drumsticks
1 tsp. cayenne pepper
2 tbsp. mustard powder
2 tbsp. oregano
2 tbsp. thyme
3 tbsp. coconut milk
1 large egg, lightly beaten
⅓ cup cauliflower
⅓ cup oats
Pepper and salt to taste

Instructions

1.Pre-heat the Air Fryer to 350°F.
2.Sprinkle salt and pepper over the chicken drumsticks and massage the coconut milk into them.
3.Put all the ingredients except the egg into the food processor and pulse to create a bread crumb-like mixture.

4.Transfer to a bowl.
5.In a separate bowl, put the beaten egg. Coat each chicken drumstick in the bread crumb mixture before dredging it in the egg. Roll it in the bread crumbs once more.
6.Put the coated chicken drumsticks in Air Fryer basket and cook for 20 minutes. Serve hot.

Bacon-Wrapped Chicken

Prep + Cook Time: 20 minutes | Servings: 6

Ingredients

1 chicken breast, cut into 6 pieces
6 rashers back bacon
1 tbsp. soft cheese

Instructions

1.Put the bacon rashers on a flat surface and cover one side with the soft cheese.
2.Lay the chicken pieces on each bacon rasher. Wrap the bacon around the chicken and use a toothpick stick to hold each one in place. Put them in Air Fryer basket.
3.Air fry at 350°F for 15 minutes.

Family Farm's Chicken Wings

Prep + Cook Time: 20 minutes | Servings: 6

Ingredients

6 chicken wings
1 tbsp. honey
2 cloves garlic, chopped
1 tsp. red chili flakes
2 tbsp. Worcestershire sauce
Pepper and salt to taste

Instructions

1.Place all the ingredients, except for the chicken wings, in a bowl and combine well.
2.Coat the chicken with the mixture and refrigerate for 1 hour.
3.Put the marinated chicken wings in the Air Fryer basket and spritz with cooking spray.
4.Air fry the chicken wings at 320°F for 8 minutes. Raise the temperature to 350°F and cook for an additional 4 minutes. Serve hot.

Chicken Surprise

Prep + Cook Time: 30 minutes | Servings: 2

Ingredients
2 chicken breasts, boneless and skinless
2 large eggs
½ cup skimmed milk
6 tbsp. soy sauce
1 cup flour
1 tsp. smoked paprika
1 tsp. salt
¼ tsp. black pepper
½ tsp. garlic powder
1 tbsp. olive oil
4 hamburger buns

Instructions
1.Slice the chicken breast into 2 – 3 pieces.
2.Place in a large bowl and drizzle with the soy sauce. Sprinkle on the smoked paprika, black pepper, salt, and garlic powder and mix well.
3.Allow to marinate for 30 – 40 minutes.
4.In the meantime, combine the eggs with the milk in a bowl. Put the flour in a separate bowl.
5.Dip the marinated chicken into the egg mixture before coating it with the flour. Cover each piece of chicken evenly.
6.Pre-heat the Air Fryer to 380°F.
7.Drizzle on the olive oil and put chicken pieces in the fryer.
8.Cook for 10 – 12 minutes. Flip the chicken once throughout the cooking process.
9.Toast the hamburger buns and put each slice of chicken between two buns to make a sandwich. Serve with ketchup or any other sauce of your choice.

Lemon & Garlic Chicken

Prep + Cook Time: 25 minutes | Servings: 1

Ingredients
1 chicken breast
1 tsp. garlic, minced
1 tbsp. chicken seasoning
1 lemon juice
Handful black peppercorns
Pepper and salt to taste

Instructions
1.Pre-heat the Air Fryer to 350°F.
2.Sprinkle the chicken with pepper and salt. Massage the chicken seasoning into the chicken breast, coating it well, and lay the seasoned chicken on a sheet of aluminum foil.
3.Top the chicken with the garlic, lemon juice, and black peppercorns. Wrap the foil to seal the chicken tightly.
4.Cook the chicken in the fryer basket for 15 minutes.

Cajun Seasoned Chicken

Prep + Cook Time: 15 minutes | Servings: 2

Ingredients
2 boneless chicken breasts
3 tbsp. Cajun spice

Instructions
1.Coat both sides of the chicken breasts with Cajun spice. Put the seasoned chicken in Air Fryer basket.
2.Air fry at 350°F for 10 minutes, ensuring they are cooked through before slicing up and serving.

Chicken Fillets

Prep + Cook Time: 30 minutes | Servings: 3

Ingredients
8 pieces of chicken fillet [approximately 3 x 1 x 1-inch dimensions]
1 egg
1 oz. salted butter, melted
1 cup friendly bread crumbs
1 tsp. garlic powder
½ cup parmesan cheese
1 tsp. Italian herbs

Instructions
1.Cover the chicken pieces in the whisked egg, melted butter, garlic powder, and Italian herbs. Allow to marinate for about 10 minutes.
2.In a bowl, mix together the Panko bread crumbs and parmesan. Use this mixture to coat the marinated chicken.
3.Put the aluminum foil in your Air Fryer basket.
4.Set the fryer to 390°F and briefly allow to warm. Line the basket with aluminum foil.
5.Place 4 pieces of the chicken in the basket. Cook for 6 minutes until golden brown. Don't turn the chicken over.
6.Repeat with the rest of the chicken pieces.
7.Serve the chicken fillets hot.

Asian Style Chicken

Prep + Cook Time: 25 minutes | Servings: 3

Ingredients
1 lb. skinless and boneless chicken breasts
3 garlic cloves, minced
1 tbsp. grated ginger
¼ tsp. ground black pepper
½ cup soy sauce
½ cup pineapple juice
1 tbsp. olive oil
2 tbsp. sesame seeds

Instructions
1.Mix together all of the ingredients except for the chicken in a large bowl.
2.Slice up the chicken breasts and coat in the mixture. Allow to marinade for at least 30 – 40 minutes.
3.Transfer the marinated chicken to the Air Fryer and cook at 380°F for about 10 – 15 minutes.
4.Top with sesame seeds before serving.

Whole Chicken

Prep + Cook Time: 30 minutes | Servings: 2

Ingredients
1 lb. whole chicken
1 lemon, juiced
1 tsp. lemon zest
1 tbsp. soy sauce
1 ½ tbsp. honey

Instructions
1.Place all of the ingredients in a bowl and combine well. Refrigerate for 1 hour.
2.Put the marinated chicken in the Air Fryer baking pan. Air fry at 320°F for 18 minutes.
3.Raise the heat to 350°F and cook for another 10 minutes or until chicken has turned light brown.

Honey & Garlic Chicken Wings

Prep + Cook Time: 25 minutes | Servings: 4

Ingredients
16 chicken wings
½ tsp. salt
¾ cup potato starch
¼ cup butter, melted
4 cloves garlic, minced
¼ cup honey

Instructions
1.Pre-heat your Air Fryer to 370°F.
2.Put the chicken wings in a bowl and cover them well with the potato starch.
3.Spritz a baking dish with cooking spray.
4.Transfer the wings to the dish, place inside the fryer and cook for 5 minutes.
5.In the meantime, mix together the rest of the ingredients with a whisk.
6.Top the chicken with this mixture and allow to cook for another 10 minutes before serving.

Buffalo Chicken Wings

Prep + Cook Time: 37 minutes | Servings: 3

Ingredients
2 lb. chicken wings
1 tsp. salt
¼ tsp. black pepper
1 cup buffalo sauce

Instructions
1.Wash the chicken wings and pat them dry with clean kitchen towels.
2.Place the chicken wings in a large bowl and sprinkle on salt and pepper.
3.Pre-heat the Air Fryer to 380°F.
4.Place the wings in the fryer and cook for 15 minutes, giving them an occasional stir throughout.
5.Place the wings in a bowl. Pour over the buffalo sauce and toss well to coat.
6.Put the chicken back in the Air Fryer and cook for a final 5 – 6 minutes.

Chicken Meatballs

Prep + Cook Time: 20 minutes | Servings: 10

Ingredients
2 chicken breasts
1 tbsp. mustard powder
1 tbsp. cumin
1 tbsp. basil
1 tbsp. thyme
1 tsp. chili powder
3 tbsp. soy sauce
2 tbsp. honey
1 onion, diced
Pepper and salt to taste

Instructions
1.Blend the chicken in your food processor to make a mince. Place the rest of the ingredients in the processor and pulse to combine well.
2.Shape the mixture into several small meatballs and place each one in the basket of the Air Fryer.
3.Air fry at 350°F for 15 minutes. Serve hot.

Chicken Legs

Prep + Cook Time: 35 minutes | Servings: 4

Ingredients
3 chicken legs, bone-in, with ski
3 chicken thighs, bone-in, with skin
2 cups flour
1 cup buttermilk
1 tsp. salt
1 tsp. ground black pepper
1 tsp. garlic powder
1 tsp. onion powder
1 tsp. ground cumin
2 tbsp. extra virgin olive oil

Instructions
1.Wash the chicken, dry it, and place it in a large bowl.
2.Pour the buttermilk over the chicken and refrigerate for 2 hours.
3.In a separate bowl, combine the flour with all of the seasonings.
4.Dip the chicken into the flour mixture. Dredge it the buttermilk before rolling it in the flour again.
5.Pre-heat the Air Fryer to 360°F
6.Put the chicken legs and thighs in the fryer basket. Drizzle on the olive oil and cook for roughly 20 minutes, flipping each piece of chicken a few times throughout the cooking time, until cooked through and crisped up.

Beastly BBQ Drumsticks

Prep + Cook Time: 45 minutes | Servings: 4

Ingredients
4 chicken drumsticks
½ tbsp. mustard
1 clove garlic, crushed
1 tsp. chili powder
2 tsp. sugar
1 tbsp. olive oil
Freshly ground black pepper

Instructions
1.Pre-heat the Air Fryer to 390°F.
2.Mix together the garlic, sugar, mustard, a pinch of salt, freshly ground pepper, chili powder and oil.
3.Massage this mixture into the drumsticks and leave to marinate for a minimum of 20 minutes.
4.Put the drumsticks in the fryer basket and cook for 10 minutes.
5.Bring the temperature down to 300°F and continue

to cook the drumsticks for a further10 minutes. When cooked through, serve with bread and corn salad.

Turkey Loaf

Prep + Cook Time: 50 minutes | Servings: 4

Ingredients
2/3 cup of finely chopped walnuts
1 egg
1 tbsp. organic tomato paste
1 ½ lb. turkey breast, diced
1 tbsp. Dijon mustard
½ tsp. dried savory or dill
1 tbsp. onion flakes
½ tsp. ground allspice
1 small garlic clove, minced
½ tsp. sea salt
¼ tsp. black pepper
1 tbsp. liquid aminos
2 tbsp. grated parmesan cheese

Instructions
1.Pre-heat Air Fryer to 375°F.
2.Coat the inside of a baking dish with a little oil.
3.Mix together the egg, dill, tomato paste, liquid aminos, mustard, salt, dill, garlic, pepper and allspice using a whisk. Stir in the diced turkey, followed by the walnuts, cheese and onion flakes.
4.Transfer the mixture to the greased baking dish and bake in the Air Fryer for 40 minutes.
5.Serve hot.

Charcoal Chicken

Prep + Cook Time: 20 minutes | Servings: 2

Ingredients
2 medium skinless, boneless chicken breasts
½ tsp. salt
3 tbsp. Cajun spice
1 tbsp. olive oil

Instructions
1.Massage the salt and Cajun spice into the chicken breasts. Drizzle with olive oil.
2.Pre-heat the Air Fryer to 370°F.
3.Place the chicken in the fryer and cook for 7 minutes.
4.Flip both chicken breasts over and cook for an additional 3 – 4 minutes.
5.Slice up before serving.

Battered Chicken Thighs
Prep + Cook Time: 4 hours 45 minutes | Servings: 4

Ingredients
2 cups buttermilk
3 tsp. salt
1 tsp. cayenne pepper
1 tbsp. paprika
1 ½ lb. chicken thighs
2 tsp. black pepper
2 cups flour
1 tbsp. garlic powder
1 tbsp. baking powder

Instructions
1.Put the chicken thighs in a large bowl.
2.In a separate bowl, combine the buttermilk, salt, cayenne, and black pepper.
3.Coat the thighs with the buttermilk mixture. Place a sheet of aluminum foil over the bowl and set in the refrigerator for 4 hours.
4.Pre-heat your Air Fryer to 400°F.
5.Combine together the flour, baking powder, and paprika in a shallow bowl. Cover a baking dish with a layer of parchment paper.
6.Coat the chicken thighs in the flour mixture and bake in the fryer for 10 minutes. Turn the thighs over and air fry for another 8 minutes. You will have to do this in two batches.

Chicken Bites
Prep + Cook Time: 30 minutes | Servings: 4

Ingredients
1 lb. skinless, boneless chicken breasts
¼ cup blue cheese salad dressing
¼ cup blue cheese, crumbled
½ cup sour cream
1 cup friendly bread crumbs
1 tbsp. olive oil
½ tsp. salt
¼ tsp. black pepper

Instructions
1.In a large bowl, combine the salad dressing, sour cream, and blue cheese.
2.In a separate bowl, combine the bread crumbs, olive oil, salt and pepper.
3.Chop the chicken breast into 1 - 2-inch pieces and coat in the bread crumbs.
4.Pre-heat the Air Fryer to 380°F.
5.Place the chicken bites in your fryer's basket.
6.Cook for 12 – 15 minutes. When cooked through and crispy, serve with the sauce of your choice.

Coconut Chicken
Prep + Cook Time: 45 minutes | Servings: 2 – 4

Ingredients
3 pcs whole chicken leg [skinless or with skin, it's up to you]

1.8 oz. pure coconut paste [alternatively, 1.8 oz. coconut milk]
4 – 5 tsp. ground turmeric
1.8 oz. old ginger
1.8 oz. galangal [a.k.a. lengkuas]
¾ tbsp. salt

Instructions
1.Mix together all of the ingredients, except for the chicken.
2.Slice a few slits into the chicken leg, mainly around the thick parts. This will help the chicken absorb the marinade.
3.Coat the chicken in the mixture and set aside to absorb.
4.Pre-heat the Air Fryer at 375°F.
5.Air fry the chicken for 20 – 25 minutes, turning it once halfway through, until golden brown.

Simple Turkey Breasts
Prep + Cook Time: 35 minutes | Servings: 5

Ingredients
6 – 7 lb. skinless, boneless turkey breast
2 tsp. salt
1 tsp. black pepper
½ tsp. dried cumin
2 tbsp. olive oil

Instructions
1.Massage all of the other ingredients into the turkey breast.
2.Pre-heat the Air Fryer to 340°F,
3.Cook the turkey breast for 15 minutes. Turn it over and cook for an additional 10 – 15 minutes, until cooked through and crispy.
4.Slice and serve the turkey with rice or fresh vegetables.

Chicken Wrapped in Bacon
Prep + Cook Time: 25 minutes | Servings: 6

Ingredients
6 rashers unsmoked back bacon
1 small chicken breast
1 tbsp. garlic soft cheese

Instructions
1.Cut the chicken breast into six bite-sized pieces.
2.Spread the soft cheese across one side of each slice of bacon.
3.Put the chicken on top of the cheese and wrap the bacon around it, holding it in place with a toothpick.
4.Transfer the wrapped chicken pieces to the Air Fryer and cook for 15 minutes at 350°F.

Chicken, Rice & Vegetables

Prep + Cook Time: 30 minutes | Servings: 4

Ingredients

1 lb. skinless, boneless chicken breasts
½ lb. button mushrooms, sliced
1 medium onion, chopped
1 package [10 oz.] Alfredo sauce
2 cups cooked rice
½ tsp. dried thyme
1 tbsp. olive oil
Salt and black pepper to taste

Instructions

1. Slice up the chicken breasts into 1-inch cubes.
2. In a large bowl, combine all of the ingredients. Sprinkle on salt and dried thyme and mix again.
3. Pre-heat the Air Fryer to 370°F and drizzle the basket with the olive oil.
4. Place the chicken and vegetables in the fryer and cook for 10 – 12 minutes. Stir the contents now and again.
5. Pour in the Alfredo sauce and allow to cook for an additional 3 – 4 minutes.
6. Serve with rice if desired.

Breadcrumb Turkey Breasts

Prep + Cook Time: 25 minutes | Servings: 6

Ingredients

6 turkey breasts
1 stick butter, melted
1 tsp. salt
2 cups friendly breadcrumbs
½ tsp. cayenne pepper
½ tsp. black pepper

Instructions

1. Put the breadcrumbs, half a teaspoon of the salt, a quarter teaspoon of the pepper, and the cayenne pepper in a large bowl. Combine well.
2. In a separate bowl, sprinkle the melted butter with the rest of the salt and pepper.
3. Coat the turkey breasts with the butter using a brush. Roll the turkey in the bread crumbs and transfer to a lined baking dish. Place in the Air Fryer.
4. Air fry at 390°F for 15 minutes.

Chicken Escallops

Prep + Cook Time: 45 minutes | Servings: 4

Ingredients

4 skinless chicken breasts
6 sage leaves

¼ cup friendly bread crumbs
2 eggs, beaten
½ cup flour
¼ cup parmesan cheese
Cooking spray

Instructions

1. Cut the chicken breasts into thin slices.
2. In a bowl, combine the sage and parmesan. Add in the flour, beaten eggs, salt and pepper and mix well.
3. Cover the chicken in the mixture before rolling it in the bread crumbs.
4. Grease the pan with the cooking spray.
5. Pre-heat your Air Fryer to 390°F and cook the chicken for 20 minutes, until it turns golden. Serve with rice.

Turkey & Maple Mustard

Prep + Cook Time: 70 minutes | Servings: 6

Ingredients

5 lb. whole turkey breast
1 tbsp. olive oil
1 tsp. dried thyme
½ tsp. smoked paprika
½ tsp. dried sage
1 tsp. sea salt
½ tsp. black pepper
1 tbsp. unsalted butter, melted
2 tbsp. Dijon mustard
¼ cup maple syrup

Instructions

1. Pre-heat the fryer to 350°F.
2. Brush the turkey breast with the olive oil.
3. Mix together the thyme, paprika, sage, salt, and pepper. Coat the turkey breast all over with this mixture.
4. Put the turkey breast in the Air Fryer basket and allow to cook for 25 minutes.
5. Flip it over and cook on the other side for a further 12 minutes.
6. Turn it once again and cook for another 12 minutes.
7. Check the temperature with a meat thermometer and ensure it has reached 165°F before removing it from the fryer.
8. In the meantime, combine the maple syrup, mustard, and melted butter in a saucepan over a medium heat. Stir continuously until a smooth consistency is achieved.
9. Pour the sauce over the cooked turkey in the fryer.
10. Cook for a final 5 minutes, ensuring the turkey turns brown and crispy.
11. Allow the turkey to rest, under a layer of aluminum foil, before carving up and serving.

Chicken Wings

Prep + Cook Time: 55 minutes | Servings: 4

Ingredients
3 lb. bone-in chicken wings
¾ cup flour
1 tbsp. old bay seasoning
4 tbsp. butter
Couple fresh lemons

Instructions
1. In a bowl, combine the all-purpose flour and Old Bay seasoning.
2. Toss the chicken wings with the mixture to coat each one well.
3. Pre-heat the Air Fryer to 375°F.
4. Give the wings a shake to shed any excess flour and place each one in the Air Fryer. You may have to do this in multiple batches, so as to not overlap any.
5. Cook for 30 – 40 minutes, shaking the basket frequently, until the wings are cooked through and crispy.
6. In the meantime, melt the butter in a frying pan over a low heat. Squeeze one or two lemons and add the juice to the pan. Mix well.
7. Serve the wings topped with the sauce.

Mozzarella Turkey Rolls

Prep + Cook Time: 20 minutes | Servings: 4

Ingredients
4 slices turkey breast
1 cup sliced fresh mozzarella
1 tomato, sliced
½ cup fresh basil
4 chive shoots

Instructions
1. Pre-heat your Air Fryer to 390°F.
2. Lay the slices of mozzarella, tomato and basil on top of each turkey slice.
3. Roll the turkey up, enclosing the filling well, and secure by tying a chive shoot around each one.
4. Put in the Air Fryer and cook for 10 minutes. Serve with a salad if desired.

Sage & Onion Turkey Balls

Prep + Cook Time: 40 minutes | Servings: 2

Ingredients
3.5 oz. turkey mince
½ small onion, diced
1 medium egg
1 tsp. sage
½ tsp. garlic, pureed
3 tbsp. friendly bread crumbs
Salt to taste
Pepper to taste

Instructions
1. Put all of the ingredients in a bowl and mix together well.
2. Take equal portions of the mixture and mold each one into a small ball. Transfer to the Air Fryer and cook for 15 minutes at 350°F.
3. Serve with tartar sauce and mashed potatoes.

Chicken Nuggets

Prep + Cook Time: 30 minutes | Servings: 4

Ingredients
½ lb. chicken breast, cut into pieces
1 tsp. parsley
1 tsp. paprika
1 tbsp. olive oil
2 eggs, beaten
1 tsp. tomato ketchup
1 tsp. garlic, minced
½ cup friendly bread crumbs
Pepper and salt to taste

Instructions
1. In a bowl, combine the bread crumbs, olive oil, paprika, pepper, and salt.
2. Place the chicken, ketchup, one egg, garlic, and parsley in a food processor and pulse together.
3. Put the other egg in a bowl.
4. Shape equal amounts of the pureed chicken into nuggets. Dredge each one in the egg before coating it in bread crumbs.
5. Put the coated chicken nuggets in the Air Fryer basket and cook at 390°F for 10 minutes.
6. Serve the nuggets hot.

Cracked Chicken Tenders

Prep + Cook Time: 30 minutes | Servings: 4

Ingredients

2 lb. skinless and boneless chicken tenders
3 large eggs
6 tbsp. skimmed milk
½ cup flour
1 cup friendly bread crumbs
¼ tsp. black pepper
1 tsp. salt
2 tbsp. olive oil

Instructions

1.In a large bowl, combine the bread crumbs and olive oil.
2.In a separate bowl, stir together the eggs and milk using a whisk. Sprinkle in the salt and black pepper.
3.Put the flour in a third bowl.
4.Slice up the chicken tenders into 1-inch strips. Coat each piece of chicken in the flour, before dipping it into the egg mixture, followed by the bread crumbs.
5.Pre-heat the Air Fryer to 380°F.
6.Cook the coated chicken tenders for about 13 – 15 minutes, shaking the basket a few times to ensure they turn crispy. Serve hot, with mashed potatoes and a dipping sauce if desired.

Randy's Roasted Chicken

Prep + Cook Time: 55 minutes | Servings: 4

Ingredients

5 – 7 lb. whole chicken with skin
1 tsp. garlic powder
1 tsp. onion powder
½ tsp. dried thyme
½ tsp. dried basil
½ tsp. dried rosemary
½ tsp. black pepper
2 tsp. salt
2 tbsp. extra virgin olive oil

Instructions

1.Massage the salt, pepper, herbs, and olive oil into the chicken. Allow to marinade for a minimum of 20 – 30 minutes.
2.In the meantime, pre-heat the Air Fryer to 340 F.
3.Place the chicken in the fryer and cook for 18 – 20 minutes.
4.Flip the chicken over and cook for an additional 20 minutes.
5.Leave the chicken to rest for about 10 minutes before carving and serving.

Herbed Chicken

Prep + Cook Time: 40 minutes | Servings: 6

Ingredients

4 lb. chicken wings
6 tbsp. red wine vinegar
6 tbsp. lime juice
1 tsp. fresh ginger, minced
1 tbsp. sugar
1 tsp. thyme, chopped
½ tsp. white pepper
¼ tsp. ground cinnamon
1 habanero pepper, chopped
6 garlic cloves, chopped
2 tbsp. soy sauce
2 ½ tbsp. olive oil
¼ tsp. salt

Instructions

1.Place all of the ingredients in a bowl and combine well, ensuring to coat the chicken entirely.
2.Put the chicken in the refrigerator to marinate for 1 hour.
3.Pre-heat the Air Fryer to 390°F.
4.Put half of the marinated chicken in the fryer basket and cook for 15 minutes, shaking the basket once throughout the cooking process.
5.Repeat with the other half of the chicken.
6.Serve hot.

Rosemary Chicken

Prep + Cook Time: 30 minutes | Servings: 2

Ingredients

¾ lb. chicken
½ tbsp. olive oil
1 tbsp. soy sauce
1 tsp. fresh ginger, minced
1 tbsp. oyster sauce
3 tbsp. sugar
1 tbsp. fresh rosemary, chopped
½ fresh lemon, cut into wedges

Instructions

1.In a bowl, combine the chicken, oil, soy sauce, and ginger, coating the chicken well.
2.Refrigerate for 30 minutes.
3.Pre-heat the Air Fryer to 390°F for 3 minutes.
4.Place the chicken in the baking pan, transfer to the fryer and cook for 6 minutes.
5.In the meantime, put the rosemary, sugar, and oyster sauce in a bowl and mix together.
6.Add the rosemary mixture in the fryer over the chicken and top the chicken with the lemon wedges.
7.Resume cooking for another 13 minutes, turning the chicken halfway through.

Chicken Strips

Prep + Cook Time: 25 minutes | Servings: 2

Ingredients
1 chicken breast, cut into strips
1 egg, beaten
¼ cup flour
¾ cup friendly bread crumbs
1 tsp. mix spice
1 tbsp. plain oats
1 tbsp. desiccated coconut
Pepper and salt to taste

Instructions
1. In a bowl, mix together the bread crumbs, mix spice, oats, coconut, pepper, and salt.
2. Put the beaten egg in a separate bowl. Pour the flour into a shallow dish.
3. Roll the chicken strips in the flour. Dredge each one in the egg and coat with the bread crumb mixture. Put the coated chicken strips in the Air Fryer basket and air fry at 350°F for 8 minutes.
4. Reduce the heat to 320°F and cook for another 4 minutes. Serve hot.

Grandma's Chicken

Prep + Cook Time: 20 minutes | Servings: 4

Ingredients
12 oz. chicken breast, diced
6 oz. general Tso sauce
½ tsp. white pepper
¼ cup milk
1 cup cornstarch

Instructions
1. Place the chicken and milk in a bowl.
2. Separate the milk from the chicken and coat the chicken with cornstarch.
3. Put the chicken in the Air Fryer basket and air fry at 350°F for 12 minutes.
4. Plate up the chicken and season with the white pepper.
5. Pour the Tso sauce over the chicken before serving.

Worcestershire Chicken Wings

Prep + Cook Time: 40 minutes | Servings: 6

Ingredients
6 chicken wings
1 ½ tbsp. Worcestershire sauce
1 tbsp. sugar
Juice and zest of 1 orange
½ tsp. thyme, dried
½ tsp. sage
1 tsp. mint
1 tsp. basil
½ tsp. oregano
1 tsp. parsley
1 tsp. rosemary
Salt and pepper to taste

Instructions
1. Combine all of the ingredients in a bowl, coating the chicken wings well with the other ingredients.
2. Refrigerate the marinated chicken for 30 minutes.
3. Pre-heat the Air Fryer to 350°F.
4. Wrap the marinated chicken in a sheet of aluminum foil, ensuring to seal with the juices. Put the wrapped chicken in Air Fryer basket and cook at 350°F for 20 minutes.
5. Unfold the foil, remove the orange zest and air fry the chicken wings at 350°F for a further 15 minutes. Serve hot.

Lime & Honey Chicken Wings

Prep + Cook Time: 7 hours | Servings: 2

Ingredients
16 winglets
½ tsp. sea salt
2 tbsp. light soya sauce
¼ tsp. white pepper powder
½ crush black pepper
2 tbsp. honey
2 tbsp. lime juice

Instructions
1. Place all of the ingredients in a glass dish. Coat the winglets well and allow to marinate in the refrigerator for a minimum of 6 hours.
2. Allow to return to room temperature for 30 minutes.
3. Put the wings in the Air Fryer and air fry at 355°F for 6 minutes. Turn each wing over before cooking for another 6 minutes.
4. Allow the chicken to cool before serving with a wedge of lemon.

Chicken Kebabs

Prep + Cook Time: 30 minutes | Servings: 3

Ingredients
1 lb. chicken breasts, diced
5 tbsp. honey
½ cup soy sauce
6 large mushrooms, cut in halves
3 medium bell peppers, cut
1 small zucchini, cut into rings
2 medium tomatoes, cut into rings
Salt and pepper to taste
¼ cup sesame seeds
1 tbsp. olive oil

Instructions
1. Cube the chicken breasts and place them in a large bowl.
2. Season with some salt and pepper. Drizzle over one tablespoon of olive oil and mix well.
3. Pour in the honey and soy sauce, and add in the sesame seeds.
4. Leave to marinate for 15 – 30 minutes.
5. Slice up the vegetables.
6. Thread the chicken and vegetables on wooden skewers, in alternating patterns.
7. Pre-heat the Air Fryer to 340°F
8. Put the chicken kebabs into the fryer basket.
9. Cook for about 15 minutes, flipping once during cooking. Serve once crispy and brown.

Chicken Tenderloins

Prep + Cook Time: 25 minutes | Servings: 4

Ingredients
8 chicken tenderloins
1 egg, beaten
2 tbsp. olive oil
1 cup friendly bread crumbs
Pepper and salt to taste

Instructions
1. Pre-heat the Air Fryer to 350°F.
2. Combine the friendly bread crumbs, olive oil, pepper, and salt in a shallow dish.
3. Put the beaten egg in separate dish.
4. Dip the chicken tenderloins into the egg before rolling them in the bread crumbs.
5. Transfer to the Air Fryer basket. Air fry the chicken for 12 minutes.

Buffalo Wings

Prep + Cook Time: 35 min. + [2 - 12 hours marinate] | Servings: 4

Ingredients
2 lb. chicken wings, without the wing tips
¼ cup + ¼ cup hot sauce, separately
3 + 3 tbsp. melted butter, separately
Sea salt to taste
Blue cheese, optional
Celery sticks, optional

Instructions
1. Prepare the chicken wings by separating the drumettes from the wingettes and put them into a bowl.
2. In a separate bowl, thoroughly combine 3 tablespoons of melted butter and ¼ cup of hot sauce.
3. Use this mixture to coat the chicken and marinate for 2 hours or overnight if possible.
4. Briefly pre-heat the Air Fryer to 400°F.
5. Divide the chicken into 2 batches. Put the first batch in the Air Fryer and cook for about 12 minutes. Give the basket a good shake at the halfway point. Repeat with the second batch.
6. Combine the cooked batches and return them to the Air Fryer, cooking for an additional 2 minutes.
7. In the meantime, make the sauce by stirring together the remaining 3 tablespoons of butter and ¼ cup of hot sauce.
8. Coat the cooked wings in the sauce before serving with a side of celery sticks and blue cheese if desired.

Moroccan Chicken

Prep + Cook Time: 25 minutes | Servings: 2

Ingredients
½ lb. shredded chicken
1 cup broth
1 carrot
1 broccoli, chopped
Pinch of cinnamon
Pinch of cumin
Pinch of red pepper
Pinch of sea salt

Instructions
1. In a bowl, cover the shredded chicken with cumin, red pepper, sea salt and cinnamon.
2. Chop up the carrots into small pieces. Put the carrot and broccoli into the bowl with the chicken.
3. Add the broth and stir everything well. Set aside for about 30 minutes.
4. Transfer to the Air Fryer. Cook for about 15 minutes at 390°F. Serve hot.

Chinese Chicken Wings

Prep + Cook Time: 45 minutes | Servings: 4

Ingredients
8 chicken wings
2 tbsp. five spice
2 tbsp. soy sauce
1 tbsp. mixed spices
Salt and pepper to taste

Instructions
1.In a bowl, mix together all of the ingredients.
2.Cover the base of the fryer with an aluminum foil and pre-heat the fryer to 360°F.
3.Add in some oil and pour in the mixture. Cook for 15 minutes.
4.Turn up the heat to 390°F, turn the chicken wings and cook for another 5 minutes. Serve with mayo dip if desired.

Chicken & Potatoes

Prep + Cook Time: 45 minutes | Servings: 6

Ingredients
1 lb. potatoes
2 lb. chicken
2 tbsp. olive oil
Pepper and salt to taste

Instructions
1.Pre-heat the Air Fryer to 350°F.
2.Place the chicken in Air Fryer basket along with the potatoes. Sprinkle on the pepper and salt.
3.Add a drizzling of the olive oil, making sure to cover the chicken and potatoes well.
4.Cook for 40 minutes.

Chicken Tenders

Prep + Cook Time: 30 minutes | Servings: 4

Ingredients
1 lb. chicken tenders
1 tsp. ginger, minced
4 garlic cloves, minced
2 tbsp. sesame oil
6 tbsp. pineapple juice
2 tbsp. soy sauce
½ tsp. pepper

Instructions
1.Put all of the ingredients, except for the chicken, in a bowl and combine well.
2.Thread the chicken onto skewers and coat with the seasonings. Allow to marinate for 2 hours.

3.Pre-heat the Air Fryer to 350°F.
4.Put the marinated chicken in fryer basket and cook for 18 minutes. Serve hot.

Lime Dijon Chicken

Prep + Cook Time: 20 minutes | Servings: 6

Ingredients
8 chicken drumsticks
1 lime juice
1 lime zest
Kosher salt to taste
1 tbsp. light mayonnaise
¾ tsp. black pepper
1 clove garlic, crushed
3 tbsp. Dijon mustard
1 tsp. dried parsley

Instructions
1.Pre-heat the Air Fryer to 375°F.
2.Remove the chicken skin and sprinkle the chicken with the salt.
3.In a bowl, mix the Dijon mustard with the lime juice, before stirring in the lime zest, pepper, parsley and garlic.
4.Cover the chicken with the lime mixture. Allow it to marinate for roughly 10 - 15 minutes.
5.Drizzle some oil in the bottom of your Air Fryer. Transfer the chicken drumsticks inside and cook for 5 minutes.
6.Give the basket a shake and fry for an additional 5 minutes.
7.Serve immediately, with a side of mayo.

Fried Chicken Thighs

Prep + Cook Time: 35 minutes | Servings: 4

Ingredients
4 chicken thighs
1 ½ tbsp. Cajun seasoning
1 egg, beaten
½ cup flour
1 tsp. seasoning salt

Instructions
1.Pre-heat the Air Fryer to 350°F.
2.In a bowl combine the flour, Cajun seasoning, and seasoning salt.
3.Place the beaten egg in another bowl.
4.Coat the chicken with the flour before dredging it in the egg. Roll once more in the flour.
5.Put the chicken in the Air Fryer and cook for 25 minutes. Serve hot.

Chapter 6 Fish and Seafood

Thai Shrimp Skewers with Peanut Dipping Sauce

Prep time: 15 minutes | Cook time: 6 minutes | Serves 2

Salt and pepper, to taste
12 ounces (340 g) extra-large shrimp, peeled and deveined
1 tablespoon vegetable oil
1 teaspoon honey
½ teaspoon grated lime zest plus 1 tablespoon juice, plus lime wedges for serving

6 (6-inch) wooden skewers
3 tablespoons creamy peanut butter
3 tablespoons hot tap water
1 tablespoon chopped fresh cilantro
1 teaspoon fish sauce

1. Preheat the air fryer to 400ºF (204ºC).
2. Dissolve 2 tablespoons salt in 1 quart cold water in a large container. Add shrimp, cover, and refrigerate for 15 minutes.
3. Remove shrimp from brine and pat dry with paper towels. Whisk oil, honey, lime zest, and ¼ teaspoon pepper together in a large bowl. Add shrimp and toss to coat. Thread shrimp onto skewers, leaving about ¼ inch between each shrimp (3 or 4 shrimp per skewer).
4. Arrange 3 skewers in air fryer basket, parallel to each other and spaced evenly apart. Arrange remaining 3 skewers on top, perpendicular to the bottom layer. Air fry until shrimp are opaque throughout, 6 to 8 minutes, flipping and rotating skewers halfway through cooking.
5. Whisk peanut butter, hot tap water, lime juice, cilantro, and fish sauce together in a bowl until smooth. Serve skewers with peanut dipping sauce and lime wedges.

Air Fryer Fish Sticks

Prep time: 10 minutes | Cook time: 10 to 12 minutes | Serves 4

Salt and pepper, to taste
1½ pounds (680g) skinless haddock fillets, ¾ inch thick, sliced into 4-inch strips
2 cups panko bread crumbs

1 tablespoon vegetable oil
¼ cup all-purpose flour
¼ cup mayonnaise
2 large eggs
1 tablespoon Old Bay seasoning
Vegetable oil spray

1. Dissolve ¼ cup salt in 2 quarts cold water in a large container. Add the haddock, cover, and let sit for 15 minutes.
2. Toss the panko with the oil in a bowl until evenly coated. Microwave, stirring frequently, until light golden brown, 2 to 4 minutes; transfer to a shallow dish. Whisk the flour, mayonnaise, eggs, Old Bay, ⅛ teaspoon salt, and ⅛ teaspoon pepper together in a second shallow dish.
3. Set a wire rack in a rimmed baking sheet and spray with vegetable oil spray. Remove the haddock from the brine and thoroughly pat dry with paper towels. Working with 1 piece at a time, dredge the haddock in the egg mixture, letting excess drip off, then coat with the panko mixture, pressing gently to adhere. Transfer the fish sticks to the prepared rack and freeze until firm, about 1 hour.
4. Preheat the air fryer to 400ºF (204ºC). Lightly spray the air fryer basket with vegetable oil spray. Arrange up to 5 fish sticks in the prepared basket, spaced evenly apart. Air fry until fish sticks are golden and register 140ºF (60ºC), 10 to 12 minutes, flipping and rotating fish sticks halfway through cooking.
5. Serve warm.

Roasted Cod with Lemon-Garlic Potatoes

Prep time: 10 minutes | Cook time: 28 minutes | Serves 2

3 tablespoons unsalted butter, softened, divided
2 garlic cloves, minced
1 lemon, grated to yield 2 teaspoons zest and sliced ¼ inch thick
Salt and pepper, to taste
1 large russet potato (12 ounce / 340-g), unpeeled, sliced ¼ inch thick
1 tablespoon minced fresh parsley, chives, or tarragon
2 (8-ounce / 227-g) skinless cod fillets, 1¼ inches thick
Vegetable oil spray

1. Preheat the air fryer to 400ºF (204ºC).
2. Make foil sling for air fryer basket by folding 1 long sheet of aluminum foil so it is 4 inches wide. Lay sheet of foil widthwise across basket, pressing foil into and up sides of basket. Fold excess foil as needed so that edges of foil are flush with top of basket. Lightly spray the foil and basket with vegetable oil spray.
3. Microwave 1 tablespoon butter, garlic, 1 teaspoon lemon zest, ¼ teaspoon salt, and ⅛ teaspoon pepper in a medium bowl, stirring once, until the butter is melted and the mixture is fragrant, about 30 seconds. Add the potato slices and toss to coat. Shingle the potato slices on sling in prepared basket to create 2 even layers. Air fry until potato slices are spotty brown and just tender, 16 to 18 minutes, using a sling to rotate potatoes halfway through cooking.
4. Combine the remaining 2 tablespoons butter, remaining 1 teaspoon lemon zest, and parsley in a small bowl. Pat the cod dry with paper towels and season with salt and pepper. Place the fillets, skinned-side down, on top of potato slices, spaced evenly apart. (Tuck thinner tail ends of fillets under themselves as needed to create uniform pieces.) Dot the fillets with the butter mixture and top with the lemon slices. Return the basket to the air fryer and air fry until the cod flakes apart when gently prodded with a paring knife and registers 140ºF (60ºC), 12 to 15 minutes, using a sling to rotate the potato slices and cod halfway through cooking.
5. Using a sling, carefully remove potatoes and cod from air fryer. Cut the potato slices into 2 portions between fillets using fish spatula. Slide spatula along underside of potato slices and transfer with cod to individual plates. Serve.

Orange-Mustard Glazed Salmon

Prep time: 10 minutes | Cook time: 10 minutes | Serves 2

1 tablespoon orange marmalade
¼ teaspoon grated orange zest plus 1 tablespoon juice
2 teaspoons whole-grain mustard
2 (8-ounce / 227-g) skin-on salmon fillets, 1½ inches thick
Salt and pepper, to taste
Vegetable oil spray

1. Preheat the air fryer to 400ºF (204ºC).
2. Make foil sling for air fryer basket by folding 1 long sheet of aluminum foil so it is 4 inches wide. Lay sheet of foil widthwise across basket, pressing foil into and up sides of basket. Fold excess foil as needed so that edges of foil are flush with top of basket. Lightly spray foil and basket with vegetable oil spray.
3. Combine marmalade, orange zest and juice, and mustard in bowl. Pat salmon dry with paper towels and season with salt and pepper. Brush tops and sides of fillets evenly with glaze. Arrange fillets skin side down on sling in prepared basket, spaced evenly apart. Air fry salmon until center is still translucent when checked with the tip of a paring knife and registers 125ºF (52ºC) (for medium-rare), 10 to 14 minutes, using sling to rotate fillets halfway through cooking.
4. Using the sling, carefully remove salmon from air fryer. Slide fish spatula along underside of fillets and transfer to individual serving plates, leaving skin behind. Serve.

Moroccan Spiced Halibut with Chickpea Salad

Prep time: 15 minutes | Cook time: 12 minutes | Serves 2

¾ teaspoon ground coriander
½ teaspoon ground cumin
¼ teaspoon ground ginger
⅛ teaspoon ground cinnamon
Salt and pepper, to taste
2 (8-ounce / 227-g) skinless halibut fillets, 1¼ inches thick
4 teaspoons extra-virgin olive oil,
divided, plus extra for drizzling
1 (15-ounce / 425-g) can chickpeas, rinsed
1 tablespoon lemon juice, plus lemon wedges for serving
1 teaspoon harissa
½ teaspoon honey
2 carrots, peeled and shredded
2 tablespoons chopped fresh mint, divided
Vegetable oil spray

1. Preheat the air fryer to 300ºF (149ºC).
2. Make foil sling for air fryer basket by folding 1 long sheet of aluminum foil so it is 4 inches wide. Lay sheet of foil widthwise across basket, pressing foil into and up sides of basket. Fold excess foil as needed so that edges of foil are flush with top of basket. Lightly spray foil and basket with vegetable oil spray.
3. Combine coriander, cumin, ginger, cinnamon, ⅛ teaspoon salt, and ⅛ teaspoon pepper in a small bowl. Pat halibut dry with paper towels, rub with 1 teaspoon oil, and sprinkle all over with spice mixture. Arrange fillets skinned side down on sling in prepared basket, spaced evenly apart. Bake until halibut flakes apart when gently prodded with a paring knife and registers 140ºF (60ºC), 12 to 16 minutes, using the sling to rotate fillets halfway through cooking.
4. Meanwhile, microwave chickpeas in medium bowl until heated through, about 2 minutes. Stir in remaining 1 tablespoon oil, lemon juice, harissa, honey, ⅛ teaspoon salt, and ⅛ teaspoon pepper. Add carrots and 1 tablespoon mint and toss to combine. Season with salt and pepper, to taste.
5. Using sling, carefully remove halibut from air fryer and transfer to individual plates. Sprinkle with remaining 1 tablespoon mint and drizzle with extra oil to taste. Serve with salad and lemon wedges.

Trout Amandine with Lemon Butter Sauce

Prep time: 20 minutes | Cook time:8 minutes | Serves 4

Trout Amandine:

⅔ cup toasted almonds
⅓ cup grated Parmesan cheese
1 teaspoon salt
½ teaspoon freshly ground black pepper
2 tablespoons butter, melted
4 (4-ounce / 113-g) trout fillets, or salmon fillets
Cooking spray

Lemon Butter Sauce:

8 tablespoons (1 stick) butter, melted
2 tablespoons freshly squeezed lemon juice
½ teaspoon Worcestershire
sauce
½ teaspoon salt
½ teaspoon freshly ground black pepper
¼ teaspoon hot sauce

1. In a blender or food processor, pulse the almonds for 5 to 10 seconds until finely processed. Transfer to a shallow bowl and whisk in the Parmesan cheese, salt, and pepper. Place the melted butter in another shallow bowl.
2. One at a time, dip the fish in the melted butter, then the almond mixture, coating thoroughly.
3. Preheat the air fryer to 300ºF (149ºC). Line the air fryer basket with parchment paper.
4. Place the coated fish on the parchment and spritz with oil.
5. Bake for 4 minutes. Flip the fish, spritz it with oil, and bake for 4 minutes more until the fish flakes easily with a fork.
6. In a small bowl, whisk the butter, lemon juice, Worcestershire sauce, salt, pepper, and hot sauce until blended.
7. Serve with the fish.

Sole and Asparagus Bundles

Prep time: 10 minutes | Cook time: 14 minutes | Serves 2

8 ounces (227 g) asparagus, trimmed
1 teaspoon extra-virgin olive oil, divided
Salt and pepper, to taste
4 (3-ounce / 85-g) skinless sole or flounder fillets, ⅛ to ¼ inch thick
4 tablespoons

unsalted butter, softened
1 small shallot, minced
1 tablespoon chopped fresh tarragon
¼ teaspoon lemon zest plus ½ teaspoon juice
Vegetable oil spray

1. Preheat the air fryer to 300ºF (149ºC).
2. Toss asparagus with ½ teaspoon oil, pinch salt, and pinch pepper in a bowl. Cover and microwave until bright green and just tender, about 3 minutes, tossing halfway through microwaving. Uncover and set aside to cool slightly.
3. Make foil sling for air fryer basket by folding 1 long sheet of aluminum foil so it is 4 inches wide. Lay sheet of foil widthwise across basket, pressing foil into and up sides of basket. Fold excess foil as needed so that edges of foil are flush with top of basket. Lightly spray foil and basket with vegetable oil spray.
4. Pat sole dry with paper towels and season with salt and pepper. Arrange fillets skinned side up on cutting board, with thicker ends closest to you. Arrange asparagus evenly across base of each fillet, then tightly roll fillets away from you around asparagus to form tidy bundles.
5. Rub bundles evenly with remaining ½ teaspoon oil and arrange seam side down on sling in prepared basket. Bake until asparagus is tender and sole flakes apart when gently prodded with a paring knife, 14 to 18 minutes, using a sling to rotate bundles halfway through cooking.
6. Combine butter, shallot, tarragon, and lemon zest and juice in a bowl. Using sling, carefully remove sole bundles from air fryer and transfer to individual plates. Top evenly with butter mixture and serve.

Crab Cakes with Lettuce and Apple Salad

Prep time: 10 minutes | Cook time: 13 minutes | Serves 2

8 ounces (227 g) lump crab meat, picked over for shells
2 tablespoons panko bread crumbs
1 scallion, minced
1 large egg
1 tablespoon mayonnaise
1½ teaspoons Dijon mustard
Pinch of cayenne pepper
2 shallots, sliced

thin
1 tablespoon extra-virgin olive oil, divided
1 teaspoon lemon juice, plus lemon wedges for serving
⅛ teaspoon salt
Pinch of pepper
½ (3-ounce / 85-g) small head Bibb lettuce, torn into bite-size pieces
½ apple, cored and sliced thin

1. Preheat the air fryer to 400ºF (204ºC).
2. Line large plate with triple layer of paper towels. Transfer crab meat to prepared plate and pat dry with additional paper towels. Combine panko, scallion, egg, mayonnaise, mustard, and cayenne in a bowl. Using a rubber spatula, gently fold in crab meat until combined; discard paper towels. Divide crab mixture into 4 tightly packed balls, then flatten each into 1-inch-thick cake (cakes will be delicate). Transfer cakes to plate and refrigerate until firm, about 10 minutes.
3. Toss shallots with ½ teaspoon oil in separate bowl; transfer to air fryer basket. Air fry until shallots are browned, 5 to 7 minutes, tossing once halfway through cooking. Return shallots to now-empty bowl and set aside.
4. Arrange crab cakes in air fryer basket, spaced evenly apart. Return basket to air fryer and air fry until crab cakes are light golden brown on both sides, 8 to 10 minutes, flipping and rotating cakes halfway through cooking.
5. Meanwhile, whisk remaining 2½ teaspoons oil, lemon juice, salt, and pepper together in large bowl. Add lettuce, apple, and shallots and toss to coat. Serve crab cakes with salad, passing lemon wedges separately.

Crab Cakes with Sriracha Mayonnaise

Prep time: 15 minutes | Cook time: 10 minutes | Serves 4

Sriracha Mayonnaise:

1 cup mayonnaise
1 tablespoon sriracha

1½ teaspoons freshly squeezed lemon juice

Crab Cakes:

1 teaspoon extra-virgin olive oil
¼ cup finely diced red bell pepper
¼ cup diced onion
¼ cup diced celery
1 pound (454 g) lump crab meat
1 teaspoon Old Bay seasoning

1 egg
1½ teaspoons freshly squeezed lemon juice
1¾ cups panko bread crumbs, divided
Vegetable oil, for spraying

1. Mix the mayonnaise, sriracha, and lemon juice in a small bowl. Place ²/₃ cup of the mixture in a separate bowl to form the base of the crab cakes. Cover the remaining sriracha mayonnaise and refrigerate. (This will become dipping sauce for the crab cakes once they are cooked.)
2. Heat the olive oil in a heavy-bottomed, medium skillet over medium-high heat. Add the bell pepper, onion, and celery and sauté for 3 minutes. Transfer the vegetables to the bowl with the reserved ²/₃ cup of sriracha mayonnaise. Mix in the crab, Old Bay seasoning, egg, and lemon juice. Add 1 cup of the panko. Form the crab mixture into 8 cakes. Dredge the cakes in the remaining ¾ cup of panko, turning to coat. Place on a baking sheet. Cover and refrigerate for at least 1 hour and up to 8 hours.
3. Preheat the air fryer to 375ºF (191ºC). Spray the air fryer basket with oil. Working in batches as needed so as not to overcrowd the basket, place the chilled crab cakes in a single layer in the basket. Spray the crab cakes with oil. Bake until golden brown, 8 to 10 minutes, carefully turning halfway through cooking. Remove to a platter and keep warm. Repeat with the remaining crab cakes as needed. Serve the crab cakes immediately with sriracha mayonnaise dipping sauce.

Remoulade Crab Cakes

Prep time: 15 minutes | Cook time: 10 minutes | Serves 4

Remoulade:

¾ cup mayonnaise
2 teaspoons Dijon mustard
1½ teaspoons yellow mustard
1 teaspoon vinegar
¼ teaspoon hot

sauce
1 teaspoon tiny capers, drained and chopped
¼ teaspoon salt
⅛ teaspoon ground black pepper

Crab Cakes:

1 cup bread crumbs, divided
2 tablespoons mayonnaise
1 scallion, finely chopped
6 ounces (170 g) crab meat
2 tablespoons pasteurized egg

product (liquid eggs in a carton)
2 teaspoons lemon juice
½ teaspoon red pepper flakes
½ teaspoon Old Bay seasoning
Cooking spray

1. Preheat the air fryer to 400ºF (204ºC).
2. In a small bowl, whisk to combine the mayonnaise, Dijon mustard, yellow mustard, vinegar, hot sauce, capers, salt, and pepper.
3. Refrigerate for at least 1 hour before serving.
4. Place a parchment liner in the air fryer basket.
5. In a large bowl, mix to combine ½ cup of bread crumbs with the mayonnaise and scallion. Set the other ½ cup of bread crumbs aside in a small bowl.
6. Add the crab meat, egg product, lemon juice, red pepper flakes, and Old Bay seasoning to the large bowl, and stir to combine.
7. Divide the crab mixture into 4 portions, and form into patties.
8. Dredge each patty in the remaining bread crumbs to coat.
9. Place the prepared patties on the liner in the air fryer in a single layer.
10. Spray lightly with cooking spray and air fry for 5 minutes. Flip the crab cakes over, air fry for another 5 minutes, until golden, and serve.

Jalea

Prep time: 20 minutes | Cook time: 10 minutes | Serves 4

Salsa Criolla:

½ red onion, thinly sliced
2 tomatoes, diced
1 serrano or jalapeño pepper, deseeded and diced

1 clove garlic, minced
¼ cup chopped fresh cilantro
Pinch of kosher salt
3 limes

Fried Seafood:

1 pound (454 g) firm, white-fleshed fish such as cod (add an extra ½-pound /227-g fish if not using shrimp)
20 large or jumbo shrimp, shelled and deveined
¼ cup all-purpose flour
¼ cup cornstarch
1 teaspoon garlic powder

1 teaspoon kosher salt
¼ teaspoon cayenne pepper
2 cups panko bread crumbs
2 eggs, beaten with 2 tablespoons water
Vegetable oil, for spraying
Mayonnaise or tartar sauce, for serving (optional)

1. To make the Salsa Criolla, combine the red onion, tomatoes, pepper, garlic, cilantro, and salt in a medium bowl. Add the juice and zest of 2 of the limes. Refrigerate the salad while you make the fish.
2. To make the seafood, cut the fish fillets into strips approximately 2 inches long and 1 inch wide. Place the flour, cornstarch, garlic powder, salt, and cayenne pepper on a plate and whisk to combine. Place the panko on a separate plate. Dredge the fish strips in the seasoned flour mixture, shaking off any excess. Dip the strips in the egg mixture, coating them completely, then dredge in the panko, shaking off any excess. Place the fish strips on a plate or rack. Repeat with the shrimp, if using.
3. Spray the air fryer basket with oil, and preheat the air fryer to 400ºF (204ºC). Working in 2 or 3 batches, arrange the fish and shrimp in a single layer in the basket, taking care not to crowd the basket. Spray with oil. Air fry for 5 minutes, then flip and air fry for another

4 to 5 minutes until the outside is brown and crisp and the inside of the fish is opaque and flakes easily with a fork. Repeat with the remaining seafood.
4. Place the fried seafood on a platter. Use a slotted spoon to remove the salsa criolla from the bowl, leaving behind any liquid that has accumulated. Place the salsa criolla on top of the fried seafood. Serve immediately with the remaining lime, cut into wedges, and mayonnaise or tartar sauce as desired.

Roasted Salmon Fillets

Prep time: 5 minutes | Cook time: 10 minutes | Serves 2

2 (8-ounce / 227 -g) skin-on salmon fillets, 1½ inches thick
1 teaspoon

vegetable oil
Salt and pepper, to taste
Vegetable oil spray

1. Preheat the air fryer to 400ºF (204ºC).
2. Make foil sling for air fryer basket by folding 1 long sheet of aluminum foil so it is 4 inches wide. Lay sheet of foil widthwise across basket, pressing foil into and up sides of basket. Fold excess foil as needed so that edges of foil are flush with top of basket. Lightly spray foil and basket with vegetable oil spray.
3. Pat salmon dry with paper towels, rub with oil, and season with salt and pepper. Arrange fillets skin side down on sling in prepared basket, spaced evenly apart. Air fry salmon until center is still translucent when checked with the tip of a paring knife and registers 125ºF (52ºC) (for medium-rare), 10 to 14 minutes, using sling to rotate fillets halfway through cooking.
4. Using the sling, carefully remove salmon from air fryer. Slide fish spatula along underside of fillets and transfer to individual serving plates, leaving skin behind. Serve.

Swordfish Skewers with Caponata

Prep time: 15 minutes | Cook time: 20 minutes | Serves 2

1 (10-ounce / 283-g) small Italian eggplant, cut into 1-inch pieces
6 ounces (170 g) cherry tomatoes
3 scallions, cut into 2 inches long
2 tablespoons extra-virgin olive oil, divided
Salt and pepper, to taste
12 ounces (340 g) skinless swordfish steaks, 1¼ inches thick, cut into 1-inch
pieces
2 teaspoons honey, divided
2 teaspoons ground coriander, divided
1 teaspoon grated lemon zest, divided
1 teaspoon juice
4 (6-inch) wooden skewers
1 garlic clove, minced
½ teaspoon ground cumin
1 tablespoon chopped fresh basil

1. Preheat the air fryer to 400ºF (204ºC).
2. Toss eggplant, tomatoes, and scallions with 1 tablespoon oil, ¼ teaspoon salt, and ⅛ teaspoon pepper in bowl; transfer to air fryer basket. Air fry until eggplant is softened and browned and tomatoes have begun to burst, about 14 minutes, tossing halfway through cooking. Transfer vegetables to cutting board and set aside to cool slightly.
3. Pat swordfish dry with paper towels. Combine 1 teaspoon oil, 1 teaspoon honey, 1 teaspoon coriander, ½ teaspoon lemon zest, ⅛ teaspoon salt, and pinch pepper in a clean bowl. Add swordfish and toss to coat. Thread swordfish onto skewers, leaving about ¼ inch between each piece (3 or 4 pieces per skewer).
4. Arrange skewers in air fryer basket, spaced evenly apart. (Skewers may overlap slightly.) Return basket to air fryer and air fry until swordfish is browned and registers 140ºF (60ºC), 6 to 8 minutes, flipping and rotating skewers halfway through cooking.
5. Meanwhile, combine remaining 2 teaspoons oil, remaining 1 teaspoon honey, remaining 1 teaspoon coriander, remaining ½ teaspoon lemon zest, lemon juice, garlic, cumin, ¼ teaspoon salt, and ⅛ teaspoon pepper in large bowl.

Microwave, stirring once, until fragrant, about 30 seconds. Coarsely chop the cooked vegetables, transfer to bowl with dressing, along with any accumulated juices, and gently toss to combine. Stir in basil and season with salt and pepper to taste. Serve skewers with caponata.

Fish Sandwich with Tartar Sauce

Prep time: 10 minutes | Cook time: 17 minutes | Serves 2

Tartar Sauce:
½ cup mayonnaise
2 tablespoons dried minced onion
1 dill pickle spear, finely chopped
2 teaspoons pickle juice
¼ teaspoon salt
⅛ teaspoon ground black pepper

Fish:
2 tablespoons all-purpose flour
1 egg, lightly beaten
1 cup panko
2 teaspoons lemon
pepper
2 tilapia fillets
Cooking spray
2 hoagie rolls

1. Preheat the air fryer to 400ºF (204ºC).
2. In a small bowl, combine the mayonnaise, dried minced onion, pickle, pickle juice, salt, and pepper.
3. Whisk to combine and chill in the refrigerator while you make the fish.
4. Place a parchment liner in the air fryer basket.
5. Scoop the flour out onto a plate; set aside.
6. Put the beaten egg in a medium shallow bowl.
7. On another plate, mix to combine the panko and lemon pepper.
8. Dredge the tilapia fillets in the flour, then dip in the egg, and then press into the panko mixture.
9. Place the prepared fillets on the liner in the air fryer in a single layer.
10. Spray lightly with cooking spray and air fry for 8 minutes. Carefully flip the fillets, spray with more cooking spray, and air fry for an additional 9 minutes, until golden and crispy.
11. Place each cooked fillet in a hoagie roll, top with a little bit of tartar sauce, and serve.

Bacon-Wrapped Scallops

Prep time: 10 minutes | Cook time: 12 minutes | Serves 4

12 slices bacon
24 large sea scallops, tendons removed
1 teaspoon plus 2 tablespoons extra-virgin olive oil, divided
Salt and pepper, to taste
6 (6-inch) wooden skewers

1 tablespoon cider vinegar
1 teaspoon Dijon mustard
5 ounces (142 g) baby spinach
1 fennel bulb, stalks discarded, bulb halved, cored, and sliced thin
5 ounces (142 g) raspberries

1. Preheat the air fryer to 350ºF (177ºC).
2. Line large plate with 4 layers of paper towels and arrange 6 slices bacon over towels in a single layer. Top with 4 more layers of paper towels and remaining 6 slices bacon. Cover with 2 layers of paper towels, place a second large plate on top, and press gently to flatten. Microwave until fat begins to render but bacon is still pliable, about 5 minutes.
3. Pat scallops dry with paper towels and toss with 1 teaspoon oil, ⅛ teaspoon salt, and ⅛ teaspoon pepper in a bowl until evenly coated. Arrange 2 scallops side to side, flat side down, on the cutting board. Starting at narrow end, wrap 1 slice bacon tightly around sides of scallop bundle. (Bacon should overlap slightly; trim excess as needed.) Thread scallop bundle onto skewer through bacon. Repeat with remaining scallops and bacon, threading 2 bundles onto each skewer.
4. Arrange 3 skewers in air fryer basket, parallel to each other and spaced evenly apart. Arrange remaining 3 skewers on top, perpendicular to the bottom layer. Bake until bacon is crisp and scallops are firm and centers are opaque, 12 to 16 minutes, flipping and rotating skewers halfway through cooking.
5. Meanwhile, whisk remaining 2 tablespoons oil, vinegar, mustard, ⅛ teaspoon salt, and ⅛ teaspoon pepper in large serving bowl until combined. Add spinach, fennel, and raspberries and gently toss to coat. Serve skewers with salad.

Baja Fish Tacos

Prep time: 15 minutes | Cook time: 10 minutes | Serves 4

Fried Fish:
1 pound (454 g) tilapia fillets (or other mild white fish)
½ cup all-purpose flour
1 teaspoon garlic powder
1 teaspoon kosher

salt
¼ teaspoon cayenne pepper
½ cup mayonnaise
3 tablespoons milk
1¾ cups panko bread crumbs
Vegetable oil, for spraying

Tacos:
8 corn tortillas
¼ head red or green cabbage, shredded
1 ripe avocado, halved and each half cut into 4 slices
12 ounces (340

g) pico de gallo or other fresh salsa
Dollop of Mexican crema
1 lime, cut into wedges

1. To make the fish, cut the fish fillets into strips 3 to 4 inches long and 1 inch wide. Combine the flour, garlic powder, salt, and cayenne pepper on a plate and whisk to combine. In a shallow bowl, whisk the mayonnaise and milk together. Place the panko on a separate plate. Dredge the fish strips in the seasoned flour, shaking off any excess. Dip the strips in the mayonnaise mixture, coating them completely, then dredge in the panko, shaking off any excess. Place the fish strips on a plate or rack.
2. Preheat the air fryer to 400ºF (204ºC). Working in batches, spray half the fish strips with oil and arrange them in the air fryer basket, taking care not to crowd them. Air fry for 4 minutes, then flip and air fry for another 3 to 4 minutes until the outside is brown and crisp and the inside is opaque and flakes easily with a fork. Repeat with the remaining strips.
3. Heat the tortillas in the microwave or on the stovetop. To assemble the tacos, place 2 fish strips inside each tortilla. Top with shredded cabbage, a slice of avocado, pico de gallo, and a dollop of crema. Serve with a lime wedge on the side.

Confetti Salmon Burgers

Prep time: 10 minutes | Cook time: 12 minutes | Serves 4

14 ounces (397 g) cooked fresh or canned salmon, flaked with a fork
¼ cup minced scallion, white and light green parts only
¼ cup minced red bell pepper
¼ cup minced celery
2 small lemons

1 teaspoon crab boil seasoning such as Old Bay
½ teaspoon kosher salt
½ teaspoon black pepper
1 egg, beaten
½ cup fresh bread crumbs
Vegetable oil, for spraying

1. In a large bowl, combine the salmon, vegetables, the zest and juice of 1 of the lemons, crab boil seasoning, salt, and pepper. Add the egg and bread crumbs and stir to combine. Form the mixture into 4 patties weighing approximately 5 ounces (142 g) each. Chill until firm, about 15 minutes.
2. Preheat the air fryer to 400ºF (204ºC).
3. Spray the salmon patties with oil on all sides and spray the air fryer basket to prevent sticking. Air fry for 12 minutes, flipping halfway through, until the burgers are browned and cooked through. Cut the remaining lemon into 4 wedges and serve with the burgers. Serve immediately.

Pecan-Crusted Tilapia

Prep time: 10minutes | Cook time: 10 minutes | Serves 4

1¼ cups pecans
¾ cup panko bread crumbs
½ cup all-purpose flour
2 tablespoons Cajun seasoning
2 eggs, beaten with

2 tablespoons water
4 (6-ounce/ 170-g) tilapia fillets
Vegetable oil, for spraying
Lemon wedges, for serving

1. Grind the pecans in the food processor until they resemble coarse meal. Combine the ground pecans with the panko on a plate. On a second plate, combine the flour and Cajun seasoning. Dry the tilapia fillets using paper towels

and dredge them in the flour mixture, shaking off any excess. Dip the fillets in the egg mixture and then dredge them in the pecan and panko mixture, pressing the coating onto the fillets. Place the breaded fillets on a plate or rack.
2. Preheat the air fryer to 375ºF (191ºC). Spray both sides of the breaded fillets with oil. Carefully transfer 2 of the fillets to the air fryer basket and air fry for 9 to 10 minutes, flipping once halfway through, until the flesh is opaque and flaky. Repeat with the remaining fillets.
3. Serve immediately with lemon wedges.

Oyster Po'Boy

Prep time: 20 minutes | Cook time: 5 minutes | Serves 4

¾ cup all-purpose flour
¼ cup yellow cornmeal
1 tablespoon Cajun seasoning
1 teaspoon salt
2 large eggs, beaten
1 teaspoon hot sauce
1 pound (454 g) pre-shucked oysters

1 (12-inch) French baguette, quartered and sliced horizontally
Tartar Sauce, as needed
2 cups shredded lettuce, divided
2 tomatoes, cut into slices
Cooking spray

1. In a shallow bowl, whisk the flour, cornmeal, Cajun seasoning, and salt until blended. In a second shallow bowl, whisk together the eggs and hot sauce.
2. One at a time, dip the oysters in the cornmeal mixture, the eggs, and again in the cornmeal, coating thoroughly.
3. Preheat the air fryer to 400ºF (204ºC). Line the air fryer basket with parchment paper.
4. Place the oysters on the parchment and spritz with oil.
5. Air fry for 2 minutes. Shake the basket, spritz the oysters with oil, and air fry for 3 minutes more until lightly browned and crispy.
6. Spread each sandwich half with Tartar Sauce. Assemble the po'boys by layering each sandwich with fried oysters, ½ cup shredded lettuce, and 2 tomato slices.
7. Serve immediately.

Tuna-Stuffed Quinoa Patties

Prep time: 10 minutes | Cook time: 15 minutes | Serves 4

12 ounces (340 g) quinoa	2 to 3 lemons
4 slices white bread with crusts removed	Kosher salt and pepper, to taste
½ cup milk	1¼ cups panko bread crumbs
3 eggs	Vegetable oil, for spraying
10 ounces (283 g) tuna packed in olive oil, drained	Lemon wedges, for serving

1. Rinse the quinoa in a fine-mesh sieve until the water runs clear. Bring 4 cups of salted water to a boil. Add the quinoa, cover, and reduce heat to low. Simmer the quinoa covered until most of the water is absorbed and the quinoa is tender, 15 to 20 minutes. Drain and allow to cool to room temperature. Meanwhile, soak the bread in the milk.
2. Mix the drained quinoa with the soaked bread and 2 of the eggs in a large bowl and mix thoroughly. In a medium bowl, combine the tuna, the remaining egg, and the juice and zest of 1 of the lemons. Season well with salt and pepper. Spread the panko on a plate.
3. Scoop up approximately ½ cup of the quinoa mixture and flatten into a patty. Place a heaping tablespoon of the tuna mixture in the center of the patty and close the quinoa around the tuna. Flatten the patty slightly to create an oval-shaped croquette. Dredge both sides of the croquette in the panko. Repeat with the remaining quinoa and tuna.
4. Spray the air fryer basket with oil to prevent sticking, and preheat the air fryer to 400ºF (204ºC). Arrange 4 or 5 of the croquettes in the basket, taking care to avoid overcrowding. Spray the tops of the croquettes with oil. Air fry for 8 minutes until the top side is browned and crispy. Carefully turn the croquettes over and spray the second side with oil. Air fry until the second side is browned and crispy, another 7 minutes. Repeat with the remaining croquettes.
5. Serve the croquetas warm with plenty of lemon wedges for spritzing.

Salmon Burgers

Prep time: 15 minutes | Cook time: 12 minutes | Serves 5

Lemon-Caper Rémoulade:

½ cup mayonnaise	chopped fresh parsley
2 tablespoons minced drained capers	2 teaspoons fresh lemon juice
2 tablespoons	

Salmon Patties:

1 pound (454 g) wild salmon fillet, skinned and pin bones removed	1 large egg, lightly beaten
	1 tablespoon Dijon mustard
6 tablespoons panko bread crumbs	1 teaspoon fresh lemon juice
¼ cup minced red onion plus ¼ cup slivered for serving	1 tablespoon chopped fresh parsley
1 garlic clove, minced	½ teaspoon kosher salt

For Serving:

5 whole wheat potato buns or gluten-free buns	10 butter lettuce leaves

1. For the lemon-caper rémoulade: In a small bowl, combine the mayonnaise, capers, parsley, and lemon juice and mix well.
2. For the salmon patties: Cut off a 4-ounce / 113-g piece of the salmon and transfer to a food processor. Pulse until it becomes pasty. With a sharp knife, chop the remaining salmon into small cubes.
3. In a medium bowl, combine the chopped and processed salmon with the panko, minced red onion, garlic, egg, mustard, lemon juice, parsley, and salt. Toss gently to combine. Form the mixture into 5 patties about ¾ inch thick. Refrigerate for at least 30 minutes.
4. Preheat the air fryer to 400ºF (204ºC).
5. Working in batches, place the patties in the air fryer basket. Air fry for about 12 minutes, gently flipping halfway, until golden and cooked through.
6. To serve, transfer each patty to a bun. Top each with 2 lettuce leaves, 2 tablespoons of the rémoulade, and the slivered red onions.

Salmon Patties

Prep time: 10 minutes | Cook time: 8 minutes | Serves 4

2 (5-ounce / 142 g) cans salmon, flaked
2 large eggs, beaten
1/3 cup minced onion
2/3 cup panko bread crumbs
1½ teaspoons Italian-Style seasoning
1 teaspoon garlic powder
Cooking spray

1. In a medium bowl, stir together the salmon, eggs, and onion.
2. In a small bowl, whisk the bread crumbs, Italian-Style seasoning, and garlic powder until blended. Add the bread crumb mixture to the salmon mixture and stir until blended. Shape the mixture into 8 patties.
3. Preheat the air fryer to 350ºF (177ºC). Line the air fryer basket with parchment paper.
4. Working in batches as needed, place the patties on the parchment and spritz with oil.
5. Bake for 4 minutes. Flip, spritz the patties with oil, and bake for 4 to 8 minutes more, until browned and firm. Serve.

Fried Shrimp

Prep time: 15 minutes | Cook time: 5 minutes | Serves 4

½ cup self-rising flour
1 teaspoon paprika
1 teaspoon salt
½ teaspoon freshly ground black pepper
1 large egg, beaten
1 cup finely crushed panko bread crumbs
20 frozen large shrimp (about 1-pound / 907-g), peeled and deveined
Cooking spray

1. In a shallow bowl, whisk the flour, paprika, salt, and pepper until blended. Add the beaten egg to a second shallow bowl and the bread crumbs to a third.
2. One at a time, dip the shrimp into the flour, the egg, and the bread crumbs, coating thoroughly.
3. Preheat the air fryer to 400ºF (204ºC). Line the air fryer basket with parchment paper.

4. Place the shrimp on the parchment and spritz with oil.
5. Air fry for 2 minutes. Shake the basket, spritz the shrimp with oil, and air fry for 3 minutes more until lightly browned and crispy. Serve hot.

Crispy Coconut Shrimp

Prep time: 15 minutes | Cook time: 8 minutes | Serves 4

Sweet Chili Mayo:
3 tablespoons mayonnaise
3 tablespoons Thai sweet chili sauce
1 tablespoon Sriracha sauce

Shrimp:
2/3 cup sweetened shredded coconut
2/3 cup panko bread crumbs
Kosher salt, to taste
2 tablespoons all-purpose or gluten-free flour
2 large eggs
24 extra-jumbo shrimp (about 1 pound / 454 g), peeled and deveined
Cooking spray

1. In a medium bowl, combine the mayonnaise, Thai sweet chili sauce, and Sriracha and mix well.
2. In a medium bowl, combine the coconut, panko, and ¼ teaspoon salt. Place the flour in a shallow bowl. Whisk the eggs in another shallow bowl.
3. Season the shrimp with ⅛ teaspoon salt. Dip the shrimp in the flour, shaking off any excess, then into the egg. Coat in the coconut-panko mixture, gently pressing to adhere, then transfer to a large plate. Spray both sides of the shrimp with oil.
4. Preheat the air fryer to 360ºF (182ºC).
5. Working in batches, arrange a single layer of the shrimp in the air fryer basket. Air fry for about 8 minutes, flipping halfway, until the crust is golden brown and the shrimp are cooked through.
6. Serve with the sweet chili mayo for dipping.

Blackened Fish

Prep time: 15 minutes | Cook time: 8 minutes | Serves 4

1 large egg, beaten
Blackened seasoning, as needed
2 tablespoons light

brown sugar
4 (4-ounce / 113- g) tilapia fillets
Cooking spray

1. In a shallow bowl, place the beaten egg. In a second shallow bowl, stir together the Blackened seasoning and the brown sugar.
2. One at a time, dip the fish fillets in the egg, then the brown sugar mixture, coating thoroughly.
3. Preheat the air fryer to 300ºF (149ºC). Line the air fryer basket with parchment paper.
4. Place the coated fish on the parchment and spritz with oil.
5. Bake for 4 minutes. Flip the fish, spritz it with oil, and bake for 4 to 6 minutes more until the fish is white inside and flakes easily with a fork.
6. Serve immediately.

Crawfish Creole Casserole

Prep time: 20 minutes | Cook time: 25 minutes | Serves 4

1½ cups crawfish meat
½ cup chopped celery
½ cup chopped onion
½ cup chopped green bell pepper
2 large eggs, beaten
1 cup half-and-half
1 tablespoon butter,

melted
1 tablespoon cornstarch
1 teaspoon Creole seasoning
¾ teaspoon salt
½ teaspoon freshly ground black pepper
1 cup shredded Cheddar cheese
Cooking spray

1. In a medium bowl, stir together the crawfish, celery, onion, and green pepper.
2. In another medium bowl, whisk the eggs, half-and-half, butter, cornstarch, Creole seasoning, salt, and pepper until blended. Stir the egg mixture into the crawfish mixture. Add the cheese and stir to combine.

3. Preheat the air fryer to 300ºF (149ºC). Spritz a baking pan with oil.
4. Transfer the crawfish mixture to the prepared pan and place it in the air fryer basket.
5. Bake for 25 minutes, stirring every 10 minutes, until a knife inserted into the center comes out clean.
6. Serve immediately.

Fried Catfish with Dijon Sauce

Prep time: 20 minutes | Cook time: 7 minutes | Serves 4

4 tablespoons butter, melted
2 teaspoons Worcestershire sauce, divided
1 teaspoon lemon pepper
1 cup panko bread

crumbs
4 (4-ounce / 113-g) catfish fillets
Cooking spray
½ cup sour cream
1 tablespoon Dijon mustard

1. In a shallow bowl, stir together the melted butter, 1 teaspoon of Worcestershire sauce, and the lemon pepper. Place the bread crumbs in another shallow bowl.
2. One at a time, dip both sides of the fillets in the butter mixture, then the bread crumbs, coating thoroughly.
3. Preheat the air fryer to 300ºF (149ºC). Line the air fryer basket with parchment paper.
4. Place the coated fish on the parchment and spritz with oil.
5. Bake for 4 minutes. Flip the fish, spritz it with oil, and bake for 3 to 6 minutes more, depending on the thickness of the fillets, until the fish flakes easily with a fork.
6. In a small bowl, stir together the sour cream, Dijon, and remaining 1 teaspoon of Worcestershire sauce. This sauce can be made 1 day in advance and refrigerated before serving. Serve with the fried fish.

Cajun Fish Fillets

Prep time: 15 minutes | Cook time: 6 minutes | Serves 4

¾ cup all-purpose flour
¼ cup yellow cornmeal
1 large egg, beaten

¼ cup Cajun seasoning
4 (4-ounce / 113-g) catfish fillets
Cooking spray

1. In a shallow bowl, whisk the flour and cornmeal until blended. Place the egg in a second shallow bowl and the Cajun seasoning in a third shallow bowl.
2. One at a time, dip the catfish fillets in the breading, the egg, and the Cajun seasoning, coating thoroughly.
3. Preheat the air fryer to 300ºF (149ºC). Line the air fryer basket with parchment paper.
4. Place the coated fish on the parchment and spritz with oil.
5. Bake for 3 minutes. Flip the fish, spritz it with oil, and bake for 3 to 5 minutes more until the fish flakes easily with a fork and reaches an internal temperature of 145ºF (63ºC). Serve warm.

New Orleans-Style Crab Cakes

Prep time: 10 minutes | Cook time: 8 to 10 minutes | Serves 4

1¼ cups bread crumbs
2 teaspoons Creole Seasoning
1 teaspoon dry mustard
1 teaspoon salt
1 teaspoon freshly ground black pepper

1½ cups crab meat
2 large eggs, beaten
1 teaspoon butter, melted
$1/_3$ cup minced onion
Cooking spray
Pecan Tartar Sauce, for serving

1. Preheat the air fryer to 350ºF (177ºC). Line the air fryer basket with parchment paper.
2. In a medium bowl, whisk the bread crumbs, Creole Seasoning, dry mustard, salt, and pepper until blended. Add the crab meat, eggs, butter, and onion. Stir until blended. Shape the crab mixture into 8 patties.

3. Place the crab cakes on the parchment and spritz with oil.
4. Air fry for 4 minutes. Flip the cakes, spritz them with oil, and air fry for 4 to 6 minutes more until the outsides are firm and a fork inserted into the center comes out clean. Serve with the Pecan Tartar Sauce.

Traditional Tuna Melt

Prep time: 10 minutes | Cook time: 12 minutes | Serves 2

2 cans unsalted albacore tuna, drained
½ cup mayonnaise
½ teaspoon salt
¼ teaspoon ground black pepper
4 slices sourdough

bread
4 pieces sliced Cheddar cheese
2 tablespoons crispy fried onions
Cooking spray
¼ teaspoon granulated garlic

1. Preheat the air fryer to 390ºF (199ºC).
2. In a medium bowl, combine the tuna, mayonnaise, salt, and pepper, and mix well. Set aside.
3. Assemble the sandwiches by laying out the bread and then adding 1 slice of cheese on top of each piece.
4. Sprinkle the fried onions on top of the cheese on 2 of the slices of bread.
5. Divide the tuna between the 2 slices of bread with the onions.
6. Take the remaining 2 slices of bread that have only cheese on them, and place them cheese-side down on top of the tuna.
7. Place one sandwich in the air fryer basket, spray with cooking spray, and air fry for 6 minutes.
8. Using a spatula, flip the sandwich over, spray it again, and air fry for another 6 minutes, or until golden brown. Sprinkle with the garlic immediately after removing from the air fryer basket. Repeat with the other sandwich.
9. Allow the sandwiches to sit for 1 to 2 minutes before cutting and serving.
10. Serve immediately.

Lemony Shrimp and Zucchini

Prep time: 15 minutes | Cook time: 7 to 8 minutes | Serves 4

1¼ pounds (567 g) extra-large raw shrimp, peeled and deveined
2 medium zucchini (about 8 ounces / 227 g each), halved lengthwise and cut into ½-inch-thick slices
1½ tablespoons olive oil

½ teaspoon garlic salt
1½ teaspoons dried oregano
⅛ teaspoon crushed red pepper flakes (optional)
Juice of ½ lemon
1 tablespoon chopped fresh mint
1 tablespoon chopped fresh dill

1. Preheat the air fryer to 350ºF (177ºC).
2. In a large bowl, combine the shrimp, zucchini, oil, garlic salt, oregano, and pepper flakes (if using) and toss to coat.
3. Working in batches, arrange a single layer of the shrimp and zucchini in the air fryer basket. Air fry for 7 to 8 minutes, shaking the basket halfway, until the zucchini is golden and the shrimp are cooked through.
4. Transfer to a serving dish and tent with foil while you air fry the remaining shrimp and zucchini.
5. Top with the lemon juice, mint, and dill and serve.

Tandoori-Spiced Salmon and Potatoes

Prep time: 10 minutes | Cook time: 28 minutes | Serves 2

1 pound (454 g) fingerling potatoes
2 tablespoons vegetable oil, divided
Kosher salt and freshly ground black pepper, to taste
1 teaspoon ground turmeric
1 teaspoon ground

cumin
1 teaspoon ground ginger
½ teaspoon smoked paprika
¼ teaspoon cayenne pepper
2 (6-ounce / 170-g) skin-on salmon fillets

1. Preheat the air fryer to 375ºF (191ºC).
2. In a bowl, toss the potatoes with 1 tablespoon of the oil until evenly coated. Season with salt and pepper. Transfer the potatoes to the air fryer and air fry for 20 minutes.
3. Meanwhile, in a bowl, combine the remaining 1 tablespoon oil, the turmeric, cumin, ginger, paprika, and cayenne. Add the salmon fillets and turn in the spice mixture until fully coated all over.
4. After the potatoes have cooked for 20 minutes, place the salmon fillets, skin-side up, on top of the potatoes, and continue cooking until the potatoes are tender, the salmon is cooked, and the salmon skin is slightly crisp.
5. Transfer the salmon fillets to two plates and serve with the potatoes while both are warm.

Spanish Garlic Shrimp

Prep time: 10 minutes | Cook time: 10 to 15 minutes | Serves 4

2 teaspoons minced garlic
2 teaspoons lemon juice
2 teaspoons olive oil
½ to 1 teaspoon

crushed red pepper
12 ounces (340 g) medium shrimp, deveined, with tails on
Cooking spray

1. In a medium bowl, mix together the garlic, lemon juice, olive oil, and crushed red pepper to make a marinade.
2. Add the shrimp and toss to coat in the marinade. Cover with plastic wrap and place the bowl in the refrigerator for 30 minutes.
3. Preheat the air fryer to 400ºF (204ºC). Spray the air fryer basket lightly with cooking spray.
4. Place the shrimp in the air fryer basket. Air fry for 5 minutes. Shake the basket and air fry until the shrimp are cooked through and nicely browned, an additional 5 to 10 minutes. Cool for 5 minutes before serving.

Tortilla Shrimp Tacos

Prep time: 10 minutes | Cook time: 6 minutes | Serves 4

Spicy Mayo:

3 tablespoons mayonnaise
1 tablespoon

Louisiana-style hot pepper sauce

Cilantro-Lime Slaw:

2 cups shredded green cabbage
½ small red onion, thinly sliced
1 small jalapeño, thinly sliced

2 tablespoons chopped fresh cilantro
Juice of 1 lime
¼ teaspoon kosher salt

Shrimp:

1 large egg, beaten
1 cup crushed tortilla chips
24 jumbo shrimp (about 1 pound / 454 g), peeled and

deveined
⅛ teaspoon kosher salt
Cooking spray
8 corn tortillas, for serving

1. For the spicy mayo: In a small bowl, mix the mayonnaise and hot pepper sauce.
2. For the cilantro-lime slaw: In a large bowl, toss together the cabbage, onion, jalapeño, cilantro, lime juice, and salt to combine. Cover and refrigerate to chill.
3. For the shrimp: Place the egg in a shallow bowl and the crushed tortilla chips in another. Season the shrimp with the salt. Dip the shrimp in the egg, then in the crumbs, pressing gently to adhere. Place on a work surface and spray both sides with oil.
4. Preheat the air fryer to 360ºF (182ºC).
5. Working in batches, arrange a single layer of the shrimp in the air fryer basket. Air fry for 6 minutes, flipping halfway, until golden and cooked through in the center.
6. To serve, place 2 tortillas on each plate and top each with 3 shrimp. Top each taco with ¼ cup slaw, then drizzle with spicy mayo.

Crab Cake Sandwich

Prep time: 15 minutes | Cook time: 10 minutes | Serves 4

Crab Cakes:

½ cup panko bread crumbs
1 large egg, beaten
1 large egg white
1 tablespoon mayonnaise
1 teaspoon Dijon mustard
¼ cup minced fresh parsley
1 tablespoon fresh lemon juice

½ teaspoon Old Bay seasoning
⅛ teaspoon sweet paprika
⅛ teaspoon kosher salt
Freshly ground black pepper, to taste
10 ounces (283 g) lump crab meat
Cooking spray

Cajun Mayo:

¼ cup mayonnaise
1 tablespoon minced dill pickle
1 teaspoon fresh

lemon juice
¾ teaspoon Cajun seasoning

For Serving:

4 Boston lettuce leaves

4 whole wheat potato buns or gluten-free buns

1. For the crab cakes: In a large bowl, combine the panko, whole egg, egg white, mayonnaise, mustard, parsley, lemon juice, Old Bay, paprika, salt, and pepper to taste and mix well. Fold in the crab meat, being careful not to over mix. Gently shape into 4 round patties, about ½ cup each, ¾ inch thick. Spray both sides with oil.
2. Preheat the air fryer to 370ºF (188ºC).
3. Working in batches, place the crab cakes in the air fryer basket. Air fry for about 10 minutes, flipping halfway, until the edges are golden.
4. Meanwhile, for the Cajun mayo: In a small bowl, combine the mayonnaise, pickle, lemon juice, and Cajun seasoning.
5. To serve: Place a lettuce leaf on each bun bottom and top with a crab cake and a generous tablespoon of Cajun mayonnaise. Add the bun top and serve.

Blackened Shrimp Tacos

Prep time: 10 minutes | Cook time: 10 to 15 minutes | Serves 4

12 ounces (340 g) medium shrimp, deveined, with tails off
1 teaspoon olive oil
1 to 2 teaspoons Blackened seasoning
8 corn tortillas, warmed
1 (14-ounce / 397-g) bag coleslaw mix
2 limes, cut in half
Cooking spray

1. Preheat the air fryer to 400ºF (204ºC).
2. Spray the air fryer basket lightly with cooking spray.
3. Dry the shrimp with a paper towel to remove excess water.
4. In a medium bowl, toss the shrimp with olive oil and Blackened seasoning.
5. Place the shrimp in the air fryer basket and air fry for 5 minutes. Shake the basket, lightly spray with cooking spray, and cook until the shrimp are cooked through and starting to brown, 5 to 10 more minutes.
6. Fill each tortilla with the coleslaw mix and top with the blackened shrimp. Squeeze fresh lime juice over top and serve.

Blackened Salmon

Prep time: 10 minutes | Cook time: 5 to 7 minutes | Serves 4

Salmon:
1 tablespoon sweet paprika
½ teaspoon cayenne pepper
1 teaspoon garlic powder
1 teaspoon dried oregano
1 teaspoon dried thyme
¾ teaspoon kosher salt
⅛ teaspoon freshly ground black pepper
Cooking spray
4 (6 ounces / 170 g each) wild salmon
fillets
Cucumber-Avocado Salsa:
2 tablespoons chopped red onion
1½ tablespoons fresh lemon juice
1 teaspoon extra-virgin olive oil
¼ teaspoon plus ⅛ teaspoon kosher salt
Freshly ground black pepper, to taste
4 Persian cucumbers, diced
6 ounces (170 g) Hass avocado, diced

1. For the salmon: In a small bowl, combine the paprika, cayenne, garlic powder, oregano, thyme, salt, and black pepper. Spray both sides of the fish with oil and rub all over. Coat the fish all over with the spices.
2. For the cucumber-avocado salsa: In a medium bowl, combine the red onion, lemon juice, olive oil, salt, and pepper. Let stand for 5 minutes, then add the cucumbers and avocado.
3. Preheat the air fryer to 400ºF (204ºC).
4. Working in batches, arrange the salmon fillets skin side down in the air fryer basket. Air fry for 5 to 7 minutes, or until the fish flakes easily with a fork, depending on the thickness of the fish.
5. Serve topped with the salsa.

Lime-Chili Shrimp Bowl

Prep time: 10 minutes | Cook time: 10 to 15 minutes | Serves 4

2 teaspoons lime juice
1 teaspoon olive oil
1 teaspoon honey
1 teaspoon minced garlic
1 teaspoon chili powder
Salt, to taste
12 ounces (340 g) medium shrimp, peeled and deveined
2 cups cooked brown rice
1 (15-ounce / 425-g) can seasoned black beans, warmed
1 large avocado, chopped
1 cup sliced cherry tomatoes
Cooking spray

1. Preheat the air fryer to 400ºF (204ºC). Spray the air fryer basket lightly with cooking spray.
2. In a medium bowl, mix together the lime juice, olive oil, honey, garlic, chili powder, and salt to make a marinade.
3. Add the shrimp and toss to coat evenly in the marinade.
4. Place the shrimp in the air fryer basket. Air fry for 5 minutes. Shake the basket and air fry until the shrimp are cooked through and starting to brown, an additional 5 to 10 minutes.
5. To assemble the bowls, spoon ¼ of the rice, black beans, avocado, and cherry tomatoes into each of four bowls. Top with the shrimp and serve.

Fish Croquettes with Lemon-Dill Aioli

Prep time: 15 minutes | Cook time: 10 minutes | Serves 4

Croquettes:

3 large eggs, divided
12 ounces (340 g) raw cod fillet, flaked apart with two forks
¼ cup 1% milk
½ cup boxed instant mashed potatoes
2 teaspoons olive oil
1/3 cup chopped fresh dill
1 shallot, minced
1 large garlic clove, minced

¾ cup plus 2 tablespoons bread crumbs, divided
1 teaspoon fresh lemon juice
1 teaspoon kosher salt
½ teaspoon dried thyme
¼ teaspoon freshly ground black pepper
Cooking spray

Lemon-Dill Aioli:

5 tablespoons mayonnaise
Juice of ½ lemon

1 tablespoon chopped fresh dill

1. For the croquettes: In a medium bowl, lightly beat 2 of the eggs. Add the fish, milk, instant mashed potatoes, olive oil, dill, shallot, garlic, 2 tablespoons of the bread crumbs, lemon juice, salt, thyme, and pepper. Mix to thoroughly combine. Place in the refrigerator for 30 minutes.
2. For the lemon-dill aioli: In a small bowl, combine the mayonnaise, lemon juice, and dill. Set aside.
3. Measure out about 3½ tablespoons of the fish mixture and gently roll in your hands to form a log about 3 inches long. Repeat to make a total of 12 logs.
4. Beat the remaining egg in a small bowl. Place the remaining ¾ cup bread crumbs in a separate bowl. Dip the croquettes in the egg, then coat in the bread crumbs, gently pressing to adhere. Place on a work surface and spray both sides with cooking spray.
5. Preheat the air fryer to 350ºF (177ºC).
6. Working in batches, arrange a single layer of the croquettes in the air fryer basket. Air fry for about 10 minutes, flipping halfway, until golden.
7. Serve with the aioli for dipping.

Garlic Scallops

Prep time: 10 minutes | Cook time: 10 to 15 minutes | Serves 4

2 teaspoons olive oil
1 packet dry zesty Italian dressing mix
1 teaspoon minced garlic

16 ounces (454 g) small scallops, patted dry
Cooking spray

1. Preheat the air fryer to 400ºF (204ºC).
2. Spray the air fryer basket lightly with cooking spray.
3. In a large zip-top plastic bag, combine the olive oil, Italian dressing mix, and garlic.
4. Add the scallops, seal the zip-top bag, and coat the scallops in the seasoning mixture.
5. Place the scallops in the air fryer basket and lightly spray with cooking spray.
6. Air fry for 5 minutes, shake the basket, and air fry for 5 to 10 more minutes, or until the scallops reach an internal temperature of 120ºF (49ºC).
7. Serve immediately.

Garlic-Lemon Tilapia

Prep time: 5 minutes | Cook time: 10 to 15 minutes | Serves 4

1 tablespoon lemon juice
1 tablespoon olive oil
1 teaspoon minced

garlic
½ teaspoon chili powder
4 (6-ounce / 170-g) tilapia fillets

1. Preheat the air fryer to 380ºF (193ºC). Line the air fryer basket with parchment paper.
2. In a large, shallow bowl, mix together the lemon juice, olive oil, garlic, and chili powder to make a marinade. Place the tilapia fillets in the bowl and coat evenly.
3. Place the fillets in the basket in a single layer, leaving space between each fillet. You may need to cook in more than one batch.
4. Air fry until the fish is cooked and flakes easily with a fork, 10 to 15 minutes.
5. Serve hot.

Seasoned Breaded Shrimp

Prep time: 15 minutes | Cook time: 10 to 15 minutes | Serves 4

2 teaspoons Old Bay seasoning, divided
½ teaspoon garlic powder
½ teaspoon onion powder
1 pound (454 g) large shrimp, deveined, with tails on
2 large eggs
½ cup whole-wheat panko bread crumbs
Cooking spray

1. Preheat the air fryer to 380ºF (193ºC).
2. Spray the air fryer basket lightly with cooking spray.
3. In a medium bowl, mix together 1 teaspoon of Old Bay seasoning, garlic powder, and onion powder. Add the shrimp and toss with the seasoning mix to lightly coat.
4. In a separate small bowl, whisk the eggs with 1 teaspoon water.
5. In a shallow bowl, mix together the remaining 1 teaspoon Old Bay seasoning and the panko bread crumbs.
6. Dip each shrimp in the egg mixture and dredge in the bread crumb mixture to evenly coat.
7. Place the shrimp in the air fryer basket, in a single layer. Lightly spray the shrimp withcooking spray. You many need to cook the shrimp in batches.
8. Air fry for 10 to 15 minutes, or until the shrimp is cooked through and crispy, shaking the basket at 5-minute intervals to redistribute and evenly cook.
9. Serve immediately.

Roasted Fish with Almond-Lemon Crumbs

Prep time: 10 minutes | Cook time: 7 to 8 minutes | Serves 4

½ cup raw whole almonds
1 scallion, finely chopped
Grated zest and juice of 1 lemon
½ tablespoon extra-virgin olive oil
¾ teaspoon kosher salt, divided
Freshly ground black pepper, to taste
4 (6 ounces / 170 g each) skinless fish fillets
Cooking spray
1 teaspoon Dijon mustard

1. In a food processor, pulse the almonds to coarsely chop. Transfer to a small bowl and add the scallion, lemon zest, and olive oil. Season with ¼ teaspoon of the salt and pepper to taste and mix to combine.
2. Spray the top of the fish with oil and squeeze the lemon juice over the fish. Season with the remaining ½ teaspoon salt and pepper to taste. Spread the mustard on top of the fish. Dividing evenly, press the almond mixture onto the top of the fillets to adhere.
3. Preheat the air fryer to 375ºF (191ºC).
4. Working in batches, place the fillets in the air fryer basket in a single layer. Air fry for 7 to 8 minutes, until the crumbs start to brown and the fish is cooked through.
5. Serve immediately.

Country Shrimp

Prep time: 10 minutes | Cook time: 15 to 20 minutes | Serves 4

1 pound (454 g) large shrimp, deveined, with tails on
1 pound (454 g) smoked turkey sausage, cut into thick slices
2 corn cobs, quartered
1 zucchini, cut into bite-sized pieces
1 red bell pepper, cut into chunks
1 tablespoon Old Bay seasoning
2 tablespoons olive oil
Cooking spray

1. Preheat the air fryer to 400ºF (204ºC). Spray the air fryer basket lightly with cooking spray.
2. In a large bowl, mix the shrimp, turkey sausage, corn, zucchini, bell pepper, and Old Bay seasoning, and toss to coat with the spices. Add the olive oil and toss again until evenly coated.
3. Spread the mixture in the air fryer basket in a single layer. You will need to cook in batches.
4. Air fry for 15 to 20 minutes, or until cooked through, shaking the basket every 5 minutes for even cooking.
5. Serve immediately.

Spicy Orange Shrimp

Prep time: 20 minutes | Cook time: 10 to 15 minutes | Serves 4

1/3 cup orange juice
3 teaspoons minced garlic
1 teaspoon Old Bay seasoning
1/4 to 1/2 teaspoon cayenne pepper

1 pound (454 g) medium shrimp, peeled and deveined, with tails off
Cooking spray

1. In a medium bowl, combine the orange juice, garlic, Old Bay seasoning, and cayenne pepper.
2. Dry the shrimp with paper towels to remove excess water.
3. Add the shrimp to the marinade and stir to evenly coat. Cover with plastic wrap and place in the refrigerator for 30 minutes so the shrimp can soak up the marinade.
4. Preheat the air fryer to 400ºF (204ºC). Spray the air fryer basket lightly with cooking spray.
5. Place the shrimp into the air fryer basket. Air fry for 5 minutes. Shake the basket and lightly spray with olive oil. Air fry until the shrimp are opaque and crisp, 5 to 10 more minutes.
6. Serve immediately.

Roasted Cod with Sesame Seeds

Prep time: 5 minutes | Cook time: 7 to 9 minutes | Makes 1 fillet

1 tablespoon reduced-sodium soy sauce
2 teaspoons honey
Cooking spray

6 ounces (170 g) fresh cod fillet
1 teaspoon sesame seeds

1. Preheat the air fryer to 360ºF (182ºC).
2. In a small bowl, combine the soy sauce and honey.
3. Spray the air fryer basket with cooking spray, then place the cod in the basket, brush with the soy mixture, and sprinkle sesame seeds on top. Roast for 7 to 9 minutes or until opaque.
4. Remove the fish and allow to cool on a wire rack for 5 minutes before serving.

Air Fried Spring Rolls

Prep time: 10 minutes | Cook time: 17 to 22 minutes | Serves 4

2 teaspoons minced garlic
2 cups finely sliced cabbage
1 cup matchstick cut carrots
2 (4-ounce / 113-g) cans tiny shrimp, drained

4 teaspoons soy sauce
Salt and freshly ground black pepper, to taste
16 square spring roll wrappers
Cooking spray

1. Preheat the air fryer to 370ºF (188ºC).
2. Spray the air fryer basket lightly with cooking spray. Spray a medium sauté pan with cooking spray.
3. Add the garlic to the sauté pan and cook over medium heat until fragrant, 30 to 45 seconds. Add the cabbage and carrots and sauté until the vegetables are slightly tender, about 5 minutes.
4. Add the shrimp and soy sauce and season with salt and pepper, then stir to combine. Sauté until the moisture has evaporated, 2 more minutes. Set aside to cool.
5. Place a spring roll wrapper on a work surface so it looks like a diamond. Place 1 tablespoon of the shrimp mixture on the lower end of the wrapper.
6. Roll the wrapper away from you halfway, then fold in the right and left sides, like an envelope. Continue to roll to the very end, using a little water to seal the edge. Repeat with the remaining wrappers and filling.
7. Place the spring rolls in the air fryer basket in a single layer, leaving room between each roll. Lightly spray with cooking spray. You may need to cook them in batches.
8. Air fry for 5 minutes. Turn the rolls over, lightly spray with cooking spray, and air fry until heated through and the rolls start to brown, 5 to 10 more minutes. Cool for 5 minutes before serving.

Cajun-Style Fish Tacos

Prep time: 5 minutes | Cook time: 10 to 15 minutes | Serves 6

2 teaspoons avocado oil
1 tablespoon Cajun seasoning
4 tilapia fillets
1 (14-ounce / 397-
g) package coleslaw mix
12 corn tortillas
2 limes, cut into wedges

1. Preheat the air fryer to 380ºF (193ºC). Line the air fryer basket with parchment paper.
2. In a medium, shallow bowl, mix the avocado oil and the Cajun seasoning to make a marinade. Add the tilapia fillets and coat evenly.
3. Place the fillets in the basket in a single layer, leaving room between each fillet. You may need to cook in batches.
4. Air fry until the fish is cooked and easily flakes with a fork, 10 to 15 minutes.
5. Assemble the tacos by placing some of the coleslaw mix in each tortilla. Add $1/_3$ of a tilapia fillet to each tortilla. Squeeze some lime juice over the top of each taco and serve.

Marinated Salmon Fillets

Prep time: 10 minutes | Cook time: 15 to 20 minutes | Serves 4

¼ cup soy sauce
¼ cup rice wine vinegar
1 tablespoon brown sugar
1 tablespoon olive oil
1 teaspoon mustard powder
1 teaspoon ground
ginger
½ teaspoon freshly ground black pepper
½ teaspoon minced garlic
4 (6-ounce / 170-g) salmon fillets, skin-on
Cooking spray

1. In a small bowl, combine the soy sauce, rice wine vinegar, brown sugar, olive oil, mustard powder, ginger, black pepper, and garlic to make a marinade.
2. Place the fillets in a shallow baking dish and pour the marinade over them. Cover the baking dish and marinate for at least 1 hour in the refrigerator, turning the fillets occasionally to keep them coated in the marinade.
3. Preheat the air fryer to 370ºF (188ºC). Spray the air fryer basket lightly with cooking spray.
4. Shake off as much marinade as possible from the fillets and place them, skin-side down, in the air fryer basket in a single layer. You may need to cook the fillets in batches.
5. Air fry for 15 to 20 minutes for well done. The minimum internal temperature should be 145ºF (63ºC) at the thickest part of the fillets.
6. Serve hot.

Homemade Fish Sticks

Prep time: 15 minutes | Cook time: 10 to 15 minutes | Serves 4

4 fish fillets
½ cup whole-wheat flour
1 teaspoon seasoned salt
2 eggs
1½ cups whole-wheat panko bread crumbs
½ tablespoon dried parsley flakes
Cooking spray

1. Preheat the air fryer to 400ºF (204ºC). Spray the air fryer basket lightly with cooking spray.
2. Cut the fish fillets lengthwise into "sticks."
3. In a shallow bowl, mix the whole-wheat flour and seasoned salt.
4. In a small bowl, whisk the eggs with 1 teaspoon of water.
5. In another shallow bowl, mix the panko bread crumbs and parsley flakes.
6. Coat each fish stick in the seasoned flour, then in the egg mixture, and dredge them in the panko bread crumbs.
7. Place the fish sticks in the air fryer basket in a single layer and lightly spray the fish sticks with cooking spray. You may need to cook them in batches.
8. Air fry for 5 to 8 minutes. Flip the fish sticks over and lightly spray with the cooking spray. Air fry until golden brown and crispy, 5 to 7 more minutes.
9. Serve warm.

Crispy Catfish Strips

Prep time: 5 minutes | Cook time: 16 to 18 minutes | Serves 4

1 cup buttermilk	1 cup cornmeal
5 catfish fillets, cut into 1½-inch strips	1 tablespoon Creole, Cajun, or Old Bay seasoning
Cooking spray	

1. Pour the buttermilk into a shallow baking dish. Place the catfish in the dish and refrigerate for at least 1 hour to help remove any fishy taste.
2. Preheat the air fryer to 400ºF (204ºC). Spray the air fryer basket lightly with cooking spray.
3. In a shallow bowl, combine cornmeal and Creole seasoning.
4. Shake any excess buttermilk off the catfish. Place each strip in the cornmeal mixture and coat completely. Press the cornmeal into the catfish gently to help it stick.
5. Place the strips in the air fryer basket in a single layer. Lightly spray the catfish with cooking spray. You may need to cook the catfish in more than one batch.
6. Air fry for 8 minutes. Turn the catfish strips over and lightly spray with cooking spray. Air fry until golden brown and crispy, 8 to 10 more minutes.
7. Serve warm.

Tuna Patty Sliders

Prep time: 15 minutes | Cook time: 10 to 15 minutes | Serves 4

3 (5-ounce / 142-g) cans tuna, packed in water	1 tablespoon sriracha
⅔ cup whole-wheat panko bread crumbs	¾ teaspoon black pepper
⅓ cup shredded Parmesan cheese	10 whole-wheat slider buns
	Cooking spray

1. Preheat the air fryer to 350ºF (177ºC).
2. Spray the air fryer basket lightly with cooking spray.
3. In a medium bowl combine the tuna, bread crumbs, Parmesan cheese, sriracha, and black pepper and stir to combine.

4. Form the mixture into 10 patties.
5. Place the patties in the air fryer basket in a single layer. Spray the patties lightly with cooking spray. You may need to cook them in batches.
6. Air fry for 6 to 8 minutes. Turn the patties over and lightly spray with cooking spray. Air fry until golden brown and crisp, another 4 to 7 more minutes. Serve warm.

Sesame Glazed Salmon

Prep time: 5 minutes | Cook time: 12 to 16 minutes | Serves 4

3 tablespoons soy sauce	garlic
1 tablespoon rice wine or dry sherry	¼ teaspoon minced ginger
1 tablespoon brown sugar	4 (6-ounce / 170-g) salmon fillets, skin-on
1 tablespoon toasted sesame oil	½ tablespoon sesame seeds
1 teaspoon minced	Cooking spray

1. In a small bowl, mix the soy sauce, rice wine, brown sugar, toasted sesame oil, garlic, and ginger.
2. Place the salmon in a shallow baking dish and pour the marinade over the fillets. Cover and refrigerate for at least 1 hour, turning the fillets occasionally to coat in the marinade.
3. Preheat the air fryer to 370ºF (188ºC). Spray the air fryer basket lightly with cooking spray.
4. Shake off as much marinade as possible and place the fillets, skin-side down, in the air fryer basket in a single layer. Reserve the marinade. You may need to cook them in batches.
5. Air fry for 8 to 10 minutes. Brush the tops of the salmon fillets with the reserved marinade and sprinkle with sesame seeds.
6. Increase the temperature to 400ºF (204ºC) and air fry for 2 to 5 more minutes for medium, 1 to 3 minutes for medium rare, or 4 to 6 minutes for well done.
7. Serve warm.

Simple Salmon Patty Bites

Prep time: 15 minutes | Cook time: 10 to 15 minutes | Serves 4

4 (5-ounce / 142-g) cans pink salmon, skinless, boneless in water, drained
2 eggs, beaten
1 cup whole-wheat panko bread crumbs
4 tablespoons finely minced red bell pepper
2 tablespoons parsley flakes
2 teaspoons Old Bay seasoning
Cooking spray

1. Preheat the air fryer to 360ºF (182ºC).
2. Spray the air fryer basket lightly with cooking spray.
3. In a medium bowl, mix the salmon, eggs, panko bread crumbs, red bell pepper, parsley flakes, and Old Bay seasoning.
4. Using a small cookie scoop, form the mixture into 20 balls.
5. Place the salmon bites in the air fryer basket in a single layer and spray lightly with cooking spray. You may need to cook them in batches.
6. Air fry until crispy for 10 to 15 minutes, shaking the basket a couple of times for even cooking.
7. Serve immediately.

Classic Shrimp Empanadas

Prep time: 10 minutes | Cook time: 8 minutes | Serves 5

½ pound (227g) raw shrimp, peeled, deveined and chopped
¼ cup chopped red onion
1 scallion, chopped
2 garlic cloves, minced
2 tablespoons minced red bell pepper
2 tablespoons chopped fresh cilantro
½ tablespoon fresh lime juice
¼ teaspoon sweet paprika
⅛ teaspoon kosher salt
⅛ teaspoon crushed red pepper flakes (optional)
1 large egg, beaten
10 frozen Goya Empanada Discos, thawed
Cooking spray

1. In a medium bowl, combine the shrimp, red onion, scallion, garlic, bell pepper, cilantro, lime juice, paprika, salt, and pepper flakes (if using).

2. In a small bowl, beat the egg with 1 teaspoon water until smooth.
3. Place an empanada disc on a work surface and put 2 tablespoons of the shrimp mixture in the center. Brush the outer edges of the disc with the egg wash. Fold the disc over and gently press the edges to seal. Use a fork and press around the edges to crimp and seal completely. Brush the tops of the empanadas with the egg wash.
4. Preheat the air fryer to 380ºF (193ºC).
5. Spray the bottom of the air fryer basket with cooking spray to prevent sticking. Working in batches, arrange a single layer of the empanadas in the air fryer basket and air fry for about 8 minutes, flipping halfway, until golden brown and crispy.
6. Serve hot.

Cajun-Style Salmon Burgers

Prep time: 10 minutes | Cook time: 10 to 15 minutes | Serves 4

4 (5-ounce / 142-g) cans pink salmon in water, any skin and bones removed, drained
2 eggs, beaten
1 cup whole-wheat bread crumbs
4 tablespoons light mayonnaise
2 teaspoons Cajun seasoning
2 teaspoons dry mustard
4 whole-wheat buns
Cooking spray

1. In a medium bowl, mix the salmon, egg, bread crumbs, mayonnaise, Cajun seasoning, and dry mustard. Cover with plastic wrap and refrigerate for 30 minutes.
2. Preheat the air fryer to 360ºF (182ºC). Spray the air fryer basket lightly with cooking spray.
3. Shape the mixture into four ½-inch-thick patties about the same size as the buns.
4. Place the salmon patties in the air fryer basket in a single layer and lightly spray the tops with cooking spray. You may need to cook them in batches.
5. Air fry for 6 to 8 minutes. Turn the patties over and lightly spray with cooking spray. Air fry until crispy on the outside, 4 to 7 more minutes.
6. Serve on whole-wheat buns.

Vegetable and Fish Tacos

Prep time: 10 minutes | Cook time: 9 to 12 minutes | Serves 4

1 pound (454 g) white fish fillets
2 teaspoons olive oil
3 tablespoons freshly squeezed lemon juice, divided
1½ cups chopped red cabbage
1 large carrot, grated
½ cup low-sodium salsa
⅓ cup low-fat Greek yogurt
4 soft low-sodium whole-wheat tortillas

1. Preheat the air fryer to 400ºF (204ºC).
2. Brush the fish with the olive oil and sprinkle with 1 tablespoon of lemon juice. Air fry in the air fryer basket for 9 to 12 minutes, or until the fish just flakes when tested with a fork.
3. Meanwhile, in a medium bowl, stir together the remaining 2 tablespoons of lemon juice, the red cabbage, carrot, salsa, and yogurt.
4. When the fish is cooked, remove it from the air fryer basket and break it up into large pieces.
5. Offer the fish, tortillas, and the cabbage mixture, and let each person assemble a taco.
6. Serve immediately.

Shrimp Dejonghe Skewers

Prep time: 10 minutes | Cook time: 15 minutes | Serves 4

2 teaspoons sherry
3 tablespoons unsalted butter, melted
1 cup panko bread crumbs
3 cloves garlic, minced
⅓ cup minced flat-leaf parsley, plus more for garnish
1 teaspoon kosher salt
Pinch of cayenne pepper
1½ pounds (680 g) shrimp, peeled and deveined
Vegetable oil, for spraying
Lemon wedges, for serving

1. Stir the sherry and melted butter together in a shallow bowl or pie plate and whisk until combined. Set aside. Whisk together the panko, garlic, parsley, salt, and cayenne pepper on a large plate or shallow bowl.

2. Thread the shrimp onto metal skewers designed for the air fryer or bamboo skewers, 3 to 4 per skewer. Dip 1 shrimp skewer in the butter mixture, then dredge in the panko mixture until each shrimp is lightly coated. Place the skewer on a plate or rimmed baking sheet and repeat the process with the remaining skewers.
3. Preheat the air fryer to 350ºF (177ºC). Arrange 4 skewers in the air fryer basket. Spray the skewers with oil and air fry for 8 minutes, until the bread crumbs are golden brown and the shrimp are cooked through. Transfer the cooked skewers to a serving plate and keep warm while cooking the remaining 4 skewers in the air fryer.
4. Sprinkle the cooked skewers with additional fresh parsley and serve with lemon wedges if desired.

Green Curry Shrimp

Prep time: 15 minutes | Cook time: 5 minutes | Serves 4

1 to 2 tablespoons Thai green curry paste
2 tablespoons coconut oil, melted
1 tablespoon half-and-half or coconut milk
1 teaspoon fish sauce
1 teaspoon soy sauce
1 teaspoon minced fresh ginger
1 clove garlic, minced
1 pound (454 g) jumbo raw shrimp, peeled and deveined
¼ cup chopped fresh Thai basil or sweet basil
¼ cup chopped fresh cilantro

1. In a baking pan, combine the curry paste, coconut oil, half-and-half, fish sauce, soy sauce, ginger, and garlic. Whisk until well combined.
2. Add the shrimp and toss until well coated. Marinate at room temperature for 15 to 30 minutes.
3. Preheat the air fryer to 400ºF (204ºC).
4. Place the pan in the air fryer basket. Air fry for 5 minutes, stirring halfway through the cooking time.
5. Transfer the shrimp to a serving bowl or platter. Garnish with the basil and cilantro. Serve immediately.

Crunchy Air Fried Cod Fillets

Prep time: 10 minutes | Cook time: 12 minutes | Serves 2

¹/₃ cup panko bread crumbs
1 teaspoon vegetable oil
1 small shallot, minced
1 small garlic clove, minced
½ teaspoon minced fresh thyme
Salt and pepper, to taste
1 tablespoon minced
fresh parsley
1 tablespoon mayonnaise
1 large egg yolk
¼ teaspoon grated lemon zest, plus lemon wedges for serving
2 (8-ounce / 227-g) skinless cod fillets, 1¼ inches thick
Vegetable oil spray

1. Preheat the air fryer to 300°F (149°C).
2. Make foil sling for air fryer basket by folding 1 long sheet of aluminum foil so it is 4 inches wide. Lay sheet of foil widthwise across basket, pressing foil into and up sides of basket. Fold excess foil as needed so that edges of foil are flush with top of basket. Lightly spray the foil and basket with vegetable oil spray.
3. Toss the panko with the oil in a bowl until evenly coated. Stir in the shallot, garlic, thyme, ¼ teaspoon salt, and ⅛ teaspoon pepper. Microwave, stirring frequently, until the panko is light golden brown, about 2 minutes. Transfer to a shallow dish and let cool slightly; stir in the parsley. Whisk the mayonnaise, egg yolk, lemon zest, and ⅛ teaspoon pepper together in another bowl.
4. Pat the cod dry with paper towels and season with salt and pepper. Arrange the fillets, skinned-side down, on plate and brush tops evenly with mayonnaise mixture. (Tuck thinner tail ends of fillets under themselves as needed to create uniform pieces.) Working with 1 fillet at a time, dredge the coated side in panko mixture, pressing gently to adhere. Arrange the fillets, crumb-side up, on sling in the prepared basket, spaced evenly apart.
5. Bake for 12 to 16 minutes, using a sling to rotate fillets halfway through cooking. Using a sling, carefully remove cod from air fryer. Serve with the lemon wedges.

Cornmeal-Crusted Trout Fingers

Prep time: 15 minutes | Cook time: 6 minutes | Serves 2

½ cup yellow cornmeal, medium or finely ground (not coarse)
¹/₃ cup all-purpose flour
1½ teaspoons baking powder
1 teaspoon kosher salt, plus more as needed
½ teaspoon freshly ground black pepper, plus more as needed
⅛ teaspoon cayenne pepper
¾ pound (340 g)
skinless trout fillets, cut into strips 1 inch wide and 3 inches long
3 large eggs, lightly beaten
Cooking spray
½ cup mayonnaise
2 tablespoons capers, rinsed and finely chopped
1 tablespoon fresh tarragon
1 teaspoon fresh lemon juice, plus lemon wedges, for serving

1. Preheat the air fryer to 400°F (204°C).
2. In a large bowl, whisk together the cornmeal, flour, baking powder, salt, black pepper, and cayenne. Dip the trout strips in the egg, then toss them in the cornmeal mixture until fully coated. Transfer the trout to a rack set over a baking sheet and liberally spray all over with cooking spray.
3. Transfer half the fish to the air fryer and air fry until the fish is cooked through and golden brown, about 6 minutes. Transfer the fish sticks to a plate and repeat with the remaining fish.
4. Meanwhile, in a bowl, whisk together the mayonnaise, capers, tarragon, and lemon juice. Season the tartar sauce with salt and black pepper.
5. Serve the trout fingers hot along with the tartar sauce and lemon wedges.

Catfish

Prep + Cook Time: 30 minutes | Servings: 4

Ingredients
2 catfish fillets [catfish]
1 medium egg, beaten
1 cup friendly bread crumbs
1 cup tortilla chips
1 lemon, juiced and peeled
1 tsp. parsley
Salt and pepper to taste

Instructions
1.Slice up the catfish fillets neatly and drizzle lightly with the lemon juice.
2.In a separate bowl, combine the bread crumbs with the lemon rind, parsley, tortillas, salt and pepper. Pour into your food processor and pulse.
3.Put the fillets in a tray and spread it evenly across the base. Pour the mixture over the fish to cover well.
4.Transfer to your Air Fryer and cook at 350°F for 15 minutes. Serve with chips and a refreshing drink.

Fish Fillets

Prep + Cook Time: 25 minutes | Servings: 4

Ingredients
4 fish fillets
1 egg, beaten
1 cup bread crumbs
4 tbsp. olive oil
Pepper and salt to taste

Instructions
1.Pre-heat the Air Fryer at 350°F.
2.In a shallow dish, combine together the bread crumbs, oil, pepper, and salt.
3.Pour the beaten egg into a second dish.
4.Dredge each fish fillet in the egg before rolling them in the bread crumbs. Place in the Air Fryer basket.
5.Allow to cook in the Air Fryer for 12 minutes.

Bean Burritos

Prep + Cook Time: 15 minutes | Servings: 4

Ingredients
4 tortillas
1 can beans
1 cup cheddar cheese, grated
¼ tsp. paprika
¼ tsp. chili powder
¼ tsp. garlic powder
Salt and pepper to taste

Instructions
1.Pre-heat the Air Fryer to 350°F.
2.In a bowl, mix together the paprika, chili powder, garlic powder, salt and pepper.
3.Fill each tortilla with an equal portion of beans before adding the spice mixture and the cheddar cheese. Roll the tortilla wraps into burritos.

4.Cover the base of a baking dish with parchment paper.
5.Transfer the burritos to the baking dish.
6.Put in the Air Fryer and cook for roughly 5 minutes. Serve hot.

Fishman Cakes

Prep + Cook Time: 35 minutes | Servings: 4

Ingredients
2 cups white fish
1 cup potatoes, mashed
1 tsp. mix herbs
1 tsp. mix spice
1 tsp. coriander
1 tsp. Worcestershire sauce
2 tsp. chili powder
1 tsp. milk
1 tsp. butter
1 small onion, diced
¼ cup bread crumbs
Pepper and salt to taste

Instructions
1.Place all of the ingredients in a bowl and combine.
2.Using your hands, mold equal portions of the mixture into small patties and refrigerate for 2 hours.
3.Put the fish cakes in the Air Fryer basket and cook at 400°F for 15 minutes. Serve hot.

Sunday's Salmon

Prep + Cook Time: 20 minutes | Servings: 3

Ingredients
½ lb. salmon fillet, chopped
2 egg whites
2 tbsp. chives, chopped
2 tbsp. garlic, minced
½ cup onion, chopped
2/3 cup carrots, grated
2/3 cup potato, grated
½ cup friendly bread crumbs
¼ cup flour
Pepper and salt

Instructions
1.In a shallow dish, combine the bread crumbs with the pepper and salt.
2.Pour the flour into another dish.
3.In a third dish, add the egg whites.
4.Put all of the other ingredients in a large mixing bowl and stir together to combine.
5.Using your hands, shape equal amounts of the mixture into small balls. Roll each ball in the flour before dredging it in the egg and lastly covering it with bread crumbs. Transfer all the coated croquettes to the Air Fryer basket and air fry at 320°F for 6 minutes.
6.Reduce the heat to 350°F and allow to cook for another 4 minutes.
7.Serve hot.

Whitefish Cakes

Prep + Cook Time: 1 hr. 20 minutes | Servings: 4

Ingredients
1 ½ cups whitefish fillets, minced
1 ½ cups green beans, finely chopped
½ cup scallions, chopped
1 chili pepper, deveined and minced
1 tbsp. red curry paste
1 tsp. sugar
1 tbsp. fish sauce
2 tbsp. apple cider vinegar
1 tsp. water
Sea salt flakes, to taste
½ tsp. cracked black peppercorns
1 ½ teaspoons butter, at room temperature
1 lemon

Instructions
1. Place all of the ingredients a bowl, following the order in which they are listed.
2. Combine well with a spatula or your hands.
3. Mold the mixture into several small cakes and refrigerate for 1 hour.
4. Put a piece of aluminum foil in the cooking basket and lay the cakes on top.
5. Cook at 390°F for 10 minutes. Turn each fish cake over before air-frying for another 5 minutes.
6. Serve the fish cakes with a side of cucumber relish.

Marinated Sardines

Prep + Cook Time: 1 hr. 15 minutes | Servings: 4

Ingredients
¾ lb. sardines, cleaned and rinsed
Salt and ground black pepper, to taste
1 tsp. smoked cayenne pepper
1 tbsp. lemon juice
1 tbsp. soy sauce
2 tbsp. olive oil
For the Potatoes:
8 medium Russet potatoes, peeled and quartered
½ stick melted butter
Salt and pepper, to taste
1 tsp. granulated garlic

Instructions
1. Dry the sardines with a paper towel.
2. Cover the sardines in the salt, black pepper, cayenne pepper, lemon juice, soy sauce, and olive oil, and leave to marinate for half an hour.
3. Air-fry the sardines at 350°F for roughly 5 minutes.
4. Raise the heat to 385°F and cook for an additional 7 - 8 minutes. Remove the sardines and plate up.
5. Wipe the cooking basket clean and pour in the potatoes, butter, salt, pepper, and garlic.
6. Roast at 390°F for 30 minutes. Serve the vegetables and the sardines together.

Halibut Steaks

Prep + Cook Time: 15 minutes | Servings: 4

Ingredients
1 lb. halibut steaks
Salt and pepper to taste
1 tsp. dried basil
2 tbsp. honey
¼ cup vegetable oil
2 ½ tbsp. Worcester sauce
1 tbsp. freshly squeezed lemon juice
2 tbsp. vermouth
1 tbsp. fresh parsley leaves, coarsely chopped

Instructions
1. Put all of the ingredients in a large bowl. Combine and cover the fish completely with the seasoning.
2. Transfer to your Air Fryer and cook at 390°F for 5 minutes.
3. Turn the fish over and allow to cook for a further 5 minutes.
4. Ensure the fish is cooked through, leaving it in the fryer for a few more minutes if necessary.
5. Serve with a side of potato salad.

Fisherman's Fish Fingers

Prep + Cook Time: 40 minutes | Servings: 4

Ingredients
¾ lb. fish, cut into fingers
1 cup friendly bread crumbs
2 tsp. mixed herbs
¼ tsp. baking soda
2 eggs, beaten
3 tsp. flour
2 tbsp. Maida
1 tsp. garlic ginger puree
½ tsp. black pepper
2 tsp. garlic powder
½ tsp. red chili flakes
½ tsp. turmeric powder
2 tbsp. lemon juice
½ tsp. salt

Instructions
1. Put the fish, garlic ginger puree, garlic powder, red chili flakes, turmeric powder, lemon juice, 1 teaspoon of the mixed herbs, and salt in a bowl and combine well.
2. In a separate bowl, combine the flour, Maida, and baking soda.
3. In a third bowl pour in the beaten eggs.
4. In a fourth bowl, stir together the bread crumbs, black pepper, and another teaspoon of mixed herbs.
5. Pre-heat the Air Fryer to 350°F.
6. Coat the fish fingers in the flour. Dredge in the egg, then roll in the breadcrumb mixture.
7. Put the fish fingers in the fryer's basket and allow to cook for 10 minutes, ensuring they crisp up nicely.

Fish Taco

Prep + Cook Time: 30 minutes | Servings: 4

Ingredients
12 oz. cod filet
1 cup friendly bread crumbs
4 – 6 friendly flour tortillas
1 cup tempura butter
½ cup salsa
½ cup guacamole
2 tbsp. freshly chopped cilantro
½ tsp. salt
¼ tsp. black pepper
Lemon wedges for garnish

Instructions
1. Slice the cod filets lengthwise and sprinkle salt and pepper on all sides.
2. Put the tempura butter in a bowl and coat each cod piece in it. Dip the fillets into the bread crumbs.
3. Pre-heat the Air Fryer to 340°F.
4. Fry the cod sticks for about 10 – 13 minutes in the fryer. Flip each one once while cooking.
5. In the meantime, coat one side of each tortilla with an even spreading of guacamole.
6. Put a cod stick in each tortilla and add the chopped cilantro and salsa on top. Lightly drizzle over the lemon juice. Fold into tacos.

Crispy Fish Fillet

Prep + Cook Time: 15 minutes | Servings: 4

Ingredients
2 fish fillets, each sliced into 4 pieces
1 tbsp. lemon juice
1 tsp. chili powder
4 tbsp. mayonnaise
3 tbsp. cornmeal
¼ tsp. black pepper
4 tbsp. flour
¼ tsp. salt

Instructions
1. Pre-heat the Air Fryer at 400°F.
2. Combine together the flour, pepper, cornmeal, salt, and chili powder.
3. In a shallow bowl, stir together the lemon juice and mayonnaise.
4. Coat the fillets in the mayonnaise mixture, before covering with the flour mixture.

5. Put the coated fish into the fryer's basket and cook for 5 minutes, ensuring they crisp up nicely. Serve hot.

Crispy Shrimp

Prep + Cook Time: 20 minutes | Servings: 8

Ingredients
2 lb. shrimp, peeled and deveined
4 egg whites
2 tbsp. olive oil
1 cup flour
½ tsp. cayenne pepper
1 cup friendly bread crumbs
Salt and pepper to taste

Instructions
1. Combine together the flour, pepper, and salt in a shallow bowl.
2. In a separate bowl mix the egg whites using a whisk.
3. In a third bowl, combine the bread crumbs, cayenne pepper, and salt.
4. Pre-heat your Air Fryer to 400°F.
5. Cover the shrimp with the flour mixture before dipping it in the egg white and lastly rolling in the bread crumbs.
6. Put the coated shrimp in the fryer's basket and top with a light drizzle of olive oil. Air fry the shrimp at 400°F for 8 minutes, in multiple batches if necessary.

Fish Sticks

Prep + Cook Time: 20 minutes | Servings: 4

Ingredients
1 lb. tilapia fillets, cut into strips
1 large egg, beaten
2 tsp. Old Bay seasoning
1 tbsp. olive oil
1 cup friendly bread crumbs

Instructions
1. Pre-heat the Air Fryer at 400°F.
2. In a shallow dish, combine together the bread crumbs, Old Bay, and oil. Put the egg in a small bowl.
3. Dredge the fish sticks in the egg. Cover them with bread crumbs and put them in the fryer's basket.
4. Cook the fish for 10 minutes or until they turn golden brown.
5. Serve hot.

Crab Herb Croquettes

Prep + Cook Time: 30 minutes | Servings: 6

Ingredients
1 lb. crab meat
1 cup friendly bread crumbs
2 egg whites
½ tsp. parsley
¼ tsp. chives
¼ tsp. tarragon
2 tbsp. celery, chopped
¼ cup red pepper, chopped
1 tsp. olive oil
½ tsp. lime juice
4 tbsp. sour cream
4 tbsp. mayonnaise
¼ cup onion, chopped
¼ tsp. salt

Instructions
1. Put the bread crumbs and salt in a bowl.
2. Pour the egg whites in a separate bowl.
3. Place the rest of the ingredients in a third bowl and combine thoroughly.
4. Using your hands, shape equal amounts of the mixture into small balls and dredge each ball in the egg white before coating with the bread crumbs.
5. Put the croquettes in the Air Fryer basket and cook at 400°F for 18 minutes. Serve hot.

Broiled Tilapia

Prep + Cook Time: 10 minutes | Servings: 4

Ingredients
1 lb. tilapia fillets
½ tsp. lemon pepper
Salt to taste

Instructions
1. Spritz the Air Fryer basket with some cooking spray.
2. Put the tilapia fillets in basket and sprinkle on the lemon pepper and salt.
3. Cook at 400°F for 7 minutes.
4. Serve with a side of vegetables.

Crab Legs

Prep + Cook Time: 20 minutes | Servings: 3

Ingredients
3 lb. crab legs

¼ cup salted butter, melted and divided
½ lemon, juiced
¼ tsp. garlic powder

Instructions
1. In a bowl, toss the crab legs and two tablespoons of the melted butter together. Place the crab legs in the basket of the fryer.
2. Cook at 400°F for fifteen minutes, giving the basket a good shake halfway through.
3. Combine the remaining butter with the lemon juice and garlic powder.
4. Crack open the cooked crab legs and remove the meat. Serve with the butter dip on the side and enjoy!

Crusty Pesto Salmon

Prep + Cook Time: 15 minutes | Servings: 2

Ingredients
¼ cup s, roughly chopped
¼ cup pesto
2 x 4-oz. salmon fillets
2 tbsp. unsalted butter, melted

Instructions
1. Mix the s and pesto together.
2. Place the salmon fillets in a round baking dish, roughly six inches in diameter.
3. Brush the fillets with butter, followed by the pesto mixture, ensuring to coat both the top and bottom. Put the baking dish inside the fryer.
4. Cook for twelve minutes at 390°F.
5. The salmon is ready when it flakes easily when prodded with a fork. Serve warm.

Buttery Cod

Prep + Cook Time: 12 minutes | Servings: 2

Ingredients
2 x 4-oz. cod fillets
2 tbsp. salted butter, melted
1 tsp. Old Bay seasoning
½ medium lemon, sliced

Instructions
1. Place the cod fillets in a baking dish.
2. Brush with melted butter, season with Old Bay, and top with some lemon slices.
3. Wrap the fish in aluminum foil and put into your fryer.
4. Cook for eight minutes at 350°F.
5. The cod is ready when it flakes easily. Serve hot.

Sesame Tuna Steak

Prep + Cook Time: 12 minutes | Servings: 2

Ingredients

1 tbsp. coconut oil, melted
2 x 6-oz. tuna steaks
½ tsp. garlic powder
2 tsp. black sesame seeds
2 tsp. white sesame seeds

Instructions

1.Apply the coconut oil to the tuna steaks with a brunch, then season with garlic powder.
2.Combine the black and white sesame seeds. Embed them in the tuna steaks, covering the fish all over. Place the tuna into your air fryer.
3.Cook for eight minutes at 400°F, turning the fish halfway through.
4.The tuna steaks are ready when they have reached a temperature of 145°F. Serve straightaway.

Lemon Garlic Shrimp

Prep + Cook Time: 15 minutes | Servings: 2

Ingredients

1 medium lemon
½ lb. medium shrimp, shelled and deveined
½ tsp. Old Bay seasoning
2 tbsp. unsalted butter, melted
½ tsp. minced garlic

Instructions

1.Grate the rind of the lemon into a bowl. Cut the lemon in half and juice it over the same bowl. Toss in the shrimp, Old Bay, and butter, mixing everything to make sure the shrimp is completely covered.
2.Transfer to a round baking dish roughly six inches wide, then place this dish in your fryer.
3.Cook at 400°F for six minutes. The shrimp is cooked when it turns a bright pink color.
4.Serve hot, drizzling any leftover sauce over the shrimp.

Foil Packet Salmon

Prep + Cook Time: 15 minutes | Servings: 2

Ingredients

2 x 4-oz. skinless salmon fillets
2 tbsp. unsalted butter, melted
½ tsp. garlic powder
1 medium lemon
½ tsp. dried dill

Instructions

1.Take a sheet of aluminum foil and cut into two squares measuring roughly 5" x 5". Lay each of the salmon fillets at the center of each piece. Brush both fillets with a tablespoon of bullet and season with a quarter-teaspoon of garlic powder.
2.Halve the lemon and grate the skin of one half over the fish. Cut four half-slices of lemon, using two to top each fillet. Season each fillet with a quarter-teaspoon of dill.
3.Fold the tops and sides of the aluminum foil over the fish to create a kind of packet. Place each one in the fryer.
4.Cook for twelve minutes at 400°F.
5.The salmon is ready when it flakes easily. Serve hot.

Foil Packet Lobster Tail

Prep + Cook Time: 15 minutes | Servings: 2

Ingredients

2 x 6-oz. lobster tail halves
2 tbsp. salted butter, melted
½ medium lemon, juiced
½ tsp. Old Bay seasoning
1 tsp. dried parsley

Instructions

1.Lay each lobster on a sheet of aluminum foil. Pour a light drizzle of melted butter and lemon juice over each one, and season with Old Bay.
2.Fold down the sides and ends of the foil to seal the lobster. Place each one in the fryer.
3.Cook at 375°F for twelve minutes.
4.Just before serving, top the lobster with dried parsley.

Avocado Shrimp

Prep + Cook Time: 20 minutes | Servings: 2

Ingredients

½ cup onion, chopped
2 lb. shrimp
1 tbsp. seasoned salt
1 avocado
½ cup pecans, chopped

Instructions

1.Pre-heat the fryer at 400°F.
2.Put the chopped onion in the basket of the fryer and spritz with some cooking spray. Leave to cook for five minutes.
3.Add the shrimp and set the timer for a further five minutes. Sprinkle with some seasoned salt, then allow to cook for an additional five minutes.
4.During these last five minutes, halve your avocado and remove the pit. Cube each half, then scoop out the flesh.
5.Take care when removing the shrimp from the fryer. Place it on a dish and top with the avocado and the chopped pecans.

Lemon Butter Scallops

Prep + Cook Time: 30 minutes | Servings: 1

Ingredients
1 lemon
1 lb. scallops
½ cup butter
¼ cup parsley, chopped

Instructions
1.Juice the lemon into a Ziploc bag.
2.Wash your scallops, dry them, and season to taste. Put them in the bag with the lemon juice. Refrigerate for an hour.
3.Remove the bag from the refrigerator and leave for about twenty minutes until it returns to room temperature. Transfer the scallops into a foil pan that is small enough to be placed inside the fryer.
4.Pre-heat the fryer at 400°F and put the rack inside.
5.Place the foil pan on the rack and cook for five minutes.
6.In the meantime, melt the butter in a saucepan over a medium heat. Zest the lemon over the saucepan, then add in the chopped parsley. Mix well.
7.Take care when removing the pan from the fryer. Transfer the contents to a plate and drizzle with the lemon-butter mixture. Serve hot.

Cheesy Lemon Halibut

Prep + Cook Time: 20 minutes | Servings: 2

Ingredients
1 lb. halibut fillet
½ cup butter
2 ½ tbsp. mayonnaise
2 ½ tbsp. lemon juice
¾ cup parmesan cheese, grated

Instructions
1.Pre-heat your fryer at 375°F.
2.Spritz the halibut fillets with cooking spray and season as desired.
3.Put the halibut in the fryer and cook for twelve minutes.
4.In the meantime, combine the butter, mayonnaise, and lemon juice in a bowl with a hand mixer. Ensure a creamy texture is achieved.
5.Stir in the grated parmesan.
6.When the halibut is ready, open the drawer and spread the butter over the fish with a butter knife. Allow to cook for a further two minutes, then serve hot.

Spicy Mackerel

Prep + Cook Time: 20 minutes | Servings: 2

Ingredients
2 mackerel fillets
2 tbsp. red chili flakes
2 tsp. garlic, minced
1 tsp. lemon juice

Instructions
1.Season the mackerel fillets with the red pepper flakes, minced garlic, and a drizzle of lemon juice. Allow to sit for five minutes.
2.Preheat your fryer at 350°F.
3.Cook the mackerel for five minutes, before opening the drawer, flipping the fillets, and allowing to cook on the other side for another five minutes.
4.Plate the fillets, making sure to spoon any remaining juice over them before serving.

Thyme Scallops

Prep + Cook Time: 12 minutes | Servings: 1

Ingredients
1 lb. scallops
Salt and pepper
½ tbsp. butter
½ cup thyme, chopped

Instructions
1.Wash the scallops and dry them completely. Season with pepper and salt, then set aside while you prepare the pan.
2.Grease a foil pan in several spots with the butter and cover the bottom with the thyme. Place the scallops on top.
3.Pre-heat the fryer at 400°F and set the rack inside.
4.Place the foil pan on the rack and allow to cook for seven minutes.
5.Take care when removing the pan from the fryer and transfer the scallops to a serving dish. Spoon any remaining butter in the pan over the fish and enjoy.

Creamy Salmon

Prep + Cook Time: 20 minutes | Servings: 2

Ingredients
¾ lb. salmon, cut into 6 pieces
¼ cup yogurt
1 tbsp. olive oil
1 tbsp. dill, chopped
3 tbsp. sour cream
Salt to taste

Instructions
1 Sprinkle some salt on the salmon.
2 Put the salmon slices in the Air Fryer basket and add in a drizzle of olive oil.
3 Air fry the salmon at 285°F for 10 minutes.
4 In the meantime, combine together the cream, dill, yogurt, and salt.
5 Plate up the salmon and pour the creamy sauce over it. Serve hot.

Fried Cajun Shrimp

Prep + Cook Time: 10 minutes | Servings: 4

Ingredients
1 ¼ lb. shrimp, peeled and deveined
½ tsp. old bay seasoning
¼ tsp. cayenne pepper
1 tbsp. olive oil
½ tsp. paprika
¼ tsp. salt

Instructions
1 Pre-heat the Air Fryer to 400°F.
2 Place all of the ingredients in a bowl and mix well to coat the shrimp evenly.
3 Put the seasoned shrimp in the fryer's basket and air fry for 5 minutes. Serve hot.

Grilled Salmon Fillets

Prep + Cook Time: 20 minutes | Servings: 2

Ingredients
2 salmon fillets
⅓ cup of water
⅓ cup of light soy sauce
⅓ cup sugar
2 tbsp. olive oil
Black pepper and salt to taste
Garlic powder [optional]

Instructions
1 Sprinkle some salt and pepper on top of the salmon fillets. Season with some garlic powder if desired.
2 In a medium bowl, mix together the remaining ingredients with a whisk and use this mixture to coat the salmon fillets. Leave to marinate for 2 hours.
3 Pre-heat the Air Fryer at 355°F.
4 Remove any excess liquid from the salmon fillets and transfer to the fryer. Cook for 8 minutes before serving warm.

Prawns

Prep + Cook Time: 30 minutes | Servings: 4

Ingredients
1 lb. prawns, peeled
1 lb. bacon slices

Instructions
Pre-heat the Air Fryer to 400°F.
Wrap the bacon slices around the prawns and put them in fryer's basket.
Air fry for 5 minutes and serve hot.

Chunky Fish

Prep + Cook Time: 10 minutes + chilling time | Servings: 4

Ingredients
2 cans canned fish
2 celery stalks, trimmed and finely chopped
1 egg, whisked
1 cup friendly bread crumbs
1 tsp. whole-grain mustard
½ tsp. sea salt
¼ tsp. freshly cracked black peppercorns
1 tsp. paprika

Instructions
1 Combine all of the ingredients in the order in which they appear. Mold the mixture into four equal-sized cakes. Leave to chill in the refrigerator for 50 minutes.
2 Put on an Air Fryer grill pan. Spritz all sides of each cake with cooking spray.
3 Grill at 360°F for 5 minutes. Turn the cakes over and resume cooking for an additional 3 minutes.
4 Serve with mashed potatoes if desired.

Glazed Halibut Steak

Prep + Cook Time: 70 minutes | Servings: 3

Ingredients
1 lb. halibut steak
2/3 cup low-sodium soy sauce
½ cup mirin
2 tbsp. lime juice
¼ cup sugar
¼ tsp. crushed red pepper flakes
¼ cup orange juice
1 garlic clove, smashed
¼ tsp. ginger, ground

Instructions
1 Make the teriyaki glaze by mixing together all of the ingredients except for the halibut in a saucepan.
2 Bring it to a boil and lower the heat, stirring constantly until the mixture reduces by half. Remove from the heat and leave to cool.
3 Pour half of the cooled glaze into a Ziploc bag. Add in the halibut, making sure to coat it well in the sauce. Place in the refrigerator for 30 minutes.
4 Pre-heat the Air Fryer to 390°F.
5 Put the marinated halibut in the fryer and allow to cook for 10 – 12 minutes.
6 Use any the remaining glaze to lightly brush the halibut steak with.
7 Serve with white rice or shredded vegetables.

Breadcrumbed Fish

Prep + Cook Time: 25 minutes | Servings: 2 – 4

Ingredients
4 tbsp. vegetable oil
5 oz. friendly bread crumbs
1 egg
4 medium fish fillets

Instructions
1 Pre-heat your Air Fryer to 350°F.
2 In a bowl, combine the bread crumbs and oil.
3 In a separate bowl, stir the egg with a whisk. Dredge each fish fillet in the egg before coating it in the crumbs mixture. Put them in Air Fryer basket.
4 Cook for 12 minutes and serve hot.

Cajun Lemon Salmon

Prep + Cook Time: 15 minutes | Servings: 1

Ingredients
1 salmon fillet
1 tsp. Cajun seasoning
½ lemon, juiced
¼ tsp. sugar
2 lemon wedges, for serving

Instructions
1 Pre-heat the Air Fryer to 350°F.
2 Combine the lemon juice and sugar.
3 Cover the salmon with the sugar mixture.
4 Coat the salmon with the Cajun seasoning.
5 Line the base of your fryer with a sheet of parchment paper.
6 Transfer the salmon to the fryer and allow to cook for 7 minutes.

Breaded Salmon

Prep + Cook Time: 25 minutes | Servings: 4

Ingredients
2 cups friendly bread crumbs
4 fillets of salmon
1 cup Swiss cheese, shredded
2 eggs, beaten

Instructions
1 Pre-heat your Air Fryer to 390°F.
2 Dredge the salmon fillets into the eggs. Add the Swiss cheese on top of each fillet.
3 Coat all sides of the fish with bread crumbs. Put in an oven safe dish, transfer to the fryer, and cook for 20 minutes.

Asian Style Fish

Prep + Cook Time: 35 minutes | Servings: 2

Ingredients
1 medium sea bass, halibut or fish cutlet [11 – 12 oz.]
1 tomato, cut into quarters
1 lime, cut thinly
1 stalk green onion, chopped
3 slices of ginger, julienned
2 garlic cloves, minced
1 chili, sliced
2 tbsp. cooking wine
1 tbsp. olive oil
Steamed rice [optional]

Instructions
1 Fry the ginger and garlic in the oil until they turn golden brown.
2 Pre-heat the Air Fryer to 360°F.
3 Wash and dry the fish. Halve it, ensuring each half is small enough to fit inside the fryer.
4 Put the fish in the basket of the fryer. Pour in a drizzle of the cooking wine.
5 Place the tomato and lime slices on top of the fish slices.
6 Add the garlic ginger oil mixture on top, followed by the green onion and chili slices.
7 Top with a sheet of aluminum foil. Cook for 15 minutes, or longer if necessary.
8 Serve hot with a side of steamed rice if desired.

Seafood Fritters

Prep + Cook Time: 50 minutes | Servings: 2 – 4

Ingredients
2 cups clam meat
1 cup shredded carrot
½ cup shredded zucchini
1 cup flour, combined with 3/4 cup water to make a batter
2 tbsp. olive oil
¼ tsp. pepper

Instructions
1 Pre-heat your Air Fryer to 390°F.
2 Combine the clam meat with the olive oil, shredded carrot, pepper and zucchini.
3 Using your hands, shape equal portions of the mixture into balls and roll each ball in the chickpea mixture.
4 Put the balls in the fryer and cook for 30 minutes, ensuring they turn nice and crispy before serving.

Calamari

Prep + Cook Time: 25 minutes | Servings: 2

Ingredients
1 cup club soda
½ lb. calamari tubes [or tentacles], about ¼ inch wide, rinsed and dried
½ cup honey
1 – 2 tbsp. sriracha
1 cup flour
Sea salt to taste
Red pepper and black pepper to taste
Red pepper flakes to taste

Instructions
1 In a bowl, cover the calamari rings with club soda and mix well. Leave to sit for 10 minutes.
2 In another bowl, combine the flour, salt, red and black pepper.
3 In a third bowl mix together the honey, pepper flakes, and Sriracha to create the sauce.
4 Remove any excess liquid from the calamari and coat each one with the flour mixture.
5 Spritz the fryer basket with the cooking spray.
6 Arrange the calamari in the basket, well-spaced out and in a single layer.
7 Cook at 380°F for 11 minutes, shaking the basket at least two times during the cooking time.
8 Take the calamari out of the fryer, coat it with half of the sauce and return to the fryer. Cook for an additional 2 minutes.
9 Plate up the calamari and pour the rest of the sauce over it.

Salmon & Dill Sauce

Prep + Cook Time: 45 minutes | Servings: 4

Ingredients
For the Salmon:
1 ½ lb. salmon
1 tsp. olive oil
1 pinch salt
For the Dill Sauce:
½ cup non-fat Greek yogurt
½ cup sour cream
Pinch of salt
2 tbsp. dill, finely chopped

Instructions
1 Pre-heat the Air Fryer to 270°F.
2 Slice the salmon into four 6-oz. pieces and pour a light drizzling of olive oil over each slice. Sprinkle on the salt.
3 Put the salmon in the cooking basket and allow to cook for 20 - 23 minutes.
4 Prepare the dill sauce by mixing together the yogurt, sour cream, chopped dill and salt.
5 Pour the sauce over the salmon and top with another sprinkling of chopped dill before serving.

Black Cod

Prep + Cook Time: 30 minutes | Servings: 2

Ingredients
2 [6- to 8-oz.] fillets of black cod or sablefish
Salt
Freshly ground black pepper
Olive oil
1 cup grapes, halved
1 small bulb fennel, sliced ¼-inch thick
½ cup pecans
3 cups shredded kale
2 tsp. white balsamic vinegar or white wine vinegar
2 tbsp. extra-virgin olive oil

Instructions
1 Pre-heat the Air Fryer to 400°F.
2 Sprinkle the cod fillets with salt and pepper and drizzle some olive oil over the fish.
3 Put the fish skin-side-down in the Air Fryer basket. Air fry for 10 minutes. Transfer the fillets to a side plate and loosely cover with aluminum foil.
4 Coat the grapes, fennel and pecans with a drizzle of olive oil and sprinkle on some salt and pepper.
5 Place the grapes, fennel and pecans in the fryer's basket and cook for 5 minutes at 400°F. Shake the basket occasionally throughout the cooking time.
6 Put the grapes, fennel and pecans in a bowl and add the kale.
7 Pour over the balsamic vinegar and olive oil and sprinkle with salt and pepper as desired. Serve with the fish and enjoy.

Tilapia Fillets

Prep + Cook Time: 25 minutes | Servings: 3

Ingredients
1 lb. tilapia fillets, sliced
4 wheat buns
2 egg yolks
1 tbsp. fish sauce
2 tbsp. mayonnaise
3 sweet pickle relish
1 tbsp. hot sauce
1 tbsp. nectar

Instructions
1 In a bowl, mix together the egg yolks and fish sauce.
2 Throw in the mayonnaise, sweet pickle relish, hot sauce and nectar.
3 Transfer the mixture to a round baking tray.
4 Put it in the Air Fryer and line the sides with the tilapia fillets. Cook for 15 minutes at 300°F.
5 Remove and serve on hamburger buns if desired.

Salmon Mixed Eggs

Prep + Cook Time: 25 minutes | Servings: 2

Ingredients
1 lb. salmon, cooked
2 eggs
1 onion, chopped
1 cup celery, chopped
1 tbsp. oil
Salt and pepper to taste

Instructions
1 In a bowl, mix the eggs with a whisk. Stir in the celery, onion, salt and pepper.
2 Grease a round baking tray with the oil. Transfer the egg mixture to the tray. Cook in the Air Fryer on 300°F for 10 minutes.
3 Serve with cooked salmon.

Cajun Salmon

Prep + Cook Time: 20 minutes | Servings: 1

Ingredients
1 salmon fillet
Cajun seasoning
Light sprinkle of sugar
¼ lemon, juiced, to serve

Instructions
1 Pre-heat Air Fryer to 355°F.
2 Lightly cover all sides of the salmon with Cajun seasoning. Sprinkle conservatively with sugar.
3 For a salmon fillet about three-quarters of an inch thick, cook in the fryer for 7 minutes, skin-side-up on the grill pan.
4 Serve with the lemon juice.

Fish Fingers

Prep + Cook Time: 40 minutes | Servings: 2

Ingredients
2 eggs
10 oz. fish, such as mackerel, cut into fingers
½ tsp. Turmeric Powder
½ Lemon, juiced
1 + 1 tsp. mixed dried herbs
1 + 1 tsp. Garlic Powder, separately
½ tsp. Red Chili Flakes
1 cup friendly bread crumbs
2 tbsp. Maida
3 tsp. flour

¼ tsp. baking soda
1 tsp. ginger garlic paste
½ tsp. black pepper
½ tsp. sea salt
1 – 2 tbsp. olive oil
Ketchup or tartar sauce [optional]

Instructions
1 Put the fish fingers in a bowl. Cover with 1 teaspoon of mixed herbs, 1 teaspoon of garlic powder, salt, red chili flakes, turmeric powder, black pepper, ginger garlic paste, and lemon juice. Leave to absorb for at least 10 minutes.
2 In a separate bowl, mix together the flour and baking soda. Crack the eggs in the mixture and stir again.
3 Throw in the marinated fish and set aside again for at least 10 minutes.
4 Combine the bread crumbs and the remaining teaspoon of mixed herbs and teaspoon of garlic powder.
5 Roll the fish sticks with the bread crumb and herb mixture.
6 Pre-heat the Air Fyer at 360°F.
7 Line the basket of the fryer with a sheet of aluminum foil. Place the fish fingers inside the fryer and pour over a drizzle of the olive oil.
8 Cook for 10 minutes, ensuring the fish is brown and crispy before serving. Enjoy with ketchup or tartar sauce if desired.

Mediterranean Salad

Prep + Cook Time: 15 minutes | Servings: 2

Ingredients
1 cup cooked quinoa
1 red bell pepper, chopped
2 prosciutto slices, chopped
¼ cup chopped kalamata olives
½ cup crumbled feta cheese
1 tsp. olive oil
1 tsp. dried oregano
6 cherry tomatoes, halved
Salt and pepper, to taste

Instructions
1 Pre-heat your Air Fryer to 350°F.
2 Drizzle the inside of the fryer with the olive oil. Place the red bell pepper inside and allow to cook for roughly 2 minutes. Put the prosciutto slices in the fryer and cook for an additional 3 minutes.
3 Put the ham and pepper in an oven-proof bowl and remove any excess grease. Combine with the remaining ingredients, save for the tomatoes.
4 Finally, stir in the cherry tomato halves.

Crispy Calamari

Prep + Cook Time: 15 minutes | Servings: 4

Ingredients
1 lb. fresh squid
Salt and pepper
2 cups flour
1 cup water
2 cloves garlic, minced
½ cup mayonnaise

Instructions
1. Remove the skin from the squid and discard any ink. Slice the squid into rings and season with some salt and pepper.
2. Put the flour and water in separate bowls. Dip the squid firstly in the flour, then into the water, then into the flour again, ensuring that it is entirely covered with flour.
3. Pre-heat the fryer at 400°F. Put the squid inside and cook for six minutes.
4. In the meantime, prepare the aioli by combining the garlic with the mayonnaise in a bowl.
5. Once the squid is ready, plate up and serve with the aioli.

Filipino Bistek

Prep + Cook Time: 10 minutes + marinating time | Servings: 4

Ingredients
2 milkfish bellies, deboned and sliced into 4 portions
¾ tsp. salt
¼ tsp. ground black pepper
¼ tsp. cumin powder
2 tbsp. calamansi juice
2 lemongrass, trimmed and cut crosswise into small pieces
½ cup tamari sauce
2 tbsp. fish sauce [Patis]
2 tbsp. sugar
1 tsp. garlic powder
½ cup chicken broth
2 tbsp. olive oil

Instructions
1. Dry the fish using some paper towels.
2. Put the fish in a large bowl and coat with the rest of the ingredients. Allow to marinate for 3 hours in the refrigerator.
3. Cook the fish steaks on an Air Fryer grill basket at 340°F for 5 minutes.
4. Turn the steaks over and allow to grill for an additional 4 minutes. Cook until medium brown.
5. Serve with steamed white rice.

Saltine Fish Fillets

Prep + Cook Time: 15 minutes | Servings: 4

Ingredients
1 cup crushed saltines
¼ cup extra-virgin olive oil
1 tsp. garlic powder
½ tsp. shallot powder
1 egg, well whisked
4 white fish fillets
Salt and ground black pepper to taste
Fresh Italian parsley to serve

Instructions
1. In a shallow bowl, combine the crushed saltines and olive oil.
2. In a separate bowl, mix together the garlic powder, shallot powder, and the beaten egg.
3. Sprinkle a good amount of salt and pepper over the fish, before dipping each fillet into the egg mixture.
4. Coat the fillets with the crumb mixture.
5. Air fry the fish at 370°F for 10 - 12 minutes.
6. Serve with fresh parsley.

Cod Nuggets

Prep + Cook Time: 25 minutes | Servings: 4

Ingredients
1 lb. cod fillet, cut into chunks
1 tbsp. olive oil
1 cup cracker crumbs
1 tbsp. egg and water
½ cup flour
Salt and pepper

Instructions
1. Place the cracker crumbs and oil in food processor and pulse together. Sprinkle the cod pieces with salt and pepper.
2. Roll the cod pieces in the flour before dredging them in egg and coating them in the cracker crumbs.
3. Pre-heat the Air Fryer to 350°F.
4. Put the fish in the basket and air fry to 350°F for 15 minutes or until a light golden-brown color is achieved.
5. Serve hot.

Sweet Potatoes & Salmon

Prep + Cook Time: 45 minutes | Servings: 4

Ingredients
For the Salmon Fillets:
4 x 6-oz. skin-on salmon fillets
1 tbsp. extra-virgin olive oil
1 tsp. celery salt
¼ tsp. ground black pepper, or more to taste
2 tbsp. capers
Pinch of dry mustard
Pinch of ground mace
1 tsp. smoked cayenne pepper
For the Potatoes:
4 sweet potatoes, peeled and cut into wedges
1 tbsp. sesame oil
Kosher salt and pepper, to taste

Instructions
1. Coat all sides of the salmon filets with a brushing of oil. Cover with all the seasonings for the fillets.
2. Air-fry at 360°F for 5 minutes, flip them over, and proceed to cook for 5 more minutes.
3. In the meantime, coat the sweet potatoes with the sesame oil, salt, and pepper.
4. Cook the potatoes at 380°F for 15 minutes.
5. Turn the potatoes over and cook for another 15 - 20 minutes.
6. Serve the potatoes and salmon together.

Grilled Shrimp

Prep + Cook Time: 35 minutes | Servings: 4

Ingredients
18 shrimps, shelled and deveined
2 tbsp. freshly squeezed lemon juice
½ tsp. hot paprika
½ tsp. salt
1 tsp. lemon-pepper seasoning
2 tbsp. extra-virgin olive oil
2 garlic cloves, peeled and minced
1 tsp. onion powder
¼ tsp. cumin powder
½ cup fresh parsley, coarsely chopped

Instructions
1. Put all the ingredients in a bowl, making sure to coat the shrimp well. Refrigerate for 30 minutes.
2. Pre-heat the Air Fryer at 400°F
3. Air-fry the shrimp for 5 minutes, ensuring that the shrimps turn pink.
4. Serve with pasta or rice.

Homemade Cod Fillets

Prep + Cook Time: 15 minutes | Servings: 4

Ingredients
4 cod fillets
¼ tsp. fine sea salt
¼ tsp. ground black pepper, or more to taste
1 tsp. cayenne pepper
½ cup non-dairy milk
½ cup fresh Italian parsley, coarsely chopped
1 tsp. dried basil
½ tsp. dried oregano
1 Italian pepper, chopped
4 garlic cloves, minced

Instructions
1. Lightly grease a baking dish with some vegetable oil.
2. Coat the cod fillets with salt, pepper, and cayenne pepper.
3. Blend the rest of the ingredients in a food processor. Cover the fish fillets in this mixture.
4. Transfer the fillets to the Air Fryer and cook at 380°F for 10 to 12 minutes, ensure the cod is flaky before serving.

Christmas Flounder

Prep + Cook Time: 15 minutes + marinating time | Servings: 4

Ingredients
4 flounder fillets
Sea salt and freshly cracked mixed peppercorns, to taste
1 ½ tbsp. dark sesame oil
2 tbsp. sake
¼ cup soy sauce
1 tbsp. grated lemon rind
2 garlic cloves, minced
1 tsp. sugar
Fresh chopped chives, to serve

Instructions
1. Put all of the ingredients, except for the chives, in a large bowl. Coat the fillets well with the seasoning.
2. Refrigerate for 2 hours to let it marinate.
3. Place the fish fillets in the Air Fryer cooking basket and cook at 360°F for 10 to 12 minutes, turning once during the cooking time.
4. Simmer the rest of the marinade over a medium-to-low heat, stirring constantly, allowing it to thicken.
5. Plate up the flounder and add the glaze on top. Serve with fresh chives.

Salmon Patties

Prep + Cook Time: 20 minutes | Servings: 4

Ingredients
1 egg
14 oz. canned salmon, drained
4 tbsp. flour
4 tbsp. cup cornmeal
4 tbsp. onion, minced
½ tsp. garlic powder
2 tbsp. mayonnaise
Salt and pepper to taste

Instructions
1. Flake apart the salmon with a fork.
2. Put the flakes in a bowl and combine with the garlic powder, mayonnaise, flour, cornmeal, egg, onion, pepper, and salt.
3. Use your hands to shape equal portions of the mixture into small patties and put each one in the Air Fryer basket.
4. Air fry the salmon patties at 350°F for 15 minutes. Serve hot.

Lemon Fish

Prep + Cook Time: 25 minutes | Servings: 2

Ingredients
2 tsp. green chili sauce
2 tsp. oil
2 egg white
Salt to taste
1 tsp. red chili sauce
2 – 3 lettuce leaves
4 tsp. flour
2 lemons
¼ cup sugar
4 fish fillets

Instructions
1. Slice up one of the lemons and set aside.
2. Boil a half-cup water in a saucepan. Stir in the sugar, ensuring it dissolves completely.
3. Put 1 cup of the flour, salt, green chili sauce, 2 teaspoons of oil and the egg white in a bowl and combine well.
4. Add 3 tbsp. of water and mix with a whisk until a smooth, thick consistency is achieved. Evenly spread the refined flour across a plate.
5. Dredge the fish fillets in the batter and cover with the refined flour.
6. Coat the Air Fryer's basket with a brushing of oil. Put the fish fillets in the basket and cook at 180°F for 10 – 15 minutes.
7. Add salt to the saucepan and combine well. Pour in the corn flour slurry and mix once more.
8. Add in the red chili sauce and stir.
9. Add the lemon slices. Squeeze the juice of the other

lemon into the saucepan. Continue to cook, ensuring the sauce thickens well, stirring all the time.
10. Take the fish out of the fryer, coat with a light brushing of oil and return to the fryer basket.
11. Allow to cook for 5 additional minutes.
12. Shred up the lettuce leaves with your hands and arrange them on a serving platter.
13. Serve the fish over the lettuce and with the lemon sauce drizzled on top.

Jumbo Shrimp

Prep + Cook Time: 10 minutes | Servings: 4

Ingredients
12 jumbo shrimps
½ tsp. garlic salt
¼ tsp. freshly cracked mixed peppercorns
For the Sauce:
1 tsp. Dijon mustard
4 tbsp. mayonnaise
1 tsp. lemon zest
1 tsp. chipotle powder
½ tsp. cumin powder

Instructions
1. Sprinkle the garlic salt over the shrimp and coat with the cracked peppercorns.
2. Fry the shrimp in the cooking basket at 395°F for 5 minutes.
3. Turn the shrimp over and allow to cook for a further 2 minutes.
4. In the meantime, mix together all ingredients for the sauce with a whisk.
5. Serve over the shrimp.

Cod

Prep + Cook Time: 20 minutes | Servings: 5

Ingredients
1 lb. cod
3 tbsp. milk
1 cup meal
2 cups friendly bread crumbs
2 large eggs, beaten
½ tsp. pepper
¼ tsp. salt

Instructions
1. Combine together the milk and eggs in a bowl.
2. In a shallow dish, stir together bread crumbs, pepper, and salt.
3. Pour the meal into a second shallow dish.
4. Coat the cod sticks with the meal before dipping each one in the egg and rolling in bread crumbs.
5. Put the fish sticks in the Air Fryer basket. Cook at 350°F for 12 minutes, shaking the basket halfway through cooking.

Cheese Tilapia

Prep + Cook Time: 20 minutes | Servings: 4

Ingredients
1 lb. tilapia fillets
¾ cup parmesan cheese, grated
1 tbsp. parsley, chopped
2 tsp. paprika
1 tbsp. olive oil
Pepper and salt to taste

Instructions
1.Pre-heat the Air Fryer to 400°F.
2.In a shallow dish, combine together the paprika, grated cheese, pepper, salt and parsley.
3.Pour a light drizzle of olive oil over the tilapia fillets. Cover the fillets with the paprika and cheese mixture.
4.Lay the fillets on a sheet of aluminum foil and transfer to the Air Fryer basket. Fry for 10 minutes. Serve hot.

Cheese Crust Salmon

Prep + Cook Time: 20 minutes | Servings: 5

Ingredients
2 lb. salmon fillet
2 garlic cloves, minced
¼ cup fresh parsley, chopped
½ cup parmesan cheese, grated
Salt and pepper to taste

Instructions
1.Pre-heat the Air Fryer to 350°F.
2.Lay the salmon, skin-side-down, on a sheet of aluminum foil. Place another sheet of foil on top.
3.Transfer the salmon to the fryer and cook for 10 minutes.
4.Remove the salmon from the fryer. Take off the top layer of foil and add the minced garlic, parmesan cheese, pepper, salt and parsley on top of the fish.
5.Return the salmon to the Air Fryer and resume cooking for another minute.

Parmesan Crusted Tilapia

Prep + Cook Time: 15 minutes | Servings: 4

Ingredients
¾ cup grated parmesan cheese
4 tilapia fillets
1 tbsp. olive oil
1 tbsp. chopped parsley
2 tsp. paprika
Pinch garlic powder

Instructions
1 Pre-heat your Air Fryer at 350°F.
2 Coat each of the tilapia fillets with a light brushing of olive oil.
3 Combine all of the other ingredients together in a bowl.
4 Cover the fillets with the parmesan mixture.
5 Line the base of a baking dish with a sheet of parchment paper and place the fillets in the dish.
6 Transfer to the Air Fryer and cook for 5 minutes. Serve hot.

Salmon Croquettes

Prep + Cook Time: 15 minutes | Servings: 4

Ingredients
1 lb. can red salmon, drained and mashed
⅓ cup olive oil
2 eggs, beaten
1 cup friendly bread crumbs
½ bunch parsley, chopped

Instructions
1 Pre-heat the Air Fryer to 400°F.
2 In a mixing bowl, combine together the drained salmon, eggs, and parsley.
3 In a shallow dish, stir together the bread crumbs and oil to combine well.
4 Mold equal-sized amounts of the mixture into small balls and coat each one with bread crumbs.
5 Put the croquettes in the fryer's basket and air fry for 7 minutes.

Chapter 7 Casseroles, Frittatas, and Quiches

Spinach Casserole

Prep time: 10 minutes | Cook time: 20 minutes | Serves 4

1 (13.5-ounce / 383-g) can spinach, drained and squeezed
1 cup cottage cheese
2 large eggs, beaten
¼ cup crumbled feta cheese
2 tablespoons all-purpose flour

2 tablespoons butter, melted
1 clove garlic, minced, or more to taste
1 ½ teaspoons onion powder
⅛ teaspoon ground nutmeg
Cooking spray

1. Preheat the air fryer to 375ºF (191ºC). Grease an 8-inch pie pan with cooking spray and set aside.
2. Combine spinach, cottage cheese, eggs, feta cheese, flour, butter, garlic, onion powder, and nutmeg in a bowl. Stir until all ingredients are well incorporated. Pour into the prepared pie pan.
3. Air fry until the center is set, 18 to 20 minutes.
4. Serve warm.

Creamy Tomato Casserole

Prep time: 5 minutes | Cook time: 30 minutes | Serves 4

5 eggs
2 tablespoons heavy cream
3 tablespoons chunky tomato

sauce
2 tablespoons grated Parmesan cheese, plus more for topping

1. Preheat the air fryer to 350ºF (177ºC).
2. Combine the eggs and cream in a bowl.
3. Mix in the tomato sauce and add the cheese.
4. Spread into a glass baking dish and bake in the preheated air fryer for 30 minutes.
5. Top with extra cheese and serve.

Cheesy Bacon Quiche

Prep time: 15 minutes | Cook time: 20 minutes | Serves 4

1 tablespoon olive oil
1 shortcrust pastry
3 tablespoons Greek yogurt
½ cup grated Cheddar cheese
3 ounces (85 g) chopped bacon

4 eggs, beaten
¼ teaspoon garlic powder
Pinch of black pepper
¼ teaspoon onion powder
¼ teaspoon sea salt
Flour, for sprinkling

1. Preheat the air fryer to 330ºF (166ºC).
2. Take 8 ramekins and grease with olive oil. Coat with a sprinkling of flour, tapping to remove any excess.
3. Cut the shortcrust pastry in 8 and place each piece at the bottom of each ramekin.
4. Put all the other ingredients in a bowl and combine well. Spoon equal amounts of the filling into each piece of pastry.
5. Bake the ramekins in the air fryer for 20 minutes.
6. Serve warm.

Easy Mac & Cheese

Prep time: 10 minutes | Cook time: 10 minutes | Serves 2

1 cup cooked macaroni
1 cup grated Cheddar cheese
½ cup warm milk

Salt and ground black pepper, to taste
1 tablespoon grated Parmesan cheese

1. Preheat the air fryer to 350ºF (177ºC).
2. In a baking dish, mix all the ingredients, except for Parmesan.
3. Put the dish inside the air fryer and bake for 10 minutes.
4. Add the Parmesan cheese on top and serve.

Chicken and Mushroom Casserole

Prep time: 15 minutes | Cook time: 20 minutes | Serves 4

4 chicken breasts
1 tablespoon curry powder
1 cup coconut milk
Salt, to taste
1 broccoli, cut into florets
1 cup mushrooms
½ cup shredded Parmesan cheese
Cooking spray

1. Preheat the air fryer to 350ºF (177ºC). Spritz a casserole dish with cooking spray.
2. Cube the chicken breasts and combine with curry powder and coconut milk in a bowl. Season with salt.
3. Add the broccoli and mushroom and mix well.
4. Pour the mixture into the casserole dish. Top with the cheese.
5. Transfer to the air fryer and bake for about 20 minutes.
6. Serve warm.

Western Prosciutto Casserole

Prep time: 5 minutes | Cook time: 10 minutes | Serves 2

1 cup day-old whole grain bread, cubed
3 large eggs, beaten
2 tablespoons water
⅛ teaspoon kosher salt
1 ounce (28 g) prosciutto, roughly chopped
1 ounce (28 g) Pepper Jack cheese, roughly chopped
1 tablespoon chopped fresh chives
Nonstick cooking spray

1. Preheat the air fryer to 360ºF (182ºC).
2. Spray a baking pan with nonstick cooking spray, then place the bread cubes in the pan. Transfer the baking pan to the air fryer.
3. In a medium bowl, stir together the beaten eggs and water, then stir in the kosher salt, prosciutto, cheese, and chives.
4. Pour the egg mixture over the bread cubes and bake for 10 minutes, or until the eggs are set and the top is golden brown.
5. Serve warm.

Mini Quiche Cups

Prep time: 15 minutes | Cook time: 16 minutes | Makes 10 quiche cups

4 ounces (113 g) ground pork sausage
3 eggs
¾ cup milk
Cooking spray
4 ounces (113 g) sharp Cheddar cheese, grated

Special Equipment:
20 foil muffin cups

1. Preheat the air fryer to 390ºF (199ºC). Spritz the air fryer basket with cooking spray.
2. Divide sausage into 3 portions and shape each into a thin patty.
3. Put patties in air fryer basket and air fry for 6 minutes.
4. While sausage is cooking, prepare the egg mixture. Combine the eggs and milk in a large bowl and whisk until well blended. Set aside.
5. When sausage has cooked fully, remove patties from the basket, drain well, and use a fork to crumble the meat into small pieces.
6. Double the foil cups into 10 sets. Remove paper liners from the top muffin cups and spray the foil cups lightly with cooking spray.
7. Divide crumbled sausage among the 10 muffin cup sets.
8. Top each with grated cheese, divided evenly among the cups.
9. Put 5 cups in air fryer basket.
10. Pour egg mixture into each cup, filling until each cup is at least ²/₃ full.
11. Bake for 8 minutes and test for doneness. A knife inserted into the center shouldn't have any raw egg on it when removed.
12. Repeat steps 8 through 11 for the remaining quiches.
13. Serve warm.

Shrimp Quiche

Prep time: 15 minutes | Cook time: 20 minutes | Serves 2

2 teaspoons vegetable oil
4 large eggs
½ cup half-and-half
4 ounces (113 g) raw shrimp, chopped
1 cup shredded Parmesan or Swiss cheese
¼ cup chopped

scallions
1 teaspoon sweet smoked paprika
1 teaspoon herbes de Provence
1 teaspoon black pepper
½ to 1 teaspoon kosher salt

1. Preheat the air fryer to 300ºF (149ºC). Generously grease a round baking pan with 4-inch sides with vegetable oil.
2. In a large bowl, beat together the eggs and half-and-half. Add the shrimp, ¾ cup of the cheese, the scallions, paprika, herbes de Provence, pepper, and salt. Stir with a fork to thoroughly combine. Pour the egg mixture into the prepared pan.
3. Put the pan in the air fryer basket and bake for 20 minutes. After 17 minutes, sprinkle the remaining ¼ cup cheese on top and bake for the remaining 3 minutes, or until the cheese has melted, the eggs are set, and a toothpick inserted into the center comes out clean.
4. Serve the quiche warm.

Ritzy Vegetable Frittata

Prep time: 15 minutes | Cook time: 21 minutes | Serves 2

4 eggs
¼ cup milk
Sea salt and ground black pepper, to taste
1 zucchini, sliced
½ bunch asparagus, sliced
½ cup mushrooms, sliced
½ cup spinach, shredded

½ cup red onion, sliced
½ tablespoon olive oil
5 tablespoons feta cheese, crumbled
4 tablespoons Cheddar cheese, grated
¼ bunch chives, minced

1. In a bowl, mix the eggs, milk, salt and pepper.
2. Over a medium heat, sauté the vegetables for 6 minutes with the olive oil in a nonstick pan.
3. Put some parchment paper in the base of a baking tin. Pour in the vegetables, followed by the egg mixture. Top with the feta and grated Cheddar.
4. Preheat the air fryer to 320ºF (160ºC).
5. Transfer the baking tin to the air fryer and bake for 15 minutes. Remove the frittata from the air fryer and leave to cool for 5 minutes.
6. Top with the minced chives and serve.

Shrimp Green Casserole

Prep time: 15 minutes | Cook time: 22 minutes | Serves 4

1 pound (454 g) shrimp, cleaned and deveined
2 cups cauliflower, cut into florets
2 green bell pepper,

sliced
1 shallot, sliced
2 tablespoons sesame oil
1 cup tomato paste
Cooking spray

1. Preheat the air fryer to 360ºF (182ºC). Spritz a baking pan with cooking spray.
2. Arrange the shrimp and vegetables in the baking pan. Then, drizzle the sesame oil over the vegetables. Pour the tomato paste over the vegetables.
3. Bake for 10 minutes in the preheated air fryer. Stir with a large spoon and bake for a further 12 minutes.
4. Serve warm.

Chapter 8 Desserts

Simple Apple Turnovers

Prep time: 10 minutes | Cook time: 10 minutes | Serves 4

1 apple, peeled, quartered, and thinly sliced
½ teaspoons pumpkin pie spice
Juice of ½ lemon
1 tablespoon granulated sugar
Pinch of kosher salt
6 sheets phyllo dough

1. Preheat the air fryer to 330°F (166°C).
2. In a medium bowl, combine the apple, pumpkin pie spice, lemon juice, granulated sugar, and kosher salt.
3. Cut the phyllo dough sheets into 4 equal pieces and place individual tablespoons of apple filling in the center of each piece, then fold in both sides and roll from front to back.
4. Spray the air fryer basket with nonstick cooking spray, then place the turnovers in the basket and bake for 10 minutes or until golden brown.
5. Remove the turnovers from the air fryer and allow to cool on a wire rack for 10 minutes before serving.

Cinnamon Almonds

Prep time: 5 minutes | Cook time: 8 minutes | Serves 4

1 cup whole almonds
2 tablespoons salted butter, melted
1 tablespoon sugar
½ teaspoon ground cinnamon

1. Preheat the air fryer to 300°F (149°C).
2. In a medium bowl, combine the almonds, butter, sugar, and cinnamon. Mix well to ensure all the almonds are coated with the spiced butter.
3. Transfer the almonds to the air fryer basket and shake so they are in a single layer. Bake for 8 minutes, stirring the almonds halfway through the cooking time.
4. Let cool completely before serving.

Oatmeal Raisin Bars

Prep time: 15 minutes | Cook time: 15 minutes | Serves 8

$1/_3$ cup all-purpose flour
¼ teaspoon kosher salt
¼ teaspoon baking powder
¼ teaspoon ground cinnamon
¼ cup light brown sugar, lightly packed
¼ cup granulated sugar
½ cup canola oil
1 large egg
1 teaspoon vanilla extract
$1 1/_3$ cups quick-cooking oats
$1/_3$ cup raisins

1. Preheat the air fryer to 360°F (182°C).
2. In a large bowl, combine the all-purpose flour, kosher salt, baking powder, ground cinnamon, light brown sugar, granulated sugar, canola oil, egg, vanilla extract, quick-cooking oats, and raisins.
3. Spray a baking pan with nonstick cooking spray, then pour the oat mixture into the pan and press down to evenly distribute. Place the pan in the air fryer and bake for 15 minutes or until golden brown.
4. Remove from the air fryer and allow to cool in the pan on a wire rack for 20 minutes before slicing and serving.

Pumpkin Pudding

Prep time: 10 minutes | Cook time: 15 minutes | Serves 4

3 cups pumpkin purée
3 tablespoons honey
1 tablespoon ginger
1 tablespoon cinnamon
1 teaspoon clove
1 teaspoon nutmeg
1 cup full-fat cream
2 eggs
1 cup sugar

1. Preheat the air fryer to 390°F (199°C).
2. In a bowl, stir all the ingredients together to combine.
3. Scrape the mixture into the a greased dish and transfer to the air fryer. Bake for 15 minutes. Serve warm.

Bourbon Bread Pudding

Prep time: 10 minutes | Cook time: 20 minutes | Serves 4

3 slices whole grain bread, cubed
1 large egg
1 cup whole milk
2 tablespoons bourbon
½ teaspoons vanilla extract
¼ cup maple syrup, divided
½ teaspoons ground cinnamon
2 teaspoons sparkling sugar

1. Preheat the air fryer to 270ºF (132ºC).
2. Spray a baking pan with nonstick cooking spray, then place the bread cubes in the pan.
3. In a medium bowl, whisk together the egg, milk, bourbon, vanilla extract, 3 tablespoons of maple syrup, and cinnamon. Pour the egg mixture over the bread and press down with a spatula to coat all the bread, then sprinkle the sparkling sugar on top and bake for 20 minutes.
4. Remove the pudding from the air fryer and allow to cool in the pan on a wire rack for 10 minutes. Drizzle the remaining 1 tablespoon of maple syrup on top. Slice and serve warm.

Apple, Peach, and Cranberry Crisp

Prep time: 10 minutes | Cook time: 12 minutes | Serves 8

1 apple, peeled and chopped
2 peaches, peeled and chopped
1/3 cup dried cranberries
2 tablespoons honey
1/3 cup brown sugar
¼ cup flour
½ cup oatmeal
3 tablespoons softened butter

1. Preheat the air fryer to 370ºF (188ºC).
2. In a baking pan, combine the apple, peaches, cranberries, and honey, and mix well.
3. In a medium bowl, combine the brown sugar, flour, oatmeal, and butter, and mix until crumbly. Sprinkle this mixture over the fruit in the pan.
4. Bake for 10 to 12 minutes or until the fruit is bubbly and the topping is golden brown. Serve warm.

Brazilian Pineapple Bake

Prep time: 5 minutes | Cook time: 16 minutes | Serves 4

½ cup brown sugar
2 teaspoons ground cinnamon
1 small pineapple, peeled, cored, and
cut into spears
3 tablespoons unsalted butter, melted

1. Preheat the air fryer to 400ºF (204ºC).
2. In a small bowl, mix the brown sugar and cinnamon until thoroughly combined.
3. Brush the pineapple spears with the melted butter. Sprinkle the cinnamon-sugar over the spears, pressing lightly to ensure it adheres well.
4. Put the spears in the air fryer basket in a single layer. (Depending on the size of the air fryer, you may have to do this in batches.) Bake for 10 minutes for the first batch (6 to 8 minutes for the next batch, as the air fryer will be preheated). Halfway through the cooking time, brush the spears with butter.
5. The pineapple spears are done when they are heated through and the sugar is bubbling. Serve hot.

Jelly Doughnuts

Prep time: 5 minutes | Cook time: 5 minutes | Serves 8

1 (16.3-ounce / 462-g) package large refrigerator biscuits
Cooking spray
1¼ cups good-quality raspberry jam
Confectioners' sugar, for dusting

1. Preheat the air fryer to 350ºF (177ºC).
2. Separate biscuits into 8 rounds. Spray both sides of rounds lightly with oil.
3. Spray the basket with oil and place 3 to 4 rounds in the basket. Air fry for 5 minutes, or until golden brown. Transfer to a wire rack; let cool. Repeat with the remaining rounds.
4. Fill a pastry bag, fitted with small plain tip, with raspberry jam; use tip to poke a small hole in the side of each doughnut, then fill the centers with the jam. Dust doughnuts with confectioners' sugar.
5. Serve immediately.

Applesauce and Chocolate Brownies

Prep time: 10 minutes | Cook time: 15 minutes | Serves 8

¼ cup unsweetened cocoa powder
¼ cup all-purpose flour
¼ teaspoon kosher salt
½ teaspoons baking powder
3 tablespoons unsalted butter, melted

½ cup granulated sugar
1 large egg
3 tablespoons unsweetened applesauce
¼ cup miniature semisweet chocolate chips
Coarse sea salt, to taste

1. Preheat the air fryer to 300ºF (149ºC).
2. In a large bowl, whisk together the cocoa powder, all-purpose flour, kosher salt, and baking powder.
3. In a separate large bowl, combine the butter, granulated sugar, egg, and applesauce, then use a spatula to fold in the cocoa powder mixture and the chocolate chips until well combined.
4. Spray a baking pan with nonstick cooking spray, then pour the mixture into the pan. Place the pan in the air fryer and bake for 15 minutes or until a toothpick comes out clean when inserted in the middle.
5. Remove the brownies from the air fryer, sprinkle some coarse sea salt on top, and allow to cool in the pan on a wire rack for 20 minutes before cutting and serving.

Pineapple Galette

Prep time: 10 minutes | Cook time: 40 minutes | Serves 2

¼ medium-size pineapple, peeled, cored, and cut crosswise into ¼-inch-thick slices
2 tablespoons dark rum
1 teaspoon vanilla extract
½ teaspoon kosher salt
Finely grated zest of

½ lime
1 store-bought sheet puff pastry, cut into an 8-inch round
3 tablespoons granulated sugar
2 tablespoons unsalted butter, cubed and chilled
Coconut ice cream, for serving

1. Preheat the air fryer to 310ºF (154ºC).
2. In a small bowl, combine the pineapple slices, rum, vanilla, salt, and lime zest and let stand for at least 10 minutes to allow the pineapple to soak in the rum.
3. Meanwhile, press the puff pastry round into the bottom and up the sides of a round metal cake pan and use the tines of a fork to dock the bottom and sides.
4. Arrange the pineapple slices on the bottom of the pastry in more or less a single layer, then sprinkle with the sugar and dot with the butter. Drizzle with the leftover juices from the bowl. Put the pan in the air fryer and bake until the pastry is puffed and golden brown and the pineapple is lightly caramelized on top, about 40 minutes.
5. Transfer the pan to a wire rack to cool for 15 minutes. Unmold the galette from the pan and serve warm with coconut ice cream.

Easy Almond Shortbread

Prep time: 5 minutes | Cook time: 12 minutes | Serves 8

½ cup (1 stick) unsalted butter
½ cup sugar
1 teaspoon pure

almond extract
1 cup all-purpose flour

1. Preheat the air fryer to 375ºF (191ºC).
2. In a bowl of a stand mixer fitted with the paddle attachment, beat the butter and sugar on medium speed until fluffy, 3 to 4 minutes. Add the almond extract and beat until combined, about 30 seconds. Turn the mixer to low. Add the flour a little at a time and beat for about 2 minutes more until well incorporated.
3. Pat the dough into an even layer in a round baking pan. Put the pan in the air fryer basket and bake for 12 minutes.
4. Carefully remove the pan from air fryer basket. While the shortbread is still warm and soft, cut it into 8 wedges.
5. Let cool in the pan on a wire rack for 5 minutes. Remove the wedges from the pan and let cool on the rack before serving.

Lemony Apple Butter

Prep time: 10 minutes | Cook time: 1 hour | Makes 1¼ cups

Cooking spray
2 cups unsweetened applesauce
⅔ cup packed light brown sugar
3 tablespoons fresh lemon juice
½ teaspoon kosher salt
¼ teaspoon ground cinnamon
⅛ teaspoon ground allspice

1. Preheat the air fryer to 340ºF (171ºC).
2. Spray a metal cake pan with cooking spray. Whisk together all the ingredients in a bowl until smooth, then pour into the greased pan. Set the pan in the air fryer and bake until the apple mixture is caramelized, reduced to a thick purée, and fragrant, about 1 hour.
3. Remove the pan from the air fryer, stir to combine the caramelized bits at the edge with the rest, then let cool completely to thicken.
4. Serve immediately.

Ricotta Lemon Poppy Seed Cake

Prep time: 15 minutes | Cook time: 55 minutes | Serves 4

Unsalted butter, at room temperature
1 cup almond flour
½ cup sugar
3 large eggs
¼ cup heavy cream
¼ cup full-fat ricotta cheese
¼ cup coconut oil, melted
2 tablespoons poppy seeds
1 teaspoon baking powder
1 teaspoon pure lemon extract
Grated zest and juice of 1 lemon, plus more zest for garnish

1. Preheat the air fryer to 325ºF (163ºC).
2. Generously butter a round baking pan. Line the bottom of the pan with parchment paper cut to fit.
3. In a large bowl, combine the almond flour, sugar, eggs, cream, ricotta, coconut oil, poppy seeds, baking powder, lemon extract, lemon zest, and lemon juice. Beat with a hand mixer on medium speed until well blended and fluffy.

4. Pour the batter into the prepared pan. Cover the pan tightly with aluminum foil. Set the pan in the air fryer basket and bake for 45 minutes. Remove the foil and bake for 10 to 15 minutes more until a knife (do not use a toothpick) inserted into the center of the cake comes out clean.
5. Let the cake cool in the pan on a wire rack for 10 minutes. Remove the cake from pan and let it cool on the rack for 15 minutes before slicing.
6. Top with additional lemon zest, slice and serve.

Chocolate Cake

Prep time: 10 minutes | Cook time: 55 minutes | Serves 4

Unsalted butter, at room temperature
3 large eggs
1 cup almond flour
⅔ cup sugar
⅓ cup heavy cream
¼ cup coconut oil,
melted
¼ cup unsweetened cocoa powder
1 teaspoon baking powder
¼ cup chopped walnuts

1. Preheat the air fryer to 400ºF (204ºC).
2. Generously butter a round baking pan. Line the bottom of the pan with parchment paper cut to fit.
3. In a large bowl, combine the eggs, almond flour, sugar, cream, coconut oil, cocoa powder, and baking powder. Beat with a hand mixer on medium speed until well blended and fluffy. (This will keep the cake from being too dense, as almond flour cakes can sometimes be.) Fold in the walnuts.
4. Pour the batter into the prepared pan. Cover the pan tightly with aluminum foil. Set the pan in the air fryer basket and bake for 45 minutes. Remove the foil and bake for 10 to 15 minutes more until a knife (do not use a toothpick) inserted into the center of the cake comes out clean.
5. Let the cake cool in the pan on a wire rack for 10 minutes. Remove the cake from the pan and let cool on the rack for 20 minutes before slicing and serving.

Chickpea Brownies

Prep time: 10 minutes | Cook time: 20 minutes | Serves 6

Vegetable oil
1 (15-ounce / 425-g) can chickpeas, drained and rinsed
4 large eggs
1/3 cup coconut oil, melted
1/3 cup honey
3 tablespoons unsweetened cocoa powder
1 tablespoon espresso powder (optional)
1 teaspoon baking powder
1 teaspoon baking soda
1/2 cup chocolate chips

1. Preheat the air fryer to 325ºF (163ºC).
2. Generously grease a baking pan with vegetable oil.
3. In a blender or food processor, combine the chickpeas, eggs, coconut oil, honey, cocoa powder, espresso powder (if using), baking powder, and baking soda. Blend or process until smooth. Transfer to the prepared pan and stir in the chocolate chips by hand.
4. Set the pan in the air fryer basket and bake for 20 minutes, or until a toothpick inserted into the center comes out clean.
5. Let cool in the pan on a wire rack for 30 minutes before cutting into squares.
6. Serve immediately.

Chocolate Molten Cake

Prep time: 5 minutes | Cook time: 10 minutes | Serves 4

3.5 ounces (99 g) butter, melted
3½ tablespoons sugar
3.5 ounces (99 g) chocolate, melted
1½ tablespoons flour
2 eggs

1. Preheat the air fryer to 375ºF (191ºC).
2. Grease four ramekins with a little butter.
3. Rigorously combine the eggs, butter, and sugar before stirring in the melted chocolate.
4. Slowly fold in the flour.
5. Spoon an equal amount of the mixture into each ramekin.
6. Put them in the air fryer and bake for 10 minutes
7. Put the ramekins upside-down on plates and let the cakes fall out. Serve hot.

Simple Pineapple Sticks

Prep time: 5 minutes | Cook time: 10 minutes | Serves 4

½ fresh pineapple, cut into sticks
¼ cup desiccated coconut

1. Preheat the air fryer to 400ºF (204ºC).
2. Coat the pineapple sticks in the desiccated coconut and put each one in the air fryer basket.
3. Air fry for 10 minutes.
4. Serve immediately

Spice Cookies

Prep time: 15 minutes | Cook time: 12 minutes | Serves 4

4 tablespoons (½ stick) unsalted butter, at room temperature
2 tablespoons agave nectar
1 large egg
2 tablespoons water
2½ cups almond flour
½ cup sugar
2 teaspoons ground ginger
1 teaspoon ground cinnamon
½ teaspoon freshly grated nutmeg
1 teaspoon baking soda
¼ teaspoon kosher salt

1. Preheat the air fryer to 325ºF (163ºC).
2. Line the bottom of the air fryer basket with parchment paper cut to fit.
3. In a large bowl using a hand mixer, beat together the butter, agave, egg, and water on medium speed until fluffy.
4. Add the almond flour, sugar, ginger, cinnamon, nutmeg, baking soda, and salt. Beat on low speed until well combined.
5. Roll the dough into 2-tablespoon balls and arrange them on the parchment paper in the basket. (They don't really spread too much, but try to leave a little room between them.) Bake for 12 minutes, or until the tops of cookies are lightly browned.
6. Transfer to a wire rack and let cool completely.
7. Serve immediately

Baked Apples

Prep time: 5 minutes | Cook time: 10 minutes | Serves 4

4 small apples, cored and cut in half
2 tablespoons salted butter or coconut oil, melted
2 tablespoons sugar
1 teaspoon apple pie spice
Ice cream, heavy cream, or whipped cream, for serving

1. Preheat the air fryer to 350ºF (177ºC).
2. Put the apples in a large bowl. Drizzle with the melted butter and sprinkle with the sugar and apple pie spice. Use the hands to toss, ensuring the apples are evenly coated.
3. Put the apples in the air fryer basket and bake for 10 minutes. Pierce the apples with a fork to ensure they are tender.
4. Serve with ice cream, or top with a splash of heavy cream or a spoonful of whipped cream.

Pecan and Cherry Stuffed Apples

Prep time: 10 minutes | Cook time: 20 minutes | Serves 4

4 apples (about 1¼ pounds / 567 g)
¼ cup chopped pecans
1/3 cup dried tart cherries
1 tablespoon melted
butter
3 tablespoons brown sugar
¼ teaspoon allspice
Pinch salt
Ice cream, for serving

1. Cut off top ½ inch from each apple; reserve tops. With a melon baller, core through stem ends without breaking through the bottom. (Do not trim bases.)
2. Preheat the air fryer to 350ºF (177ºC). Combine pecans, cherries, butter, brown sugar, allspice, and a pinch of salt. Stuff mixture into the hollow centers of the apples. Cover with apple tops. Put in the air fryer basket, using tongs. Air fry for 20 to 25 minutes, or just until tender.
3. Serve warm with ice cream.

Berry Crumble

Prep time: 10 minutes | Cook time: 15 minutes | Serves 4

For the Filling:
2 cups mixed berries
2 tablespoons sugar
1 tablespoon
cornstarch
1 tablespoon fresh lemon juice

For the Topping:
¼ cup all-purpose flour
¼ cup rolled oats
1 tablespoon sugar
2 tablespoons cold
unsalted butter, cut into small cubes
Whipped cream or ice cream (optional)

1. Preheat the air fryer to 400ºF (204ºC).
2. For the filling: In a round baking pan, gently mix the berries, sugar, cornstarch, and lemon juice until thoroughly combined.
3. For the topping: In a small bowl, combine the flour, oats, and sugar. Stir the butter into the flour mixture until the mixture has the consistency of bread crumbs.
4. Sprinkle the topping over the berries.
5. Put the pan in the air fryer basket and air fry for 15 minutes. Let cool for 5 minutes on a wire rack.
6. Serve topped with whipped cream or ice cream, if desired.

Chocolate Croissants

Prep time: 5 minutes | Cook time: 24 minutes | Serves 8

1 sheet frozen puff pastry, thawed
1/3 cup chocolate-
hazelnut spread
1 large egg, beaten

1. On a lightly floured surface, roll puff pastry into a 14-inch square. Cut pastry into quarters to form 4 squares. Cut each square diagonally to form 8 triangles.
2. Spread 2 teaspoons chocolate-hazelnut spread on each triangle; from wider end, roll up pastry. Brush egg on top of each roll.
3. Preheat the air fryer to 375ºF (191ºC). Air fry rolls in batches, 3 or 4 at a time, 8 minutes per batch, or until pastry is golden brown.
4. Cool on a wire rack; serve while warm or at room temperature.

Lemony Blackberry Crisp

Prep time: 5 minutes | Cook time: 20 minutes | Serves 1

2 tablespoons lemon juice
1/3 cup powdered erythritol
1/4 teaspoon
xantham gum
2 cup blackberries
1 cup crunchy granola

1. Preheat the air fryer to 350°F (177°C).
2. In a bowl, combine the lemon juice, erythritol, xantham gum, and blackberries. Transfer to a round baking dish and cover with aluminum foil.
3. Put the dish in the air fryer and bake for 12 minutes.
4. Take care when removing the dish from the air fryer. Give the blackberries a stir and top with the granola.
5. Return the dish to the air fryer and bake for an additional 3 minutes, this time at 320°F (160°C). Serve once the granola has turned brown and enjoy.

Cardamom and Vanilla Custard

Prep time: 5 minutes | Cook time: 25 minutes | Serves 2

1 cup whole milk
1 large egg
2 tablespoons plus 1 teaspoon sugar
1/4 teaspoon vanilla
bean paste or pure vanilla extract
1/4 teaspoon ground cardamom, plus more for sprinkling

1. Preheat the air fryer to 350°F (177°C).
2. In a medium bowl, beat together the milk, egg, sugar, vanilla, and cardamom.
3. Put two ramekins in the air fryer basket. Divide the mixture between the ramekins. Sprinkle lightly with cardamom. Cover each ramekin tightly with aluminum foil. Bake for 25 minutes, or until a toothpick inserted in the center comes out clean.
4. Let the custards cool on a wire rack for 5 to 10 minutes.
5. Serve warm, or refrigerate until cold and serve chilled.

Chocolate and Peanut Butter Lava Cupcakes

Prep time: 10 minutes | Cook time: 10 to 13 minutes | Serves 8

Nonstick baking spray with flour
1 1/3 cups chocolate cake mix
1 egg
1 egg yolk
1/4 cup safflower oil
1/4 cup hot water
1/3 cup sour cream
3 tablespoons peanut butter
1 tablespoon powdered sugar

1. Preheat the air fryer to 350°F (177°C).
2. Double up 16 foil muffin cups to make 8 cups. Spray each lightly with nonstick spray; set aside.
3. In a medium bowl, combine the cake mix, egg, egg yolk, safflower oil, water, and sour cream, and beat until combined.
4. In a small bowl, combine the peanut butter and powdered sugar and mix well. Form this mixture into 8 balls.
5. Spoon about 1/4 cup of the chocolate batter into each muffin cup and top with a peanut butter ball. Spoon remaining batter on top of the peanut butter balls to cover them.
6. Arrange the cups in the air fryer basket, leaving some space between each. Bake for 10 to 13 minutes or until the tops look dry and set.
7. Let the cupcakes cool for about 10 minutes, then serve warm.

Honey-Roasted Pears

Prep time: 5 minutes | Cook time: 20 minutes | Serves 4

2 large Bosc pears, halved and deseeded
3 tablespoons honey
1 tablespoon unsalted butter
½ teaspoon ground

cinnamon
¼ cup walnuts, chopped
¼ cup part skim low-fat ricotta cheese, divided

1. Preheat the air fryer to 350ºF (177ºC).
2. In a baking pan, place the pears, cut side up.
3. In a small microwave-safe bowl, melt the honey, butter, and cinnamon. Brush this mixture over the cut sides of the pears.
4. Pour 3 tablespoons of water around the pears in the pan. Roast the pears for 20 minutes, or until tender when pierced with a fork and slightly crisp on the edges, basting once with the liquid in the pan.
5. Carefully remove the pears from the pan and place on a serving plate. Drizzle each with some liquid from the pan, sprinkle the walnuts on top, and serve with a spoonful of ricotta cheese.

Oatmeal and Carrot Cookie Cups

Prep time: 10 minutes | Cook time: 8 minutes | Makes 16 cups

3 tablespoons unsalted butter, at room temperature
¼ cup packed brown sugar
1 tablespoon honey
1 egg white
½ teaspoon vanilla extract

$1/_3$ cup finely grated carrot
½ cup quick-cooking oatmeal
$1/_3$ cup whole-wheat pastry flour
½ teaspoon baking soda
¼ cup dried cherries

1. Preheat the air fryer to 350ºF (177ºC)
2. In a medium bowl, beat the butter, brown sugar, and honey until well combined.
3. Add the egg white, vanilla, and carrot. Beat to combine.
4. Stir in the oatmeal, pastry flour, and baking soda.
5. Stir in the dried cherries.

6. Double up 32 mini muffin foil cups to make 16 cups. Fill each with about 4 teaspoons of dough. Bake the cookie cups, 8 at a time, for 8 minutes, or until light golden brown and just set. Serve warm.

Rich Chocolate Cookie

Prep time: 10 minutes | Cook time: 9 minutes | Serves 4

Nonstick baking spray with flour
3 tablespoons softened butter
$1/_3$ cup plus 1 tablespoon brown sugar
1 egg yolk
½ cup flour

2 tablespoons ground white chocolate
¼ teaspoon baking soda
½ teaspoon vanilla
¾ cup chocolate chips

1. Preheat the air fryer to 350ºF (177ºC).
2. In a medium bowl, beat the butter and brown sugar together until fluffy. Stir in the egg yolk.
3. Add the flour, white chocolate, baking soda, and vanilla, and mix well. Stir in the chocolate chips.
4. Line a baking pan with parchment paper. Spray the parchment paper with nonstick baking spray with flour.
5. Spread the batter into the prepared pan, leaving a ½-inch border on all sides.
6. Bake for about 9 minutes or until the cookie is light brown and just barely set.
7. Remove the pan from the air fryer and let cool for 10 minutes. Remove the cookie from the pan, remove the parchment paper, and let cool on a wire rack.
8. Serve immediately.

Curry Peaches, Pears, and Plums

Prep time: 5 minutes | Cook time: 5 minutes | Serves 6 to 8

2 peaches
2 firm pears
2 plums
2 tablespoons

melted butter
1 tablespoon honey
2 to 3 teaspoons
curry powder

1. Preheat the air fryer to 325ºF (163ºC).
2. Cut the peaches in half, remove the pits, and cut each half in half again. Cut the pears in half, core them, and remove the stem. Cut each half in half again. Do the same with the plums.
3. Spread a large sheet of heavy-duty foil on the work surface. Arrange the fruit on the foil and drizzle with the butter and honey. Sprinkle with the curry powder.
4. Wrap the fruit in the foil, making sure to leave some air space in the packet.
5. Put the foil package in the basket and bake for 5 to 8 minutes, shaking the basket once during the cooking time, until the fruit is soft.
6. Serve immediately.

Orange Cake

Prep time: 10 minutes | Cook time: 23 minutes | Serves 8

Nonstick baking
spray with flour
1¼ cups all-purpose
flour
$^1/_3$ cup yellow
cornmeal
¾ cup white sugar
1 teaspoon baking

soda
¼ cup safflower oil
1¼ cups orange
juice, divided
1 teaspoon vanilla
¼ cup powdered
sugar

1. Preheat the air fryer to 350ºF (177ºC).
2. Spray a baking pan with nonstick spray and set aside.
3. In a medium bowl, combine the flour, cornmeal, sugar, baking soda, safflower oil, 1 cup of the orange juice, and vanilla, and mix well.
4. Pour the batter into the baking pan and place in the air fryer. Bake for 23 minutes or until a toothpick inserted in the center of the cake comes out clean.

5. Remove the cake from the basket and place on a cooling rack. Using a toothpick, make about 20 holes in the cake.
6. In a small bowl, combine remaining ¼ cup of orange juice and the powdered sugar and stir well. Drizzle this mixture over the hot cake slowly so the cake absorbs it.
7. Cool completely, then cut into wedges to serve.

Graham Cracker Cheesecake

Prep time: 10 minutes | Cook time: 20 minutes | Serves 8

1 cup graham
cracker crumbs
3 tablespoons
softened butter
1½ (8-ounce / 227-
g) packages cream
cheese, softened

$^1/_3$ cup sugar
2 eggs
1 tablespoon flour
1 teaspoon vanilla
¼ cup chocolate
syrup

1. For the crust, combine the graham cracker crumbs and butter in a small bowl and mix well. Press into the bottom of a baking pan and put in the freezer to set.
2. For the filling, combine the cream cheese and sugar in a medium bowl and mix well. Beat in the eggs, one at a time. Add the flour and vanilla.
3. Preheat the air fryer to 450ºF (232ºC).
4. Remove $^2/_3$ cup of the filling to a small bowl and stir in the chocolate syrup until combined.
5. Pour the vanilla filling into the pan with the crust. Drop the chocolate filling over the vanilla filling by the spoonful. With a clean butter knife, stir the fillings in a zigzag pattern to marbleize them.
6. Bake for 20 minutes or until the cheesecake is just set.
7. Cool on a wire rack for 1 hour, then chill in the refrigerator until the cheesecake is firm.
8. Serve immediately.

Banana and Walnut Cake

Prep time: 10 minutes | Cook time: 25 minutes | Serves 6

1 pound (454 g) bananas, mashed
8 ounces (227 g) flour
6 ounces (170 g) sugar
3.5 ounces (99 g)
walnuts, chopped
2.5 ounces (71 g) butter, melted
2 eggs, lightly beaten
¼ teaspoon baking soda

1. Preheat the air fryer to 355ºF (179ºC).
2. In a bowl, combine the sugar, butter, egg, flour, and baking soda with a whisk. Stir in the bananas and walnuts.
3. Transfer the mixture to a greased baking dish. Put the dish in the air fryer and bake for 10 minutes.
4. Reduce the temperature to 330ºF (166ºC) and bake for another 15 minutes. Serve hot.

Fried Golden Bananas

Prep time: 5 minutes | Cook time: 7 minutes | Serves 6

1 large egg
¼ cup cornstarch
¼ cup plain bread crumbs
3 bananas, halved
crosswise
Cooking oil
Chocolate sauce, for drizzling

1. Preheat the air fryer to 350ºF (177ºC).
2. In a small bowl, beat the egg. In another bowl, place the cornstarch. Put the bread crumbs in a third bowl.
3. Dip the bananas in the cornstarch, then the egg, and then the bread crumbs.
4. Spray the air fryer basket with cooking oil.
5. Put the bananas in the basket and spray them with cooking oil. Air fry for 5 minutes.
6. Open the air fryer and flip the bananas. Air fry for an additional 2 minutes.
7. Transfer the bananas to plates. Drizzle the chocolate sauce over the bananas, and serve.

Pineapple and Chocolate Cake

Prep time: 10 minutes | Cook time: 35 to 40 minutes | Serves 4

2 cups flour
4 ounces (113 g) butter, melted
¼ cup sugar
½ pound (227 g) pineapple, chopped
½ cup pineapple
juice
1 ounce (28 g) dark chocolate, grated
1 large egg
2 tablespoons skimmed milk

1. Preheat the air fryer to 370ºF (188ºC).
2. Grease a cake tin with a little oil or butter.
3. In a bowl, combine the butter and flour to create a crumbly consistency.
4. Add the sugar, chopped pineapple, juice, and grated dark chocolate and mix well.
5. In a separate bowl, combine the egg and milk. Add this mixture to the flour mixture and stir well until a soft dough forms.
6. Pour the mixture into the cake tin and transfer to the air fryer.
7. Bake for 35 to 40 minutes.
8. Serve immediately.

Chocolate S'mores

Prep time: 5 minutes | Cook time: 3 minutes | Serves 12

12 whole cinnamon graham crackers
2 (1.55-ounce / 44-g) chocolate bars,
broken into 12 pieces
12 marshmallows

1. Preheat the air fryer to 350ºF (177ºC).
2. Halve each graham cracker into 2 squares.
3. Put 6 graham cracker squares in the air fryer. Do not stack. Put a piece of chocolate into each. Bake for 2 minutes.
4. Open the air fryer and add a marshmallow onto each piece of melted chocolate. Bake for 1 additional minute.
5. Remove the cooked s'mores from the air fryer, then repeat steps 2 and 3 for the remaining 6 s'mores.
6. Top with the remaining graham cracker squares and serve.

Black Forest Pies

Prep time: 10 minutes | Cook time: 15 minutes | Serves 6

3 tablespoons milk or dark chocolate chips
2 tablespoons thick, hot fudge sauce
2 tablespoons chopped dried cherries

1 (10-by-15-inch) sheet frozen puff pastry, thawed
1 egg white, beaten
2 tablespoons sugar
½ teaspoon cinnamon

1. Preheat the air fryer to 350ºF (177ºC).
2. In a small bowl, combine the chocolate chips, fudge sauce, and dried cherries.
3. Roll out the puff pastry on a floured surface. Cut into 6 squares with a sharp knife.
4. Divide the chocolate chip mixture into the center of each puff pastry square. Fold the squares in half to make triangles. Firmly press the edges with the tines of a fork to seal.
5. Brush the triangles on all sides sparingly with the beaten egg white. Sprinkle the tops with sugar and cinnamon.
6. Put in the air fryer basket and bake for 15 minutes or until the triangles are golden brown. The filling will be hot, so cool for at least 20 minutes before serving.

Pear and Apple Crisp

Prep time: 10 minutes | Cook time: 20 minutes | Serves 6

½ pound (227 g) apples, cored and chopped
½ pound (227 g) pears, cored and chopped
1 cup flour
1 cup sugar
1 tablespoon butter
1 teaspoon ground

cinnamon
¼ teaspoon ground cloves
1 teaspoon vanilla extract
¼ cup chopped walnuts
Whipped cream, for serving

1. Preheat the air fryer to 340ºF (171ºC).
2. Lightly grease a baking dish and place the apples and pears inside.

3. Combine the rest of the ingredients, minus the walnuts and the whipped cream, until a coarse, crumbly texture is achieved.
4. Pour the mixture over the fruits and spread it evenly. Top with the chopped walnuts.
5. Bake for 20 minutes or until the top turns golden brown.
6. Serve at room temperature with whipped cream.

Chocolate Coconut Brownies

Prep time: 15 minutes | Cook time: 15 minutes | Serves 8

½ cup coconut oil
2 ounces (57 g) dark chocolate
1 cup sugar
2½ tablespoons water
4 whisked eggs
¼ teaspoon ground cinnamon
½ teaspoons ground

anise star
¼ teaspoon coconut extract
½ teaspoons vanilla extract
1 tablespoon honey
½ cup flour
½ cup desiccated coconut
Sugar, for dusting

1. Preheat the air fryer to 355ºF (179ºC).
2. Melt the coconut oil and dark chocolate in the microwave.
3. Combine with the sugar, water, eggs, cinnamon, anise, coconut extract, vanilla, and honey in a large bowl.
4. Stir in the flour and desiccated coconut. Incorporate everything well.
5. Lightly grease a baking dish with butter. Transfer the mixture to the dish.
6. Put the dish in the air fryer and bake for 15 minutes.
7. Remove from the air fryer and allow to cool slightly.
8. Take care when taking it out of the baking dish. Slice it into squares.
9. Dust with sugar before serving.

Mini Strawberry Pies

Prep + Cook Time: 15 minutes | Servings: 8

Ingredients
1 cup sugar
¼ tsp. ground cloves
1/8 tsp. cinnamon powder
1 tsp. vanilla extract
1 [12-oz.] can biscuit dough
12 oz. strawberry pie filling
¼ cup butter, melted

Instructions
1. In a bowl, mix together the sugar, cloves, cinnamon, and vanilla.
2. With a rolling pin, roll each piece of the biscuit dough into a flat, round circle.
3. Spoon an equal amount of the strawberry pie filling onto the center of each biscuit.
4. Roll up the dough. Dip the biscuits into the melted butter and coat them with the sugar mixture.
5. Coat with a light brushing of non-stick cooking spray on all sides.
6. Transfer the cookies to the Air Fryer and bake them at 340°F for roughly 10 minutes, or until a golden-brown color is achieved.
7. Allow to cool for 5 minutes before serving.

Coconut Brownies

Prep + Cook Time: 15 minutes | Servings: 8

Ingredients
½ cup coconut oil
2 oz. dark chocolate
1 cup sugar
2 ½ tbsp. water
4 whisked eggs
¼ tsp. ground cinnamon
½ tsp. ground anise star
¼ tsp. coconut extract
½ tsp. vanilla extract
1 tbsp. honey
½ cup flour
½ cup desiccated coconut
sugar, to dust

Instructions
1. Melt the coconut oil and dark chocolate in the microwave.
2. Combine with the sugar, water, eggs, cinnamon, anise, coconut extract, vanilla, and honey in a large bowl.
3. Stir in the flour and desiccated coconut. Incorporate everything well.
4. Lightly grease a baking dish with butter. Transfer the mixture to the dish.
5. Place the dish in the Air Fryer and bake at 355°F for 15 minutes.
6. Remove from the fryer and allow to cool slightly.
7. Take care when taking it out of the baking dish. Slice it into squares.
8. Dust with sugar before serving.

Banana & Vanilla Pastry Puffs

Prep + Cook Time: 15 minutes | Servings: 8

Ingredients
1 package [8-oz.] crescent dinner rolls, refrigerated
1 cup milk
4 oz. instant vanilla pudding
4 oz. cream cheese, softened
2 bananas, peeled and sliced
1 egg, lightly beaten

Instructions
1. Roll out the crescent dinner rolls and slice each one into 8 squares.
2. Mix together the milk, pudding, and cream cheese using a whisk.
3. Scoop equal amounts of the mixture into the pastry squares. Add the banana slices on top.
4. Fold the squares around the filling, pressing down on the edges to seal them.
5. Apply a light brushing of the egg to each pastry puff before placing them in the Air Fryer.
6. Air bake at 355°F for 10 minutes.

Double Chocolate Cake

Prep + Cook Time: 45 minutes | Servings: 8

Ingredients
½ cup sugar
1 ¼ cups flour
1 tsp. baking powder
⅓ cup cocoa powder
¼ tsp. ground cloves
1/8 tsp. freshly grated nutmeg
Pinch of table salt
1 egg
¼ cup soda of your choice
¼ cup milk
½ stick butter, melted
2 oz. bittersweet chocolate, melted
½ cup hot water

Instructions
1. In a bowl, thoroughly combine the dry ingredients.
2. In another bowl, mix together the egg, soda, milk, butter, and chocolate.
3. Combine the two mixtures. Add in the water and stir well.
4. Take a cake pan that is small enough to fit inside your Air Fryer and transfer the mixture to the pan.
5. Place a sheet of foil on top and bake at 320°F for 35 minutes.
6. Take off the foil and bake for further 10 minutes.
7. Frost the cake with buttercream if desired before serving.

Banana Oatmeal Cookies

Prep + Cook Time: 20 minutes | Servings: 6

Ingredients
2 cups quick oats
¼ cup milk
4 ripe bananas, mashed
¼ cup coconut, shredded

Instructions
1. Pre-heat the Air Fryer to 350°F.
2. Combine all of the ingredients in a bowl.
3. Scoop equal amounts of the cookie dough onto a baking sheet and put it in the Air Fryer basket.
4. Bake the cookies for 15 minutes.

Sugar Butter Fritters

Prep + Cook Time: 30 minutes | Servings: 16

Ingredients
For the dough:
4 cups flour
1 tsp. kosher salt
1 tsp. sugar
3 tbsp. butter, at room temperature
1 packet instant yeast
1 ¼ cups lukewarm water
For the Cakes
1 cup sugar
Pinch of cardamom
1 tsp. cinnamon powder
1 stick butter, melted

Instructions
1. Place all of the ingredients in a large bowl and combine well.
2. Add in the lukewarm water and mix until a soft, elastic dough forms.
3. Place the dough on a lightly floured surface and lay a greased sheet of aluminum foil on top of the dough. Refrigerate for 5 to 10 minutes.
4. Remove it from the refrigerator and divide it in two. Mold each half into a log and slice it into 20 pieces.
5. In a shallow bowl, combine the sugar, cardamom and cinnamon.
6. Coat the slices with a light brushing of melted butter and the sugar.
7. Spritz Air Fryer basket with cooking spray.
8. Transfer the slices to the fryer and air fry at 360°F for roughly 10 minutes. Turn each slice once during the baking time.
9. Dust each slice with the sugar before serving.

Pear & Apple Crisp with Walnuts

Prep + Cook Time: 25 minutes | Servings: 6

Ingredients
½ lb. apples, cored and chopped
½ lb. pears, cored and chopped
1 cup flour
1 cup sugar
1 tbsp. butter
1 tsp. ground cinnamon
¼ tsp. ground cloves
1 tsp. vanilla extract
¼ cup chopped walnuts
Whipped cream, to serve

Instructions
1. Lightly grease a baking dish and place the apples and pears inside.
2. Combine the rest of the ingredients, minus the walnuts and the whipped cream, until a coarse, crumbly texture is achieved.
3. Pour the mixture over the fruits and spread it evenly. Top with the chopped walnuts.
4. Air bake at 340°F for 20 minutes or until the top turns golden brown.
5. When cooked through, serve at room temperature with whipped cream.

Sweet & Crisp Bananas

Prep + Cook Time: 20 minutes | Servings: 4

Ingredients
4 ripe bananas, peeled and halved
1 tbsp. meal
1 tbsp. cashew, crushed
1 egg, beaten
1 ½ tbsp. coconut oil
¼ cup flour
1 ½ tbsp. sugar
½ cup friendly bread crumbs

Instructions
1. Put the coconut oil in a saucepan and heat over a medium heat. Stir in the bread crumbs and cook, stirring continuously, for 4 minutes.
2. Transfer the bread crumbs to a bowl.
3. Add in the meal and crushed cashew. Mix well.
4. Coat each of the banana halves in the corn flour, before dipping it in the beaten egg and lastly coating it with the bread crumbs.
5. Put the coated banana halves in the Air Fryer basket. Season with the sugar.
6. Air fry at 350°F for 10 minutes.

Shortbread Fingers

Prep + Cook Time: 20 minutes | Servings: 10

Ingredients
1 ½ cups butter
1 cup flour
¾ cup sugar
Cooking spray

Instructions
1. Pre-heat your Air Fryer to 350°F.
2. In a bowl. combine the flour and sugar.
3. Cut each stick of butter into small chunks. Add the chunks into the flour and the sugar.
4. Blend the butter into the mixture to combine everything well.
5. Use your hands to knead the mixture, forming a smooth consistency.
6. Shape the mixture into 10 equal-sized finger shapes, marking them with the tines of a fork for decoration if desired.
7. Lightly spritz the Air Fryer basket with the cooking spray. Place the cookies inside, spacing them out well.
8. Bake the cookies for 12 minutes.
9. Let cool slightly before serving. Alternatively, you can store the cookies in an airtight container for up to 3 days.

Coconut & Banana Cake

Prep + Cook Time: 1 hour 15 minutes | Servings: 5

Ingredients
2/3 cup sugar, shaved
2/3 cup unsalted butter
3 eggs
1 ¼ cup flour
1 ripe banana, mashed
½ tsp. vanilla extract
1/8 tsp. baking soda
Sea salt to taste
Topping Ingredients
sugar to taste, shaved
Walnuts to taste, roughly chopped
Bananas to taste, sliced

Instructions
1. Pre-heat the Air Fryer to 360°F.
2. Mix together the flour, baking soda, and a pinch of sea salt.
3. In a separate bowl, combine the butter, vanilla extract and sugar using an electrical mixer or a blender, to achieve a fluffy consistency. Beat in the eggs one at a time.
4. Throw in half of the flour mixture and stir thoroughly. Add in the mashed banana and continue to mix. Lastly, throw in the remaining half of the flour mixture and

combine until a smooth batter is formed.
5. Transfer the batter to a baking tray and top with the banana slices.
6. Scatter the chopped walnuts on top before dusting with the sugar
7. Place a sheet of foil over the tray and pierce several holes in it.
8. Put the covered tray in the Air Fryer. Cook for 48 minutes.
9. Decrease the temperature to 320°F, take off the foil, and allow to cook for an additional 10 minutes until golden brown.
10. Insert a skewer or toothpick in the center of the cake. If it comes out clean, the cake is ready.

Roasted Pumpkin Seeds & Cinnamon

Prep + Cook Time: 35 minutes | Servings: 2

Ingredients
1 cup pumpkin raw seeds
1 tbsp. ground cinnamon
2 tbsp. sugar
1 cup water
1 tbsp. olive oil

Instructions
1. In a frying pan, combine the pumpkin seeds, cinnamon and water.
2. Boil the mixture over a high heat for 2 - 3 minutes.
3. Pour out the water and place the seeds on a clean kitchen towel, allowing them to dry for 20 - 30 minutes.
4. In a bowl, mix together the sugar, dried seeds, a pinch of cinnamon and one tablespoon of olive oil.
5. Pre-heat the Air Fryer to 340°F.
6. Place the seed mixture in the fryer basket and allow to cook for 15 minutes, shaking the basket periodically throughout.

Pineapple Sticks

Prep + Cook Time: 20 minutes | Servings: 4

Ingredients
½ fresh pineapple, cut into sticks
¼ cup desiccated coconut

Instructions
1. Pre-heat the Air Fryer to 400°F.
2. Coat the pineapple sticks in the desiccated coconut and put each one in the Air Fryer basket.
3. Air fry for 10 minutes.

Sponge Cake
Prep + Cook Time: 50 minutes | Servings: 8

Ingredients
For the Cake:
9 oz. sugar
9 oz. butter
3 eggs
9 oz. flour
1 tsp. vanilla extract
Zest of 1 lemon
1 tsp. baking powder
For the Frosting
Juice of 1 lemon
Zest of 1 lemon
1 tsp. yellow food coloring
7 oz. sugar
4 egg whites

Instructions
1. Pre-heat your Air Fryer to 320°F.
2. Use an electric mixer to combine all of the cake ingredients.
3. Grease the insides of two round cake pans.
4. Pour an equal amount of the batter into each pan.
5. Place one pan in the fryer and cook for 15 minutes, before repeating with the second pan.
6. In the meantime, mix together all of the frosting ingredients.
7. Allow the cakes to cool. Spread the frosting on top of one cake and stack the other cake on top.

Apple Wedges
Prep + Cook Time: 25 minutes | Servings: 4

Ingredients
4 large apples
2 tbsp. olive oil
½ cup dried apricots, chopped
1 – 2 tbsp. sugar
½ tsp. ground cinnamon

Instructions
1. Peel the apples and slice them into eight wedges. Throw away the cores.
2. Coat the apple wedges with the oil.
3. Place each wedge in the Air Fryer and cook for 12 - 15 minutes at 350°F.
4. Add in the apricots and allow to cook for a further 3 minutes.
5. Stir together the sugar and cinnamon. Sprinkle this mixture over the cooked apples before serving.

Chocolate Lava Cake
Prep + Cook Time: 20 minutes | Servings: 4

Ingredients
1 cup dark cocoa candy melts

1 stick butter
2 eggs
4 tbsp. sugar
1 tbsp. honey
4 tbsp. flour
Pinch of kosher salt
Pinch of ground cloves
¼ tsp. grated nutmeg
¼ tsp. cinnamon powder

Instructions
1. Spritz the insides of four custard cups with cooking spray.
2. Melt the cocoa candy melts and butter in the microwave for 30 seconds to 1 minute.
3. In a large bowl, combine the eggs, sugar and honey with a whisk until frothy. Pour in the melted chocolate mix.
4. Throw in the rest of the ingredients and combine well with an electric mixer or a manual whisk.
5. Transfer equal portions of the mixture into the prepared custard cups.
6. Place in the Air Fryer and air bake at 350°F for 12 minutes.
7. Remove from the Air Fryer and allow to cool for 5 to 6 minutes.
8. Place each cup upside-down on a dessert plate and let the cake slide out. Serve with fruits and chocolate syrup if desired.

English Lemon Tarts
Prep + Cook Time: 30 minutes | Servings: 4

Ingredients
½ cup butter
½ lb. flour
2 tbsp. sugar
1 large lemon, juiced and zested
2 tbsp. lemon curd
Pinch of nutmeg

Instructions
1. In a large bowl, combine the butter, flour and sugar until a crumbly consistency is achieved.
2. Add in the lemon zest and juice, followed by a pinch of nutmeg. Continue to combine. If necessary, add a couple tablespoons of water to soften the dough.
3. Sprinkle the insides of a few small pastry tins with flour. Pour equal portions of the dough into each one and add sugar or lemon zest on top.
4. Pre-heat the Air Fryer to 360°F.
5. Place the lemon tarts inside the fryer and allow to cook for 15 minutes.

Cheesecake Cups

Prep + Cook Time: 10 minutes | Servings: 4

Ingredients
8 oz cream cheese, softened
2 oz heavy cream
1 tsp Sugar Glycerite
1 tsp Splenda
1 tsp vanilla flavoring (Frontier Organic)

Instructions
1. Combine all the ingredients.
2. Whip until a pudding consistency is achieved.
3. Divide in cups.
4. Refrigerate until served!

Strawberry Shake

Prep + Cook Time: 5 minutes | Servings: 1

Ingredients
3/4 cup coconut milk (from the carton)
¼ cup heavy cream
7 ice cubes
2 tbsp sugar-free strawberry Torani syrup
¼ tsp Xanthan Gum

Instructions
1. Combine all the ingredients into blender.
2. Blend for 1-2 minutes.
3. Serve!

Raspberry Pudding Surprise

Prep + Cook Time: 40 minutes | Servings: 1

Ingredients
3 tbsp chia seeds
½ cup unsweetened milk
1 scoop chocolate protein powder
¼ cup raspberries, fresh or frozen
1 tsp honey

Instructions
1. Combine the milk, protein powder and chia seeds together.
2. Let rest for 5 minutes before stirring.
3. Refrigerate for 30 minutes.
4. Top with raspberries.
5. Serve!

Vanilla Bean Dream

Prep + Cook Time: 35 minutes | Servings: 1

Ingredients
½ cup extra virgin coconut oil, softened
½ cup coconut butter, softened
Juice of 1 lemon
Seeds from ½ a vanilla bean

Instructions
1. Whisk the ingredients in an easy-to-pour cup.
2. Pour into a lined cupcake or loaf pan.
3. Refrigerate for 20 minutes. Top with lemon zest.
4. Serve!

White Chocolate Berry Cheesecake

Prep + Cook Time: 5-10 minutes | Servings: 4

Ingredients
8 oz cream cheese, softened
2 oz heavy cream
½ tsp Splenda
1 tsp raspberries
1 tbsp Da Vinci Sugar-Free syrup, white chocolate flavor

Instructions
1. Whip together the ingredients to a thick consistency.
2. Divide in cups.
3. Refrigerate.
4. Serve!

Coconut Pillow

Prep + Cook Time: 1-2 days | Servings: 4

Ingredients
1 can unsweetened coconut milk
Berries of choice
Dark chocolate

Instructions
1. Refrigerate the coconut milk for 24 hours.
2. Remove it from your refrigerator and whip for 2-3 minutes.
3. Fold in the berries.
4. Season with the chocolate shavings.
5. Serve!

Coffee Surprise

Prep + Cook Time: 5 minutes | Servings: 1

Ingredients
2 heaped tbsp flaxseed, ground
100ml cooking cream 35% fat
½ tsp cocoa powder, dark and unsweetened
1 tbsp goji berries
Freshly brewed coffee

Instructions
1.Mix together the flaxseeds, cream and cocoa and coffee.
2.Season with goji berries.
3.Serve!

Chocolate Cheesecake

Prep + Cook Time: 60 minutes | Servings: 4

Ingredients
4 oz cream cheese
½ oz heavy cream
1 tsp Sugar Glycerite
1 tsp Splenda
1 oz Enjoy Life mini chocolate chips

Instructions
1.Combine all the ingredients except the chocolate to a thick consistency.
2.Fold in the chocolate chips.
3.Refrigerate in serving cups.
4.Serve!

Crusty

Prep + Cook Time: 60 minutes | Servings: 3

Ingredients
2 cups flour
4 tsp melted butter
2 large eggs
½ tsp salt

Instructions
1.Mix together the flour and butter.
2.Add in the eggs and salt and combine well to form a dough ball.
3.Place the dough between two pieces of parchment paper. Roll out to 10" by 16" and ¼ inch thick.
4.Serve!

Chocolate Peanut Butter Cups

Prep + Cook Time: 70 minutes | Servings: 2

Ingredients
1 stick unsalted butter
1 oz / 1 cube unsweetened chocolate
5 packets Sugar in the Raw
1 tbsp heavy cream
4 tbsp peanut butter

Instructions
1.In a microwave, melt the butter and chocolate.
2.Add the Sugar.
3.Stir in the cream and peanut butter.
4.Line the muffin tins. Fill the muffin cups.
5.Freeze for 60 minutes.
6.Serve!

Macaroon Bites

Prep + Cook Time: 30 minutes | Servings: 2

Ingredients
4 egg whites
½ tsp vanilla
½ tsp EZ-Sweet (or equivalent of 1 cup artificial sweetener)
4½ tsp water
1 cup unsweetened coconut

Instructions
1.Preheat your fryer to 375°F/190°C.
2.Combine the egg whites, liquids and coconut.
3.Put into the fryer and reduce the heat to 325°F/160°C.
4.Bake for 15 minutes.
5.Serve!

Choco-berry Fudge Sauce

Prep + Cook Time: 30 minutes | Servings: 2

Ingredients
4 oz cream cheese, softened
1-3.5 oz 90% chocolate Lindt bar, chopped
¼ cup powdered erythritol
¼ cup heavy cream
1 tbsp Monin sugar-free raspberry syrup

Instructions
1.In a large skillet, melt together the cream cheese and chocolate.
2.Stir in the sweetener.
3.Remove from the heat and allow to cool.
4.Once cool, mix in the cream and syrup.
5.Serve!

Choco-Coconut Puddin

Prep + Cook Time: 65 minutes | Servings: 1

Ingredients

1 cup coconut milk
2 tbsp cacao powder or organic cocoa
½ tsp Sugar powder extract or 2 tbsp honey/maple syrup
½ tbsp quality gelatin
1 tbsp water

Instructions

1. On a medium heat, combine the coconut milk, cocoa and sweetener.
2. In a separate bowl, mix in the gelatin and water.
3. Add to the pan and stir until fully dissolved.
4. Pour into small dishes and refrigerate for 1 hour.
5. Serve!

Strawberry Frozen Dessert

Prep + Cook Time: 45 minutes | Servings: 1

Ingredients

½ cup sugar-free strawberry preserves
½ cup Sugar in the Raw or Splenda
2 cups Fage Total 0% Greek Yogurt
Ice cream maker

Instructions

1. In a food processor, purée the strawberries. Add the strawberry preserves.
2. Add the Greek yogurt and fully mix.
3. Put into the ice cream maker for 25-30 minute.
4. Serve!

Berry Layer Cake

Prep + Cook Time: 8 minutes | Servings: 1

Ingredients

¼ lemon pound cake
¼ cup whipping cream
½ tsp Truvia
1/8 tsp orange flavor
1 cup of mixed berries

Instructions

1. Using a sharp knife, divide the lemon cake into small cubes.
2. Dice the strawberries.
3. Combine the whipping cream, Truvia, and orange flavor.
4. Layer the fruit, cake and cream in a glass.
5. Serve!

Chocolate Pudding

Prep + Cook Time: 50 minutes | Servings: 1

Ingredients

3 tbsp chia seeds
1 cup unsweetened milk
1 scoop cocoa powder
¼ cup fresh raspberries
½ tsp honey

Instructions

1. Mix together all of the ingredients in a large bowl.
2. Let rest for 15 minutes but stir halfway through.
3. Stir again and refrigerate for 30 minutes. Garnish with raspberries.
4. Serve!

Cranberry Cream Surprise

Prep + Cook Time: 30 minutes | Servings: 1

Ingredients

1 cup mashed cranberries
½ cup Confectioner's Style Swerve
2 tsp natural cherry flavoring
2 tsp natural rum flavoring
1 cup organic heavy cream

Instructions

1. Combine the mashed cranberries, sweetener, cherry and rum flavorings.
2. Cover and refrigerate for 20 minutes.
3. Whip the heavy cream until soft peaks form.
4. Layer the whipped cream and cranberry mixture.
5. Top with fresh cranberries, mint leaves or grated dark chocolate.
6. Serve!

Banana Chocolate Cake

Prep + Cook Time: 30 minutes | Servings: 10

Ingredients
1 stick softened butter
½ cup sugar
1 egg
1 bananas, mashed
2 tbsp. maple syrup
2 cups flour
¼ tsp. anise star, ground
¼ tsp. ground mace
¼ tsp. ground cinnamon
¼ tsp. crystallized ginger
½ tsp. vanilla paste
Pinch of kosher salt
½ cup cocoa powder

Instructions
1. Beat together the softened butter and sugar to combine well.
2. Mix together the egg, mashed banana and maple syrup using a whisk.
3. Combine the two mixtures, stirring well until pale and creamy.
4. Add in the flour, anise star, mace, cinnamon, crystallized ginger, vanilla paste, salt, and cocoa powder. Mix well to form the batter.
5. Grease two cake pans with cooking spray.
6. Transfer the batter into the cake pans and place them in the Air Fryer.
7. Cook at 330°F for 30 minutes. Frost with chocolate glaze if desired

Lemon Butter Pound Cake

Prep + Cook Time: 2 hours 20 minutes | Servings: 8

Ingredients
1 stick softened butter
1 cup sugar
1 medium egg
1 ¼ cups flour
1 tsp. butter flavoring
1 tsp. vanilla essence
Pinch of salt
¾ cup milk
Grated zest of 1 medium-sized lemon
For the Glaze:

2 tbsp. freshly squeezed lemon juice

Instructions
1. In a large bowl, use a creamer to mix together the butter and sugar. Fold in the egg and continue to stir.
2. Add in the flour, butter flavoring, vanilla essence, and salt, combining everything well.
3. Pour in the milk, followed by the lemon zest, and continue to mix.
4. Lightly brush the inside of a cake pan with the melted butter.
5. Pour the cake batter into the cake pan.
6. Place the pan in the Air Fryer and bake at 350°F for 15 minutes.
7. After removing it from the fryer, run a knife around the edges of the cake to loosen it from the pan and transfer it to a serving plate.
8. Leave it to cool completely.
9. In the meantime, make the glaze by combining with the lemon juice.
10. Pour the glaze over the cake and let it sit for a further 2 hours before serving.

Fried Pineapple Rings

Prep + Cook Time: 10 minutes | Servings: 6

Ingredients
2/3 cup flour
½ tsp. baking powder
½ tsp. baking soda
Pinch of kosher salt
½ cup water
1 cup rice milk
½ tsp. ground cinnamon
¼ tsp. ground anise star
½ tsp. vanilla essence
4 tbsp. sugar
¼ cup unsweetened flaked coconut
1 medium pineapple, peeled and sliced

Instructions
1. Mix together all of the ingredients, minus the pineapple.
2. Cover the pineapple slices with the batter.
3. Place the slices in the Air Fryer and cook at 380°F for 6 - 8 minutes.
4. Pour a drizzling of maple syrup over the pineapple and serve with a side of vanilla ice cream.

Hazelnut Brownie Cups

Prep + Cook Time: 30 minutes | Servings: 12

Ingredients
6 oz. semisweet chocolate chips
1 stick butter, at room temperature
1 cup sugar
2 large eggs
¼ cup red wine
¼ tsp. hazelnut extract
1 tsp. pure vanilla extract
¾ cup flour
2 tbsp. cocoa powder
½ cup ground hazelnuts
Pinch of kosher salt

Instructions
1. Melt the butter and chocolate chips in the microwave.
2. In a large bowl, combine the sugar, eggs, red wine, hazelnut and vanilla extract with a whisk. Pour in the chocolate mix.
3. Add in the flour, cocoa powder, ground hazelnuts, and a pinch of kosher salt, continuing to stir until a creamy, smooth consistency is achieved.
4. Take a muffin tin and place a cupcake liner in each cup. Spoon an equal amount of the batter into each one.
5. Air bake at 360°F for 28 - 30 minutes, cooking in batches if necessary.
6. Serve with a topping of ganache if desired.

Swirled German Cake

Prep + Cook Time: 25 minutes | Servings: 8

Ingredients
1 cup flour
1 tsp. baking powder
1 cup sugar
1/8 tsp. kosher salt
¼ tsp. ground cinnamon
¼ tsp. grated nutmeg
1 tsp. orange zest
1 stick butter, melted
2 eggs
1 tsp. pure vanilla extract
¼ cup milk
2 tbsp. unsweetened cocoa powder

Instructions
1. Take a round pan that is small enough to fit inside your Air Fryer and lightly grease the inside with oil.
2. In a bowl, use an electric mixer to combine the flour, baking powder, sugar, salt, cinnamon, nutmeg, and orange zest.
3. Fold in the butter, eggs, vanilla, and milk, incorporating everything well.
4. Spoon a quarter-cup of the batter to the baking pan.
5. Stir the cocoa powder into the rest of the batter.
6. Use a spoon to drop small amounts of the brown batter into the white batter. Swirl them together with a knife.
7. Place the pan in the Air Fryer and cook at 360°F for about 15 minutes.
8. Remove the pan from the fryer and leave to cool for roughly 10 minutes.

Oatmeal Apple & Plum Crumble

Prep + Cook Time: 20 minutes | Servings: 6

Ingredients
¼ lb. plums, pitted and chopped
¼ lb. Braeburn apples, cored and chopped
1 tbsp. fresh lemon juice
2 ½ oz. sugar
1 tbsp. honey
½ tsp. ground mace
½ tsp. vanilla paste
1 cup fresh cranberries
⅓ cup oats
2/3 cup flour
½ stick butter, chilled
1 tbsp. cold water

Instructions
1. Coat the plums and apples with the lemon juice, sugar, honey, and ground mace.
2. Lightly coat the inside of a cake pan with cooking spray.
3. Pour the fruit mixture into the pan.
4. In a bowl, mix together all of the other ingredients, combining everything well.
5. Use a palette knife to spread this mixture evenly over the fruit.
6. Place the pan in the Air Fryer and air bake at 390°F for 20 minutes. Ensure the crumble is cooked through before serving.

Dunky Dough Dippers & Chocolate Sauce

Prep + Cook Time: 45 minutes | Servings: 5

Ingredients
¾ cup sugar
1 lb. friendly bread dough
1 cup heavy cream
12 oz. high quality semi-sweet chocolate chips
½ cup butter, melted
2 tbsp. extract

Instructions
1. Pre-heat the Air Fryer to 350°F.
2. Coat the inside of the basket with a little melted butter.
3. Halve and roll up the dough to create two 15-inch logs. Slice each log into 20 disks.
4. Halve each disk and twist it 3 or 4 times.
5. Lay out a cookie sheet and lay the twisted dough pieces on top. Brush the pieces with some more melted butter and sprinkle on the sugar.
6. Place the sheet in the fryer and air fry for 5 minutes. Flip the dough twists over, and brush the other side with more butter. Cook for an additional 3 minutes. It may be necessary to complete this step in batches.
7. In the meantime, make the chocolate sauce. Firstly, put the heavy cream into a saucepan over the medium heat and allow it to simmer.
8. Put the chocolate chips into a large bowl and add the simmering cream on top. Whisk the chocolate chips everything together until a smooth consistency is achieved. Stir in 2 tablespoons of extract.
9. Transfer the baked cookies in a shallow dish, pour over the rest of the melted butter and sprinkle on the sugar.
10. Drizzle on the chocolate sauce before serving.

Peach Crumble

Prep + Cook Time: 35 minutes | Servings: 6

Ingredients
1 ½ lb. peaches, peeled and chopped
2 tbsp. lemon juice
1 cup flour
1 tbsp. water
½ cup sugar
5 tbsp. cold butter
Pinch of sea salt

Instructions
1. Mash the peaches a little with a fork to achieve a lumpy consistency.
2. Add in two tablespoons of sugar and the lemon juice.
3. In a bowl, combine the flour, salt, and sugar. Throw in a tablespoon of water before adding in the cold butter, mixing until crumbly.
4. Grease the inside of a baking dish and arrange the berries at the bottom. Top with the crumbs.
5. Transfer the dish to the Air Fryer and air fry for 20 minutes at 390°F.

Banana Walnut Cake

Prep + Cook Time: 55 minutes | Servings: 6

Ingredients
16 oz. bananas, mashed
8 oz. flour
6 oz. sugar
3.5 oz. walnuts, chopped
2.5 oz. butter
2 eggs
¼ tsp. baking soda

Instructions
1. Coat the inside of a baking dish with a little oil.
2. Pre-heat the Air Fryer at 355°F.
3. In a bowl combine the sugar, butter, egg, flour and soda using a whisk. Throw in the bananas and walnuts.
4. Transfer the mixture to the dish. Place the dish in the fryer and cook for 10 minutes.
5. Reduce the heat to 330°F and cook for another 15 minutes. Serve hot.

Cheesy Lemon Cake

Prep + Cook Time: 60 minutes | Servings: 6

Ingredients
17.5 oz. ricotta cheese
5.4 oz. sugar
3 eggs
3 tbsp. flour
1 lemon, juiced and zested
2 tsp. vanilla extract [optional]

Instructions
1. Pre-heat Air Fryer to 320°F.
2. Combine all of the ingredients until a creamy consistency is achieved.
3. Place the mixture in a cake tin.
4. Transfer the tin to the fryer and cook the cakes for 25 minutes.
5. Remove the cake from the fryer, allow to cool, and serve.

Chocolate Brownies & Caramel Sauce

Prep + Cook Time: 45 minutes | Servings: 4

Ingredients
½ cup butter, plus more for greasing the pan
1 ¾ oz. unsweetened chocolate
1 cup sugar
2 medium eggs, beaten
1 cup flour
2 tsp. vanilla
2 tbsp. water
2/3 cup milk

Instructions
1. In a saucepan over a medium heat, melt the butter and chocolate together.
2. Take the saucepan off the heat and stir in the sugar, eggs, flour, and vanilla, combining everything well.
3. Pre-heat your Air Fryer to 350°F.
4. Coat the inside of a baking dish with a little butter. Transfer the batter to the dish and place inside the fryer.
5. Bake for 15 minutes.
6. In the meantime, prepare the caramel sauce. In a small saucepan, slowly bring the water to a boil. Cook for around 3 minutes, until the mixture turns light brown.
7. Lower the heat and allow to cook for another two minutes. Gradually add in the rest of the butter. Take the saucepan off the heat and allow the caramel to cool.
8. When the brownies are ready, slice them into squares. Pour the caramel sauce on top and add on some sliced banana if desired before serving.

Pumpkin Cinnamon Pudding

Prep + Cook Time: 25 minutes | Servings: 4

Ingredients
3 cups pumpkin puree
3 tbsp. honey
1 tbsp. ginger
1 tbsp. cinnamon
1 tsp. clove
1 tsp. nutmeg
1 cup full-fat cream
2 eggs
1 cup sugar

Instructions
1. Pre-heat your Air Fryer to 390°F.
2. In a bowl, stir all of the ingredients together to combine.
3. Grease the inside of a small baking dish.
4. Pour the mixture into the dish and transfer to the fryer. Cook for 15 minutes. Serve with whipped cream if desired.

Banana Walnut Bread

Prep + Cook Time: 40 minutes | Servings: 1 loaf

Ingredients
7 oz. flour
¼ tsp. baking powder
2.5 oz. butter
5.5 oz. sugar
2 medium eggs
14 oz. bananas, peeled
2.8 oz. chopped walnuts

Instructions
1. Pre-heat the Air Fryer to 350°F.
2. Take a baking tin small enough to fit inside the Air Fryer and grease the inside with butter.
3. Mix together the flour and the baking powder in a bowl.
4. In a separate bowl, beat together the sugar and butter until fluffy and pale. Gradually add in the flour and egg. Stir.
5. Throw in the walnuts and combine again.
6. Mash the bananas using a fork and transfer to the bowl. Mix once more, until everything is incorporated.
7. Pour the mixture into the tin, place inside the fryer and cook for 10 minutes.

Peach Slices

Prep + Cook Time: 40 minutes | Servings: 4

Ingredients
4 cups peaches, sliced
2 – 3 tbsp. sugar
2 tbsp. flour
⅓ cup oats
2 tbsp. unsalted butter
¼ tsp. vanilla extract
1 tsp. cinnamon

Instructions
1. In a large bowl, combine the peach slices, sugar, vanilla extract, and cinnamon. Pour the mixture into a baking tin and place it in the Air Fryer.
2. Cook for 20 minutes on 290°F.
3. In the meantime, combine the oats, flour, and unsalted butter in a separate bowl.
4. Once the peach slices cooked, pour the butter mixture on top of them.
5. Cook for an additional 10 minutes at 300 - 310°F.
6. Remove from the fryer and allow to crisp up for 5 – 10. Serve with ice cream if desired.

Vanilla Souffle

Prep + Cook Time: 50 minutes | Servings: 6

Ingredients
¼ cup flour
¼ cup butter, softened
1 cup whole milk
¼ cup sugar
2 tsp. vanilla extract
1 vanilla bean
5 egg whites
4 egg yolks
1 oz. sugar
1 tsp. cream of tartar

Instructions
1.Mix together the flour and butter to create a smooth paste.
2.In a saucepan, heat up the milk. Add the ¼ cup sugar and allow it to dissolve.
3.Put the vanilla bean in the mixture and bring it to a boil.
4.Pour in the flour-butter mixture. Beat the contents of the saucepan thoroughly with a wire whisk, removing all the lumps.
5.Reduce the heat and allow the mixture to simmer and thicken for a number of minutes.
6.Take the saucepan off the heat. Remove the vanilla bean and let the mixture cool for 10 minutes in an ice bath.
7.In the meantime, grease six 3-oz. ramekins or soufflé dishes with butter and add a sprinkling of sugar to each one.
8.In a separate bowl quickly, rigorously stir the egg yolks and vanilla extract together. Combine with the milk mixture.
9.In another bowl, beat the egg whites, 1 oz. sugar and cream of tartar to form medium stiff peaks.
10.Fold the egg whites into the soufflé base. Transfer everything to the ramekins, smoothing the surfaces with a knife or the back of a spoon.
11.Pre-heat the Air Fryer to 330°F.
12.Put the ramekins in the cooking basket and cook for 14 – 16 minutes. You may need to complete this step in multiple batches.
13.Serve the soufflés topped with powdered sugar and with a side of chocolate sauce.

Butter Marshmallow Fluff Turnover

Prep + Cook Time: 35 minutes | Servings: 4

Ingredients
4 sheets filo pastry, defrosted
4 tbsp. chunky peanut butter
4 tsp. marshmallow fluff
2 oz. butter, melted
Pinch of sea salt

Instructions
1.Pre-heat the Air Fryer to 360°F.
2.Roll out the pastry sheets. Coat one with a light brushing of butter.
3.Lay a second pastry sheet on top of the first one. Brush once again with butter. Repeat until all 4 sheets have been used.
4.Slice the filo layers into four strips, measuring roughly 3 inches x 12 inches.
5.Spread one tablespoon of peanut butter and one teaspoon of marshmallow fluff on the underside of each pastry strip.
6.Take the tip of each sheet and fold it backwards over the filling, forming a triangle. Repeat this action in a zigzag manner until the filling is completely enclosed.
7.Seal the ends of each turnover with a light brushing of butter.
8.Put the turnovers in the fryer basket and cook for 3 – 5 minutes, until they turn golden brown and puffy.
9.Sprinkle a little sea salt over each turnover before serving.

Chocolate-Covered Maple Bacon

Prep + Cook Time: 25 minutes | Servings: 4

Ingredients
8 slices sugar-free bacon
1 tbsp. granular erythritol
1/3 cup low-carb sugar-free chocolate chips
1 tsp. coconut oil
½ tsp. maple extract

Instructions
1.Place the bacon in the fryer's basket and add the erythritol on top. Cook for six minutes at 350°F and turn the bacon over. Leave to cook another six minutes or until the bacon is sufficiently crispy.
2.Take the bacon out of the fryer and leave it to cool.
3.Microwave the chocolate chips and coconut oil together for half a minute. Remove from the microwave and mix together before stirring in the maple extract.
4.Set the bacon flat on a piece of parchment paper and pour the mixture over. Allow to harden in the refrigerator for roughly five minutes before serving.

Sugar Pork Rinds

Prep + Cook Time: 10 minutes | Servings: 2

Ingredients
2 oz. pork rinds
2 tsp. unsalted butter, melted
¼ cup powdered erythritol
½ tsp. ground cinnamon

Instructions
1. Coat the rinds with the melted butter.
2. In a separate bowl, combine the erythritol and cinnamon and pour over the pork rinds, ensuring the rinds are covered completely and evenly.
3. Transfer the pork rinds into the fryer and cook at 400°F for five minutes.

Toasted Coconut Flakes

Prep + Cook Time: 5 minutes | Servings: 1

Ingredients
1 cup unsweetened coconut flakes
2 tsp. coconut oil, melted
¼ cup granular erythritol
Salt

Instructions
In a large bowl, combine the coconut flakes, oil, granular erythritol, and a pinch of salt, ensuring that the flakes are coated completely.
Place the coconut flakes in your fryer and cook at 300°F for three minutes, giving the basket a good shake a few times throughout the cooking time. Fry until golden and serve.

Blackberry Crisp

Prep + Cook Time: 18 minutes | Servings: 1

Ingredients
2 tbsp. lemon juice
1/3 cup powdered erythritol
¼ tsp. xantham gum
2 cup blackberries
1 cup crunchy granola

Instructions
1. In a bowl, combine the lemon juice, erythritol, xantham gum, and blackberries. Transfer to a round baking dish about six inches in diameter and seal with aluminum foil.
2. Put the dish in the fryer and leave to cook for twelve minutes at 350°F.

3. Take care when removing the dish from the fryer. Give the blackberries another stir and top with the granola.
4. Return the dish to the fryer and cook for an additional three minutes, this time at 320°F. Serve once the granola has turned brown and enjoy.

Churros

Prep + Cook Time: 15 minutes | Servings: 1

Ingredients
½ cup water
¼ cup butter
½ cup flour
3 eggs
2 ½ tsp. sugar

Instructions
1. In a saucepan, bring the water and butter to a boil. Once it is bubbling, add the flour and mix to create a doughy consistency.
2. Remove from the heat, allow to cool, and crack the eggs into the saucepan. Blend with a hand mixer until the dough turns fluffy.
3. Transfer the dough into a piping bag.
4. Pre-heat the fryer at 380°F.
5. Pipe the dough into the fryer in several three-inch-long segments. Cook for ten minutes before removing from the fryer and coating in the sugar.
6. Serve with the low-carb chocolate sauce of your choice.

Peanut Butter Cookies

Prep + Cook Time: 15 minutes | Servings: 1

Ingredients
¼ tsp. salt
4 tbsp. erythritol
½ cup peanut butter
1 egg

Instructions
1. Combine the salt, erythritol, and peanut butter in a bowl, incorporating everything well. Break the egg over the mixture and mix to create a dough.
2. Flatten the dough using a rolling pin and cut into shapes with a knife or cookie cutter. Make a crisscross on the top of each cookie with a fork.
3. Pre-heat your fryer at 360°F.
4. Once the fryer has warmed up, put the cookies inside and leave to cook for ten minutes. Take care when taking them out and allow to cook before enjoying.

Avocado Pudding

Prep + Cook Time: 5 minutes | Servings: 1

Ingredients
Avocado
3 tsp. liquid Sugar
1 tbsp. cocoa powder
4 tsp. unsweetened milk
¼ tsp. vanilla extract

Instructions
1.Pre-heat your fryer at 360°F.
2.Halve the avocado, twist to open, and scoop out the pit.
3.Spoon the flesh into a bowl and mash it with a fork. Throw in the Sugar, cocoa powder, milk, and vanilla extract, and combine everything with a hand mixer.
4.Transfer this mixture to the basket of your fryer and cook for three minutes.

Chia Pudding

Prep + Cook Time: 10 minutes | Servings: 1

Ingredients
cup chia seeds
1 cup unsweetened coconut milk
1 tsp. liquid Sugar
1 tbsp. coconut oil
1 tsp. butter

Instructions
1.Pre-heat the fryer at 360°F.
2.In a bowl, gently combine the chia seeds with the milk and Sugar, before mixing the coconut oil and butter. Spoon seven equal-sized portions into seven ramekins and set these inside the fryer.
3.Cook for four minutes. Take care when removing the ramekins from the fryer and allow to cool for four minutes before serving.

Bacon Cookies

Prep + Cook Time: 15 minutes | Servings: 2

Ingredients
¼ tsp. ginger
1/5 tsp. baking soda
2/3 cup peanut butter
2 tbsp. Swerve
3 slices bacon, cooked and chopped

Instructions
1.In a bowl, mix the ginger, baking soda, peanut butter, and Swerve together, making sure to combine everything well.
2.Stir in the chopped bacon.
3.With clean hands, shape the mixture into a cylinder and cut in six. Press down each slice into a cookie with your palm.
4.Pre-heat your fryer at 350°F.

5.When the fryer is warm, put the cookies inside and cook for seven minutes. Take care when taking them out of the fryer and allow to cool before serving.

Blueberry Pancakes

Prep + Cook Time: 20 minutes | Servings: 4

Ingredients
½ tsp. vanilla extract
2 tbsp. honey
½ cup blueberries
½ cup sugar
2 cups + 2 tbsp. flour
3 eggs, beaten
1 cup milk
1 tsp. baking powder
Pinch of salt

Instructions
1.Pre-heat the Air Fryer to 390°F.
2.In a bowl, mix together all of the dry ingredients.
3.Pour in the wet ingredients and combine with a whisk, ensuring the mixture becomes smooth.
4.Roll each blueberry in some flour to lightly coat it before folding it into the mixture. This is to ensure they do not change the color of the batter.
5.Coat the inside of a baking dish with a little oil or butter.
6.Spoon several equal amounts of the batter onto the baking dish, spreading them into pancake-shapes and ensuring to space them out well. This may have to be completed in two batches.
7.Place the dish in the fryer and bake for about 10 minutes.

New England Pumpkin Cake

Prep + Cook Time: 50 minutes | Servings: 4

Ingredients
1 large egg
½ cup skimmed milk
7 oz. flour
2 tbsp. sugar
5 oz. pumpkin puree
Pinch of salt
Pinch of cinnamon [if desired]
Cooking spray

Instructions
1.Stir together the pumpkin puree and sugar in a bowl. Crack in the egg and combine using a whisk until smooth.
2.Add in the flour and salt, stirring constantly. Pour in the milk, ensuring to combine everything well.
3.Spritz a baking tin with cooking spray.
4.Transfer the batter to the baking tin.
5.Pre-heat the Air Fryer to 350°F.
6.Put the tin in the Air Fryer basket and bake for 15 minutes.

Mixed Berry Puffed Pastry

Prep + Cook Time: 20 minutes | Servings: 3

Ingredients
3 pastry dough sheets
½ cup mixed berries, mashed
1 tbsp. honey
2 tbsp. cream cheese
3 tbsp. chopped walnuts
¼ tsp. vanilla extract

Instructions
1. Pre-heat your Air Fryer to 375°F.
2. Roll out the pastry sheets and spread the cream cheese over each one.
3. In a bowl, combine the berries, vanilla extract and honey.
4. Cover a baking sheet with parchment paper.
5. Spoon equal amounts of the berry mixture into the center of each sheet of pastry. Scatter the chopped walnuts on top.
6. Fold up the pastry around the filling and press down the edges with the back of a fork to seal them.
7. Transfer the baking sheet to the Air Fryer and cook for approximately 15 minutes.

Cherry Pie

Prep + Cook Time: 35 minutes | Servings: 8

Ingredients
1 tbsp. milk
2 ready-made pie crusts
21 oz. cherry pie filling
1 egg yolk

Instructions
1. Pre-heat the Air Fryer to 310°F.
2. Coat the inside of a pie pan with a little oil or butter and lay one of the pie crusts inside. Use a fork to pierce a few holes in the pastry.
3. Spread the pie filling evenly over the crust.
4. Slice the other crust into strips and place them on top of the pie filling to make the pie look more homemade.
5. Place in the Air Fryer and cook for 15 minutes.

Apple Pie

Prep + Cook Time: 25 minutes | Servings: 7

Ingredients
2 large apples
½ cup flour
2 tbsp. unsalted butter
1 tbsp. sugar
½ tsp. cinnamon

Instructions
1. Pre-heat the Air Fryer to 360°F
2. In a large bowl, combine the flour and butter. Pour in the sugar, continuing to mix.

3. Add in a few tablespoons of water and combine everything to create a smooth dough.
4. Grease the insides of a few small pastry tins with butter. Divide the dough between each tin and lay each portion flat inside.
5. Peel, core and dice up the apples. Put the diced apples on top of the pastry and top with a sprinkling of sugar and cinnamon.
6. Place the pastry tins in your Air Fryer and cook for 15 - 17 minutes.
7. Serve with whipped cream or ice cream if desired.

Chocolate Molten Lava Cake

Prep + Cook Time: 25 minutes | Servings: 4

Ingredients
3 ½ oz. butter, melted
3 ½ tbsp. sugar
3 ½ oz. chocolate, melted
1 ½ tbsp. flour
2 eggs

Instructions
1. Pre-heat the Air Fryer to 375°F.
2. Grease four ramekins with a little butter.
3. Rigorously combine the eggs and butter before stirring in the melted chocolate.
4. Slowly fold in the flour.
5. Spoon an equal amount of the mixture into each ramekin.
6. Put them in the Air Fryer and cook for 10 minutes
7. Place the ramekins upside-down on plates and let the cakes fall out. Serve hot.

Pineapple Cake

Prep + Cook Time: 40 minutes | Servings: 4

Ingredients
2 cups flour
¼ lb. butter
¼ cup sugar
½ lb. pineapple, chopped
½ cup pineapple juice
1 oz. dark chocolate, grated
1 large egg
2 tbsp. skimmed milk

Instructions
1. Pre-heat the Air Fryer to 370°F.
2. Grease a cake tin with a little oil or butter.
3. In a bowl, combine the butter and flour to create a crumbly consistency.
4. Add in the sugar, diced pineapple, juice, and crushed dark chocolate and mix well.
5. In a separate bowl, combine the egg and milk. Add this mixture to the flour and stir well until a soft dough forms.
6. Pour the mixture into the cake tin and transfer to the Air Fryer.
7. Cook for 35 - 40 minutes.

Glazed Donuts

Prep + Cook Time: 25 minutes | Servings: 2 – 4

Ingredients
1 can [8 oz.] refrigerated croissant dough
Cooking spray
1 can [16 oz.] vanilla frosting

Instructions
1.Cut the croissant dough into 1-inch-round slices. Make a hole in the center of each one to create a donut.
2.Put the donuts in the Air Fryer basket, taking care not to overlap any, and spritz with cooking spray. You may need to cook everything in multiple batches.
3.Cook at 400°F for 2 minutes. Turn the donuts over and cook for another 3 minutes.
4.Place the rolls on a paper plate.
5.Microwave a half-cup of frosting for 30 seconds and pour a drizzling of the frosting over the donuts before serving.

Apple Dumplings

Prep + Cook Time: 40 minutes | Servings: 2

Ingredients
2 tbsp. sultanas
2 sheets puff pastry
2 tbsp. butter, melted
2 small apples
1 tbsp. sugar

Instructions
1.Pre-heat your Air Fryer to 350°F
2.Peel the apples and remove the cores.
3.In a bowl, stir together the sugar and the sultanas.
4.Lay one apple on top of each pastry sheet and stuff the sugar and sultanas into the holes where the cores used to be.
5.Wrap the pastry around the apples, covering them completely.
6.Put them on a sheet of aluminum foil and coat each dumpling with a light brushing of melted butter
7.Transfer to the Air Fryer and bake for 25 minutes until a golden brown color is achieved and the apples have softened inside.

Bananas & Ice Cream

Prep + Cook Time: 25 minutes | Servings: 2

Ingredients
2 large bananas
1 tbsp. butter
1 tbsp. sugar
2 tbsp. friendly bread crumbs
Vanilla ice cream for serving

Instructions
1.Place the butter in the Air Fryer basket and allow it to melt for 1 minute at 350°F.
2.Combine the sugar and bread crumbs in a bowl.
3.Slice the bananas into 1-inch-round pieces. Drop them into the sugar mixture and coat them well.
4.Place the bananas in the Air Fryer and cook for 10 – 15 minutes.
5.Serve warm, with ice cream on the side if desired.

Raspberry Muffins

Prep + Cook Time: 35 minutes | Servings: 10

Ingredients
1 egg
1 cup frozen raspberries, coated with some flour
1 ½ cups flour
½ cup sugar
⅓ cup vegetable oil
2 tsp. baking powder
Yogurt, as needed
1 tsp. lemon zest
2 tbsp. lemon juice
Pinch of sea salt

Instructions
1.Pre-heat the Air Fryer to 350°F
2.Place all of the dry ingredients in a bowl and combine well.
3.Beat the egg and pour it into a cup. Mix it with the oil and lemon juice. Add in the yogurt, to taste.
4.Mix together the dry and wet ingredients.
5.Add in the lemon zest and raspberries.
6.Coat the insides of 10 muffin tins with a little butter.
7.Spoon an equal amount of the mixture into each muffin tin.
8.Transfer to the fryer, and cook for 10 minutes, in batches if necessary.

Pecan Pie

Prep + Cook Time: 1 hour 10 minutes | Servings: 4

Ingredients
1x 8-inch pie dough
½ tsp. cinnamon
¾ tsp. vanilla extract
2 eggs
¾ cup maple syrup
1/8 tsp. nutmeg
2 tbsp. butter
1 tbsp. butter, melted
2 tbsp. sugar
½ cup chopped pecans

Instructions
1.Pre-heat the Air Fryer to 370°F.
2.In a small bowl, coat the pecans in the melted butter.
3.Transfer the pecans to the Air Fryer and allow them to toast for about 10 minutes.
4.Put the pie dough in a greased pie pan and add the pecans on top.
5.In a bowl, mix together the rest of the ingredients. Pour this over the pecans.
6.Place the pan in the fryer and bake for 25 minutes.

Orange Carrot Cake

Prep + Cook Time: 30 minutes | Servings: 8

Ingredients
2 large carrots, peeled and grated
1 ¾ cup flour
¾ cup sugar
2 eggs
10 tbsp. olive oil
2 cups sugar
1 tsp. mixed spice
2 tbsp. milk
4 tbsp. melted butter
1 small orange, rind and juice

Instructions
1.Set the Air Fryer to 360°F and allow to heat up for 10 minutes.
2.Place a baking sheet inside the tin.
3.Combine the flour, sugar, grated carrots, and mixed spice.
4.Pour the milk, beaten eggs, and olive oil into the middle of the batter and mix well.
5.Pour the mixture in the tin, transfer to the fryer and cook for 5 minutes.
6.Lower the heat to 320°F and allow to cook for an additional 5 minutes.
7.In the meantime, prepare the frosting by combining the melted butter, orange juice, rind, and sugar until a smooth consistency is achieved.
8.Remove the cake from the fryer, allow it to cool for several minutes and add the frosting on top.

Chocolate Cookies

Prep + Cook Time: 30 minutes | Servings: 8

Ingredients
3 oz. sugar
4 oz. butter
1 tbsp. honey
6 oz. flour
1 ½ tbsp. milk
2 oz. chocolate chips

Instructions
1.Pre-heat the Air Fryer to 350°F.
2.Mix together the sugar and butter using an electric mixer, until a fluffy texture is achieved.
3.Stir in the remaining ingredients, minus the chocolate chips.
4.Gradually fold in the chocolate chips.
5.Spoon equal portions of the mixture onto a lined baking sheet and flatten out each one with a spoon. Ensure the cookies are not touching.
6.Place in the fryer and cook for 18 minutes.

Butter Cake

Prep + Cook Time: 25 minutes | Servings: 2

Ingredients
1 egg
1 ½ cup flour
7 tbsp. butter, at room temperature
6 tbsp. milk
6 tbsp. sugar
Pinch of sea salt
Cooking spray
Dusting of sugar to serve

Instructions
1.Pre-heat the Air Fryer to 360°F.
2.Spritz the inside of a small ring cake tin with cooking spray.
3.In a bowl, combine the butter and sugar using a whisk.
4.Stir in the egg and continue to mix everything until the mixture is smooth and fluffy.
5.Pour the flour through a sieve into the bowl.
6.Pour in the milk, before adding a pinch of salt, and combine once again to incorporate everything well.
7.Pour the batter into the tin and use the back of a spoon to made sure the surface is even.
8.Place in the fryer and cook for 15 minutes.
9.Before removing it from the fryer, ensure the cake is cooked through by inserting a toothpick into the center and checking that it comes out clean.
10.Allow the cake to cool and serve.

Easy Chocolate Donuts

Prep time: 5 minutes | Cook time: 8 minutes | Serves 8

1 (8-ounce / 227-g) can jumbo biscuits
Cooking oil

Chocolate sauce, for drizzling

1. Preheat the air fryer to 375ºF (191ºC)
2. Separate the biscuit dough into 8 biscuits and place them on a flat work surface. Use a small circle cookie cutter or a biscuit cutter to cut a hole in the center of each biscuit. You can also cut the holes using a knife.
3. Spray the air fryer basket with cooking oil.
4. Put 4 donuts in the air fryer. Do not stack. Spray with cooking oil. Air fry for 4 minutes.
5. Open the air fryer and flip the donuts. Air fry for an additional 4 minutes.
6. Remove the cooked donuts from the air fryer, then repeat steps 3 and 4 for the remaining 4 donuts.
7. Drizzle chocolate sauce over the donuts and enjoy while warm.

Cinnamon and Pecan Pie

Prep time: 10 minutes | Cook time: 25 minutes | Serves 4

1 pie dough
½ teaspoons cinnamon
¾ teaspoon vanilla extract
2 eggs
¾ cup maple syrup

⅛ teaspoon nutmeg
3 tablespoons melted butter, divided
2 tablespoons sugar
½ cup chopped pecans

1. Preheat the air fryer to 370ºF (188ºC).
2. In a small bowl, coat the pecans in 1 tablespoon of melted butter.
3. Transfer the pecans to the air fryer and air fry for about 10 minutes.
4. Put the pie dough in a greased pie pan and add the pecans on top.
5. In a bowl, mix the rest of the ingredients. Pour this over the pecans.
6. Put the pan in the air fryer and bake for 25 minutes.
7. Serve immediately.

Chapter 9 Wraps and Sandwiches

Nugget and Veggie Taco Wraps

Prep time: 5 minutes | Cook time: 15 minutes | Serves 4

1 tablespoon water
4 pieces commercial vegan nuggets, chopped
1 small yellow onion, diced
1 small red bell

pepper, chopped
2 cobs grilled corn kernels
4 large corn tortillas
Mixed greens, for garnish

1. Preheat the air fryer to 400ºF (204ºC).
2. Over a medium heat, sauté the nuggets in the water with the onion, corn kernels and bell pepper in a skillet, then remove from the heat.
3. Fill the tortillas with the nuggets and vegetables and fold them up. Transfer to the inside of the fryer and air fry for 15 minutes.
4. Once crispy, serve immediately, garnished with the mixed greens.

Veggie Salsa Wraps

Prep time: 5 minutes | Cook time: 7 minutes | Serves 4

1 cup red onion, sliced
1 zucchini, chopped
1 poblano pepper, deseeded and finely chopped
1 head lettuce
½ cup salsa
8 ounces (227 g) Mozzarella cheese

1. Preheat the air fryer to 390ºF (199ºC).
2. Place the red onion, zucchini, and poblano pepper in the air fryer basket and air fry for 7 minutes, or until they are tender and fragrant.
3. Divide the veggie mixture among the lettuce leaves and spoon the salsa over the top. Finish off with Mozzarella cheese. Wrap the lettuce leaves around the filling.
4. Serve immediately.

Tuna and Lettuce Wraps

Prep time: 10 minutes | Cook time: 4 to 7 minutes | Serves 4

1 pound (454 g) fresh tuna steak, cut into 1-inch cubes
1 tablespoon grated fresh ginger
2 garlic cloves, minced
½ teaspoon toasted sesame oil
4 low-sodium whole-wheat tortillas
¼ cup low-fat mayonnaise
2 cups shredded romaine lettuce
1 red bell pepper, thinly sliced

1. Preheat the air fryer to 390ºF (199ºC).
2. In a medium bowl, mix the tuna, ginger, garlic, and sesame oil. Let it stand for 10 minutes.
3. Air fry the tuna in the air fryer basket for 4 to 7 minutes, or until lightly browned.
4. Make the wraps with the tuna, tortillas, mayonnaise, lettuce, and bell pepper.
5. Serve immediately.

Chicken Pita Sandwich

Prep time: 10 minutes | Cook time: 9 to 11 minutes | Serves 4

2 boneless, skinless chicken breasts, cut into 1-inch cubes
1 small red onion, sliced
1 red bell pepper, sliced
¹/₃ cup Italian salad dressing, divided
½ teaspoon dried thyme
4 pita pockets, split
2 cups torn butter lettuce
1 cup chopped cherry tomatoes

1. Preheat the air fryer to 380ºF (193ºC).
2. Place the chicken, onion, and bell pepper in the air fryer basket. Drizzle with 1 tablespoon of the Italian salad dressing, add the thyme, and toss.
3. Bake for 9 to 11 minutes, or until the chicken is 165ºF (74ºC) on a food thermometer, stirring once during cooking time.
4. Transfer the chicken and vegetables to a bowl and toss with the remaining salad dressing.
5. Assemble sandwiches with the pita pockets, butter lettuce, and cherry tomatoes. Serve immediately.

Smoky Chicken Sandwich

Prep time: 10 minutes | Cook time: 11 minutes | Serves 2

2 boneless, skinless chicken breasts (8 ounces / 227 g each), sliced horizontally in half and separated into 4 thinner cutlets
Kosher salt and freshly ground black pepper, to taste
½ cup all-purpose flour
3 large eggs, lightly beaten
½ cup dried bread crumbs
1 tablespoon smoked paprika
Cooking spray
½ cup marinara sauce
6 ounces (170 g) smoked Mozzarella cheese, grated
2 store-bought soft, sesame-seed hamburger or Italian buns, split

1. Preheat the air fryer to 350ºF (177ºC).
2. Season the chicken cutlets all over with salt and pepper. Set up three shallow bowls: Place the flour in the first bowl, the eggs in the second, and stir together the bread crumbs and smoked paprika in the third. Coat the chicken pieces in the flour, then dip fully in the egg. Dredge in the paprika bread crumbs, then transfer to a wire rack set over a baking sheet and spray both sides liberally with cooking spray.
3. Transfer 2 of the chicken cutlets to the air fryer and air fry for 6 minutes, or until beginning to brown. Spread each cutlet with 2 tablespoons of the marinara sauce and sprinkle with one-quarter of the smoked Mozzarella. Increase the temperature to 400ºF (204ºC) and air fry for 5 minutes more, or until the chicken is cooked through and crisp and the cheese is melted and golden brown.
4. Transfer the cutlets to a plate, stack on top of each other, and place inside a bun. Repeat with the remaining chicken cutlets, marinara, smoked Mozzarella, and bun.
5. Serve the sandwiches warm.

Lettuce Fajita Meatball Wraps

Prep time: 10 minutes | Cook time: 10 minutes | Serves 4

1 pound (454 g) 85% lean ground beef
½ cup salsa, plus more for serving
¼ cup chopped onions
¼ cup diced green or red bell peppers
1 large egg, beaten
1 teaspoon fine sea salt
½ teaspoon chili powder
½ teaspoon ground cumin
1 clove garlic, minced
Cooking spray

For Serving:
8 leaves Boston lettuce
Pico de gallo or salsa
Lime slices

1. Preheat the air fryer to 350ºF (177ºC). Spray the air fryer basket with cooking spray.
2. In a large bowl, mix together all the ingredients until well combined.
3. Shape the meat mixture into eight 1-inch balls. Place the meatballs in the air fryer basket, leaving a little space between them. Air fry for 10 minutes, or until cooked through and no longer pink inside and the internal temperature reaches 145ºF (63ºC).
4. Serve each meatball on a lettuce leaf, topped with pico de gallo or salsa. Serve with lime slices.

Classic Sloppy Joes

Prep time: 10 minutes | Cook time: 17 to 19 minutes | Makes 4 large sandwiches or 8 sliders

1 pound (454 g) very lean ground beef
1 teaspoon onion powder
⅓ cup ketchup
¼ cup water
½ teaspoon celery seed
1 tablespoon lemon juice
1½ teaspoons brown sugar
1¼ teaspoons low-sodium Worcestershire sauce
½ teaspoon salt (optional)
½ teaspoon vinegar
⅛ teaspoon dry mustard
Hamburger or slider buns, for serving
Cooking spray

1. Preheat the air fryer to 390ºF (199ºC). Spray the air fryer basket with cooking spray.
2. Break raw ground beef into small chunks and pile into the basket. Roast for 5 minutes. Stir to break apart and roast for 3 minutes. Stir and roast for 2 to 4 minutes longer, or until meat is well done.
3. Remove the meat from the air fryer, drain, and use a knife and fork to crumble into small pieces.
4. Give your air fryer basket a quick rinse to remove any bits of meat.
5. Place all the remaining ingredients, except for the buns, in a baking pan and mix together. Add the meat and stir well.
6. Bake at 330ºF (166ºC) for 5 minutes. Stir and bake for 2 minutes.
7. Scoop onto buns. Serve hot.

Cheesy Chicken Sandwich

Prep time: 10 minutes | Cook time: 5 to 7 minutes | Serves 1

⅓ cup chicken, cooked and shredded
2 Mozzarella slices
1 hamburger bun
¼ cup shredded cabbage
1 teaspoon mayonnaise
2 teaspoons butter, melted
1 teaspoon olive oil
½ teaspoon balsamic vinegar
¼ teaspoon smoked paprika
¼ teaspoon black pepper
¼ teaspoon garlic powder
Pinch of salt

1. Preheat the air fryer to 370ºF (188ºC).
2. Brush some butter onto the outside of the hamburger bun.
3. In a bowl, coat the chicken with the garlic powder, salt, pepper, and paprika.
4. In a separate bowl, stir together the mayonnaise, olive oil, cabbage, and balsamic vinegar to make coleslaw.
5. Slice the bun in two. Start building the sandwich, starting with the chicken, followed by the Mozzarella, the coleslaw, and finally the top bun.
6. Transfer the sandwich to the air fryer and bake for 5 to 7 minutes.
7. Serve immediately.

Veggie Pita Sandwich

Prep time: 10 minutes | Cook time: 9 to 12 minutes | Serves 4

1 baby eggplant, peeled and chopped
1 red bell pepper, sliced
½ cup diced red onion
½ cup shredded carrot
1 teaspoon olive oil
⅓ cup low-fat Greek yogurt
½ teaspoon dried tarragon
2 low-sodium whole-wheat pita breads, halved crosswise

1. Preheat the air fryer to 390ºF (199ºC).
2. In a baking pan, stir together the eggplant, red bell pepper, red onion, carrot, and olive oil. Put the vegetable mixture into the air fryer basket and roast for 7 to 9 minutes, stirring once, until the vegetables are tender. Drain if necessary.
3. In a small bowl, thoroughly mix the yogurt and tarragon until well combined.
4. Stir the yogurt mixture into the vegetables. Stuff one-fourth of this mixture into each pita pocket.
5. Place the sandwiches in the air fryer and bake for 2 to 3 minutes, or until the bread is toasted.
6. Serve immediately.

Chicken-Lettuce Wraps

Prep time: 15 minutes | Cook time: 12 to 16 minutes | Serves 2 to 4

1 pound (454 g) boneless, skinless chicken thighs, trimmed
1 teaspoon vegetable oil
2 tablespoons lime juice
1 shallot, minced
1 tablespoon fish sauce, plus extra for serving
2 teaspoons packed brown sugar
1 garlic clove, minced
⅛ teaspoon red pepper flakes
1 mango, peeled, pitted, and cut into ¼-inch pieces
⅓ cup chopped fresh mint
⅓ cup chopped fresh cilantro
⅓ cup chopped fresh Thai basil
1 head Bibb lettuce, leaves separated (8 ounces / 227 g)
¼ cup chopped dry-roasted peanuts
2 Thai chiles, stemmed and sliced thin

1. Preheat the air fryer to 400ºF (204ºC).
2. Pat the chicken dry with paper towels and rub with oil. Place the chicken in air fryer basket and air fry for 12 to 16 minutes, or until the chicken registers 175ºF (79ºC), flipping and rotating chicken halfway through cooking.
3. Meanwhile, whisk lime juice, shallot, fish sauce, sugar, garlic, and pepper flakes together in large bowl; set aside.
4. Transfer chicken to cutting board, let cool slightly, then shred into bite-size pieces using 2 forks. Add the shredded chicken, mango, mint, cilantro, and basil to bowl with dressing and toss to coat.
5. Serve the chicken in the lettuce leaves, passing peanuts, Thai chiles, and extra fish sauce separately.

Tuna Muffin Sandwich

Prep time: 8 minutes | Cook time: 4 to 8 minutes | Serves 4

1 (6-ounce / 170-g) can chunk light tuna, drained
¼ cup mayonnaise
2 tablespoons mustard
1 tablespoon lemon juice
2 green onions, minced
3 English muffins, split with a fork
3 tablespoons softened butter
6 thin slices Provolone or Muenster cheese

1. Preheat the air fryer to 390ºF (199ºC).
2. In a small bowl, combine the tuna, mayonnaise, mustard, lemon juice, and green onions. Set aside.
3. Butter the cut side of the English muffins. Bake, butter-side up, in the air fryer for 2 to 4 minutes, or until light golden brown. Remove the muffins from the air fryer basket.
4. Top each muffin with one slice of cheese and return to the air fryer. Bake for 2 to 4 minutes or until the cheese melts and starts to brown.
5. Remove the muffins from the air fryer, top with the tuna mixture, and serve.

Cheesy Greens Sandwich

Prep time: 15 minutes | Cook time: 10 to 13 minutes | Serves 4

1½ cups chopped mixed greens
2 garlic cloves, thinly sliced
2 teaspoons olive oil
2 slices low-sodium low-fat Swiss cheese
4 slices low-sodium whole-wheat bread
Cooking spray

1. Preheat the air fryer to 400ºF (204ºC).
2. In a baking pan, mix the greens, garlic, and olive oil. Air fry for 4 to 5 minutes, stirring once, until the vegetables are tender. Drain, if necessary.
3. Make 2 sandwiches, dividing half of the greens and 1 slice of Swiss cheese between 2 slices of bread. Lightly spray the outsides of the sandwiches with cooking spray.
4. Bake the sandwiches in the air fryer for 6 to 8 minutes, turning with tongs halfway through, until the bread is toasted and the cheese melts.
5. Cut each sandwich in half and serve.

Cheesy Shrimp Sandwich

Prep time: 10 minutes | Cook time: 5 to 7 minutes | Serves 4

1¼ cups shredded Colby, Cheddar, or Havarti cheese
1 (6-ounce / 170-g) can tiny shrimp, drained
3 tablespoons mayonnaise
2 tablespoons minced green onion
4 slices whole grain or whole-wheat bread
2 tablespoons softened butter

1. Preheat the air fryer to 400ºF (204ºC).
2. In a medium bowl, combine the cheese, shrimp, mayonnaise, and green onion, and mix well.
3. Spread this mixture on two of the slices of bread. Top with the other slices of bread to make two sandwiches. Spread the sandwiches lightly with butter.
4. Air fry for 5 to 7 minutes, or until the bread is browned and crisp and the cheese is melted.
5. Cut in half and serve warm.

Bacon and Bell Pepper Sandwich

Prep time: 10 minutes | Cook time: 6 minutes | Serves 4

⅓ cup spicy barbecue sauce
2 tablespoons honey
8 slices cooked bacon, cut into thirds
1 red bell pepper, sliced
1 yellow bell pepper, sliced
3 pita pockets, cut in half
1¼ cups torn butter lettuce leaves
2 tomatoes, sliced

1. Preheat the air fryer to 350ºF (177ºC).
2. In a small bowl, combine the barbecue sauce and the honey. Brush this mixture lightly onto the bacon slices and the red and yellow pepper slices.
3. Put the peppers into the air fryer basket and roast for 4 minutes. Then shake the basket, add the bacon, and roast for 2 minutes or until the bacon is browned and the peppers are tender.
4. Fill the pita halves with the bacon, peppers, any remaining barbecue sauce, lettuce, and tomatoes, and serve immediately.

Chapter 10 Appetizers, Snacks, and Side Dishes

Bacon-Wrapped Shrimp and Jalapeño

Prep time: 20 minutes | Cook time: 26 minutes | Serves 8

24 large shrimp, peeled and deveined, about ¾ pound (340 g)
5 tablespoons barbecue sauce, divided
12 strips bacon, cut in half
24 small pickled jalapeño slices

1. Toss together the shrimp and 3 tablespoons of the barbecue sauce. Let stand for 15 minutes. Soak 24 wooden toothpicks in water for 10 minutes. Wrap 1 piece bacon around the shrimp and jalapeño slice, then secure with a toothpick.
2. Preheat the air fryer to 350ºF (177ºC).
3. Working in batches, place half of the shrimp in the air fryer basket, spacing them ½ inch apart. Air fry for 10 minutes. Turn shrimp over with tongs and air fry for 3 minutes more, or until bacon is golden brown and shrimp are cooked through.
4. Brush with the remaining barbecue sauce and serve.

Crispy Apple Chips

Prep time: 5 minutes | Cook time: 25 to 35 minutes | Serves 1

1 Honeycrisp or Pink Lady apple

1. Preheat the air fryer to 300ºF (149ºC).
2. Core the apple with an apple corer, leaving apple whole. Cut the apple into ⅛-inch-thick slices.
3. Arrange the apple slices in the basket, staggering slices as much as possible. Air fry for 25 to 35 minutes, or until the chips are dry and some are lightly browned, turning 4 times with tongs to separate and rotate them from top to bottom.
4. Place the chips in a single layer on a wire rack to cool. Apples will become crisper as they cool. Serve immediately.

Veggie Shrimp Toast

Prep time: 15 minutes | Cook time: 3 to 6 minutes | Serves 4

8 large raw shrimp, peeled and finely chopped
1 egg white
2 garlic cloves, minced
3 tablespoons minced red bell pepper
1 medium celery stalk, minced
2 tablespoons cornstarch
¼ teaspoon Chinese five-spice powder
3 slices firm thin-sliced no-sodium whole-wheat bread

1. Preheat the air fryer to 350ºF (177ºC).
2. In a small bowl, stir together the shrimp, egg white, garlic, red bell pepper, celery, cornstarch, and five-spice powder. Top each slice of bread with one-third of the shrimp mixture, spreading it evenly to the edges. With a sharp knife, cut each slice of bread into 4 strips.
3. Place the shrimp toasts in the air fryer basket in a single layer. You may need to cook them in batches. Air fry for 3 to 6 minutes, until crisp and golden brown.
4. Serve hot.

Crispy Prosciutto-Wrapped Asparagus

Prep time: 5 minutes | Cook time: 16 to 24 minutes | Serves 6

12 asparagus spears, woody ends trimmed
24 pieces thinly sliced prosciutto
Cooking spray

1. Preheat the air fryer to 360ºF (182ºC).
2. Wrap each asparagus spear with 2 slices of prosciutto, then repeat this process with the remaining asparagus and prosciutto.
3. Spray the air fryer basket with cooking spray, then place 2 to 3 bundles in the basket and air fry for 4 minutes. Repeat this process with the remaining asparagus bundles.
4. Remove the bundles and allow to cool on a wire rack for 5 minutes before serving.

Cheesy Hash Brown Bruschetta

Prep time: 5 minutes | Cook time: 6 to 8 minutes | Serves 4

4 frozen hash brown patties
1 tablespoon olive oil
1/3 cup chopped cherry tomatoes
3 tablespoons diced fresh Mozzarella
2 tablespoons grated Parmesan cheese
1 tablespoon balsamic vinegar
1 tablespoon minced fresh basil

1. Preheat the air fryer to 400ºF (204ºC).
2. Place the hash brown patties in the air fryer in a single layer. Air fry for 6 to 8 minutes, or until the potatoes are crisp, hot, and golden brown.
3. Meanwhile, combine the olive oil, tomatoes, Mozzarella, Parmesan, vinegar, and basil in a small bowl.
4. When the potatoes are done, carefully remove from the basket and arrange on a serving plate. Top with the tomato mixture and serve.

Veggie Salmon Nachos

Prep time: 10 minutes | Cook time: 9 to 12 minutes | Serves 6

2 ounces (57 g) baked no-salt corn tortilla chips
1 (5-ounce / 142-g) baked salmon fillet, flaked
1/2 cup canned low-sodium black beans, rinsed and drained
1 red bell pepper, chopped
1/2 cup grated carrot
1 jalapeño pepper, minced
1/3 cup shredded low-sodium low-fat Swiss cheese
1 tomato, chopped

1. Preheat the air fryer to 360ºF (182ºC).
2. In a baking pan, layer the tortilla chips. Top with the salmon, black beans, red bell pepper, carrot, jalapeño, and Swiss cheese.
3. Bake in the air fryer for 9 to 12 minutes, or until the cheese is melted and starts to brown.
4. Top with the tomato and serve.

Spicy Chicken Wings

Prep time: 5 minutes | Cook time: 20 minutes | Serves 2 to 4

1¼ pounds (567 g) chicken wings, separated into flats and drumettes
1 teaspoon baking powder
1 teaspoon cayenne pepper
1/4 teaspoon garlic powder
Kosher salt and freshly ground black pepper, to taste
1 tablespoon unsalted butter, melted

For serving:

Blue cheese dressing
Celery
Carrot sticks

1. Place the chicken wings on a large plate, then sprinkle evenly with the baking powder, cayenne, and garlic powder. Toss the wings with your hands, making sure the baking powder and seasonings fully coat them, until evenly incorporated. Let the wings stand in the refrigerator for 1 hour or up to overnight.
2. Preheat the air fryer to 400ºF (204ºC).
3. Season the wings with salt and black pepper, then transfer to the air fryer, standing them up on end against the air fryer basket wall and each other. Air fry for 20 minutes, or until the wings are cooked through and crisp and golden brown. Transfer the wings to a bowl and toss with the butter while they're hot.
4. Arrange the wings on a platter and serve warm with the blue cheese dressing, celery and carrot sticks.

Fast and Easy Tortilla Chips

Prep time: 5 minutes | Cook time: 3 minutes | Serves 2

8 corn tortillas
1 tablespoon olive
oil
Salt, to taste

1. Preheat the air fryer to 390ºF (199ºC).
2. Slice the corn tortillas into triangles. Coat with a light brushing of olive oil.
3. Put the tortilla pieces in the air fryer basket and air fry for 3 minutes. You may need to do this in batches.
4. Season with salt before serving.

BBQ Pork Ribs

Prep time: 5 minutes | Cook time: 35 minutes | Serves 2

1 tablespoon kosher salt
1 tablespoon dark brown sugar
1 tablespoon sweet paprika
1 teaspoon garlic powder
1 teaspoon onion powder
1 teaspoon poultry seasoning
½ teaspoon mustard powder
½ teaspoon freshly ground black pepper
2¼ pounds (1 kg) individually cut St. Louis–style pork spareribs

1. Preheat the air fryer to 350ºF (177ºC).
2. In a large bowl, whisk together the salt, brown sugar, paprika, garlic powder, onion powder, poultry seasoning, mustard powder, and pepper. Add the ribs and toss. Rub the seasonings into them with your hands until they're fully coated.
3. Arrange the ribs in the air fryer basket, standing up on their ends and leaned up against the wall of the basket and each other. Roast for 35 minutes, or until the ribs are tender inside and golden brown and crisp on the outside. Transfer the ribs to plates and serve hot.

Coconut-Crusted Shrimp

Prep time: 10 minutes | Cook time: 4 minutes | Serves 2 to 4

½ pound (227 g) medium shrimp, peeled and deveined (tails intact)
1 cup canned coconut milk
Finely grated zest of 1 lime
Kosher salt, to taste
½ cup panko bread crumbs
½ cup unsweetened shredded coconut
Freshly ground black pepper, to taste
Cooking spray
1 small or ½ medium cucumber, halved and deseeded
1 cup coconut yogurt
1 serrano chile, deseeded and minced

1. Preheat the air fryer to 400ºF (204ºC).
2. In a bowl, combine the shrimp, coconut milk, lime zest, and ½ teaspoon kosher salt. Let the shrimp stand for 10 minutes.
3. Meanwhile, in a separate bowl, stir together the bread crumbs and shredded coconut and season with salt and pepper.
4. A few at a time, add the shrimp to the bread crumb mixture and toss to coat completely. Transfer the shrimp to a wire rack set over a baking sheet. Spray the shrimp all over with cooking spray.
5. Transfer the shrimp to the air fryer and air fry for 4 minutes, or until golden brown and cooked through. Transfer the shrimp to a serving platter and season with more salt.
6. Grate the cucumber into a small bowl. Stir in the coconut yogurt and chile and season with salt and pepper. Serve alongside the shrimp while they're warm.

Shishito Peppers with Herb Dressing

Prep time: 10 minutes | Cook time: 6 minutes | Serves 2 to 4

6 ounces (170 g) shishito peppers
1 tablespoon vegetable oil
Kosher salt and freshly ground black pepper, to taste
½ cup mayonnaise
2 tablespoons finely chopped fresh basil leaves
2 tablespoons finely chopped fresh flat-leaf parsley
1 tablespoon finely chopped fresh tarragon
1 tablespoon finely chopped fresh chives
Finely grated zest of ½ lemon
1 tablespoon fresh lemon juice
Flaky sea salt, for serving

1. Preheat the air fryer to 400ºF (204ºC).
2. In a bowl, toss together the shishitos and oil to evenly coat and season with kosher salt and black pepper. Transfer to the air fryer and air fry for 6 minutes, shaking the basket halfway through, or until the shishitos are blistered and lightly charred.
3. Meanwhile, in a small bowl, whisk together the mayonnaise, basil, parsley, tarragon, chives, lemon zest, and lemon juice.
4. Pile the peppers on a plate, sprinkle with flaky sea salt, and serve hot with the dressing.

Spiced Sweet Potato Fries

Prep time: 10 minutes | Cook time: 15 minutes | Serves 2

2 tablespoons olive oil
1½ teaspoons smoked paprika
1½ teaspoons kosher salt, plus more as needed
1 teaspoon chili powder
½ teaspoon ground cumin
½ teaspoon ground turmeric
½ teaspoon mustard powder
¼ teaspoon cayenne pepper
2 medium sweet potatoes (about 10 ounces / 284 g each), cut into wedges, ½ inch thick and 3 inches long
Freshly ground black pepper, to taste
²⁄₃ cup sour cream
1 garlic clove, grated

1. Preheat the air fryer to 400°F (204°C).
2. In a large bowl, combine the olive oil, paprika, salt, chili powder, cumin, turmeric, mustard powder, and cayenne. Add the sweet potatoes, season with black pepper, and toss to evenly coat.
3. Transfer the sweet potatoes to the air fryer (save the bowl with the leftover oil and spices) and air fry for 15 minutes, shaking the basket halfway through, or until golden brown and crisp. Return the potato wedges to the reserved bowl and toss again while they are hot.
4. Meanwhile, in a small bowl, stir together the sour cream and garlic. Season with salt and black pepper and transfer to a serving dish.
5. Serve the potato wedges hot with the garlic sour cream.

Rosemary-Garlic Shoestring Fries

Prep time: 5 minutes | Cook time: 18 minutes | Serves 2

1 large russet potato (about 12 ounces / 340 g), scrubbed clean, and julienned
1 tablespoon vegetable oil
Leaves from 1 sprig fresh rosemary
Kosher salt and freshly ground black pepper, to taste
1 garlic clove, thinly sliced
Flaky sea salt, for serving

1. Preheat the air fryer to 400°F (204°C).
2. Place the julienned potatoes in a large colander and rinse under cold running water until the water runs clear. Spread the potatoes out on a double-thick layer of paper towels and pat dry.
3. In a large bowl, combine the potatoes, oil, and rosemary. Season with kosher salt and pepper and toss to coat evenly. Place the potatoes in the air fryer and air fry for 18 minutes, shaking the basket every 5 minutes and adding the garlic in the last 5 minutes of cooking, or until the fries are golden brown and crisp.
4. Transfer the fries to a plate and sprinkle with flaky sea salt while they're hot. Serve immediately.

Spiced Mixed Nuts

Prep time: 5 minutes | Cook time: 6 minutes | Makes 2 cups

½ cup raw cashews
½ cup raw pecan halves
½ cup raw walnut halves
½ cup raw whole almonds
2 tablespoons olive oil
1 tablespoon light brown sugar
1 teaspoon chopped fresh rosemary
leaves
1 teaspoon chopped fresh thyme leaves
1 teaspoon kosher salt
½ teaspoon ground coriander
¼ teaspoon onion powder
¼ teaspoon freshly ground black pepper
⅛ teaspoon garlic powder

1. Preheat the air fryer to 350°F (177°C).
2. In a large bowl, combine all the ingredients and toss until the nuts are evenly coated in the herbs, spices, and sugar.
3. Scrape the nuts and seasonings into the air fryer and air fry for 6 minutes, or until golden brown and fragrant, shaking the basket halfway through.
4. Transfer the cocktail nuts to a bowl and serve warm.

Lemony Chicken Drumsticks

Prep time: 5 minutes | Cook time: 30 minutes | Serves 2

2 teaspoons freshly ground coarse black pepper
1 teaspoon baking powder
½ teaspoon garlic powder
4 chicken drumsticks (4 ounces / 113 g each)
Kosher salt, to taste
1 lemon

1. In a small bowl, stir together the pepper, baking powder, and garlic powder. Place the drumsticks on a plate and sprinkle evenly with the baking powder mixture, turning the drumsticks so they're well coated. Let the drumsticks stand in the refrigerator for at least 1 hour or up to overnight.
2. Preheat the air fryer to 375ºF (191ºC).
3. Sprinkle the drumsticks with salt, then transfer them to the air fryer, standing them bone-end up and leaning against the wall of the air fryer basket. Air fry for 30 minutes, or until cooked through and crisp on the outside.
4. Transfer the drumsticks to a serving platter and finely grate the zest of the lemon over them while they're hot. Cut the lemon into wedges and serve with the warm drumsticks.

Baked Ricotta

Prep time: 10 minutes | Cook time: 15 minutes | Makes 2 cups

1 (15-ounce / 425-g) container whole milk Ricotta cheese
3 tablespoons grated Parmesan cheese, divided
2 tablespoons extra-virgin olive oil
1 teaspoon chopped fresh thyme leaves
1 teaspoon grated lemon zest
1 clove garlic, crushed with press
¼ teaspoon salt
¼ teaspoon pepper
Toasted baguette slices or crackers, for serving

1. Preheat the air fryer to 380ºF (193ºC).
2. To get the baking dish in and out of the air fryer, create a sling using a 24-inch length of foil, folded lengthwise into thirds.
3. Whisk together the Ricotta, 2 tablespoons of the Parmesan, oil, thyme, lemon zest, garlic, salt, and pepper. Pour into a baking dish. Cover the dish tightly with foil.
4. Place the sling under dish and lift by the ends into the air fryer, tucking the ends of the sling around the dish. Bake for 10 minutes. Remove the foil cover and sprinkle with the remaining 1 tablespoon of the Parmesan. Air fry for 5 more minutes, or until bubbly at edges and the top is browned.
5. Serve warm with toasted baguette slices or crackers.

Cayenne Sesame Nut Mix

Prep time: 10 minutes | Cook time: 2 minutes | Makes 4 cups

1 tablespoon buttery spread, melted
2 teaspoons honey
¼ teaspoon cayenne pepper
2 teaspoons sesame seeds
¼ teaspoon kosher salt
¼ teaspoon freshly ground black pepper
1 cup cashews
1 cup almonds
1 cup mini pretzels
1 cup rice squares cereal
Cooking spray

1. Preheat the air fryer to 360ºF (182ºC).
2. In a large bowl, combine the buttery spread, honey, cayenne pepper, sesame seeds, kosher salt, and black pepper, then add the cashews, almonds, pretzels, and rice squares, tossing to coat.
3. Spray a baking pan with cooking spray, then pour the mixture into the pan and bake for 2 minutes.
4. Remove the sesame mix from the air fryer and allow to cool in the pan on a wire rack for 5 minutes before serving.

Crispy Spiced Chickpeas

Prep time: 5 minutes | Cook time: 6 to 12 minutes | Makes 1½ cups

1 can (15-ounce / 425-g) chickpeas, rinsed and dried with paper towels
1 tablespoon olive oil
½ teaspoon dried rosemary
½ teaspoon dried parsley
½ teaspoon dried chives
¼ teaspoon mustard powder
¼ teaspoon sweet paprika
¼ teaspoon cayenne pepper
Kosher salt and freshly ground black pepper, to taste

1. Preheat the air fryer to 350ºF (177ºC).
2. In a large bowl, combine all the ingredients, except for the kosher salt and black pepper, and toss until the chickpeas are evenly coated in the herbs and spices.
3. Scrape the chickpeas and seasonings into the air fryer and air fry for 6 to 12 minutes, or until browned and crisp, shaking the basket halfway through.
4. Transfer the crispy chickpeas to a bowl, sprinkle with kosher salt and black pepper, and serve warm.

Peppery Chicken Meatballs

Prep time: 5 minutes | Cook time: 13 to 20 minutes | Makes 16 meatballs

2 teaspoons olive oil
¼ cup minced onion
¼ cup minced red bell pepper
2 vanilla wafers, crushed
1 egg white
½ teaspoon dried thyme
½ pound (227 g) ground chicken breast

1. Preheat the air fryer to 370ºF (188ºC).
2. In a baking pan, mix the olive oil, onion, and red bell pepper. Put the pan in the air fryer. Air fry for 3 to 5 minutes, or until the vegetables are tender.
3. In a medium bowl, mix the cooked vegetables, crushed wafers, egg white, and thyme until well combined
4. Mix in the chicken, gently but thoroughly, until everything is combined.

5. Form the mixture into 16 meatballs and place them in the air fryer basket. Air fry for 10 to 15 minutes, or until the meatballs reach an internal temperature of 165ºF (74ºC) on a meat thermometer.
6. Serve immediately.

Crispy Phyllo Artichoke Triangles

Prep time: 15 minutes | Cook time: 9 to 12 minutes | Makes 18 triangles

¼ cup Ricotta cheese
1 egg white
$^1/_3$ cup minced and drained artichoke hearts
3 tablespoons grated Mozzarella cheese
½ teaspoon dried thyme
6 sheets frozen phyllo dough, thawed
2 tablespoons melted butter

1. Preheat the air fryer to 400ºF (204ºC).
2. In a small bowl, combine the Ricotta cheese, egg white, artichoke hearts, Mozzarella cheese, and thyme, and mix well.
3. Cover the phyllo dough with a damp kitchen towel while you work so it doesn't dry out. Using one sheet at a time, place on the work surface and cut into thirds lengthwise.
4. Put about 1½ teaspoons of the filling on each strip at the base. Fold the bottom right-hand tip of phyllo over the filling to meet the other side in a triangle, then continue folding in a triangle. Brush each triangle with butter to seal the edges. Repeat with the remaining phyllo dough and filling.
5. Place the triangles in the air fryer basket. Bake, 6 at a time, for about 3 to 4 minutes, or until the phyllo is golden brown and crisp.
6. Serve hot.

Lemony Pear Chips

Prep time: 15 minutes | Cook time: 9 to 13 minutes | Serves 4

2 firm Bosc pears, cut crosswise into ⅛-inch-thick slices
1 tablespoon freshly squeezed lemon juice
½ teaspoon ground cinnamon
⅛ teaspoon ground cardamom

1. Preheat the air fryer to 380ºF (193ºC).
2. Separate the smaller stem-end pear rounds from the larger rounds with seeds. Remove the core and seeds from the larger slices. Sprinkle all slices with lemon juice, cinnamon, and cardamom.
3. Put the smaller chips into the air fryer basket. Air fry for 3 to 5 minutes, or until light golden brown, shaking the basket once during cooking. Remove from the air fryer.
4. Repeat with the larger slices, air frying for 6 to 8 minutes, or until light golden brown, shaking the basket once during cooking.
5. Remove the chips from the air fryer. Cool and serve or store in an airtight container at room temperature up for to 2 days.

Sweet Bacon Tater Tots

Prep time: 5 minutes | Cook time: 7 minutes | Serves 4

24 frozen tater tots
6 slices cooked bacon
2 tablespoons maple syrup
1 cup shredded Cheddar cheese

1. Preheat the air fryer to 400ºF (204ºC).
2. Put the tater tots in the air fryer basket. Air fry for 10 minutes, shaking the basket halfway through the cooking time.
3. Meanwhile, cut the bacon into 1-inch pieces.
4. Remove the tater tots from the air fryer basket and put into a baking pan. Top with the bacon and drizzle with the maple syrup. Air fry for 5 minutes, or until the tots and bacon are crisp.
5. Top with the cheese and air fry for 2 minutes, or until the cheese is melted.
6. Serve hot.

Air Fried Pot Stickers

Prep time: 10 minutes | Cook time: 18 to 20 minutes | Makes 30 pot stickers

½ cup finely chopped cabbage
¼ cup finely chopped red bell pepper
2 green onions, finely chopped
1 egg, beaten
2 tablespoons cocktail sauce
2 teaspoons low-sodium soy sauce
30 wonton wrappers
1 tablespoon water, for brushing the wrappers

1. Preheat the air fryer to 360ºF (182ºC).
2. In a small bowl, combine the cabbage, pepper, green onions, egg, cocktail sauce, and soy sauce, and mix well.
3. Put about 1 teaspoon of the mixture in the center of each wonton wrapper. Fold the wrapper in half, covering the filling; dampen the edges with water, and seal. You can crimp the edges of the wrapper with your fingers so they look like the pot stickers you get in restaurants. Brush them with water.
4. Place the pot stickers in the air fryer basket and air fry in 2 batches for 9 to 10 minutes, or until the pot stickers are hot and the bottoms are lightly browned.
5. Serve hot.

Bacon-Wrapped Dates

Prep time: 10 minutes | Cook time: 10 to 14 minutes | Serves 6

12 dates, pitted
6 slices high-quality bacon, cut in half
Cooking spray

1. Preheat the air fryer to 360ºF (182ºC).
2. Wrap each date with half a bacon slice and secure with a toothpick.
3. Spray the air fryer basket with cooking spray, then place 6 bacon-wrapped dates in the basket and bake for 5 to 7 minutes or until the bacon is crispy. Repeat this process with the remaining dates.
4. Remove the dates and allow to cool on a wire rack for 5 minutes before serving.

Creamy Spinach-Broccoli Dip

Prep time: 10 minutes | Cook time: 9 to 14 minutes | Serves 4

½ cup low-fat Greek yogurt
¼ cup nonfat cream cheese
½ cup frozen chopped broccoli, thawed and drained
½ cup frozen chopped spinach, thawed and drained
⅓ cup chopped red bell pepper
1 garlic clove, minced
½ teaspoon dried oregano
2 tablespoons grated low-sodium Parmesan cheese

1. Preheat the air fryer to 340ºF (171ºC).
2. In a medium bowl, blend the yogurt and cream cheese until well combined.
3. Stir in the broccoli, spinach, red bell pepper, garlic, and oregano. Transfer to a baking pan. Sprinkle with the Parmesan cheese.
4. Place the pan in the air fryer basket. Bake for 9 to 14 minutes, or until the dip is bubbly and the top starts to brown.
5. Serve immediately.

Poutine with Waffle Fries

Prep time: 10 minutes | Cook time: 15 to 17 minutes | Serves 4

2 cups frozen waffle cut fries
2 teaspoons olive oil
1 red bell pepper, chopped
2 green onions, sliced
1 cup shredded Swiss cheese
½ cup bottled chicken gravy

1. Preheat the air fryer to 380ºF (193ºC).
2. Toss the waffle fries with the olive oil and place in the air fryer basket. Air fry for 10 to 12 minutes, or until the fries are crisp and light golden brown, shaking the basket halfway through the cooking time.
3. Transfer the fries to a baking pan and top with the pepper, green onions, and cheese. Air fry for 3 minutes, or until the vegetables are crisp and tender.
4. Remove the pan from the air fryer and drizzle the gravy over the fries. Air fry for 2 minutes, or until the gravy is hot.
5. Serve immediately.

Cheesy Stuffed Mushrooms

Prep time: 10 minutes | Cook time: 8 to 12 minutes | Serves 4

16 medium button mushrooms, rinsed and patted dry
⅓ cup low-sodium salsa
3 garlic cloves, minced
1 medium onion, finely chopped
1 jalapeño pepper, minced
⅛ teaspoon cayenne pepper
3 tablespoons shredded Pepper Jack cheese
2 teaspoons olive oil

1. Preheat the air fryer to 350ºF (177ºC).
2. Remove the stems from the mushrooms and finely chop them, reserving the whole caps.
3. In a medium bowl, mix the salsa, garlic, onion, jalapeño, cayenne, and Pepper Jack cheese. Stir in the chopped mushroom stems.
4. Stuff this mixture into the mushroom caps, mounding the filling. Drizzle the olive oil on the mushrooms. Air fry the mushrooms in the air fryer basket for 8 to 12 minutes, or until the filling is hot and the mushrooms are tender.
5. Serve immediately.

Spicy Kale Chips

Prep time: 5 minutes | Cook time: 8 to 12 minutes | Serves 4

5 cups kale, large stems removed and chopped
2 teaspoons canola oil
¼ teaspoon smoked paprika
¼ teaspoon kosher salt
Cooking spray

1. Preheat the air fryer to 390ºF (199ºC).
2. In a large bowl, toss the kale, canola oil, smoked paprika, and kosher salt.
3. Spray the air fryer basket with cooking spray, then place half the kale in the basket and air fry for 2 to 3 minutes.
4. Shake the basket and air fry for 2 to 3 more minutes, or until crispy. Repeat this process with the remaining kale.
5. Remove the kale and allow to cool on a wire rack for 3 to 5 minutes before serving.

Buffalo Cauliflower with Sour Dip

Prep time: 10 minutes | Cook time: 10 to 14 minutes | Serves 6

1 large head cauliflower, separated into small florets
1 tablespoon olive oil
½ teaspoon garlic powder
⅓ cup low-sodium hot wing sauce, divided
⅔ cup nonfat Greek yogurt
½ teaspoons Tabasco sauce
1 celery stalk, chopped
1 tablespoon crumbled blue cheese

1. Preheat the air fryer to 380ºF (193ºC).
2. In a large bowl, toss the cauliflower florets with the olive oil. Sprinkle with the garlic powder and toss again to coat. Put half of the cauliflower in the air fryer basket. Air fry for 5 to 7 minutes, or until the cauliflower is browned, shaking the basket once during cooking.
3. Transfer to a serving bowl and toss with half of the wing sauce. Repeat with the remaining cauliflower and wing sauce.
4. In a small bowl, stir together the yogurt, Tabasco sauce, celery, and blue cheese. Serve the cauliflower with the dip.

Zucchini and Potato Tots

Prep time: 5 minutes | Cook time: 20 minutes | Serves 4

1 large zucchini, grated
1 medium baked potato, skin removed and mashed
¼ cup shredded Cheddar cheese
1 large egg, beaten
½ teaspoon kosher salt
Cooking spray

1. Preheat the air fryer to 390ºF (199ºC).
2. Wrap the grated zucchini in a paper towel and squeeze out any excess liquid, then combine the zucchini, baked potato, shredded Cheddar cheese, egg, and kosher salt in a large bowl.
3. Spray a baking pan with cooking spray, then place individual tablespoons of the zucchini mixture in the pan and air fry for 10 minutes. Repeat this process with the remaining mixture.
4. Remove the tots and allow to cool on a wire rack for 5 minutes before serving.

Lemony Endive in Curried Yogurt

Prep time: 5 minutes | Cook time: 10 minutes | Serves 6

6 heads endive
½ cup plain and fat-free yogurt
3 tablespoons lemon juice
1 teaspoon garlic powder
½ teaspoon curry powder
Salt and ground black pepper, to taste

1. Wash the endives, and slice them in half lengthwise.
2. In a bowl, mix together the yogurt, lemon juice, garlic powder, curry powder, salt and pepper.
3. Brush the endive halves with the marinade, coating them completely. Allow to sit for at least 30 minutes or up to 24 hours.
4. Preheat the air fryer to 320ºF (160ºC).
5. Put the endives in the air fryer basket and air fry for 10 minutes.
6. Serve hot.

Mozzarella Arancini

Prep time: 5 minutes | Cook time: 8 to 11 minutes | Makes 16 arancini

2 cups cooked rice, cooled
2 eggs, beaten
1½ cups panko bread crumbs, divided
½ cup grated Parmesan cheese
2 tablespoons minced fresh basil
16 ¾-inch cubes Mozzarella cheese
2 tablespoons olive oil

1. Preheat the air fryer to 400ºF (204ºC).
2. In a medium bowl, combine the rice, eggs, ½ cup of the bread crumbs, Parmesan cheese, and basil. Form this mixture into 16 1½-inch balls.
3. Poke a hole in each of the balls with your finger and insert a Mozzarella cube. Form the rice mixture firmly around the cheese.
4. On a shallow plate, combine the remaining 1 cup of the bread crumbs with the olive oil and mix well. Roll the rice balls in the bread crumbs to coat.
5. Air fry the arancini in batches for 8 to 11 minutes or until golden brown.
6. Serve hot.

Tortellini with Spicy Dipping Sauce

Prep time: 5 minutes | Cook time: 20 minutes | Serves 4

¾ cup mayonnaise
2 tablespoons mustard
1 egg
½ cup flour
½ teaspoon dried oregano

1½ cups bread crumbs
2 tablespoons olive oil
2 cups frozen cheese tortellini

1. Preheat the air fryer to 380ºF (193ºC).
2. In a small bowl, combine the mayonnaise and mustard and mix well. Set aside.
3. In a shallow bowl, beat the egg. In a separate bowl, combine the flour and oregano. In another bowl, combine the bread crumbs and olive oil, and mix well.
4. Drop the tortellini, a few at a time, into the egg, then into the flour, then into the egg again, and then into the bread crumbs to coat. Put into the air fryer basket, cooking in batches.
5. Air fry for about 10 minutes, shaking halfway through the cooking time, or until the tortellini are crisp and golden brown on the outside. Serve with the mayonnaise mixture.

Pigs in a Blanket

Prep time: 5 minutes | Cook time: 14 minutes | Serves 4 to 6

24 cocktail smoked sausages
6 slices deli-sliced Cheddar cheese, each cut into 8

rectangular pieces
1 (8-ounce / 227-g) tube refrigerated crescent roll dough

1. Preheat the air fryer to 350ºF (177ºC).
2. Unroll the crescent roll dough into one large sheet. If your crescent roll dough has perforated seams, pinch or roll all the perforated seams together. Cut the large sheet of dough into 4 rectangles. Then cut each rectangle into 6 pieces by making one slice lengthwise in the middle and 2 slices horizontally. You should have 24 pieces of dough.

3. Make a deep slit lengthwise down the center of the cocktail sausage. Stuff two pieces of cheese into the slit in the sausage. Roll one piece of crescent dough around the stuffed cocktail sausage, leaving the ends of the sausage exposed. Pinch the seam together. Repeat with the remaining sausages.
4. Air fry in 2 batches for 7 minutes, placing the sausages seam-side down in the basket. Serve hot.

Breaded Artichoke Hearts

Prep time: 5 minutes | Cook time: 8 minutes | Serves 14

14 whole artichoke hearts, packed in water
1 egg
½ cup all-purpose flour

⅓ cup panko bread crumbs
1 teaspoon Italian seasoning
Cooking spray

1. Preheat the air fryer to 380ºF (193ºC)
2. Squeeze excess water from the artichoke hearts and place them on paper towels to dry.
3. In a small bowl, beat the egg. In another small bowl, place the flour. In a third small bowl, combine the bread crumbs and Italian seasoning, and stir.
4. Spritz the air fryer basket with cooking spray.
5. Dip the artichoke hearts in the flour, then the egg, and then the bread crumb mixture.
6. Place the breaded artichoke hearts in the air fryer. Spray them with cooking spray. Air fry for 8 minutes, or until the artichoke hearts have browned and are crisp, flipping once halfway through.
7. Let cool for 5 minutes before serving.

Herbed Pita Chips

Prep time: 5 minutes | Cook time: 5 to 6 minutes | Serves 4

¼ teaspoon dried basil
¼ teaspoon marjoram
¼ teaspoon ground oregano
¼ teaspoon garlic powder
¼ teaspoon ground thyme
¼ teaspoon salt
2 whole 6-inch pitas, whole grain or white
Cooking spray

1. Preheat the air fryer to 330ºF (166ºC).
2. Mix all the seasonings together.
3. Cut each pita half into 4 wedges. Break apart wedges at the fold.
4. Mist one side of pita wedges with oil. Sprinkle with half of seasoning mix.
5. Turn pita wedges over, mist the other side with oil, and sprinkle with remaining seasonings.
6. Place pita wedges in air fryer basket and bake for 2 minutes.
7. Shake the basket and bake for 2 minutes longer. Shake again, and if needed, bake for 1 or 2 more minutes, or until crisp. Watch carefully because at this point they will cook very quickly.
8. Serve hot.

Cheesy Apple Roll-Ups

Prep time: 5 minutes | Cook time: 4 to 5 minutes | Makes 8 roll-ups

8 slices whole wheat sandwich bread
4 ounces (113 g) Colby Jack cheese, grated
½ small apple, chopped
2 tablespoons butter, melted

1. Preheat the air fryer to 390ºF (199ºC).
2. Remove the crusts from the bread and flatten the slices with a rolling pin. Don't be gentle. Press hard so that bread will be very thin.
3. Top bread slices with cheese and chopped apple, dividing the ingredients evenly.
4. Roll up each slice tightly and secure each with one or two toothpicks.
5. Brush outside of rolls with melted butter.
6. Place in air fryer basket and air fry for 4 to 5 minutes, or until outside is crisp and nicely browned.
7. Serve hot.

Cajun Zucchini Chips

Prep time: 5 minutes | Cook time: 15 to 16 minutes | Serves 4

2 large zucchini, cut into ⅛-inch-thick slices
2 teaspoons Cajun seasoning
Cooking spray

1. Preheat the air fryer to 370ºF (188ºC).
2. Spray the air fryer basket lightly with cooking spray.
3. Put the zucchini slices in a medium bowl and spray them generously with cooking spray.
4. Sprinkle the Cajun seasoning over the zucchini and stir to make sure they are evenly coated with oil and seasoning.
5. Place the slices in a single layer in the air fryer basket, making sure not to overcrowd. You will need to cook these in several batches.
6. Air fry for 8 minutes. Flip the slices over and air fry for an additional 7 to 8 minutes, or until they are as crisp and brown as you prefer.
7. Serve immediately.

Rosemary Baked Cashews

Prep time: 5 minutes | Cook time: 3 minutes | Makes 2 cups

2 sprigs of fresh rosemary (1 chopped and 1 whole)
1 teaspoon olive oil
1 teaspoon kosher
salt
½ teaspoon honey
2 cups roasted and unsalted whole cashews
Cooking spray

1. Preheat the air fryer to 300ºF (149ºC).
2. In a medium bowl, whisk together the chopped rosemary, olive oil, kosher salt, and honey. Set aside.
3. Spray the air fryer basket with cooking spray, then place the cashews and the whole rosemary sprig in the basket and bake for 3 minutes.
4. Remove the cashews and rosemary from the air fryer, then discard the rosemary and add the cashews to the olive oil mixture, tossing to coat.
5. Allow to cool for 15 minutes before serving.

Beef and Mango Skewers

Prep time: 10 minutes | Cook time: 4 to 7 minutes | Serves 4

¾ pound (340 g) beef sirloin tip, cut into 1-inch cubes
2 tablespoons balsamic vinegar
1 tablespoon olive oil

1 tablespoon honey
½ teaspoon dried marjoram
Pinch of salt
Freshly ground black pepper, to taste
1 mango

1. Preheat the air fryer to 390ºF (199ºC).
2. Put the beef cubes in a medium bowl and add the balsamic vinegar, olive oil, honey, marjoram, salt, and pepper. Mix well, then massage the marinade into the beef with your hands. Set aside.
3. To prepare the mango, stand it on end and cut the skin off, using a sharp knife. Then carefully cut around the oval pit to remove the flesh. Cut the mango into 1-inch cubes.
4. Thread metal skewers alternating with three beef cubes and two mango cubes.
5. Roast the skewers in the air fryer basket for 4 to 7 minutes, or until the beef is browned and at least 145ºF (63ºC).
6. Serve hot.

Spinach and Crab Meat Cups

Prep time: 10 minutes | Cook time: 10 minutes | Makes 30 cups

1 (6-ounce / 170-g) can crab meat, drained to yield ⅓ cup meat
¼ cup frozen spinach, thawed, drained, and chopped
1 clove garlic, minced
½ cup grated

Parmesan cheese
3 tablespoons plain yogurt
¼ teaspoon lemon juice
½ teaspoon Worcestershire sauce
30 mini frozen phyllo shells, thawed
Cooking spray

1. Preheat the air fryer to 390ºF (199ºC).
2. Remove any bits of shell that might remain in the crab meat.
3. Mix the crab meat, spinach, garlic, and cheese together.

4. Stir in the yogurt, lemon juice, and Worcestershire sauce and mix well.
5. Spoon a teaspoon of filling into each phyllo shell.
6. Spray the air fryer basket with cooking spray and arrange half the shells in the basket. Air fry for 5 minutes. Repeat with the remaining shells.
7. Serve immediately.

Artichoke-Spinach Dip

Prep time: 10 minutes | Cook time: 10 minutes | Makes 3 cups

1 (14-ounce / 397-g) can artichoke hearts packed in water, drained and chopped
1 (10-ounce / 284-g) package frozen spinach, thawed and drained
1 teaspoon minced garlic
2 tablespoons

mayonnaise
¼ cup nonfat plain Greek yogurt
¼ cup shredded part-skim Mozzarella cheese
¼ cup grated Parmesan cheese
¼ teaspoon freshly ground black pepper
Cooking spray

1. Preheat the air fryer to 360ºF (182ºC).
2. Wrap the artichoke hearts and spinach in a paper towel and squeeze out any excess liquid, then transfer the vegetables to a large bowl.
3. Add the minced garlic, mayonnaise, plain Greek yogurt, Mozzarella, Parmesan, and black pepper to the large bowl, stirring well to combine.
4. Spray a baking pan with cooking spray, then transfer the dip mixture to the pan and air fry for 10 minutes.
5. Remove the dip from the air fryer and allow to cool in the pan on a wire rack for 10 minutes before serving.

Bruschetta with Basil Pesto

Prep time: 10 minutes | Cook time: 5 to 11 minutes | Serves 4

8 slices French bread, ½ inch thick
2 tablespoons softened butter
1 cup shredded Mozzarella cheese
½ cup basil pesto
1 cup chopped grape tomatoes
2 green onions, thinly sliced

1. Preheat the air fryer to 350ºF (177ºC).
2. Spread the bread with the butter and place butter-side up in the air fryer basket. Bake for 3 to 5 minutes, or until the bread is light golden brown.
3. Remove the bread from the basket and top each piece with some of the cheese. Return to the basket in 2 batches and bake for 1 to 3 minutes, or until the cheese melts.
4. Meanwhile, combine the pesto, tomatoes, and green onions in a small bowl.
5. When the cheese has melted, remove the bread from the air fryer and place on a serving plate. Top each slice with some of the pesto mixture and serve.

Crispy Breaded Beef Cubes

Prep time: 10 minutes | Cook time: 12 to 16 minutes | Serves 4

1 pound (454 g) sirloin tip, cut into 1-inch cubes
1 cup cheese pasta sauce
1½ cups soft bread crumbs
2 tablespoons olive oil
½ teaspoon dried marjoram

1. Preheat the air fryer to 360ºF (182ºC).
2. In a medium bowl, toss the beef with the pasta sauce to coat.
3. In a shallow bowl, combine the bread crumbs, oil, and marjoram, and mix well. Drop the beef cubes, one at a time, into the bread crumb mixture to coat thoroughly.
4. Air fry the beef in two batches for 6 to 8 minutes, shaking the basket once during cooking time, until the beef is at least 145ºF (63ºC) and the outside is crisp and brown.
5. Serve hot.

Cheesy Steak Fries

Prep time: 5 minutes | Cook time: 20 minutes | Serves 5

1 (28-ounce / 794-g) bag frozen steak fries
Cooking spray
Salt and pepper, to taste
½ cup beef gravy
1 cup shredded Mozzarella cheese
2 scallions, green parts only, chopped

1. Preheat the air fryer to 400ºF (204ºC).
2. Place the frozen steak fries in the air fryer. Air fry for 10 minutes. Shake the basket and spritz the fries with cooking spray. Sprinkle with salt and pepper. Air fry for an additional 8 minutes.
3. Pour the beef gravy into a medium, microwave-safe bowl. Microwave for 30 seconds, or until the gravy is warm.
4. Sprinkle the fries with the cheese. Air fry for an additional 2 minutes, until the cheese is melted.
5. Transfer the fries to a serving dish. Drizzle the fries with gravy and sprinkle the scallions on top for a green garnish. Serve.

Cheesy Jalapeño Poppers

Prep time: 5 minutes | Cook time: 10 minutes | Serves 4

8 jalapeño peppers
½ cup whipped cream cheese
¼ cup shredded Cheddar cheese

1. Preheat the air fryer to 360ºF (182ºC).
2. Use a paring knife to carefully cut off the jalapeño tops, then scoop out the ribs and seeds. Set aside.
3. In a medium bowl, combine the whipped cream cheese and shredded Cheddar cheese. Place the mixture in a sealable plastic bag, and using a pair of scissors, cut off one corner from the bag. Gently squeeze some cream cheese mixture into each pepper until almost full.
4. Place a piece of parchment paper on the bottom of the air fryer basket and place the poppers on top, distributing evenly. Air fry for 10 minutes.
5. Allow the poppers to cool for 5 to 10 minutes before serving.

Air Fried Olives

Prep time: 5 minutes | Cook time: 8 minutes | Serves 4

1 (5½-ounce / 156-g) jar pitted green olives
½ cup all-purpose flour

Salt and pepper, to taste
½ cup bread crumbs
1 egg
Cooking spray

1. Preheat the air fryer to 400ºF (204ºC).
2. Remove the olives from the jar and dry thoroughly with paper towels.
3. In a small bowl, combine the flour with salt and pepper to taste. Place the bread crumbs in another small bowl. In a third small bowl, beat the egg.
4. Spritz the air fryer basket with cooking spray.
5. Dip the olives in the flour, then the egg, and then the bread crumbs.
6. Place the breaded olives in the air fryer. It is okay to stack them. Spray the olives with cooking spray. Air fry for 6 minutes. Flip the olives and air fry for an additional 2 minutes, or until brown and crisp.
7. Cool before serving.

Crispy Mozzarella Sticks

Prep time: 5 minutes | Cook time: 6 to 7 minutes | Serves 4 to 8

1 egg
1 tablespoon water
8 eggroll wraps

8 Mozzarella string cheese "sticks"

1. Preheat the air fryer to 390ºF (199ºC).
2. Beat together egg and water in a small bowl.
3. Lay out eggroll wraps and moisten edges with egg wash.
4. Place one piece of string cheese on each wrap near one end.
5. Fold in sides of eggroll wrap over ends of cheese, and then roll up.
6. Brush outside of wrap with egg wash and press gently to seal well.
7. Place in air fryer basket in a single layer and air fry for 5 minutes. Air fry for an additional 1 or 2 minutes, if necessary, or until they are golden brown and crispy.
8. Serve immediately.

Spicy Chicken Bites

Prep time: 10 minutes | Cook time: 10 to 12 minutes | Makes 30 bites

8 ounces boneless and skinless chicken thighs, cut into 30 pieces
¼ teaspoon kosher

salt
2 tablespoons hot sauce
Cooking spray

1. Preheat the air fryer to 390ºF (199ºC).
2. Spray the air fryer basket with cooking spray and season the chicken bites with the kosher salt, then place in the basket and air fry for 10 to 12 minutes or until crispy.
3. While the chicken bites cook, pour the hot sauce into a large bowl.
4. Remove the bites and add to the sauce bowl, tossing to coat. Serve warm.

Root Veggie Chips with Herb Salt

Prep time: 10 minutes | Cook time: 8 minutes | Serves 2

1 parsnip, washed
1 small beet, washed
1 small turnip, washed
½ small sweet potato, washed
1 teaspoon olive oil

Cooking spray
Herb Salt:
¼ teaspoon kosher salt
2 teaspoons finely chopped fresh parsley

1. Preheat the air fryer to 360ºF (182ºC).
2. Peel and thinly slice the parsnip, beet, turnip, and sweet potato, then place the vegetables in a large bowl, add the olive oil, and toss.
3. Spray the air fryer basket with cooking spray, then place the vegetables in the basket and air fry for 8 minutes, gently shaking the basket halfway through.
4. While the chips cook, make the herb salt in a small bowl by combining the kosher salt and parsley.
5. Remove the chips and place on a serving plate, then sprinkle the herb salt on top and allow to cool for 2 to 3 minutes before serving.

Coconut Shrimp

Prep + Cook Time: 20 minutes | Servings: 16

Ingredients
½ tsp. salt
1 lb. large shrimp [about 16 to 20 peeled/de-veined]
½ cup flour
2 egg whites
½ cup friendly (panko) bread crumbs
½ cup unsweetened coconut, shredded
Zest of 1 lime
¼ tsp. cayenne pepper
Spray can of vegetable or canola oil
Sweet chili sauce or duck sauce, to serve

Instructions
1 In a shallow dish, beat the eggs with a whisk.
2 Combine the bread crumbs, coconut, lime zest, salt and cayenne pepper in a separate dish.
3 Pre-heat the Air Fryer to 400°F.
4 Coat the shrimp in the flour. Dip the shrimp into the egg mixture, and then into the breadcrumb coconut mixture, ensuring to coat the shrimp all over.
5 Place the shrimp on a plate and spritz with oil. Move the shrimp to the basket of your fryer, taking care not to overlap the fish.
6 Air fry the shrimp for 5 - 6 minutes, ensuring that each shrimp is cooked through and firm before serving.

Tortilla Chips

Prep + Cook Time: 5 minutes | Servings: 2

Ingredients
8 corn tortillas
Salt to taste
1 tbsp. olive oil

Instructions
1 Pre-heat your Air Fryer to 390°F.
2 Slice the corn tortillas into triangles. Coat with a light brushing of olive oil.
3 Put the tortilla pieces in the wire basket and air fry for 3 minutes. You may need to do this in multiple batches.
4 Season with salt before serving.

Naan Bread Dippers

Prep + Cook Time: 50 minutes | Servings: 10

Ingredients
4 naan bread, cut into 2-inch strips
3 tbsp. butter, melted
12 oz. light cream cheese, softened
1 cup plain yogurt
2 tsp. curry powder
2 cups cooked chicken, shredded
4 scallions, minced
⅓ cup golden raisins
6 oz. Monterey Jack cheese, grated [about 2 cups]
¼ cup fresh cilantro, chopped
Salt and freshly ground black pepper
½ cup sliced s
½ cup Major Grey's Chutney

Instructions
1 Pre-heat Air Fryer to 400°F.
2 Slice up the naan in thirds lengthwise before cutting crosswise into 2-inch strips. In a bowl, toss the strips with the melted butter.
3 Move the naan strips to Air Fryer basket. Toast for 5 minutes, shaking the basket halfway through. You will have to do this in two batches.
4 Mix together the softened cream cheese and yogurt with a hand mixer or in a food processor. Add in the curry powder and combine evenly.
5 Fold in the shredded chicken, scallions, golden raisins, Monterey Jack cheese and chopped cilantro.
6 Sprinkle with salt and freshly ground black pepper as desired.
7 Pour the mixture into a 1-quart baking dish and spread out evenly. Arrange the sliced s on top. Air-fry at 300°F for 25 minutes.
8 Put a dollop of Major Grey's chutney in the center of the dip and scatter the scallions on top.
9 Serve the naan dippers with the hot dip.

Snack Mix

Prep + Cook Time: 30 minutes | Servings: 10

Ingredients
½ cup honey
3 tbsp. butter, melted
1 tsp. salt
2 cups sesame sticks
2 cup pepitas [pumpkin seeds]
2 cups granola
1 cup cashews
2 cups crispy corn puff cereal [Kix or Corn Pops]
2 cup mini pretzel crisps

Instructions
1 In a bowl, combine the honey, butter, and salt.
2 In another bowl, mix together the sesame sticks, pepitas, granola, cashews, corn puff cereal, and pretzel crisps.
3 Combine the contents of the two bowls.
4 Pre-heat your Air Fryer to 370°F.
5 Put the mixture in the fryer basket and air-fry for 10 - 12 minutes to toast the snack mixture, shaking the basket frequently. You will have to do this in two batches.
6 Place the snack mix on a cookie sheet and allow it to cool fully.
7 Store in an airtight container for up to one week. Makes a great holiday gift!

Feta Triangles

Prep + Cook Time: 55 minutes | Servings: 5

Ingredients
1 egg yolk, beaten
4 oz. feta cheese
2 tbsp. flat-leafed parsley, finely chopped
1 scallion, finely chopped
2 sheets of frozen filo pastry, defrosted
2 tbsp. olive oil ground black pepper to taste

Instructions
1 In a bowl, combine the beaten egg yolk with the feta, parsley and scallion. Sprinkle on some pepper to taste.
2 Slice each sheet of filo dough into three strips.
3 Place a teaspoonful of the feta mixture on each strip of pastry.
4 Pinch the tip of the pastry and fold it up to enclose the filling and create a triangle. Continue folding the strip in zig-zags until the filling is wrapped in a triangle. Repeat with all of the strips of pastry.
5 Pre-heat the Air Fryer to 390°F.
6 Coat the pastry with a light coating of oil and arrange in the cooking basket.
7 Place the basket in the Air Fryer and cook for 3 minutes.
8 Lower the heat to 360°F and cook for a further 2 minutes or until a golden brown color is achieved

Sage & Onion Stuffing

Prep + Cook Time: 35 minutes | Servings: 6

Ingredients
2 lb. sausage meat
½ onion
½ tsp. garlic puree
1 tsp. sage
3 tbsp. friendly bread crumbs
Pinch of salt
Black pepper

Instructions
1 Combine all of the ingredients in a large bowl.
2 Take equal portions of the mixture, mold them into medium sized balls and put them in the Air Fryer.
3 Cook at 355°F for 15 minutes.

Puppy Poppers

Prep + Cook Time: 25 minutes | Servings: 50 treats

Ingredients
½ cup unsweetened applesauce
1 cup peanut butter
2 cup oats
1 cup flour
1 tsp. baking powder

Instructions
1 Combine the applesauce and peanut butter in a bowl to create a smooth consistency.
2 Pour in the oats, flour and baking powder. Continue mixing to form a soft dough.
3 Shape a half-teaspoon of dough into a ball and continue with the rest of the dough.
4 Pre-heat the Air Fryer to 350°F.
5 Grease the bottom of the basket with oil.
6 Place the poppers in the fryer and cook for 8 minutes, flipping the balls at the halfway point. You may need to cook the poppers in batches.
7 Let the poppers cool and serve immediately or keep in an airtight container for up to 2 weeks.

Masala Cashew

Prep + Cook Time: 20 minutes | Servings: 3

Ingredients
½ lb. cashew nuts
½ tsp. garam masala powder
1 tsp. coriander powder
1 tsp. ghee
1 tsp. red chili powder
½ tsp. black pepper
2 tsp. dry mango powder
1 tsp. sea salt

Instructions
1 Put all the ingredients in a large bowl and toss together well.
2 Arrange the cashew nuts in the basket of your Air Fryer.
3 Cook at 250°F for 15 minutes until the nuts are brown and crispy.
4 Let the nuts cool before serving or transferring to an airtight container to be stored for up to 2 weeks.

Bacon Wrapped Shrimp

Prep + Cook Time: 50 minutes | Servings: 4

Ingredients
1 ¼ lb. tiger shrimp, peeled and deveined [16 pieces]
1 lb. bacon, thinly sliced, room temperature [16 slices]

Instructions
1 Wrap each bacon slice around a piece of shrimp, from the head to the tail. Refrigerate for 20 minutes.
2 Pre-heat the Air Fryer to 390°F.
3 Place the shrimp in the fryer's basket and cook for 5 – 7 minutes.
4 Allow to dry on a paper towel before serving.

Tomato & Avocado Egg Rolls

Prep + Cook Time: 20 minutes | Servings: 5

Ingredients
10 egg roll wrappers
3 avocados, peeled and pitted
1 tomato, diced
Salt and pepper, to taste

Instructions
1 Pre-heat your Air Fryer to 350°F.
2 Put the tomato and avocados in a bowl. Sprinkle on some salt and pepper and mash together with a fork until a smooth consistency is achieved.
3 Spoon equal amounts of the mixture onto the wrappers. Roll the wrappers around the filling, enclosing them entirely.
4 Transfer the rolls to a lined baking dish and cook for 5 minutes.

Cheese Boats

Prep + Cook Time: 30 minutes | Servings: 2

Ingredients
1 cup ground chicken
1 zucchini
1 ½ cups crushed tomatoes
½ tsp. salt
¼ tsp. pepper
½ tsp. garlic powder
2 tbsp. butter or olive oil
½ cup cheese, grated
¼ tsp. dried oregano

Instructions
1 Peel and halve the zucchini. Use a spoon to scoop out the flesh.
2 In a bowl, combine the ground chicken, tomato, garlic powder, butter, cheese, oregano, salt, and pepper. Fill in the hollowed-out zucchini with this mixture.
3 Transfer to the Air Fryer and bake for about 10 minutes at 400°F. Serve warm.

Eggplant

Prep + Cook Time: 45 minutes | Servings: 6

Ingredients
3 eggplants, medium
½ lemon, juiced
1 tbsp. duck fat, or coconut oil
1 tbsp. Maggi sauce
3 tsp. za'atar
1 tsp. sumac
1 tsp. garlic powder
1 tsp. onion powder
1 tsp. extra virgin olive oil
2 bay leaves

Instructions
1 Wash, dry and destem the eggplants. Chop them into 1-inch cubes.
2 In the Air Fryer basket, combine duck fat [or coconut oil], maggi sauce, za'atar, onion powder, garlic powder, sumac and bay leaves.
3 Melt the ingredients for 2 minutes at 320°F, stirring well.
4 Place the eggplant in the Air Fryer basket and allow to cook for 25 minutes.
5 In a large bowl, mix together the lemon juice and extra virgin olive oil. Add the cooked eggplant and stir to coat evenly.
6 Serve immediately with grated parmesan or fresh chopped basil if desired.

Sweet Potato Fries

Prep + Cook Time: 35 minutes | Servings: 5

Ingredients
2 large sweet potatoes
1 tbsp. extra virgin olive oil

Instructions
1 Wash the sweet potatoes. Dry and peel them before chopping them into shoestring fries. In a bowl, toss the fries with the olive oil to coat well.
2 Set your Air Fryer to 320°F and briefly allow to warm. Put the sweet potatoes in the Air Fryer basket and fry for 15 minutes, stirring them at the halfway point.
3 Once done, toss again to make sure no fries are sticking to each other.
4 Turn the heat to 350°F and cook for a further 10 minutes, again giving them a good stir halfway through the cooking time.
5 Serve your fries straightaway.

Chicken, Mushroom & Spinach Pizza

Prep + Cook Time: 25 minutes | Servings: 4

Ingredients
10 ½ oz. minced chicken
1 tsp. garlic powder
1 tsp. black pepper
2 tbsp. tomato basil sauce
5 button mushrooms, sliced thinly
Handful of spinach

Instructions
1 Pre-heat your Air Fryer at 450°F.
2 Add parchment paper onto your baking tray.
3 In a large bowl add the chicken with the black pepper and garlic powder.
4 Add one spoonful of the chicken mix onto your baking tray.
5 Flatten them into 7-inch rounds.
6 Bake in the Air Fryer for about 10 minutes.
7 Take out off the Air Fryer and add the tomato basil sauce onto each round.
8 Add the mushroom on top. Bake again for 5 minutes.
9 Serve immediately.

Turkey Sausage Patties

Prep + Cook Time: 20 minutes | Servings: 6

Ingredients
1 lb. lean ground turkey
1 tsp. olive oil
1 tbsp. chopped chives
1 small onion, diced
1 large garlic clove, chopped
¾ tsp. paprika
Kosher salt and pepper to taste
Pinch of raw sugar
1 tbsp. vinegar
1 tsp. fennel seed
Pinch of nutmeg

Instructions
1 Pre-heat the Air Fryer to 375°F.
2 Add a half-teaspoon of the oil to the fryer, along with the onion and garlic. Air fry for 30 seconds before adding in the fennel. Place everything on a plate.
3 In a bowl, combine the ground turkey with the sugar, paprika, nutmeg, vinegar, chives and the onion mixture. Divide into equal portions and shape each one into a patty.
4 Add another teaspoon of oil to the fryer. Put the patties in the fryer and cook for roughly 3 minutes.
5 Serve with salad or on hamburger buns.

Bacon Fries

Prep + Cook Time: 60 minutes | Servings: 2 – 4

Ingredients
2 large russet potatoes, peeled and cut into ½ inch sticks
5 slices of bacon, diced
2 tbsp. vegetable oil
2 ½ cups cheddar cheese, shredded
3 oz. cream cheese, melted
Salt and freshly ground black pepper
¼ cup chopped scallions
Ranch dressing

Instructions
1 Boil a large pot of salted water.
2 Briefly cook the potato sticks in the boiling water for 4 minutes.
3 Drain the potatoes and run some cold water over them in order to wash off the starch. Pat them dry with a kitchen towel.
4 Pre-heat the Air Fryer to 400°F.
5 Put the chopped bacon in the Air Fryer and air-fry for 4 minutes. Shake the basket at the halfway point.
6 Place the bacon on paper towels to drain any excess

fat and remove the grease from the Air Fryer drawer.
7 Coat the dried potatoes with oil and put them in the Air Fryer basket. Air-fry at 360°F for 25 minutes, giving the basket the occasional shake throughout the cooking time and sprinkling the fries with salt and freshly ground black pepper at the halfway point.
8 Take a casserole dish or baking pan that is small enough to fit inside your Air Fryer and place the fries inside.
9 Mix together the 2 cups of the Cheddar cheese and the melted cream cheese.
10 Pour the cheese mixture over the fries and top them with the rest of the Cheddar cheese and the cooked bacon crumbles.
11 Take absolute care when placing the baking pan inside the cooker. Use a foil sling [a sheet of aluminum foil folded into a strip about 2 inches wide by 24 inches long].
12 Cook the fries at 340°F for 5 minutes, ensuring the cheese melts.
13 Garnish the fries with the chopped scallions and serve straight from in the baking dish with some ranch dressing.

Toasted Pumpkin Seeds

Prep + Cook Time: 25 minutes | Servings: 4

Ingredients
1 ½ cups pumpkin seeds [cut a whole pumpkin & scrape out the insides
using a large spoon, separating the seeds from the flesh]
1 tsp. smoked paprika
1 ½ tsp. salt
Olive oil

Instructions
1 Run the pumpkin seeds under some cold water.
2 Over a medium heat, boil two quarts of salted water in a pot.
3 Add in the pumpkin seeds and cook in the water for 8 to 10 minutes.
4 Dump the contents of the pot into a sieve to drain the seeds. Place them on paper towels and allow them to dry for at least 20 minutes.
5 Pre-heat your Air Fryer to 350°F.
6 In a medium bowl coat the pumpkin seeds with olive oil, smoked paprika and salt.
7 Put them in the fryer's basket and air fry for at least 30 minutes until slightly browned and crispy. Shake the basket a few times during the cooking time.
8 Allow the seeds to cool. Serve with a salad or keep in an airtight container for snacking.

Banana Peppers

Prep + Cook Time: 20 minutes | Servings: 8

Ingredients
1 cup full-fat cream cheese
Cooking spray
16 avocado slices
16 slices salami
Salt and pepper to taste
16 banana peppers

Instructions
1 Pre-heat the Air Fryer to 400°F.
2 Spritz a baking tray with cooking spray.
3 Remove the stems from the banana peppers with a knife.
4 Cut a slit into one side of each banana pepper.
5 Season the cream cheese with the salt and pepper and combine well.
6 Fill each pepper with one spoonful of the cream cheese, followed by one slice of avocado.
7 Wrap the banana peppers in the slices of salami and secure with a toothpick.
8 Place the banana peppers in the baking tray and transfer it to the Air Fryer. Bake for roughly 8 - 10 minutes.

Eggplant Chips

Prep + Cook Time: 45 minutes | Servings: 4

Ingredients
2 eggplants, peeled and thinly sliced
Salt
½ cup tapioca starch
¼ cup canola oil
½ cup water
1 tsp. garlic powder
½ tsp. dried dill weed
½ tsp. ground black pepper, to taste

Instructions
1 Season the eggplant slices with salt and leave for half an hour.
2 Run them under cold water to rinse off any excess salt.
3 In a bowl, coat the eggplant slices with all of the other ingredients.
4 Cook at 390°F for 13 minutes. You may need to do this in batches.
5 Serve with the dipping sauce of your choice.

Sage Potatoes

Prep + Cook Time: 45 minutes | Servings: 8

Ingredients
1 ½ lb. fingerling potatoes, halved lengthwise
2 tbsp. melted butter
¼ cup fresh sage leaves, finely chopped
2 sprigs thyme, chopped
1 tsp. lemon zest, finely grated
¼ tsp. ground pepper
1 tbsp. sea salt flakes
½ tsp. grated ginger

Instructions
1 Place the potatoes in a bowl of cold water and allow to absorb for about half an hour.
2 Dry them with a clean kitchen towel.
3 Transfer to the Air Fryer and roast at 400°F for 15 minutes.
4 Serve with tomato ketchup and mayonnaise if desired.

Dijon & Quinoa Cocktail Meatballs

Prep + Cook Time: 20 minutes | Servings: 6

Ingredients
½ lb. ground pork
½ lb. ground beef
1 cup quinoa, cooked
1 egg, beaten
2 scallions, finely chopped
½ tsp. onion powder
1 ½ tbsp. Dijon mustard
¾ cup ketchup
1 tsp. ancho chili powder
1 tbsp. sesame oil
2 tbsp. tamari sauce
¼ cup balsamic vinegar
2 tbsp. sugar

Instructions
1 In a bowl, stir together all the ingredients and combine well.
2 Use your hands to shape equal amounts of the mixture into small meatballs.
3 Place the meatballs in the Air Fryer and cook at 370°F for 10 minutes. Give the basket a good shake and allow to cook for another 5 minutes.

Ricotta Balls

Prep + Cook Time: 25 minutes | Servings: 2 – 4

Ingredients
2 cups ricotta, grated
2 eggs, separated
2 tbsp. chives, finely chopped
2 tbsp. fresh basil, finely chopped
4 tbsp. flour
¼ tsp. salt to taste
¼ tsp. pepper powder to taste
1 tsp. orange zest, grated
For coating
¼ cup friendly bread crumbs
1 tbsp. vegetable oil

Instructions
1.Pre-heat your Air Fryer at 390°F.
2.In a bowl, combine the yolks, flour, salt, pepper, chives and orange zest. Throw in the ricotta and incorporate with your hands.
3.Mold equal amounts of the mixture into balls.
4.Mix the oil with the bread crumbs until a crumbly consistency is achieved.
5.Coat the balls in the bread crumbs and transfer each one to the fryer's basket.
6.Put the basket in the fryer. Air fry for 8 minutes or until a golden brown color is achieved.
7.Serve with a sauce of your choosing, such as ketchup.

Spiced Nuts

Prep + Cook Time: 40 minutes | Servings: 3 cups

Ingredients
1 egg white, lightly beaten
¼ cup sugar
1 tsp. salt
½ tsp. ground cinnamon
¼ tsp. ground cloves
¼ tsp. ground allspice
Pinch ground cayenne pepper
1 cup pecan halves
1 cup cashews
1 cup s

Instructions
1.In a bowl, combine the egg white with the sugar and spices.
2.Pre-heat the Air Fryer to 300°F.
3.Coat the inside of the fryer's basket with vegetable oil.
4.Cover the nuts with the spiced egg white. Place half of them in the fryer.
5.Air fry for 25 minutes, giving the nuts a few good stirs throughout the cooking time, until they are crunchy and toasted.
6.Repeat with the other half of the nuts.
7.Serve immediately or store in an airtight container for up to two weeks.

Shrimp Bites

Prep + Cook Time: 45 minutes | Servings: 10

Ingredients
1 ¼ lb. shrimp, peeled and deveined
1 tsp. paprika
½ tsp. ground black pepper
½ tsp. red pepper flakes, crushed
1 tbsp. salt
1 tsp. chili powder
1 tbsp. shallot powder
¼ tsp. cumin powder
1 ¼ lb. thin bacon slices

Instructions
1.Coat the shrimps with all of the seasonings.
2.Wrap a slice of bacon around each shrimp, and hold it in place with a toothpick. Refrigerate for half an hour.
3.Transfer to the Air Fryer and fry at 360°F for 7 - 8 minutes.

Cajun Spiced Snack

Prep + Cook Time: 30 minutes | Servings: 5

Ingredients
2 tbsp. Cajun or Creole seasoning
½ cup butter, melted
2 cups peanut
2 cups mini wheat thin crackers
2 cups mini pretzels
2 tsp. salt
1 tsp. cayenne pepper
4 cups plain popcorn
1 tsp. paprika
1 tsp. garlic
½ tsp. thyme
½ tsp. oregano
1 tsp. black pepper
½ tsp. onion powder

Instructions
1.Pre-heat the Air Fryer to 370°F.
2.In a bowl, combine the Cajun spice with the melted butter.
3.In a separate bowl, stir together the peanuts, crackers, popcorn and pretzels. Coat the snacks with the butter mixture.
4.Place in the fryer and fry for 8 - 10 minutes, shaking the basket frequently during the cooking time. You will have to complete this step in two batches.
5.Put the snack mix on a cookie sheet and leave to cool.
6.The snacks can be kept in an airtight container for up to one week.

Cheesy Broccoli Balls
Prep + Cook Time: 20 minutes | Servings: 6

Ingredients
2 eggs, well whisked
2 cups Colby cheese, shredded
1 cup flour
Seasoned salt, to taste
¼ tsp. ground black pepper, or more if preferred
1 head broccoli, chopped into florets
1 cup crushed saltines

Instructions
1.Mix together the eggs, cheese, flour, salt, pepper, and broccoli until a dough-like paste is formed.
2.Refrigerate for 1 hour. Divide the mixture evenly and mold each portion into small balls. Coat the balls in the crushed saltines and spritz them all over with cooking spray.
3.Cook at 360°F for 10 minutes. At this point, you should check how far along in the cooking process they are and allow to cook for a further 8 - 10 minutes as needed.
4.Serve with the dipping sauce of your choice.

Meatballs in Tomato Sauce
Prep + Cook Time: 35 minutes | Servings: 4

Ingredients
1 small onion, finely chopped
¾ lb. [12 oz] ground beef
1 tbsp. chopped fresh parsley
½ tbsp. chopped fresh thyme leaves
1 egg
3 tbsp. friendly bread crumbs
Pepper and salt to taste
10 oz. your favorite tomato sauce if desired

Instructions
1 Put all the ingredients in a bowl and combine well. Use your hands to mold the mixture into 10 - 12 balls.
2 Pre-heat the Air Fryer to 390°F.
3 Put the meatballs in the Air Fryer basket and place the basket in the Air Fryer. Cook the meatballs for 8 minutes.
4 Put the meatballs in an oven dish, pour in the tomato sauce and set the dish in the basket of the Air Fryer.
5 Reduce the temperature to 330°F and warm the meatballs for 5 minutes.

Amazing Blooming Onion
Prep + Cook Time: 40 minutes | Servings: 4

Ingredients
4 medium/small onions
1 tbsp. olive oil
4 dollops of butter

Instructions
1 Peel the onion. Cut off the top and bottom.
2 To make it bloom, cut as deeply as possible without slicing through it completely. 4 cuts [i.e. 8 segments] should do it.
3 Place the onions in a bowl of salted water and allow to absorb for 4 hours to help eliminate the sharp taste and induce the blooming process.
4 Pre-heat your Air Fryer to 355°F.
5 Transfer the onions to the Air Fryer. Pour over a light drizzle of olive oil and place a dollop of butter on top of each onion.
6 Cook or roast for 30 minutes. Remove the outer layer before serving if it is too brown.

Crab Croquettes
Prep + Cook Time: 5 minutes | Servings: 6

Ingredients
For the Filling:
1 lb. lump crab meat
2 egg whites, beaten
1 tbsp. olive oil
¼ cup red onion, finely chopped
¼ red bell pepper, finely chopped
2 tbsp. celery, finely chopped
¼ tsp. tarragon, finely chopped
¼ tsp. chives, finely chopped
½ tsp. parsley, finely chopped
½ tsp. cayenne pepper
¼ cup mayonnaise
¼ cup sour cream
For the Breading
3 eggs, beaten
1 cup flour
1 cup friendly bread crumbs
1 tsp. olive oil
½ tsp. salt

Instructions
1 Sauté the olive oil, onions, peppers, and celery over a medium heat, allowing to sweat until the vegetables turn translucent. This should take about 4 – 5 minutes.
2 Take off the heat and allow to cool.
3 In a food processor, pulse the bread crumbs, olive oil and salt to form a fine crumb.
4 Place the eggs, panko mixture and flour in three separate bowls.
5 Combine the crabmeat, egg whites, mayonnaise, sour cream, spices and vegetables in a large bowl.
6 Pre-heat the Air Fryer to 390°F.
7 Take equal amounts of the crab mixture and shape into golf balls. Coat the balls in the flour, before dipping them in the eggs and finally in the panko, making sure the bread crumbs stick well.
8 Put croquettes in the fryer basket in a single layer and well-spaced.
9 Cook the croquettes for 8 – 10 minutes or until a golden brown color is achieved.

Pumpkin Seeds

Prep + Cook Time: 55 minutes | Servings: 1 ½ cups

Ingredients
1 ½ cups pumpkin seeds from a large whole pumpkin
Olive oil
1 ½ tsp. salt
1 tsp. smoked paprika

Instructions
1 Boil two quarts of well-salted water in a pot. Cook the pumpkin seeds in the boiling water for 10 minutes.
2 Dump the content of the pot into a sieve and dry the seeds on paper towels for at least 20 minutes.
3 Pre-heat the Air Fryer to 350°F.
4 Cover the seeds with olive oil, salt and smoked paprika, before placing them in the Air Fryer basket.
5 Air fry for 35 minutes. Give the basket a good shake several times throughout the cooking process to ensure the pumpkin seeds are crispy and lightly browned.
6 Let the seeds cool before serving. Alternatively, you can keep them in an air-tight container or bag for snacking or for use as a yogurt topping.

Cocktail Flanks

Prep + Cook Time: 45 minutes | Servings: 4

Ingredients
1x 12-oz. package cocktail franks
1x 8-oz. can crescent rolls

Instructions
1 Drain the cocktail franks and dry with paper towels.
2 Unroll the crescent rolls and slice the dough into rectangular strips, roughly 1" by 1.5".
3 Wrap the franks in the strips with the ends poking out. Leave in the freezer for 5 minutes.
4 Pre-heat the Air Fryer to 330°F.
5 Take the franks out of the freezer and put them in the cooking basket. Cook for 6 – 8 minutes.
6 Reduce the heat to 390°F and cook for another 3 minutes or until a golden-brown color is achieved.

Garlic Mushrooms

Prep + Cook Time: 30 minutes | Servings: 4

Ingredients
16 small button mushrooms
For the Stuffing:
1 ½ slices bread
1 garlic clove, crushed
1 tbsp. flat-leafed parsley, finely chopped
Ground black pepper to taste
1 ½ tbsp. olive oil

Instructions
1 Pre-heat the Air Fryer to 390°F.
2 Blend together the bread slices, garlic, parsley and pepper until a fine crumb is formed.
3 Mix in the olive oil.
4 Remove the mushroom stalks and spoon even amounts of the filling into the caps. Press the crumbs in well to make sure none fall out
5 Put the mushroom caps in the cooking basket and place it in the Air Fryer.
6 Cook the mushrooms for 7 – 8 minutes or until they turn golden and crispy.

Curly's Cauliflower

Prep + Cook Time: 30 minutes | Servings: 4

Ingredients
4 cups bite-sized cauliflower florets
1 cup friendly bread crumbs, mixed with 1 tsp. salt
¼ cup melted butter [vegan/other]
¼ cup buffalo sauce [vegan/other]
Mayo [vegan/other] or creamy dressing for dipping

Instructions
1 In a bowl, combine the butter and buffalo sauce to create a creamy paste.
2 Completely cover each floret with the sauce.
3 Coat the florets with the bread crumb mixture. Cook the florets in the Air Fryer for approximately 15 minutes at 350°F, shaking the basket occasionally.
4 Serve with a raw vegetable salad, mayo or creamy dressing.

Fried Mushrooms

Prep + Cook Time: 40 minutes | Servings: 4

Ingredients
2 lb. button mushrooms
3 tbsp. white or French vermouth [optional]
1 tbsp. coconut oil
2 tsp. herbs of your choice
½ tsp. garlic powder

Instructions
1 Wash and dry the mushrooms. Slice them into quarters.
2 Pre-heat your Air Fryer at 320°F and add the coconut oil, garlic powder, and herbs to the basket.
3 Briefly cook the ingredients for 2 minutes and give them a stir. Put the mushrooms in the air fryer and cook for 25 minutes, stirring occasionally throughout.
4 Pour in the white vermouth and mix. Cook for an additional 5 minutes.
5 Serve hot.

Cheesy Garlic Bread

Prep + Cook Time: 20 minutes | Servings: 2

Ingredients
1 friendly baguette
4 tsp. butter, melted
3 chopped garlic cloves
5 tsp. sundried tomato pesto
1 cup mozzarella cheese, grated

Instructions
1 Cut your baguette into 5 thick round slices.
2 Add the garlic cloves to the melted butter and brush onto each slice of bread.
3 Spread a teaspoon of sun dried tomato pesto onto each slice.
4 Top each slice with the grated mozzarella.
5 Transfer the bread slices to the Air Fryer and cook them at 180°F for 6 – 8 minutes.
6 Top with some freshly chopped basil leaves, chili flakes and oregano if desired.

Stuffed Mushrooms

Prep + Cook Time: 25 minutes | Servings: 4

Ingredients
6 small mushrooms
1 tbsp. onion, peeled and diced
1 tbsp. friendly bread crumbs
1 tbsp. olive oil
1 tsp. garlic, pureed
1 tsp. parsley
Salt and pepper to taste

Instructions
1 Combine the bread crumbs, oil, onion, parsley, salt, pepper and garlic in a bowl.
2 Scoop the stalks out of the mushrooms and spoon equal portions of the crumb mixture in the caps. Transfer to the Air Fryer and cook for 10 minutes at 350°F.
3 Serve with mayo dip if desired.

Grilled Tomatoes

Prep + Cook Time: 25 minutes | Servings: 2

Ingredients
2 tomatoes, medium to large
Herbs of your choice, to taste
Pepper to taste
High quality cooking spray

Instructions
1 Wash and dry the tomatoes, before chopping them in half.
2 Lightly spritz them all over with cooking spray.
3 Season each half with herbs (oregano, basil, parsley, rosemary, thyme, sage, etc.) as desired and black pepper.
4 Put the halves in the tray of your Air Fryer. Cook for 20 minutes at 320°F, or longer if necessary. Larger tomatoes will take longer to cook.

Carrots & Rhubarb

Prep + Cook Time: 35 minutes | Servings: 4

Ingredients
1 lb. heritage carrots
1 lb. rhubarb
1 medium orange
½ cup walnuts, halved
2 tsp. walnut oil
½ tsp. sugar or a few drops of sugar extract

Instructions
1 Rinse the carrots to wash. Dry and chop them into 1-inch pieces.
2 Transfer them to the Air Fryer basket and drizzle over the walnut oil.
3 Cook at 320°F for about 20 minutes.
4 In the meantime, wash the rhubarb and chop it into ½-inch pieces.
5 Coarsely dice the walnuts.
6 Wash the orange and grate its skin into a small bowl. Peel the rest of the orange and cut it up into wedges.
7 Place the rhubarb, walnuts and sugar in the fryer and allow to cook for an additional 5 minutes.
8 Add in 2 tbsp. of the orange zest, along with the orange wedges. Serve immediately.

Broccoli

Prep + Cook Time: 30 minutes | Servings: 4

Ingredients
1 large head broccoli
½ lemon, juiced
3 cloves garlic, minced
1 tbsp. coconut oil
1 tbsp. white sesame seeds
2 tsp. Maggi sauce or other seasonings to taste

Instructions
1 Wash and dry the broccoli. Chop it up into small florets.
2 Place the minced garlic in your Air Fryer basket, along with the coconut oil, lemon juice and Maggi sauce.
3 Heat for 2 minutes at 320°F and give it a stir. Put the garlic and broccoli in the basket and cook for another 13 minutes.
4 Top the broccoli with the white sesame seeds and resume cooking for 5 more minutes, ensuring the seeds become nice and toasty.

Maple Glazed Beets

Prep + Cook Time: 60 minutes | Servings: 8

Ingredients
3 ½ lb. beetroots
4 tbsp. maple syrup
1 tbsp. coconut oil

Instructions
1 Wash and peel the beets. Cut them up into 1-inch pieces.
2 Put the coconut oil in the Air Fryer and melt for 1 minute at 320°F.
3 Place the beet cubes to the Air Fryer Basket and allow to cook for 40 minutes. Coat the beetroots in two tbsp. of the maple syrup and cook for another 10 minutes, ensuring the beets become soft.
4 Toss the cooked beets with the remaining two tbsp. of maple syrup and serve right away.

Endive Marinated in Curried Yogurt

Prep + Cook Time: 20 minutes | Servings: 6

Ingredients
6 heads endive
½ cup plain and fat-free yogurt
3 tbsp. lemon juice
1 tsp. garlic powder [or 2 minced cloves of garlic]
½ tsp. curry powder
Salt and ground black pepper to taste

Instructions
1 Wash the endives, and slice them in half lengthwise.
2 In a bowl, mix together the yogurt, lemon juice, garlic powder [or minced garlic], curry powder, salt and pepper. If you would like you marinade to be thinner, add some more lemon juice.
3 Brush the endive halves with the marinade, coating them completely. Allow to sit for a minimum of a half-hour and a maximum of one day.
4 Pre-heat Air Fryer to 320°F. Allow the endives to cook for 10 minutes and serve hot.

Tasty Tofu

Prep + Cook Time: 35 minutes | Servings: 4

Ingredients
1x 12 oz. package low-fat and extra firm tofu
2 tbsp. low-sodium soy sauce
2 tbsp. fish sauce
1 tbsp. coriander paste
1 tsp. sesame oil
1 tsp. duck fat or coconut oil
1 tsp. Maggi sauce

Instructions
1 Remove the liquid from the package of tofu and chop the tofu into 1-inch cubes. Line a plate with paper towels and spread the tofu out on top in one layer. Place another paper towel on top, followed by another plate, weighting it down with a heavier object if necessary. This is to dry the tofu out completely. Leave for a minimum of 30 minutes or a maximum of 24 hours, replacing the paper towels once or twice throughout the duration.
2 In a medium bowl, mix together the sesame oil, Maggi sauce, coriander paste, fish sauce, and soy sauce. Stir to combine fully.
3 Coat the tofu cubes with this mixture and allow to marinate for at least a half-hour, tossing the cubes a few times throughout to ensure even coating. Add another few drops of fish sauce or soy sauce to thin out the marinade if necessary.
4 Melt the duck fat/coconut oil in your Air Fryer at 350°F for about 2 minutes. Place the tofu cubes in the basket and cook for about 20 minutes or longer to achieve a crispier texture. Flip the tofu over or shake the basket every 10 minutes.
5 Serve hot with the dipping sauce of your choosing.

Roasted Peppers

Prep + Cook Time: 40 minutes | Servings: 4

Ingredients
12 medium bell peppers
1 sweet onion, small
1 tbsp. Maggi sauce
1 tbsp. extra virgin olive oil

Instructions
1 Warm up the olive oil and Maggi sauce in Air Fryer at 320°F.
2 Peel the onion, slice it into 1-inch pieces, and add it to the Air Fryer.
3 Wash and de-stem the peppers. Slice them into 1-inch pieces and remove all the seeds, with water if necessary [ensuring to dry the peppers afterwards].
4 Place the peppers in the Air Fryer.
5 Cook for about 25 minutes, or longer if desired. Serve hot.

Rosemary Green Beans

Prep + Cook Time: 10 minutes | Servings: 1

Ingredients
1 tbsp. butter, melted
2 tbsp. rosemary
½ tsp. salt
3 cloves garlic, minced
¾ cup green beans, chopped

Instructions
1.Pre-heat your fryer at 390°F.
2.Combine the melted butter with the rosemary, salt, and minced garlic. Toss in the green beans, making sure to coat them well.
3.Cook in the fryer for five minutes.

Carrot Croquettes

Prep + Cook Time: 10 minutes | Servings: 4

Ingredients
2 medium-sized carrots, trimmed and grated
2 medium-sized celery stalks, trimmed and grated
½ cup of leek, finely chopped
1 tbsp. garlic paste
¼ tsp. freshly cracked black pepper
1 tsp. fine sea salt
1 tbsp. fresh dill, finely chopped
1 egg, lightly whisked
¼ cup flour
¼ tsp. baking powder
½ cup bread crumbs [seasoned or regular]
Chive mayo to serve

Instructions
1.Drain any excess liquid from the carrots and celery by placing them on a paper towel.
2.Stir together the vegetables with all of the other ingredients, save for the bread crumbs and chive mayo.
3.Use your hands to mold 1 tablespoon of the vegetable mixture into a ball and repeat until all of the mixture has been used up. Press down on each ball with your hand or a palette knife. Cover completely with bread crumbs. Spritz the croquettes with a non-stick cooking spray.
4.Arrange the croquettes in a single layer in your Air Fryer and fry for 6 minutes at 360°F.
5.Serve warm with the chive mayo on the side.

Peppered Puff Pastry

Prep + Cook Time: 25 minutes | Servings: 4

Ingredients
1 ½ tbsp. sesame oil
1 cup white mushrooms, sliced
2 cloves garlic, minced
1 bell pepper, seeded and chopped
¼ tsp. sea salt
¼ tsp. dried rosemary
½ tsp. ground black pepper, or more to taste
11 oz. puff pastry sheets
½ cup crème fraiche
1 egg, well whisked
½ cup parmesan cheese, preferably freshly grated

Instructions
1.Pre-heat your Air Fryer to 400°F.
2.In a skillet, heat the sesame oil over a moderate heat and fry the mushrooms, garlic, and pepper until soft and fragrant.
3.Sprinkle on the salt, rosemary, and pepper.
4.In the meantime, unroll the puff pastry and slice it into 4-inch squares.
5.Spread the crème fraiche across each square.
6.Spoon equal amounts of the vegetables into the puff pastry squares. Enclose each square around the filling in a triangle shape, pressing the edges with your fingertips.
7.Brush each triangle with some whisked egg and cover with grated Parmesan.
8.Cook for 22-25 minutes.

Sautéed Green Beans

Prep + Cook Time: 12 minutes | Servings: 4

Ingredients
¾ lb. green beans, cleaned
1 tbsp. balsamic vinegar
¼ tsp. kosher salt
½ tsp. mixed peppercorns, freshly cracked
1 tbsp. butter
Sesame seeds to serve

Instructions
1.Pre-heat your Air Fryer at 390°F.
2.Combine the green beans with the rest of the ingredients, except for the sesame seeds. Transfer to the fryer and cook for 10 minutes.
3.In the meantime, heat the sesame seeds in a small skillet to toast all over, stirring constantly to prevent burning.
4.Serve the green beans accompanied by the toasted sesame seeds.

Horseradish Mayo & Gorgonzola Mushrooms

Prep + Cook Time: 15 minutes | Servings: 5

Ingredients

½ cup of bread crumbs
2 cloves garlic, pressed
2 tbsp. fresh coriander, chopped
⅓ tsp. kosher salt
½ tsp. crushed red pepper flakes
1 ½ tbsp. olive oil
20 medium-sized mushrooms, stems removed
½ cup Gorgonzola cheese, grated
¼ cup low-fat mayonnaise
1 tsp. prepared horseradish, well-drained
tbsp. fresh parsley, finely chopped

Instructions

1. Combine the bread crumbs together with the garlic, coriander, salt, red pepper, and the olive oil.
2. Take equal-sized amounts of the bread crumb mixture and use them to stuff the mushroom caps. Add the grated Gorgonzola on top of each.
3. Put the mushrooms in the Air Fryer grill pan and transfer to the fryer.
4. Grill them at 380°F for 8-12 minutes, ensuring the stuffing is warm throughout.
5. In the meantime, prepare the horseradish mayo. Mix together the mayonnaise, horseradish and parsley.
6. When the mushrooms are ready, serve with the mayo.

Scallion & Ricotta Potatoes

Prep + Cook Time: 15 minutes | Servings: 4

Ingredients

4 baking potatoes
2 tbsp. olive oil
½ cup Ricotta cheese, room temperature
2 tbsp. scallions, chopped
1 heaped tbsp. fresh parsley, roughly chopped
1 heaped tbsp. coriander, minced
2 oz. Cheddar cheese, preferably freshly grated
1 tsp. celery seeds
½ tsp. salt
½ tsp. garlic pepper

Instructions

1. Pierce the skin of the potatoes with a knife.

2. Cook in the Air Fryer basket for roughly 13 minutes at 350°F. If they are not cooked through by this time, leave for 2 – 3 minutes longer.
3. In the meantime, make the stuffing by combining all the other ingredients.
4. Cut halfway into the cooked potatoes to open them.
5. Spoon equal amounts of the stuffing into each potato and serve hot.

Low-Carb Pizza Crust

Prep + Cook Time: 20 minutes | Servings: 4

Ingredients

1 tbsp. full-fat cream cheese
½ cup whole-milk mozzarella cheese, shredded
2 tbsp. flour
1 egg white

Instructions

1. In a microwave-safe bowl, combine the cream cheese, mozzarella, and flour and heat in the microwave for half a minute. Mix well to create a smooth consistency. Add in the egg white and stir to form a soft ball of dough.
2. With slightly wet hands, press the dough into a pizza crust about six inches in diameter.
3. Place a sheet of parchment paper in the bottom of your fryer and lay the crust on top. Cook for ten minutes at 350°F, turning the crust over halfway through the cooking time.
4. Top the pizza base with the toppings of your choice and enjoy!

Bacon-Wrapped Onion Rings

Prep + Cook Time: 15 minutes | Servings: 8

Ingredients

1 large onion, peeled
8 slices sugar-free bacon
1 tbsp. sriracha

Instructions

1. Chop up the onion into slices a quarter-inch thick. Gently pull apart the rings. Take a slice of bacon and wrap it around an onion ring. Repeat with the rest of the ingredients. Place each onion ring in your fryer.
2. Cut the onion rings at 350°F for ten minutes, turning them halfway through to ensure the bacon crisps up.
3. Serve hot with the sriracha.

Croutons

Prep + Cook Time: 25 minutes | Servings: 4

Ingredients
2 slices friendly bread
1 tbsp. olive oil

Instructions
1. Cut the slices of bread into medium-size chunks.
2. Coat the inside of the Air Fryer with the oil. Set it to 390°F and allow it to heat up.
3. Place the chunks inside and shallow fry for at least 8 minutes.
4. Serve with hot soup.

Garlic Stuffed Mushrooms

Prep + Cook Time: 25 minutes | Servings: 4

Ingredients
6 small mushrooms
1 oz. onion, peeled and diced
1 tbsp. friendly bread crumbs
1 tbsp. olive oil
1 tsp. garlic, pureed
1 tsp. parsley
Salt and pepper to taste

Instructions
1. Combine the bread crumbs, oil, onion, parsley, salt, pepper and garlic in a bowl. Cut out the mushrooms' stalks and stuff each cap with the crumb mixture.
2. Cook in the Air Fryer for 10 minutes at 350°F.
3. Serve with a side of mayo dip.

Zucchini Sweet Potatoes

Prep + Cook Time: 20 minutes | Servings: 4

Ingredients
2 large-sized sweet potatoes, peeled and quartered
1 medium-sized zucchini, sliced
1 Serrano pepper, deveined and thinly sliced
1 bell pepper, deveined and thinly sliced
1 – 2 carrots, cut into matchsticks
¼ cup olive oil
1 ½ tbsp. maple syrup
½ tsp. porcini powder
¼ tsp. mustard powder
½ tsp. fennel seeds
1 tbsp. garlic powder
½ tsp. fine sea salt
¼ tsp. ground black pepper
Tomato ketchup to serve

Instructions
1. Put the sweet potatoes, zucchini, peppers, and the carrot into the basket of your Air Fryer. Coat with a drizzling of olive oil.
2. Pre-heat the fryer at 350°F.
3. Cook the vegetables for 15 minutes.
4. In the meantime, prepare the sauce by vigorously combining the other ingredients, save for the tomato ketchup, with a whisk.
5. Lightly grease a baking dish small enough to fit inside your fryer.
6. Move the cooked vegetables to the baking dish, pour over the sauce and make sure to coat the vegetables well.
7. Raise the temperature to 390°F and cook the vegetables for an additional 5 minutes.
8. Serve warm with a side of ketchup.

Cheese Lings

Prep + Cook Time: 25 minutes | Servings: 6

Ingredients
1 cup flour
small cubes cheese, grated
¼ tsp. chili powder
1 tsp. butter
Salt to taste
1 tsp. baking powder

Instructions
1. Combine all the ingredients to form a dough, along with a small amount water as necessary.
2. Divide the dough into equal portions and roll each one into a ball.
3. Pre-heat Air Fryer at 360°F.
4. Transfer the balls to the fryer and air fry for 5 minutes, stirring periodically.

Potato Side Dish

Prep + Cook Time: 30 minutes | Servings: 2

Ingredients
2 medium potatoes
1 tsp. butter
3 tbsp. sour cream
1 tsp. chives
1 ½ tbsp. cheese, grated
Salt and pepper to taste

Instructions
1. Pierce the potatoes with a fork and boil them in water until they are cooked.
2. Transfer to the Air Fryer and cook for 15 minutes at 350°F.
3. In the meantime, combine the sour cream, cheese and chives in a bowl. Cut the potatoes halfway to open them up and fill with the butter and toppings.
4. Serve with salad.

Roasted Potatoes & Cheese

Prep + Cook Time: 55 minutes | Servings: 4

Ingredients
4 medium potatoes
1 asparagus bunch
⅓ cup cottage cheese
⅓ cup low-fat crème fraiche
1 tbsp. wholegrain mustard

Instructions
1. Pour some oil into your Air Fryer and pre-heat to 390°F.
2. Cook potatoes for 20 minutes.
3. Boil the asparagus in salted water for 3 minutes.
4. Remove the potatoes and mash them with rest of ingredients. Sprinkle on salt and pepper.
5. Serve with rice.

Vegetable & Cheese Omelet

Prep + Cook Time: 15 minutes | Servings: 2

Ingredients
3 tbsp. plain milk
4 eggs, whisked
1 tsp. melted butter
Kosher salt and freshly ground black pepper, to taste
1 red bell pepper, deveined and chopped
1 green bell pepper, deveined and chopped
1 white onion, finely chopped
½ cup baby spinach leaves, roughly chopped
½ cup Halloumi cheese, shaved

Instructions
1. Grease the Air Fryer baking pan with some canola oil.
2. Place all of the ingredients in the baking pan and stir well.
3. Transfer to the fryer and cook at 350°F for 13 minutes.
4. Serve warm.

Scrambled Eggs

Prep + Cook Time: 15 minutes | Servings: 2

Ingredients
2 tbsp. olive oil, melted
4 eggs, whisked

---

5 oz. fresh spinach, chopped
1 medium-sized tomato, chopped
1 tsp. fresh lemon juice
½ tsp. coarse salt
½ tsp. ground black pepper
½ cup of fresh basil, roughly chopped

Instructions
1. Grease the Air Fryer baking pan with the oil, tilting it to spread the oil around. Pre-heat the fryer at 280°F.
2. Mix the remaining ingredients, apart from the basil leaves, whisking well until everything is completely combined.
3. Cook in the fryer for 8 - 12 minutes.
4. Top with fresh basil leaves before serving with a little sour cream if desired.

Sweet Corn Fritters

Prep + Cook Time: 20 minutes | Servings: 4

Ingredients
1 medium-sized carrot, grated
1 yellow onion, finely chopped
4 oz. canned sweet corn kernels, drained
1 tsp. sea salt flakes
1 heaping tbsp. fresh cilantro, chopped
1 medium-sized egg, whisked
2 tbsp. plain milk
1 cup of Parmesan cheese, grated
¼ cup flour
⅓ tsp. baking powder
⅓ tsp. sugar

Instructions
1. Place the grated carrot in a colander and press down to squeeze out any excess moisture. Dry it with a paper towel.
2. Combine the carrots with the remaining ingredients.
3. Mold 1 tablespoon of the mixture into a ball and press it down with your hand or a spoon to flatten it. Repeat until the rest of the mixture is used up.
4. Spritz the balls with cooking spray.
5. Arrange in the basket of your Air Fryer, taking care not to overlap any balls. Cook at 350°F for 8 to 11 minutes or until they're firm.
6. Serve warm.

Rosemary Cornbread

Prep + Cook Time: 1 hr. | Servings: 6

Ingredients
1 cup cornmeal
1 ½ cups flour
½ tsp. baking soda
½ tsp. baking powder
¼ tsp. kosher salt
1 tsp. dried rosemary
¼ tsp. garlic powder
2 tbsp. sugar
2 eggs
¼ cup melted butter
1 cup buttermilk
½ cup corn kernels

Instructions
1. In a bowl, combine all the dry ingredients. In a separate bowl, mix together all the wet ingredients. Combine the two.
2. Fold in the corn kernels and stir vigorously.
3. Pour the batter into a lightly greased round loaf pan that is lightly greased.
4. Cook for 1 hour at 380°F.

Veggie Rolls

Prep + Cook Time: 30 minutes | Servings: 6

Ingredients
2 potatoes, mashed
¼ cup peas
¼ cup carrots, mashed
1 small cabbage, sliced
¼ beans
2 tbsp. sweetcorn
1 small onion, chopped
1 tsp. capsicum
1 tsp. coriander
2 tbsp. butter
Ginger
Garlic to taste
½ tsp. masala powder
½ tsp. chili powder
½ cup bread crumbs
1 packet spring roll sheets
½ cup cornstarch slurry

Instructions
1. Boil all the vegetables in water over a low heat. Rinse and allow to dry.
2. Unroll the spring roll sheets and spoon equal amounts of vegetable onto the center of each one. Fold into spring rolls and coat each one with the slurry and bread crumbs.
3. Pre-heat the Air Fryer to 390°F. Cook the rolls for 10 minutes.
4. Serve with a side of boiled rice.

Grilled Cheese

Prep + Cook Time: 25 minutes | Servings: 2

Ingredients
4 slices bread
½ cup sharp cheddar cheese
¼ cup butter, melted

Instructions
1. Pre-heat the Air Fryer at 360°F.
2. Put cheese and butter in separate bowls.
3. Apply the butter to each side of the bread slices with a brush.
4. Spread the cheese across two of the slices of bread and make two sandwiches. Transfer both to the fryer.
5. Cook for 5 – 7 minutes or until a golden brown color is achieved and the cheese is melted.

Potato Gratin

Prep + Cook Time: 55 minutes | Servings: 6

Ingredients
½ cup milk
7 medium russet potatoes, peeled
1 tsp. black pepper
½ cup cream
½ cup semi-mature cheese, grated
½ tsp. nutmeg

Instructions
1. Pre-heat the Air Fryer to 390°F.
2. Cut the potatoes into wafer-thin slices.
3. In a bowl, combine the milk and cream and sprinkle with salt, pepper, and nutmeg as desired.
4. Use the milk mixture to coat the slices of potatoes. Place in an 8" heat-resistant baking dish. Top the potatoes with the rest of the cream mixture.
5. Put the baking dish into the basket of the fryer and cook for 25 minutes.
6. Pour the cheese over the potatoes.
7. Cook for an additional 10 minutes, ensuring the top is nicely browned before serving.

Roasted Vegetables

Prep + Cook Time: 30 minutes | Servings: 6

Ingredients
1 ⅓ cup small parsnips
1 ⅓ cup celery [3 – 4 stalks]
2 red onions
1 ⅓ cup small butternut squash
1 tbsp. fresh thyme needles
1 tbsp. olive oil
Salt and pepper to taste

Instructions
1.Pre-heat the Air Fryer to 390°F.
2.Peel the parsnips and onions and cut them into 2-cm cubes. Slice the onions into wedges.
3.Do not peel the butternut squash. Cut it in half, de-seed it, and cube.
4.Combine the cut vegetables with the thyme, olive oil, salt and pepper.
5.Put the vegetables in the basket and transfer the basket to the Air Fryer.
6.Cook for 20 minutes, stirring once throughout the cooking time, until the vegetables are nicely browned and cooked through.

Sweet Potato Curry Fries

Prep + Cook Time: 55 minutes | Servings: 4

Ingredients
2.2 lb. sweet potatoes
1 tsp. curry powder
2 tbsp. olive oil
Salt to taste

Instructions
1.Pre-heat Air Fryer to 390°F.
2.Wash the sweet potatoes before slicing them into matchsticks.
3.Drizzle the oil in the pan, place the fries inside and bake for 25 minutes.
4.Sprinkle with curry and salt before serving with ketchup if desired.

Smoked BBQ Toasted s

Prep + Cook Time: 10 minutes | Servings: 1

Ingredients
2 tsp. coconut oil, melted
¼ tsp. smoked paprika
1 tsp. chili powder
¼ tsp. cumin
1 cup raw s

Instructions
1.Mix the melted coconut oil with the paprika, chili powder, and cumin. Place the s in a large bowl and pour the coconut oil over them, tossing them to cover them evenly.
2.Place the s in the basket of your fryer and spread them out across the base.
3.Cook for six minutes at 320°F, giving the basket an occasional shake to make sure everything is cooked evenly.
4.Leave to cool and serve.

Roasted Eggplant

Prep + Cook Time: 20 minutes | Servings: 1

Ingredients
1 large eggplant
2 tbsp. olive oil
¼ tsp. salt
½ tsp. garlic powder

Instructions
1.Prepare the eggplant by slicing off the top and bottom and cutting it into slices around a quarter-inch thick.
2.Apply olive oil to the slices with a brush, coating both sides. Season each side with sprinklings of salt and garlic powder.
3.Place the slices in the fryer and cook for fifteen minutes at 390°F.
4.Serve right away.

Low-Carb Pita Chips

Prep + Cook Time: 15 minutes | Servings: 1

Ingredients
1 cup mozzarella cheese, shredded
1 egg
¼ cup blanched finely ground flour
½ oz. pork rinds, finely ground

Instructions
1.Melt the mozzarella in the microwave. Add the egg, flour, and pork rinds and combine together to form a smooth paste. Microwave the cheese again if it begins to set.
2.Put the dough between two sheets of parchment paper and use a rolling pin to flatten it out into a rectangle. The thickness is up to you. With a sharp knife, cut into the dough to form triangles. It may be necessary to complete this step-in multiple batches.
3.Place the chips in the fryer and cook for five minutes at 350°F. Turn them over and cook on the other side for another five minutes, or until the chips are golden and firm.
4.Allow the chips to cool and harden further. They can be stored in an airtight container.

Flatbread

Prep + Cook Time: 20 minutes | Servings: 1

Ingredients
1 cup mozzarella cheese, shredded
¼ cup blanched finely ground flour
1 oz. full-fat cream cheese, softened

Instructions
1.Microwave the mozzarella for half a minute until melted. Combine with the flour to achieve a smooth consistency, before adding the cream cheese. Keep mixing to create a dough, microwaving the mixture again if the cheese begins to harden.
2.Divide the dough into two equal pieces. Between two sheets of parchment paper, roll out the dough until it is about a quarter-inch thick. Cover the bottom of your fryer with another sheet of parchment.
3.Transfer the dough into the fryer and cook at 320°F for seven minutes. You may need to complete this step in two batches. Make sure to turn the flatbread halfway through cooking. Take care when removing it from the fryer and serve warm.

Buffalo Cauliflower

Prep + Cook Time: 10 minutes | Servings: 1

Ingredients
½ packet dry ranch seasoning
2 tbsp. salted butter, melted
Cauliflower florets
¼ cup buffalo sauce

Instructions
1.In a bowl, combine the dry ranch seasoning and butter. Toss with the cauliflower florets to coat and transfer them to the fryer.
2.Cook at 400°F for five minutes, shaking the basket occasionally to ensure the florets cook evenly.
3.Remove the cauliflower from the fryer, pour the buffalo sauce over it, and enjoy.

Brussels Sprout Chips

Prep + Cook Time: 15 minutes | Servings: 1

Ingredients
1 lb. Brussels sprouts

1 tbsp. coconut oil, melted
1 tbsp. unsalted butter, melted

Instructions
1.Prepare the Brussels sprouts by halving them, discarding any loose leaves.
2.Combine with the melted coconut oil and transfer to your air fryer.
3.Cook at 400°F for ten minutes, giving the basket a good shake throughout the cooking time to brown them up if desired.
4.The sprouts are ready when they are partially caramelized. Remove them from the fryer and serve with a topping of melted butter before serving.

Cauliflower Tots

Prep + Cook Time: 20 minutes | Servings: 8

Ingredients
1 large head cauliflower
½ cup parmesan cheese, grated
1 cup mozzarella cheese, shredded
1 tsp. seasoned salt
1 egg

Instructions
1.Place a steamer basket over a pot of boiling water, ensuring the water is not high enough to enter the basket.
2.Cut up the cauliflower into florets and transfer to the steamer basket. Cover the pot with a lid and leave to steam for seven minutes, making sure the cauliflower softens.
3.Place the florets on a cheesecloth and leave to cool. Remove as much moisture as possible. This is crucial as it ensures the cauliflower will harden.
4.In a bowl, break up the cauliflower with a fork.
5.Stir in the parmesan, mozzarella, seasoned salt, and egg, incorporating the cauliflower well with all of the other ingredients. Make sure the mixture is firm enough to be moldable.
6.Using your hand, mold about two tablespoons of the mixture into tots and repeat until you have used up all of the mixture. Put each tot into your air fryer basket. They may need to be cooked in multiple batches.
7.Cook at 320°F for twelve minutes, turning them halfway through. Ensure they are brown in color before serving.

Herbed Garlic Radishes
Prep + Cook Time: 15 minutes | Servings: 2

Ingredients
1 lb. radishes
2 tbsp. unsalted butter, melted
¼ tsp. dried oregano
½ tsp. dried parsley
½ tsp. garlic powder

Instructions
1. Prepare the radishes by cutting off their tops and bottoms and quartering them.
2. In a bowl, combine the butter, dried oregano, dried parsley, and garlic powder. Toss with the radishes to coat.
3. Transfer the radishes to your air fryer and cook at 350°F for ten minutes, shaking the basket at the halfway point to ensure the radishes cook evenly through. The radishes are ready when they begin to turn brown.

Jicama Fries
Prep + Cook Time: 25 minutes | Servings: 1

Ingredients
1 small jicama, peeled
¼ tsp. onion powder
¾ tsp. chili powder
¼ tsp. garlic powder
¼ tsp. ground black pepper

Instructions
1. To make the fries, cut the jicama into matchsticks of your desired thickness.
2. In a bowl, toss them with the onion powder, chili powder, garlic powder, and black pepper to coat. Transfer the fries into the basket of your air fryer.
3. Cook at 350°F for twenty minutes, giving the basket an occasional shake throughout the cooking process. The fries are ready when they are hot and golden in color. Enjoy!

Crumbed Beans
Prep + Cook Time: 10 minutes | Servings: 4

Ingredients
½ cup flour
1 tsp. smoky chipotle powder
½ tsp. ground black pepper
1 tsp. sea salt flakes
2 eggs, beaten
½ cup crushed saltines
10 oz. wax beans

Instructions
1. Combine the flour, chipotle powder, black pepper, and salt in a bowl. Put the eggs in a second bowl. Place the crushed saltines in a third bowl.
2. Wash the beans with cold water and discard any tough strings.
3. Coat the beans with the flour mixture, before dipping them into the beaten egg. Lastly cover them with the crushed saltines.
4. Spritz the beans with a cooking spray.
5. Air-fry at 360°F for 4 minutes. Give the cooking basket a good shake and continue to cook for 3 minutes. Serve hot.

Colby Potato Patties
Prep + Cook Time: 15 minutes | Servings: 8

Ingredients
2 lb. white potatoes, peeled and grated
½ cup scallions, finely chopped
½ tsp. freshly ground black pepper, or more to taste
1 tbsp. fine sea salt
½ tsp. hot paprika
2 cups Colby cheese, shredded
¼ cup canola oil
1 cup crushed crackers

Instructions
1. Boil the potatoes until soft. Dry them off and peel them before mashing thoroughly, leaving no lumps.
2. Combine the mashed potatoes with scallions, pepper, salt, paprika, and cheese.
3. Mold the mixture into balls with your hands and press with your palm to flatten them into patties.
4. In a shallow dish, combine the canola oil and crushed crackers. Coat the patties in the crumb mixture.
5. Cook the patties at 360°F for about 10 minutes, in multiple batches if necessary.
6. Serve with tabasco mayo or the sauce of your choice.

Turkey Garlic Potatoes
Prep + Cook Time: 45 minutes | Servings: 2

Ingredients
3 unsmoked turkey strips
6 small potatoes
1 tsp. garlic, minced
2 tsp. olive oil
Salt to taste
Pepper to taste

Instructions
1. Peel the potatoes and cube them finely.
2. Coat in 1 teaspoon of oil and cook in the Air Fryer for 10 minutes at 350°F.
3. In a separate bowl, slice the turkey finely and combine with the garlic, oil, salt and pepper. Pour the potatoes into the bowl and mix well.
4. Lay the mixture on some silver aluminum foil, transfer to the fryer and cook for about 10 minutes.
5. Serve with raita.

Hollandaise Sauce

Prep + Cook Time: 2 minutes | Servings: 8

Ingredients
8 large egg yolks
½ tsp salt
2 tbsp fresh lemon juice
1 cup unsalted butter

Instructions
1.Combine the egg yolks, salt, and lemon juice in a blender until smooth.
2.Put the butter in your microwave for around 60 seconds, until melted and hot.
3.Turn the blender on a low speed and slowly pour in the butter until the sauce begins to thicken.
4.Serve!

Granny's Green Beans

Prep + Cook Time: 10 minutes | Servings: 4

Ingredients
1 lb green beans, trimmed
1 cup butter
2 cloves garlic, minced
1 cup toasted pine nuts

Instructions
1.Boil a pot of water.
2.Add the green beans and cook until tender for 5 minutes.
3.Heat the butter in a large skillet over a high heat. Add the garlic and pine nuts and sauté for 2 minutes or until the pine nuts are lightly browned.
4.Transfer the green beans to the skillet and turn until coated.
5.Serve!

Mini Pepper Poppers

Prep + Cook Time: 10 minutes | Servings: 4

Ingredients
8 mini sweet peppers
¼ cup pepper jack cheese, shredded
4 slices sugar-free bacon, cooked and crumbled
4 oz. full-fat cream cheese, softened

Instructions
1.Prepare the peppers by cutting off the tops and halving them lengthwise. Then take out the membrane and the seeds.
2.In a small bowl, combine the pepper jack cheese, bacon, and cream cheese, making sure to incorporate everything well
3.Spoon equal-sized portions of the cheese-bacon mixture into each of the pepper halves.
4.Place the peppers inside your fryer and cook for eight minutes at 400°F. Take care when removing them from the fryer and enjoy warm.

Bacon-Wrapped Jalapeno Popper

Prep + Cook Time: 20 minutes | Servings: 4

Ingredients
6 jalapenos
1/3 cup medium cheddar cheese, shredded
¼ tsp. garlic powder
3 oz. full-fat cream cheese
12 slices sugar-free bacon

Instructions
1.Prepare the jalapenos by slicing off the tops and halving each one lengthwise. Take care when removing the seeds and membranes, wearing gloves if necessary.
2.In a microwavable bowl, combine the cheddar cheese, garlic powder, and cream cheese. Microwave for half a minute and mix again, before spoon equal parts of this mixture into each of the jalapeno halves.
3.Take a slice of bacon and wrap it around one of the jalapeno halves, covering it entirely. Place it in the basket of your fryer. Repeat with the rest of the bacon and jalapenos.
4.Cook at 400°F for twelve minutes, flipping the peppers halfway through in order to ensure the bacon gets crispy. Make sure not to let any of the contents spill out of the jalapeno halves when turning them.
5.Eat the peppers hot or at room temperature.

Cheesy Bacon Bread

Prep + Cook Time: 25 minutes | Servings: 2

Ingredients
4 slices sugar-free bacon, cooked and chopped
2 eggs
¼ cup pickled jalapenos, chopped
¼ cup parmesan cheese, grated
2 cups mozzarella cheese, shredded

Instructions
1. Add all of the ingredients together in a bowl and mix together.
2. Cut out a piece of parchment paper that will fit the base of your fryer's basket. Place it inside the fryer
3. With slightly wet hands, roll the mixture into a circle. You may have to form two circles to cook in separate batches, depending on the size of your fryer.
4. Place the circle on top of the parchment paper inside your fryer. Cook at 320°F for ten minutes.
5. Turn the bread over and cook for another five minutes.
6. The bread is ready when it is golden and cooked all the way through. Slice and serve warm.

Mozzarella Sticks

Prep + Cook Time: 60 minutes | Servings: 4

Ingredients
6 x 1-oz. mozzarella string cheese sticks
1 tsp. dried parsley
½ oz. pork rinds, finely ground
½ cup parmesan cheese, grated
2 eggs

Instructions
1. Halve the mozzarella sticks and freeze for forty-five minutes. Optionally you can leave them longer and place in a Ziploc bag to prevent them from becoming freezer burned.
2. In a small bowl, combine the dried parsley, pork rinds, and parmesan cheese.
3. In a separate bowl, beat the eggs with a fork.
4. Take a frozen mozzarella stick and dip it into the eggs, then into the pork rind mixture, making sure to coat it all over. Proceed with the rest of the cheese sticks, placing each coated stick in the basket of your air fryer.
5. Cook at 400°F for ten minutes, until they are golden brown.
6. Serve hot, with some homemade marinara sauce if desired.

Beef Jerky

Prep + Cook Time: 250 minutes | Servings: 4

Ingredients
¼ tsp. garlic powder
¼ tsp. onion powder
¼ cup soy sauce
2 tsp. Worcestershire sauce
1 lb. flat iron steak, thinly sliced

Instructions
1. In a bowl, combine the garlic powder, onion powder, soy sauce, and Worcestershire sauce. Marinade the beef slices with the mixture in an airtight bag, shaking it well to ensure the beef is well-coated. Leave to marinate for at least two hours
2. Place the meat in the basket of your air fryer, making sure it is evenly spaced. Cook the beef slices in more than one batch if necessary.
3. Cook for four hours at 160°F.
4. Allow to cool before serving. You can keep the jerky in an airtight container for up to a week, if you can resist it that long.

Bacon-Wrapped Brie

Prep + Cook Time: 15 minutes | Servings: 1

Ingredients
4 slices sugar-free bacon
8 oz. brie cheese

Instructions
1. On a cutting board, lay out the slices of bacon across each other in a star shape (two Xs overlaid). Then place the entire round of brie in the center of this star.
2. Lift each slice of bacon to wrap it over the brie and use toothpicks to hold everything in place. Cut up a piece of parchment paper to fit in your fryer's basket and place it inside, followed by the wrapped brie, setting it in the center of the sheet of parchment.
3. Cook at 400°F for seven minutes. Turn the brie over and cook for a further three minutes.
4. It is ready once the bacon is crispy and cheese is melted on the inside.
5. Slice up the brie and enjoy hot.

Crust-less Meaty Pizza

Prep + Cook Time: 15 minutes | Servings: 1

Ingredients
½ cup mozzarella cheese, shredded
2 slices sugar-free bacon, cooked and crumbled
¼ cup ground sausage, cooked
7 slices pepperoni
1 tbsp. parmesan cheese, grated

Instructions
1.Spread the mozzarella across the bottom of a six-inch cake pan. Throw on the bacon, sausage, and pepperoni, then add a sprinkle of the parmesan cheese on top. Place the pan inside your air fryer.
2.Cook at 400°F for five minutes. The cheese is ready once brown in color and bubbly. Take care when removing the pan from the fryer and serve.

Radish Chips

Prep + Cook Time: 15 minutes | Servings: 1

Ingredients
2 cups water
1 lb. radishes
½ tsp. garlic powder
¼ tsp. onion powder
2 tbsp. coconut oil, melted

Instructions
1.Boil the water over the stove.
2.In the meantime, prepare the radish chips. Slice off the tops and bottoms and, using a mandolin, shave into thin slices of equal size. Alternatively, this step can be completed using your food processor if it has a slicing blade.
3.Put the radish chips in the pot of boiling water and allow to cook for five minutes, ensuring they become translucent. Take care when removing from the water and place them on a paper towel to dry.
4.Add the radish chips, garlic powder, onion powder, and melted coconut oil into a bowl and toss to coat. Transfer the chips to your fryer.
5.Cook at 320°F for five minutes, occasionally giving the basket a good shake to ensure even cooking. The chips are done when cooked through and crispy. Serve immediately.

Parmesan Zucchini Chips

Prep + Cook Time: 10 minutes | Servings: 1

Ingredients
2 medium zucchini
1 oz. pork rinds, finely ground
½ cup parmesan cheese, grated
1 egg

Instructions
1.Cut the zucchini into slices about a quarter-inch thick. Lay on a paper towel to dry.
2.In a bowl, combine the ground pork rinds and the grated parmesan.
3.In a separate bowl, beat the egg with a fork.
4.Take a zucchini slice and dip it into the egg, then into the pork rind-parmesan mixture, making sure to coat it evenly. Repeat with the rest of the slices. Lay them in the basket of your fryer, taking care not to overlap. This step may need to be completed in more than one batch.
5.Cook at 320°F for five minutes. Turn the chips over and allow to cook for another five minutes.
6.Allow to cool to achieve a crispier texture or serve warm. Enjoy!

Buffalo Cauliflower

Prep + Cook Time: 10 minutes | Servings: 1

Ingredients
½ packet dry ranch seasoning
2 tbsp. salted butter, melted
Cauliflower florets
¼ cup buffalo sauce

Instructions
1.In a bowl, combine the dry ranch seasoning and butter. Toss with the cauliflower florets to coat and transfer them to the fryer.
2.Cook at 400°F for five minutes, shaking the basket occasionally to ensure the florets cook evenly.
3.Remove the cauliflower from the fryer, pour the buffalo sauce over it, and enjoy.

Zesty Cilantro Roasted Cauliflower

Prep + Cook Time: 10 minutes | Servings: 2

Ingredients
2 cups cauliflower florets, chopped
2 tbsp. coconut oil, melted
2 ½ tsp. taco seasoning mix
1 medium lime
2 tbsp. cilantro, chopped

Instructions
1.Mix the cauliflower with the melted coconut oil and the taco seasoning, ensuring to coat the florets all over.
2.Cook at 350°F for seven minutes, shaking the basket a few times through the cooking time. Then transfer the cauliflower to a bowl.
3.Squeeze the lime juice over the cauliflower and season with the cilantro. Toss once more to coat and enjoy.

Chipotle Jicama Hash

Prep + Cook Time: 15 minutes | Servings: 2

Ingredients
4 slices bacon, chopped
12 oz jicama, peeled and diced
4 oz purple onion, chopped
1 oz green bell pepper (or poblano), seeded and chopped
4 tbsp Chipotle mayonnaise

Instructions
1. Using a skillet, brown the bacon on a high heat.
2. Remove and place on a towel to drain the grease.
3. Use the remaining grease to fry the onions and jicama until brown.
4. When ready, add the bell pepper and cook the hash until tender.
5. Transfer the hash onto two plates and serve each plate with 4 tablespoons of Chipotle mayonnaise.

Fried Queso Blanco

Prep + Cook Time: 170 minutes | Servings: 4

Ingredients
5 oz queso blanco
1 ½ tbsp olive oil
3 oz cheese
2 oz olives
1 pinch red pepper flakes

Instructions
1. Cube some cheese and freeze it for 1-2 hours.
2. Pour the oil in a skillet and heat to boil over a medium temperature.
3. Add the cheese cubes and heat till brown.
4. Combine the cheese together using a spatula and flatten.
5. Cook the cheese on both sides, flipping regularly.
6. While flipping, fold the cheese into itself to form crispy layers.
7. Use a spatula to roll it into a block.
8. Remove it from the pan, allow it to cool, cut it into small cubes, and serve.

Spinach with Bacon & Shallots

Prep + Cook Time: 30 minutes | Servings: 4

Ingredients
16 oz raw spinach
½ cup chopped white onion
½ cup chopped shallot
½ pound raw bacon slices
2 tbsp butter

Instructions
1. Slice the bacon strips into small narrow pieces.
2. In a skillet, heat the butter and add the chopped onion, shallots and bacon.
3. Sauté for 15-20 minutes or until the onions start to caramelize and the bacon is cooked.
4. Add the spinach and sauté on a medium heat. Stir frequently to ensure the leaves touch the skillet while cooking.
5. Cover and steam for around 5 minutes, stir and continue until wilted.
6. Serve!

Bacon-Wrapped Sausage Skewers

Prep + Cook Time: 8 minutes | Servings: 2

Ingredients
5 Italian chicken sausages
10 slices bacon

Instructions
1. Preheat your air fryer to 370°F/190°C.
2. Cut the sausage into four pieces.
3. Slice the bacon in half.
4. Wrap the bacon over the sausage.
5. Skewer the sausage.
6. Fry for 4-5 minutes until browned.

Roasted Brussels Sprouts & Bacon

Prep + Cook Time: 45 minutes | Servings: 2

Ingredients
24 oz brussels sprouts
¼ cup fish sauce
¼ cup bacon grease
6 strips bacon
Pepper to taste

Instructions
1. De-stem and quarter the brussels sprouts.
2. Mix them with the bacon grease and fish sauce.
3. Slice the bacon into small strips and cook.
4. Add the bacon and pepper to the sprouts.
5. Spread onto a greased pan and cook at 450°F/230°C for 35 minutes.
6. Stir every 5 minute or so.
7. Broil for a few more minutes and serve.

Ham & Cheese Rolls

Prep + Cook Time: 5 minutes | Servings: 4

Ingredients
16 slices ham
1 package chive and onion cream cheese (8 oz)
16 slices thin Swiss cheese

Instructions
1. Place the ham on a chopping board.
2. Dry the slices with a paper towel.
3. Thinly spread 2 teaspoons of Swiss cheese over each slice of ham.
4. On the clean section of ham, add a half inch slice of cheese.
5. On the cheese side, fold the ham over the cheese and roll it up.
6. Leave it as is, or slice into smaller rolls.

Hillbilly Cheese Surprise

Prep + Cook Time: 40 minutes | Servings: 6

Ingredients
4 cups broccoli florets
¼ cup ranch dressing
½ cup sharp cheddar cheese, shredded
¼ cup heavy whipping cream
Kosher salt and pepper to taste

Instructions
1. Preheat your fryer to 375°F/190°C.
2. In a bowl, combine all of the ingredients until the broccoli is well-covered.
3. In a casserole dish, spread out the broccoli mixture.
4. Bake for 30 minutes.
5. Take out of your fryer and mix.
6. If the florets are not tender, bake for another 5 minutes until tender.
7. Serve!

Parmesan & Garlic Cauliflower

Prep + Cook Time: 40 minutes | Servings: 4

Ingredients
3/4 cup cauliflower florets
2 tbsp butter
1 clove garlic, sliced thinly
2 tbsp shredded parmesan
1 pinch of salt

Instructions
1. Preheat your fryer to 350°F/175°C.
2. On a low heat, melt the butter with the garlic for 5-10 minutes.
3. Strain the garlic in a sieve.
4. Add the cauliflower, parmesan and salt.
5. Bake for 20 minutes or until golden.

Jalapeño Guacamole

Prep + Cook Time: 30 minutes | Servings: 4

Ingredients
2 Hass avocados, ripe
¼ red onion
1 jalapeño
1 tbsp fresh lime juice
Sea salt

Instructions
1. Spoon the avocado innings into a bowl.
2. Dice the jalapeño and onion.
3. Mash the avocado to the desired consistency.
4. Add in the onion, jalapeño and lime juice.
5. Sprinkle with salt.

Green Beans & s

Prep + Cook Time: 15 minutes | Servings: 4

Ingredients
1 lb fresh green beans, trimmed
2 tbsp butter
¼ cup sliced s
2 tsp lemon pepper

Instructions
1. Steam the green beans for 8 minutes, until tender, then drain.
2. On a medium heat, melt the butter in a skillet.
3. Sauté the s until browned.
4. Sprinkle with salt and pepper.
5. Mix in the green beans.

Sugar Snap Bacon

Prep + Cook Time: 10 minutes | Servings: 4

Ingredients
3 cups sugar snap peas
½ tbsp lemon juice
2 tbsp bacon fat
2 tsp garlic
½ tsp red pepper flakes

Instructions
1. In a skillet, cook the bacon fat until it begins to smoke.
2. Add the garlic and cook for 2 minutes.
3. Add the sugar peas and lemon juice.
4. Cook for 2-3 minutes.
5. Remove and sprinkle with red pepper flakes and lemon zest.
6. Serve!

Carrots & Cumin

Prep + Cook Time: 25 minutes | Servings: 4

Ingredients

2 cups carrots, peeled and chopped
1 tsp. cumin seeds
1 tbsp. olive oil
¼ cup coriander

Instructions

1. Cover the carrots with the cumin and oil.
2. Transfer to the Air Fryer and cook at 390°F for 12 minutes.
3. Season with the coriander before serving.

Cheese Sticks

Prep + Cook Time: 15 minutes | Servings: 4

Ingredients

1 lb. mozzarella cheese
2 eggs, beaten
1 tsp. cayenne pepper
1 cup friendly bread crumbs
1 tsp. onion powder
1 tsp. garlic powder
1 cup flour
½ tsp. salt

Instructions

1. Slice the mozzarella cheese into 3- x ½-inch sticks.
2. Put the beaten eggs in a bowl.
3. Pour the flour into a shallow dish.
4. In a second bowl combine the bread crumbs, cayenne pepper, onion powder, garlic powder, and salt.
5. Dredge the mozzarella strips in the beaten egg before coating it in the flour. Dip it in the egg again. Lastly, press it into the bread crumbs.
6. Refrigerate for 20 minutes.
7. Pre-heat the Air Fryer to 400°F.
8. Spritz the Air Fryer basket with cooking spray.
9. Put the coated cheese sticks in the Air Fryer basket and cook for 5 minutes. Serve immediately.

Onion Rings

Prep + Cook Time: 25 minutes | Servings: 2

Ingredients

1 large onion, cut into slices

1 egg, beaten
¾ cup friendly bread crumbs
1 cup milk
1 tsp. baking powder
1 ¼ cup flour
1 tsp. salt

Instructions

1. Pre-heat the Air Fryer for 5 minutes.
2. In a small bowl, combine the baking powder, flour, and salt
3. In a second bowl, stir together the milk and egg using a whisk.
4. Put the bread crumbs in a shallow dish.
5. Coat each slice of onion with the flour, then dredge it in the egg mixture. Lastly, press it into the breadcrumbs.
6. Transfer the coated onion rings to the Air Fryer basket and cook at
7. 350°F for 10 minutes.

Vegan Veggie Dish

Prep + Cook Time: 30 minutes | Servings: 4

Ingredients

1 large zucchini, sliced
3 – 4 cherry tomatoes on the vine
1 medium carrot, peeled and cubed
1 large parsnip, peeled and cubed
1 green pepper, sliced
1 tsp. mustard
1 tsp. mixed herbs
2 cloves garlic, crushed
2 tbsp. honey
3+3 tbsp. olive oil, separately
Sea salt to taste
Black pepper to taste

Instructions

1. Place the slices of zucchini, green pepper, parsnip, carrot and cherry tomatoes inside the Air Fryer.
2. Pour 3 tablespoons of oil over the vegetables and cook at 360°F for 15 minutes.
3. In the meantime, make the marinade by mixing together all of the other ingredients in the Air Fryer baking dish.
4. Transfer the cooked vegetables to the baking dish and coat it completely with the marinade. Season with pepper and salt as desired.
5. Return to the fryer and cook at 390°F for 5 minutes. Serve hot.

Tofu

Prep + Cook Time: 20 minutes | Servings: 4

Ingredients
15 oz. extra firm tofu, drained and cut into cubes
1 tsp. chili flakes
¾ cup cornstarch
¼ cup cornmeal
Pepper to taste
Salt to taste

Instructions
1.In a bowl, combine the cornmeal, cornstarch, chili flakes, pepper, and salt.
2.Coat the tofu cubes completely with the mixture.
3.Pre-heat your Air Fryer at 350°F.
4.Spritz the basket with cooking spray.
5.Transfer the coated tofu to the basket and air fry for 8 minutes, shaking the basket at the 4-minute mark.

Friday's Fries

Prep + Cook Time: 25 minutes | Servings: 2

Ingredients
1 large eggplant, cut into 3-inch slices
¼ cup water
1 tbsp. olive oil
¼ cup cornstarch
¼ tsp. salt

Instructions
1.Pre-heat the Air Fryer to 400°F.
2.In a bowl, combine the water, olive oil, cornstarch, and salt.
3.Coat the sliced eggplant with the mixture.
4.Put the coated eggplant slices in the Air Fryer basket and cook for 20 minutes.

Sweet Potato Bites

Prep + Cook Time: 30 minutes | Servings: 2

Ingredients
2 sweet potatoes, diced into 1-inch cubes
1 tsp. red chili flakes
2 tsp. cinnamon
2 tbsp. olive oil
2 tbsp. honey
½ cup fresh parsley, chopped

Instructions
1.Pre-heat the Air Fryer at 350°F.

2.Place all of the ingredients in a bowl and stir well to coat the sweet potato cubes entirely.
3.Put the sweet potato mixture into the Air Fryer basket and cook for 15 minutes.

Kale Chips

Prep + Cook Time: 15 minutes | Servings: 2

Ingredients
1 head kale
1 tbsp. olive oil
1 tsp. soy sauce

Instructions
1.De-stem the head of kale and shred each leaf into a 1 ½" piece. Wash and dry well.
2.Toss the kale with the olive oil and soy sauce to coat it completely.
3.Transfer to the Air Fryer and cook at 390°F for 2 to 3 minutes, giving the leaves a good toss at the halfway mark.

Stuffed Tomatoes

Prep + Cook Time: 30 minutes | Servings: 4

Ingredients
4 large tomatoes, without tops, seeds, or pith
1 clove garlic, crushed
1 onion, cubed
1 cup frozen peas
2 cups cooked rice, cold
1 tbsp. soy sauce
1 carrot, cubed
1 tbsp. olive oil
Parsley to taste, roughly chopped
Cooking spray

Instructions
1.Fry up the rice in a pan with the olive oil over a low heat.
2.Add in the cubed onion, carrots, crushed garlic, and frozen peas and allow to cook for 2 minutes, stirring occasionally.
3.Pour in the soy sauce and toss to coat. Remove the pan from the heat.
4.Pre-heat the Air Fryer to 360°F.
5.Stuff each tomato with the rice and vegetables
6.Put the tomatoes in the Air Fryer and cook for 20 minutes.
7.Garnish the cooked tomatoes with the chopped parsley and serve.

Mix Nuts

Prep + Cook Time: 15 minutes | Servings: 8

Ingredients
2 cup mixed nuts
1 tsp. chipotle chili powder
1 tsp. ground cumin
1 tbsp. butter, melted
1 tsp. pepper
1 tsp. salt

Instructions
1. In a bowl, combine all of the ingredients, coating the nuts well.
2. Set your Air Fryer to 350°F and allow to heat for 5 minutes.
3. Place the mixed nuts in the fryer basket and roast for 4 minutes, shaking the basket halfway through the cooking time.

Cheesy Potatoes

Prep + Cook Time: 20 minutes | Servings: 4

Ingredients
11 oz. potatoes, diced and boiled
1 egg yolk
2 tbsp. flour
3 tbsp. parmesan cheese
3 tbsp. friendly bread crumbs, tossed with a little oil
Pepper to taste
Nutmeg to taste
Salt to taste

Instructions
1. Pre-heat Air Fryer at 390°F.
2. Mash up the potatoes and combine with all of the ingredients, minus the bread crumbs.
3. Shape equal amounts of the mixture into medium-sized balls and roll each one in the bread crumbs.
4. Place the potato balls in the fryer and cook for 4 minutes.

Baked Potatoes

Prep + Cook Time: 45 minutes | Servings: 3

Ingredients
3 Idaho or russet baking potatoes, washed
2 cloves garlic, crushed
1 tbsp. olive oil
1 tbsp. sea salt
Parsley, roughly chopped
Sour cream to taste

Instructions
1. Pierce each potato several times with a fork.
2. Sprinkle the potatoes with salt and coat with the garlic puree and olive oil.
3. Place the potatoes in the Air Fryer basket and cook at 390°F for 35 - 40 minutes until soft. Serve with parsley and sour cream, or whatever toppings you desire.

Baby Corn

Prep + Cook Time: 20 minutes | Servings: 4

Ingredients
8 oz. baby corns, boiled
1 cup flour
1 tsp. garlic powder
½ tsp. carom seeds
¼ tsp. chili powder
Pinch of baking soda
Salt to taste

Instructions
1. In a bowl, combine the flour, chili powder, garlic powder, cooking soda, salt and carom seed. Add in a little water to create a batter-like consistency.
2. Coat each baby corn in the batter.
3. Pre-heat the Air Fryer at 350°F.
4. Cover the Air Fryer basket with aluminum foil before laying the coated baby corns on top of the foil.
5. Cook for 10 minutes.

French Fries

Prep + Cook Time: 25 minutes | Servings: 4

Ingredients
1 lb. russet potatoes
1 tsp. salt
½ tsp. black pepper
1 tbsp. olive oil

Instructions
1. In a pot filled with water, blanch the potatoes until softened.
2. Remove from the heat and allow to cool. Slice the potatoes into matchstick shapes.
3. Place them in a large bowl and coat with the olive oil, salt and pepper.
4. Pre-heat the Air Fryer to 390°F.
5. Cook the French fries for about 15 minutes, giving the basket a shake now and again throughout the cooking time. Serve with freshly chopped herbs if desired.

Roasted Corn

Prep + Cook Time: 15 minutes | Servings: 8

Ingredients
4 fresh ears of corn
2 to 3 tsp. vegetable oil
Salt and pepper to taste

Instructions
1. Remove the husks from the corn, before washing and drying the corn. Slice up the corn to fit your Air Fryer basket if necessary.
2. Pour a drizzling of vegetable oil over the corn, coating it well. Sprinkle on salt and pepper.
3. Place in the fryer and cook at 400°F for about 10 minutes.

Roasted Carrots

Prep + Cook Time: 20 minutes | Servings: 2

Ingredients
1 tbsp. olive oil
3 cups baby carrots or carrots, cut into large chunks
1 tbsp. honey
Salt and pepper to taste

Instructions
1. In a bowl, coat the carrots with the honey and olive oil before sprinkling on some salt and pepper.
2. Place into the Air Fryer and cook at 390°F for 12 minutes. Serve hot.

Fried Kale Chips

Prep + Cook Time: 10 minutes | Servings: 2

Ingredients
1 head kale, torn into 1 ½-inch pieces
1 tbsp. olive oil
1 tsp. soy sauce

Instructions
1. Wash and dry the kale pieces.
2. Transfer the kale to a bowl and coat with the soy sauce and oil.
3. Place it in the Air Fryer and cook at 400°F for 3 minutes, tossing it halfway through the cooking process.

Orange Cauliflower

Prep + Cook Time: 30 minutes | Servings: 2

Ingredients
½ lemon, juiced

1 head cauliflower
½ tbsp. olive oil
1 tsp. curry powder
Sea salt to taste
Ground black pepper to taste

Instructions
1. Wash the cauliflower. Cut out the leaves and core.
2. Chop the cauliflower into equally-sized florets.
3. Coat the inside of the Air Fryer with the oil and allow it to warm up for about 2 minutes at 390°F.
4. In a bowl, mix together the fresh lemon juice and curry powder. Add in the cauliflower florets. Sprinkle in the pepper and salt and mix again, coating the florets well.
5. Transfer to the fryer, cook for 20 minutes, and serve warm.

Lemon Green Beans

Prep + Cook Time: 20 minutes | Servings: 4

Ingredients
1 lemon, juiced
1 lb. green beans, washed and destemmed
¼ tsp. extra virgin olive oil
Sea salt to taste
Black pepper to taste

Instructions
1. Pre-heat the Air Fryer to 400°F.
2. Put the green beans in your Air Fryer basket and drizzle the lemon juice over them.
3. Sprinkle on the pepper and salt. Pour in the oil, and toss to coat the green beans well.
4. Cook for 10 – 12 minutes and serve warm.

Broccoli Florets

Prep + Cook Time: 20 minutes | Servings: 4

Ingredients
1 lb. broccoli, cut into florets
1 tbsp. lemon juice
1 tbsp. olive oil
1 tbsp. sesame seeds
3 garlic cloves, minced

Instructions
1. In a bowl, combine all of the ingredients, coating the broccoli well.
2. Transfer to the Air Fryer basket and air fry at 400°F for 13 minutes.

Avocado Fries

Prep + Cook Time: 20 minutes | Servings: 4

Ingredients
½ cup panko
½ tsp. salt
1 whole avocado
1 oz. aquafaba

Instructions
1.In a shallow bowl, stir together the panko and salt.
2.In a separate shallow bowl, add the aquafaba.
3.Dip the avocado slices into the aquafaba, before coating each one in the panko.
4.Place the slices in your Air Fryer basket, taking care not to overlap any. Air fry for 10 minutes at 390°F.

Oriental Spinach Samosa

Prep + Cook Time: 45 minutes | Servings: 2

Ingredients
¾ cup boiled and blended spinach puree
¼ cup green peas
½ tsp. sesame seeds
Ajwain, salt, chaat masala, chili powder to taste
2 tsp. olive oil
1 tsp. chopped fresh coriander leaves
1 tsp. garam masala
¼ cup boiled and cut potatoes
½ 1 cup flour
½ tsp. cooking soda

Instructions
1.In a bowl, combine the Ajwain, flour, cooking soda and salt to form a dough-like consistency. Pour in one teaspoon of the oil and the spinach puree. Continue to mix the dough, ensuring it is smooth.
2.Refrigerate for 20 minutes. Add another teaspoon of oil to a saucepan and sauté the potatoes and peas for 5 minutes.
3.Stir in the sesame seeds, coriander, and any other spices you desire.
4.Use your hands to shape equal sized amounts of the dough into small balls. Mold these balls into cone-shapes.
5.Fill each cone with the potatoes and peas mixture and seal.
6.Pre-heat your Air Fryer to 390°F.
7.Put the samosas in the basket and cook for 10 minutes.
8.Serve the samosas with the sauce of your choice.

Tomatoes & Herbs

Prep + Cook Time: 30 minutes | Servings: 2

Ingredients
2 large tomatoes, washed and cut into halves
Herbs, such as oregano, basil, thyme, rosemary, sage to taste
Cooking spray
Pepper to taste
Parmesan, grated [optional]
Parsley, minced [optional]

Instructions
1.Spritz both sides of each tomato half with a small amount of cooking spray.
2.Coat the tomatoes with a light sprinkling of pepper and the herbs of your choice.
3.Place the tomatoes in the basket, cut-side-up. Cook at 320°F for 20 minutes, or longer if necessary.
4.Serve hot, at room temperature, or chilled as a refreshing summer snack. Optionally, you can garnish them with grated Parmesan and minced parsley before serving.

Vegetable Fritters

Prep + Cook Time: 15 minutes | Servings: 4

Ingredients
1 cup bell peppers, deveined and chopped
1 tsp. sea salt flakes
1 tsp. cumin
¼ tsp. paprika
½ cup shallots, chopped
2 cloves garlic, minced
1 ½ tbsp. fresh chopped cilantro
1 egg, whisked
¾ cup Cheddar cheese, grated
¼ cup cooked quinoa
¼ cup flour

Instructions
1.In a bowl, combine all of the ingredients well.
2.Divide the mixture into equal portions and shape each one into a ball. Use your palm to flatten each ball very slightly to form patties.
3.Lightly coat the patties with a cooking spray.
4.Put the patties in your Air Fryer cooking basket, taking care not to overlap them.
5.Cook at 340°F for 10 minutes, turning them over halfway through.

Flax Cheese Chips

Prep + Cook Time: 20 minutes | Servings: 2

Ingredients
1 ½ cup cheddar cheese
4 tbsp ground flaxseed meal
Seasonings of your choice

Instructions
1. Preheat your fryer to 425°F/220°C.
2. Spoon 2 tablespoons of cheddar cheese into a mound, onto a non-stick pad.
3. Spread out a pinch of flax seed on each chip.
4. Season and bake for 10-15 minutes.

Country Style Chard

Prep + Cook Time: 5 minutes | Servings: 2

Ingredients
4 slices bacon, chopped
2 tbsp butter
2 tbsp fresh lemon juice
½ tsp garlic paste
1 bunch Swiss chard, stems removed, leaves cut into 1-inch pieces

Instructions
1. On a medium heat, cook the bacon in a skillet until the fat begins to brown.
2. Melt the butter in the skillet and add the lemon juice and garlic paste.
3. Add the chard leaves and cook until they begin to wilt.
4. Cover and turn up the heat to high.
5. Cook for 3 minutes.
6. Mix well, sprinkle with salt and serve.

Baked Tortillas

Prep + Cook Time: 30 minutes | Servings: 4

Ingredients
1 large head of cauliflower divided into florets.
4 large eggs
2 garlic cloves (minced)
1 ½ tsp herbs (whatever your favorite is - basil, oregano, thyme)
½ tsp salt

Instructions
1. Preheat your fryer to 375°F/190°C.
2. Put parchment paper on two baking sheets.
3. In a food processor, break down the cauliflower into rice.
4. Add ¼ cup water and the riced cauliflower to a saucepan.
5. Cook on a medium high heat until tender for 10 minutes. Drain.
6. Dry with a clean kitchen towel.
7. Mix the cauliflower, eggs, garlic, herbs and salt.
8. Make 4 thin circles on the parchment paper.
9. Bake for 20 minutes, until dry.

Homemade Mayonnaise

Prep + Cook Time: 30 minutes | Servings: 4

Ingredients
1 large egg
Juice from 1 lemon.
1 tsp dry mustard
½ tsp black pepper
1 cup avocado oil

Instructions
1. Combine the egg and lemon juice in a container and let sit for 20 minutes.
2. Add the dry mustard, pepper, and avocado oil.
3. Insert an electric whisk into the container.
4. Blend for 30 seconds.
5. Transfer to a sealed container and store in your refrigerator.

Fried Green Tomatoes

Prep + Cook Time: 10 minutes | Servings: 2

Ingredients
2 medium green tomatoes
1 egg
¼ cup blanched finely ground flour
1/3 cup parmesan cheese, grated

Instructions
1. Slice the tomatoes about a half-inch thick.
2. Crack the egg into a bowl and beat it with a whisk. In a separate bowl, mix together the flour and parmesan cheese.
3. Dredge the tomato slices in egg, then dip them into the flour-cheese mixture to coat. Place each slice into the fryer basket. They may need to be cooked in multiple batches.
4. Cook at 400°F for seven minutes, turning them halfway through the cooking time, and then serve warm.

Avocado Sticks

Prep + Cook Time: 10 minutes | Servings: 2

Ingredients
2 avocados
4 egg yolks
1 ½ tbsp. water
Salt and pepper
1 cup flour
1 cup herbed butter

Instructions
1. Halve the avocados, twist to open, and take out the pits. Cut each half into three equal slices.
2. In a bowl, combine the egg yolks and water. Season with salt and pepper to taste and whisk together.
3. Pour the flour into a shallow bowl.
4. Coat each slice of avocado in the flour, then in the egg, before dipping it in the flour again. Ensure the flour coats the avocado well and firmly.
5. Pre-heat the fryer at 400°F. When it is warm, put the avocados inside and cook for eight minutes.
6. Take care when removing the avocados from the fryer and enjoy with a side of the herbed butter.

Cheesy Cauliflower Bites

Prep + Cook Time: 20 minutes | Servings: 3

Ingredients
2 cup cauliflower florets
¾ cup cheddar cheese, shredded
½ cup onion, chopped
1 tsp. seasoning salt
2 tbsp. butter, melted
2 cloves garlic, minced

Instructions
1. Pulse the cauliflower florets in the food processor until they become crumbly. Use a cheesecloth to remove all the moisture from the cauliflower.
2. In a bowl, combine the cauliflower with the cheese, onion, seasoning salt, and melted butter. With your hands, roll the mixture into balls.
3. Pre-heat the fryer at 400°F.
4. Fry the balls for fourteen minutes, leaving them in the fryer for an additional two minutes if you like them browner. Serve hot.

Brussels Sprouts with Cheese Sauce

Prep + Cook Time: 10 minutes | Servings: 2

Ingredients
¾ cups Brussels sprouts
1 tbsp. extra virgin olive oil
¼ tsp. salt
¼ cup mozzarella cheese, shredded

Instructions
1. Halve the Brussels sprouts and drizzle with the olive oil. Season with salt and toss to coat.
2. Pre-heat your fryer at 375°F. When warm, transfer the Brussels sprouts inside and add the shredded mozzarella on top.
3. Cook for five minutes, serving when the cheese is melted.

Vegetable Mix

Prep + Cook Time: 45 minutes | Servings: 4

Ingredients
3.5 oz. radish
½ tsp. parsley
3.5 oz. celeriac
1 yellow carrot
1 orange carrot
1 red onion
3.5 oz. pumpkin
3.5 oz. parsnips
Salt to taste
Epaulette pepper to taste
1 tbsp. olive oil
4 cloves garlic, unpeeled

Instructions
1. Peel and slice up all the vegetables into 2- to 3-cm pieces.
2. Pre-heat your Air Fryer to 390°F.
3. Pour in the oil and allow it to warm before placing the vegetables in the fryer, followed by the garlic, salt and pepper.
4. Roast for 18 – 20 minutes.
5. Top with parsley and serve hot with rice if desired.

Potato Chips

Prep + Cook Time: 45 minutes | Servings: 4

Ingredients
2 large potatoes, peel and sliced
1 tbsp. rosemary
3.5 oz. sour cream
¼ tsp. salt

Instructions
1. Place the potato slices in water and allow to absorb for 30 minutes.
2. Drain the potato slices and transfer to a large bowl. Toss with the rosemary, sour cream, and salt.
3. Pre-heat the Air Fryer to 320°F
4. Put the coated potato slices in the fryer's basket and cook for 35 minutes. Serve hot.

Brussels Sprouts

Prep + Cook Time: 15 minutes | Servings: 2

Ingredients
2 cups Brussels sprouts, sliced in half
1 tbsp. balsamic vinegar
1 tbsp. olive oil
¼ tsp. salt

Instructions
1. Toss all of the ingredients together in a bowl, coating the Brussels sprouts well.
2. Place the sprouts in the Air Fryer basket and air fry at 400°F for 10 minutes, shaking the basket at the halfway point.

Garlic Potatoes

Prep + Cook Time: 40 minutes | Servings: 4

Ingredients
1 lb. russet baking potatoes
1 tbsp. garlic powder
1 tbsp. freshly chopped parsley
½ tsp. salt
¼ tsp. black pepper
1 – 2 tbsp. olive oil

Instructions
1. Wash the potatoes and pat them dry with clean paper towels.
2. Pierce each potato several times with a fork.
3. Place the potatoes in a large bowl and season with the garlic powder, salt and pepper.
4. Pour over the olive oil and mix well.
5. Pre-heat the Air Fryer to 360°F.
6. Place the potatoes in the fryer and cook for about 30 minutes, shaking the basket a few times throughout the cooking time.
7. Garnish the potatoes with the chopped parsley and serve with butter, sour cream or another dipping sauce if desired.

Zucchini Rolls

Prep + Cook Time: 15 minutes | Servings: 2 – 4

Ingredients
3 zucchinis, sliced thinly lengthwise with a mandolin or very sharp knife
1 tbsp. olive oil
1 cup goat cheese
¼ tsp. black pepper

Instructions
1. Preheat your Air Fryer to 390°F.
2. Coat each zucchini strip with a light brushing of olive oil.
3. Combine the sea salt, black pepper and goat cheese.
4. Scoop a small, equal amount of the goat cheese onto the center of each strip of zucchini. Roll up the strips and secure with a toothpick.
5. Transfer to the Air Fryer and cook for 5 minutes until the cheese is warm and the zucchini slightly crispy. If desired, add some tomato sauce on top.

Asparagus

Prep + Cook Time: 15 minutes | Servings: 4

Ingredients
10 asparagus spears, woody end cut off
1 clove garlic, minced
4 tbsp. olive oil
Pepper to taste
Salt to taste

Instructions
1. Set the Air Fryer to 400°F and allow to heat for 5 minutes.
2. In a bowl, combine the garlic and oil.
3. Cover the asparagus with this mixture and put it in the fryer basket. Sprinkle over some pepper and salt.
4. Cook for 10 minutes and serve hot.

Zucchini Chips

Prep + Cook Time: 30 minutes | Servings: 2

Ingredients
3 medium zucchini, sliced
1 tsp. parsley, chopped
3 tbsp. parmesan cheese, grated
Pepper to taste
Salt to taste

Instructions
1. Pre-heat the Air Fryer to 425°F.
2. Put the sliced zucchini on a sheet of baking paper and spritz with cooking spray.
3. Combine the cheese, pepper, parsley, and salt. Use this mixture to sprinkle over the zucchini.
4. Transfer to the Air Fryer and cook for 25 minutes, ensuring the zucchini slices have crisped up nicely before serving.

Sweet Potato Wedges

Prep + Cook Time: 25 minutes | Servings: 2

Ingredients
2 large sweet potatoes, cut into wedges
1 tbsp. olive oil
1 tsp. chili powder
1 tsp. mustard powder
1 tsp. cumin
1 tbsp. Mexican seasoning
Pepper to taste
Salt to taste

Instructions
1.Pre-heat the Air Fryer at 350°F.
2.Place all of the ingredients into a bowl and combine well to coat the sweet potatoes entirely.
3.Place the wedges in the Air Fryer basket and air fry for 20 minutes, shaking the basket at 5-minute intervals.

Potato Wedges

Prep + Cook Time: 30 minutes | Servings: 4

Ingredients
4 medium potatoes, cut into wedges
1 tbsp. Cajun spice
1 tbsp. olive oil
Pepper to taste
Salt to taste

Instructions
1.Place the potato wedges in the Air Fryer basket and pour in the olive oil.
2.Cook wedges at 370°F for 25 minutes, shaking the basket twice throughout the cooking time.
3.Put the cooked wedges in a bowl and coat them with the Cajun spice, pepper, and salt. Serve warm.

Banana Chips

Prep + Cook Time: 20 minutes | Servings: 3

Ingredients
2 large raw bananas, peel and sliced
½ tsp. red chili powder
1 tsp. olive oil
¼ tsp. turmeric powder
1 tsp. salt

Instructions
1.Put some water in a bowl along with the turmeric powder and salt.
2.Place the sliced bananas in the bowl and allow to soak for 10 minutes.
3.Dump the contents into a sieve to strain the banana slices before drying them with a paper towel.
4.Pre-heat the Air Fryer to 350°F.
5.Put the banana slices in a bowl and coat them with the olive oil, chili powder and salt.
6.Transfer the chips to the fryer basket and air fry for 15 minutes.

Honey Carrots

Prep + Cook Time: 20 minutes | Servings: 4

Ingredients
1 tbsp. honey
3 cups baby carrots or carrots, cut into bite-size pieces
1 tbsp. olive oil
Sea salt to taste
Ground black pepper to taste

Instructions
1.In a bowl, combine the carrots, honey, and olive oil, coating the carrots completely. Sprinkle on some salt and ground black pepper.
2.Transfer the carrots to the Air Fryer and cook at 390°F for 12 minutes. Serve immediately.

Potato Totes

Prep + Cook Time: 20 minutes | Servings: 2

Ingredients
1 large potato, diced
1 tsp. onion, minced
1 tsp. olive oil
Pepper to taste
Salt to taste

Instructions
1.Boil the potatoes in a saucepan of water over a medium-high heat.
2.Strain the potatoes, transfer them to bowl, and mash them thoroughly.
3.Combine with the olive oil, onion, pepper and salt in mashed potato.
4.Shape equal amounts of the mixture into small tots and place each one in the Air Fryer basket. Cook at 380°F for 8 minutes.
5.Give the basket a good shake and cook for an additional 5 minutes before serving.

Honey Sriracha Chicken Wings

Prep time: 5 minutes | Cook time: 30 minutes | Serves 4

1 tablespoon Sriracha hot sauce
1 tablespoon honey
1 garlic clove, minced
½ teaspoon kosher salt
16 chicken wings and drumettes
Cooking spray

1. Preheat the air fryer to 360ºF (182ºC).
2. In a large bowl, whisk together the Sriracha hot sauce, honey, minced garlic, and kosher salt, then add the chicken and toss to coat.
3. Spray the air fryer basket with cooking spray, then place 8 wings in the basket and air fry for 15 minutes, turning halfway through. Repeat this process with the remaining wings.
4. Remove the wings and allow to cool on a wire rack for 10 minutes before serving.

Crispy Cajun Dill Pickle Chips

Prep time: 5 minutes | Cook time: 10 minutes | Makes 16 slices

¼ cup all-purpose flour
½ cup panko bread crumbs
1 large egg, beaten
2 teaspoons Cajun seasoning
2 large dill pickles, sliced into 8 rounds each
Cooking spray

1. Preheat the air fryer to 390ºF (199ºC).
2. Place the all-purpose flour, panko bread crumbs, and egg into 3 separate shallow bowls, then stir the Cajun seasoning into the flour.
3. Dredge each pickle chip in the flour mixture, then the egg, and finally the bread crumbs. Shake off any excess, then place each coated pickle chip on a plate.
4. Spritz the air fryer basket with cooking spray, then place 8 pickle chips in the basket and air fry for 5 minutes, or until crispy and golden brown. Repeat this process with the remaining pickle chips.
5. Remove the chips and allow to slightly cool on a wire rack before serving.

Chapter 11 Fast and Easy Everyday Favorites

Air Fried Broccoli

Prep time: 5 minutes | Cook time: 6 minutes | Serves 1

4 egg yolks
¼ cup butter, melted
2 cups coconut flower
Salt and pepper, to taste
2 cups broccoli florets

1. Preheat the air fryer to 400ºF (204ºC).
2. In a bowl, whisk the egg yolks and melted butter together. Throw in the coconut flour, salt and pepper, then stir again to combine well.
3. Dip each broccoli floret into the mixture and place in the air fryer basket. Air fry for 6 minutes in batches if necessary. Take care when removing them from the air fryer and serve immediately.

Rosemary and Orange Roasted Chickpeas

Prep time: 5 minutes | Cook time: 10 to 12 minutes | Makes 4 cups

4 cups cooked chickpeas
2 tablespoons vegetable oil
1 teaspoon kosher salt
1 teaspoon cumin
1 teaspoon paprika
Zest of 1 orange
1 tablespoon chopped fresh rosemary

1. Preheat the air fryer to 400ºF (204ºC).
2. Make sure the chickpeas are completely dry prior to roasting. In a medium bowl, toss the chickpeas with oil, salt, cumin, and paprika.
3. Working in batches, spread the chickpeas in a single layer in the air fryer basket. Air fry for 10 to 12 minutes until crisp, shaking once halfway through.
4. Return the warm chickpeas to the bowl and toss with the orange zest and rosemary. Allow to cool completely.
5. Serve.

Spinach and Carrot Balls

Prep time: 10 minutes | Cook time: 10 minutes | Serves 4

2 slices toasted bread
1 carrot, peeled and grated
1 package fresh spinach, blanched and chopped
½ onion, chopped
1 egg, beaten
½ teaspoon garlic powder
1 teaspoon minced garlic
1 teaspoon salt
½ teaspoon black pepper
1 tablespoon nutritional yeast
1 tablespoon flour

1. Preheat the air fryer to 390ºF (199ºC).
2. In a food processor, pulse the toasted bread to form bread crumbs. Transfer into a shallow dish or bowl.
3. In a bowl, mix together all the other ingredients.
4. Use your hands to shape the mixture into small-sized balls. Roll the balls in the bread crumbs, ensuring to cover them well.
5. Put in the air fryer basket and air fry for 10 minutes.
6. Serve immediately.

Buttery Sweet Potatoes

Prep time: 5 minutes | Cook time: 10 minutes | Serves 4

2 tablespoons butter, melted
1 tablespoon light brown sugar
2 sweet potatoes, peeled and cut into ½-inch cubes
Cooking spray

1. Preheat the air fryer to 400ºF (204ºC). Line the air fryer basket with parchment paper.
2. In a medium bowl, stir together the melted butter and brown sugar until blended. Toss the sweet potatoes in the butter mixture until coated.
3. Place the sweet potatoes on the parchment and spritz with oil.
4. Air fry for 5 minutes. Shake the basket, spritz the sweet potatoes with oil, and air fry for 5 minutes more until they're soft enough to cut with a fork.
5. Serve immediately.

Simple and Easy Croutons

Prep time: 5 minutes | Cook time: 8 minutes | Serves 4

2 slices friendly bread
1 tablespoon olive oil
Hot soup, for serving

1. Preheat the air fryer to 390ºF (199ºC).
2. Cut the slices of bread into medium-size chunks.
3. Brush the air fryer basket with the oil.
4. Place the chunks inside and air fry for at least 8 minutes.
5. Serve with hot soup.

Carrot and Celery Croquettes

Prep time: 10 minutes | Cook time: 6 minutes | Serves 4

2 medium-sized carrots, trimmed and grated
2 medium-sized celery stalks, trimmed and grated
½ cup finely chopped leek
1 tablespoon garlic paste
¼ teaspoon freshly cracked black pepper
1 teaspoon fine sea salt
1 tablespoon finely chopped fresh dill
1 egg, lightly whisked
¼ cup flour
¼ teaspoon baking powder
½ cup bread crumbs
Cooking spray
Chive mayo, for serving

1. Preheat the air fryer to 360ºF (182ºC).
2. Drain any excess liquid from the carrots and celery by placing them on a paper towel.
3. Stir together the vegetables with all of the other ingredients, save for the bread crumbs and chive mayo.
4. Use your hands to mold 1 tablespoon of the vegetable mixture into a ball and repeat until all of the mixture has been used up. Press down on each ball with your hand or a palette knife. Cover completely with bread crumbs. Spritz the croquettes with cooking spray.
5. Arrange the croquettes in a single layer in the air fryer basket and air fry for 6 minutes.
6. Serve warm with the chive mayo on the side.

Cheesy Potato Patties

Prep time: 5 minutes | Cook time: 10 minutes | Serves 8

2 pounds (907 g) white potatoes
½ cup finely chopped scallions
½ teaspoon freshly ground black pepper, or more to taste
1 tablespoon fine
sea salt
½ teaspoon hot paprika
2 cups shredded Colby cheese
¼ cup canola oil
1 cup crushed crackers

1. Preheat the air fryer to 360ºF (182ºC).
2. Boil the potatoes until soft. Dry them off and peel them before mashing thoroughly, leaving no lumps.
3. Combine the mashed potatoes with scallions, pepper, salt, paprika, and cheese.
4. Mold the mixture into balls with your hands and press with your palm to flatten them into patties.
5. In a shallow dish, combine the canola oil and crushed crackers. Coat the patties in the crumb mixture.
6. Bake the patties for about 10 minutes, in multiple batches if necessary.
7. Serve hot.

Corn Fritters

Prep time: 15 minutes | Cook time: 8 minutes | Serves 6

1 cup self-rising flour
1 tablespoon sugar
1 teaspoon salt
1 large egg, lightly
beaten
¼ cup buttermilk
¾ cup corn kernels
¼ cup minced onion
Cooking spray

1. Preheat the air fryer to 350ºF (177ºC). Line the air fryer basket with parchment paper.
2. In a medium bowl, whisk the flour, sugar, and salt until blended. Stir in the egg and buttermilk. Add the corn and minced onion. Mix well. Shape the corn fritter batter into 12 balls.
3. Place the fritters on the parchment and spritz with oil. Bake for 4 minutes. Flip the fritters, spritz them with oil, and bake for 4 minutes more until firm and lightly browned.
4. Serve immediately.

Sweet Corn and Carrot Fritters

Prep time: 10 minutes | Cook time: 8 to 11 minutes | Serves 4

1 medium-sized carrot, grated
1 yellow onion, finely chopped
4 ounces (113 g) canned sweet corn kernels, drained
1 teaspoon sea salt flakes
1 tablespoon chopped fresh cilantro
1 medium-sized egg, whisked
2 tablespoons plain milk
1 cup grated Parmesan cheese
¼ cup flour
$^1/_3$ teaspoon baking powder
$^1/_3$ teaspoon sugar
Cooking spray

1. Preheat the air fryer to 350ºF (177ºC).
2. Place the grated carrot in a colander and press down to squeeze out any excess moisture. Dry it with a paper towel.
3. Combine the carrots with the remaining ingredients.
4. Mold 1 tablespoon of the mixture into a ball and press it down with your hand or a spoon to flatten it. Repeat until the rest of the mixture is used up.
5. Spritz the balls with cooking spray.
6. Arrange in the air fryer basket, taking care not to overlap any balls. Bake for 8 to 11 minutes, or until they're firm.
7. Serve warm.

Bacon-Wrapped Beef Hot Dog

Prep time: 5 minutes | Cook time: 10 minutes | Serves 4

4 slices sugar-free bacon
4 beef hot dogs

1. Preheat the air fryer to 370ºF (188ºC).
2. Take a slice of bacon and wrap it around the hot dog, securing it with a toothpick. Repeat with the other pieces of bacon and hot dogs, placing each wrapped dog in the air fryer basket.
3. Bake for 10 minutes, turning halfway through.
4. Once hot and crispy, the hot dogs are ready to serve.

Bistro Potato Wedges

Prep time: 10 minutes | Cook time: 13 minutes | Serves 4

1 pound (454 g) fingerling potatoes, cut into wedges
1 teaspoon extra-virgin olive oil
½ teaspoon garlic powder
Salt and pepper, to taste
½ cup raw cashews, soaked in water
overnight
½ teaspoon ground turmeric
½ teaspoon paprika
1 tablespoon nutritional yeast
1 teaspoon fresh lemon juice
2 tablespoons to ¼ cup water

1. Preheat the air fryer to 400ºF (204ºC).
2. In a bowl, toss together the potato wedges, olive oil, garlic powder, and salt and pepper, making sure to coat the potatoes well.
3. Transfer the potatoes to the air fryer basket and air fry for 10 minutes.
4. In the meantime, prepare the cheese sauce. Pulse the cashews, turmeric, paprika, nutritional yeast, lemon juice, and water together in a food processor. Add more water to achieve your desired consistency.
5. When the potatoes are finished cooking, transfer to a bowl and add the cheese sauce on top. Air fry for an additional 3 minutes.
6. Serve hot.

Simple Pea Delight

Prep time: 5 minutes | Cook time: 15 minutes | Serves 2 to 4

1 cup flour
1 teaspoon baking powder
3 eggs
1 cup coconut milk
1 cup cream cheese
3 tablespoons pea
protein
½ cup chicken or turkey strips
Pinch of sea salt
1 cup Mozzarella cheese

1. Preheat the air fryer to 390ºF (199ºC).
2. In a large bowl, mix all ingredients together using a large wooden spoon.
3. Spoon equal amounts of the mixture into muffin cups and bake for 15 minutes.
4. Serve immediately.

Cheesy Sausage Balls

Prep time: 5 minutes | Cook time: 15 minutes | Serves 6

12 ounces (340 g) Jimmy Dean's Sausage
6 ounces (170 g)
shredded Cheddar cheese
10 Cheddar cubes

1. Preheat the air fryer to 375ºF (191ºC).
2. Mix the shredded cheese and sausage.
3. Divide the mixture into 12 equal parts to be stuffed.
4. Add a cube of cheese to the center of the sausage and roll into balls.
5. Air fry for 15 minutes, or until crisp.
6. Serve immediately.

Baked Halloumi with Greek Salsa

Prep time: 15 minutes | Cook time: 6 minutes | Serves 4

Salsa:
1 small shallot, finely diced
3 garlic cloves, minced
2 tablespoons fresh lemon juice
2 tablespoons extra-virgin olive oil
1 teaspoon freshly cracked black pepper
Pinch of kosher salt
½ cup finely diced English cucumber
1 plum tomato, deseeded and finely diced
2 teaspoons chopped fresh parsley
1 teaspoon snipped fresh dill
1 teaspoon snipped fresh oregano

Cheese:
8 ounces (227 g) Halloumi cheese, sliced into ½-inch-
thick pieces
1 tablespoon extra-virgin olive oil

1. Preheat the air fryer to 375ºF (191ºC).
2. For the salsa: Combine the shallot, garlic, lemon juice, olive oil, pepper, and salt in a medium bowl. Add the cucumber, tomato, parsley, dill, and oregano. Toss gently to combine; set aside.
3. For the cheese: Place the cheese slices in a medium bowl. Drizzle with the olive oil. Toss gently to coat. Arrange the cheese in a single layer in the air fryer basket. Bake for 6 minutes.
4. Divide the cheese among four serving plates. Top with the salsa and serve immediately.

Baked Cheese Sandwich

Prep time: 5 minutes | Cook time: 8 minutes | Serves 2

2 tablespoons mayonnaise
4 thick slices sourdough bread
4 thick slices Brie cheese
8 slices hot capicola

1. Preheat the air fryer to 350ºF (177ºC).
2. Spread the mayonnaise on one side of each slice of bread. Place 2 slices of bread in the air fryer basket, mayonnaise-side down.
3. Place the slices of Brie and capicola on the bread and cover with the remaining two slices of bread, mayonnaise-side up.
4. Bake for 8 minutes, or until the cheese has melted.
5. Serve immediately.

Pomegranate Avocado Fries

Prep time: 5 minutes | Cook time: 7 to 8 minutes | Serves 4

1 cup panko bread crumbs
1 teaspoon kosher salt, plus more for sprinkling
1 teaspoon garlic powder
½ teaspoon cayenne pepper
2 ripe but firm avocados
1 egg, beaten with 1 tablespoon water
Cooking spraying
Pomegranate molasses, for serving

1. Preheat the air fryer to 375ºF (191ºC).
2. Whisk together the panko, salt, and spices on a plate. Cut each avocado in half and remove the pit. Cut each avocado half into 4 slices and scoop the slices out with a large spoon, taking care to keep the slices intact.
3. Dip each avocado slice in the egg wash and then dredge it in the panko. Place the breaded avocado slices on a plate.
4. Working in 2 batches, arrange half of the avocado slices in a single layer in the air fryer basket. Spray lightly with oil. Bake the slices for 7 to 8 minutes, turning once halfway through. Remove the cooked slices to a platter and repeat with the remaining avocado slices.
5. Sprinkle the warm avocado slices with salt and drizzle with pomegranate molasses. Serve immediately.

Easy Roasted Asparagus

Prep time: 5 minutes | Cook time: 6 minutes | Serves 4

1 pound (454 g) asparagus, trimmed and halved crosswise
1 teaspoon extra-
virgin olive oil
Salt and pepper, to taste
Lemon wedges, for serving

1. Preheat the air fryer to 400ºF (204ºC).
2. Toss the asparagus with the oil, ⅛ teaspoon salt, and ⅛ teaspoon pepper in bowl. Transfer to air fryer basket.
3. Place the basket in air fryer and roast for 6 to 8 minutes, or until tender and bright green, tossing halfway through cooking.
4. Season with salt and pepper and serve with lemon wedges.

Baked Chorizo Scotch Eggs

Prep time: 5 minutes | Cook time: 15 to 20 minutes | Makes 4 eggs

1 pound (454 g) Mexican chorizo or other seasoned sausage meat
4 soft-boiled eggs plus 1 raw egg
1 tablespoon water
½ cup all-purpose flour
1 cup panko bread crumbs
Cooking spray

1. Divide the chorizo into 4 equal portions. Flatten each portion into a disc. Place a soft-boiled egg in the center of each disc. Wrap the chorizo around the egg, encasing it completely. Place the encased eggs on a plate and chill for at least 30 minutes.
2. Preheat the air fryer to 360ºF (182ºC).
3. Beat the raw egg with 1 tablespoon of water. Place the flour on a small plate and the panko on a second plate. Working with 1 egg at a time, roll the encased egg in the flour, then dip it in the egg mixture. Dredge the egg in the panko and place on a plate. Repeat with the remaining eggs.
4. Spray the eggs with oil and place in the air fryer basket. Bake for 10 minutes. Turn and bake for an additional 5 to 10 minutes, or until browned and crisp on all sides.
5. Serve immediately.

Indian-Style Sweet Potato Fries

Prep time: 5 minutes | Cook time: 8 minutes | Makes 20 fries

Seasoning Mixture:
¾ teaspoon ground coriander
½ teaspoon garam masala
½ teaspoon garlic powder
½ teaspoon ground cumin
¼ teaspoon ground cayenne pepper

Fries:
2 large sweet potatoes, peeled
2 teaspoons olive oil

1. Preheat the air fryer to 400ºF (204ºC).
2. In a small bowl, combine the coriander, garam masala, garlic powder, cumin, and cayenne pepper.
3. Slice the sweet potatoes into ¼-inch-thick fries.
4. In a large bowl, toss the sliced sweet potatoes with the olive oil and the seasoning mixture.
5. Transfer the seasoned sweet potatoes to the air fryer basket and fry for 8 minutes, until crispy.
6. Serve warm.

Bacon and Green Beans

Prep time: 15 minutes | Cook time: 8 to 10 minutes | Serves 4

2 (14.5-ounce / 411-g) cans cut green beans, drained
4 bacon slices, air-fried and diced
¼ cup minced onion
1 tablespoon distilled white vinegar
1 teaspoon freshly squeezed lemon juice
½ teaspoon salt
½ teaspoon freshly ground black pepper
Cooking spray

1. Preheat the air fryer to 370ºF (188ºC).
2. Spritz a baking pan with oil. In the prepared pan, stir together the green beans, bacon, onion, vinegar, lemon juice, salt, and pepper until blended.
3. Place the pan on the air fryer basket.
4. Air fry for 4 minutes. Stir the green beans and air fry for 4 to 6 minutes more until soft.
5. Serve immediately.

Easy Devils on Horseback

Prep time: 5 minutes | Cook time: 7 minutes | Serves 12

24 petite pitted prunes (4½ ounces / 128 g)
¼ cup crumbled blue cheese, divided
8 slices center-cut bacon, cut crosswise into thirds

1. Preheat the air fryer to 400ºF (204ºC).
2. Halve the prunes lengthwise, but don't cut them all the way through. Place ½ teaspoon of cheese in the center of each prune. Wrap a piece of bacon around each prune and secure the bacon with a toothpick.
3. Working in batches, arrange a single layer of the prunes in the air fryer basket. Air fry for about 7 minutes, flipping halfway, until the bacon is cooked through and crisp.
4. Let cool slightly and serve warm.

Crunchy Fried Okra

Prep time: 5 minutes | Cook time: 8 to 10 minutes | Serves 4

1 cup self-rising yellow cornmeal
1 teaspoon Italian-style seasoning
1 teaspoon paprika
1 teaspoon salt
½ teaspoon freshly ground black pepper
2 large eggs, beaten
2 cups okra slices
Cooking spray

1. Preheat the air fryer to 400ºF (204ºC). Line the air fryer basket with parchment paper.
2. In a shallow bowl, whisk the cornmeal, Italian-style seasoning, paprika, salt, and pepper until blended. Place the beaten eggs in a second shallow bowl.
3. Add the okra to the beaten egg and stir to coat. Add the egg and okra mixture to the cornmeal mixture and stir until coated.
4. Place the okra on the parchment and spritz it with oil.
5. Air fry for 4 minutes. Shake the basket, spritz the okra with oil, and air fry for 4 to 6 minutes more until lightly browned and crispy.
6. Serve immediately.

Bacon-Wrapped Jalapeño Poppers

Prep time: 5 minutes | Cook time: 12 minutes | Serves 6

6 large jalapeños
4 ounces (113 g) ⅓-less-fat cream cheese
¼ cup shredded reduced-fat sharp

Cheddar cheese
2 scallions, green tops only, sliced
6 slices center-cut bacon, halved

1. Preheat the air fryer to 325ºF (163ºC).
2. Wearing rubber gloves, halve the jalapeños lengthwise to make 12 pieces. Scoop out the seeds and membranes and discard.
3. In a medium bowl, combine the cream cheese, Cheddar, and scallions. Using a small spoon or spatula, fill the jalapeños with the cream cheese filling. Wrap a bacon strip around each pepper and secure with a toothpick.
4. Working in batches, place the stuffed peppers in a single layer in the air fryer basket. Bake for about 12 minutes, until the peppers are tender, the bacon is browned and crisp, and the cheese is melted.
5. Serve warm.

Air Fried Green Tomatoes

Prep time: 5 minutes | Cook time: 6 to 8 minutes | Serves 4

4 medium green tomatoes
⅓ cup all purpose flour
2 egg whites
¼ cup almond milk
1 cup ground

almonds
½ cup panko bread crumbs
2 teaspoons olive oil
1 teaspoon paprika
1 clove garlic, minced

1. Preheat the air fryer to 400ºF (204ºC).
2. Rinse the tomatoes and pat dry. Cut the tomatoes into ½-inch slices, discarding the thinner ends.
3. Put the flour on a plate. In a shallow bowl, beat the egg whites with the almond milk until frothy. And in another plate, combine the almonds, bread crumbs, olive oil, paprika, and garlic and mix well.
4. Dip the tomato slices into the flour, then into the egg white mixture, then into the almond mixture to coat.

5. Place four of the coated tomato slices in the air fryer basket. Air fry for 6 to 8 minutes, or until the tomato coating is crisp and golden brown. Repeat with remaining tomato slices and serve immediately.

Purple Potato Chips with Rosemary

Prep time: 10 minutes | Cook time: 9 to 14 minutes | Serves 6

1 cup Greek yogurt
2 chipotle chiles, minced
2 tablespoons adobo sauce
1 teaspoon paprika
1 tablespoon lemon juice
10 purple fingerling

potatoes
1 teaspoon olive oil
2 teaspoons minced fresh rosemary leaves
⅛ teaspoon cayenne pepper
¼ teaspoon coarse sea salt

1. Preheat the air fryer to 400ºF (204ºC).
2. In a medium bowl, combine the yogurt, minced chiles, adobo sauce, paprika, and lemon juice. Mix well and refrigerate.
3. Wash the potatoes and dry them with paper towels. Slice the potatoes lengthwise, as thinly as possible. You can use a mandoline, a vegetable peeler, or a very sharp knife.
4. Combine the potato slices in a medium bowl and drizzle with the olive oil; toss to coat.
5. Air fry the chips, in batches, in the air fryer basket, for 9 to 14 minutes. Use tongs to gently rearrange the chips halfway during cooking time.
6. Sprinkle the chips with the rosemary, cayenne pepper, and sea salt. Serve with the chipotle sauce for dipping.

Beef Bratwursts

Prep time: 5 minutes | Cook time: 15 minutes | Serves 4

4 (3-ounce / 85-g) beef bratwursts

1. Preheat the air fryer to 375ºF (191ºC).
2. Place the beef bratwursts in the air fryer basket and air fry for 15 minutes, turning once halfway through.
3. Serve hot.

Herb-Roasted Veggies

Prep time: 10 minutes | Cook time: 14 to 18 minutes | Serves 4

1 red bell pepper, sliced
1 (8-ounce / 227-g) package sliced mushrooms
1 cup green beans, cut into 2-inch pieces
1/3 cup diced red onion
3 garlic cloves, sliced
1 teaspoon olive oil
½ teaspoon dried basil
½ teaspoon dried tarragon

1. Preheat the air fryer to 350ºF (177ºC).
2. In a medium bowl, mix the red bell pepper, mushrooms, green beans, red onion, and garlic. Drizzle with the olive oil. Toss to coat.
3. Add the herbs and toss again.
4. Place the vegetables in the air fryer basket. Roast for 14 to 18 minutes, or until tender. Serve immediately.

Classic Mexican Street Corn

Prep time: 5 minutes | Cook time: 7 minutes | Serves 4

4 medium ears corn, husked
Cooking spray
2 tablespoons mayonnaise
1 tablespoon fresh lime juice
½ teaspoon ancho chile powder
¼ teaspoon kosher salt
2 ounces (57 g) crumbled Cotija or Feta cheese
2 tablespoons chopped fresh cilantro

1. Preheat the air fryer to 375ºF (191ºC).
2. Spritz the corn with cooking spray. Working in batches, arrange the ears of corn in the air fryer basket in a single layer. Air fry for about 7 minutes, flipping halfway, until the kernels are tender when pierced with a paring knife. When cool enough to handle, cut the corn kernels off the cob.
3. In a large bowl, mix together mayonnaise, lime juice, ancho powder, and salt. Add the corn kernels and mix to combine. Transfer to a serving dish and top with the Cotija and cilantro. Serve immediately.

Scalloped Veggie Mix

Prep time: 10 minutes | Cook time: 15 minutes | Serves 4

1 Yukon Gold potato, thinly sliced
1 small sweet potato, peeled and thinly sliced
1 medium carrot, thinly sliced
¼ cup minced onion
3 garlic cloves, minced
¾ cup 2 percent milk
2 tablespoons cornstarch
½ teaspoon dried thyme

1. Preheat the air fryer to 380ºF (193ºC).
2. In a baking pan, layer the potato, sweet potato, carrot, onion, and garlic.
3. In a small bowl, whisk the milk, cornstarch, and thyme until blended. Pour the milk mixture evenly over the vegetables in the pan.
4. Bake for 15 minutes. Check the casserole—it should be golden brown on top, and the vegetables should be tender.
5. Serve immediately.

Peppery Brown Rice Fritters

Prep time: 10 minutes | Cook time: 8 to 10 minutes | Serves 4

1 (10-ounce / 284-g) bag frozen cooked brown rice, thawed
1 egg
3 tablespoons brown rice flour
1/3 cup finely grated carrots
1/3 cup minced red bell pepper
2 tablespoons minced fresh basil
3 tablespoons grated Parmesan cheese
2 teaspoons olive oil

1. Preheat the air fryer to 380ºF (193ºC).
2. In a small bowl, combine the thawed rice, egg, and flour and mix to blend.
3. Stir in the carrots, bell pepper, basil, and Parmesan cheese.
4. Form the mixture into 8 fritters and drizzle with the olive oil.
5. Put the fritters carefully into the air fryer basket. Air fry for 8 to 10 minutes, or until the fritters are golden brown and cooked through.
6. Serve immediately.

Cheesy Baked Grits

Prep time: 10 minutes | Cook time: 12 minutes | Serves 6

¾ cup hot water
2 (1-ounce / 28-g) packages instant grits
1 large egg, beaten
1 tablespoon butter, melted
2 cloves garlic, minced
½ to 1 teaspoon red pepper flakes
1 cup shredded Cheddar cheese or jalapeño Jack cheese

1. Preheat the air fryer to 400ºF (204ºC).
2. In a baking pan, combine the water, grits, egg, butter, garlic, and red pepper flakes. Stir until well combined. Stir in the shredded cheese.
3. Place the pan in the air fryer basket and air fry for 12 minutes, or until the grits have cooked through and a knife inserted near the center comes out clean.
4. Let stand for 5 minutes before serving.

Indian Masala Omelet

Prep time: 10 minutes | Cook time: 12 minutes | Serves 2

4 large eggs
½ cup diced onion
½ cup diced tomato
¼ cup chopped fresh cilantro
1 jalapeño, deseeded and finely chopped
½ teaspoon ground turmeric
½ teaspoon kosher salt
½ teaspoon cayenne pepper
Olive oil, for greasing the pan

1. Preheat the air fryer to 250ºF (121ºC). Generously grease a 3-cup Bundt pan.
2. In a large bowl, beat the eggs. Stir in the onion, tomato, cilantro, jalapeño, turmeric, salt, and cayenne.
3. Pour the egg mixture into the prepared pan. Place the pan in the air fryer basket. Bake for 12 minutes, or until the eggs are cooked through. Carefully unmold and cut the omelet into four pieces.
4. Serve immediately.

Traditional Queso Fundido

Prep time: 10 minutes | Cook time: 25 minutes | Serves 4

4 ounces (113 g) fresh Mexican chorizo, casings removed
1 medium onion, chopped
3 cloves garlic, minced
1 cup chopped tomato
2 jalapeños, deseeded and diced
2 teaspoons ground cumin
2 cups shredded Oaxaca or Mozzarella cheese
½ cup half-and-half
Celery sticks or tortilla chips, for serving

1. Preheat the air fryer to 400ºF (204ºC).
2. In a baking pan, combine the chorizo, onion, garlic, tomato, jalapeños, and cumin. Stir to combine.
3. Place the pan in the air fryer basket. Air fry for 15 minutes, or until the sausage is cooked, stirring halfway through the cooking time to break up the sausage.
4. Add the cheese and half-and-half; stir to combine. Air fry for 10 minutes, or until the cheese has melted.
5. Serve with celery sticks or tortilla chips.

Cheesy Chile Toast

Prep time: 5 minutes | Cook time: 5 minutes | Serves 1

2 tablespoons grated Parmesan cheese
2 tablespoons grated Mozzarella cheese
2 teaspoons salted butter, at room temperature
10 to 15 thin slices serrano chile or jalapeño
2 slices sourdough bread
½ teaspoon black pepper

1. Preheat the air fryer to 325ºF (163ºC).
2. In a small bowl, stir together the Parmesan, Mozzarella, butter, and chiles.
3. Spread half the mixture onto one side of each slice of bread. Sprinkle with the pepper. Place the slices, cheese-side up, in the air fryer basket. Bake for 5 minutes, or until the cheese has melted and started to brown slightly.
4. Serve immediately.

Cheesy Jalapeño Poppers

Prep time: 5 minutes | Cook time: 25 minutes | Serves 6

2 slices bacon, halved
¾ cup whole milk ricotta cheese
½ cup shredded sharp Cheddar cheese
1 green onion, finely chopped
¼ teaspoon salt
6 large jalapeños, halved lengthwise and deseeded
½ cup finely crushed potato chips

1. Preheat the air fryer to 400ºF (204ºC).
2. Lay bacon in single layer in basket. Air fry for 5 minutes, or until crisp. Remove bacon and place on paper towels to drain. When cool, finely chop.
3. Stir together ricotta, Cheddar, green onion, bacon, and salt. Spoon into jalapeños; top with potato chips.
4. Place half the jalapeños in the basket and air fry for 8 minutes, or until tender. Repeat with the remaining jalapeños.
5. Serve immediately.

Simple Sweet Potato Soufflé

Prep time: 10 minutes | Cook time: 30 minutes | Serves 4

1 sweet potato, baked and mashed
2 tablespoons unsalted butter, divided
1 large egg, separated
¼ cup whole milk
½ teaspoon kosher salt

1. Preheat the air fryer to 330ºF (166ºC).
2. In a medium bowl, combine the sweet potato, 1 tablespoon of melted butter, egg yolk, milk, and salt. Set aside.
3. In a separate medium bowl, whisk the egg white until stiff peaks form.
4. Using a spatula, gently fold the egg white into the sweet potato mixture.
5. Coat the inside of four 3-inch ramekins with the remaining 1 tablespoon of butter, then fill each ramekin halfway full. Place 2 ramekins in the air fryer basket and bake for 15 minutes. Repeat this process with the remaining ramekins.
6. Remove the ramekins from the air fryer and allow to cool on a wire rack for 10 minutes before serving

Beet Salad with Lemon Vinaigrette

Prep time: 10 minutes | Cook time: 12 to 15 minutes | Serves 4

6 medium red and golden beets, peeled and sliced
1 teaspoon olive oil
¼ teaspoon kosher
salt
½ cup crumbled Feta cheese
8 cups mixed greens
Cooking spray

Vinaigrette:
2 teaspoons olive oil
2 tablespoons
chopped fresh chives
Juice of 1 lemon

1. Preheat the air fryer to 360ºF (182ºC).
2. In a large bowl, toss the beets, olive oil, and kosher salt.
3. Spray the air fryer basket with cooking spray, then place the beets in the basket and air fry for 12 to 15 minutes or until tender.
4. While the beets cook, make the vinaigrette in a large bowl by whisking together the olive oil, lemon juice, and chives.
5. Remove the beets from the air fryer, toss in the vinaigrette, and allow to cool for 5 minutes. Add the Feta and serve on top of the mixed greens.

Air-Fried Chicken Wings

Prep time: 5 minutes | Cook time: 19 minutes | Serves 6

2 pounds (907 g) chicken wings, tips
removed
⅛ teaspoon salt

1. Preheat the air fryer to 400ºF (204ºC). Season the wings with salt.
2. Working in 2 batches, place half the chicken wings in the basket and air fry for 15 minutes, or until the skin is browned and cooked through, turning the wings with tongs halfway through cooking.
3. Combine both batches in the air fryer and air fry for 4 minutes more. Transfer to a large bowl and serve immediately.

Chapter 12 Holiday Specials

Whole Chicken Roast

Prep time: 10 minutes | Cook time: 1 hour | Serves 6

1 teaspoon salt
1 teaspoon Italian seasoning
½ teaspoon freshly ground black pepper
½ teaspoon paprika
½ teaspoon garlic powder
½ teaspoon onion powder
2 tablespoons olive oil, plus more as needed
1 (4-pound / 1.8-kg) fryer chicken

1. Preheat the air fryer to 360ºF (182ºC).
2. Grease the air fryer basket lightly with olive oil.
3. In a small bowl, mix the salt, Italian seasoning, pepper, paprika, garlic powder, and onion powder.
4. Remove any giblets from the chicken. Pat the chicken dry thoroughly with paper towels, including the cavity.
5. Brush the chicken all over with the olive oil and rub it with the seasoning mixture.
6. Truss the chicken or tie the legs with butcher's twine. This will make it easier to flip the chicken during cooking.
7. Put the chicken in the air fryer basket, breast-side down. Air fry for 30 minutes. Flip the chicken over and baste it with any drippings collected in the bottom drawer of the air fryer. Lightly brush the chicken with olive oil.
8. Air fry for 20 minutes. Flip the chicken over one last time and air fry until a thermometer inserted into the thickest part of the thigh reaches at least 165ºF (74ºC) and it's crispy and golden, 10 more minutes. Continue to cook, checking every 5 minutes until the chicken reaches the correct internal temperature.
9. Let the chicken rest for 10 minutes before carving and serving.

Bourbon Monkey Bread

Prep time: 15 minutes | Cook time: 25 minutes | Serves 6 to 8

1 (16.3-ounce / 462-g) can store-bought refrigerated biscuit dough
¼ cup packed light brown sugar
1 teaspoon ground cinnamon
½ teaspoon freshly grated nutmeg
½ teaspoon ground ginger
½ teaspoon kosher salt
¼ teaspoon ground allspice
⅛ teaspoon ground cloves
4 tablespoons (½ stick) unsalted butter, melted
½ cup powdered sugar
2 teaspoons bourbon
2 tablespoons chopped candied cherries
2 tablespoons chopped pecans

1. Preheat the air fryer to 310ºF (154ºC).
2. Open the can and separate the biscuits, then cut each into quarters. Toss the biscuit quarters in a large bowl with the brown sugar, cinnamon, nutmeg, ginger, salt, allspice, and cloves until evenly coated. Transfer the dough pieces and any sugar left in the bowl to a round cake pan, metal cake pan, or foil pan and drizzle evenly with the melted butter. Put the pan in the air fryer and bake until the monkey bread is golden brown and cooked through in the middle, about 25 minutes. Transfer the pan to a wire rack and let cool completely. Unmold from the pan.
3. In a small bowl, whisk the powdered sugar and the bourbon into a smooth glaze. Drizzle the glaze over the cooled monkey bread and, while the glaze is still wet, sprinkle with the cherries and pecans to serve.

Lush Snack Mix

Prep time: 10 minutes | Cook time: 10 minutes | Serves 10

½ cup honey
3 tablespoons butter, melted
1 teaspoon salt
2 cups sesame sticks
2 cup pumpkin

seeds
2 cups granola
1 cup cashews
2 cups crispy corn puff cereal
2 cup mini pretzel crisps

1. In a bowl, combine the honey, butter, and salt.
2. In another bowl, mix the sesame sticks, pumpkin seeds, granola, cashews, corn puff cereal, and pretzel crisps.
3. Combine the contents of the two bowls.
4. Preheat the air fryer to 370°F (188°C).
5. Put the mixture in the air fryer basket and air fry for 10 to 12 minutes to toast the snack mixture, shaking the basket frequently. Do this in two batches.
6. Put the snack mix on a cookie sheet and allow it to cool fully.
7. Serve immediately.

Holiday Spicy Beef Roast

Prep time: 10 minutes | Cook time: 45 minutes | Serves 8

2 pounds (907 g) roast beef, at room temperature
2 tablespoons extra-virgin olive oil
1 teaspoon sea salt flakes
1 teaspoon black

pepper, preferably freshly ground
1 teaspoon smoked paprika
A few dashes of liquid smoke
2 jalapeño peppers, thinly sliced

1. Preheat the air fryer to 330°F (166°C).
2. Pat the roast dry using kitchen towels. Rub with extra-virgin olive oil and all seasonings along with liquid smoke.
3. Roast for 30 minutes in the preheated air fryer. Turn the roast over and roast for additional 15 minutes.
4. Check for doneness using a meat thermometer and serve sprinkled with sliced jalapeños. Bon appétit!

Hearty Honey Yeast Rolls

Prep time: 10 minutes | Cook time: 20 minutes | Makes 8 rolls

¼ cup whole milk, heated to 115°F (46°C) in the microwave
½ teaspoon active dry yeast
1 tablespoon honey
²/₃ cup all-purpose flour, plus more for dusting

½ teaspoon kosher salt
2 tablespoons unsalted butter, at room temperature, plus more for greasing
Flaky sea salt, to taste

1. In a large bowl, whisk together the milk, yeast, and honey and let stand until foamy, about 10 minutes.
2. Stir in the flour and salt until just combined. Stir in the butter until absorbed. Scrape the dough onto a lightly floured work surface and knead until smooth, about 6 minutes. Transfer the dough to a lightly greased bowl, cover loosely with a sheet of plastic wrap or a kitchen towel, and let sit until nearly doubled in size, about 1 hour.
3. Uncover the dough, lightly press it down to expel the bubbles, then portion it into 8 equal pieces. Prep the work surface by wiping it clean with a damp paper towel (if there is flour on the work surface, it will prevent the dough from sticking lightly to the surface, which helps it form a ball). Roll each piece into a ball by cupping the palm of the hand around the dough against the work surface and moving the heel of the hand in a circular motion while using the thumb to contain the dough and tighten it into a perfectly round ball. Once all the balls are formed, nestle them side by side in the air fryer basket.
4. Cover the rolls loosely with a kitchen towel or a sheet of plastic wrap and let sit until lightly risen and puffed, 20 to 30 minutes.
5. Preheat the air fryer to 270°F (132°C).
6. Uncover the rolls and gently brush with more butter, being careful not to press the rolls too hard. Air fry until the rolls are light golden brown and fluffy, about 12 minutes.
7. Remove the rolls from the air fryer and brush liberally with more butter, if you like, and sprinkle each roll with a pinch of sea salt. Serve warm.

Mushroom and Green Bean Casserole

Prep time: 10 minutes | Cook time: 15 minutes | Serves 4

4 tablespoons unsalted butter
¼ cup diced yellow onion
½ cup chopped white mushrooms
½ cup heavy whipping cream
1 ounce (28 g) full-
fat cream cheese
½ cup chicken broth
¼ teaspoon xanthan gum
1 pound (454 g) fresh green beans, edges trimmed
½ ounce (14 g) pork rinds, finely ground

1. In a medium skillet over medium heat, melt the butter. Sauté the onion and mushrooms until they become soft and fragrant, about 3 to 5 minutes.
2. Add the heavy whipping cream, cream cheese, and broth to the pan. Whisk until smooth. Bring to a boil and then reduce to a simmer. Sprinkle the xanthan gum into the pan and remove from heat.
3. Preheat the air fryer to 320ºF (160ºC).
4. Chop the green beans into 2-inch pieces and place into a baking dish. Pour the sauce mixture over them and stir until coated. Top the dish with ground pork rinds. Put into the air fryer basket and bake for 15 minutes.
5. Top will be golden and green beans fork-tender when fully cooked. Serve warm.

Eggnog Bread

Prep time: 10 minutes | Cook time: 18 minutes | Serves 6 to 8

1 cup flour, plus more for dusting
¼ cup sugar
1 teaspoon baking powder
¼ teaspoon salt
¼ teaspoon nutmeg
½ cup eggnog
1 egg yolk
1 tablespoon plus 1 teaspoon butter, melted
¼ cup pecans
¼ cup chopped candied fruit (cherries, pineapple, or mixed fruits)
Cooking spray

1. Preheat the air fryer to 360ºF (182ºC).
2. In a medium bowl, stir together the flour, sugar, baking powder, salt, and nutmeg.
3. Add eggnog, egg yolk, and butter. Mix well but do not beat.
4. Stir in nuts and fruit.
5. Spray a baking pan with cooking spray and dust with flour.
6. Spread batter into prepared pan and bake for 18 minutes or until top is dark golden brown and bread starts to pull away from sides of pan.
7. Serve immediately.

Hasselback Potatoes

Prep time: 5 minutes | Cook time: 50 minutes | Serves 4

4 russet potatoes, peeled
Salt and freshly ground black pepper,
to taste
¼ cup grated Parmesan cheese
Cooking spray

1. Preheat the air fryer to 400ºF (204ºC).
2. Spray the air fryer basket lightly with cooking spray.
3. Make thin parallel cuts into each potato, ⅛-inch to ¼-inch apart, stopping at about ½ of the way through. The potato needs to stay intact along the bottom.
4. Spray the potatoes with cooking spray and use the hands or a silicone brush to completely coat the potatoes lightly in oil.
5. Put the potatoes, sliced side up, in the air fryer basket in a single layer. Leave a little room between each potato. Sprinkle the potatoes lightly with salt and black pepper.
6. Air fry for 20 minutes. Reposition the potatoes and spritz lightly with cooking spray again. Air fry until the potatoes are fork-tender and crispy and browned, another 20 to 30 minutes.
7. Sprinkle the potatoes with Parmesan cheese and serve.

Air Fried Spicy Olives

Prep time: 10 minutes | Cook time: 5 minutes | Serves 4

12 ounces (340 g) pitted black extra-large olives
¼ cup all-purpose flour
1 cup panko bread crumbs
2 teaspoons dried thyme
1 teaspoon red pepper flakes
1 teaspoon smoked paprika
1 egg beaten with 1 tablespoon water
Vegetable oil for spraying

1. Preheat the air fryer to 400ºF (204ºC).
2. Drain the olives and place them on a paper towel–lined plate to dry.
3. Put the flour on a plate. Combine the panko, thyme, red pepper flakes, and paprika on a separate plate. Dip an olive in the flour, shaking off any excess, then coat with egg mixture. Dredge the olive in the panko mixture, pressing to make the crumbs adhere, and place the breaded olive on a platter. Repeat with the remaining olives.
4. Spray the olives with oil and place them in a single layer in the air fryer basket. Work in batches if necessary so as not to overcrowd the basket. Air fry for 5 minutes until the breading is browned and crispy. Serve warm

Chapter 13 Sauces, Dips, and Dressings

Cashew Pesto

Prep time: 10 minutes | Cook time: 0 minutes | Makes 1 cup

¼ cup raw cashews	oil
Juice of 1 lemon	4 cups basil leaves,
2 garlic cloves	packed
⅓ red onion (about	1 cup wheatgrass
2 ounces / 56 g in	¼ cup water
total)	¼ teaspoon salt
1 tablespoon olive	

1. Put the cashews in a heatproof bowl and add boiling water to cover. Soak for 5 minutes and then drain.
2. Put all ingredients in a blender and blend for 2 to 3 minutes or until fully combined.

Red Buffalo Sauce

Prep time: 5 minutes | Cook time: 20 minutes | Makes 2 cups

¼ cup olive oil	ounces / 56 g in
4 garlic cloves,	total)
roughly chopped	1 cup water
1 (5-ounce / 142-	½ cup apple cider
g) small red onion,	vinegar
roughly chopped	½ teaspoon salt
6 red chiles, roughly	½ teaspoon freshly
chopped (about 2	ground black pepper

1. In a large nonstick sauté pan, heat ¼ cup olive oil over medium-high heat. Once it's hot, add the garlic, onion, and chiles. Cook for 5 minutes, stirring occasionally, until onion are golden brown.
2. Add the water and bring to a boil. Cook for about 10 minutes or until the water has nearly evaporated.
3. Transfer the cooked onion and chile mixture to a food processor or blender and blend briefly to combine. Add the apple cider vinegar, salt, and pepper. Blend again for 30 seconds.
4. Using a mesh sieve, strain the sauce into a bowl. Use a spoon or spatula to scrape and press all the liquid from the pulp.

Cauliflower Alfredo Sauce

Prep time: 2 minutes | Cook time: 0 minutes | Makes 4 cups

2 tablespoons olive oil	into florets
6 garlic cloves,	1 teaspoon salt
minced	¼ teaspoon freshly
3 cups unsweetened	ground black pepper
almond milk	Juice of 1 lemon
1 (1-pound / 454-g)	4 tablespoons
head cauliflower, cut	nutritional yeast

1. In a medium saucepan, heat the olive oil over medium-high heat. Add the garlic and sauté for 1 minute or until fragrant. Add the almond milk, stir, and bring to a boil.
2. Gently add the cauliflower. Stir in the salt and pepper and return to a boil. Continue cooking over medium-high heat for 5 minutes or until the cauliflower is soft. Stir frequently and reduce heat if needed to prevent the liquid from boiling over.
3. Carefully transfer the cauliflower and cooking liquid to a food processor, using a slotted spoon to scoop out the larger pieces of cauliflower before pouring in the liquid. Add the lemon and nutritional yeast and blend for 1 to 2 minutes until smooth.
4. Serve immediately.

Ginger Sweet Sauce

Prep time: 5 minutes | Cook time: 5 minutes | Makes ⅔ cup

3 tablespoons ketchup	minced fresh ginger root
2 tablespoons water	2 teaspoons soy
2 tablespoons maple syrup	sauce (or tamari, which is a gluten-
1 tablespoon rice vinegar	free option)
2 teaspoons peeled	1 teaspoon cornstarch

1. In a small saucepan over medium heat, combine all the ingredients and stir continuously for 5 minutes, or until slightly thickened. Enjoy warm or cold.

Avocado Dressing

Prep time: 5 minutes | Cook time: 0 minutes | Makes 12 tablespoons

1 large avocado, pitted and peeled
½ cup water
2 tablespoons tahini
2 tablespoons freshly squeezed lemon juice
1 teaspoon dried basil
1 teaspoon white wine vinegar
1 garlic clove
¼ teaspoon pink Himalayan salt
¼ teaspoon freshly ground black pepper

1. Combine all the ingredients in a food processor and blend until smooth.

Dijon and Balsamic Vinaigrette

Prep time: 5 minutes | Cook time: 0 minutes | Makes 12 tablespoons

6 tablespoons water
4 tablespoons Dijon mustard
4 tablespoons balsamic vinegar
1 teaspoon maple syrup
½ teaspoon pink Himalayan salt
¼ teaspoon freshly ground black pepper

1. In a bowl, whisk together all the ingredients.

Hemp Dressing

Prep time: 5 minutes | Cook time: 0 minutes | Makes 12 tablespoons

½ cup white wine vinegar
¼ cup tahini
¼ cup water
1 tablespoon hemp seeds
½ tablespoon freshly squeezed lemon juice
1 teaspoon garlic powder
1 teaspoon dried oregano
1 teaspoon dried basil
1 teaspoon red pepper flakes
½ teaspoon onion powder
½ teaspoon pink Himalayan salt
½ teaspoon freshly ground black pepper

1. In a bowl, combine all the ingredients and whisk until mixed well.

Lemony Tahini

Prep time: 5 minutes | Cook time: 0 minutes | Serves 4

¾ cup water
½ cup tahini
3 garlic cloves, minced
Juice of 3 lemons
½ teaspoon pink Himalayan salt

1. In a bowl, whisk together all the ingredients until mixed well.

Cashew Mayo

Prep time: 5 minutes | Cook time: 0 minutes | Makes 18 tablespoons

1 cup cashews, soaked in hot water for at least 1 hour
¼ cup plus 3 tablespoons milk
1 tablespoon apple cider vinegar
1 tablespoon freshly squeezed lemon juice
1 tablespoon Dijon mustard
1 tablespoon aquafaba
⅛ teaspoon pink Himalayan salt

1. In a food processor, combine all the ingredients and blend until creamy and smooth.

Mushroom Apple Gravy

Prep time: 5 minutes | Cook time: 10 minutes | Serves 4

2 cups vegetable broth
½ cup finely chopped mushrooms
2 tablespoons whole wheat flour
1 tablespoon unsweetened applesauce
1 teaspoon onion powder
½ teaspoon dried thyme
¼ teaspoon dried rosemary
⅛ teaspoon pink Himalayan salt
Freshly ground black pepper, to taste

1. In a nonstick saucepan over medium-high heat, combine all the ingredients and mix well. Bring to a boil, stirring frequently, reduce the heat to low, and simmer, stirring constantly, until it thickens.

Balsamic Dressing

Prep time: 5 minutes | Cook time: 0 minutes | Makes 1 cup

2 tablespoons Dijon mustard
¼ cup balsamic

vinegar
¾ cup olive oil

1. Put all ingredients in a jar with a tight-fitting lid. Put on the lid and shake vigorously until thoroughly combined. Refrigerate until ready to use and shake well before serving.

Pico de Gallo

Prep time: 5 minutes | Cook time: 0 minutes | Serves 2

3 large tomatoes, chopped
½ small red onion, diced
⅛ cup chopped fresh cilantro
3 garlic cloves, chopped

2 tablespoons chopped pickled jalapeño pepper
1 tablespoon lime juice
¼ teaspoon pink Himalayan salt (optional)

1. In a medium bowl, combine all the ingredients and mix with a wooden spoon.

Cashew Ranch Dressing

Prep time: 15 minutes | Cook time: 0 minutes | Serves 12

1 cup cashews, soaked in warm water for at least 1 hour
½ cup water
2 tablespoons freshly squeezed lemon juice

1 tablespoon vinegar
1 teaspoon garlic powder
1 teaspoon onion powder
2 teaspoons dried dill

1. In a food processor, combine the cashews, water, lemon juice, vinegar, garlic powder, and onion powder. Blend until creamy and smooth. Add the dill and pulse a few times until combined.

Hummus

Prep time: 5 minutes | Cook time: 0 minutes | Serves 2

1 (19-ounce / 539-g) can chickpeas, drained and rinsed
¼ cup tahini
3 tablespoons cold water
2 tablespoons freshly squeezed lemon juice

1 garlic clove
½ teaspoon turmeric powder
⅛ teaspoon black pepper
Pinch pink Himalayan salt, to taste

1. Combine all the ingredients in a food processor and blend until smooth.

Cashew Vodka Sauce

Prep time: 15 minutes | Cook time: 5 minutes | Makes 3 cups

¾ cup raw cashews
¼ cup boiling water
1 tablespoon olive oil
4 garlic cloves, minced
1½ cups unsweetened

almond milk
1 tablespoon arrowroot powder
1 teaspoon salt
1 tablespoon nutritional yeast
1¼ cups marinara sauce

1. Put the cashews in a heatproof bowl and add boiling water to cover. Let soak for 10 minutes. Drain the cashews and place them in a blender. Add ¼ cup boiling water and blend for 1 to 2 minutes or until creamy. Set aside.
2. In a small saucepan, heat the olive oil over medium heat. Add the garlic and sauté for 2 minutes until golden. Whisk in the almond milk, arrowroot powder, and salt. Bring to a simmer. Continue to simmer, whisking frequently, for about 5 minutes or until the sauce thickens.
3. Carefully transfer the hot almond milk mixture to the blender with the cashews. Blend for 30 seconds to combine, then add the nutritional yeast and marinara sauce. Blend for 1 minute or until creamy.

Appendix 1: Measurement Conversion Chart

VOLUME EQUIVALENTS(DRY)

US STANDARD	METRIC (APPROXIMATE)
1/8 teaspoon	0.5 mL
1/4 teaspoon	1 mL
1/2 teaspoon	2 mL
3/4 teaspoon	4 mL
1 teaspoon	5 mL
1 tablespoon	15 mL
1/4 cup	59 mL
1/2 cup	118 mL
3/4 cup	177 mL
1 cup	235 mL
2 cups	475 mL
3 cups	700 mL
4 cups	1 L

WEIGHT EQUIVALENTS

US STANDARD	METRIC (APPROXIMATE)
1 ounce	28 g
2 ounces	57 g
5 ounces	142 g
10 ounces	284 g
15 ounces	425 g
16 ounces (1 pound)	455 g
1.5 pounds	680 g
2 pounds	907 g

VOLUME EQUIVALENTS(LIQUID)

US STANDARD	US STANDARD (OUNCES)	METRIC (APPROXIMATE)
2 tablespoons	1 fl.oz.	30 mL
1/4 cup	2 fl.oz.	60 mL
1/2 cup	4 fl.oz.	120 mL
1 cup	8 fl.oz.	240 mL
1 1/2 cup	12 fl.oz.	355 mL
2 cups or 1 pint	16 fl.oz.	475 mL
4 cups or 1 quart	32 fl.oz.	1 L
1 gallon	128 fl.oz.	4 L

TEMPERATURES EQUIVALENTS

FAHRENHEIT(F)	CELSIUS(C) (APPROXIMATE)
225 °F	107 °C
250 °F	120 °C
275 °F	135 °C
300 °F	150 °C
325 °F	160 °C
350 °F	180 °C
375 °F	190 °C
400 °F	205 °C
425 °F	220 °C
450 °F	235 °C
475 °F	245 °C
500 °F	260 °C

Appendix 2: Air Fryer Cooking Chart

Beef

Item	Temp (°F)	Time (mins)	Item	Temp (°F)	Time (mins)
Beef Eye Round Roast (4 lbs.)	400 °F	45 to 55	Meatballs (1-inch)	370 °F	7
Burger Patty (4 oz.)	370 °F	16 to 20	Meatballs (3-inch)	380 °F	10
Filet Mignon (8 oz.)	400 °F	18	Ribeye, bone-in (1-inch, 8 oz)	400 °F	10 to 15
Flank Steak (1.5 lbs.)	400 °F	12	Sirloin steaks (1-inch, 12 oz)	400 °F	9 to 14
Flank Steak (2 lbs.)	400 °F	20 to 28			

Chicken

Item	Temp (°F)	Time (mins)	Item	Temp (°F)	Time (mins)
Breasts, bone in (1 ¼ lb.)	370 °F	25	Legs, bone-in (1 ¾ lb.)	380 °F	30
Breasts, boneless (4 oz)	380 °F	12	Thighs, boneless (1 ½ lb.)	380 °F	18 to 20
Drumsticks (2 ½ lb.)	370 °F	20	Wings (2 lb.)	400 °F	12
Game Hen (halved 2 lb.)	390 °F	20	Whole Chicken	360 °F	75
Thighs, bone-in (2 lb.)	380 °F	22	Tenders	360 °F	8 to 10

Pork & Lamb

Item	Temp (°F)	Time (mins)	Item	Temp (°F)	Time (mins)
Bacon (regular)	400 °F	5 to 7	Pork Tenderloin	370 °F	15
Bacon (thick cut)	400 °F	6 to 10	Sausages	380 °F	15
Pork Loin (2 lb.)	360 °F	55	Lamb Loin Chops (1-inch thick)	400 °F	8 to 12
Pork Chops, bone in (1-inch, 6.5 oz)	400 °F	12	Rack of Lamb (1.5 – 2 lb.)	380 °F	22

Fish & Seafood

Item	Temp (°F)	Time (mins)	Item	Temp (°F)	Time (mins)
Calamari (8 oz)	400 °F	4	Tuna Steak	400 °F	7 to 10
Fish Fillet (1-inch, 8 oz)	400 °F	10	Scallops	400 °F	5 to 7
Salmon, fillet (6 oz)	380 °F	12	Shrimp	400 °F	5
Swordfish steak	400 °F	10			

Vegetables					
INGREDIENT	AMOUNT	PREPARATION	OIL	TEMP	COOK TIME
Asparagus	2 bunches	Cut in half, trim stems	2 Tbsp	420°F	12-15 mins
Beets	1½ lbs	Peel, cut in ½-inch cubes	1Tbsp	390°F	28-30 mins
Bell peppers (for roasting)	4 peppers	Cut in quarters, remove seeds	1Tbsp	400°F	15-20 mins
Broccoli	1 large head	Cut in 1-2-inch florets	1Tbsp	400°F	15-20 mins
Brussels sprouts	1lb	Cut in half, remove stems	1Tbsp	425°F	15-20 mins
Carrots	1lb	Peel, cut in ¼-inch rounds	1 Tbsp	425°F	10-15 mins
Cauliflower	1 head	Cut in 1-2-inch florets	2 Tbsp	400°F	20-22 mins
Corn on the cob	7 ears	Whole ears, remove husks	1 Tbps	400°F	14-17 mins
Green beans	1 bag (12 oz)	Trim	1 Tbps	420°F	18-20 mins
Kale (for chips)	4 oz	Tear into pieces,remove stems	None	325°F	5-8 mins
Mushrooms	16 oz	Rinse, slice thinly	1 Tbps	390°F	25-30 mins
Potatoes, russet	1½ lbs	Cut in 1-inch wedges	1 Tbps	390°F	25-30 mins
Potatoes, russet	1lb	Hand-cut fries, soak 30 mins in cold water, then pat dry	½ -3 Tbps	400°F	25-28 mins
Potatoes, sweet	1lb	Hand-cut fries, soak 30 mins in cold water, then pat dry	1 Tbps	400°F	25-28 mins
Zucchini	1lb	Cut in eighths lengthwise, then cut in half	1 Tbps	400°F	15-20 mins

Printed in Great Britain
by Amazon

11708296R00167